STUDY GUIDE

STUDY GUIDE

to accompany

MACROECONOMICS

THIRD EDITION

Krugman | Wells

Elizabeth Sawyer Kelly
University of Wisconsin-Madison

WORTH PUBLISHERS

Study Guide
by Elizabeth Sawyer Kelly
to accompany
Krugman/Wells: Macroeconomics, Third Edition

ISBN 13: 978-1-4641-0407-7
ISBN 10: 1-4641-0407-7

First Printing

Printed in the United States of America

Worth Publishers
41 Madison Avenue
New York, NY 10010
www.wortheconomics.com

Contents

Key to Corresponding Chapter Numbers

	Macroeconomics	*Economics*	*Microeconomics*
First Principles	Chapter 1	Chapter 1	Chapter 1
Economic Models: Trade-offs and Trade	Chapter 2	Chapter 2	Chapter 2
Supply and Demand	Chapter 3	Chapter 3	Chapter 3
Price Controls and Quotas: Meddling with Markets	Chapter 4 (modified)	Chapter 5	Chapter 5
International Trade	Chapter 5	Chapter 8	Chapter 8
Macroeconomics: The Big Picture	Chapter 6	Chapter 21	
GDP and CPI: Tracking the Macroeconomy	Chapter 7	Chapter 22	
Unemployment and Inflation	Chapter 8	Chapter 23	
Long-Run Economic Growth	Chapter 9	Chapter 24	
Savings, Investment Spending, and the Financial System	Chapter 10	Chapter 25	
Income and Expenditure	Chapter 11	Chapter 26	
Aggregate Demand and Aggregate Supply	Chapter 12	Chapter 27	
Fiscal Policy	Chapter 13	Chapter 28	
Money, Banking, and the Federal Reserve System	Chapter 14	Chapter 29	
Monetary Policy	Chapter 15	Chapter 30	
Inflation, Disinflation, and Deflation	Chapter 16	Chapter 31	
Crises and Consequences	Chapter 17	Chapter 32	
Macroeconomics: Events and Ideas	Chapter 18	Chapter 33	
Open-Economy Macroeconomics	Chapter 19	Chapter 34	

Preface

This Study Guide is designed for use with *Macroeconomics, **Third Edition*** by Paul Krugman and Robin Wells. It is intended to help you evaluate your understanding of the material covered in the textbook and thereby reinforce the key concepts you need to learn.

For each chapter, the Study Guide is organized as follows:

Before You Read the Chapter
- Summary: an opening paragraph that provides a brief overview of the chapter.
- Objectives: a numbered list outlining and describing the material that you should have learned in the chapter. These objectives can be easily used as a study tool.
- Key Terms: a list of bold key terms with their definitions. This section includes room for note taking.

After You Read the Chapter
- Tips: a numbered list of learning tips with graphical analysis.
- Worked Problems: a new set of worked-out problems that take the student step-by-step through a particular problem/exercise.
- Problems and Exercises: a set of 10–15 comprehensive problems.

Before You Take the Test
- Chapter Review Questions: a set of approximately 30 multiple-choice questions that focus on the key concepts from the text that you should grasp after reading the chapter. These questions are designed for quick exam preparation.

Answer Key
- Answers to Problems and Exercises: detailed solutions to the Problems and Exercises in the Study Guide.
- Answers to Chapter Review Questions: solutions to the multiple-choice questions in the Study Guide—along with thorough explanations.

Answers as well as explanatory solutions can be found at the end of each chapter. Students often use an answer section to simply check if they have gotten the "right" answer. I caution you to use the answer section accompanying each chapter with an eye to getting the highest possible value from the exercises provided. In economics, the reasoning used in coming to conclusions and correctly modeling the problems are as important as coming to an accurate answer. Explanations for each problem have been provided in order for you to check that your understanding of the concepts has been appropriately applied.

The study of economics has the potential of altering the way you evaluate and understand the world. I hope that your use of this guide will help you in your study of basic macroeconomics principles and will provide a jumping-off point for further study in the economics field.

Elizabeth Sawyer Kelly

STUDY GUIDE

chapter 1

First Principles

BEFORE YOU READ THE CHAPTER

Summary

This chapter provides a brief overview of twelve general principles underlying the study of economics. These principles are explored and discussed at greater length as you work your way through the text. This first chapter indicates the breadth and depth of economics as a course of study by delineating these twelve principles, which describe how individuals make choices and how individual choices interact.

Chapter Objectives

This chapter introduces a set of principles that will guide your study of economics.

Objective #1. Resources—land, labor, capital, and human capital—are scarce, so individuals as well as societies must make choices about how to use these resources.

Objective #2. The opportunity cost, or the real cost of something, is what you must give up to get it.

Objective #3. Decisions about how much to produce and how much to consume are made at the margin. These decisions invariably involve a trade-off, or a comparison of the costs and benefits of producing more or consuming more.

Objective #4. People usually exploit opportunities to make themselves better off—in other words, people respond to incentives.

Objective #5. There are gains from trade.

Objective #6. Markets move toward equilibrium, a situation in which no individual would be better off doing something different.

Objective #7. Resources should be used as efficiently as possible to achieve society's goals. However, there is a trade-off between efficiency and equity: decisions based solely on efficiency may be highly inequitable.

Objective #8. Markets usually lead to efficiency.

Objective #9. When markets fail to achieve efficiency, government intervention can improve society's welfare. Markets may fail due to (1) the existence of side effects from individual actions that are not accounted for in the market; (2) the prevention of mutually beneficial trades by an individual or individuals so they can capture a greater share of resources; or (3) the inability to produce some goods, due to the nature of these goods, efficiently by the market.

Objective #10. One person's spending is another person's income.

Objective #11. Spending sometimes gets out of line with the economy's capacity to produce goods and services. It is possible for the economy's spending to be less than, or greater than, the current level of production.

Objective #12. Government policies can change the level of spending in an economy.

Key Terms

Notes

individual choice the decision by an individual of what to do, which necessarily involves a decision of what not to do.

resource anything, such as land, labor, and capital, that can be used to produce something else; includes natural resources (from the physical environment) and human resources (labor, skill, intelligence).

scarce in short supply; a *resource* is scarce when there is not enough of the resources available to satisfy all the various ways a society wants to use them.

opportunity cost the real cost of an item: what you must give up in order to get it.

trade-off a comparison of costs and benefits of doing something.

marginal decision a decision made at the "margin" of an activity to do a bit more or a bit less of an activity.

marginal analysis the study of *marginal decisions*.

incentive anything that offers rewards to people who change their behavior.

interaction (of choices) my choices affect your choices, and vice versa; a feature of most economic situations. The results of this interaction are often quite different from what the individuals intend.

trade in a market *economy,* individuals provide goods and services to others and receive goods and services in return.

Key Terms *(continued)*

gains from trade by dividing tasks and trading, people can get more of what they want through *trade* than they could if they tried to be self-sufficient.

specialization each person specializes in the task that he or she is good at performing.

equilibrium an economic situation in which no individual would be better off doing something different.

efficient description of a market or *economy* that takes all opportunities to make some people better off without making other people worse off.

equity fairness; everyone gets his or her fair share. Since people can disagree about what is "fair," equity is not as well defined a concept as efficiency.

■ AFTER YOU READ THE CHAPTER

Tips

Tip #1. The study of economics is cumulative. You should master each topic as it is presented since later topics build on earlier topics.

Tip #2. Pay attention to new vocabulary and make sure you know, understand, and can apply these terms. Your instructor will expect you to do more than just define the terms: you must also be able to indicate through your work an ability to apply these terms in a meaningful manner.

Tip #3. Plan to spend time every day studying economics. Review your lecture notes, review the vocabulary, work on the practice questions, and identify what questions you have about the material. Once you formulate your questions, seek out answers by returning to your text, your lecture notes, your classmates, or your professor.

Tip #4. Think about the topics that might be on an exam and the kinds of questions that might be asked about these topics—questions that are strictly definitional, questions that apply the definitions in a problem-solving setting, and questions that force you to really think about the material and apply your knowledge. Most college-level exams include questions designed to make you think about the material.

Tip #5. You might find it helpful to create a set of flash cards to help you study. For this chapter the set of flash cards would include a card for each principle and a card for each new vocabulary word. On the vocabulary cards, put the word on one side of the card and its definition on the other. In the upper corner of each card, note the chapter the card comes from—

for example, you might write "Ch. 1" on the cards for this chapter to remind you where this material was first presented. Then, make a point of reviewing these flash cards throughout the day until you feel confident you have absorbed this material.

Tip #6. Your study of economics is applicable to the real world. As you read or listen to the news, try to apply your new knowledge of economics to your understanding of these world events.

WORKED PROBLEMS

1. In each of the following situations identify the cost or the benefit that the market does not take into account in determining the optimal amount of the good. For example, when Joe drives to work during rush hour, his driving adds to the traffic congestion: Joe imposes a cost on all the other drivers that the market and Joe do not take into account when deciding whether he should drive during rush hour.
    a. Mary drinks several alcoholic drinks and then gets into her car to drive home. Mary's actions increase the risk of car accidents that may injure Mary as well as other people. In addition, Mary's actions may also lead to other types of property damage.
    b. Jerry picks up litter along his route to work.
    c. Sarah decides to paint the outside of her house lime green. Most of Sarah's neighbors strongly dislike her choice of color since they fear that their property values are apt to fall after Sarah paints her home lime green.
    d. Ying smokes two packs of cigarettes a day at her place of employment even though she knows smoking will likely create health consequences for her as well as anyone else who breathes her second-hand smoke.

    STEP 1: For each of the situations think about a cost or a benefit that the transaction involves that will not be considered by the market.

    Review the section "Interaction: How Economics Work" on pages 11–17.

    a. Mary imposes a cost on other members of society when she drinks and then drives. Her driving while intoxicated poses distinct risks to her and to others who may be on her route. Mary, if intoxicated, may make poor decisions that result in a car accident that may injure her as well as other individuals. Her driving while impaired also poses greater risk of property damage due to driving error.

    b. Jerry provides a benefit to other members of society when he collects litter: thanks to Jerry's uncompensated efforts, the route is aesthetically more pleasing to everyone traveling the route.

    c. Sarah imposes a cost on her neighbors when she paints the exterior of her house lime green. Her actions are apt to decrease the property values of her neighbors.

    d. Ying imposes a cost on society by her choice of smoking: she is likely to experience greater health risks and costs that will not necessarily be borne just by her. In addition, her actions result in air pollution that creates costs to those who are not smoking but who are exposed to Ying's smoking.

2. This chapter introduces four general principles that underlie the economics of individual choice: (1) resources are scarce; (2) the real cost of something is what you must give up to get it; (3) "how much?" is a decision at the margin; and (4)

people usually exploit opportunities to make themselves better off. In each of the following situations identify which of these principles is being illustrated. More than one principle may be illustrated in a particular example.

   a. Peter is trying to decide whether he should spend the afternoon working on the sailboat he is building or whether he should spend the afternoon studying for his economics exam.

   b. Carolyn has realized that she can earn $20 an hour babysitting while attending law school. Any other job she might be able to fit into her schedule would only pay $15 an hour.

   c. Katherine would like to fly to Costa Rica for a week and she would like to replace her snow tires on her car. Either choice Katherine makes will cost $400 and she only has $400 to spend.

   d. Mark decides to work as a canoe guide for the summer and therefore turns down the opportunity of working in Arizona.

   e. Susie is debating how many servings of cake she is going to eat at her cousin's wedding reception.

STEP 1: **For each of the situations think about which principle or principles apply to the scenario.**

Review the section "Principles that Underlie Individual Choice: The Core of Economics" on pages 6–11.

a. Faced with this decision, Peter is aware that resources are scarce and that he has only one afternoon available and thus cannot do both activities. He also recognizes that the real cost of doing something is measured by what must be given up: he can work on his sailboat but the cost to him of this choice is not studying for his economics exam. Or, he can study for his economics exam, but the cost to him of this choice is not working on his boat.

b. Carolyn when deciding to babysit is exploiting the opportunity to make herself better off. Babysitting offers her the highest wage per hour that she can command while in law school.

c. Katherine faces scarce resources (only $400) as well as the recognition that the real cost of doing something is measured by what must be given up. Katherine can go to Costa Rica, but she must give up new snow tires in order to take the trip.

d. Since Mark must choose between the canoe guide position and the job in Arizona, he is faced with the first and second principle: resources are scarce (he has limited available time) and the real cost of doing something is measured by what must be given up.

e. Susie's decision about how much wedding cake to eat is a decision made at the margin: Susie considers how much enjoyment or benefit she will get from an additional piece of cake versus the cost of eating another piece. If the benefit is greater than the cost, then Susie will eat an additional piece of cake.

3. In January 2009, Flight 1549, the "Miracle on the Hudson," crashed after Canadian geese struck the airplane. Amazingly no one on board was killed, but the accident did lead to the Federal Aviation Administration ordering a review of wildlife hazards at all major American airports. In some locales substantial populations of Canadian geese were identified and orders were made to kill these geese. The "how much?" principle is useful in analyzing many situations. Use this principle to provide an analysis of the steps you would advocate that officials take in deciding what the optimal number of geese is for an airport.

STEP 1: In formulating your answer to this question, think about the benefit of a small change in the number of geese and the cost of this small change in the number of geese.

Review the section "'How Much?' Is a Decision at the Margin" on pages 8–9.

The "how much?" principle advises that each decision should be made at the margin where we consider the benefit of a small change relative to the cost of that small change. In the case of the Canadian geese, we would want to start with an analysis of the cost of the current flock sizes as it relates to aviation operation, and then consider what the marginal benefit of a reduction in the Canadian geese population in the area would be, as well as what the marginal cost of that reduction would be. Provided that the marginal benefit was greater than the marginal cost, then it would make sense to reduce the Canadian geese population. But, if the marginal benefit proved smaller than the marginal cost, then it would not make sense to reduce the Canadian geese population.

4. Suppose you are on a Board of Directors for an organization and that your Board is currently trying to hire an Administrative Assistant to assist in a broad range of responsibilities for your group. You advertise the job, its responsibilities, and its salary range and then you begin to receive applications from prospective employees. In reviewing the resumes, you realize that none of the applicants has the necessary experience or skill set that you seek. Analyze this situation and what you think you should do to rectify it.

STEP 1: Think about which principle or principles is applicable to this question as you formulate your answer.

Review the section "Markets Move Toward Equilibrium" on pages 13–14. Recall the statement, "markets usually reach equilibrium via changes in prices, which rise or fall until no opportunities for individuals to make themselves better off remain" (page 13) when answering this question.

People applying for the job know what skills you are looking for and what the salary range is. If you are not getting applicants with those skills, it suggests that you are offering a salary that is too low. By adjusting the salary level upward you should begin to see a group of prospective employees that possess greater skills and more experience.

5. Suppose that a new government is elected and that on taking office these political leaders mandate that everyone in their society receive the same wage per hour. Discuss the equity of this decision as well as its efficiency.

STEP 1: One of the ideas that your course of study in economics will expose you to is the trade-off between equity and efficiency. A policy may prove to be highly efficient but inequitable or highly equitable but quite inefficient. In the example, identify both the equity and efficiency aspects of the proposed policy.

Review the section "Resources Should Be Used as Efficiently as Possible to Achieve Society's Goals" on pages 14–15.

With regard to equity, this mandate seeks to treat everyone equally: all people get the same wage per hour irrespective of what work they are doing. Some members of this society might feel that this is still inequitable since, for example, some jobs are harder to perform than others, some jobs require far more training than others, and some jobs are riskier than others. Income equity among all members of a society poses some definitional and operational challenges. With regard to efficiency, if everyone receives the same wage per hour, then there will be little incentive to work hard. Most members of the society will choose to work less intensely, and this will therefore result in less total output for the society and a reduction in overall living standard.

6. In recent months, the U.S. government has sought to keep interest rates low through the actions of the Federal Reserve Bank as well as by implementing a major government spending program. Briefly discuss what the intent of these programs has been.

STEP 1: **Identify which of the principles introduced in the chapter seem most relevant with regard to this question.**

Review the section "Economy-Wide Interactions" on pages 18-20. In particular play close attention to the sections "Overall Spending Sometimes Gets Out of Line with the Economy's Productive Capacity" on pages 18-19 and "Government Policies Can Change Spending" on page 19.

In light of the financial crisis that began in 2007, the government has tried to pursue monetary and fiscal policies that would soften the recessionary impact. By pursuing monetary policies that would keep interest rates low, the Federal Reserve Bank hoped to stimulate consumer and business spending that is affected by the level of the interest rate. In addition, the government increased its expenditures on goods and services in order to help maintain a higher level of spending than would otherwise have occurred during the months after the financial crisis.

Problems and Exercises

1. For each of the following situations describe the opportunity costs of each decision.

    a. Sarah considers two options for Saturday night: she can attend a concert that costs $10 per ticket or she can go to the free movie offered at the student union. She decides to attend the concert.

    b. A new business in town debates paying $20,000 for a prime location versus $10,000 for a less perfect location. The business estimates that it will eventually serve the same number of customers in either location, but that it will take 6 months before the suboptimal location provides the same outcome as the prime location. The business decides to purchase the $10,000 property.

    c. Jamie is given a choice for his next holiday from school: he can be an unpaid intern at a company or he can earn $2,000 working as a camp counselor. He decides to take the internship.

d. Roberto is studying for two midterms this week. He figures he has 20 available hours to study for both midterms. If he studies all 20 hours for the economics exam he will undoubtedly get an A on the exam, but he will at best make a C on his organic chemistry test. If he studies all 20 hours for the organic chemistry test he will get an A on the organic chemistry exam, but he will likely earn a D on his economics test. Roberto decides to devote all of his available time to economics since he has determined that he does not wish to pursue a premed major.

2. The following table presents the possible combinations of study time available to Roberto this week as he prepares for his two midterms (one in economics and the other in organic chemistry). Assume Roberto has 20 hours available to study and that he will use all 20 hours studying economics and chemistry.

Hours of study time spent on economics	Hours of study time spent on organic chemistry	Grade in economics	Grade in organic chemistry
0	20	60	90
5	15	70	85
10	10	80	75
15	5	86	73
20	0	90	70

Roberto currently plans to study 10 hours for economics and 10 hours for organic chemistry.

a. If he alters his plan and studies 15 hours for economics, what is the opportunity cost of that decision?

b. If he alters his plan and studies 15 hours for organic chemistry, what is the opportunity cost of that decision?

c. If he alters his plan and studies 20 hours for economics, what is the opportunity cost of that decision?

d. If he alters his plan and studies 20 hours for organic chemistry, what is the opportunity cost of that decision?

3. a. Joe is trying to decide whether to have another piece of cake at dinner tonight. Describe how Joe can use the principle of marginal analysis to decide whether to eat this piece of cake.

    b. A local government is debating whether to institute a stricter recycling ordinance for their community. Suppose the cost of the additional recycling restrictions is $500,000 a year due to the need to have additional labor and capital available to meet the demands of the new ordinance. This community uses marginal analysis to make their decisions and decides to adopt this stricter recycling ordinance. What do you know about the benefits this community will receive from implementing this ordinance?

    c. Susy is recovering from knee surgery and has a number of exercises she needs to do each day to enhance that recovery. These exercises are tedious and at times painful. If Susy uses the principle of marginal analysis to make her decisions, what must be true about the costs and benefits of doing these exercises if Susy is to do them on a daily basis?

4. The two health insurance organizations in a community are trying to encourage their members to embrace healthier lifestyles. Healthlines is willing to pay 25% of the class fee for exercise classes offered at the local gym. Longhealth is willing to refund 50% of the class fee at the end of the class, provided that the instructor signs a form verifying that the member has attended at least 80% of the classes. Which fee structure is likely to result in the larger improvement in lifestyle choices? Explain the reasoning that underlies your answer.

5. Matt and Sarah are teenagers in Everycity, USA. Both of their families are concerned about their teenagers staying out late. Matt's family has a rule that if he returns home after midnight (even one minute late!) he loses his driving privileges for two weeks and cannot go out during that time. Sarah's family does not have a rule. Instead, before she goes out for the evening, Sarah and her family negotiate an expected time of return and Sarah then strives to honor this agreement. When she is running later than expected she calls her family so they will not be unduly worried. Compare and contrast these two approaches, paying particular attention to the set of incentives that the two approaches offer Matt and Sarah.

6. Suppose that Bill and Mary are the only individuals living in a community and that this community has no contact with the rest of the world. Bill grows tomatoes and corn while Mary grows wheat and onions. How does trade between Bill and Mary benefit both of them?

7. Wisconsin produces cheese and corn while Georgia produces peaches and peanuts. How does trade between these two states benefit the individuals who live in these two states?

8. a. Pedro enjoys getting a cup of coffee on his way to campus each morning. He can get a cup at Joe's for $1.50 or he can get a cup at Mary's for $2.00. The coffee is equivalent at both places and the waiting time in line is equivalent as well. Is this an equilibrium situation? Explain your answer.

    b. Suzanne cats a hamburger for lunch every Wednesday. She can purchase her hamburger at the Big Bun for $5.50 or she can purchase a similar hamburger at The Real McCoy for $7.00. Is this an equilibrium situation? Explain your answer.

9. a. The cafeteria at your college offers two desserts each night: soft-serve ice cream and some kind of cake or pie. Each night the cafeteria runs out of the soft-serve ice cream and finds that it has a surplus of the cake or pie. Is this situation efficient? Explain your answer.

b. A community provides bus service to its residents and charges $2.00 per ride. At this price, 98% of residents refuse to ride the buses and instead drive their cars. The community has serious air pollution problems from automobile emissions. Is this an efficient situation? Explain your answer.

c. A community ponders implementing a no-smoking ordinance that would eliminate smoking in all businesses, government offices, and public places. Smokers are upset and argue that their rights are being violated by this proposed ordinance. An independent analyst estimates that the benefits of the ordinance will be $100,000 a year while the cost of implementing the ordinance will be $40,000. Would it be efficient to implement the ordinance? Explain your answer.

10. France is debating a change in their unemployment insurance policy. Historically the country has been willing to provide generous benefits to the unemployed for a substantial period. The country is now debating whether to reduce the length of time that unemployed people can collect these benefits. Comment on the efficiency and equity aspects of this proposed change in policy.

11. The government of a country decides to mandate that all people younger than twenty-five years old must be in school and must pursue a college education. The government also passes the necessary legislation to fund this education for all of its citizens. Comment on the efficiency and equity aspects of this proposed policy.

12. Government sometimes intervenes to alter people's decisions. For each of the following situations comment on how the government intervention provides an incentive to change behavior and what the desired change in behavior is.

a. The government offers a free bus pass to all citizens living in metropolitan areas.

b. The government offers individuals an income tax refund of $2,000 a year if they reduce the number of cars they own in their household by one car.

c. The government requires all children younger than sixteen years old to be in school, and failure to comply results in the child's guardian being sent to jail.

d. The college you attend requires you to have an up-to-date immunization record before you can move into your dormitory.

13. A community sits on a rocky seacoast and each year several large ships run up against the rocks and sink. The community would benefit from installing a lighthouse, but the lighthouse has not been built because no individuals are willing to pay for the construction of this lighthouse, knowing that once the lighthouse is built they can enjoy the lighthouse even if they did not contribute to its construction. Is there a solution to this problem? Explain your answer.

14. An economy experiences a recession in which the level of production of goods and services is lower than the level the economy is capable of producing. As the level of production falls, people decrease their level of spending. What can you conclude in general about the level of people's income in this economy?

15. An economy has a fixed amount of resources available to it during any given period. If there is too much spending in the economy during this time, how will the economy respond?

16. What can the government do to alter the level of spending during a recession? What can the government do to alter the level of spending during a period of inflation?

BEFORE YOU TAKE THE TEST

Chapter Review Questions

1. Camillo is offered two jobs: one pays a salary of $30,000 per year and offers four weeks of vacation, and the other job pays a salary of $32,000 per year and offers two weeks of vacation. What is the opportunity cost for Camillo of taking the job offering $32,000 per year?

a. $2,000 plus two weeks of vacation per year

b. $2,000 per year

c. two weeks of vacation per year

d. $30,000 plus two weeks of vacation per year

2. Ning decides to attend a special speaker presentation tonight at her college instead of staying in her dorm and listening to her music collection. Which of the following statements is true?

a. Ning faces no opportunity cost with regard to her decision since listening to music or attending the speaker are both free events.

b. The opportunity cost of Ning's decision is so small that it is not worth calculating.

c. The opportunity cost of Ning's decision is the loss of her evening of music listening.

d. The opportunity cost of Ning's decision includes the cost associated with hearing the speaker.

3. A firm is debating the purchase of an additional piece of machinery. The firm estimates that the machine will enable them to increase their revenue by $1,000 a month, but it will increase their monthly costs by $750. This firm applies the principle of marginal analysis and decides that

a. it should purchase the machine since the benefits from this additional equipment exceed the costs.

b. it should not purchase the machine since the benefits from this additional equipment are less than the costs.

4. Marie is training for a triathlon. She will need to be able to swim, bike, and run to compete successfully. On Tuesdays, Thursdays, and Saturdays she always swims, while on Mondays and Fridays she runs. On Wednesdays she bikes. On Sundays she can choose to rest, bike, swim, or run. When Marie chooses to rest on Sundays it must be the case that

a. Marie is lazy and not pushing herself to her fullest potential.

b. Marie perceives that the benefit of a day of rest exceeds the cost of a day of rest.

c. Marie has lost sight of her goal to compete successfully in the triathlon.

d. Marie is not able to compare the benefits and costs associated with biking, swimming, and running.

5. Scarcity of resources implies that
   a. people can do whatever they want and do not need to worry about making choices.
   b. life involves making choices about how to best use these scarce resources.
   c. societies need to invest time and money to discover more resources.
   d. only very wealthy individuals are not constrained by their resources.

6. Each day people make decisions about what to wear, what to eat, or where to work
   a. since they all face constraints that mean they cannot do everything they would like to do.
   b. without regard to the level of resources that are available to them.

7. The university in Smart, USA, has a parking problem and is looking into programs to alleviate the parking shortage. Which of the following ideas is likely to decrease by the greatest amount the number of cars parking on campus each day?
   a. Faculty and staff at the university all receive free parking permits.
   b. Faculty and staff at the university all pay a set fee per year for parking permits.
   c. Faculty and staff at the university must pay an hourly fee for each hour that they park on campus.
   d. Faculty and staff are exempt from any parking policies at the university since they need to be able to come to campus to do their jobs.

8. Salespeople working at Department Store of Suburbia are offered two compensation plans. Plan A pays the worker $4.00 per hour plus a 5% sales commission on the total dollar value of sales that this worker makes. Plan B pays the worker $6.00 per hour and does not include a sales commission. Total sales per hour per salesperson averages $100. Which of the following statements is true?
   a. Plan A will result in the salespeople being less helpful to customers than does plan B.
   b. Plan A will result in the salespeople being more helpful to customers than does plan B.

9. Trade between two individuals
   a. rarely is beneficial.
   b. usually benefits only one of the trading partners.
   c. usually requires some form of coercion.
   d. is beneficial to both of the individuals.

10. Trade between two countries
    a. always benefits the economically wealthier country more than the economically weaker country.
    b. usually benefits only one of the trading partners.
    c. usually is the result of some form of coercion.
    d. is beneficial to both of the countries.

11. An equilibrium
    a. is a situation in which people have exploited all opportunities to make themselves better off.
    b. is a situation in which no individual would be better off doing something different.
    c. usually is reached through changes in prices, which increase or decrease until there are no longer opportunities for individuals to make themselves better off.
    d. Answers (a), (b), and (c) are all true.

12. A situation is efficient when
   a. it is producing the maximum gains from trade that are possible given the resources available.
   b. the price of the good under consideration is as low as possible.
   c. one person is made better off even if some other person is made worse off.
   d. one group of people are made better off even if it harms some other group of people.

13. A college keeps its library open all night throughout the semester even though students study in the library after midnight only in the weeks immediately before midterms and final exams. This situation is
   a. efficient, since no one can be made better off with the available resources.
   b. inefficient, since the college could close the library after midnight for those weeks that are not right before the midterms or final exams and use the freed-up resources to provide other, more highly valued, services.
   c. too much of an administrative headache to solve.
   d. equitable, since it does not discriminate between different weeks in the semester.

14. A government policy gives everyone under thirty years of age a subsidy no matter what their level of income. From the perspective of the people under thirty, this policy
   a. may be equitable, since it guarantees everyone under thirty the same level of subsidy, but it is probably not efficient.
   b. is efficient, since the government simply writes a check for the same amount to everyone under thirty.

15. A government policy gives everyone under thirty years of age a subsidy no matter what their level of income. But, if you are a member of the ethnic group that runs the government you receive a subsidy that is twice the size of the subsidy paid to people who do not belong to this ethnic group. From the perspective of the people under thirty, this policy
   a. is inequitable, since the individual's ethnic identity alters the level of the subsidy available to the individual.
   b. is equitable, since each person under thirty is treated the same as every other person under thirty in their ethnic group.

16. Government intervention in a market
   a. is never a good idea.
   b. can improve an outcome if the market fails to provide the good or the right amount of the good.
   c. should not occur if there are side payments from the provision of the good that the market does not include.
   d. always reduces the level of efficiency.

17. When one group of people in an economy decreases their spending, this will
   a. have no effect on the level of income of other people in the economy.
   b. increase the level of income of other people in the economy.
   c. decrease the level of income of other people in the economy.
   d. lead to inflationary pressures in this economy.

18. When one group of people in an economy increases their spending, this will
    a. have no effect on the level of income of other people in the economy.
    b. increase the level of income of other people in the economy.
    c. decrease the level of income of other people in the economy.
    d. lead to inflationary pressures in this economy.

19. When there is too much spending in an economy relative to production, this leads to
    a. a recession in that economy.
    b. inflation in that economy.

20. In a recession, the government can increase the level of spending in the economy by
    a. decreasing taxes.
    b. decreasing government spending.

█ ANSWER KEY

Answers to Problems and Exercises

1. **a.** Sarah's decision to attend the concert has two opportunity costs: attending the concert means that she will be unable to attend the movie, and in addition, to attend the concert she must pay $10 for a ticket. Her decision to attend the concert means that she is giving up whatever she could have purchased with the $10.

b. The business gives up $10,000 to get the property, but this is not an opportunity cost since the business must have a business location to exist. However, there is an opportunity cost to this decision: the business gives up the additional business it would have gotten at the prime location during the first six months.

c. When he decides to take the internship, Jamie incurs an opportunity cost of $2,000, since he is giving up this income to work in the intern position.

d. Roberto's opportunity cost with regard to his studying is his diminished grade in organic chemistry. (Obviously Roberto might want to consider some combination of studying that allows him to prepare for both exams, but this question did not offer that possibility.)

2. Remember that opportunity cost measures what is given up, so when Roberto studies more for his economics exam, he is giving up time he could devote to his organic chemistry exam. This decision will therefore affect his organic chemistry grade. Similarly, if Roberto devotes more time to studying for his organic chemistry exam, then he will be giving up points on his economics exam.

a. The opportunity cost of studying 15 hours for the economics exam instead of 10 hours is two points on the organic chemistry exam.

b. The opportunity cost of studying 15 hours for the organic chemistry exam instead of 10 hours is ten points on the economics exam.

c. The opportunity cost of studying 20 hours for the economics exam instead of 10 hours is five points on the organic chemistry exam.

d. The opportunity cost of studying 20 hours for the organic chemistry exam instead of 10 hours is twenty points on the economics exam.

3. **a.** Joe will want to think about the benefits of eating another slice of cake (tastes good, delays the start of his studying, prolongs the amount of time he can spend with his friends) to the costs of eating another slice of cake (an additional hour of exercise to maintain a steady weight, a feeling of guilt, an unhealthy balance in his diet). If Joe decides that the costs associated with the additional slice of cake outweigh the benefits, he will decide not to eat the cake. But if he decides that the benefits outweigh the costs, he will eat the cake.

b. Since the community enacts the ordinance, it must be the case that the benefits from the new ordinance outweigh the costs; in other words, the community must anticipate that this ordinance will generate more than $500,000 worth of benefits to their community.

c. Susy must perceive that the benefits of doing the exercises each day are greater than the costs of doing them every day.

4. Longhealth's policy rewards people who not only sign up for the class but also participate in the class. If the goal is to alter people's lifestyle choices toward more exercise, then Longhealth's policy offers the better set of incentives. Although Healthlines subsidizes the exercise class, it does not provide any incentive to ensure that members actually attend and participate in the class.

5. The incentives Matt faces are quite clear: being late carries a major penalty, so Matt will try hard to make sure he gets home on time. This may lead Matt to drive faster than is optimal in order to avoid his family's wrath. Unfortunately, the set of incentives offered to Matt may get him home early on most nights, but it may also result in a tragic outcome if he is running late. Sarah, on the other hand, faces a set of incentives that encourages her growth by forecasting what she is going to do, taking responsibility for what she is doing, and recognizing that even a well-planned evening may run late. Sarah knows that she is responsible for getting in at the time she agreed to, but she also knows that if she is running late she need not speed to get home.

6. Without trade, Bill would have only tomatoes and corn to eat; by trading, Bill gets more variety in his diet. This argument is also true for Mary, who would have only wheat and onions to eat if she did not trade with Bill.

7. Without trade, both states would have less variety in the goods available to their residents. With trade, Wisconsin residents can enjoy Georgia peaches and peanuts and Georgia residents can enjoy Wisconsin cheese and corn.

8. **a.** This is not an equilibrium situation. If the coffee is equivalent and the waiting times the same, then people should go to Joe's for the less expensive cup of coffee. One would anticipate that over time the price at Mary's will fall and that the price of Joe's will rise until the two prices converge.

   b. This is not an equilibrium situation. If the hamburgers are equivalent, then people should go to the Big Bun for the less expensive hamburger. One would anticipate that over time the price of hamburgers at the two restaurants will converge at a single price.

9. **a.** This is not an efficient situation since clearly the cafeteria is failing to provide the type of dessert that is preferred by the students. The cafeteria could make students better off by providing a larger amount of soft-serve ice cream and a smaller amount of cake or pie.

   b. If we assume that the air pollution seriously affects the quality of life in this community, then this is not an efficient situation. If the community drove less and rode the bus more, then the quality of life would be enhanced in the community and people would be better off. The community might be able to move toward this outcome by reducing the price of bus transportation dramatically and by instituting other types of charges for those who opt to travel by car.

   c. Yes, it would be efficient to implement this ordinance. It would even be possible to compensate the smokers for their loss of rights and still have the benefits from the ordinance exceed the costs of the ordinance.

10. The proposed policy moves the country toward a more efficient outcome, since a reduction in the length of time that unemployed people can collect benefits will encourage the unemployed to resume work and therefore result in fewer wasted resources. People may feel that this policy change is unfair, however, since historically the country has been willing to provide more generous support to the unemployed.

11. Because this policy covers all individuals within the designated group, it is equitable, but it is highly inefficient since it requires everyone to do the same thing regardless of their interests and abilities. The policy also requires a large amount of resources to implement that the government could use in alternative ways. For example, the government might want to provide job training in fields that would be beneficial to the economy but are not taught in a college curriculum (for example, carpentry, mechanical repair, drafting).

12. **a.** The government subsidizes bus ridership by providing free bus passes, which reduces the cost of riding the bus while increasing the cost of using a car. The government wishes to encourage people to use the bus system more and the private transportation system less.

    b. The government provides a financial reward for altering your household's car usage. By reducing the number of cars in each household, the government hopes to reduce the number of miles driven and the emissions from automobiles.

    c. The government's incentive here is a negative incentive. Guardians do not wish to serve time in jail, and their wish to avoid this outcome will result in their children going to school.

    d. The college wants to reduce the risk of transmission of highly communicable diseases in the dormitories. They limit your ability to engage in student activities until you can provide proof that you are immunized.

13. In this case, the lighthouse will not be built through the contributions of individuals in the community. The market will fail to provide the lighthouse, but the government can intervene by imposing a tax for the construction of the lighthouse and then providing these funds to the community for the construction.

14. When people reduce their spending and purchase fewer goods and services, the level of income that other people in the economy earn is reduced since the purchases by one group of people represent income for another group of people. In a recession, the level of spending and the level of income fall in an economy.

15. With a fixed amount of resources in an economy during a given period, there is a limit to the amount of goods and services the economy can produce. If spending is greater than this economic capacity, then this puts pressure on the prices of goods and services to rise, leading to inflationary pressures. Too much spending in an economy results in inflation.

16. A recession implies that the level of spending in the economy is too low. The government can stimulate spending by decreasing the level of taxes, by increasing the level of government spending, or by having the central bank increase the money supply. When there is inflation in an economy, the government can slow down spending by increasing the level of taxes, by decreasing the level of government spending, or by having the central bank decrease the money supply. The textbook will discuss these issues in much greater detail in subsequent chapters.

Answers to Chapter Review Questions

1. **Answer c.** The opportunity cost of taking the job includes what must be given up. In this case, Camillo is giving up two weeks of vacation since the other job offers four weeks of vacation instead of two weeks. He is not giving up any salary when he selects the job paying $32,000.

2. **Answer c.** Ning's opportunity cost is measured by what she must give up when she chooses to do something else. In this case, when Ning decides to attend the lecture she is giving up a night of listening to music in her dorm room.

3. **Answer a.** The firm should purchase this equipment since the addition to revenue ($1,000 a month) is greater than the addition to cost ($750 a month).

4. **Answer b.** In making a decision about whether to run, swim, bike, or rest, Marie should compare the benefits she gets from additional exercise to the costs she incurs from this additional exercise. When she elects to rest, she perceives that the additional costs of the exercise exceed the additional benefits of the exercise.

5. **Answer b.** When resources are scarce, this implies that people and societies must make decisions about how to use those scarce resources since the scarcity of resources is a constraint on production and consumption.

6.   **Answer a.** People must make decisions every day because they do not have an infinite amount of time, income, or resources that would allow them to do everything they might want to do.

7.   **Answer c.** To get the university community to curtail their parking on campus by the greatest amount, the university should adopt a program that makes drivers aware of the cost of bringing a car on campus every time they drive on campus. Thus, charging an hourly parking fee is the best choice offered, since this fee will serve to remind drivers that bringing a car to campus will cost them something each time they drive on campus and park. In contrast, a single annual fee does not reward the purchaser for reducing the number of times they park on campus during the year; free parking indicates that parking on campus does not cost anything and will result in people parking on campus more often; and exempting the staff from parking fees eliminates incentives to get staff to think about alternatives to driving on campus and parking.

8.   **Answer b.** When salespeople are awarded the base salary plus a commission, they are encouraged to be helpful to shoppers in the hope of boosting their sales figures. When offered a flat hourly rate, they have no incentive to provide helpful service beyond the minimum required by the store, since their compensation will not be affected by their extra effort.

9.   **Answer d.** Individuals who elect to trade with each other do so because the trade is beneficial to them. As long as trade is a choice, then the decision to trade with each other must indicate that the trade is beneficial to both parties.

10. **Answer d.** Countries that elect to trade with each other do so because the trade is beneficial to them. As long as trade is a choice, then the decision to trade with each other must indicate that the trade is beneficial to both parties.

11. **Answer d.** All three of these responses describe equilibrium. They are true either by definition or by implication.

12. **Answer a.** Answers (c) and (d) are essentially the same answer, with answer (c) focusing on the individual while answer (d) focuses on the group: both are incorrect. That leaves answers (a) and (b): a situation is efficient when no one can be made better off through a different outcome. This implies that the maximum gains from trade are achieved when a situation is efficient, and this does not necessarily occur when price is as low as possible.

13. **Answer b.** Since college students do not use the library throughout the semester in the early morning hours, the college is not using its scarce resources efficiently when it elects to keep the library open all night. It would be more efficient to open the library all night only during those weeks when students would actually avail themselves of these hours.

14. **Answer a.** This policy treats everyone under thirty equally and so it is an equitable policy from that perspective. However, the policy is not efficient since it does not consider whether this is an efficient use of the resources involved.

15. **Answer a.** This policy is not equitable since it does not treat everyone under thirty equally: instead it discriminates on the basis of ethnicity.

16. **Answer b.** This is a definitional statement. Answer (a) is incorrect since there are times when government intervention is helpful (for example, regulation of certain industries or laws restricting pollution); answer (c) is incorrect since government intervention may be called for when there are side payments that the market does not account for; and answer (d) is incorrect since there are occasions when government intervention can improve the efficiency of the market.

17. **Answer c.** This is true by definition. If spending is reduced by one group in an economy, then some other individuals in the economy will not receive as much income as they initially did due to this reduction in spending.

18. **Answer b.** This is true by definition. An increase in spending in an economy indicates that some people in that economy will receive that additional spending and, hence, their incomes will rise.

19. **Answer b.** When spending increases at a faster pace than the production of goods and services, then this leads to upward pressure on the prices of those goods and services. Hence, this spending will lead to inflation.

20. **Answer a.** If the government decreases taxes, this tax decrease results in people having higher net incomes and, therefore, more income available to spend. This leads to greater spending. In contrast, if the government decreases government spending, there is less spending in the economy.

chapter 2

Economic Models:
Trade-offs and Trade

■ BEFORE YOU READ THE CHAPTER

Summary

This chapter introduces the concept of model building and then discusses two different economic models, the model of production possibility frontiers and the model of comparative advantage. Models are a simplified representation of reality, and the study of economic models will be a crucial aspect of your study of economics. The two models presented in this chapter provide a simplified framework for discussing the concept of opportunity cost, trade-offs, scarcity, efficiency, and gains from trade. This chapter uses the production possibility frontier model to discuss comparative advantage and the gains that are possible through trade. The chapter also presents the circular flow diagram as a way to describe a simple economy and, in addition, discusses the distinction between positive and normative economics.

Chapter Objectives

Objective #1. A model is a simplified representation of reality that is used to better understand real-life situations. Underlying every model is a set of assumptions.

Objective #2. The production possibility frontier is a model that represents the production possibilities available to an individual or to an economy. The production possibility frontier model assumes that the individual (or country) has a set amount of resources, a set level of technology, and a set amount of time, and then the production possibility frontier delineates a set of points that indicate the maximum amount of two goods that can be produced by this individual (or country) given their resources, technology, and available time. For simplicity, this Study Guide refers to production possibility frontiers in terms of production by countries rather than individuals, but the arguments made from the perspective of countries also hold for individuals. Figure 2.1 illustrates a linear production possibility frontier for a country, where the frontier indicates the maximum amount of goods X and Y that can be produced from the available resources and technology. Points A and B are points that lie on the production possibility frontier and are feasible production points for this country. Points C and D are points that lie inside the production possibility frontier: this country can produce these points—they are feasible—but the country is not using its available resources fully. Points C and D are therefore feasible points, but not efficient points. Points *E* and *F* lie outside the production possibility frontier and are therefore not feasible points of production for this country.

Figure 2.1

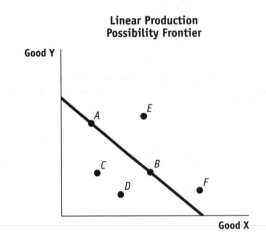

Linear Production
Possibility Frontier

Objective #3. The simplest version of this production possibility frontier model assumes that the frontier is linear and thus has a constant slope. This implies that the opportunity cost of producing another unit of the good measured on the *x*-axis stays the same as you move along the production possibility frontier. In Figure 2.2 the opportunity cost of moving from point *A* to point *B* and the opportunity cost of moving from point *C* to point *D* are illustrated. Remember that opportunity cost measures what you give up to get something: thus, when moving from point *A* to point *B*, opportunity cost is measured in terms of good Y, the good you give up to get more of good X; whereas, when moving from point *C* to point *D*, opportunity cost is measured in terms of good X, the good you give up to get more of good Y. The lines that are bold in Figure 2.2 indicate the opportunity cost of moving from point *A* to point *B* or from point *C* to point *D*.

Figure 2.2

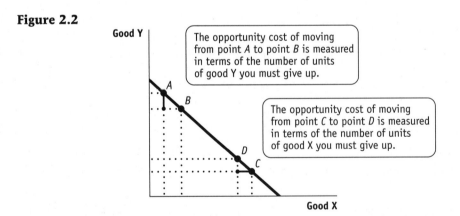

The opportunity cost of moving from point *A* to point *B* is measured in terms of the number of units of good Y you must give up.

The opportunity cost of moving from point *C* to point *D* is measured in terms of the number of units of good X you must give up.

Objective #4. A more realistic production possibility frontier is one that is bowed out from the origin: this implies that as the country produces more and more of one of the goods, the opportunity cost of producing this good increases. The production possibility frontier has this shape due to specialization of resources: some of the resources available to the country are more suited to produce good X than they are good Y. When the country decides to increase the production of one type of good, the first few units can be produced at relatively low opportunity cost since resources can be shifted from the production of one good to the production of the other good that are not particularly well suited to the production of the first good. However, the opportunity cost eventually will rise since the increased production of this good eventually will require the use of resources that are ill-suited to produce this good. Figure 2.3 illustrates a bowed-out production possibility frontier and the opportunity cost of getting one more unit of the good measured on the *x*-axis. Notice that as we get more and more units of good X, the opportunity cost of each additional unit of X is larger than the opportunity cost of the preceding unit.

Figure 2.3

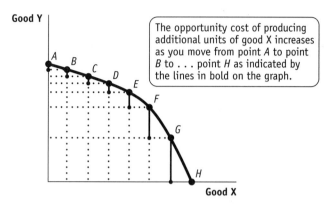

Good Y

The opportunity cost of producing additional units of good X increases as you move from point *A* to point *B* to . . . point *H* as indicated by the lines in bold on the graph.

Good X

Objective #5. There are two types of efficiency to discuss with respect to production possibility frontiers: productive efficiency and allocative efficiency. Productive efficiency refers to producing at a point that lies on the production possibility frontier. Points that lie inside the frontier are inefficient, since it is possible to increase the level of production from the given set of resources. Allocative efficiency refers to producing the right mix of goods from the available resources. For an economy to be allocatively efficient it must allocate its resources in such a way as to make consumers as well off as possible. Another way of saying this is that an allocatively efficient economy produces the mix of goods that people want.

Objective #6. For an economy to be efficient it must achieve productive and allocative efficiency: it must not waste resources and it must produce the right mix of goods.

Objective #7. The production possibility frontier illustrates scarcity in that there are points of production that cannot be produced because the level of resources and/or technology constrain production. The production possibility frontier illustrates trade-offs: getting more of good X requires giving up some of good Y.

Objective #8. Economic growth can be illustrated with the production possibility frontier model. When the frontier shifts away from the origin, this means that the represented economy can now produce more of good X and good Y. The production possibility frontier shifts out when there are increases in resources or increases in the available level of technology.

Objective #9. The model of production possibility frontiers can also be used to illustrate the gains from trade, which is referred to as the model of comparative advantage. This model assumes that there are two countries, that there are two goods that the countries produce, and that each country has a set amount of resources, technology, and time available to them. Furthermore, this model assumes that the two countries have different opportunity costs of production. In this model, countries benefit from specializing in the production of that good for which they have the comparative advantage, or lower opportunity cost of production, and then trade with each other. Countries do not have to have absolute advantage in production to benefit from trade: the benefits from trade only require that countries have different opportunity costs of production for the two goods and that each country specialize in producing the good that it can produce at lower opportunity cost relative to the other country.

Objective #10. The simple circular flow diagram of the economy can be used to describe the relationship between firms and households. In this simple circular-flow diagram, households provide factors of production to firms, while firms provide goods and services to households.

Objective #11. Positive economics is factual and descriptive, whereas normative economics is about what ought to be or what should be. Positive economics is objective and can be tested for accuracy, and it often involves forecasting. Normative economics is subjective and prescriptive, and it is value based. However, it is possible to rank normative policies designed to achieve a certain prescription on the basis of the efficiency of each policy.

Objective #12. Economists may come to different conclusions because they have different values or because they use different economic models.

Key Terms

model a simplified representation of a real situation that is used to better understand real-life situations.

other things equal assumption in the development of a model, the assumption that all relevant factors except the one under study remain unchanged.

production possibility frontier illustrates the trade-offs facing an economy that produces only two goods. It shows the maximum quantity of one good that can be produced for any given quantity produced of the other.

factors of production the *resources* used to produce goods and services. Labor and capital are examples of factors.

technology the technical means for producing goods and services.

comparative advantage the advantage conferred on an individual or nation in producing a good or service if the *opportunity cost* of producing the good or service is lower for that individual or nation than for other producers.

absolute advantage the advantage conferred on an individual in an activity if he or she can do it better than other people.

barter people directly exchange goods or services that they have for goods or services that they want.

circular-flow diagram represents the transactions in an *economy* by two kinds of flows around a circle: flows of physical things such as goods or labor in one direction and flows of money to pay for these physical things in the opposite direction.

household a person or a group of people that share their income.

firm an organization that produces goods and services for sale.

markets for goods and services markets in which *firms* sell goods and services that they produce to *households*.

factor markets markets in which *firms* buy the *resources* they need to produce goods and services.

Notes

Key Terms *(continued)*

income distribution the way in which total income is divided among the owners of the various factors of production.

positive economics the branch of economic analysis that describes the way the *economy* actually works.

normative economics the branch of economic analysis that makes prescriptions about the way the *economy* should work.

forecast a simple prediction of the future.

variable a quantity that can take on more than one value.

horizontal axis the horizontal number line of a graph along which values of the *x*-variable are measured; also referred to as the *x-axis.*

x-axis the horizontal number line of a graph along which values of the *x*-variable are measured; also referred to as the *horizontal axis.*

vertical axis the vertical number line of a graph along which values of the *y*-variable are measured; also referred to as the *y-axis.*

y-axis the vertical number line of a graph along which values of the *y*-variable are measured; also referred to as the *vertical axis.*

origin the point where the axes of a two-variable graph meet.

causal relationship the relationship between two variables in which the value taken by one variable directly influences or determines the value taken by the other variable.

independent variable the determining variable in a causal relationship.

dependent variable the determined variable in a causal relationship.

curve a line on a graph, which may be curved or straight, that depicts a relationship between two variables.

linear relationship the relationship between two variables in which the *slope* is constant and therefore is depicted on a graph by a *curve* that is a straight line.

nonlinear relationship the relationship between two variables in which the *slope* is not constant and therefore is depicted on a graph by a *curve* that is not a straight line.

positive relationship a relationship between two variables in which an increase in the value of one variable is associated with an increase in the value of the other variable. It is illustrated by a *curve* that slopes upward from left to right.

negative relationship a relationship between two variables in which an increase in the value of one variable is associated with a decrease in the value of the other variable. It is illustrated by a *curve* that slopes downward from left to right.

horizontal intercept the point at which a *curve* hits the *horizontal axis;* it indicates the value of the *x*-variable when the value of the *y*-variable is zero.

Notes

Key Terms *(continued)*

vertical intercept the point at which a *curve* hits the *vertical axis;* it shows the value of the *y*-variable when the value of the *x*-variable is zero.

slope a measure of how steep a line or curve is. The slope of a line is measured by "rise over run"—the change in the *y*-variable between two points on the line divided by the change in the *x*-variable between those same two points.

nonlinear curve a curve in which the *slope* is not the same between every pair of points.

absolute value the value of a number without regard to a plus or minus sign.

tangent line a straight line that just touches a *nonlinear curve* at a particular point; the *slope* of the tangent line is equal to the slope of the nonlinear curve at that point.

maximum the highest point on a *nonlinear curve*, where the *slope* changes from positive to negative.

minimum the lowest point on a *nonlinear curve*, where the *slope* changes from negative to positive.

time-series graph a two-variable graph that has dates on the *horizontal axis* and values of a variable that occurred on those dates on the *vertical axis.*

scatter diagram a graph that shows points that correspond to actual observations of the *x*- and *y*-variables; a *curve* is usually fitted to the scatter of points to indicate the trend in the data.

pie chart a circular graph that shows how some total is divided among its components, usually expressed in percentages.

bar graph a graph that uses bars of varying height or length to show the comparative sizes of different observations of a variable.

truncated cut; in a truncated axis, some of the range of values are omitted, usually to save space.

omitted variable an unobserved *variable* that, through its influence on other variables, creates the erroneous appearance of a direct *causal relationship* among those variables.

reverse causality the error committed when the true direction of causality between two *variables* is reversed, and the *independent variable* and the *dependent variable* are incorrectly identified.

■ AFTER YOU READ THE CHAPTER

Tips

Tip #1.   This chapter introduces the concept of models. This is a crucial concept that forms the basis of the majority of material you will study in the rest of the course. In working with models it is important to understand the simplifying assumptions underlying whatever model you are using.

Tip #2.   Many of the models you will encounter in this course make the other-things-equal assumption, which means that the model considers only one change at a time while holding everything else constant. Make sure you understand this basic assumption before working with the models introduced in the chapter.

Tip #3.   Economic models can be described verbally, but they can also be represented by graphs or equations. You will want to be comfortable working with all three types of representations. The appendix to Chapter 2 provides an introduction to graphs in economics.

Tip #4.   Throughout the course you will find it helpful to be able to sketch graphs to illustrate the ideas you are analyzing. You should practice making precise, numerically significant graphs, but you also should practice less formal graphs that sketch the nature of the relationship rather than the precise mathematical relationship.

Tip #5.   Opportunity cost can be measured using the production possibility frontier model. To do this calculation pick a point on the production possibility frontier and identify how much of each good is being produced. Then pick a second point on the production possibility frontier and identify the new levels of production. The opportunity cost is measured as the number of units of the good you must give up to get more of the other good. Note that both points must be on the production possibility frontier. Figure 2.4 illustrates the measurement of opportunity cost when moving from point A to point B. In this example, the opportunity cost is measured as the amount of good Y, $Y_1 - Y_2$, that must be given up to increase the production of good X from its initial value of X_1 to the new level X_2. The bold line indicates the amount of good Y that is given up to increase the production of good X from X_1 to X_2.

Figure 2.4

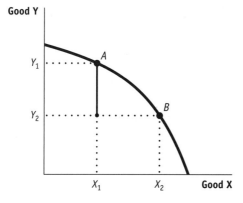

Tip #6.   You should practice working with the models and with specific techniques introduced with each model. For instance, you should be comfortable calculating opportunity cost using the production possibility frontier model. You also should be comfortable comparing the opportunity cost of production for two countries and deciding which good each country should specialize in producing.

Tip #7. If you are using flash cards, make sure you include the following cards: (a) a linear production possibility frontier indicating feasible and infeasible points as well as efficient and inefficient points, (b) a production possibility frontier bowed out from the origin showing these same concepts, and (c) an example of comparative advantage that illustrates two countries and then calculates each country's comparative advantage. Also, don't forget to include a card for each new vocabulary word as well as the chapter heading on each card.

Tip #8. Calculating opportunity cost in a problem is often challenging for students initially. Let's explore a fail-safe method for this calculation based on a linear production possibility frontier (this is the type of production possibility frontier that we will use in the comparative advantage model). First, construct the production possibility frontier and, since it is linear, calculate the slope of the frontier. Then use this slope measure to generate the opportunity costs you want: the opportunity cost of producing one more unit of the good measured on the x-axis is given by the slope, since the slope tells us the change in the y-variable divided by the change in the x-variable. Thus, if the slope of the production possibility frontier is −2, then the opportunity cost of producing an additional unit of good X is 2 units of good Y. To find the opportunity cost of the good produced on the y-axis, we simply need to use the reciprocal of the slope. Thus, if the slope of the linear production possibility frontier is −2, then the opportunity cost of producing one more unit of good Y is ½ unit of good X, since this is the amount of good X we must give up to get one more unit of good Y. The problems in this chapter will give you a chance to practice this reasoning and this technique.

Tip #9. Once you can calculate the opportunity cost of producing good X or good Y, then you can compare the opportunity costs faced by two countries. The model of comparative advantage illustrates that countries will benefit from trade when they specialize and produce the good that has the lowest opportunity cost of production relative to the other country.

WORKED PROBLEMS

1. People often face trade-offs about the use of their resources. In this problem, Joe can produce either bicycles or sweaters. The following points lie on Joe's production possibility frontier and represent points where Joe is maximizing his production of the two goods given his available resources, technology, and time. Assume that Joe's production possibility frontier for these two goods is linear.

Production point	Bicycles per year	Sweaters per year
A	160	20
B	120	40
C	60	70
D	40	80

a. Draw a graph of Joe's production possibility frontier. In your graph measure bicycles on the y-axis and sweaters on the x-axis.

STEP 1: Draw a graph of Joe's production possibility frontier using the given points in the table. The following figure provides a graph of the Joe's production possibility frontier based upon the points given in the provided table.

Review the section "Models in Economics: Some Important Examples" on pages 26–39, the section "Trade-offs: The Production Possibility Frontier" on pages 27–32 (along with Figure 2-1), and the section "How Graphs Work" on pages 49–52.

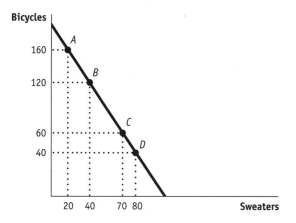

b. Write an equation for Joe's production possibility frontier.

STEP 2: Use the slope-intercept form to write an equation for Joe's production possibility frontier. The slope-intercept form is given as $y = mx + b$, where y is the variable measured on the vertical axis (in this case bicycles, B), x is the variable measured on the horizontal axis (in this case sweaters, S), m is the slope of the equation, and b is the y-intercept.

Review "Chapter 2 Appendix: Graphs in Economics" on pages 49–64.

To write the equation for Joe's production possibility frontier, you will need to know the slope of the frontier as well as the y-intercept for the frontier. Since the frontier is linear, the slope will be constant and equal to the change in the bicycles divided by the change in sweaters. Thus, moving from point A to point B, the slope is equal to $(160 - 120)/(20 - 40) = -2$. To find the y-intercept, you can use the general formula for a linear equation, $y = mx + b$, and substitute in the slope measure you just computed for m, and replace the y and x with B and S (where B is the number of bicycles and S is the number of sweaters). Thus, $y = mx + b$ is now $B = -2S + b$. To find the y-intercept, b, you need to replace (S,B) with values that you know are on the line. For example, you know that point A is on the line and that point A consists of 20 sweaters and 160 bicycles. Thus, $B = -2S + b$ can be written as $160 = -2(20) + b$. Solving for b, you will find that $b = 200$. You can use any of the points you are given in the table to find this y-intercept: the only requirement is that the point must lie on the production possibility frontier. The following figure illustrates Joe's production possibility frontier while identifying both the y-intercept and the x-intercept (to find the x-intercept, use the basic formula $B = -2S + 200$ and substitute $B = 0$ into this equation: thus, $S = 100$).

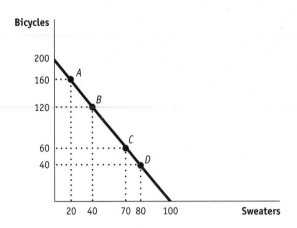

c. Consider each of the following production points and determine whether the production point is (1) feasible and efficient; (2) feasible and inefficient; or (3) infeasible (that is, the point lies beyond the production possibility frontier). Hint: you may find the equation you wrote in part (b) helpful in determining the attributes of these production points.

   i. 30 sweaters and 150 bicycles

   ii. 15 sweaters and 170 bicycles

   iii. 90 sweaters and 15 bicycles

   iv. 75 sweaters and 55 bicycles

STEP 3: Using the equation for Joe's production possibility frontier you found in part (b), check each of the previously mentioned points to see if they lie on his production possibility frontier, lie beyond his production possibility frontier, or lie inside his production possibility frontier.

Review the section "Trade-offs: The Production Possibility Frontier" on pages 27–32 and the section "Efficiency" on pages 29–30.

   i. This point is infeasible. To see this, use the equation you found in part (b) and plug in the value for S. Thus, $B = -2S + 200$ and you are told that sweater production is 30. So, $B = -2(30) + 200 = 140$. The maximum number of bicycles that can be produced when 30 sweaters are produced is 140 and not 150. The point (30, 150) lies beyond Joe's production possibility frontier and therefore is not feasible.

   ii. This point is feasible and efficient. To see this, use the equation from part (b) and this point. Thus, $B = -2(15) + 200 = 170$. The point (15, 170) lies on Joe's production possibility frontier: it is both feasible and efficient.

   iii. This point is feasible but inefficient. To see this, use the equation from part (b) and this point. Thus, $B = -2(90) + 200 = 20$. The point (90, 15) lies inside Joe's production possibility frontier since the point (90, 20) lies on his frontier. This point is therefore feasible but inefficient.

   iv. This point is infeasible. To see this, use the equation from part (b) and this point. Thus, $B = -2(75) + 200 = 50$. The point (75, 55) lies outside Joe's production possibility frontier since the point (75, 50) lies on his frontier. This point is therefore not feasible.

   d. Suppose that Joe experiences an improvement in his sweater-making technology so that he can now produce twice as many sweaters as he could initially. Assume that his ability to produce bicycles has not changed. Draw this new production possibility frontier for Joe and then write an equation for this new production possibility frontier.

STEP 4: Draw Joe's new production possibility frontier and compare it to his original production possibility frontier.

Review the section "Economic Growth" on pages 31–32 (along with Figure 2-3).

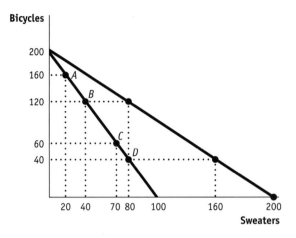

The equation for this new production possibility frontier is $B = -S + 200$.

2. The following graph depicts Susie's production possibility frontier for producing widgets and gadgets. In this problem assume that Susie is initially producing only widgets and no gadgets.

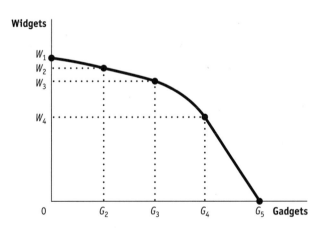

Use this graph to evaluate Susie's opportunity cost of moving from one point of her production possibility frontier to another point on her production possibility frontier.

    a. What is Susie's opportunity cost of producing G_2 units of gadgets if she is currently producing zero gadgets?

STEP 1: For questions (a), (b), and (c), refer to the previous graph and measure Susie's opportunity cost by what she must give up when moving from one point on her production possibility frontier to another point on her production possibility frontier.

Review the section "Opportunity Cost" on pages 30–31 (along with Figure 2-2).

The opportunity cost of producing G_2 units of gadgets is the number of widgets that must be given up. Initially Susie is producing W_1 widgets and 0 gadgets. When Susie moves along her production possibility frontier to produce G_2 units of gadgets, she finds that she must decrease her widget production to W_2. The opportunity cost of this gadget production is therefore equal to $(W_1 - W_2)$ units of widgets.

b. Suppose that Susie is now producing G_2 units of gadgets and that she is producing at a point on her production possibility frontier. What is the opportunity cost of producing G_3 units of gadgets?

The opportunity cost of producing G_3 units of gadgets is the number of widgets that must be given up. Using the same logic as in the answer to part (a), this opportunity cost can be calculated as the distance $(W_2 - W_3)$ since this distance measures the number of widgets that Susie must give up in order to increase her gadget production from G_2 units to G_3 units.

c. Suppose that Susie is now producing G_3 units of gadgets and that she is producing at a point on her production possibility frontier. What is the opportunity cost of producing G_4 units of gadgets?

The opportunity cost of producing G_4 units of gadgets is the number of widgets that must be given up. Using the same logic as in the answer to part (a), this opportunity cost can be calculated as the distance $(W_3 - W_4)$ since this distance measures the number of widgets that Susie must give up in order to increase her gadget production from G_3 to G_4 units.

d. What happens to Susie's opportunity cost of producing gadgets as she decides to produce increasing amounts of gadgets? Provide a verbal explanation and then use the preceding graph to illustrate what happens to Susie's opportunity cost as she produces more and more gadgets.

STEP 2: Refer to the graph and use it to see what happens to Susie's opportunity cost as she increases her production of gadgets by one unit at a time starting with zero units of gadgets. Remember that her opportunity cost of producing a gadget is measured by the number of widgets she must give up.

Review the section "Opportunity Cost" (along with Figure 2-2) on pages 30–31.

As Susie produces more and more gadgets, her opportunity cost increases. Since her production possibility frontier is bowed outward from the origin, this indicates that Susie's available resources are specialized, with some of those resources being more suited to widget production while others are more suited to gadget production. This idea of increasing opportunity cost is illustrated on the following graph.

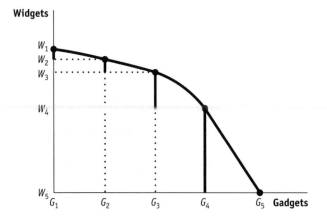

Notice that the bold vertical lines get longer and longer as we move from 0 units of gadgets to a larger level of gadget production (e.g., G_4). The length of the bold vertical lines measures the opportunity cost of that level of gadget production: for example, the opportunity cost of moving from 0 units of gadgets to G_2 units of gadgets is given by the vertical distance ($W_1 - W_2$).

e. Suppose that Susie had initially produced only gadgets and no widgets. Does the opportunity cost of producing widgets increase as Susie increases her widget production by one unit at a time from 0 units of widgets to W_1 units of widgets? Use a graph to illustrate your answer.

STEP 3: Now, you want to use the graph to think about moving from the point that corresponds to G_5 units of gadgets and 0 units of widgets to the point that corresponds to 0 units of gadgets and W_1 units of widgets. As you move upward along the curve increasing widget production by one unit at a time, remember that the opportunity cost of this increased widget production will be measured by the number of gadgets that must be given up.

Review the section "Opportunity Cost" (along with Figure 2-2) on pages 30–31.

The law of increasing opportunity cost holds if Susie moves from producing only gadgets to producing a mix of gadgets and widgets. The following graph illustrates this idea by considering changing the production of widgets by one unit at a time. Notice that in this case the opportunity cost is measured as a horizontal distance since increasing widget production implies giving up gadget production: thus, the opportunity cost of producing widgets is measured by the number of gadgets that must be given up.

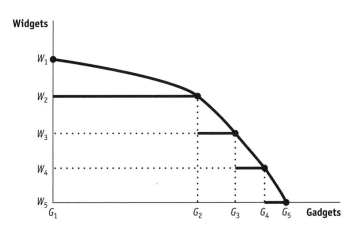

3. The following provides a numerical example of how trade is advantageous to two countries that decide to trade with each other. Suppose there are two countries, Arcadia and Supreme, that produce bricks and windows. Arcadia and Supreme use only labor to produce these two goods, and each country has 200 units of available labor. The following table provides information about the number of hours of labor needed in each country to produce one unit of bricks or one unit of windows.

	Hours of labor to produce one brick	Hours of labor to produce one window
Arcadia	2 hours of labor	4 hours of labor
Supreme	5 hours of labor	2 hours of labor

Use the table's information to draw production possibility frontiers for Arcadia and for Supreme. In your graph, measure bricks on the *x*-axis and windows on the *y*-axis. Then use your graph to find each country's opportunity cost of producing one brick. Identify each country's comparative advantage. Finally, calculate a range of prices for one brick in terms of windows.

STEP 1: Draw and label the production possibility frontiers for Arcadia and Supreme.

Review the section "Trade-offs: The Production Possibility Frontier" on pages 27–32 (along with Figure 2-1).

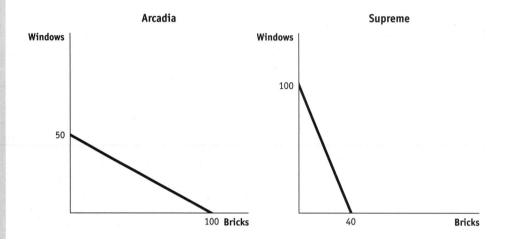

STEP 2: Find each country's opportunity cost of producing one brick, as measured by the number of windows that must be given up when the country produces one additional brick.

Review the section "Trade-offs: The Production Possibility Frontier" on pages 27–32 (along with Figure 2-1) and the section "Opportunity Cost" on pages 30–31.

The opportunity cost of producing one brick for Arcadia is ½ window. To see this, remember that the slope of the production possibility frontier tells you how many units of the good on the *y*-axis must be given up in order to get one more unit of the good on the *x*-axis. Since the slope of Arcadia's production possibility frontier is equal to –1/2, we know that the opportunity cost of one more brick is equal to ½ window. The opportunity cost of producing one brick for Supreme is 2.5 windows.

STEP 3: Identify each country's comparative advantage by comparing their opportunity cost of production for each good: a country has the comparative advantage in producing the good when its opportunity cost of producing the good is lower than the other country's opportunity cost of producing the good.

Review the section "Comparative Advantage and Gains from Trade" on pages 33–36 (along with Figure 2-5 and Table 2-2).

Arcadia has the comparative advantage in producing bricks since Arcadia can produce an additional brick at lower opportunity cost than can Supreme. One additional brick costs Arcadia ½ window, while it costs Supreme 2.5 windows: Arcadia can produce bricks at lower opportunity cost and therefore has a comparative advantage in brick production.

STEP 4: Find the range of prices for one brick in terms of windows.

Review the section "Comparative Advantage and Gains from Trade" on pages 33–36 (along with Figure 2-5 and Table 2-6).

Arcadia is willing to produce bricks for any price equal to or greater than ½ window. Supreme is willing to purchase one brick for any price equal to or less than 2.5 windows. The range of prices for one brick will therefore fall between ½ window and 2.5 windows.

4. All countries face scarcity of resources and must therefore make tough decisions about what they should produce. Consider the following example about the allocation of resources toward health care. Suppose that a kidney transplant costs $50,000, while immunizations against major childhood diseases cost $500 per child. Assume that a country has a total of $10 million available for these two programs and that there is no issue with regard to procuring the necessary kidneys for transplants. Use the provided information to construct the country's production possibility frontier, placing childhood immunizations on the horizontal axis and kidney transplants on the vertical axis. Use your graph to measure the opportunity cost of producing an additional kidney transplant as well as the opportunity cost of producing an additional childhood immunization. Use this example to discuss the trade-offs that an economy faces with regard to the production of these two goods.

STEP 1: Use the given information to construct a production possibility frontier for these two goods. Then use this figure to measure the opportunity cost of producing an additional unit of either good.

Review the section "Trade-offs: The Production Possibility Frontier" on pages 27–32 (along with Figure 2-1).

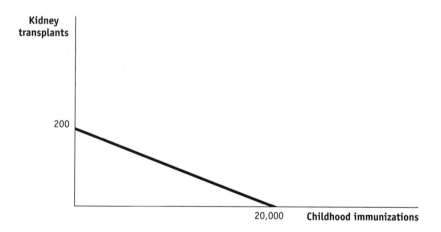

The opportunity cost of a kidney transplant is 100 immunizations. The opportunity cost of an immunization is (1/100) of a kidney transplant.

STEP 2: Use this example to discuss the trade-offs an economy faces with regard to the production of these two goods.

Review the section "Efficiency" on pages 29–30 and the section "Opportunity Cost" on pages 30–31.

If a country is faced with a limited amount of resources, it cannot produce an unlimited amount of goods and services. In this example, the country has only so many financial resources available for the production of kidney transplants and immunizations: the country will have to decide how to allocate these scarce resources, and in allocating these scarce resources it will face a trade-off where the decision to produce more kidney transplants implies a decision to provide fewer immunizations and vice versa.

5. In your study of economics it is helpful to practice certain mathematical techniques. With this example, practice the mathematics reviewed in the Appendix to Chapter 2. Use the production possibility frontier you constructed in problem 4 to determine whether the following production combinations are feasible and efficient (that is, the point lies on the production possibility frontier), are feasible and inefficient (that is, the combination lies inside the production possibility frontier), or are not feasible (that is, the combination lies beyond the production possibility frontier).
   a. 400 immunizations and 190 kidney transplants
   b. 10,000 immunizations and 100 kidney transplants
   c. 1,800 immunizations and 182 kidney transplants
   d. 3,200 immunizations and 170 kidney transplants

STEP 1: Write a mathematical equation expressing the relationship between kidney transplants (K) and childhood immunizations (I). Use this equation to evaluate each of the preceding combinations.

Review the section "Trade-offs: The Production Possibility Frontier" on pages 27–32, the section "Two-Variable Graphs" on pages 49–51, and the section "Curves on a Graph" on pages 51–52.

The equation for the linear production possibility frontier you found in problem 4 is $K = 200 - (1/100) I$, where K is kidney transplants and I is immunizations.
   a. You can then substitute the immunization value into the formula to calculate the maximum number of kidney transplants that are possible given this level of immunizations. Thus, $K = 200 - (1/100)(400)$, or $K = 196$. The combination of 400 immunizations and 190 kidney transplants must be feasible but inefficient since it is possible to produce 400 immunizations and 196 kidney transplants.
   b. Use the same technique: when this economy produces 10,000 immunizations, it can produce a maximum of 100 kidney transplants. This combination is feasible and efficient.
   c. Use the same technique: when this economy produces 1,800 immunizations, it can produce a maximum of 182 kidney transplants. This combination is feasible and efficient.
   d. Use the same technique: when this economy produces 3,200 immunizations, it can produce a maximum of 168 kidney transplants. The combination of 3,200 immunizations and 170 kidney transplants is not feasible.

6. Let's continue practicing the interpretation of the numerical relationship depicted in a production possibility frontier. Using the production possibility frontier you constructed in problem 4, determine the maximum number of kidney transplants this country can produce this year given the following levels of childhood immunizations.
   a. 3,000 immunizations
   b. 4,500 immunizations
   c. 6,800 immunizations
   d. 18,000 immunizations

STEP 1: Use the mathematical equation expressing the relationship between kidney transplants (K) and childhood immunizations (I) that you wrote in problem (5). Use this equation to evaluate the maximum number of kidney transplants this economy can produce when it produces a given level of childhood immunizations.

Review the on "Trade-offs: The Production Possibility Frontier" on pages 27–32, the section "Two-Variable Graphs" on pages 49–51, and the section "Curves on a Graph" on pages 51–52.

The equation for the linear production possibility frontier you found in problem (4) is $K = 200 - (1/100)\ I$, where K is kidney transplants and I is immunizations.

   a. Substitute the immunization value into the formula to calculate the maximum number of kidney transplants that are possible given this level of immunizations. Thus, $K = 200 - (1/100)(3{,}000) = 170$ kidney transplants.

   b. Use the same technique to determine the maximum number of kidney transplants this country can produce when it produces 4,500 immunizations: the maximum number of kidney transplants it can produce is 155.

   c. Use the same technique to determine the maximum number of kidney transplants this country can produce when it produces 6,800 immunizations: the maximum number of kidney transplants it can produce is 132.

   d. Use the same technique to determine the maximum number of kidney transplants this country can produce when it produces 18,000 immunizations: the maximum number of kidney transplants it can produce is 20.

Problems and Exercises

1.   Suppose that you wish to travel from your college campus to a nearby community. You go online to download a map to guide you on your trip. How is this map an example of a model? How does it simplify reality? How do you evaluate whether or not your map helps you better understand the world?

2. The production possibilities frontier model holds resources, technology, and the time period constant in order to construct a path of points that represents the maximum amount of two goods an economy can produce given the constraints of their resources and technology during the given time period. This model allows us to consider the effect of an increase in resources while holding everything else constant. In this example, what is it that we are holding constant? Describe the effect of this change in resources on this economy's production possibility frontier

3. Suppose you are stranded on an island by yourself and must therefore produce all the goods you consume. You consume clams and mangos exclusively. If you devote all your available time to harvesting clams, you can harvest 100 clams in a week. If you devote all your available time to collecting mangos, you can find 200 mangos in a week.

   a. Imagine it is possible for you to divide your time between harvesting clams and collecting mangos and that you can even find fractional amounts of both goods. Draw a sketch of your production possibility frontier for a week, placing mangos on the x-axis and clams on the y-axis.

Clams per week

Mangos per week

b. Now, sketch your production possibility frontier for a two-week period. Describe what happens to your production possibility frontier when you increase the amount of time available for production.

Clams per two-week period

Mangos per two-week period

c. Now, imagine you invent a clam rake that enhances your ability to harvest clams. With this invention you are able to increase your clam harvest to a maximum of 200 clams a week if you spend all your time on clams. Your invention has no effect on your ability to collect mangos. Sketch your new production possibility frontier. Describe in words the effect of a change in technology that affects the ability to produce one of the goods, but not both of the goods.

Clams per week

Mangos per week

d. Suppose you have your clam rake and, in addition, you procure knowledge over time that enhances your ability to collect mangos. Your ability to gather mangos increases to 300 mangos a week due to this knowledge. Sketch your new production possibility frontier based on this knowledge and your use of the clam rake. In effect you have experienced a change in technology that has a positive effect on the production of both goods. Describe in words the effect of this change on the production possibility frontier.

Clams per week

Mangos per week

4. Let's return to the example given in problem 3.

a. What is the opportunity cost of harvesting a clam, given the original information in problem 3?

b. What is the opportunity cost of collecting a mango, given the original information in problem 3?

c. What is the slope of the production possibility frontier that you sketched in your answer to problem 3a? How does this slope measure relate to the answers you provide in parts (a) and (b) of this question?

d. What happened to the slope of the production possibility frontier once you invent the clam rake (question 3c)? What happens to the opportunity cost of harvesting clams once you invent the clam rake? What happens to the opportunity cost of collecting mangos once you invent the clam rake?

5. The country of Orange manufactures sofas and lamps. With its available resources and technology, Orange can manufacture in a year 1,000 sofas and 0 lamps or 0 sofas and 250 lamps. It can also manufacture any combination of sofas and lamps that lie on the straight line connecting these two points.

   a. Sketch Orange's production possibility frontier, placing sofas on the *y*-axis and lamps on the *x*-axis.

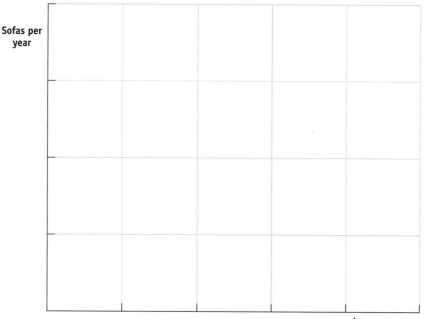

Sofas per year

Lamps per year

   b. Fill in the following table by listing some of the feasible and efficient combinations of production available to Orange each year given its resources and technology.

Combination	Number of lamps possible	Number of sofas possible
A	0	
B	50	
C		500
D		200
E	225	
F	250	

   c. What is the slope of the production possibility frontier for Orange?

   d. What is the opportunity cost of producing one additional sofa for Orange?

   e. What is the opportunity cost of producing one additional lamp for Orange?

f. What is the value of the *y*-intercept for Orange? (Hint: in this example the *y*-intercept is the number of sofas Orange can produce if it does not produce anything else.)

g. Write an equation for the production possibility frontier for Orange using *S* to stand for sofas and *L* to stand for lamps. Write this equation in *y*-intercept form. (Hint: this means that the equation will be written with *S* on the left-hand side of the equation, where the *S* stands for the value of the variable measured on the vertical axis of your sketch.) Verify that each of the combinations you found in part (b) of this problem are true in the equation you wrote.

6. The country of Utopia produces two goods from its available resources and technology. The only resource that Utopia has is labor. It takes 3 hours of labor to produce 2 widgets and 4 hours of labor to produce 1 gadget. For this question assume that the production possibility frontier for Utopia is a straight line.

a. Sketch the production possibility frontier for the country of Utopia. (Hint: to do this you must first decide on a relevant time period. You might pick 120 hours, or 1,200 hours, or 1.2 million hours as your labor constraint, for example, and then you would sketch your production possibility frontier based on this amount of available time and labor.) Draw your production possibility frontier with widgets on the *y*-axis and gadgets on the *x*-axis.

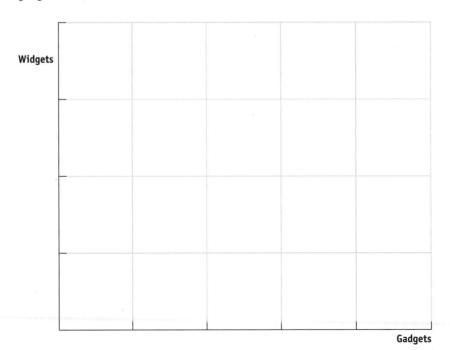

b. What is the slope of your production possibility frontier?

c. What is the opportunity cost of producing an additional widget in Utopia?

d. What is the opportunity cost of producing an additional gadget in Utopia?

7. The country of Jonesville produces two goods from its available resources and technology. The only resource that Jonesville has is labor. The following table gives the amount of labor necessary to produce a widget or a gadget. For this question assume that the production possibility frontier for Jonesville is a straight line.

	Number of hours of labor needed to produce a gadget	Number of hours of labor needed to produce a widget
Jonesville	2	5

a. Suppose that you want to draw a production possibility frontier for Jonesville. What must you do first to draw your sketch?

b. Sketch the production possibility frontier for Jonesville assuming that Jonesville has 120 hours of labor available. Place gadgets on the *x*-axis and widgets on the *y*-axis.

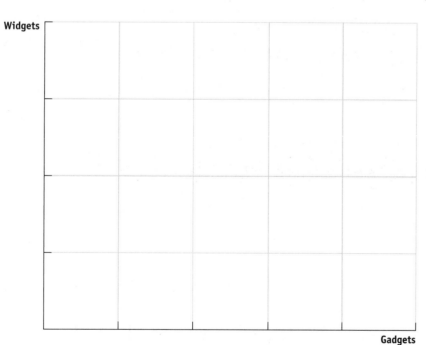

Widgets

Gadgets

c. What is the slope of the production possibility frontier?

d. What is the opportunity cost of producing an additional gadget?

e. What is the opportunity cost of producing an additional widget?

f. Suppose that Jonesville has 240 hours of labor instead of 120 hours of labor. Does this affect the opportunity cost of producing widgets or gadgets? Explain your answer.

8. The following table provides six possible production combinations that Smithtown can produce from their available resources and technology during this year. Assume that Smithtown only produces bicycles and tents from their available resources.

Combination	Bicycles	Tents
A	100	0
B	90	10
C	70	25
D	40	36
E	10	42
F	0	44

a. Sketch Smithtown's production possibility frontier. Measure bicycles along the *x*-axis and tents along the *y*-axis.

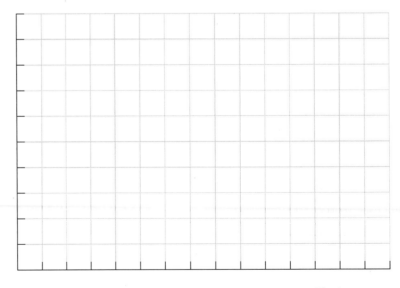

Tents per year

Bicycles per year

b. Suppose Smithtown is currently producing at combination C. If Smithtown chooses to produce at combination B, what is the opportunity cost of moving from combination C to combination B?

c. Suppose Smithtown is currently producing at combination C. If Smithtown chooses to produce at combination D, what is the opportunity cost of moving from combination C to combination D?

d. Smithtown's production possibility frontier is not linear. Provide an explanation for why the production possibility frontier is not linear.

9. Suppose an economy produces two goods in a year using its available resources and technology. This economy's resources are specialized.
   a. Describe the general shape of this economy's production possibility frontier.

   b. If this economy currently produces only one of these two goods, what do you know must be true about the opportunity cost of producing more and more units of the good that is not being currently produced?

   c. If this economy is to be productively efficient, what must be true about its production of these two goods?

   d. If this economy is to be allocatively efficient, what must be true about its production of these two goods?

e. Suppose this economy is deemed to be efficient. What must occur for this statement to be true?

10. Economists believe that specialization and trade are beneficial when they are based on comparative advantage. Briefly explain why economists believe this to be true.

11. There are two islands in the middle of the ocean and these two islands produce fish and baskets. Big Island can produce either 100 fish per day and 0 baskets per day or 0 fish per day and 200 baskets per day. Big Island can also produce any combination of fish and baskets that lies on their linear production possibility frontier. Small Island can produce either 80 fish per day and 0 baskets per day or 0 fish per day and 80 baskets per day. Like Big Island, Small Island has a linear production possibility frontier.

a. Sketch two graphs. Sketch Big Island's production possibility frontier on the first graph and sketch Small Island's production possibility frontier on the second graph. Place fish/day on the *y*-axis and baskets/day on the *x*-axis.

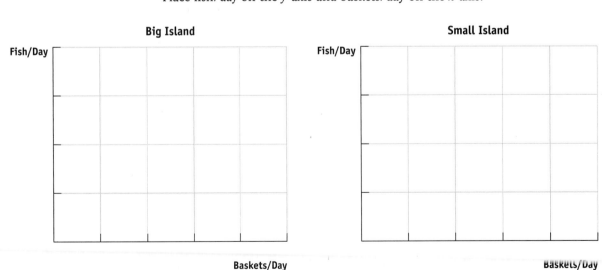

b. What is the slope of Big Island's production possibility frontier?

c. What is the slope of Small Island's production possibility frontier?

d. What is the opportunity cost of producing an additional basket on Big Island? What is the opportunity cost of producing an additional basket on Small Island? Which island can produce baskets at lower opportunity cost?

e. What is the opportunity cost of producing an additional fish on Big Island? What is the opportunity cost of producing an additional fish on Small Island? Which island can produce fish at lower opportunity cost?

f. What good should Big Island specialize in producing?

g. What good should Small Island specialize in producing?

12. There are two islands in the middle of the ocean, and these two islands produce fish and baskets. Big Island can produce either 100 fish per day and 0 baskets per day or 0 fish per day and 200 baskets per day. Big Island can also produce any combination of fish and baskets that includes these two combinations and lies on their linear production possibility frontier. Small Island can produce either 80 fish per day and 0 baskets per day or 0 fish per day and 80 baskets per day. Like Big Island, Small Island has a linear production possibility frontier. Currently there is no trade between the two islands. The current production for both islands is given in the following table.

Initial production	Fish	Baskets
Big Island	80	40
Small Island	30	50
Total production	110	90

a. Is Big Island producing at a productively efficient point? Explain your answer.

b. Is Small Island producing at a productively efficient point? Explain your answer.

Referring back to question 11, let's analyze what happens to total production if these islands decide to specialize and trade according to their comparative advantage.

c. Suppose that Big Island decides to produce 50 baskets instead of 40 baskets. How many fish will Big Island be able to produce if its basket production is increased to 50 baskets?

d. Suppose that Small Island decides to produce 40 fish instead of 30 fish. How many baskets will Small Island be able to produce if its fish production is increased to 40 fish?

e. Fill in the following table showing the new levels of production given the information in parts (c) and (d).

New production	Fish	Baskets
Big Island		50
Small Island	40	
Total production		

f. Do specialization and trade benefit both islands in this example? Explain your answer.

Referring back to question 11, let's analyze what happens to total production if these islands decide to specialize and trade without regard to their comparative advantage.

g. Suppose that Big Island decides to produce 30 baskets instead of 40 baskets. How many fish will Big Island be able to produce if its basket production is decreased to 30 baskets?

h. Suppose that Small Island decides to produce 20 fish instead of 30 fish. How many baskets will Small Island be able to produce if its fish production is decreased to 20 fish?

i. Fill in the following table showing the new levels of production given the information in parts (g) and (h).

New production	Fish	Baskets
Big Island		30
Small Island	20	
Total production		

j. Do specialization and trade benefit both islands in this example? Explain your answer.

k. What must be true for specialization and trade to be beneficial? (Hint: think about the two examples in this problem and how they differ before you write your answer.)

13. Suppose that Jane and Bob live on an island far away from any other countries. Jane and Bob both produce widgets and gadgets from their available resources, but they do not currently trade with each other. The table that follows gives the number of hours of labor needed to produce one widget or one gadget for Bob and Jane. For this example let's assume that Jane and Bob each have 120 hours of labor time.

	Hours of labor needed to produce a widget	Hours of labor needed to produce a gadget
Bob	2	4
Jane	3	1.5

a. Sketch two graphs: on the first graph draw Bob's production possibility frontier and on the second graph draw Jane's production possibility frontier. Place widgets on the *y*-axis and gadgets on the *x*-axis. Label both graphs carefully.

Bob's Production Possibility Frontier

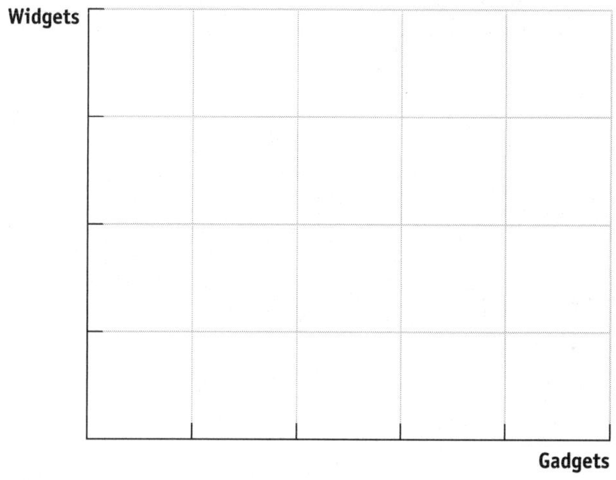

Widgets

Gadgets

Jane's Production Possibility Frontier

Widgets

Gadgets

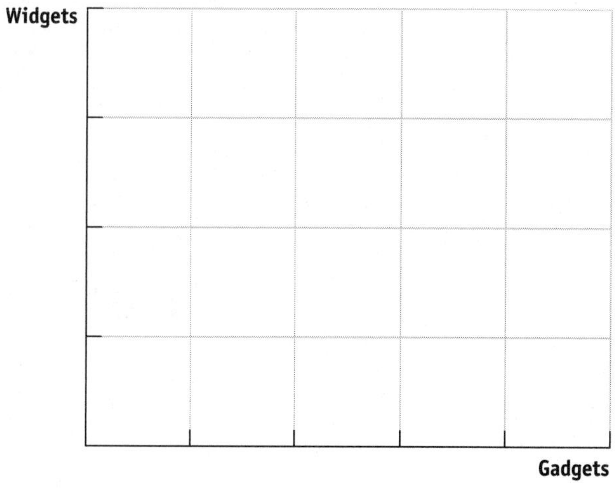

b. Suppose that Bob and Jane devote half of their labor time to producing gadgets and half to producing widgets. Fill in the following table based on this allocation of labor.

Initial production	Widgets	Gadgets
Bob		
Jane		
Total production		

c. What is Bob's opportunity cost of producing an additional gadget? What is Jane's opportunity cost of producing an additional gadget? Who can produce gadgets at lower opportunity cost?

d. What is Bob's opportunity cost of producing an additional widget? What is Jane's opportunity cost of producing an additional widget? Who can produce widgets at lower opportunity cost?

e. Bob and Jane decide to specialize and trade. What good should Bob specialize in producing?

f. Bob and Jane decide to specialize and trade. What good should Jane specialize in producing?

g. Bob and Jane specialize according to their comparative advantage and give us this partially filled-in table that provides some information about their production. Fill in the missing information on the table assuming that Bob and Jane are both productively efficient.

New production	Widgets	Gadgets
Bob	46	
Jane		60
Total production		

14. Decide whether each of the following statements is a normative statement or a positive statement, then explain your answer.

a. The gasoline tax is projected to yield $10 million in tax revenue next year.

b. If the gasoline tax was raised by 10 cents per gallon, the tax revenue from this tax would increase by 4%.

c. The state should raise the gasoline tax for the coming year. An increase in the tax will reduce congestion and smog, which is more important than the cost to commuters if they shift from private car transportation to public transportation.

d. Mandatory school enhances the work skills of students.

e. The age of mandatory school attendance should be extended, since this will provide greater benefits to our economy.

f. An extension of mandatory school attendance will increase government education costs by $2 million for the state.

15. Economists sometimes disagree about positive economics, but more often they disagree about normative economics. Briefly define both of these terms and then explain why economists do not always agree.

16. Why must the circular-flow diagram include two flows moving in opposite directions? In your answer identify what each of these flows is.

17. Suppose you are told that each additional inch of height results in an increase of five pounds in weight. What can you conclude from this information about the relationship between height and weight?

18. Suppose you are told that the points $(x, y) = (15, 30)$ and $(x, y) = (-5, 10)$ both sit on the same straight line.

    a. From this information, calculate the slope of the line.

    b. Draw a quick sketch of this line and be sure to mark and identify both of these two points on the line.

    c. Write an equation for this line.

    d. What is the y-intercept of this line?

19. Suppose that you know that the slope of a straight line is -10 and the line also contains the point $(x, y) = (10, 0)$.

    a. What is the equation for this line given this information?

    b. What is the x-intercept of this line?

    c. What is the y-intercept of this line?

■ BEFORE YOU TAKE THE TEST

Chapter Review Questions

1. Models
   a. are an exact replica of reality.
   b. bear no resemblance to real life.
   c. are a simplification of the real world.
   d. are made more complicated by the assumptions that underlie the model.

2. There are a limited number of possible economic models.
   a. True   b. False

3. The other-things-equal assumption means that
   a. all economic models hold the same variables constant.
   b. all economic models change only one variable at a time, and that variable is always the same for all economic models.
   c. only one variable is allowed to change in a model at a time so that the analyst using the model can focus on the effect of that change on the model.
   d. lots of variables are allowed to change in a model at one time so that the analyst using the model can focus on the effect of all these changes on a single variable of interest.

4. Suppose Mike has a linear production possibility frontier in the production of potatoes and tomatoes. If Mike devotes all his time to the production of potatoes, he can produce 1,000 pounds of potatoes a year; if he devotes all his time to the production of tomatoes, he can produce 2,000 pounds of tomatoes a year. Which of the following combinations of potatoes and tomatoes are not feasible for Mike?
   a. 1,000 pounds of potatoes and 2,000 pounds of tomatoes per year
   b. 1,000 pounds of potatoes and 0 pounds of tomatoes per year
   c. 0 pounds of potatoes and 2,000 pounds of tomatoes per year
   d. 500 pounds of potatoes and 1,000 pounds of tomatoes per year

5. Suppose Mike has a linear production possibility frontier in the production of potatoes and tomatoes. If Mike devotes all his time to the production of potatoes, he can produce 1,000 pounds of potatoes a year; if he devotes all his time to the production of tomatoes, he can produce 2,000 pounds of tomatoes a year. Which of the following combinations of potatoes and tomatoes are not efficient for Mike?
   a. 500 pounds of potatoes and 500 pounds of tomatoes per year
   b. 500 pounds of potatoes and 1,000 pounds of tomatoes per year
   c. 750 pounds of potatoes and 500 pounds of tomatoes per year
   d. 250 pounds of potatoes and 1,500 pounds of tomatoes per year

6. Utopia has a linear production possibility frontier in the production of widgets and gadgets. It can produce three gadgets per hour of labor time or four widgets per hour of labor time. What is the opportunity cost of producing one widget in Utopia?
   a. 3 gadgets   c. 0.75 gadget
   b. 4 widgets   d. 1.33 gadgets

7. Jonesville produces widgets and gadgets and its production possibility frontier is linear. The following table provides the number of units of labor necessary to produce 1 gadget or 1 widget in Jonesville.

	Number of hours of labor needed to produce a gadget	Number of hours of labor needed to produce a widget
Jonesville	5	10

Suppose that Jonesville has 100 hours of labor. What is the maximum number of widgets it can produce?

a. 10 widgets   c. 1 widget
b. 20 widgets   d. 100 widgets

8. Jonesville produces widgets and gadgets and its production possibility frontier is linear. The following table provides the number of units of labor necessary to produce 1 gadget or 1 widget in Jonesville.

	Number of hours of labor needed to produce a gadget	Number of hours of labor needed to produce a widget
Jonesville	5	10

Suppose that Jonesville has 100 hours of labor. What is the maximum number of widgets and gadgets it can produce if it devotes half of its labor time to the production of gadgets and half of its labor time to the production of widgets?

a. 20 gadgets and 5 widgets   c. 5 gadgets and 20 widgets
b. 10 gadgets and 5 widgets   d. 5 gadgets and 10 widgets

9. Jonesville produces widgets and gadgets and its production possibility frontier is linear. The following table provides the number of units of labor necessary to produce 1 gadget or 1 widget in Jonesville.

	Number of hours of labor needed to produce a gadget	Number of hours of labor needed to produce a widget
Jonesville	5	10

Suppose that Jonesville initially has 100 hours of labor. What happens to the opportunity cost of producing a widget if Jonesville's labor resource increases to 200 hours of labor?

a. The opportunity cost of producing a widget decreases.
b. The opportunity cost of producing a widget increases.
c. The opportunity cost of producing a widget does not change.
d. The opportunity cost of producing a widget may increase, decrease, or remain unchanged depending on the number of gadgets that are produced in Jonesville.

10. Jonesville produces widgets and gadgets and its production possibility frontier is linear. The following table provides the number of units of labor necessary to produce 1 gadget or 1 widget in Jonesville.

	Number of hours of labor needed to produce a gadget	Number of hours of labor needed to produce a widget
Jonesville	5	10

Suppose that Jonesville has 100 hours of labor. Which of the following combinations of gadgets and widgets is not feasible for Jonesville to produce?

a. 4 gadgets and 8 widgets   c. 8 gadgets and 6 widgets

b. 7 gadgets and 7 widgets   d. 0 gadgets and 10 widgets

11. Utopia has a linear production possibility frontier in the production of widgets and gadgets. It can produce 3 gadgets per hour of labor time or 4 widgets per hour of labor time. Suppose that Utopia has 120 hours of labor time and that it chooses to divide its labor time equally between the production of widgets and gadgets. What is the maximum number of widgets Utopia can produce given this decision?

a. 480 widgets   c. 60 widgets

b. 240 widgets   d. 15 widgets

12. Suburbia has a production possibility frontier bowed out from the origin for the two goods, guns and butter, that Suburbia produces from its available resources and technology. The following table describes six points that lie on Suburbia's production possibility frontier.

Combination	Number of guns	Pounds of butter
A	0	80
B	10	75
C	20	65
D	30	50
E	40	30
F	50	0

Suppose Suburbia is initially producing at point D. What is the opportunity cost of moving to point E?

a. 10 guns

b. 40 guns

c. 20 pounds of butter

d. 30 pounds of butter

13. Suburbia has a production possibility frontier bowed out from the origin for the two goods, guns and butter, that Suburbia produces from its available resources and technology. The following table describes six points that lie on Suburbia's production possibility frontier.

Combination	Number of guns	Pounds of butter
A	0	80
B	10	75
C	20	65
D	30	50
E	40	30
F	50	0

Suppose Suburbia is initially producing at point D. What is the opportunity cost of moving to point B?

a. 25 pounds of butter

b. 20 guns

c. 10 guns

d. 75 pounds of butter

14. Suburbia has a production possibility frontier bowed out from the origin for the two goods, guns and butter, that Suburbia produces from its available resources and technology. The following table describes six points that lie on Suburbia's production possibility frontier.

Combination	Number of guns	Pounds of butter
A	0	80
B	10	75
C	20	65
D	30	50
E	40	30
F	50	0

Suburbia is currently producing 50 pounds of butter and 20 guns. This combination is

a. allocatively efficient, since butter is tastier than guns.

b. productively efficient, since it is a feasible point for Suburbia to produce.

c. infeasible, because Suburbia cannot produce this combination given its resources and technology.

d. feasible but inefficient, since it is a combination that lies inside the production possibility frontier.

15. Which of the following statements is true?

  I. Points that lie on the production possibility frontier are allocatively efficient.

  II. Points that lie on the production possibility frontier are productively efficient.

a. Statement I is true.

b. Statement II is true.

c. Statements I and II are true.

d. Statements I and II are false.

16. An economy is allocatively efficient provided that
   a. it produces at any point along its production possibility frontier.
   b. it produces the right mix of goods from its available resources.
   c. no resources are wasted.
   d. all of the statements are true about allocative efficiency.

17. Suppose there are two countries, Texia and Urbania, that produce food and clothing and currently do not trade. Both countries have linear production possibility frontiers. Texia, if it devotes all of its resources to food production, can produce 1,000 units of food this year and 0 units of clothing. If Texia devotes all of its resources to clothing production this year, it can produce 500 units of clothing and 0 units of food. Urbania can either produce 500 units of food this year and 0 units of clothing, or it can produce 200 units of clothing this year and 0 units of food. _____ has the absolute advantage in the production of clothing and _____ has the absolute advantage in the production of food.
   a. Texia; Texia   c. Urbania; Texia
   b. Texia; Urbania   d. Urbania; Urbania

18. Suppose there are two countries, Texia and Urbania, that produce food and clothing and currently do not trade. Both countries have linear production possibility frontiers. Texia, if it devotes all of its resources to food production, can produce 1,000 units of food this year and 0 units of clothing. If Texia devotes all of its resources to clothing production this year, it can produce 500 units of clothing and 0 units of food. Urbania can either produce 500 units of food this year and 0 units of clothing, or it can produce 200 units of clothing this year and 0 units of food. _____ has the comparative advantage in the production of clothing and _____ has the comparative advantage in the production of food.
   a. Texia; Texia   c. Urbania; Texia
   b. Texia; Urbania   d. Urbania; Urbania

19. Suppose there are two countries, Texia and Urbania, that produce food and clothing and currently do not trade. Both countries have linear production possibility frontiers. Texia, if it devotes all of its resources to food production, can produce 1,000 units of food this year and 0 units of clothing. If Texia devotes all of its resources to clothing production this year, it can produce 500 units of clothing and 0 units of food. Urbania can either produce 500 units of food this year and 0 units of clothing, or it can produce 200 units of clothing this year and 0 units of food. Each country devotes half of its resources to the production of food and half of its resources to the production of clothing. Total clothing production is equal to _____ and total food production is equal to _____.
   a. 600; 500   c. 100; 250
   b. 250; 500   d. 350; 750

20. Suppose there are two countries, Texia and Urbania, that produce food and clothing and initially do not trade. Both countries have linear production possibility frontiers. Texia, if it devotes all of its resources to food production, can produce 1,000 units of food this year, and 0 units of clothing. If Texia devotes all of its resources to clothing production this year, it can produce 500 units of clothing and 0 units of food. Urbania can either produce 500 units of food this year and 0 units of clothing, or it can produce 200 units of clothing this year and 0 units of food. Suppose that Texia and Urbania decide to specialize and trade. If Texia increases its clothing production to a total of 400 units, how many units of food will Texia be able to produce if it is productively efficient?
   a. 100 units   c. 300 units
   b. 200 units   d. 400 units

21. Specialization and trade benefit
    a. usually only one of the trading partners.
    b. the wealthier country more than the poorer country.
    c. the poorer country more than the wealthier country.
    d. both countries if they specialize according to their comparative advantage.

22. Which of the following statements is true about positive economics?
    I. Positive economics is about how the world should work.
    II. Positive economics is about how the world works.
    III. Positive economics is descriptive.
    a. Statements I, II, and III are all true.
    b. Statements I and III are true.
    c. Statements II and III are true.
    d. Statement II is true.

23. Which of the following statements is an example of normative economics?
    I. The United States should pass a value-added tax, since this is a tax that will work best for the country.
    II. A value-added tax will add $10 billion to the administrative costs of the U.S. tax system.
    III. A value-added tax will increase the economic burden of taxes on poor people by 15%.
    a. Statements I, II, and III are all examples of normative economics.
    b. Statements I and III are examples of normative economics.
    c. Statements I and II are examples of normative economics.
    d. Statement I is an example of normative economics.

24. In the simple circular-flow diagram presented in the chapter there are only two types of inhabitants in the economy. These two types are
    a. money earners and money savers.
    b. households and firms.
    c. resources and outputs.
    d. governments and individuals.

25. The simple circular-flow diagram presented in the chapter illustrates two markets: the markets for
    a. households and firms.
    b. government services and foreign produced goods.
    c. money and physical times.
    d. goods and services and the market for factors of production.

26. A positively sloped line indicates that as one variable increases, the other variable
    a. stays the same.
    b. increases.
    c. decreases.
    d. may increase, decrease, or remain unchanged.

27. A negatively sloped line indicates that as one variable increases, the other variable
    a. stays the same.
    b. increases.
    c. decreases.
    d. may increase, decrease, or remain the same.

ANSWER KEY

Answers to Problems and Exercises

1. The map is an example of a model because it simplifies the real world while trying to enable the user to better understand that world. It simplifies the real world by leaving out many things—for example, your map may only show the main roads in your community, or it might leave out major landmarks that you might find helpful, such as park and school names. The map is helpful to you provided it enables you to get from your starting point to your destination. Although it simplifies the real world, it should still provide key insights into that world.

2. Technology and the time period are being held constant so that we can focus on the effect of a change in the level of resources on this economy's production possibility frontier. If resources increase, we would expect the production possibility frontier to shift out because the economy should be able to produce more of both goods now that there are more resources to work with.

3. a.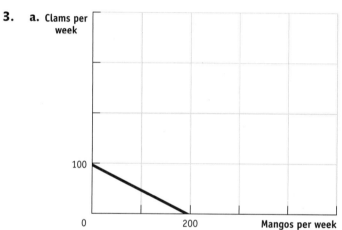

b. An increase in the time period, holding everything else constant, increases the level of production.

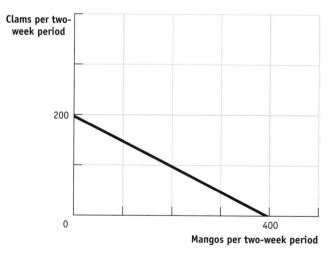

c. The invention of the clam rake shifts the production possibilities frontier out along the clam axis since it is now possible to produce more clams in the same time period.

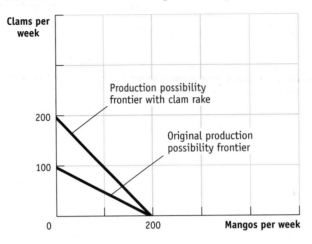

d. Technological change shifts the production possibility frontier away from the origin and therefore results in the possibility of greater production of both goods.

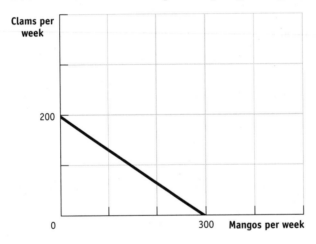

4. a. The opportunity cost of harvesting a clam is measured in terms of the number of mangos you must give up when you harvest a clam. In the original example, you must give up 2 mangos for every clam you harvest.

b. The opportunity cost of collecting a mango is measured in terms of the number of clams you must give up when you collect a mango. In the original example, you must give up ½ clam for every mango you collect.

c. The slope of the production possibility frontier is –½ (remember, you calculate this as the rise/run, or the change in the y-variable divided by the change in the x-variable). The slope tells us what the change in the y-variable is for a 1-unit change in the x-variable. In this case, the slope tells us what the change in the number of clams is for a 1-unit change in mangos: when mango collection increases by 1 unit, then clam harvesting decreases by ½ unit; when mango collection decreases by 1 unit, then clam harvesting increases by ½ unit. The negative sign of the slope tells us that these two variables move in opposite directions: an increase in mangos requires a decrease in clams, or a decrease in mangos requires an increase in clams. The slope measure tells us what the opportunity cost of one more mango is, since mangos are measured on the horizontal axis in this example. If we take the reciprocal of the slope (in this case, –2), it would give us the opportunity cost of producing one more unit of the good on the y-axis. In this case harvesting one more clam has an opportunity cost of 2 mangos since that is the amount of mangos we must give up to get one more clam.

d. The invention of the clam rake changed the slope of the production possibility frontier from –½ to –1 and therefore changed the opportunity cost of producing both goods. The opportunity cost of collecting a mango is now 1 clam and the opportunity cost of harvesting one clam is 1 mango.

5. a.

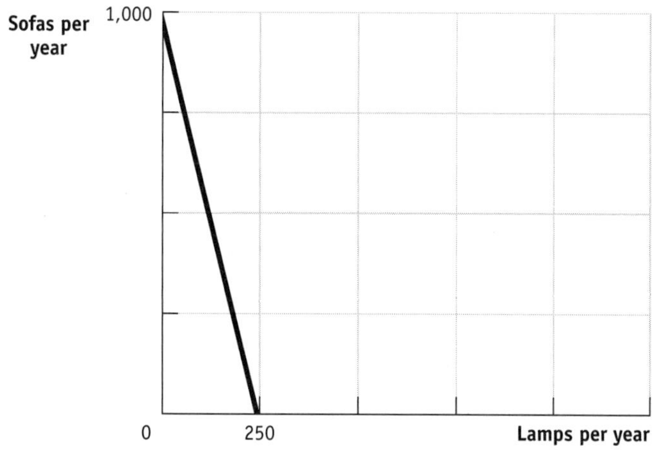

b.

Combination	Number of lamps possible	Number of sofas possible
A	0	1,000
B	50	800
C	125	500
D	200	200
E	225	100
F	250	0

c. The slope of the production possibility frontier is –4 (you can find this by looking at the rise/run, or in this case, –1,000/250).

d. The opportunity cost of producing one more sofa is ¼ lamp. (Hint: remember that because sofas are measured on the y-axis, you can find the opportunity cost by taking the reciprocal of the slope measure.)

e. The opportunity cost of producing one more lamp is 4 sofas. (Hint: remember that because lamps are measured on the x-axis, you can find the opportunity cost by using the slope measure.)

f. The y-intercept is 1,000, since if Orange uses all of its resources and technology to produce sofas, this is the maximum number of sofas it can produce in a year.

g. The equation for Orange's production possibility frontier is $S = 1,000 - 4L$. You can verify that all the combinations work in this equation by substituting the value of the number of lamps in one of the combinations and verifying that the equation generates the number of sofas you found in the table. For example, if L equals 225, then $S = 1,000 - 4(225)$ or $S = 100$ (the value you found in the table).

6. a. To draw the production possibility frontier, you first need to identify the number of hours of labor that Utopia has available. Since it takes 3 hours of labor to produce 2 widgets (or 1.5 hours of labor to produce 1 widget) and 4 hours of labor to produce 1 gadget, you will find it helpful to select an amount of time that is divisible by both three and four. So, for instance, 12 hours would work, as would 120 hours, or 240 hours, or an infinite number of other numbers that are divisible by both three and four. For our sketch let's suppose that there are 120 hours of labor available to Utopia and that its citizens can produce either widgets or gadgets or some combination of the two goods. If they devote all of their labor time to widget production, they can produce 80 widgets since (120 hours of labor/3 hours of labor) × (2 widgets) = 80 widgets. If they devote all of their labor time to gadget production, they can produce 30 gadgets since (120 hours of labor/4 hours of labor) × (1 gadget) = 30 gadgets. The following graph illustrates Utopia's production possibility frontier.

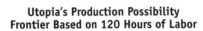

Utopia's Production Possibility Frontier Based on 120 Hours of Labor

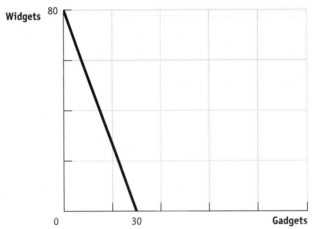

The values of your intercepts will be different depending on the number of hours of labor you assume Utopia has, but the slope of the production possibility frontier should be the same as in the figure shown.

b. The slope of the production possibility frontier is −8/3.

c. The opportunity cost of producing an additional widget in Utopia is 3/8 gadget.

d. The opportunity cost of producing an additional gadget in Utopia is 8/3 widget.

7. a. You must first decide how much labor Jonesville has so that you can calculate the maximum amount of widgets and gadgets Jonesville can produce. Since you know gadgets take 2 hours of labor and widgets take 5 hours of labor, you will want to pick a number of hours that is divisible by both two and five. For example, 10 hours would work, or 100 hours, or 20 hours, or 2,000 hours—there is an infinite number of labor quantities that would work in constructing this production possibility frontier.

b.

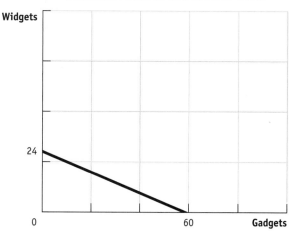

**Production Possibility Frontier for
Jonesville Based on 120 Hours of Labor**

c. The slope of the production possibility frontier is −24/60, or −4/10, or −0.4.

d. Recall that you can use the slope measure to quickly find the opportunity cost of producing one more unit of the good measured on the *x*-axis. To produce one more gadget, you must give up 0.4 widget, therefore the opportunity cost of an additional gadget is 0.4 widget.

e. Recall that you can use the reciprocal of the slope measure to quickly find the opportunity cost of producing one more unit of the good measured on the *y*-axis. To produce one more widget, you must give up 1/0.4 gadgets, therefore the opportunity cost of an additional widget is 2.5 gadgets.

f. If Jonesville has an increase in the amount of labor available to use in producing gadgets and widgets, it can produce more gadgets and more widgets. That is, Jonesville's production possibility frontier will shift out from the origin. But the slope of the new production possibility frontier will be the same as the one drawn based upon 120 hours of labor, thus the opportunity cost of producing widgets or gadgets will not change for Jonesville.

8. a.

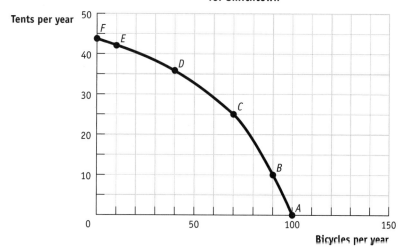

**Production Possibility Frontier
for Smithtown**

b. The opportunity cost of moving from point *C* to point *B* is measured in terms of the number of units of production you give up. In this case you give up 15 tents, so this is the opportunity cost.

c. The opportunity cost of moving from point *C* to point *D* is 30 bicycles.

d. Smithtown's resources are not equally well suited to produce bicycles and tents. If Smithtown initially devotes all of its resources to producing bicycles, then some of its resources that are currently going into the production of bicycles are not particularly productive at producing bicycles. Smithtown can move some of these resources away from bicycle production and into tent production without decreasing its bicycle production significantly. However, as Smithtown decides to produce more and more tents, this will eventually require moving resources that are well suited to bicycle production into tent production where they are less productive. This specialization of resources results in a production possibility frontier that is bowed out from the origin.

9. **a.** This economy's production possibility frontier must be bowed out from the origin if the economy's resources are specialized: this implies that the opportunity cost of producing more and more units of one of the goods increases because increased production of this good requires the economy to use resources that would be more productive producing the other good.

b. The opportunity cost of producing more and more units of the good will increase due to the shape of the production possibility frontier, which is bowed out from the origin.

c. To be productively efficient, this economy must be producing at a point that is located on the production possibility frontier.

d. To be allocatively efficient, this economy must be producing at a point that represents the optimal mix of these two goods for the economy.

e. To be efficient, the economy must be both productively and allocatively efficient—that is, it must produce not only on the production possibility frontier, but it must also produce the right mix of goods.

10. Economists believe that specialization and trade based on comparative advantage result in a greater level of production than is possible without specialization and trade. Economists argue that, so long as opportunity costs differ, specialization in the production of the good that has a lower opportunity cost will enhance the overall level of production available and will therefore be beneficial.

11. **a.**

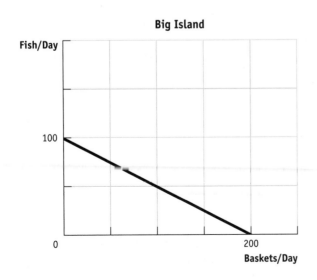

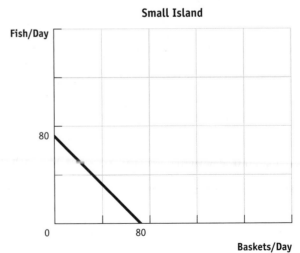

b. The slope of Big Island's production possibility frontier is –1/2.

c. The slope of Small Island's production possibility frontier is –1.

d. The opportunity cost of producing an additional basket for Big Island is ½ fish. The opportunity cost of producing an additional basket for Small Island is 1 fish. Big Island can produce an additional basket at a lower opportunity cost than can Small Island.

e. The opportunity cost of producing an additional fish for Big Island is 2 baskets. The opportunity cost of producing an additional fish for Small Island is 1 basket. Small Island can produce an additional fish at a lower opportunity cost than can Big Island.

f. Big Island should specialize in producing baskets, since it can produce baskets at a lower opportunity cost than can Small Island.

g. Small Island should specialize in producing fish, since it can produce fish at a lower opportunity cost than can Big Island.

12. a. Big Island is producing at a productively efficient point because 80 fish and 40 baskets lies on its linear production possibility frontier.

b. Small Island is producing at a productively efficient point because 30 fish and 50 baskets lies on its linear production possibility frontier.

c. Big Island will be able to produce 75 fish. The easiest way to calculate this answer is to write an equation for Big Island's production possibility frontier: $F = (-1/2)B + 100$, where F is the symbol for fish and B is the symbol for baskets. Thus, if $B = 50$ then F must equal 75 according to this equation.

d. Small Island will be able to produce 40 baskets. The easiest way to calculate this answer is to write an equation for Small Island's production possibility frontier: $F = (-1)B + 80$, where F stands for fish and B stands for baskets. Thus, if $F = 40$ then B must equal 40.

e.

New production	Fish	Baskets
Big Island	75	50
Small Island	40	40
Total production	115	90

f. Specialization and trade are beneficial to both islands since the total production of fish is increased to 115 fish instead of the original 110. This change in fish production does not change the level of basket production. Thus, the two islands can increase the amount of goods available to them if they specialize according to their comparative advantage and then trade with each other.

g. Big Island will be able to produce 85 fish. The easiest way to calculate this answer is to write an equation for Big Island's production possibility frontier: $F = (-1/2)B + 100$, where F is the symbol for fish and B is the symbol for baskets. Thus, if $B = 30$ then F must equal 85 according to this equation.

h. Small Island will be able to produce 60 baskets. The easiest way to calculate this answer is to write an equation for Small Island's production possibility frontier: $F = (-1)B + 80$, where F stands for fish and B stands for baskets. Thus, if $F = 20$ then B must equal 60.

i.

New production	Fish	Baskets
Big Island	85	30
Small Island	20	60
Total production	105	90

j. Specialization and trade are not beneficial to both islands in this example since the total production of fish decreased to 105 fish instead of the original 110. This change in fish production does not change the level of basket production. Thus, the two islands decrease the amount of goods available to them when they specialize and trade with each other without paying attention to their comparative advantage.

k. For specialization and trade to be beneficial for two countries, they must have different opportunity costs of production, and they must also specialize according to their comparative advantage.

13. a.

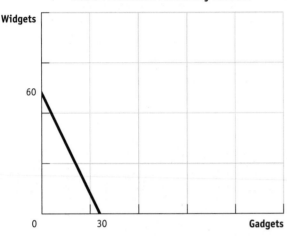

Bob's Production Possibility Frontier

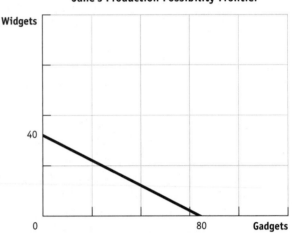

Jane's Production Possibility Frontier

b.

Initial production	Widgets	Gadgets
Bob	30	15
Jane	20	40
Total production	50	55

c. Bob's opportunity cost of producing an additional gadget is 2 widgets, whereas Jane's opportunity cost of producing an additional gadget is ½ widget. Jane can produce gadgets at a lower opportunity cost than can Bob.

d. Bob's opportunity cost of producing an additional widget is ½ gadget, whereas Jane's opportunity cost of producing an additional widget is 2 gadgets. Bob can produce widgets at a lower opportunity cost than can Jane.

e. Bob should specialize in producing widgets.

f. Jane should specialize in producing gadgets.

g.

Initial production	Widgets	Gadgets
Bob	46	7
Jane	10	60
Total production	56	67

14. a. Positive: this statement is a forecast of the tax revenue from the gasoline tax. It is verifiable and hence positive.

b. Positive: this is also a forecast, and although it may be wrong, it can be verified through the data once the data is available.

c. Normative: this is a value statement that reflects one person's viewpoint of the way the world should work. It is not refutable since it reflects a person's opinion and not a set of facts.

d. Positive: this statement can be tested for its accuracy.

e. Normative: this statement reflects the opinions of the speaker.

f. Positive: this is a forecast.

15. Positive economics is descriptive, whereas normative economics is prescriptive—that is, positive economics is objective and expresses how the world works, while normative economics is subjective and expresses how the world should work. Economists may differ because of positive economics: they may use different models with different assumptions that lead to different conclusions. Economists may also disagree over normative economics: economists may not share the same values and will therefore reach different conclusions about how the world should work. Economists can evaluate alternative policies in terms of their efficiency at reaching stated goals.

16. The circular-flow diagram is a simplified representation of the economy. There is a flow of physical items like goods, services, labor, and raw materials that moves in one direction around the circle and there is a flow of money to pay for these physical things that moves in the opposite direction around the circle.

17. Height and weight are positively related: this implies that as height increases, weight increases or as height decreases, weight decreases. A graph of the relationship between height and weight would show an upward-sloping line.

18. a. The slope of the line is equal to the rise/run = (the change in Y)/(the change in X) = $(30 - 10)/[15 - (-5)] = 20/(20) = 1$.

b.

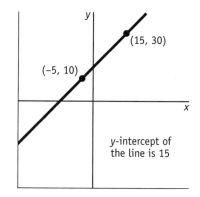

y-intercept of the line is 15

c. The general slope intercept form of an equation is $y = mx + b$ where m is the slope of the line and b is the y-intercept of the line. We know from part (a) that the slope of the line is 1. Hence, $y = x + b$. To find b, use one of the given points. Thus, $30 = 15 + b$ implies that b is equal to 15. The equation for the line is therefore $y = x + 15$.

d. From part (c) we know that the y-intercept of the line is 15.

19. a. To find the equation for this line, recall that the general slope intercept form is $y = mx + b$ where m is the slope and b is the y-intercept. You know that the slope is equal to -10, so you can rewrite this equation as $y = -10x + b$. To find b, simply substitute the point $(x, y) = (10, 0)$ into this equation. Thus, $0 = -10(10) + b$, or $b = 100$. The equation for the line is therefore $y = -10x + 100$.

b. The y-intercept for this line is 100 since when x is equal to zero, the y value is 100.

c. To find the x-intercept of the line, you could use the equation from part (a): $y = -10x + 100$ and use 0 as the value for y. When y is equal to zero, then x is equal to 10. Alternatively, you might recognize that the point $(x, y) = (10, 0)$ already tells you the x-intercept: when the value of y is zero, then the value of x is 10.

Answers to Chapter Review Questions

1. **Answer c.** This is a simple definition of "model."

2. **Answer b.** This is not a true statement since there are an infinite number of possible models. Models can vary, for example, due to their focus of attention, their underlying assumptions, and their degree of complexity.

3. **Answer c.** The assumption "other things equal" implies that everything else is being held equal or constant while considering the effect of changing one variable. Answer (a) is incorrect since different economic models have different economic variables. Answer (b) is incorrect since different variables may be varied in different models or even within a particular model. Answer (d) is incorrect with regard to the other-things-equal assumption, which is used to isolate the effect of a single change on the rest of the model.

4. **Answer a.** Mike can produce 1,000 pounds of potatoes and 0 pounds of tomatoes a year or he can produce 2,000 pounds of tomatoes and 0 pounds of potatoes a year. His resources do not allow him to produce a combination of 1,000 pounds of potatoes and 2,000 pounds of tomatoes in a year. Thus, answer (a) is not feasible, while answers (b) and (c) are feasible. Answer (d) is also feasible since if Mike devotes half of his resources this year to producing potatoes and half of his resources this year to producing tomatoes, he will be able to produce 500 pounds of potatoes and 1,000 pounds of tomatoes this year.

5. **Answer a.** Any combination of production of potatoes and tomatoes that lies on Mike's linear production possibility frontier is an efficient combination. An inefficient combination must lie inside his production possibility frontier. His linear production possibility frontier includes the two points (1,000 pounds of potatoes, 0 pounds of tomatoes) and (0 pounds of potatoes, 2,000 pounds of tomatoes), and we can use these two points to write an equation for his production possibility frontier. If potatoes are measured on the y-axis and are denoted by P, and tomatoes are measured on the x-axis and denoted by T, then Mike's production possibility frontier is $P = 1,000 - \frac{1}{2}T$. Substitute the number of tomatoes provided in each answer into this equation to calculate the number of potatoes Mike can produce when he produces that level of tomatoes. Thus, for answer (b), when Mike produces 1,000 pounds of tomatoes, the equation states that he will be able to produce 500 pounds of potatoes, which is the number of potatoes given in answer (b). Answers (c) and (d) also fit the equation. Thus, answers (b), (c), and (d) all identify production combinations that are on the production possibility frontier. But answer (a) does not fit the equation: when Mike produces 500 pounds of tomatoes, the equation says that he will be able to produce 750 pounds of potatoes, while answer (a) says that he will produce 500 pounds of potatoes. The combination in answer (a) is a combination that lies inside Mike's production possibility frontier.

6. **Answer c.** Since in Utopia 4 widgets can be produced in the same amount of labor time as 3 gadgets, then 1 widget can be produced in the same amount of labor time as $\frac{3}{4}$ gadget. Thus, the opportunity cost of producing 1 widget is measured by the number of gadgets that must be given up, in this case $\frac{3}{4}$ of a gadget.

7. **Answer a.** Jonesville uses all of its labor to produce widgets. With 100 hours of labor, it can produce 10 widgets since the production of each widget takes 10 hours of labor.

8. **Answer b.** When Jonesville devotes 50 hours of labor to widget production, it can produce 5 widgets. When Jonesville devotes 50 hours of labor to gadget production, it can produce 10 gadgets. Thus, when Jonesville divides its labor evenly between widget and gadget production, the maximum number of gadgets it can produce is 10 while the maximum number of widgets it can produce is 5.

9. **Answer c.** Since the number of hours needed to produce each widget and each gadget has not changed in Jonesville, the opportunity cost of producing these goods does not change. Jonesville does see its linear production possibility frontier shift out due to the

increase in the amount of available labor, but the new production possibility frontier has the same slope as the original production possibility frontier.

10. **Answer b.** A combination of gadgets and widgets is not feasible for Jonesville if that combination lies outside of its production possibility frontier. If gadgets are measured on the vertical axis and widgets are measured on the horizontal axis, then the production possibility frontier can be written as $G = 20 - 2W$, where G is the symbol for gadgets and W is the symbol for widgets. Answer (a) lies on the production possibility frontier since $G = 20 - 2(8) = 4$. Answer (c) lies on the production possibility frontier since $G = 20 - 2(6) = 8$. Answer (d) lies on the production possibility frontier since $G = 20 - 2(10) = 0$. Answer (b) does not lie on the production possibility frontier nor does it lie inside the production possibility frontier: $G = 20 - 2(7) = 6$, but the answer in (b) has gadgets equal to 7 and not 6. The combination of 7 widgets and 7 gadgets lies beyond the production possibility frontier for Jonestown.

11. **Answer b.** Utopia plans to devote 60 hours of labor to the production of widgets. If the production of 4 widgets takes 1 hour of labor time, then 60 hours of labor is enough labor to produce 240 widgets.

12. **Answer c.** The opportunity cost of moving from point D to point E is measured by what Suburbia must give up when it makes this move. At point D, Suburbia has 50 pounds of butter, while at point E Suburbia has only 30 pounds of butter; thus, when moving from point D to point E, Suburbia must give up 20 pounds of butter. Notice that when measuring the opportunity cost of moving from one point of a production possibility frontier to another point on the production possibility frontier, it is important to provide the unit of measurement as well as the numerical value.

13. **Answer b.** The opportunity cost of moving from point D to point B is measured by what Suburbia must give up when it makes this move. In this case, Suburbia is giving up guns to get more butter. Moving from point D to point B, Suburbia gives up 20 guns.

14. **Answer d.** From the table, we know that Suburbia can produce 50 pounds of butter and 30 guns (point D on the production possibility frontier). When Suburbia produces 50 pounds of butter and 20 guns, it is producing at a point that is inside its production possibility frontier and hence it is producing at a feasible but inefficient point, since the point does not lie on the production possibility frontier. Alternatively, Suburbia could produce 20 guns and 65 pounds of butter (point C) according to the table. Its choice of 20 guns and 50 pounds of butter is also not efficient from this perspective.

15. **Answer b.** Allocative efficiency focuses on producing the right mix of goods and services. Without additional information, we cannot identify which point is the allocatively efficient point on the production possibility frontier. Productively efficient refers to the maximum production feasible from the available resources. All points on the production possibility frontier are productively efficient.

16. **Answer b.** This is true by definition.

17. **Answer a.** Given the resources that Texia and Urbania have this year, Texia is able to produce more food and more clothing than Urbania this year.

18. **Answer b.** For every unit of clothing that Texia produces it must give up 2 units of food, while for Urbania the opportunity cost of producing 1 unit of clothing is 2.5 units of food. Thus, the opportunity cost of producing clothing is lower for Texia than it is for Urbania. Texia therefore has the comparative advantage in producing clothing while Urbania has the comparative advantage in producing food.

19. **Answer d.** When Texia devotes half of its resources to food production and half of its resources to clothing production, it can produce 500 units of food and 250 units of clothing. When Urbania devotes half of its resources to food production and half of its

resources to clothing production, it can produce 250 units of food and 100 units of clothing. Thus, under this arrangement, total food production is 750 units and total clothing production is 350 units.

20. **Answer b.** Texia's production possibility frontier can be written as $F = 1,000 - 2C$, where F is the number of units of food and C is the number of units of clothing. When Texia produces 400 units of clothing, the maximum amount of food it can produce is 200 units: $F = 1,000 - 2(400) = 200$.

21. **Answer d.** The logic of comparative advantage is that both trading parties benefit through specialization and trade based on their comparative advantage.

22. **Answer c.** Positive economics is objective, factual, and can be subject to proof. In contrast, normative economics is subjective and expresses what ought to happen or what should happen. Statements II and III are both statements that describe positive economics, since positive economics describes and analyzes how the world works.

23. **Answer d.** Normative economics is subjective and value oriented. Both statements II and III are positive statements that can be evaluated as to their factual accuracy. Statement I is a normative statement since it expresses someone's subjective opinion and therefore cannot be proven true or false.

24. **Answer b.** The simple circular-flow diagram depicts the relationship between households and firms with firms providing goods and services to households, while households provide factors of production to firms.

25. **Answer d.** There are two markets represented in the simple circular-flow diagram: the market for goods and services where households buy the goods and services they want from firms; and the market for factors of production where firms buy the resources they need to produce goods and services.

26. **Answer b.** A positively sloped line is one in which the relationship between the two variables depicted is such that an increase in the value of one variable is accompanied by an increase in the value of the other variable. Or, conversely, a decrease in the value of one variable is accompanied by a decrease in the value of the other variable.

27. **Answer c.** A negatively sloped line indicates that the two variables are inversely related: as the value of one variable increases, the value of the other variable decreases.

3

Supply and Demand

■ BEFORE YOU READ THE CHAPTER

Summary

Chapter 3 describes a competitive market and then develops the model of supply and demand for this type of market. The chapter describes the demand and supply curves, explains the distinction between movements along a curve versus a shift of the curve, discusses the primary determinants of supply and demand, and defines the meaning of equilibrium in this model. The chapter also discusses how a market eliminates shortages and surpluses through changes in price and quantity so that the market returns to its equilibrium.

Chapter Objectives

Objective #1. A competitive market is a market that has many buyers and many sellers of the same good or service. No buyer or seller can affect the price of the good or service in a competitive market.

Objective #2. A demand schedule shows the relationship between possible prices of the good or service and the quantity of that good or service demanded at those different prices. As the price increases, the quantity demanded decreases: price and quantity demanded are inversely related to each other. A demand curve is the graphical representation of the demand schedule. The demand curve is drawn with the price of the good on the vertical axis and the quantity demanded on the horizontal axis. Demand curves usually slope downward: this is referred to as the "law of demand." Demand refers to the entire demand curve, while quantity demanded refers to a specific quantity demanded at a specific price. Figure 3.1 illustrates a demand curve as well as the quantity demanded (Q_1) at the price (P_1). Notice that as the price of the good decreases from P_1 to P_2, the quantity demanded increases from Q_1 to Q_2, thus illustrating the inverse relationship between the quantity demanded of the good and the price of the good.

Figure 3.1

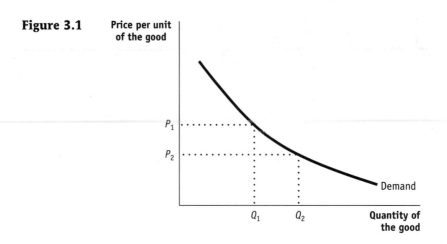

Objective #3. The quantity demanded depends on many factors, but the primary determinants of the quantity demanded are the price of the good, the changes in the price of related goods, and changes in income, tastes, expectations, and the number of consumers. A change in the price of the good, holding everything else constant, will cause a movement along the curve and a change in the quantity demanded. A change in any other determinant of demand, holding everything else constant, will cause a shift in the demand curve. At any given price, the quantity demanded will increase when demand shifts to the right and decrease when demand shifts to the left. Figure 3.1 illustrates the concept of a movement along the demand curve. Holding everything else constant, an increase (or decrease) in the price of the good will cause the quantity demanded to decrease (or increase). There is a movement along the demand curve. But, if the price is held constant and some other factor that influences demand changes, then there will be a shift in the demand curve. Figure 3.2 illustrates an increase in demand where the demand curve shifts from D_1 to D_2: at every price, a greater quantity of the good is demanded since demand has increased (the quantity demanded changes from Q_1 to Q_2). For example, suppose tastes and preferences for the good increases, holding everything else constant: this will cause the demand curve to shift to the right as illustrated in Figure 3.2.

Figure 3.2

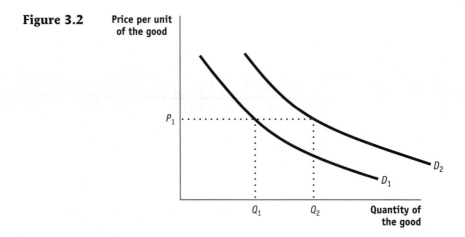

Objective #4. The chapter discusses several kinds of specific types of goods.

- Two goods are substitutes if a decrease in the price of one of the goods causes a decrease in the demand for the other good. As the price of the first good decreases, people increase the quantity of this good they demand, which results in a reduction in the overall demand for the other, substitute good. Two goods are complements if a decrease in the price of one of the goods causes an increase in the demand for the other good. As the price of the first good decreases, people increase the quantity of this good they demand, which results in an increase in the overall demand for the other, complementary, good.

- A good is a normal good if a decrease in income causes a decrease in the demand for the good. A good is an inferior good if a decrease in income causes an increase in the demand for the good.

Objective #5.   A market demand curve illustrates the combined quantity demanded by all consumers in the market. The market demand curve is found by horizontally adding together the individual demand curves. At each price the quantity demanded by each individual is added together to give the total quantity demanded at that price. Figure 3.3 illustrates this horizontal summation of the individual demand curves to create a market demand curve. For simplicity, it assumes there are only two demanders of the good in the market. The figure illustrates the demand for each of these individuals and then, for the market demand curve, it adds up the quantity demanded by the two individuals at a particular price. By repeating this horizontal addition for different prices, it is possible to create the market demand curve. Notice that the market demand curve depicted in Figure 3.3 is composed of two straight line segments: when the price is equal to or greater than P_2, Individual Two does not demand the good: the good is too expensive. Thus, the market demand is composed of a segment from P_1 to P_2 that just reflects Individual One's demand, while the segment starting at P_2, and for all prices lower than P_2, includes demand from both Individual One and Individual Two.

Figure 3.3

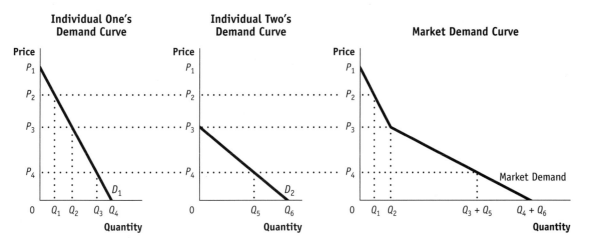

Objective #6.   The quantity of a good or service supplied by a producer depends on the price producers are offered for their product. The supply schedule illustrates the relationship between various prices and the quantity of the good supplied at each of these prices. Generally speaking, the quantity supplied increases as the price increases, holding everything else constant. A supply curve is the graphical representation of a supply schedule. Usually a supply curve is upward sloping: the quantity supplied increases as the price increases. Figure 3.4 illustrates a supply curve as well as the quantity supplied (Q_1) at the price (P_1). Notice that as the price of the good decreases from P_1 to P_2, the quantity supplied decreases from Q_1 to Q_2 thus illustrating the positive relationship between the quantity supplied of the good and the price of the good.

Figure 3.4

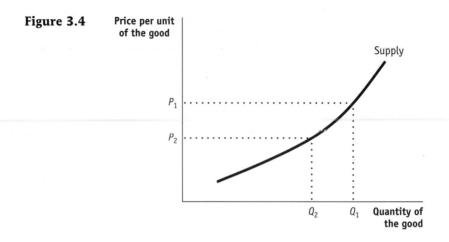

Objective #7. The quantity supplied depends on many factors, but the primary determinants of the quantity supplied are the price of the good, the price of its inputs, the price of related goods, and changes in technology, expectations, and the number of producers. A change in the price of the good causes a movement along the supply curve; a change in one of the other supply determinants, other than price, causes a shift in the supply curve. A rightward shift in the supply curve is an increase in supply; a leftward shift in the supply curve is a decrease in supply. An increase in the price of inputs, holding everything else constant, will cause a decrease in supply. This means that the supply curve shifts to the left, and at every price the quantity supplied is now less than it was initially. Figure 3.4 illustrates the concept of a movement along the supply curve. Holding everything else constant, an increase (or decrease) in the price of the good will cause the quantity supplied to increase (or decrease). There is a movement along the supply curve. But if the price is held constant and some other factor that influences supply changes, then there will be a shift in the supply curve. Figure 3.5 illustrates an increase in supply where the supply curve shifts from S_1 to S_2. At every price, a greater quantity of the good is supplied since supply has increased (the quantity supplied changes from Q_1 to Q_2). For example, suppose the price of an input decreases, holding everything else constant: this will cause the supply curve to shift to the right, as illustrated in Figure 3.5. But if the price is held constant and some other factor that influences supply changes, then there will be a shift in the supply curve.

Figure 3.5

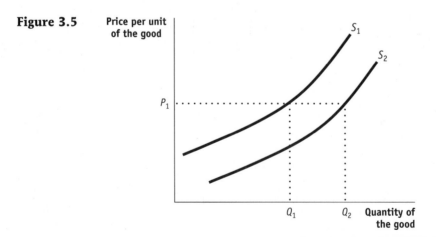

Objective #8. Two goods are substitutes in production when an increase in the price of one of these goods results in greater production of this good and reduced production of the other good. Two goods are complements in production when an increase in the price of one of these goods results in greater production of both goods.

Objective #9.   The market supply curve is found by horizontally adding together the individual supply curves. At each price, the quantity supplied by each firm is added together to create the market supply curve. As the number of individual producers increases there is an increase in supply. Figure 3.6 illustrates this horizontal summation of the individual supply curves to create a market supply curve. For simplicity it assumes there are only two providers of the good in the market. The figure illustrates the supply curve for each of these two firms. Then, for the market supply curve, it adds up the quantity supplied by the two firms at a particular price. By repeating this horizontal addition for different prices, it is possible to create the market supply curve. Notice that the market supply curve depicted in Figure 3.6 is composed of two straight line segments: when the price is equal to or less than P_1, Firm Two does not supply the good: the price is too low for the firm to be willing to supply the good. Thus, the market supply is composed of a segment for prices up to P_1 that just reflects Firm One's supply, while the segment starting at P_1, and for all prices greater than P_1, includes supply from both Firm One and Firm Two.

Figure 3.6

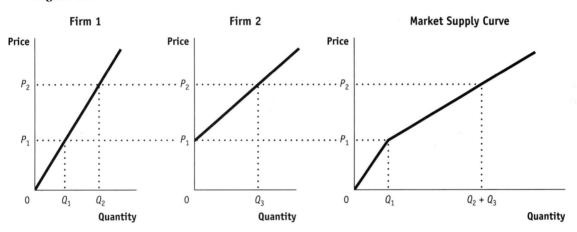

Objective #10. A competitive market is in equilibrium at the price at which the quantity demanded equals the quantity supplied. This price is called the equilibrium price. The quantity associated with this equilibrium price is called the equilibrium quantity. The equilibrium price is the market-clearing price, since at this price the quantity demanded equals the quantity supplied. The equilibrium in a market occurs at the point of intersection between the demand and supply curves. Figure 3.7 illustrates a market in equilibrium. At price P_1, the quantity demanded (Q_d) of the good is equal to the quantity supplied (Q_s) of the good.

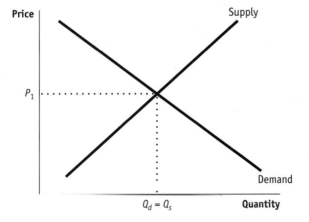

Figure 3.7

Objective #11. At a given price, if the quantity supplied of the good is greater than the quantity demanded of the good, there is a surplus, or excess supply, in the market. If there is excess supply, prices will fall until the quantity supplied equals the quantity demanded. At a given price, if the quantity supplied of the good is less than the quantity demanded of the good, there is a shortage, or excess demand, in the market. If there is excess demand, prices will rise until the quantity supplied equals the quantity demanded. Figure 3.8 illustrates disequilibrium: when the price is P_2, there is excess supply in the market since the quantity supplied of the good is equal to Q_2, while the quantity demanded in the market is equal to Q_3; when the price is P_3, there is excess demand in the market since the quantity supplied of the good is equal to Q_4, while the quantity demanded in the market is equal to Q_5. When there is excess supply in the market, price decreases until the market is restored to equilibrium: note that as the price decreases from P_2 toward P_1, there is a movement along both the demand and the supply curves. When there is excess demand in the market, price increases until the market is restored to equilibrium: note that as the price increases from P_3 toward P_1, there is a movement along both the demand and the supply curve.

Figure 3.8

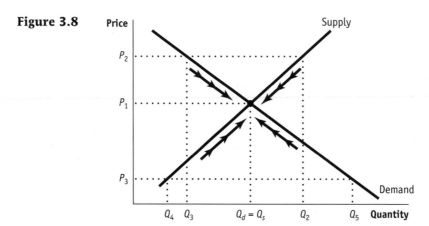

Objective #12. A shift in the demand curve, holding everything else constant, causes a change in the equilibrium price and quantity. The shift in the demand curve causes a movement along the supply curve. An increase in demand leads to a rise in both the equilibrium price and equilibrium quantity. A decrease in demand leads to a fall in both the equilibrium price and equilibrium quantity. A shift in the supply curve, holding everything else constant, causes a change in the equilibrium price and quantity. The shift in the supply curve causes a movement along the demand curve. An increase in supply leads to a fall in the equilibrium price and a rise in the equilibrium quantity. A decrease in supply leads to a rise in the equilibrium price and a fall in the equilibrium quantity. Figure 3.9 illustrates the effect of an increase in demand on the market equilibrium: the increase in demand causes both the equilibrium price and the equilibrium quantity to increase. Figure 3.10 illustrates the effect of an increase in supply on the market equilibrium: the increase in demand causes the equilibrium price to decrease, while the equilibrium quantity increases.

Figure 3.9

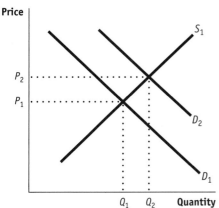

Figure 3.10

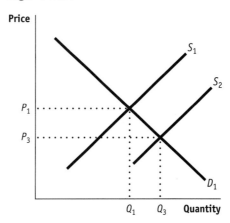

Objective #13. If demand and supply both change simultaneously but without specific information about the relative magnitude of these changes, there will be ambiguity about the value of either the new equilibrium price or the new equilibrium quantity. The four possible outcomes of these changes are summarized in Table 3.1.

Table 3.1

Shift in demand	Shift in supply	Effect on equilibrium price	Effect on equilibrium quantity
Right	Left	Increase	Ambiguous
Right	Right	Ambiguous	Increase
Left	Left	Ambiguous	Decrease
Left	Right	Decrease	Ambiguous

Figure 3.11 illustrates the first case in Table 3.1. Both the demand and the supply curves shift: the demand curve shifts to the right and the supply curve to the left. Figure 3.11 illustrates three possible outcomes that might occur with these two simultaneous shifts: note that in each illustration we know with certainty that the equilibrium price increases, but when we compare the three illustrations we see that the equilibrium quantity may increase, decrease, or remain the same. You should practice by drawing the other three examples given in the table.

Figure 3.11

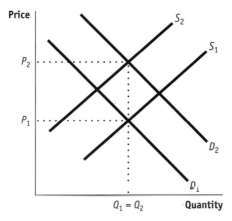

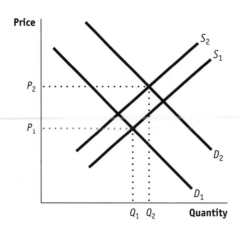

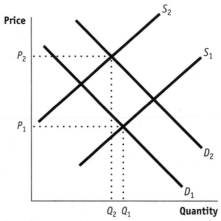

Key Terms

competitive market a market in which there are many buyers and sellers of the same good or service, none of whom can influence the price at which the good or service is sold.

supply and demand model a model of how a *competitive market* works.

demand schedule a list or table showing how much of a good or service consumers will want to buy at different prices.

quantity demanded the actual amount of a good or service consumers are willing to buy at some specific price.

demand curve a graphical representation of the *demand schedule,* showing the relationship between quantity demanded and price.

law of demand a higher price for a good or service, other things equal, leads people to demand a smaller quantity of that good or service.

shift of the demand curve a change in the *quantity* demanded at any given price, represented graphically by the change of the original *demand curve* to a new position, denoted by a new demand curve.

movement along the demand curve a change in the *quantity demanded* of a good that results from a change in the price of that good.

Notes

Key Terms *(continued)*

substitutes pairs of goods for which a rise in the price of one of the goods leads to an increase in the demand for the other good.

complements pairs of goods for which a rise in the price of one good leads to a decrease in the demand for the other good.

normal good a good for which a rise in income increases the demand for that good—the "normal" case.

inferior good a good for which a rise in income decreases the demand for the good.

individual demand curve a graphical representation of the relationship between *quantity demanded* and price for an individual consumer.

quantity supplied the actual amount of a good or service producers are willing to sell at some specific price.

supply schedule a list or table showing how much of a good or service producers will supply at different prices.

supply curve a graphical representation of the *supply schedule,* showing the relationship between *quantity supplied* and price.

shift of the supply curve a change in the *quantity supplied* of a good or service at any given price, represented graphically by the change of the original *supply curve* to a new position, denoted by a new supply curve.

movement along the supply curve a change in the *quantity supplied* of a good that results from a change in the price of that good.

input a good or service used to produce another good or service.

individual supply curve a graphical representation of the relationship between *quantity supplied* and price for an individual producer.

equilibrium price the price at which the market is in *equilibrium,* that is, the quantity of a good or service demanded equals the quantity of that good or service supplied; also referred to as the *market-clearing price.*

equilibrium quantity the quantity of a good or service bought and sold at the *equilibrium (or market-clearing) price.*

market-clearing price the price at which the market is in *equilibrium,* that is, the quantity of a good or service demanded equals the quantity of that good or service supplied; also referred to as the *equilibrium price.*

surplus the excess of a good or service that occurs when the quantity supplied exceeds the quantity demanded; surpluses occur when the price is above the *equilibrium price.*

shortage the insufficiency of a good or service that occurs when the quantity demanded exceeds the quantity supplied; shortages occur when the price is below the *equilibrium price.*

AFTER YOU READ THE CHAPTER

Tips

Tip #1. A full understanding of this chapter is critical for your study of economics. The model of supply and demand is used repeatedly in a variety of settings throughout the remainder of this course. You should work with the material in this chapter until you are confident that you know it well and that you understand the techniques, vocabulary, and information in the chapter. Pay particular attention to the distinction between supply and the quantity supplied, demand and the quantity demanded, and shifts of a curve versus movements along a curve. You also should know the determinants of demand and the determinants of supply, and fully understand the meaning of equilibrium in a market and how to find the equilibrium price and equilibrium quantity.

Tip #2. A demand curve is usually downward sloping. The negative slope of a demand curve implies that the quantity demanded of a good or service is inversely related to its price. Another way to express this idea is that as the price of the good decreases, holding everything else constant, consumers will want to buy more units of the good. Figure 3.12 illustrates this law of demand: at P_1, Q_1 units of the good are demanded; as the price of the good falls from P_1 to P_2, the quantity demanded of the good increases from Q_1 to Q_2.

Figure 3.12

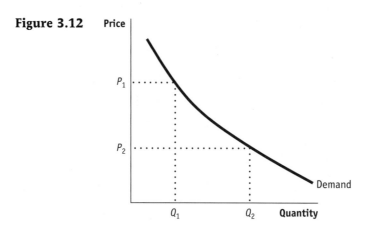

Tip #3. A supply curve is usually upward sloping. The positive slope of a supply curve implies that the quantity supplied of a good or service is directly related to its price. Another way to express this idea is that as the price of the good decreases, holding everything else constant, producers will want to supply fewer units of the good. Figure 3.13 illustrates this idea: at P_1, Q_1 units of the good are supplied; as the price of the good falls from P_1 to P_2, the quantity supplied of the good decreases from Q_1 to Q_2.

Figure 3.13

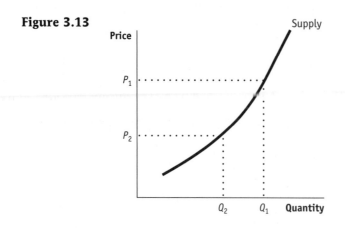

Tip #4. A demand curve illustrates the relationship between the price of the good and the quantity demanded at each specific price. In drawing the demand curve, the other determinants of demand are held constant; this constancy is referred to as the other-things-equal assumption. This assumption allows economists to consider a change in a single variable while holding all other potentially important variables constant. In the examples throughout the remainder of the course, we typically consider a single change in a situation while holding the other variables constant. Students often struggle with this concept and have trouble working with the model of supply and demand because they do not limit themselves to considering a single change at a time.

Tip #5. Besides the price of the good, the quantity demanded of a good is affected by the following variables: changes in the price of related goods, changes in income, changes in tastes and preferences, changes in expectations, and changes in the number of consumers. You will need to know this list of variables as well as how each of these variables affects the demand curve.

Tip #6. A supply curve illustrates the relationship between the price of the good and the quantity supplied at each specific price. In drawing the supply curve, the other determinants of supply are held constant; this constancy is another example of the other-things-equal assumption.

Tip #7. Besides the price of the good, the quantity supplied of a good is affected by the following variables: changes in input prices, changes in the price of related goods, and changes in technology, expectations, and the number of producers. You need to know this list of variables as well as how each of these variables affects the supply curve.

Tip #8. Economists make a distinction between demand and the quantity demanded. The quantity demanded refers to a specific quantity associated with a specific price (as in Figure 3.12, where Q_1 is associated with P_1 and Q_2 is associated with P_2). Demand refers to the entire demand curve. Although this may sound like a matter of semantics, economists view this distinction as highly important. Economists make the same distinction between supply and the quantity supplied. The quantity supplied refers to a specific quantity associated with a specific price (as in Figure 3.13, where Q_1 is associated with P_1 and Q_2 is associated with P_2). Supply refers to the entire supply curve.

Tip #9. Economists also make a distinction between a movement along a curve and a shift of the curve. A movement along a curve is caused by a change in the good's price, while a shift in a curve is caused by a change in some variable other than the price of the good.

- Figure 3.14 illustrates this distinction for a demand curve. There is a movement from point A to point B when the price decreases from P_1 to P_2, and there is a shift in the demand curve from D_1 to D_2 due to a change in some other determinant of demand. A shift causes the quantity demanded of the good to change at every price—for example, at P_1 in Figure 3.14, the shift causes the quantity demanded to increase from Q_1 to Q_3 (compare point A to point C). Figure 3.14 illustrates an increase in demand when the demand curve shifts to the right from D_1 to D_2. A decrease in demand would be illustrated by the demand curve shifting to the left (in Figure 3.14, this would be a shift from D_2 to D_1).

Figure 3.14

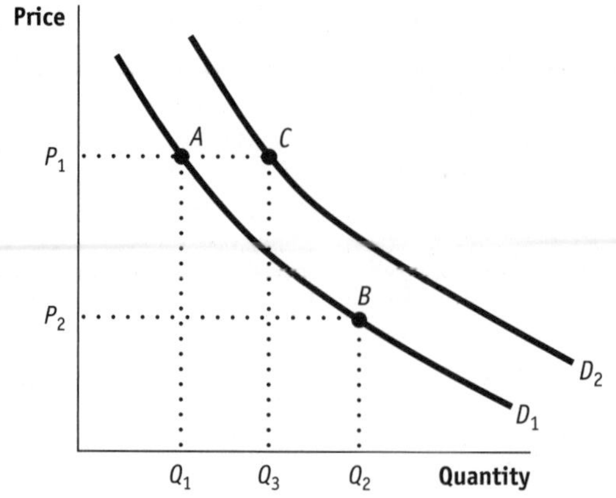

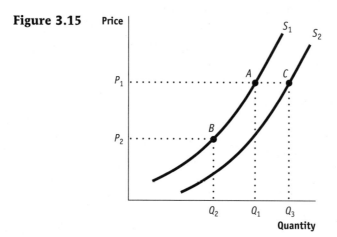

- Figure 3.15 illustrates this distinction for a supply curve. There is a movement from point A to point B when the price decreases from P_1 to P_2, and there is a shift in the supply curve from S_1 to S_2 due to a change in some other determinant of supply. A shift causes the quantity supplied of the good to change at every price—for example, at P_1 in Figure 3.15, the shift causes the quantity supplied to increase from Q_1 to Q_3 (compare point A to point C). Figure 3.15 illustrates an increase in supply when the supply curve shifts to the right from S_1 to S_2. A decrease in supply would be illustrated by the supply curve shifting to the left (in Figure 3.15 this would be a shift from S_2 to S_1).

Figure 3.15

Tip #10. Students initially find it easier to understand the concepts of substitutes and complements if they think about concrete examples. (In Chapter 6, the concept of cross-price elasticity of demand will provide a formal way to determine if two goods are substitutes or complements.) For example, consider soft drinks and popcorn. Two different brands of soft drinks are substitutes: holding all other demand determinants constant, if the price of one brand increases, then the demand for the other soft drink will increase since it is now relatively cheaper and the two goods can easily serve as substitutes for each other. In contrast, if the price of soft drinks increases, holding everything else constant, then the demand for popcorn will decrease. Popcorn and soft drinks are consumed together: they are complements to each other, which implies that if one of these goods gets more expensive (and therefore, you move upward along that good's demand curve), the quantity demanded of that good decreases. This in turn leads to a decrease in the demand for the complementary good. Questions about substitutes and complements are far easier to interpret if you take the time to think of two specific goods.

Tip #11. You will find it easier to understand questions about normal and inferior goods if you think of specific examples. (In Chapter 6, the concept of income elasticity of demand will provide a formal way to determine if a good is a normal or an inferior good.) A normal good is a good that you will choose to increase the quantity demanded at every price as your income increases (demand shifts to the right as income increases). For example, as your income increases you will increase the quantity demanded of vacations, car travel, and recreation. An inferior good is a good that you will choose to decrease the quantity demanded at every price as your income increases (demand shifts to the left as income increases). For example, as your income increases you will likely consume fewer fast-food restaurant meals or generic pasta dinners.

Tip #12. A shift in the demand or supply curve causes a movement along the supply or demand curve. Figure 3.16 illustrates this idea for a demand curve shift. Notice that when demand shifts to the left (a decrease in demand) this causes a movement along the supply curve: the equilibrium price falls from P_1 to P_2 and the equilibrium quantity falls from Q_1 to Q_2.

Figure 3.16

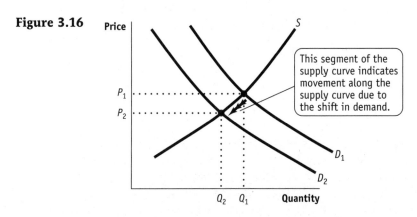

Figure 3.17 illustrates this idea for a supply curve shift. Notice that when supply shifts to the right (an increase in supply) this causes a movement along the demand curve: the equilibrium price falls from P_1 to P_2 and the equilibrium quantity increases from Q_1 to Q_2.

Figure 3.17

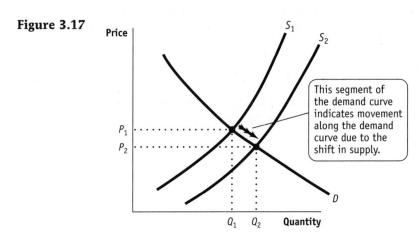

Tip #13. The market equilibrium occurs at the point of intersection of the demand and supply curves. Figure 3.18 indicates that equilibrium at point E, where the equilibrium price is P_1 and the equilibrium quantity is Q_1. If the price is greater than the equilibrium price, there is excess supply, or a surplus, in the market. Figure 3.18 illustrates a situation of excess supply at the price P_2. Note that at price P_2 the quantity supplied is Q_3, while the quantity demanded is Q_2. If the price is less than the equilibrium price, there is excess demand, or a shortage, in the market. Figure 3.18 illustrates a situation of excess demand at the price P_3. Note that at price P_3 the quantity supplied is Q_5, while the quantity demanded is Q_4.

Figure 3.18

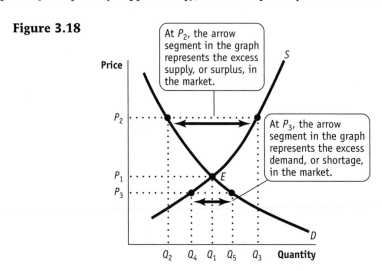

Tip #14. If you are given an equation for the demand curve and an equation for the supply curve, you can solve these two equations for the equilibrium price and equilibrium quantity. For example, suppose demand is given by the equation $P = 10 - Q$ and supply is given by the equation $P = Q$. To find the equilibrium, recall that in equilibrium the quantity demanded equals the quantity supplied; thus, $10 - Q = Q$, or the equilibrium quantity equals 5. Replace Q in either equation with 5 and you will find that the equilibrium price is 5.

Tip #15. Often a quick sketch of a demand and supply curve is all that you need to answer questions about the effect of a change in the market on the equilibrium price or equilibrium quantity. Practice drawing a quick representation of the demand and supply curves as you do this chapter's problems, recognizing that you do not always need a precisely plotted graph to find a solution or to guide your solution of a problem.

Tip #16. As always, if you are making a set of flash cards, make one for each new definition or concept and then review these cards (as well as the cards from the earlier chapters).

WORKED PROBLEMS

1. The supply and demand model is often used to analyze the effect of a change in the market on the equilibrium price and quantity of a good. Consider each of the following markets and the given situation to determine whether the demand and/or supply curve shift(s), and what the impact on the equilibrium price and equilibrium quantity will be relative to the initial equilibrium price and equilibrium quantity. For any shift in the demand or supply curve, indicate whether the curve shifts to the left or to the right. The examples are given in a table to help you consolidate your answers.

Market under consideration	Situation	Shift or movement along the demand curve	Shift or movement along the supply curve	Effect on equilibrium price	Effect on equilibrium quantity
Automobile market	War in the Middle East disrupts petroleum exports substantially				
Pizza market	Price of cheese increases				
Shampoo market	Health advisors release study showing danger of frequent hair washing				
Oil market	Oil-producing countries form cartel and agree to restrict output				
Insulation market	Homeowners granted tax credit for installing home insulation				

STEP 1: For each of the situations, draw the initial market situation and then label the initial equilibrium price and equilibrium quantity.

Review the section "Supply, Demand, and Equilibrium" on pages 83–88.

STEP 2: Next look at the situation and decide whether the situation will cause a movement or a shift of the demand curve, or a movement or a shift of the supply curve. Draw the appropriate shift on your base graph.

Review the section "Shifts of the Demand Curve" on pages 68-70, the section "Understanding Shifts of the Demand Curve" on pages 70-75, the section "Shifts of the Supply Curve" on pages 77-78, and the section "Understanding Shifts of the Supply Curve" on pages 78-80.

STEP 3: Mark the new equilibrium price and equilibrium quantity and then compare the new equilibrium to the initial equilibrium. For example, when war in the Middle East disrupts petroleum exports substantially, this will cause the price of gas to rise, and since cars and gas are complements, the demand for cars will shift to the left due to the increase in the price of gas. As demand shifts left, there is a movement along the supply curve resulting in a reduction in the equilibrium quantity and the equilibrium price of cars.

Review the section "Changes in Supply and Demand" on pages 88-94.

STEP 4: Record your answers on the given table.

Market under consideration	Situation	Shift or movement along the demand curve	Shift or movement along the supply Curve	Effect on equilibrium price	Effect on equilibrium quantity
Automobile market	War in the Middle East disrupts petroleum exports substantially	Demand shifts left as the price of gas rises: cars and gas are complements	Movement along the supply curve as price falls	Decrease in the price of cars	Decrease in the quantity of cars
Pizza market	Price of cheese increases	Movement along the demand curve as price increases	Supply shifts left since cheese is an input in making pizza	Increase in the price of pizza	Decrease in the quantity of pizza
Shampoo market	Health advisors release study showing danger of frequent hair washing	Demand shifts left due to change in tastes and preferences for washing hair: people wish to wash their hair less often at any price of shampoo after the study	Movement along the supply curve as the price of shampoo falls	Decrease in the price of shampoo	Decrease in the quantity of shampoo

Market under consideration	Situation	Shift or movement along the demand curve	Shift or movement along the supply curve	Effect on equilibrium price	Effect on equilibrium quantity
Oil market	Oil-producing countries form cartel and agree to restrict output	Movement along the demand curve due to the shift in the supply curve	Supply shifts left due to the cartel restricting output at every price	Increase in the price of oil	Decrease in the quantity of oil
Insulation market	Homeowners granted tax credit for installing home insulation	Demand shifts right due to the government subsidizing consumption of home insulation: at every price, the quantity of insulation demanded increases	Movement along the supply curve due to the shift in the demand curve	Increase in the price of home insulation	Increase in the quantity of home insulation

2. In the market for corn flakes, the price of cardboard used in packing the cereal has risen at the same time that the Surgeon General releases a report detailing the dangers of a diet high in corn products. What happens to the equilibrium price and equilibrium quantity relative to the equilibrium before these two changes?

STEP 1: First identify that there are two different changes occurring in the market for corn flakes: the price of cardboard used in packing the cereal is increasing and the Surgeon General has released a report that reveals the danger of eating corn products. In this question you will want to model each of these changes to see what the overall effect is in the market for corn flakes.

Review the section "Simultaneous Shifts of Supply and Demand Curves" on pages 90–94.

STEP 2: Draw the initial market situation and label the initial equilibrium price and equilibrium quantity. The figure that follows illustrates the initial situation.

Review the section "Supply, Demand, and Equilibrium" on pages 83–88.

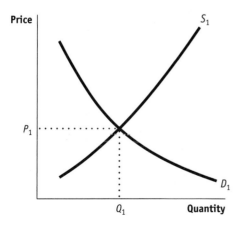

STEP 3: Consider the change in the price of cardboard: this is an input used to produce a box of corn flakes, and thus an increase in the price of cardboard will cause the supply curve for corn flakes to shift to the left. Draw the appropriate shift on your base graph and label it clearly. The figure that follows illustrates this shift.

Review the section "Shifts of the Supply Curve" on pages 77–78 and the section "Understanding Shifts of the Supply Curve" on pages 78–80.

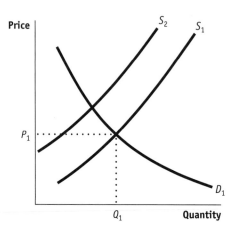

STEP 4: Next, consider the Surgeon General's report: people will decrease the quantity of corn flakes they demand at every price once this report is released. This will cause the demand curve to shift to the left. But we are not told the magnitude of the shift: a small shift will cause the equilibrium price to rise while the equilibrium quantity will fall (the intersection of D_2 and S_2, with the equilibrium occurring at Q_2 and P_2); a moderate shift might cause the equilibrium price to remain at its initial level, while the equilibrium quantity falls (the intersection of D_2' and S_2, with the equilibrium occurring at Q_2' and $P_2' = P_1$); and a large shift would cause the equilibrium price to fall, while the equilibrium quantity also falls (the intersection of D_2'' and S_2, with the equilibrium occurring at Q_2'' and P_2''). Price is therefore indeterminate, while quantity will definitely decrease with these two changes in the market for corn flakes. Study the following figure carefully to see this concept.

Review the section "Shifts of the Demand Curve" on pages 68–70, the section "Understanding Shifts of the Demand Curve" on pages 70–75, the section "Changes in Supply and Demand" on pages 88–94, and the section "Simultaneous Shifts of Supply and Demand Curves" on pages 90–94.

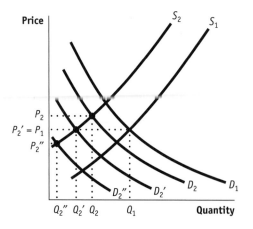

3. In the market for chocolate, people read that the consumption of chocolate has major health benefits. At the same time, the cost of growing and harvesting cocoa beans increases. What happens to the equilibrium price and equilibrium quantity relative to the equilibrium before these two changes?

STEP 1: First, identify that there are two different changes occurring in the market for chocolate: eating chocolate provides health benefits and the cost of growing and harvesting cocoa beans increases. In this question, you will want to model each of these changes to see what the overall effect is in the market for chocolate.

Review the section "Simultaneous Shifts of Supply and Demand Curves" on pages 90-94.

STEP 2: Draw the initial market situation and label the initial equilibrium price and equilibrium quantity. The following figure illustrates the initial situation.

Review the section "Supply, Demand, and Equilibrium" on pages 83-88.

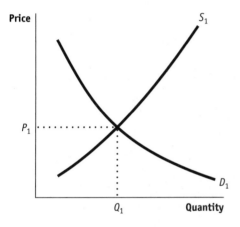

STEP 3: Consider the change in the cost of growing and harvesting cocoa beans: cocoa beans are an input used to produce chocolate, and thus an increase in the price of cocoa beans will cause the supply curve for chocolate to shift to the left. Draw the appropriate shift on your base graph and label it clearly. The figure that follows illustrates this shift.

Review the section "Shifts of the Supply Curve" on pages 77-78 and the section "Understanding Shifts of the Supply Curve" on pages 78-80.

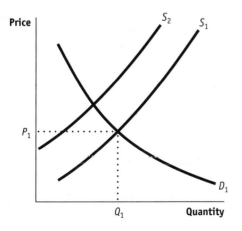

STEP 4: Next, consider the health benefits from consuming chocolate: this will cause the quantity demanded of chocolate to increase at every price. Thus, the demand curve for chocolate will shift to the right. But we are not told the magnitude of the shift:

- A small shift will cause the equilibrium price to rise while the equilibrium quantity will fall (the intersection of D_2 and S_2, with the equilibrium occurring at Q_2 and P_2)

- A moderate shift might cause the equilibrium price to rise while the equilibrium quantity remains at its initial level (the intersection of D_2' and S_2, with the equilibrium occurring at P_2' and $Q_2' = Q_1$)

- A large shift would cause the equilibrium price to rise while the equilibrium quantity also rises (the intersection of D_2'' and S_2, with the equilibrium occurring at Q_2'' and P_2'').

Price will definitely increase while quantity is indeterminate with these two changes in the market for chocolate.

Study the following figure carefully to see this concept.

Review the section "Shifts of the Demand Curve" on pages 68–70, the section "Understanding Shifts of the Demand Curve" on pages 70–75, the section "Changes in Supply and Demand" on pages 88–94, and the section "Simultaneous Shifts of Supply and Demand Curves" on pages 90–94.

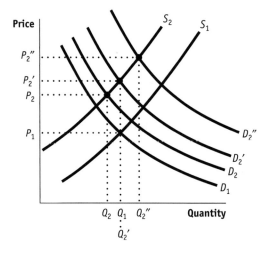

4.   Suppose you are told that the initial demand curve for good X is $P = 100 - Q$. You are then told that incomes increase in this economy and that good X is a normal good. If you know that the quantity demanded of good X changes by 5 units at every price, what is the equation for the new demand curve?

STEP 1: Start by drawing a graph of the initial demand curve. The figure that follows illustrates this demand curve.

Review the section "The Demand Schedule and the Demand Curve" on pages 67–68 (along with Figure 3-1 on page 67).

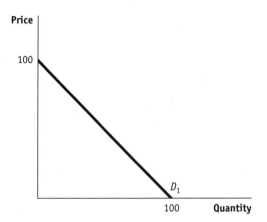

STEP 2: You are told that incomes increase in this economy and that this is a normal good. A change in income will cause the demand curve to shift: since incomes increase and the good is a normal good, the demand curve will shift to the right.

Review the section "Shifts of the Demand Curve" on pages 68–70.

STEP 3: Calculate the exact location of the new demand curve. You know that, at every price, 5 more units are being demanded than were demanded initially. Thus, if the price was initially $0, the quantity demanded was initially 100 units (use the demand equation to get the quantity demanded when the price is $0). Now, at a price of $0, the original 100 units plus an additional 5 units will be demanded. Thus, you know that the point $(Q,P) = (105, \$0)$ sits on the new demand curve. The new demand curve has the same slope as the original demand curve, so all you need to find is the new y-intercept: use the point you know that is on the new demand curve to find this y-intercept. Thus, $P = b - Q$, and when $Q = 105$ and $P = \$0$, then $b = 105$. Thus, the new demand equation is $P = 105 - Q$. The figure that follows illustrates the new demand curve, D_2, along with the initial demand curve. Alternatively, the initial demand curve can be written as $Q = 100 - P$. The new demand curve has the same slope as the initial demand curve and an x-intercept of 105: thus, the new demand curve can be written as $Q = 105 - P$.

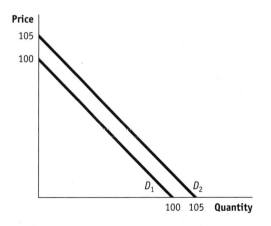

5. Suppose you are told that each firm in an industry is identical and that there are two firms in the industry. Furthermore, you are told that one firm's supply curve is given by the equation $P = 10 + 2Q$. Find the market supply curve in this industry.

STEP 1: To find the market supply curve, you will want to horizontally add all the individual supply curves of the firms in the industry. This will be relatively easy if you draw three horizontally aligned graphs where the first graph illustrates firm 1's supply curve, the second graph illustrates firm 2's supply curve, and the third graph illustrates the market supply curve. The following figure represents this concept.

Review the section "Shifts of the Supply Curve" on pages 77–78 (along with Figure 3-10 on page 80).

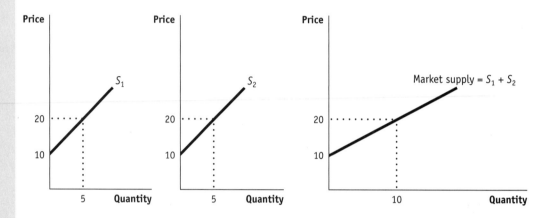

STEP 2: To find the market supply curve, you will want to horizontally add all the individual supply curves of the firms in the industry. Use your sketch to help you write this equation.

Review the section "Shifts of the Supply Curve" on pages 77–78 (along with Figure 3-10 on page 80).

From the third graph you can see that the y-intercept is 10. You can also calculate the slope of the market supply curve as the change in price divided by the change in quantity. Using the points (0,10) and (10,20), the slope is equal to 1. The market supply curve can thus be written as $P = Q + 10$.

Problems and Exercises

1. Why is the assumption that there are many buyers and many sellers in a competitive market important?

2. You are given the following information about demand in the competitive market for bicycles.

Price per bicycle	Quantity of bicycles demanded per week
$100	0
80	100
60	200
40	500
20	800
0	1,000

a. Graph this demand schedule placing price on the vertical axis and quantity on the horizontal axis.

Demand Curve

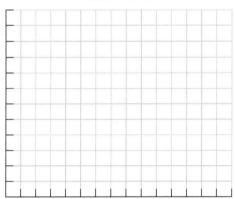

Price

Quantity per week

b. Suppose the price is initially $40. If the price rises by $20, what happens to the quantity demanded?

c. Suppose the price is initially $40. If the price falls by $40, what happens to the quantity demanded?

3. For each of the situations in the following table, fill in the missing information. First, determine whether the situation causes a shift or a movement along the demand curve; then, if it causes a shift, determine whether the demand curve shifts to the right or to the left.

Situation	Specified market	Movement or shift	Rightward or leftward shift in demand
People's income increases	Market for exotic vacations		
People's income decreases	Market for goods sold in secondhand shops		
Price of bicycles increases	Market for bicycles		
Price of tennis balls increases	Market for tennis racquets		
Price of movie tickets decreases	Popcorn at movie theaters		
Popularity of music-playing device increases	Market for music-playing device		
Popularity of branded clothing items decreases	Market for brand-name designer clothing		
Winter clothing to go on sale next month	Market for winter clothing		
Increase in urban residents	Market for apartments in urban areas		

4. Suppose a market has three consumers (this will simplify the work you need to do!): Joe, Maria, and Chao. Their demand schedules are given in the following table.

Price	Quantity demanded by Joe	Quantity demanded by Maria	Quantity demanded by Chao
$0	10	20	5
1	8	16	4
2	6	12	3
3	4	8	2
4	2	4	1

a. In the following graphs, sketch a graph of Joe's demand curve, Maria's demand curve, and Chao's demand curve. Then sketch the market demand curve based on the demand of these three individuals.

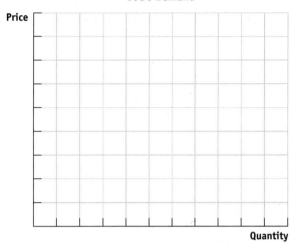

Joe's Demand

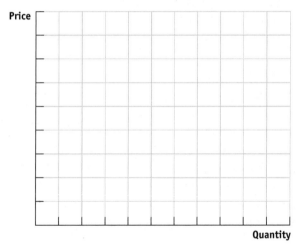

Maria's Demand

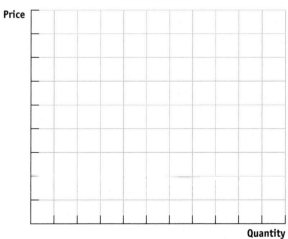

Chao's Demand

Market Demand

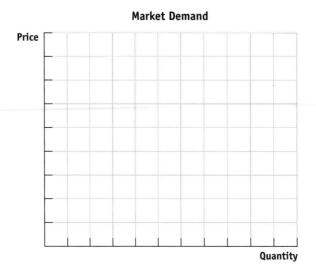

b. Summarize the market demand curve you found by filling in the following table.

Price	Quantity demanded in market
$0	
1	
2	
3	
4	

5. The following graph represents the supply curve for the production of widgets in Town Center.

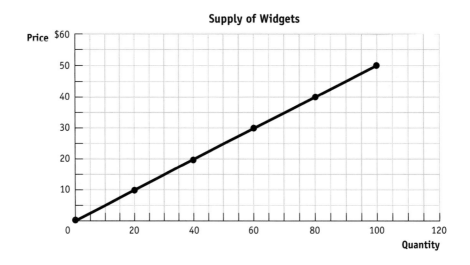

Supply of Widgets

a. At a price of $20, how many widgets are producers willing to supply?

b. At a price of $40, how many widgets are producers willing to supply?

c. Suppose there are ten widget producers in Town Center and that the price of widgets is $50. If each widget producer produces exactly the same number of widgets as every other widget producer, how many widgets will each producer produce at this price?

d. Suppose the price is initially $30 but then falls to $20. What is the change in the quantity supplied?

e. Suppose the price is initially $30 but then increases to $50. What is the change in the quantity supplied?

f. What price must suppliers receive to be willing to supply 80 widgets?

g. What price must suppliers receive to be willing to supply 40 widgets?

h. What does the slope of a typical supply curve imply about the relationship between price and the quantity supplied?

6. For each of the situations in the following table, fill in the missing information: first, determine whether the situation causes a shift or a movement along the supply curve; then, if it causes a shift, determine whether the supply curve shifts to the right or to the left.

Situation	Specified market	Movement or shift	Rightward or leftward shift in supply
Labor costs for air travel and cruise ships increase	Market for exotic vacations		
Prices of office equipment and phone service rise by 40%	Market for call center services		
Price of bicycles increases	Market for bicycles		
Price of leather boots increases	Market for beef products		
Price of leather boots increases	Market for leather belts		
New technology for music-playing device revealed	Market for music-playing devices		
Price of brand-name designer clothing increases	Market for brand-name designer clothing		
Stock market prices expected to fall next quarter	Stock market today		
Increase in number of coffee shop owners in the metro area	Market for coffee shops in the metro area		

7. The following table provides the demand and supply schedules for Healthy Snacks, Inc.

Price	Quantity demanded	Quantity supplied
$ 0	1,000	0
10	800	125
20	600	275
30	400	400
40	200	550
50	0	675

a. Draw a sketch of the demand and supply curves for Healthy Snacks, Inc. Don't worry about drawing a precise graph but instead focus on drawing a simple rendering of the underlying relationships captured in the previous table. This drawing should be accurate with regard to *x*-intercepts and *y*-intercepts and it should also indicate the point of equilibrium.

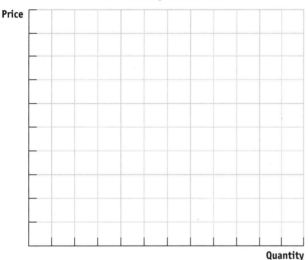

Demand and Supply Curves for Healthy Snacks, Inc.

Price

Quantity

b. From the table, what are the equilibrium price and the equilibrium quantity in this market? Indicate these on your graph.

c. Fill in the following table based on the data given to you. Assume that for each row in the table, the price is as given and that you are calculating the number of units of excess demand or excess supply. (Hint: some of the cells in your table will be left empty—for example, if there is excess supply, then there isn't excess demand.)

Price	Excess Demand	Excess Supply
$ 0		
10		
20		
30		
40		
50		

d. Why is a situation of excess demand referred to as a shortage? Explain using a simple graph to illustrate your answer.

e. Why is a situation of excess supply referred to as a surplus? Explain using a simple graph to illustrate your answer.

8. Use the following graph to answer this next set of questions. The graph illustrates the competitive market for garbage cans in Cleantopia.

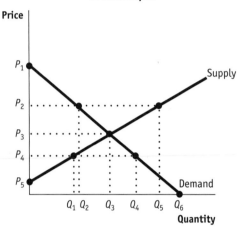

Market for Garbage Cans in Cleantopia

a. What is the equilibrium price in this market?

b. What is the equilibrium quantity in this market?

c. Suppose the current price of garbage cans in Cleantopia is P_2. Describe this market in detail and explain what you think will happen in this market.

d. Suppose the current price of garbage cans in Cleantopia is P_4. Describe this market in detail and explain what you think will happen in this market.

e. Suppose at the current market price the quantity demanded equals Q_4. Describe this market and identify the quantity supplied given this information. What do you expect will happen in this market?

f. Suppose at the current market price the quantity supplied equals Q_5. Describe this market and identify the quantity demanded given this information. What do you expect will happen in this market?

g. At what price is the quantity demanded equal to zero? What does it mean to have the quantity demanded equal to zero?

h. At what price is the quantity supplied equal to zero? What does it mean to have the quantity supplied equal to zero?

9.   The competitive market for bicycles in Pedal City is described by the demand curve $P = 2,000 - 2Q$ and the supply curve $P = 6Q$. There are 20 bicycle manufacturers in Pedal City and each of these manufacturers produces the same number of bicycles as every other manufacturer.

a. Using the two equations for the demand and supply curves, fill in the following table describing the demand and supply schedules for bicycles in Pedal City.

Price	Quantity demanded	Quantity supplied
$ 0		
240		
480		
720		
960		
1,200		
1,440		
1,680		
1,920		

b. Examine the table you created in (a) and provide a range of prices that you expect the equilibrium price to fall between. Why do you expect the equilibrium price to fall within this range?

c. Sketch a graph of the demand and supply curves for bicycles in Pedal City.

Market for Bicycles in Pedal City

Price

Quantity

d. If the current price for bicycles is $240, how many bicycles will be supplied in Pedal City and how many bicycles will a single manufacturer produce? At a price of $240, how many bicycles will be demanded? At a price of $240, is the market in equilibrium? Explain your answer.

e. If the current price for bicycles is $480, how many bicycles will be supplied in Pedal City and how many bicycles will a single manufacturer produce? At a price of $480, how many bicycles will be demanded? At a price of $480, is the market in equilibrium? Explain your answer.

f. If the current price for bicycles is $1,680, how many bicycles will be supplied in Pedal City and how many bicycles will a single manufacturer produce? At a price of $1,680, how many bicycles will be demanded? At a price of $1,680, is the market in equilibrium? Explain your answer.

g. Calculate the equilibrium price and the equilibrium quantity in the market for bicycles in Pedal City.

10. For each of the following situations, sketch a graph of the initial market demand (D_1) and supply (S_1) curves and indicate the initial equilibrium price (P_1) and equilibrium quantity (Q_1). Then sketch any changes in the market demand (D_2) and supply (S_2) curves and indicate the new equilibrium price (P_2) and equilibrium quantity (Q_2). For each situation, identify which curve(s) shift and whether there is a movement along the demand or supply curves.

a. The price of gasoline increases by 40%. What happens in the market for bicycles?

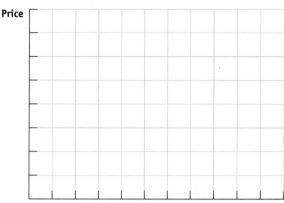

b. The price of gasoline increases by 40%. What happens in the market for fuel-inefficient SUVs?

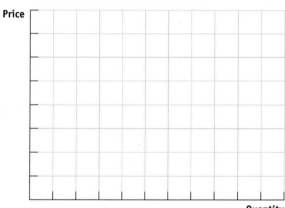

c. New technology for music-playing devices is developed. What happens in the market for music-playing devices?

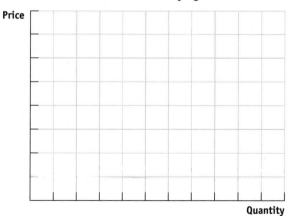

d. The price of labor decreases. What happens in the market for fast-food restaurants?

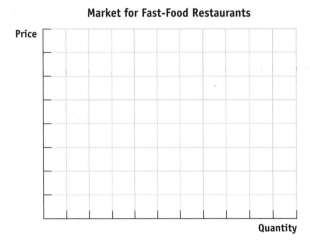

Market for Fast-Food Restaurants

e. Income increases and good X is a normal good. What happens in the market for good X?

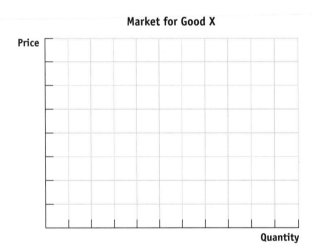

Market for Good X

f. Income increases and good X is an inferior good. What happens in the market for good X?

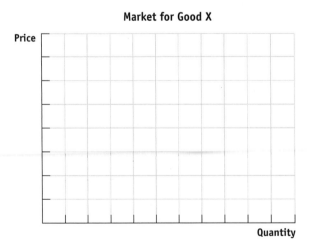

Market for Good X

11. You are given the following information about the demand and supply schedules for gadgets in Micro Town. Assume that gadgets in Micro Town are produced in a competitive market.

Price	Quantity demanded	Quantity supplied
$ 0	100	0
2	80	20
4	60	40
6	40	60
8	20	80
10	0	100

a. From the data provided in the table, write an equation expressing the demand schedule and an equation expressing the supply schedule.

b. Using the equations you wrote in part (a), find the equilibrium price and the equilibrium quantity in this market.

c. Now suppose that the quantity demanded increases by 20 units at every price and that the quantity supplied increases by 40 units at every price. What happens to the equilibrium price and equilibrium quantity in this market relative to the initial levels of the equilibrium price and equilibrium quantity? (Hint: you might find it helpful to draw a sketch of the original demand curve and then the new demand curve to help guide you in your work. Then, once you have the new demand curve equation, you could draw a sketch of the original supply curve and the new supply curve to help you calculate the new supply curve equation.)

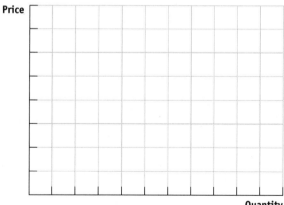

d. Now suppose that the quantity demanded increases by the same amount as in part (c), but that the quantity supplied increases by only 10 units at every price. What happens to the equilibrium price and the equilibrium quantity in this market relative to the initial levels of the equilibrium price and equilibrium quantity?

e. In parts (c) and (d), the demand and supply curves shifted to the right. If you knew the direction of these shifts, but did not know the size or magnitude of the shift, what would you know about the new equilibrium price and quantity?

12. Let's generalize the findings of question 11 for four different situations in which both the demand and supply curves shift at the same time. In each of these situations we assume that we know the direction of the shift but not the size of the shift. Fill in the following table for each of the possible situations. The first situation (the one in question 11) has already been done for you.

Situation	Effect on equilibrium price	Effect on equilibrium quantity
Demand shifts to the right and supply shifts to the right	May increase, decrease, or remain the same	Increases
Demand shifts to the left and supply shifts to the left		
Demand shifts to the right and supply shifts to the left		
Demand shifts to the left and supply shifts to the right		

BEFORE YOU TAKE THE TEST

Chapter Review Questions

1. Competitive markets are characterized as having
   a. many buyers and a single seller.
   b. many buyers and a few sellers.
   c. many buyers and many sellers.
   d. a few buyers and many sellers.

2. Sue goes to the store to purchase a bottle of shampoo. When she gets to the store she discovers that her brand of shampoo is on sale for $4 a bottle instead of the usual $5.99 per bottle. According to the law of demand, we can expect that
   a. Sue will purchase one bottle of shampoo.
   b. Sue will not purchase the shampoo.
   c. Sue will likely purchase more than one bottle of shampoo.
   d. Sue will substitute away from her usual brand of shampoo and instead purchase an alternative brand.

3. The law of demand states that the quantity demanded is an inverse function of its price. This means that
   a. as price increases, the quantity demanded decreases.
   b. as price increases, the quantity demanded increases.
   c. the demand curve shifts to the left with increases in price.
   d. the demand curve shifts to the right with increases in price.

4. Consider the market for mangos. Suppose researchers discover that eating mangos generates large health benefits. Which of the following statements is true?
   a. This discovery will not affect the market for mangos.
   b. This discovery will cause the demand for mangos to shift to the right.
   c. This discovery will cause the price of mangos to decrease due to a movement along the demand curve for mangos.
   d. This discovery will cause a movement along the demand curve for mangos.

5. Consider the demand curve for automobiles. An increase in the price of automobiles due to a leftward shift in the supply curve will
   a. cause a movement along the demand curve for automobiles.
   b. result in an increase in the quantity of automobiles demanded.
   c. have no effect on the quantity of automobiles demanded since the change occurred on the supply side of the model.
   d. Answers (a) and (b) are both true statements.

6. The prices of flat-screen TVs are expected to fall next year. Which of the following statements about the market for flat-screen TVs this year are true?
   I. Consumers will decrease their demand for flat-screen TVs at all prices this year in anticipation of the decrease in flat-screen TV prices next year.
   II. Flat-screen TV prices today are likely to decrease due to these expectations.
   III. Flat-screen TV prices today are likely to increase due to these expectations.
   a. Statement I is true.
   b. Statement II is true.
   c. Statement III is true.
   d. Statements I and II are true.
   e. Statements I and III are true.

7. Peanut butter and jelly are considered to be complements in the diet of many people. Holding everything else constant, if the price of peanut butter increases, then the demand for
   a. peanut butter will shift to the left.
   b. peanut butter will shift to the right.
   c. jelly will shift to the left.
   d. jelly will shift to the right.

8. Ham and turkey are considered to be substitutes in the diet of many people. Holding everything else constant, if the price of ham decreases, then the demand for
   a. turkey will shift to the left.
   b. turkey will shift to the right.
   c. ham will shift to the left.
   d. ham will shift to the right.

9. Consider two goods: good X and good Y. Holding everything else constant, the price of good Y increases and the demand for good X decreases. Good X and good Y are
   a. complements.
   b. substitutes.
   c. not related to each other.

10. Consider two goods: good X and good Y. Holding everything else constant, the price of good Y decreases and the demand for good X decreases. Good X and good Y are
    a. complements.
    b. substitutes.
    c. not related to each other.

11. Holding everything else constant, Jon's income increases. If Jon's demand for good X decreases, then it must be the case that good X is a(n)
    a. inferior good.
    b. normal good.
    c. complement.
    d. substitute.

12. Jon's income increases by 10% this year while his purchases of steak increase by 4% this year over last year's purchases of steak. Holding everything else constant, Jon considers steak to be a(n)
    a. inferior good.
    b. normal good.
    c. complement.
    d. substitute.

13. Smalltown experiences an increase in its population due to the economic opportunities available in Smalltown. This event is likely to
    a. cause the demand curve for many products in Smalltown to shift to the right.
    b. cause the demand curve for many products in Smalltown to shift to the left.
    c. have little effect on the demand for products in Smalltown.
    d. cause the supply curve for many products in Smalltown to shift to the left.

14. A market is initially composed of 100 buyers. Holding everything else constant, if an additional 100 buyers join this market, then this will
    a. have no effect on the market demand curve since there is a limit to how many units of the good can be demanded at any price.
    b. cause the market demand curve to shift to the left since the good's price will necessarily increase when there are more buyers.
    c. cause the market demand curve to shift to the right as the additional demand of these new consumers is added to the initial demand curve.
    d. cause a movement along the demand curve as the price of the good rises due to the increase in the number of buyers.

15. Consider a market composed of three consumers: Peter, Anya, and Pablo. The market demand schedule is given in the table that follows. Which of the possible individual demand schedules provided in the answer selection is most likely to correspond to this market demand schedule?

Price	Market quantity demanded
$10	100
20	75
30	50
40	25

a.

Price	Quantity demanded by Peter	Quantity demanded by Anya	Quantity demanded by Pablo
$10	25	25	40
20	20	20	35
30	15	14	16
40	10	10	5

b.

Price	Quantity demanded by Peter	Quantity demanded by Anya	Quantity demanded by Pablo
$10	25	25	50
20	20	15	35
30	15	10	25
40	10	10	5

c.

Price	Quantity demanded by Peter	Quantity demanded by Anya	Quantity demanded by Pablo
$10	25	25	55
20	15	20	35
30	10	15	20
40	5	10	5

d.

Price	Quantity demanded by Peter	Quantity demanded by Anya	Quantity demanded by Pablo
$10	25	25	50
20	20	20	35
30	15	15	20
40	10	10	5

16. Consider a supply curve. When the price of the good increases, then this results in a movement along the supply curve resulting in a greater
a. supply of the good.
b. quantity supplied.

17. The cost of ground beef used to produce Fast Wally's hamburgers increases. Holding everything else constant, this will result

  a. in the supply curve shifting to the left.

  b. in the supply curve shifting to the right.

  c. in a movement along the supply curve to a smaller quantity supplied.

  d. in a movement along the supply curve to a greater quantity supplied.

18. The cost of raw materials used to produce Ever Strong Batteries decreases. Holding everything else constant, this will result

  a. in the supply curve shifting to the left.

  b. in the supply curve shifting to the right.

  c. in a movement along the supply curve to a smaller quantity supplied.

  d. in a movement along the supply curve to a greater quantity supplied.

19. Input prices decrease for a manufacturer. Holding everything else constant, this implies that at any given price the manufacturer will supply

  a. more of the good.

  b. less of the good.

20. A manufacturer produces two different products from its fixed set of resources. When the manufacturer increases the production of the first good, it must necessarily reduce the level of production of the second good due to these fixed resources. These two goods are

  a. complements in production.

  b. substitutes in production.

21. A sawmill operator produces lumber used in the construction industry as well as sawdust used for pet bedding. An increase in the supply of lumber is likely to

  a. increase the supply of sawdust, since lumber and sawdust are complements in production.

  b. decrease the supply of sawdust, since lumber and sawdust are complements in production.

  c. increase the supply of sawdust, since lumber and sawdust are substitutes in production.

  d. decrease the supply of sawdust, since lumber and sawdust are substitutes in production.

22. Research and development result in the discovery of a new technology for electricity generation. Holding everything else constant, this discovery will

  a. increase the supply of electricity.

  b. increase the quantity supplied of electricity.

  c. decrease the supply of electricity.

  d. decrease the quantity supplied of electricity.

23. The sawmill industry expects lumber prices to rise next year due to growing demand for the construction of new homes. Holding everything else constant, this expectation will shift

  a. the supply curve for lumber this year to the left.

  b. the supply curve for lumber this year to the right.

24. The following graph illustrates the supply curve for the competitive market for widgets. Currently there are 16 producers in this market and each producer produces exactly the same number of widgets as every other producer. Suppose the price of widgets is $40. If all the producers continue to produce the same number as every other producer, what will be the level of production for each producer?

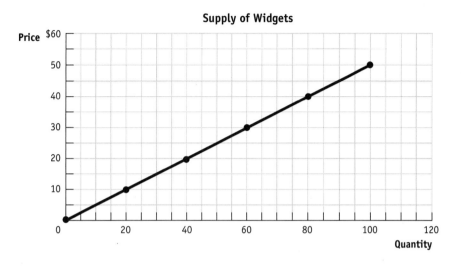

Supply of Widgets

a. 8 widgets
b. 10 widgets
c. 5 widgets
d. 20 widgets

25. The market demand curve for a product is the horizontal summation of the individual demand curves for the product, holding the
a. quantity demanded constant.
b. price constant.

26. Which of the following statements is true about equilibrium in a competitive market for a good?
  I. In equilibrium, the quantity demanded equals the quantity supplied.
  II. The equilibrium price and the equilibrium quantity correspond to the price and quantity at which the demand curve intersects the supply curve.
  III. In equilibrium, every consumer who wishes to consume the product is satisfied.
a. Statement I is true.
b. Statement II is true.
c. Statement III is true.
d. Statements I and II are true.
e. Statements I, II, and III are true.

27. The competitive market for widgets is described by the following table.

Price	Quantity demanded	Quantity supplied
$ 0	400	0
20	300	100
40	200	200
60	100	300
80	0	400

If the current price is $20, then there is a(n)
a. excess supply of 200 widgets.
b. shortage of 200 widgets.
c. excess demand of 100 widgets.
d. surplus of 100 widgets.

28. The competitive market for widgets is described by the following table.

Price	Quantity demanded	Quantity supplied
$ 0	400	0
20	300	100
40	200	200
60	100	300
80	0	400

If the current price is $60, then there is a(n)
a. excess supply of 200 widgets.
b. excess demand of 200 widgets.
c. shortage of 100 widgets.
d. surplus of 100 widgets.

29. The competitive market for widgets is described by the following table.

Price	Quantity demanded	Quantity supplied
$ 0	400	0
20	300	100
40	200	200
60	100	300
80	0	400

The equilibrium quantity in this market is _____ and the equilibrium price is _____ .

a. 300 widgets; $20
b. 200 widgets; $20
c. 200 widgets; $40
d. 200 widgets; $60

30. The competitive market for widgets is described by the following table. Furthermore, you are told that both the demand curve and the supply curve are linear.

Price	Quantity demanded	Quantity supplied
$ 0	400	0
20	300	100
40	200	200
60	100	300
80	0	400

Which of the following equations is the demand equation for widgets?

a. $Q = 80 - 5P$
b. $P = 80 - 5Q$
c. $Q = 400 - 5P$
d. $Q = 1/5P$

31. The competitive market for widgets is described by the following table. Furthermore, you are told that both the demand curve and the supply curve are linear.

Price	Quantity demanded	Quantity supplied
$ 0	400	0
20	300	100
40	200	200
60	100	300
80	0	400

Which of the following equations is the supply equation for widgets?

a. $P = 5Q$
b. $P = 1/5Q$
c. $Q = 1/5P$
d. $Q = 100 + 1/5Q$

32. Use the following graph of a competitive market for candles to answer this question.

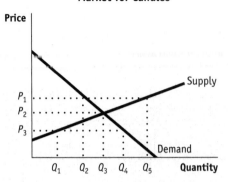

Market for Candles

At a price of P_1, there is an

a. excess supply of the good equal to $Q_2 - Q_5$.

b. excess supply of the good equal to $Q_5 - Q_2$.

c. excess supply of the good equal to $Q_3 - Q_2$.

d. excess demand for the good equal to $Q_3 - Q_2$.

33. Use the following graph of a competitive market for candles to answer this question.

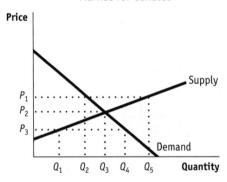

Market for Candles

At a price of P_3, there is an

a. excess demand for the good of $Q_4 - Q_1$.

b. excess demand for the good of $Q_1 - Q_4$.

c. excess demand for the good of $Q_3 - Q_2$.

d. excess supply of the good of $Q_3 - Q_2$.

34. In the competitive market for candles, there is an increase in the number of people purchasing candles and a decrease in the cost of beeswax, a major ingredient in the production of candles. Which of the following statements is true?

a. The equilibrium price and the equilibrium quantity of candles will increase.

b. The equilibrium price and the equilibrium quantity of candles will decrease.

c. The equilibrium price may increase, decrease, or remain the same, but the equilibrium quantity will increase.

d. The equilibrium quantity may increase, decrease, or remain the same, but the equilibrium price will increase.

35. Consumers in Mayville consider houses and apartments to be substitutes. There is an increase in the price of houses in Mayville at the same time three new apartment buildings are opened in Mayville. In the market for apartments in Mayville
   a. the equilibrium price will rise relative to its level before these two events.
   b. the equilibrium price will fall relative to its level before these two events.
   c. the equilibrium quantity will rise relative to its level before these two events.
   d. the equilibrium quantity will fall relative to its level before these two events.

36. The production of good X requires labor inputs and therefore the price of good X is directly affected by labor costs. Suppose that the price of labor increases while simultaneously people's income rises. If good X is a normal good, then we know in the market for good X
   a. the equilibrium price will increase and the equilibrium quantity may increase, decrease, or remain the same relative to their initial levels.
   b. the equilibrium price will decrease and the equilibrium quantity may increase, decrease, or remain the same relative to their initial levels.
   c. the equilibrium quantity will increase and the equilibrium price may increase, decrease, or remain the same relative to their initial levels.
   d. the equilibrium quantity will decrease and the equilibrium price may increase, decrease, or remain the same relative to their initial levels.

37. People's income rises, while simultaneously there is a technological advance in the production of good X. Good X is an inferior good. Given this information we know in the market for good X
   a. the equilibrium price will increase and the equilibrium quantity may increase, decrease, or remain the same relative to their initial levels.
   b. the equilibrium price will decrease and the equilibrium quantity may increase, decrease, or remain the same relative to their initial levels.
   c. the equilibrium quantity will increase and the equilibrium price may increase, decrease, or remain the same relative to their initial levels.
   d. the equilibrium quantity will decrease and the equilibrium price may increase, decrease, or remain the same relative to their initial levels.

38. The price of bubble gum increases at the same time that sugar, a major ingredient in candy, gets more expensive. If candy and bubble gum are substitutes, what happens to the equilibrium price and the equilibrium quantity in the market for candy?
   a. The equilibrium price will increase and the equilibrium quantity may increase, decrease, or remain the same relative to their initial levels.
   b. The equilibrium price will decrease and the equilibrium quantity may increase, decrease, or remain the same relative to their initial levels.
   c. The equilibrium quantity will increase and the equilibrium price may increase, decrease, or remain the same relative to their initial levels.
   d. The equilibrium quantity will decrease and the equilibrium price may increase, decrease, or remain the same relative to their initial levels.

◼ ANSWER KEY

Answers to Problems and Exercises

1. This assumption results in a market situation in which no buyer (or group of buyers) and no seller (or group of sellers) can affect the market price. In a competitive market, the interaction of demand and supply determines the equilibrium price and the equilibrium quantity rather than the behavior of a particular buyer and/or seller.

2. **a.**

Demand Curve

b. If the price rises to $60, the quantity demanded will fall by 300 units, from 500 bicycles to 200 bicycles.

c. If the price falls to $0, the quantity demanded will increase by 500 units, from 500 bicycles to 1,000 bicycles.

3.

Situation	Specified market	Movement or shift	Rightward or leftward shift in demand
People's income increases	Market for exotic vacations	Shift	Rightward
People's income decreases	Market for goods sold in secondhand shops	Shift	Rightward
Price of bicycles increases	Market for bicycles	Movement	
Price of tennis balls increases	Market for tennis racquets	Shift	Leftward
Price of movie tickets decreases	Popcorn at movie theaters	Shift	Rightward
Popularity of music-playing device increases	Market for music-playing device	Shift	Rightward
Popularity of branded clothing items decreases	Market for brand-name designer clothing	Shift	Leftward
Winter clothing to go on sale next month	Market for winter clothing	Shift	Leftward
Increase in urban residents	Market for apartments in urban areas	Shift	Rightward

4.   **a.** Note: these sketches are not drawn to scale since they are meant to be a guide rather than a perfect mathematical rendering of the data in the table. To find the market demand curve, hold price constant and ask how many units are demanded by all the consumers at this price. For example, at a price of $3, Joe demands 4 units, Maria demands 8 units, and Chao demands 2 units for a total market demand of 14 units at a price of $3. Repeat this for another price (e.g., for a price of $4, Joe demands 2 units, Maria demands 4 units, and Chao demands 1 unit for a total market demand of 7 units).

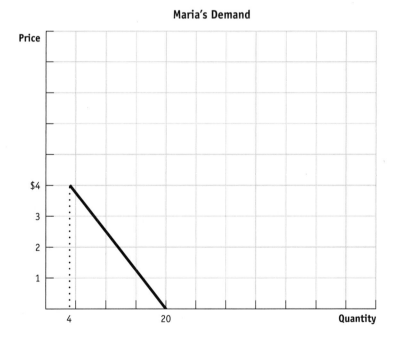

Chao's Demand

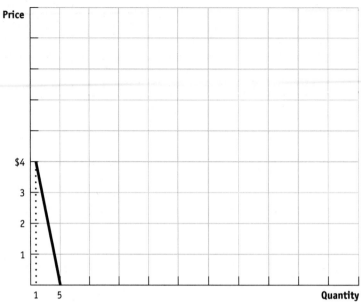

Market Demand

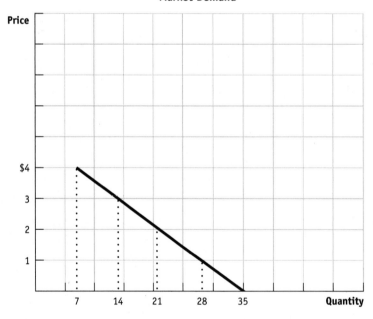

b. Summarize the market demand curve you found by filling in the following table.

Price	Quantity demanded in market
$0	35
1	28
2	21
3	14
4	7

5. **a.** At a price of $20, producers are willing to supply 40 units.

   b. At a price of $40, producers are willing to supply 80 units.

   c. At a price of $50, 100 widgets are supplied. Thus, if there are ten producers producing exactly the same number of widgets, then each producer must produce 10 widgets.

   d. When price falls from $30 to $20, the number of widgets supplied decreases by 20 widgets (from 60 widgets to 40 widgets).

   e. When price rises from $30 to $50, the number of widgets supplied increases by 40 widgets (from 60 widgets to 100 widgets).

   f. Suppliers are willing to supply 80 widgets if the price is $40.

   g. Suppliers are willing to supply 40 widgets if the price is $20.

   h. The typical supply curve is upward sloping: its slope is positive. This implies that the quantity supplied increases when price increases and that the quantity supplied decreases when price decreases.

6.

Situation	Specified market	Movement or shift	Rightward or leftward shift in supply
Labor costs for air travel and cruise ships increase	Market for exotic vacations	Shift	Leftward
Prices of office equipment and phone service rise by 40%	Market for call center services	Shift	Leftward
Price of bicycles increases	Market for bicycles	Movement	
Price of leather boots increases	Market for beef products	Shift	Rightward
Price of leather boots increases	Market for leather belts	Shift	Leftward
New technology for music-playing device revealed	Market for music-playing devices	Shift	Rightward
Price of brand-name designer clothing increases	Market for brand-name designer clothing	Movement	
Stock market prices expected to fall next quarter	Stock market today	Shift	Rightward
Increase in number of coffee shop owners in the metro area	Market for coffee shops in the metro area	Shift	Rightward

7. a.,b. Equilibrium occurs at the price at which the quantity demanded equals the quantity supplied. From the following table, we can see that the quantity demanded equals the quantity supplied at a price of $30. The equilibrium price is thus $30 and the equilibrium quantity is 400 units. This point is illustrated in the graph in part (d).

c.

Price	Excess demand	Excess supply
$ 0	1,000 units	
10	675 units	
20	325 units	
30	Equilibrium	Equilibrium
40		350 units
50		675 units

d. When there is excess demand this means that the quantity demanded by consumers is greater than the quantity supplied by producers. The market for some reason does not provide an adequate amount of the good, and thus there is a shortage of the good. The figure following illustrates a shortage at a price of P_1. Note that at P_1, the quantity demanded is Q_1, the quantity supplied is Q_2, and the excess demand is equal to $Q_1 - Q_2$. When a market has excess demand, this implies that the current price of the good is less than the market-clearing price.

**Illustration of a Situation of
Excess Demand, or a Shortage**

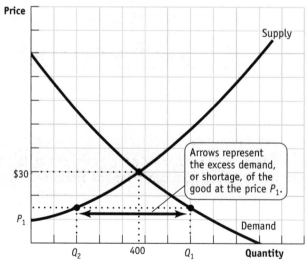

e. When there is excess supply this means that the quantity demanded by consumers is less than the quantity supplied by producers. The market for some reason provides too much of the good, and thus there is a surplus of the good. The following figure illustrates a surplus at a price of P_1. Note that at P_1, the quantity demanded is Q_1, the quantity supplied is Q_2, and the excess supply is equal to $Q_2 - Q_1$. When a market has excess supply of a good, this implies that the current price in the market is greater than the market-clearing price.

Illustration of a Situation of Excess Supply, or a Surplus

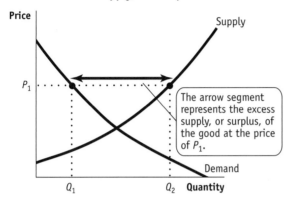

8. a. The equilibrium price in this market is P_3 since the quantity demanded (Q_3) equals the quantity supplied (Q_3) at this price.

b. Q_3.

c. At P_2 there is an excess supply, or surplus, of the good, since the quantity supplied equals Q_5 while the quantity demanded equals Q_2. The price should fall toward the equilibrium price. As the price falls, consumers will increase the quantity demanded of the good while producers will decrease the quantity supplied of the good until the price reaches the point where the quantity demanded equals the quantity supplied.

d. At P_4 there is an excess demand, or shortage, for the good, since the quantity supplied equals Q_1 while the quantity demanded equals Q_4. The price should rise toward the equilibrium price. As the price increases, consumers will reduce the quantity demanded of the good while producers will increase the quantity supplied of the good until the price reaches the point where the quantity demanded equals the quantity supplied.

e. When the quantity demanded is equal to Q_4, this implies that the current price in the market is P_4, which is the situation of excess demand described in part (d).

f. When the quantity supplied is equal to Q_5, this implies that the current price in the market is P_2, which is the situation of excess supply described in part (c).

g. At P_1 the quantity demanded is equal to zero. This implies that at a price of P_1 the price is too high for consumers to be willing to demand the product.

h. At P_5 the quantity supplied is equal to zero. This implies that at a price of P_5 the price is too low for producers to be willing to supply the good.

9. a.

Price	Quantity demanded	Quantity supplied
$ 0	1,000	0
240	880	40
480	760	80
720	640	120
960	520	160
1,200	400	200
1,440	280	240
1,680	160	280
1,920	40	320

b. Examination of the previous table reveals that prices less than or equal to $1,440 result in a situation of excess demand, while prices greater than or equal to $1,680 result in a situation of excess supply. Thus, the equilibrium price will fall somewhere in the range of $1,440 to $1,680 in this market.

c.

Market for Bicycles in Pedal City

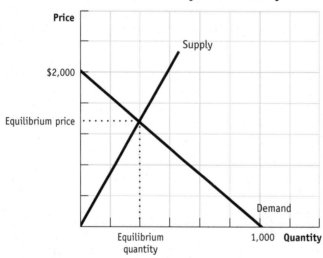

d. At a price of $240, 40 bicycles will be supplied and each manufacturer will produce 2 bicycles. At a price of $240, 880 bicycles will be demanded. The market is not in equilibrium since there is an excess demand for bicycles.

e. At a price of $480, 80 bicycles will be supplied and each manufacturer will produce 4 bicycles. At a price of $480, 760 bicycles will be demanded. The market is not in equilibrium since there is an excess demand for bicycles.

f. At a price of $1,680, 280 bicycles will be supplied and each manufacturer will produce 14 bicycles. At a price of $1,680, 160 bicycles will be demanded. The market is not in equilibrium since there is an excess supply of bicycles.

g. Since $P = 2,000 - 2Q$ and $P = 6Q$, we can use this information to write $2,000 - 2Q = 6Q$. Solving this equation gives us the equilibrium quantity of 250 bicycles. Substituting this quantity into either the demand equation or the supply equation yields the equilibrium price: $P = 2,000 - 2(250) = $1,500$, or $P = 6(250) = $1,500$.

10. a. Gasoline and bicycles are substitutes for each other. When the price of gasoline rises, people substitute away from gasoline toward bicycle transportation. This is illustrated in the following graph with the demand curve for bicycles shifting to the right, resulting in a higher equilibrium price (P_2) and a higher equilibrium quantity (Q_2). Note that there is a shift in the demand curve and a movement along the supply curve.

Market for Bicycles

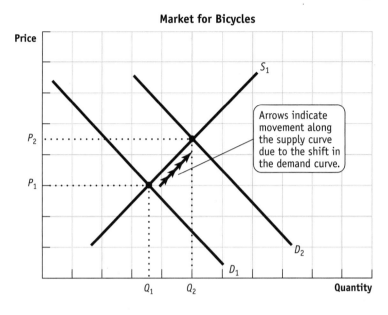

b. Gasoline and SUVs are complements for each other. When the price of gasoline rises, people find that driving SUVs is relatively more expensive and therefore decrease their demand for SUVs at every price. This is illustrated in the following graph with the demand curve for SUVs shifting to the left, resulting in a lower equilibrium price (P_2) and a lower equilibrium quantity (Q_2). Note that there is a shift in the demand curve and a movement along the supply curve.

Market for SUVs

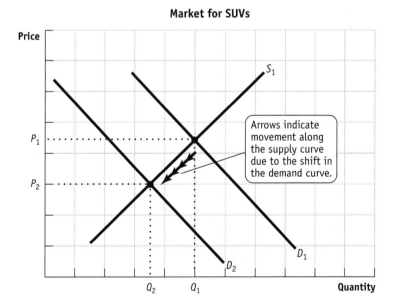

c. New technology shifts the supply curve to the right from S_1 to S_2. This causes a movement along the demand curve and results in a decrease in the equilibrium price and an increase in the equilibrium quantity. This is illustrated in the following graph.

Market for Music-Playing Devices

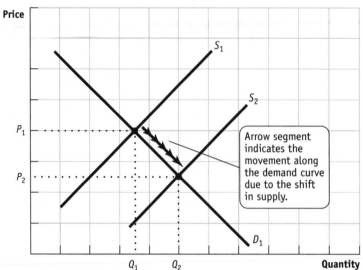

d. When the price of labor decreases, this causes the supply of the good to shift to the right since labor is an input in the production of fast-food meals. This results in a movement along the demand curve and a decrease in the equilibrium price and an increase in the equilibrium quantity.

Market for Fast-Food Restaurants

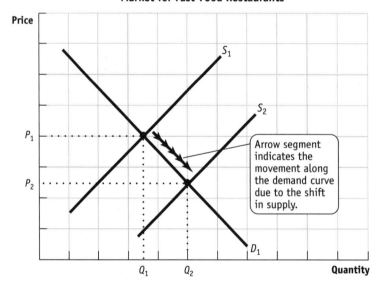

e. An increase in income shifts the demand curve to the right if the good is a normal good. This shift in demand causes a movement along the supply curve and an increase in both the equilibrium price and the equilibrium quantity.

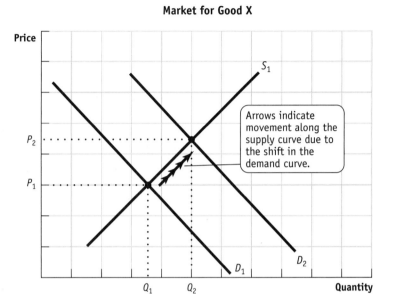

Market for Good X

f. An increase in income shifts the demand curve to the left if the good is an inferior good. This shift in demand causes a movement along the supply curve and a decrease in both the equilibrium price and the equilibrium quantity. The following graph illustrates this situation.

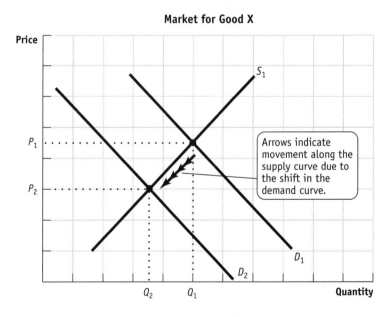

Market for Good X

11. a. The demand equation is $P = 10 - (1/10)Q$ and the supply equation is $P = (1/10)Q$.

   b. Solving the two equations from part (a), we find that the equilibrium price equals $5 and the equilibrium quantity equals 50.

c. To find the new equilibrium price and quantity, we need to know the new demand and supply curves. Draw a sketch of the original demand curve and the new demand curve (shifted to the right at every price by 20 units) to guide you in your calculations. The following figure illustrates this sketch.

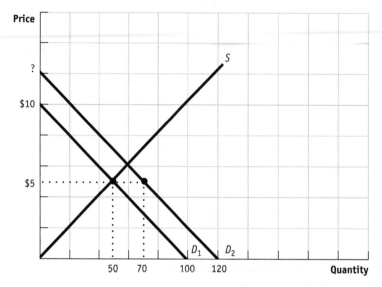

We know from part (b) that the initial equilibrium is at price $5 and the equilibrium quantity is 50, which gives us two points on the new demand curve: (70, 5) and (120, 0). We also know that the new demand curve is parallel to the original demand curve and thus has the same slope as the original demand curve. But we do not know the y-intercept for the new demand curve. To find the equation, let's write the new equation as $P = b - (1/10)Q$. This equation has the same slope as the original demand curve, but has not yet identified the y-intercept. To find the value of b, let's substitute the coordinates of one of the points we know is on D_2: thus, using (70, 5) yields $5 = b - (1/10)70$, or $b = 12$. So our new demand curve equation is $P = 12 - (1/10)Q$. Use the same technique to find the new supply curve equation. The graph that follows sketches the original demand and supply curve and also the new supply curve, which illustrates an increase of 40 units in the quantity supplied at every price. We know the coordinates of two points on this new supply curve—(40, 0) and (90, 5)—and we also know that the new supply curve has the same slope as the original supply curve. So we can rewrite the new supply curve as $P = b + (1/10)Q$ and then use one of our known points to solve for b, the y-intercept. Thus, using (90, 5) we get $5 = b + (1/10)90$, or $b = -4$, and the new supply curve is $P = (1/10)Q - 4$.

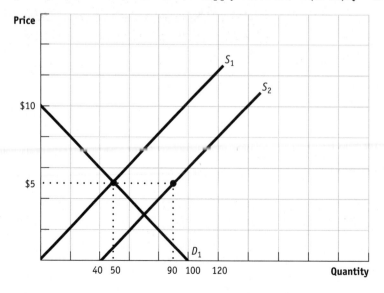

Using the new demand curve and new supply curve, we can easily solve for the equilibrium price and the equilibrium quantity in this market. Since $P = 12 - (1/10)Q$ and $P = (1/10)Q - 4$, we have $12 - (1/10)Q = (1/10)Q - 4$, or the equilibrium quantity (Q) equals 80. Then replacing Q with 80 in either the demand or supply equation, we find that the equilibrium price (P) equals 4. In this case, the equilibrium price decreases relative to its initial level, while the equilibrium quantity increases relative to its initial level.

d. Since the change in the quantity demanded at each price is the same as in part (c), we know that the new demand curve can be written as $P = 12 - (1/10)Q$. But we need to use the same technique as we employed in part (c) to find the new supply curve. When you do this, you will find that the new supply curve equation is $P = (1/10)Q - 1$. Solving these two equations for the equilibrium price and the equilibrium quantity, we find that the new equilibrium price is 5.5 while the new equilibrium quantity is 65 units. In this case, the equilibrium price and the equilibrium quantity increase relative to their initial quantities.

e. You would know with certainty that the equilibrium quantity increased, but you would not know if the equilibrium price increased, decreased, or remained the same, since you do not know the magnitude of the shifts in the demand and supply curves.

12.

Situation	Effect on equilibrium price	Effect on equilibrium quantity
Demand shifts to the right and supply shifts to the right	May increase, decrease, or remain the same	Increases
Demand shifts to the left and supply shifts to the left	May increase, decrease, or remain the same	Decreases
Demand shifts to the right and supply shifts to the left	Increases	May increase, decrease, or remain the same
Demand shifts to the left and supply shifts to the right	Decreases	May increase, decrease, or remain the same

Answers to Chapter Review Questions

1. **Answer c.** This is a definitional statement.

2. **Answer c.** The law of demand states that as the price of the good decreases, the quantity demanded of the good increases. Since the shampoo is on sale, its price has fallen and the law of demand suggests that the quantity demanded should therefore increase.

3. **Answer a.** This is a definitional statement. An inverse function of two variables means that an increase in one of the variables will result in a decrease in the other variable, or a decrease in one of the variables will result in an increase in the other variable. The law of demand states that as the price of the good increases, the quantity demanded of the good decreases; thus, price and quantity are inversely related.

4. **Answer b.** This research finding is likely to result in an increase in tastes and preferences for mangos, which will cause the demand curve for mangos to shift to the right.

5. **Answer a.** A leftward shift in the supply curve holding everything else constant will cause the price of the good to increase. This increase in price will result in a movement along the demand curve, since as the price increases, the quantity demanded of the good decreases.

6. **Answer d.** The expected fall in flat-screen TV prices next year will cause the demand curve for flat-screen TVs this year to shift to the left as consumers decrease the quantity of flat-screen TVs they demand at every price. This will result in a movement along the supply curve for flat-screen TVs this year. This price expectation should result in a decrease in the price of flat-screen TVs this year.

7. **Answer c.** Since peanut butter and jelly are considered complements in this example, an increase in the price of peanut butter will cause the demand curve for jelly to shift to the left, since as fewer units of peanut butter are demanded due to the higher price of peanut butter, fewer units of jelly will also be demanded at any given price for jelly.

8. **Answer a.** Since ham and turkey are substitutes, when the price of ham decreases, this causes the quantity of ham demanded to increase. As more units of ham are demanded, fewer units of turkey are demanded at every price. The demand for turkey therefore shifts to the left.

9. **Answer a.** As the price of good Y increases, this results in a decrease in the quantity demanded of good Y. Since the demand for good X decreases, this implies that good Y and good X are consumed together; thus good X and good Y are complements.

10. **Answer b.** As the price of good Y decreases, this results in an increase in the quantity demanded of good Y. Since the demand for good X increases when the quantity demanded of good Y decreases, this implies that good X is a substitute for good Y.

11. **Answer a.** When Jon's income increases, the quantity of good X he demands at any given price falls, which implies that good X is an inferior good.

12. **Answer b.** Both Jon's income and the quantity of steak he demands increases; therefore steak is a normal good.

13. **Answer a.** An increase in population shifts the demand curve to the right, as the increase in population implies a larger number of consumers of the product.

14. **Answer c.** An increase in the number of buyers causes the quantity demanded of the good to increase at every price, and the demand curve shifts to the right.

15. **Answer d.** To find the market demand curve, hold price constant and then add the quantity of the good demanded by each of the consumers. Thus, if the price of the good is $10, then the total of Peter's, Anya's, and Pablo's demand must add up to 100 units according to the table provided in the question.

16. **Answer b.** This question is asking you to recall that a change in the price of the good, holding everything else constant, results in a movement along the curve. This movement along the curve causes a change in the quantity supplied and not a change in the supply curve.

17. **Answer a.** Ground beef is an input in the production of Fast Wally's hamburgers. When ground beef gets more expensive, this increases the cost of producing hamburgers, which causes the supply curve to shift to the left.

18. **Answer b.** When the cost of raw materials decreases, more batteries can be produced at any given price. This decrease in the cost of raw materials causes the supply curve for batteries to shift to the right.

19. **Answer a.** When input prices decrease, producers are willing to supply more units of the good at every price.

20. **Answer b.** Since an increase in the production of one of the goods results in a decrease in the production of the other good, these two goods must be substitutes in production.

21. **Answer a.** Sawdust and lumber are complements in production. As the producer increases its production of lumber, the production of sawdust is also increased since sawdust is a by-product of lumber production.

22. **Answer a.** New technology causes the supply curve to shift to the right, resulting in an increase in the quantity supplied of the good at every price.

23. **Answer a.** The sawmill industry will want to decrease the supply of lumber they provide to the market this year due to their expectation that next year's lumber prices will be higher. At every price the quantity of lumber supplied this year will be decreased, and the supply curve for lumber this year shifts to the left.

24. **Answer c.** When the price is $40, 80 widgets are produced. Since there are sixteen producers in this market and each of these producers produce the same number of widgets, this implies that each producer must be producing 5 widgets.

25. **Answer b.** This is a definitional statement. The market demand curve is found by holding price constant and then adding together the quantities demanded by each consumer in the market. This process is repeated for other prices.

26. **Answer d.** The first two statements are fairly straightforward, but statement III may be somewhat appealing at first glance. At equilibrium, however, even though the quantity demanded equals the quantity supplied, this does not imply that every potential consumer of the good is consuming the good. Those consumers who would like to consume the good, but who are unwilling to pay the equilibrium price, will not consume the good.

27. **Answer b.** At a price of $20, 300 widgets are demanded while 100 widgets are supplied. Thus, at a price of $20 there is an excess demand, or shortage, of 200 widgets.

28. **Answer a.** At a price of $60, 100 widgets are demanded while 300 widgets are supplied. Thus, at a price of $60 there is an excess supply, or surplus, of 200 widgets.

29. **Answer c.** The equilibrium quantity is the quantity at which demand equals the quantity supplied. The equilibrium quantity is 200 widgets, and the equilibrium price is $40.

30. **Answer c.** To find the demand curve, you can either plot the demand curve (although this is time consuming) or you can calculate the slope (rise/run = $-20/100 = -1/5$) and then use the slope-intercept form, $y = mx + b$, to write the equation. Thus, $P = (-1/5)Q + 80$, or solving for Q, $Q = 400 - 5P$.

31. **Answer b.** To find the supply curve, you can either plot the supply curve (although this is time consuming) or you can calculate the slope (rise/run = $20/100 = 1/5$) and then use the slope-intercept form, $y = mx + b$, to write the equation. Thus, $P = (1/5)Q + 0$.

32. **Answer b.** At P_1 the quantity demanded is Q_2 units while the quantity supplied is Q_5 units. The quantity supplied is greater than the quantity demanded at P_1: this excess supply is equal to $Q_5 - Q_2$.

33. **Answer a.** At P_3 the quantity demanded is Q_4 units while the quantity supplied is Q_1 units. The quantity demanded is greater than the quantity supplied at P_3: this excess demand is equal to $Q_4 - Q_1$.

34. **Answer c.** Since we do not know the relative magnitude of the shifts in the demand and supply curves, we cannot know for certain what happens to both the equilibrium price and the equilibrium quantity. The demand curve shifts to the right with the increase in the number of people purchasing candles, and the supply curve also shifts to the right with the decrease in the price of beeswax, one of the inputs in candle production. The equilibrium quantity will increase, but the equilibrium price may increase, decrease, or remain the same depending on the relative magnitude of the shifts in the two curves.

35. **Answer c.** The demand curve for apartments shifts to the right with the increase in the price of houses (houses and apartments are substitute goods for consumers in Mayville), while the supply curve for apartments also shifts to the right with the opening of the new apartment buildings. Since we do not know the magnitude of the shifts in the demand and supply curves, we know that the equilibrium quantity is now larger, but the equilibrium price may increase, decrease, or remain the same with these shifts in the demand and supply curves.

36. **Answer a.** The demand curve for good X shifts to the right since good X is a normal good and income has increased. At the same time, the supply curve for good X shifts to the left since the price of labor has increased. These two shifts result in the equilibrium price increasing while the equilibrium quantity may have increased, decreased, or remained the same depending on the magnitude of the shifts in the demand and supply curves.

37. **Answer b.** Since good X is an inferior good, the increase in income results in the demand curve for good X shifting to the left. At the same time, the technological advance causes the supply curve for good X to shift to the right. The equilibrium price will decrease, but the equilibrium quantity may increase, decrease, or remain the same depending on the magnitude of the shifts in the demand and supply curves.

38. **Answer a.** The supply curve for candy shifts to the left with the increase in the price of sugar, while the demand curve for candy shifts to the right with the increase in the price of bubble gum. The equilibrium price will increase, but the equilibrium quantity may increase, decrease, or remain the same depending on the magnitude of the shifts in the demand and supply curves.

chapter 4

Price Controls and Quotas: Meddling with Markets

BEFORE YOU READ THE CHAPTER

Summary

This chapter develops the ideas of price controls and quantity controls in competitive markets and then illustrates how the implementation of these types of controls reduces the efficiency of a market. In particular, the chapter discusses effective price ceilings, whereby the government sets the price of the good below the equilibrium price; effective price floors, whereby the government sets the price of the good above the equilibrium price; and quantity controls, whereby the government limits the amount of the good available to a level lower than the equilibrium level of output. The chapter also discusses the distributional impact of market interventions.

Chapter Objectives

Objective #1.   Price controls refer to the government's intervention in a market to set the price of the good or service at some level other than the equilibrium price. A price ceiling is the maximum price for a good or service allowed by the government, and a price floor is the minimum price for a good or service allowed by the government.

Objective #2.   An effective price ceiling in a competitive market creates a situation of excess quantity demanded. If the price ceiling is set above the equilibrium price in the market, the price ceiling will not be effective and therefore will have no effect on the equilibrium price and the equilibrium quantity in the market.

Objective #3.   An effective price ceiling prevents a market from being efficient because the price ceiling prevents transactions from occurring that would make some people better off without making other people worse off. In particular, an effective price ceiling prevents demanders who are willing to pay more for the good from consuming the good since the good's supply is artificially limited by the imposed price ceiling. Inefficiency arises because the price ceiling:

- reduces the quantity of the good available;
- reduces the value of total surplus;
- misallocates the good or service among consumers;
- wastes resources, as consumers spend resources searching for the good that is artificially scarce due to the price ceiling; and
- reduces the quality of the available units that would have been supplied in the absence of the price ceiling.

Objective #4.   Price ceilings provide incentives for illegal activities. Price ceilings are primarily instituted because they benefit some particular group of demanders.

Objective #5.   An effective price floor in a competitive market creates a situation of excess quantity supplied. If the price floor is set below the equilibrium price in the market, the price floor will have no effect on the equilibrium price and the equilibrium quantity in the market.

Objective #6.   An effective price floor results in market inefficiency because it prevents transactions from occurring that would make some people better off without making other people worse off. In particular, an effective price floor prevents suppliers who are willing to supply the good from selling the good since the good's demand is artificially limited by the imposed price floor. Inefficiency arises because the price floor:

- reduces the quantity of the good demanded;
- reduces the value of total surplus;
- misallocates the provision of the good or service by sellers;
- wastes resources, as suppliers search the market for a potential demander of the good; and
- increases the quality of the available units above the level that would have been demanded in the absence of the price floor.

Objective #7.   Price floors provide an incentive for illegal or black market activities, including the bribery and corruption of government officials. Price floors are primarily instituted because they benefit a particular group of sellers.

Objective #8.   The government may also implement quantity controls or a quota in a market. In this case the government sets a limit on the total quantity of the good that can be bought and sold in the market. This quantity is usually limited through the selling of licenses that legally grant the holder of the license the right to supply the good. Quantity controls always set a maximum amount allowed. To be binding in the market, the quota must be set below the equilibrium quantity.

Objective #9.   A quota or quantity control creates a wedge between the price consumers are willing to pay for the good and the price at which producers are willing to supply the good. The difference between these two prices is the quota rent, or the income that the license holder receives from their ownership of a valuable commodity (the license).

Objective #10. Quantity controls are inefficient because they prevent some mutually beneficial transactions from occurring, since the demand price for a given quantity (the quota amount) is greater than the supply price for that quantity. These missed transactions create an incentive to evade the quota limit, often through illegal activity.

Key Terms

price controls legal restrictions on how high or low a market price may go.

price ceiling a maximum price sellers are allowed to charge for a good or service; a form of *price control.*

price floor a minimum price buyers are required to pay for a good or service; a form of *price control.*

inefficient allocation to consumers a form of inefficiency in which people who want the good badly and are willing to pay a high price don't get it, and those who care relatively little about the good and are only willing to pay a low price do get it; often a result of a *price ceiling.*

wasted resources a form of inefficiency in which people expend money, effort, and time to cope with the shortages caused by a *price ceiling.*

inefficiently low quality a form of inefficiency in which sellers offer low-quality goods at a low price even though buyers would prefer a higher quality at a higher price; often a result of a *price ceiling.*

black market a market in which goods or services are bought and sold illegally, either because it is illegal to sell them at all or because the prices charged are legally prohibited by a *price ceiling.*

minimum wage a legal floor on the wage rate, which is the market price of labor.

inefficient allocation of sales among sellers a form of inefficiency in which sellers who would be willing to sell a good at the lowest price are not always those who actually manage to sell it; often the result of a *price floor.*

inefficiently high quality a form of inefficiency in which sellers offer high-quality goods at a high price even though buyers would prefer a lower quality at a lower price; often the result of a *price floor.*

quantity control an upper limit, set by the government, on the quantity of some good that can be bought or sold; also referred to as a *quota.*

quota an upper limit, set by the government, on the quantity of some good that can be bought or sold; also referred to as a *quantity control.*

quota limit the total amount of a good under a *quota* or *quantity control* that can be legally transacted.

license the right, conferred by the government, to supply a good.

demand price the price of a given quantity at which consumers will demand that quantity.

Key Terms *(continued)*

supply price the price of a given quantity at which producers will supply that quantity.

wedge the difference between the *demand price* of the quantity transacted and the *supply price* of the quantity transacted for a good when the supply of the good is legally restricted. Often created by a *quantity control,* or *quota.*

quota rent the difference between the *demand price* and the *supply price* at the *quota limit;* this difference, the earnings that accrue to the license-holder, is equal to the market price of the *license* when the license is traded.

▌ AFTER YOU READ THE CHAPTER

Tips

Tip #1. Students often find it confusing to remember the difference between a price floor and a price ceiling.

- A floor is a surface that you stand on and that is solid. A price floor is the *lowest* price that can be charged for a good. Figure 4.1 illustrates a price floor. To be effective, a price floor must be set at a price that is greater than the equilibrium price. At P_F, Q_1 units will be supplied and Q_2 units will be demanded. An effective price floor always results in a surplus of the good.

Figure 4.1

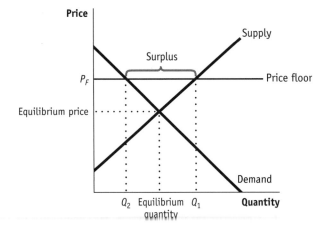

- A ceiling is a surface that you hope is solid and stays above your head. A price ceiling is the *highest* price that can be charged for a good. Figure 4.2 illustrates a price ceiling. To be effective, a price ceiling must be set at a price that is less than the equilibrium price. At P_C, Q_1 units will be supplied and Q_2 units will be demanded. An effective price ceiling always results in a shortage of the good.

Figure 4.2

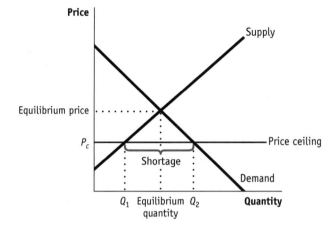

Tip #2. A quota, or quantity control, is a policy implemented by the government to set a maximum amount of the good or service that can be sold in a market. A quota has no effect if it is set at a level greater than the equilibrium quantity; to be effective a quota must be set at a level smaller than the equilibrium quantity. Figure 4.3 illustrates an effective quantity control, or quota, where the maximum allowed quantity is set by the government at Q_1. At Q_1 demanders are willing to pay P_1 for each unit of the good they consume, while suppliers are willing to supply the good at price P_2. This difference, $P_1 - P_2$, is referred to as a wedge. This wedge corresponds to the quota rent the license holder of the good receives when the quantity control is imposed in a market. This quota rent represents the additional compensation the license holder receives from selling the good in a market where the quantity of the good has been artificially restricted.

Figure 4.3

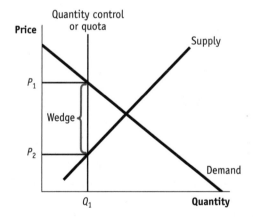

WORKED PROBLEMS

1. Consider a market for cotton in which the market demand curve is given by the equation $Q = 40,000 - 200P$ and the market supply curve is given by the equation $Q = 200P$, where Q is bales of cotton and P is the price per bale of cotton. Suppose this market is initially in equilibrium and then cotton farmers successfully lobby the legislature to impose a price floor of $150 per bale of cotton. After imposition of this price floor, what will be the price of cotton in this market, and how does this price compare with the initial equilibrium price? Identify the number of bales of cotton consumers will purchase once the price floor is implemented. How does this quantity compare with the initial equilibrium quantity in this market? What will the surplus or shortage of cotton equal with the imposition of this price floor? If the government purchases the surplus cotton, what will be the cost of this purchase to the government?

STEP 1: First draw a graph of the market for cotton and find the initial equilibrium price and quantity in this market. Use the two equations to solve for the equilibrium price and quantity.

Thus, $40,000 - 200P = 200P$, or $P = 100$. If $P = 100$, then the quantity demanded at this price can be found using the demand equation: $Q = 40,000 - 200(100)$, or $Q = 20,000$. If $P = 100$, then the quantity supplied at this price can be found using the supply equation: $Q = 200(100) = 20,000$. Since the market is in equilibrium, the quantity demanded is equal to the quantity supplied when the price is equal to 100.

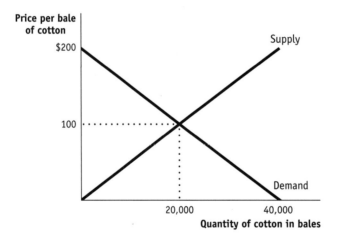

STEP 2: Draw the price floor on your graph and determine if the price floor is an effective price floor. Once you have determined if the price floor is effective, you will know whether the price in this market is the price floor price of $150 per bale or the equilibrium price of $100 per bale. Identify the number of bales of cotton that consumers demand by using the demand equation to see how many bales of cotton they are willing to demand at the new price for cotton. The effective price floor raises the price of cotton and this causes consumers to purchase fewer units of cotton.

Review the section "Price Floors" on pages 109–115 and Figure 4-6 on page 111.

Since the price floor is greater than the equilibrium price, the price floor is effective in this market. The price of cotton in this market will now be the price floor price of $150 per bale: the price of cotton is now higher than it was before the implementation of the price floor. When the price of cotton is $150 per bale, consumers are willing to purchase 10,000 bales of cotton.

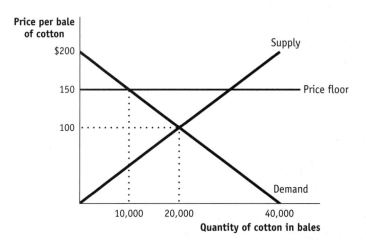

STEP 3: Identify the surplus of cotton that will be produced in this market when there is a price floor and then determine what the cost of purchasing this surplus will be for the government.

Review the section "Price Floors" on pages 109–115 and Figure 4-6 on page 111.

To find the surplus with the price floor requires identifying how many units of cotton suppliers are willing to supply at a price of $150, then subtracting out the number of units of cotton demanders are willing to demand at a price of $150. At a price of $150, suppliers are willing to supply 30,000 bales of cotton, but consumers are willing to purchase only 10,000 bales. Thus, the surplus of cotton is equal to 20,000 bales. If the government purchases this amount of cotton at $150 per bale, it will cost the government $4,500,000. The shaded area in the following graph identifies this cost to the government.

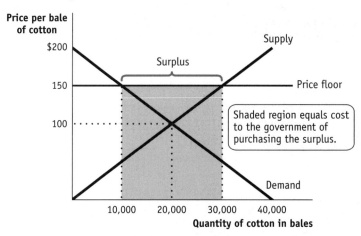

2. Consider the same market for cotton as in problem (1). Suppose this market is initially in equilibrium and then cotton farmers successfully lobby the legislature to impose a quantity control, or quota, in this market of 10,000 bales of cotton. What will the "wedge" or quota rent be equal to in this market?

STEP 1: Start by drawing a graph of the market for cotton, identifying the initial equilibrium price and quantity. From your work in problem (1), you already have identified the equilibrium price as $100 per bale of cotton and the equilibrium quantity as 20,000 bales of cotton. After labeling these points on your graph, draw the quantity control or quota on your graph. The quantity control will be a vertical line where the quantity of bales of cotton is 10,000.

Review the section "Controlling Quantities" on pages 115–120, the section "The Anatomy of Quantity Controls" on pages 116–118, and Figure 4-9 on page XXX.

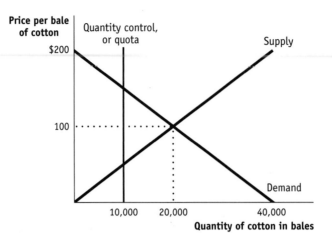

STEP 2: To find the "wedge" or quota rent, you will need to see what price consumers are willing to pay for the quota amount and what price producers must receive in order to provide the quota amount. The difference between the price consumers are willing to pay and the price producers must receive is the "wedge."

Review the section "The Anatomy of Quantity Controls" on pages 116–118 and Figure 4-9 on page XXX.

Consumers are willing to pay $150 per bale of cotton when 10,000 bales of cotton are offered in the market. Producers must receive $50 per bale of cotton if they supply 10,000 bales of cotton. The "wedge" is therefore $100, or the difference between these two prices. The following figure illustrates this wedge.

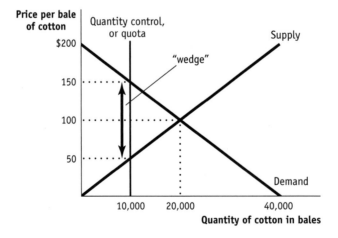

3. The following table describes several interventions in a market. Complete the table.

Situation	This is an example of a 1) Price Floor, 2) Price Ceiling, or 3) Quantity Control or Quota	What must be true for this intervention in the market to be effective?
The government decides to limit the number of taxicab licenses in Chicago		
The minimum price that can be charged for a sports car is set at $75,000 by the government		
The minimum wage that can be paid to a worker is set at $10 an hour by the government		
The maximum tuition that can be charged by a public university is set at $5,000 a year by the government		

STEP 1: To answer this question, you must first have a firm grasp of the differences among a price floor, a price ceiling, and a quantity control or quota. You need to understand what makes each of these interventions effective in the market: this will require that you understand and are comfortable with each type of market intervention.

Review the section "Price Ceilings" on pages 102–109 and Figure 4-2 on page 104. Review the section "Price Floors" on pages 109–115 and Figure 4-6 on page 111. Review the section "Controlling Quantities" on pages 115–120 and Figure 4-9 on page XXX.

A price ceiling is a maximum price that can be charged for a good. A price floor is a minimum price that can be charged for a good. A quantity control or quota is a maximum amount of the good that can be provided in the market. This maximum amount is set by the government. To fill in the second column of the table, you will want to consider each situation and determine whether the situation is one in which the government is setting a maximum price, a minimum price, or a maximum quantity.

STEP 2: For each type of market intervention by the government, you will want to think about what must be true in order for the intervention to have any impact on the market.

Review the section "Price Ceilings" on pages 102–109 and Figure 4-2 on page 104. Review the section "Price Floors" on pages 109–115 and Figure 4-6 on page 111. Review the section "Controlling Quantities" on pages 115–120 and Figure 4-9 on page XXX.

For a price ceiling to be effective, the price ceiling must be set at a price that is less than the market equilibrium amount. For a price floor to be effective, the price floor must be set at a price that is greater than the market equilibrium amount. For a quantity control or quota to have any effect on the market, the quantity control must be set at a quantity that is less than the market equilibrium quantity. The completed table follows.

Situation	This is an example of a 1) Price Floor, 2) Price Ceiling, or 3) Quantity Control or Quota	What must be true for this intervention in the market to be effective?
The government decides to limit the number of taxicab licenses in Chicago	Quantity control or quota	Quota amount must be less than the market equilibrium quantity
The minimum price that can be charged for a sports car is set at $75,000 by the government	Price floor	Price floor must be set at a price that is greater than the market equilibrium price
The minimum wage that can be paid to a worker is set at $10 an hour by the government	Price floor	Price floor must be set at a price that is greater than the market equilibrium price
The maximum tuition that can be charged by a public university is set at $5,000 a year by the government	Price ceiling	Price ceiling must be set at a price that is less than the market equilibrium price

4. Consider the market for bananas in Paradise, a small country that grows all the bananas that are eaten in Paradise. Suppose that the market for bananas in Paradise is described by the demand and supply curves that are given in the following graph. You are asked to identify the equilibrium price and quantity in this market as well as the value of consumer surplus, producer surplus, and total surplus. Paradise is considering implementing a price floor of $20 per box of bananas. How will this price floor affect consumer surplus, producer surplus, and total surplus?

STEP 1: To find the equilibrium price and quantity in this market, you will need both the equation for the demand curve and the equation for the supply curve.

The demand curve has a y-intercept of 50 and a slope equal to $-1/10$. The demand curve can be written as $P = 50 - (1/10)Q$, or $Q = 500 - 10P$. The supply curve has a y-intercept of 0 and a slope equal to $1/40$. The supply curve can be written as

$P = (1/40)Q$, or $Q = 40P$. Use these two equations to find the equilibrium price and quantity: the equilibrium price is $10 per box of bananas and the equilibrium quantity is 400 boxes of bananas.

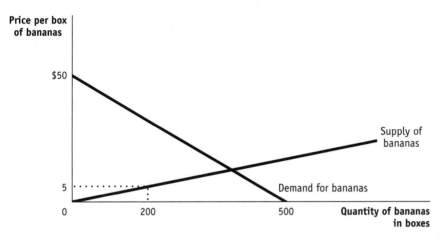

STEP 2: Identify the area of consumer surplus and the area of producer surplus, and then calculate the value of these two areas. Sum these two values to find total surplus.

Review the section "Consumer Surplus and the Demand Curve" on pages XXX–XXX and Figure 4-2 on page XXX. Review the section "Producer Surplus and the Supply Curve" on pages XXX–XXX and Figure 4-7 on page XXX.

First, identify on the graph the areas that correspond to consumer surplus and producer surplus. Then, use the formula for the area of a triangle to calculate the value of these areas. Remember that the area of a triangle is equal to (1/2) (the base of the triangle)(the height of the triangle). The following graph identifies the areas of consumer surplus and producer surplus. Recall that total surplus is just the sum of consumer and producer surplus.

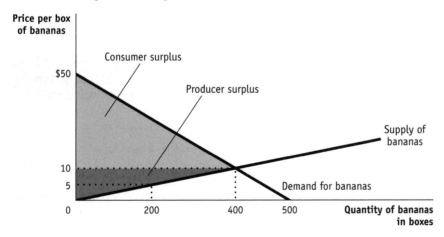

The value of consumer surplus is equal to (1/2)($50 per box of bananas – $10 per box of bananas)(400 boxes of bananas) = $8,000. The value of producer surplus is equal to (1/2)($10 per box of bananas – $0 per box of bananas)(400 boxes of bananas) = $2,000. The value of total surplus is equal to the sum of consumer plus producer surplus, or $10,000.

STEP 3: Analyze the effect of a price floor equal to $20 per box of bananas in Paradico.

Review the section "Price Floors" on pages 109–115 and Figure 4-6 on page 111.

First, check to see if the price floor is effective: recall that a price floor must be set above the equilibrium price in order for it to impact the market. In this example, the equilibrium price in the market is $10 per box of bananas, so the price floor of $20 per box of bananas will be effective. Then, determine how many bananas will be demanded at the price floor price of $20 per box of bananas. To find the number of bananas demanded when the price is $20 per box, use the demand equation. When the price is $20 per box, demanders will demand 300 boxes of bananas. Notice that suppliers need to receive a price of only $7.50 in order to be willing to supply 300 boxes of bananas.

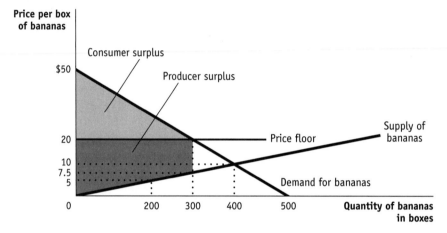

Then, determine the new areas that correspond to consumer and producer surplus. The preceding graph will help you identify these areas.

The new value for consumer surplus is equal to $4,500. The new value for producer surplus is a bit more difficult to calculate since it is composed of a rectangle and a triangle. Producer surplus will equal [($20 per box of bananas – $7.50 per box of bananas)(300 boxes of bananas) + (1/2)($7.50 per box of bananas – $0 per box of bananas)(300 boxes of bananas)], or $4,875.

Problems and Exercises

1. Use the following graph to answer the following questions.

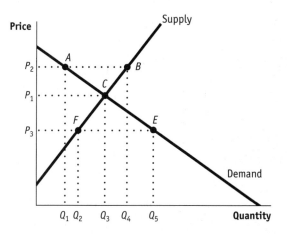

a. Identify the equilibrium price and the equilibrium quantity.

b. Suppose a price floor of P_3 is implemented by the government in this market. Describe what will happen to the price and quantity once this price floor is implemented.

c. Suppose a price floor of P_2 is implemented by the government in this market. Describe what will happen to the price and quantity once this price floor is implemented.

d. What must be true about a price floor in a market for a good or service in order for that price floor to be effective?

e. You are told that an effective price floor has been implemented in this market and that the resultant surplus is greater than $Q_4 - Q_1$. What do you know about the level of this price floor?

2. Use the following graph to answer the following questions.

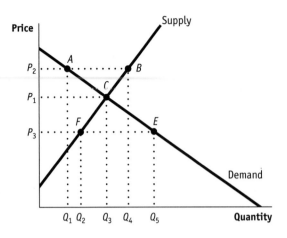

a. Identify the equilibrium price and the equilibrium quantity.

b. Suppose a price ceiling of P_2 is implemented by the government in this market. Describe what will happen to the price and quantity once this price ceiling is implemented.

c. Suppose a price ceiling of P_3 is implemented by the government in this market. Describe what will happen to the price and quantity once this price ceiling is implemented.

d. What must be true about a price ceiling in a market for a good or service in order for that price ceiling to be effective?

e. You are told that an effective price ceiling has been implemented in this market and that the resultant shortage is smaller than $Q_5 - Q_2$. What do you know about the level of this price ceiling?

3. Consider the market for housing in Metropolitan City, where all housing units are exactly the same. Currently the equilibrium price of housing is $2,000 a month and local residents consume 1,500 units of housing. The local residents argue that housing is too expensive and that an effective price ceiling should be implemented. Once the price ceiling is implemented by the local government council, only 1,200 units of housing are supplied in this market. Is this an efficient level of housing for Metropolitan City? Explain your answer. To support your answer, provide two sketches: in the first sketch indicate the equilibrium quantity, the equilibrium price, and the area of total surplus; in the second sketch indicate the price ceiling, and the area of total surplus.

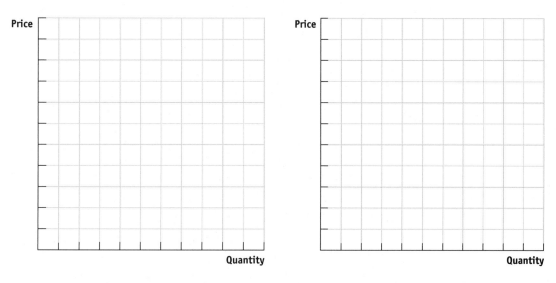

4. A price ceiling is implemented in the market for housing in Metropolitan City, where all housing units are identical. You know that before the price ceiling is implemented, the demand for housing in Metropolitan City is given by the equation $P = 1,000 - 0.1Q_D$ and the supply of housing is given by the equation $P = 200 + 0.3Q_S$.

a. Prior to the implementation of the price ceiling, what is the equilibrium price for housing in Metropolitan City and what is the equilibrium quantity of housing?

b. Fill in the following demand and supply schedules for this market, given the preceding equations.

Price	Quantity demanded	Quantity supplied
$ 200		
400		
600		
800		
1,000		

c. When the price ceiling is implemented, a housing shortage develops. This shortage is equal to 4,000 housing units. Calculate the price ceiling in this market for housing. (Hint: you may find the table from part (b) helpful in thinking about this problem.)

d. Who benefits from the imposition of the price ceiling in the market for housing in Metropolitan City?

e. Who is hurt by the imposition of a price ceiling in the market for housing in Metropolitan City?

f. Why is this price ceiling apt to result in black market activities in the market for housing? Provide at least two examples of potential black market activities.

g. Does an effective price ceiling in this market result in too many or too few resources being allocated to the market for housing in Metropolitan City? Explain your answer.

5. Farmers in Corntopia successfully lobby their government to enact a price floor for their agricultural commodity. The price floor is set at $10 above the equilibrium price. The initial demand and supply curves for agricultural production in Corntopia are as follows: $P = 100 - Q$ and $P = Q$, where price is per bushel and quantity is measured in bushels.

a. What is the level of the price floor in this market?

b. How many units of the agricultural product will be demanded and supplied at this price floor level?

c. Suppose the government purchases the surplus in this market once the price floor is implemented. What will be the cost to the government of buying this surplus?

d. Given the price floor, what is the expenditure consumers make when purchasing this commodity? Do not include in your calculation the cost to the government of buying the surplus.

e. What is total farm revenue equal to in this market once the price floor is implemented? What is the relationship between total farm revenue, consumer expenditure, and government expenditure on the good, given the price floor? Does total farm revenue increase when the government enacts a price floor? Explain your answer.

f. Who benefits from the enactment of a price floor in this market?

6. **a.** Draw a graph of the demand and supply curves given to you in problem 5. Label the equilibrium price and the equilibrium quantity on this graph. Shade in the area that corresponds to total farm revenue in this market and label this area clearly.

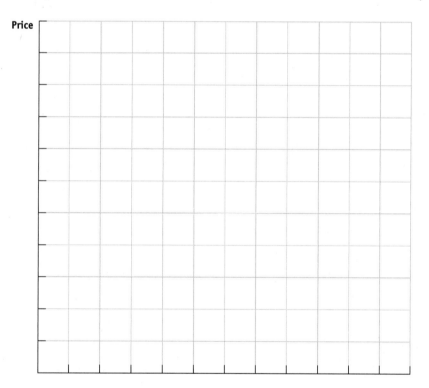

b. Redraw the graph of the demand and supply curves given to you in problem 5, and draw in a line indicating the price floor. On the graph, indicate the quantity demanded and the quantity supplied using the values you found in problem 5. Shade in and clearly label the areas that correspond to consumer expenditure on the good and government expenditure on the good, given the price floor.

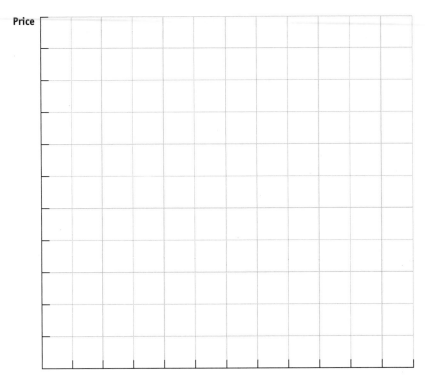

Price

Quantity

7. Consider the following graph.

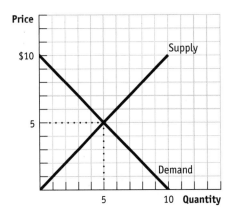

Price

$10

5

Supply

Demand

5   10   Quantity

a. What price are consumers willing to pay for this good if 1 unit of the good is produced? What price must sellers receive to be willing to sell 1 unit of the good? Given that resources are scarce, should this first unit of the good be produced? Explain your answer.

b. What price are consumers willing to pay for the second unit of the good if 2 units are produced? What price must sellers receive to be willing to sell this second unit of the good? Given that resources are scarce, should the second unit of this good be produced? Explain your answer.

c. Generalize your findings from parts (a) and (b) of this question. What is the optimal amount of the good to be produced expressed in terms of the consumers' willingness to pay and the sellers' costs?

d. If this market produces a total of 4 units of this good, are resources being underallocated or overallocated to this market? Explain your answer.

8. Consider the following graph.

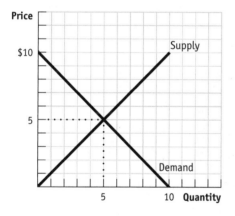

a. What price are consumers willing to pay for this good if 8 units of the good are produced? What price must sellers receive to be willing to provide 8 units of the good? Given that resources are scarce, should this market produce 8 units of the good? Explain your answer.

b. What price are consumers willing to pay if 7 units are produced? What price must sellers receive to be willing to produce 7 units of the good? Given that resources are scarce, should this market produce 7 units of the good? Explain your answer.

  c. Given your findings in parts (a) and (b), make a general statement about the optimal amount of the good to produce expressed in terms of the consumers' willingness to pay and the sellers' costs.

  d. If this market produces a total of 9 units of the good, are resources being underallocated or overallocated to this market? Explain your answer.

9. Consider the labor market in Utopia. You are told that the equilibrium wage in this market is $10 per hour and that the equilibrium amount of labor in this market is 1,000 hours of labor. Furthermore, you know that at a wage of $14 per hour, 600 hours of labor are demanded and 1,400 hours of labor are supplied. The workers in Utopia successfully lobby Utopia's government for the implementation of a price floor. This price floor results in 1,200 hours of labor being supplied and 800 hours of labor being demanded.

  a. Use the preceding information to derive the labor demand curve for Utopia. Assume this labor demand curve is linear. In your equation, abbreviate the price of labor, or its hourly wage rate, as W, and the quantity of labor demanded, measured as hours of labor, as L. (Hint: you may find sketching a graph of the preceding information helpful.)

Wage rate per hour of labor

Quantity of hours of labor

b. Use the preceding information to derive the labor supply curve for Utopia. Assume this labor supply curve is linear. In your equation, abbreviate the hourly wage rate as W and the hours of labor supplied as L.

c. What wage rate did the government set when it implemented the price floor?

d. Describe the effects of this price floor on the labor market in Utopia. Who benefits from the price floor? Who is hurt by the price floor?

10. The market for taxi rides in Metropolia this week is described in the following table. Assume that all taxi rides are the same in Metropolia.

Price of taxi rides	Quantity of taxi rides demanded per week	Quantity of taxi rides supplied per week
$ 1	200	40
2	180	60
3	160	80
4	140	100
5	120	120
6	100	140
7	80	160
8	60	180
9	40	200
10	20	220

a. What is the equilibrium price and the equilibrium quantity of taxi rides in Metropolia per week?

Suppose the government of Metropolia institutes a medallion system that limits the number of taxi rides available in Metropolia per week to 80 taxi rides.

b. At what price will consumers want to purchase 80 taxi rides per week?

    c. At what price will suppliers be willing to supply 80 taxi rides per week?

    d. What price will a taxi medallion rent for in this market? Explain your answer.

    e. Draw a graph of the taxi ride market in Metropolia. On this graph, indicate the quota limit, the demand price, the supply price, and the medallion's rental price.

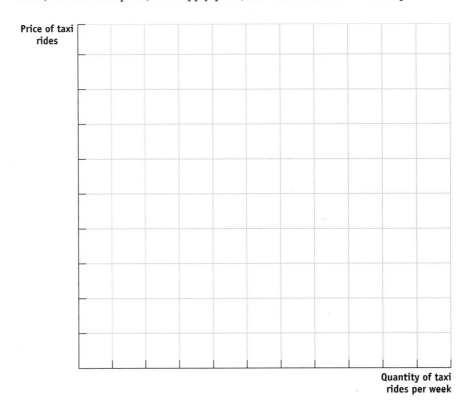

    f. What is the total value of the taxi medallions per week in Metropolia?

BEFORE YOU TAKE THE TEST

Chapter Review Questions

1. The implementation of an effective price ceiling
   a. decreases the area of producer surplus.
   b. increases the area of producer surplus.

2. The implementation of an effective price floor
  a. decreases the area of consumer surplus.
  b. increases the area of consumer surplus.

3. When demanders can make a strong moral or political case for lower prices in a market, the government may decide to enact an effective
  a. price floor.   b. price ceiling.

4. When suppliers can make a strong moral or political case for higher prices in a market, the government may decide to enact an effective
  a. price floor.   b. price ceiling.

5. Consider minimum-wage legislation requiring that all workers receive a wage payment greater than the equilibrium market wage. Which of the following two groups is more likely to have advocated for this legislation?
  a. demanders of labor   b. suppliers of labor

6. When the government intervenes in a market to regulate prices, this is an example of a
  a. quantity control.   c. price ceiling.
  b. price floor.   d. price control.

7. When the government institutes an upper limit on prices, this is referred to as a
  a. quantity control.   c. price ceiling.
  b. price floor.   d. price control.

8. When the government institutes a lower limit on prices, this is referred to as a
  a. quantity control.   c. price ceiling.
  b. price floor.   d. price control.

9. Use the information in the following table to answer the question.

Price	Quantity demanded	Quantity supplied
$ 20	200	0
40	150	50
60	100	100
80	50	150
100	0	200

If the government mandates that prices in this market can fall no lower than $50, this results in
  a. a situation of excess quantity demanded.
  b. a situation of excess quantity supplied.
  c. fewer than 100 units being supplied in this market.
  d. no effect in this market, since the equilibrium price is greater than $50.

10. Use the information in the following table to answer the question.

Price	Quantity demanded	Quantity supplied
$ 20	200	0
40	150	50
60	100	100
80	50	150
100	0	200

Suppose a price floor of $40 is implemented in this market. This results in
a. an excess demand of 100 units.
b. an excess supply of 100 units.
c. no effect in this market, since the price floor is set below the equilibrium price.
d. no effect in this market, since the price floor is set above the equilibrium price.

11. Use the information in the following table to answer the question.

Price	Quantity demanded	Quantity supplied
$ 20	200	0
40	150	50
60	100	100
80	50	150
100	0	200

Suppose a price ceiling of $40 is implemented in this market. This results in
a. an excess demand of 100 units.
b. an excess supply of 100 units.
c. no effect in this market, since the price ceiling is set below the equilibrium price.
d. a temporary shortage of the good while prices rise, and the quantity demanded and the quantity supplied adjust until they are equal.

12. Use the information in the following table to answer the question.

Price	Quantity demanded	Quantity supplied
$ 20	200	0
40	150	50
60	100	100
80	50	150
100	0	200

If the price ceiling is set at $40 in this market, then
a. too few resources are being allocated to the production of this good.
b. too many resources are being allocated to the production of this good.

13. Which of the following statements is true?

I. Price ceilings are inefficient because they result in too much of the good being produced in the market.

II. Price ceilings are inefficient because they result in the production of goods with too low a level of quality.

III. Price ceilings are inefficient because they lead to wasted resources since they increase the amount of time consumers must search for the price-controlled good.

a. Statement I is true.

b. Statement II is true.

c. Statements I and II are true.

d. Statements II and III are true.

14. Use the information in the following table to answer the question.

Price	Quantity demanded	Quantity supplied
$ 20	200	0
40	150	50
60	100	100
80	50	150
100	0	200

If the price ceiling is set at $40 in this market, the loss in total surplus in this market equals

a. $2,000.

b. $1,000.

c. $500.

d. $200.

15. An effective price ceiling typically causes an inefficient allocation of the good to

a. consumers of the good.

b. producers of the good.

16. Black market or illegal activities increase with the imposition of price controls in markets. Black markets result in

a. improving the situation of all participants in the price-controlled market.

b. worsening the situation for those people who attempt to obey the rules and restrictions imposed by the government in a price-controlled market.

c. have little or no real impact in price-controlled markets.

d. the creation of greater respect in society for the need to obey all laws.

17. Use the following graph to answer the question.

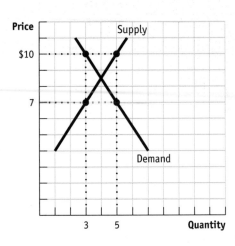

An effective price floor is implemented in the market depicted in the graph. This price floor generates an excess quantity supplied of 2 units in this market. This price floor must be equal to

a. $10.

b. $7.

18. Use the following graph to answer the question.

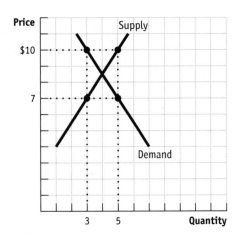

An effective price floor is enacted in this market, and with this price floor the government promises to purchase any unwanted units produced. If the price floor is set at $10, then the government will spend _____ purchasing the unwanted units of the good.

a. $50

b. $30

c. $21

d. $20

19. Use the following graph to answer the question.

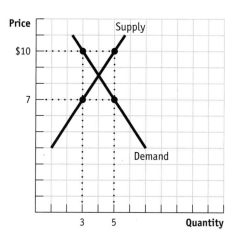

An effective price floor is enacted in this market at a price of $10. With this price floor, consumers' expenditure on this good will equal

a. $50.   c. $21.

b. $30.   d. $20.

20. Which of the following statements is true?

   a. An effective price ceiling reduces the quantity of the good available to consumers, while an effective price floor increases the quantity of the good available to consumers.

   b. An effective price floor reduces the quantity of the good available to consumers, while an effective price ceiling increases the quantity of the good available to consumers.

   c. Government intervention in markets in the form of effective price ceilings or price floors increases the quantity of the good available to consumers.

   d. Government intervention in markets in the form of effective price ceilings or price floors decreases the quantity of the good available to consumers.

21. Use the following graph to answer the question. Different areas in the graph are labeled with letters.

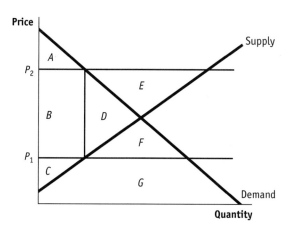

An effective price floor set at P_2 results in a loss of total surplus equal to

a. area D.   c. area E.

b. areas A and C.   d. area G.

22. When a price is artificially set above the equilibrium price in a market, who determines the quantity of the good bought and sold in the market?

a. demanders   b. suppliers

23. When suppliers determine the quantity of the good bought and sold in a market, this must be due to the imposition of an effective
   a. price floor.   b. price ceiling.

24. An effective price floor prevents suppliers from competing for customers through lower prices, so suppliers compete for customers by offering goods with
   a. greater quality than consumers desire.
   b. lower quality than consumers desire.

25. Which of the following statements is true?
   I. An effective price floor benefits some suppliers.
   II. An effective price floor benefits all demanders.
   III. An effective price floor results in a persistent surplus.
   IV. An effective price floor results in an inefficiently high level of quality in the good offered by suppliers.
   a. Statements I and III are true.
   b. Statements I, III, and IV are true.
   c. Statements III and IV are true.
   d. Statements II, III, and IV are true.

26. A quantity control or quota
   a. limits the price that suppliers can charge for the good or service in the regulated market.
   b. limits the price that demanders must pay for the good or service in the regulated market.
   c. limits the amount of the good or service available in the regulated market.
   d. increases the amount of the good or service available in the regulated market to an amount that exceeds the equilibrium quantity.

27. A quota limit imposed on a market
   a. restricts the amount of the good available in that market.
   b. results in a payment being made by the government to the license holder.
   c. places a lower limit on the amount of the good provided in the regulated market.
   d. places an upper limit on the price of the good provided in the regulated market.

28. Which of the following statements is true?
   I. Quantity controls are inefficient since they prevent mutually beneficial transactions from occurring.
   II. Quantity controls in a market result in too many resources being allocated to that market.
   III. Quantity controls result in a wedge: the price demanders are willing to pay for the last unit is less than the price suppliers must receive to produce this last unit.
   a. Statement I is true.
   b. Statement II is true.
   c. Statements I and III are true.
   d. Statements I, II, and III are true.

29. Quantity controls
   a. provide an incentive to engage in illegal activities.
   b. result in underproduction of the good or service in the market where the quota limit has been imposed.
   c. result in a less efficient outcome than the market outcome.
   d. Answers (a), (b), and (c) are all true statements.

Answers to Problems and Exercises

1.   a. The equilibrium price is P_1 and the equilibrium quantity is Q_3.

b. This is not an effective price floor since the price floor of P_3 is less than the equilibrium price P_1. Since it is a nonbinding/ineffective price floor, the equilibrium price and quantity will not change.

c. This is an effective price floor since the price floor of P_2 is greater than the equilibrium price P_1. At P_2, Q_1 units of the good will be demanded and Q_4 units of the good will be supplied. This excess supply of $Q_4 - Q_1$ will not be eliminated by price decreases since the price is artificially set at P_2 by the government and is not allowed to decrease. An effective price floor creates a situation of excess supply, or a surplus, that is not eliminated by changes in the price of the good because the price has been set at a level that is greater than the market-clearing price.

d. For a price floor to have an effect in a market, the price floor must be set at a price that is greater than the equilibrium price.

e. The price floor must be set at a price that is greater than P_2 since we know from part (c) that the surplus in the market at P_2 equals $Q_4 - Q_1$.

2.   a. The equilibrium price is P_1 and the equilibrium quantity is Q_3.

b. This is not an effective price ceiling since the price ceiling of P_2 is greater than the equilibrium price P_1. Since it is a nonbinding/ineffective price ceiling, the equilibrium price and quantity will not change.

c. This is an effective price ceiling since the price ceiling of P_3 is less than the equilibrium price P_1. At P_3, Q_5 units of the good will be demanded and Q_2 units of the good will be supplied. This excess demand of $Q_5 - Q_2$ will not be eliminated by price increases since the price is artificially set at P_3 by the government and is not allowed to increase. An effective price ceiling creates a situation of excess demand, or a shortage, that is not eliminated by changes in the price of the good because the price has been set at a level that is less than the market-clearing price.

d. For a price ceiling to have an effect in a market, the price ceiling must be set at a price that is less than the equilibrium price.

e. The price ceiling must be set at a price that is greater than P_3 but still less than the equilibrium price of P_1. We know this because when the price ceiling is set at P_3, the shortage is equal to $Q_5 - Q_2$, and the new price ceiling results in a smaller shortage than the shortage at price P_3.

3. The market is in equilibrium when there are 1,500 units of housing offered at the price of $2,000 per month, so 1,200 is not an efficient level of housing. The price ceiling forces consumers to reduce their consumption of the good from the efficient level. In the sketch below, the shaded area represents the total surplus received when 1,500 units of housing are supplied at a price of $2,000 per unit.

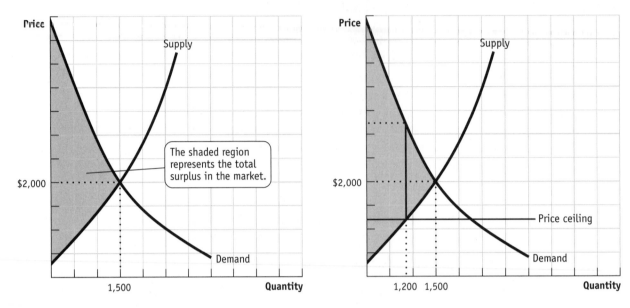

The second sketch illustrates the area of total surplus once the effective price ceiling is implemented. Notice that the area of total surplus is reduced relative to its initial level.

4. **a.** The equilibrium price is $800 per unit of housing and the equilibrium quantity of housing is 2,000 units.

   b.

Price	Quantity demanded	Quantity supplied
$ 200	8,000	0
400	6,000	666.67
600	4,000	1,333.33
800	2,000	2,000
1,000	0	2,666.67

   c. From the table in part (b), you know that a price ceiling of $400 is too low (the shortage is greater than 4,000 units of housing at this price) while a price ceiling of $600 is too high (the shortage at this price is less than 4,000 units of housing). You could try some prices between $400 and $600 or you could solve this problem algebraically. The shortage of 4,000 units is the difference between the quantity demanded and the quantity supplied at the price ceiling, or in other words, $Q_S + 4,000 = Q_D$. Thus, the demand equation can be rewritten as $P_C = 1,000 - 0.1(Q_S + 4,000)$ and the supply equation is equal to $P_C = 200 + 0.3Q_S$, where P_C is the price ceiling level. Solving this set of equations, we find that the quantity supplied is equal to 1,000 units. Thus, the quantity demanded is equal to 5,000 units while the price ceiling level is $500.

   d. The people lucky enough to get one of the housing units supplied at the price ceiling price benefit from this government intervention. These individuals pay less than the market-clearing price for their housing unit.

e. Consumers who want housing but who cannot find housing due to the price ceiling are hurt by the decision to implement the price ceiling. Additionally, as landlords fail to maintain the housing units in Metropolitan City, the whole community is affected as the general condition of the housing stock deteriorates. And if a black market develops in the housing market, this will erode the general level of lawful behavior in the community.

f. Since the quantity demanded of housing exceeds the quantity supplied of housing at the price ceiling, persistent shortages will exist in this market. Consumers eager to find housing will resort to activities that are illegal—for example, subletting housing units at rates higher than the price ceiling rate or making illegal payments to landlords.

g. Too few resources are devoted to the housing market. We know this because the effective price ceiling creates a persistent shortage in the market for housing.

5.   a. The level of the price floor in this market is $60 per bushel. To find the price floor level, first solve for the equilibrium price in the market: set demand equal to supply. Thus, $100 - Q = Q$, and thus the equilibrium quantity is 50 bushels of the agricultural commodity. We can then substitute this quantity into either the demand or supply equation to find the equilibrium price. The equilibrium price is $50 per bushel. If the price floor is set $10 above the equilibrium price, we know the price floor must be at $60 per bushel.

b. At $60 per bushel, demanders demand 40 bushels and suppliers supply 60 bushels. There is an excess supply of 20 bushels.

c. If the government buys the surplus 20 bushels at the price floor level of $60 per bushel, it will spend $1,200.

d. Consumers demand 40 bushels at the price of $60 per bushel. The expenditure by consumers on the product will equal $2,400.

e. Total farm revenue equals the total number of bushels supplied times the price floor, or (60 bushels)($60 per bushel), or $3,600. Total farm revenue equals the sum of consumer expenditure on the good plus government expenditure on the good. Total farm revenue without the price floor is equal to the equilibrium price times the equilibrium quantity, or (50 bushels) ($50 per bushel), or $2,500. Total farm revenue increases with the imposition of an effective price floor.

f. The farmers benefit from the imposition of the price floor since it increases total farm revenue.

6.   a.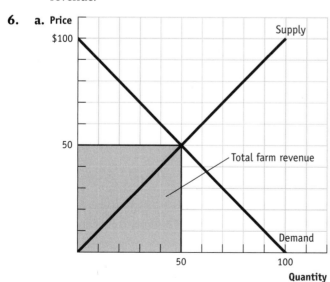

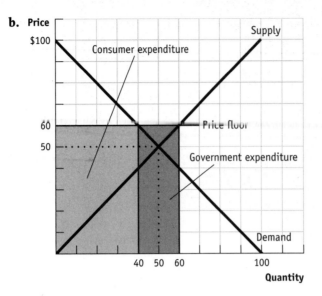

b. Price

7. **a.** To answer this set of questions, you need the demand and supply equations that correspond to the graph. Using the graph as a reference, we can write the demand equation as $P = 10 - Q$ and the supply equation as $P = Q$. Plugging a quantity value of 1 into both of these equations reveals that demanders are willing to pay $9 for the first unit and suppliers need to receive $1 to produce this first unit. Clearly this first unit should be produced since the value to the consumer ($9) exceeds the seller's cost of producing it ($1).

    b. Using the equations found in part (a), we can substitute a value of 2 for the quantity in both equations to find that demanders are willing to pay $8 for the second unit and suppliers need to receive $2 to produce the second unit. The second unit of the good should be produced since its value to consumers ($8) exceeds the seller's cost of producing it ($2).

    c. The optimal amount of the good to be produced is the amount at which the consumers' willingness to pay for the last unit exactly equals the sellers' cost of producing the last unit. So long as the value the consumers place on the good (the price they are willing to pay) exceeds the cost the sellers must receive to produce the good, not enough of the good is being produced. In this case, the optimal amount is 5 units, where the consumers' willingness to pay and the sellers' cost are equal at $5.

    d. Resources are being underallocated to this market since consumers are willing to pay $6 for the last unit produced (the fourth unit) while suppliers are willing to sell this last unit so long as the price is at least equal to $4. When the value the consumers place on the last unit produced is greater than the cost of producing this last unit, not enough of the good is being produced.

8. **a.** To answer this set of questions, you need the demand and supply equations. Using the graph as a reference, we can write the demand equation as $P = 10 - Q$ and the supply equation as $P = Q$. Plugging a quantity of 8 into both of these equations, we find that consumers are willing to pay a price of $2 for the good and sellers need to receive a price of $8 for the good to produce 8 units. Since the value the consumers place on the eighth unit ($2) is less than the sellers' cost of producing the eighth unit ($8), the eighth unit should not be produced.

b. Using the same reasoning as outlined in answer (a), we find that consumers are willing to pay $3 per unit if 7 units are produced and sellers require a price of $7 per unit to be willing to produce 7 units. Since the value of the seventh unit to the consumers ($3) is less than the cost of producing the seventh unit for the producer ($7), the seventh unit should not be produced.

c. The optimal amount of the good to produce is the amount at which the consumers' willingness to pay for the last unit exactly equals the sellers' cost of producing the last unit. So long as the value the consumers place on the good (the price they are willing to pay) is less than the cost the sellers must receive to produce the good, too much of the good is being produced. In this case, the optimal amount is 5 units, where the consumers' willingness to pay and the sellers' cost are equal at $5.

d. Resources are being overallocated to this market: too much of this good is being produced since the value consumers place on the last unit produced is less than the cost to sellers of producing the last unit.

9. **a.** The information you are given in this problem can be represented as follows:

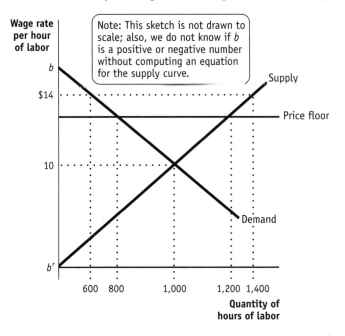

Thus, we know two points of the labor demand curve: (1,000, $10) and (600, $14). Use these two points to compute the slope of the demand curve: slope = rise/run = $(y_1 - y_2)/(x_1 - x_2) = (10 - 14)/(1{,}000 - 600) = -0.01$. The demand equation can be written as $W = b - 0.01L$. Then, use one of the points that you know is on the demand curve—either (1,000, $10) or (600, $14)—with this equation to solve for b. Thus, $W = b - 0.01L$ can be written as $10 = b - 0.01(1{,}000)$, or $b = 20$. The labor demand curve is therefore $W = 20 - 0.01L$.

b. Use a similar procedure to write the supply equation: $W = 0.01L + b'$, where b' is the y-intercept of the labor supply curve. Then use one of the points that you know is on the supply curve—either (1,000, $10) or (1,400, $14)—with this equation to identify the value of b'. Thus, $W = 0.01L + b'$ can be rewritten as $10 = 0.01(1{,}000) + b'$ and b' therefore equals 0. The labor supply equation is thus $W = 0.01L$.

c. At the price floor, we know that the quantity of labor demanded is 800 units. Substitute this number for L in the labor demand equation: $W = 20 - 0.01(800)$, or $W = \$12$ per hour of labor. To verify that the price floor has been set at a wage of $12 per hour of labor, check your answer with the labor supply equation. At the price floor, we know the quantity of labor supplied is equal to 1,200 units. Using this number for L in the labor supply equation, we find $W = 0.01(1,200)$, or $W = \$12$ per hour of labor.

d. This price floor creates a surplus of labor when the price floor is set at a wage rate of $12 per hour of labor. In a labor market, a surplus of labor implies that there is unemployment: workers who want to work (i.e., they are willing to supply their labor at the prevailing wage rate) cannot find work (i.e., there is insufficient demand for their services at the prevailing wage rate). Workers lucky enough to get a job paying $12 per hour benefit from the price floor while workers who are unable to find work at that wage rate are harmed by the price floor.

10. a. Equilibrium occurs when the quantity demanded equals the quantity supplied. From the table, we can see that the equilibrium price is $5 and the equilibrium quantity is 120 taxi rides per week.

b. Consumers will demand 80 taxi rides per week at a price of $7.

c. Suppliers are willing to supply 80 taxi rides per week for a price of $3.

d. The medallion will rent for $4 per taxi ride, or the difference between the demand price and the supply price when the quantity of taxi rides is limited to 80 rides per week.

e.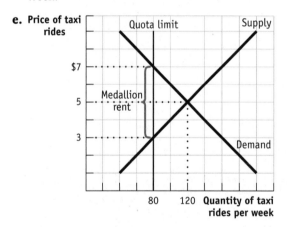

f. The taxi medallions are worth the product of the medallion rent per ride times the number of taxi rides per week. Thus, the taxi medallions' worth per week equals ($4 per taxi ride)(80 taxi rides), or $320.

Answers to Chapter Review Questions

1. **Answer a.** Since an effective price ceiling reduces the price that producers receive and consumers pay, this results in a decrease in producer surplus.

2. **Answer a.** Since an effective price floor increases the price that producers receive and consumers pay, this results in a decrease in consumer surplus.

3. **Answer b.** Demanders desire lower prices for the good and this can be achieved through the enactment of an effective price ceiling, since it reduces the price below the equilibrium price.

4. **Answer a.** Producers desire higher prices for the good and this can be achieved through the enactment of an effective price floor, since it raises the price above the equilibrium price.

5. **Answer b.** Suppliers of labor will receive this higher wage and therefore benefit from it. Demanders of labor will find that this higher wage increases the cost of hiring labor, and they will not benefit from it.

6. **Answer d.** The government can intervene in a market to regulate prices so that they are lower than the equilibrium level (an effective price ceiling) or higher than the equilibrium level (an effective price floor). Both are examples of price controls.

7. **Answer c.** An upper limit on prices establishes a price level for a product that is less than the equilibrium price and cannot be exceeded. This is an example of an effective price ceiling.

8. **Answer b.** A lower limit on prices establishes a minimum price level for a product that is in excess of the equilibrium price for that product. This is an example of an effective price floor.

9. **Answer d.** Setting a lower limit on prices of $50 in this market is an example of an ineffective price floor since a price floor of $50 is less than the equilibrium price of $60. This price floor would have no effect on the market.

10. **Answer c.** Setting a price floor of $40 in this market is an example of an ineffective price floor since a price floor of $40 is less than the equilibrium price of $60. This price floor would have no effect on the market.

11. **Answer a.** A price ceiling of $40 results in 150 units being demanded and 50 units being supplied. This is therefore a situation of excess demand of 100 units.

12. **Answer a.** At a price ceiling of $40, consumers wish to consume 150 units of the good while suppliers are only willing to supply 50 units of the good. This indicates that too few resources are being allocated to this market.

13. **Answer d.** Statement I is incorrect because price ceilings result in too little of the good being produced in the market. Statement II is correct because when price is limited to a level below the equilibrium price, producers have an incentive to reduce the quality of the product they provide to the market. Statement III is correct because an effective price ceiling results in greater costs as demanders seek out the artificially scarce good.

14. **Answer b.** The total surplus in the market when there is no price ceiling is equal to $4,000. With the imposition of the effective price ceiling the total surplus equals $3,000. To find these areas of total surplus, sketch a graph and then calculate the relevant areas. The initial total surplus is equal to (1/2)($100/unit – $20/unit)(100 units) or $4,000. The total surplus with the effective price ceiling is equal to (1/2)($100/unit –$80/unit)(50 units) + (1/2)($40/unit – $20/unit)(50 units) + ($80/unit – $40/unit)(50 units), or $3,000. The graph below illustrates this.

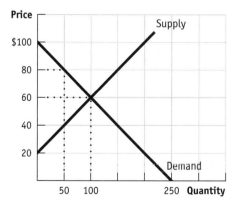

The change in total surplus is $4,000 – $3,000, or $1,000.

15. **Answer a.** An effective price ceiling limits the amount of the good available to consumers in the market by limiting the price to a level that is less than the equilibrium price. Producers produce the amount they are willing to produce at that price, and they do not expand production even though consumers are willing to consume more units of the good.

16. **Answer b.** Answers (a) and (b) are mutually exclusive: if one of these answers is correct, then the other must by necessity be incorrect. Reading answer (b) helps to identify a group that is hurt by black market activities: those individuals who decide not to engage in black market activities are left worse off because of their obedience to the rules imposed by the price-controlled market. Answer (c) is incorrect since price controls do affect markets and do have impacts when they are effective. Answer (d) is also incorrect since price-controlled markets generate black market activities, which are against the law.

17. **Answer a.** An effective price floor is the minimum price that can be charged for a good, and this price must be set above the equilibrium price. At a price of $10, the quantity demanded is 3 units while the quantity supplied is 5 units. At a price floor of $10, there will be excess supply of 2 units. The price floor must equal $10.

18. **Answer d.** At a price floor of $10, the excess supply is 2 units. If the government purchases these 2 units at $10 each, the cost to the government of this purchase is $20.

19. **Answer b.** With a $10 price floor, consumers in this market will demand 3 units of the good. Their expenditure on the good will equal ($10/unit)(3 units), or $30.

20. **Answer d.** Effective price ceilings and price floors both reduce the quantity of the good available to consumers, so answers (a), (b), and (c) are not true.

21. **Answer a.** When the price floor is set at P_2, the area of total surplus is equal to areas $A + B + C$. Without the price floor, the area of total surplus is equal to areas $A + B + C + D$. The loss in total surplus due to the imposition of the effective price floor is equal to area D.

22. **Answer a.** When the price is artificially set above the equilibrium price, demanders determine the quantity demanded in the market since they select the quantity they are willing to demand based on the price of the good.

23. **Answer b.** A price ceiling is set below the equilibrium price. This limits the price that can be charged for a good in the market. Producers take this price and then determine the number of units of the good they are willing to provide in the market at this price.

24. **Answer a.** When producers cannot compete for customers through prices, they must look for other ways to compete. One way is to offer goods of higher quality, and with an effective price floor producers will compete by offering higher-quality goods.

25. **Answer b.** Statement I is correct because those suppliers who are lucky enough to sell their good at the higher price are benefited. Statement III is also correct since an effective price floor results in excess supply of the good. Statement IV is correct as well because suppliers will compete for customers by offering higher-quality goods since they cannot compete for customers by offering lower prices. Statement II is incorrect: demanders of this good now have to pay a higher price than they would have in a freely functioning market.

26. **Answer c.** A quota control by definition is a limit on the number of units of the good that can be offered in the market. Answers (a) and (b) are both incorrect since they discuss price controls rather than quantity controls. Answer (d) is also incorrect since a quota limit reduces the amount of the good available rather than increasing the amount of the good available.

27. **Answer a.** Answer (a) is the basic definition of a quota limit. Answer (b) is incorrect since there is no assumption of the government making a payment to the license holder when there is a quota limit. Answer (c) is incorrect since a quota limit represents the maximum amount of the good allowed in a market rather than the minimum amount. Answer (d) is incorrect since it focuses on price controls rather than quantity controls.

28. **Answer a.** Statement I is correct because quantity controls restrict the amount of output to a level that is less than the equilibrium amount of output, and thus are inefficient since they prevent mutually beneficial trades from occurring. Because quantity controls restrict output, this implies that too few resources are devoted to the production of the good, so statement II is incorrect. Quantity controls do result in a wedge being created, but that wedge is the difference between the high price consumers are willing to pay and the low price producers must receive to provide the good, thus statement III is incorrect.

29. **Answer d.** Quantity controls restrict output, result in too few resources being devoted to the production of the good, and create an incentive for black market activities as consumers seek out alternative methods for getting the scarce good.

chapter 5

International Trade

BEFORE YOU READ THE CHAPTER

Summary

This chapter discusses international trade and the gains from trade that are possible through specialization according to comparative advantage. The chapter explores the sources of comparative advantage, and also provides a model to illustrate the distributional consequences of trade. This model provides a method for considering who benefits and who loses from international trade and why the benefits from trade outweigh the losses from trade. The chapter also considers the impact of tariffs and quotas and how tariffs and quotas create market inefficiencies and reduce the area of total surplus. Finally, the chapter discusses why governments engage in trade protection and the effect of international trade agreements on the international flow of goods and services.

Chapter Objectives

Objective #1. Trade is beneficial to both parties that engage in the trade, whether they are individuals or countries. Countries that specialize in producing different goods and then trade these goods with other countries benefit from this trade. Goods and services purchased from abroad are called imports, and goods and services sold abroad are called exports. Countries trade goods and services with one another, but they also invest funds: this linking of the markets for goods and services as well as financial assets between different countries is referred to as globalization.

Objective #2. A country has the comparative advantage in producing a good or service when that country can produce the good or service at a lower opportunity cost than can other countries. A simple way to model international trade is to use linear production possibility frontiers to analyze trade between two countries. The straight line production possibility frontier implies that the opportunity cost of producing the two goods does not change as the level of production of these two goods changes. This model is known as the Ricardian model of international trade.

Objective #3. Autarky refers to the situation in which a country does not engage in trade with any other countries. The Ricardian model of international trade allows a comparison to be made between a situation in which two countries trade with one another versus a situation in which the two countries act as autarkies and do not trade with each other. The Ricardian model of international trade results in the following conclusions:

- When countries specialize according to comparative advantage and then trade with one another, the total amount of goods and services produced is greater than when the countries do not engage in specialization and trade.

- No country will engage in trade unless the relative price of the good traded is less than its opportunity cost of producing the good in autarky.

Objective #4.   For example, consider two countries, country A and country B, that have linear production possibility frontiers for the production of two goods: good X and good Y. These two countries and their production possibility frontiers are illustrated in Figure 5.1.

Figure 5.1

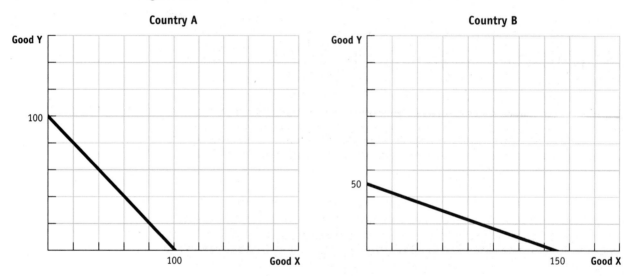

The opportunity cost of country A producing one more unit of good X is equal to 1 unit of good Y, since country A must give up 1 unit of good Y to produce an additional unit of good X according to their production possibility frontier illustrated in Figure 5.1. The opportunity cost of country B producing one more unit of good X is equal to 1/3 unit of good Y since country B must give up 1/3 unit of good Y to produce an additional unit of good X according to their production possibility frontier illustrated in Figure 5.1. Comparison of these two opportunity costs reveals that country B can produce good X at lower opportunity cost than can country A, since country B gives up fewer units of good Y to get one more unit of good X. Country B has the comparative advantage in producing good X. Country A has the comparative advantage in producing good Y, since the opportunity cost of producing 1 unit of good Y for country A is 1 unit of good X, while for country B the opportunity cost of producing 1 unit of good Y is 3 units of good X. Both countries can benefit by specializing in the production of the good they can produce at lower opportunity cost and then trading.

- As an example, suppose the two countries initially do not trade and that country A produces 50 units of good X and 50 units of good Y while country B produces 75 units of good X and 25 units of good Y. Total production without trade is summarized in the following table.

	Production of good X	Production of good Y
Country A	50	50
Country B	75	25
Total production	125	75

- Now, suppose the two countries specialize according to their comparative advantage: country A produces 0 units of good X and 100 units of good Y while country B produces 150 units of good X and 0 units of good Y. The table that follows summarizes the result of this specialization. Notice that the total production of both goods increases when the two countries specialize.

	Production of good X	Production of good Y
Country A	0	100
Country B	150	0
Total production	150	100

- Let's digress a moment and consider what would happen if the two countries specialized, but produced those goods for which they did not have the comparative advantage: this implies that country A produces good X while country B produces good Y. The table that follows summarizes what happens when countries do not specialize according to their comparative advantage: total production decreases! Specialization is beneficial only when countries produce those goods for which they have lower opportunity cost of production.

	Production of good X	Production of good Y
Country A	100	0
Country B	0	50
Total production	100	50

- Once countries decide to specialize according to comparative advantage and to trade, they then need to decide on the price of these traded goods. In our example, country A will be willing to trade good Y for any price greater than 1 unit of X (country A's opportunity cost of producing good Y). Country B, on the other hand, will be willing to trade up to 3 units of X for 1 unit of Y. Thus, country A and country B can make a mutually beneficial trade provided that the range of prices when Country A provides one unit of Y is between 1 unit of X and 3 units of X. Country A is unwilling to provide a unit of Y for less than 1 unit of X and country B is unwilling to pay more than 3 units of X for one unit of Y. Using similar reasoning, country A will be willing to trade good X for any price between 1/3 a unit of good Y and 1 unit of good Y.

Objective #5.   Gains from trade depend on comparative advantage and not absolute advantage. Comparative advantage is based on the opportunity cost of producing the good and not the absolute amount of resources used to produce the good. A country with low wage rates generally reflects low labor productivity, while a country with high wage rates reflects high labor productivity.

- One fallacy with regard to trade is the pauper labor fallacy, which is the belief that a high-wage country importing goods produced by workers in a low-wage country is an action that results in harming workers in the high-wage country.

- A second fallacy with regard to trade is the sweatshop labor fallacy, which is the belief that trade must be bad for workers in low-wage countries since the wages paid to workers in these countries is so much lower than the wages paid to workers in high-wage countries.

- Both the pauper labor fallacy and the sweatshop labor fallacy fail to recognize that trade is to the advantage of both the high-wage and the low-wage country, because both are able to achieve a higher standard of living through trade with each other.

Objective #6.   Comparative advantage arises because of differences in climate, differences in factor endowments, and differences in technology.

- Climate and seasonal differences (northern hemisphere versus southern hemisphere) play a significant role in comparative advantage, since some goods can only be produced in certain climates or during certain seasons.

- The Heckscher-Ohlin model finds that a country has a comparative advantage in producing those goods whose production is intensive in the factors that are abundant in that country compared to other countries. This finding arises because the opportunity cost of a given factor is low when that factor is relatively abundant. This argument also helps to explain incomplete specialization, which is the situation when a country continues to produce a good that it also imports. A country will engage in incomplete specialization whenever that country has factor endowments that make it economically feasible for them to produce the good. A country can still gain from trade even if it does not completely specialize.

- Technological differences can also drive comparative advantage. Technological differences may arise due to accumulated experience or because of innovations that one country has made that other countries have not adopted.

Objective #7.   The model of demand and supply can be used to analyze the benefits of international trade. Figure 5.2 illustrates a market for a country that does not trade. In this figure, domestic demand represents the total demand for this good from individuals who live in this country, while domestic supply represents the total supply of this good from firms producing this good in this country. In autarky, the equilibrium in this market would be determined by the intersection of the domestic demand curve with the domestic supply curve: P_A is the equilibrium price and Q_A is the equilibrium quantity under autarky. Consumer and producer surplus are indicated in the figure, and total surplus in this market equals the sum of consumer and producer surplus.

Figure 5.2

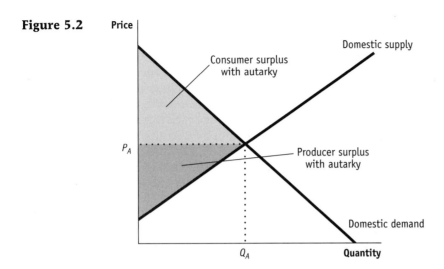

Consider what happens in this market if this country opens to trade. Suppose the world price for this good is lower than the autarky price (P_A) for this good. In Figure 5.3, this world price (P_W) is drawn on the graph. Notice that if the country opens to trade, the quantity of the good demanded domestically in this country at the world price (Q_D) will be greater than the amount of the good supplied domestically at this price (Q_S). This excess demand will be satisfied by the country importing ($Q_D - Q_S$) units of the good. Trade will also change the areas of consumer and producer surplus in this country: consumer surplus will increase as consumers get more units of the good at a lower price, while producer surplus decreases as domestic producers sell fewer units of the good at the lower price. Study Figure 5.3 carefully and recall that consumer surplus is the area that is beneath the demand curve but above the equilibrium price, while producer surplus is the area that is above the supply curve but below the equilibrium price. With trade, total surplus increases, but domestic producers of this good see a reduction in their producer surplus while domestic consumers see an increase in their consumer surplus. In the case of an imported good, domestic consumers benefit while domestic producers lose. Trade is beneficial since total surplus increases, but trade has distributional consequences as you can see from what happens to the areas of consumer and producer surplus.

Figure 5.3

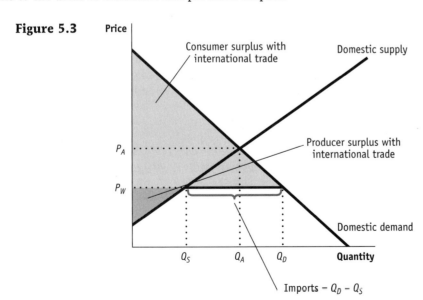

We can use the same analysis to consider the situation when the world price is greater than the autarky price. Starting from Figure 5.2, a market under autarky, let's consider a situation in which the world price exceeds the autarky price. Figure 5.4 illustrates this example: P_W is the world price and, in this case, when this country opens to trade, it finds that the quantity demanded domestically at the world price (Q_D) is less than the amount supplied domestically at this price (Q_S). This excess supply of ($Q_S - Q_D$) will be exported to other countries. Figure 5.4 also identifies the areas of consumer surplus and producer surplus once trade is allowed. As in Figure 5.3, we find that the area of total surplus is larger than in autarky. However, the distribution of the surplus has changed: in Figure 5.3, domestic consumers benefited from trade while domestic suppliers were hurt; in Figure 5.4, domestic suppliers benefit from trade while domestic consumers are hurt. In both of these examples we find that trade is beneficial since it increases total surplus, but that trade has distributional consequences.

Figure 5.4

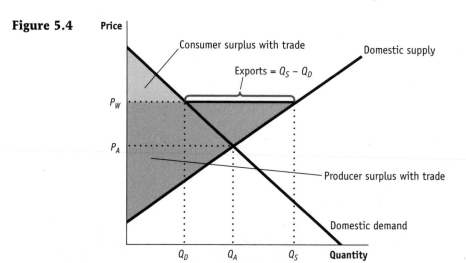

Objective #8. A country's industries can be broken down into two broad categories: exporting industries that produce goods and services to be sold abroad, and import-competing industries that produce goods and services also imported from abroad. When a country opens to trade, this leads to higher production in the exporting industries and lower production in the import-competing industries, and these changes affect the demand for factors of production in these two types of industries. The Heckscher-Ohlin model posits that international trade increases the demand for those factors of production that are relatively abundant in the country and decreases the demand for those factors of production that are relatively scarce. Thus, the price of abundant factors tends to rise while the price of scarce factors tends to fall. This price movement redistributes income toward a country's abundant factors and away from a country's less abundant factors.

Objective #9. Countries engage in trade protection, or protection, to limit the level of imports with the idea of protecting domestic producers in import-competing industries from foreign competition. Tariffs are a form of excise tax levied on the sales of imported goods, while quotas are legal limits on the quantity of a good that can be imported.

- Figure 5.5 illustrates a tariff placed on the good represented in this diagram. The tariff raises the world price of the good and therefore reduces the level of imports while simultaneously reducing the overall domestic demand for the good and increasing the domestic supply of the good. In Figure 5.5, the domestic supply and domestic demand curves are illustrated. P_W is the world price for the good with open trade, and P_T is the price of the good once the tariff is applied. At P_T, the quantity supplied domestically is Q_{ST} while the quantity demanded domestically is Q_{DT}. Thus, the level of imports with the imposition of the tariff is $(Q_{DT} - Q_{ST})$. The tariff results in a decrease in consumer surplus, an increase in producer surplus, and the capture of some of the consumer surplus as tariff revenue that the government earns. These areas are marked on the graph. In addition, the tariff results in deadweight loss: some mutually beneficial trades fail to occur and the economy wastes some resources on inefficient production since some producers produce the good even though their costs are greater than the world price of P_W. These two areas of deadweight loss are also identified on the graph. Study Figure 5.5 carefully and then compare it with Figure 5.3 to see how a tariff changes the outcome in this market. Notice that the tariff redistributes part of the consumer surplus to domestic producers and to the government as well as creates the areas of deadweight loss.

Figure 5.5

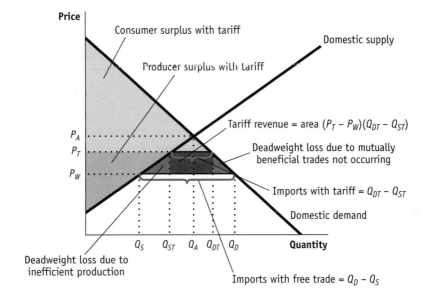

- Imposition of a quota in a market with free trade creates a limit on the number of units of the good that can be imported into the domestic market. This legal limit is typically administered through a license whereby the license holder purchases the legal right to import a certain number of units of the good into the domestic market. A quota results in a similar outcome as the tariff, but with one crucial difference. With a quota, the area labeled tariff revenue is now license-holder revenue. Instead of the government earning tax revenue from the imposition of the tariff, the quota results in the license holder earning quota rents equal to the area $(P_Q - P_W)(Q_{D\,QUOTA} - Q_{S\,QUOTA})$. The quota results in an increase in the domestic producer surplus and a decrease in the domestic consumer surplus. In addition, the quota results in the same two areas of deadweight loss that occurred with the tariff. Figure 5.6 illustrates the impact of a quota of $(Q_{D\,QUOTA} - Q_{S\,QUOTA})$ units on the market.

Figure 5.6

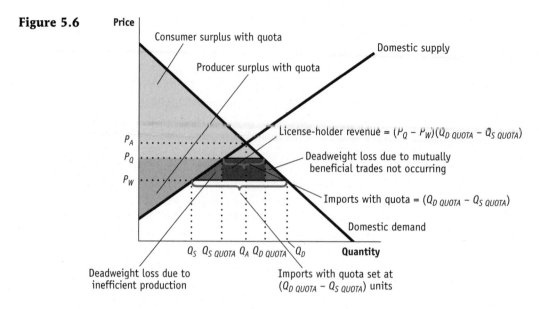

Objective #10. Advocates of tariffs and quotas offer three common arguments for trade protection: national security, job creation, and the infant industry argument. The national security argument focuses on the need to protect domestic suppliers of crucial goods from foreign competition. The job creation argument focuses on the additional jobs that are created in the import-competing industries when these industries are protected by a tariff or quota. The infant industry argument claims that newly emerging industries (those in their infancy) may need trade protection to get established. Despite these arguments, most trade protection reflects the political influence of the import-competing producers.

Objective #11. Trade protection hurts domestic consumers as well as foreign export industries. Because countries care about each other's trade policies, they engage in international trade agreements. These agreements involve treaties that pledge countries will engage in less trade protection in return for a promise from other countries that they will also engage in less trade protection. The North American Free Trade Agreement (NAFTA) and the European Union (EU) are examples of trade agreements between groups of countries. Global trade agreements that cover most of the world also are in place, and the World Trade Organization (WTO) oversees these global trade agreements. The WTO provides the framework for the extensive and complex negotiations that are involved in major international agreements; in addition, the WTO resolves disputes among its members.

Objective #12. Globalization or growing world trade has generally been seen as a positive outcome. However, concerns have arisen over the growing wage gap between more educated and less educated workers. In addition, the growth of offshore outsourcing has generated concerns about increasing economic insecurity.

Objective #13 [from Appendix]: An individual's consumer surplus is the difference between the individual's willingness to pay and the price he/she pays for the good: consumer surplus measures the net gain the consumer receives when he/she purchases the good. Total consumer surplus is the sum of the individual consumer surpluses achieved by all the buyers of the good. Total consumer surplus is equal to the area under the demand curve but above the price.

- The area of consumer surplus is a triangle for a smooth demand curve or a series of rectangles for a step-shaped demand curve.

- Holding everything else constant, a decrease in price increases consumer surplus while an increase in price decreases consumer surplus.

Objective #14 [from Appendix]: The seller's price is the lowest price the seller is willing to sell the good for. Individual producer surplus is the difference between the price the good sells for and the lowest price the seller is willing to accept for the good: individual producer surplus measures the net gain the seller receives from selling the good. Total producer surplus is the sum of the individual producer surplus achieved by all the sellers of the good. Total producer surplus is equal to the area above the supply curve but beneath the price.

- The area of producer surplus is a triangle for a smooth supply curve or a series of rectangles for a step-shaped supply curve.

- Holding everything else constant, a decrease in price decreases producer surplus and an increase in price increases producer surplus.

Objective #15 [from Appendix]: Total surplus is the sum of consumer and producer surplus. At the market equilibrium, total surplus is maximized: the market equilibrium allocates the consumption of the good among potential consumers and the sales of the good among potential sellers in order to achieve the maximum possible gains to society. In a well-functioning market, total surplus cannot be increased by reallocating consumption among consumers, reallocating sales among sellers, or by changing the quantity traded. In fact, each of these actions diminishes the level of total surplus in the market.

- Preventing a sale in a market that would have taken place in equilibrium reduces both consumer and producer surplus, resulting in a loss of total surplus. Increasing sales beyond the equilibrium quantity similarly reduces consumer surplus, producer surplus, and total surplus, since such a sale would represent a situation where the buyer's willingness to buy must be less than the seller's cost.

Key Terms

imports goods and services purchased from other countries.

exports goods and services sold to other countries.

globalization the phenomenon of growing economic linkages among countries.

Ricardian model of international trade a model that analyzes international *trade* under the assumption that *opportunity costs* are constant.

autarky a situation in which a country does not trade with other countries.

factor intensity the difference in the ratio of factors used to produce a good in various industries. For example, oil refining is capital-intensive compared to clothing manufacture because oil refiners use a higher ratio of capital to labor than do clothing producers.

Heckscher–Ohlin model a *model* of international trade in which a country has a *comparative advantage* in a good whose production is intensive in the factors that are abundantly available in that country.

domestic demand curve a *demand curve* that shows how the quantity of a good demanded by domestic consumers depends on the price of that good.

domestic supply curve a *supply curve* that shows how the quantity of a good supplied by domestic producers depends on the price of that good.

world price the price at which a good can be bought or sold abroad.

exporting industries industries that produce goods and services that are sold abroad.

import-competing industries industries that produce goods and services that are also imported.

free trade *trade* that is unregulated by government *tariffs* or other artificial barriers; the levels of *exports* and *imports* occur naturally, as a result of supply and demand.

trade protection policies that limit *imports*.

protection an alternative term for *trade protection;* policies that limit *imports*.

tariff a tax levied on *imports*.

Key Terms *(continued)*

import quota a legal limit on the quantity of a good that can be imported from abroad.

international trade agreements treaties by which countries agree to lower *trade protections* against one another.

North American Free Trade Agreement (NAFTA) a *trade* agreement among the United States, Canada, and Mexico.

European Union (EU) a customs union among 27 European nations.

World Trade Organization (WTO) an international organization of member countries that oversees *international trade agreements* and rules on disputes between countries over those agreements.

offshore outsourcing businesses hiring people in another country to perform various tasks.

willingness to pay the maximum price a consumer is prepared to pay for a good.

individual consumer surplus the net gain to an individual buyer from the purchase of a good; equal to the difference between the buyer's *willingness to pay* and the price paid.

total consumer surplus the sum of the *individual consumer surpluses* of all the buyers of a good in a market.

consumer surplus a term often used to refer both to *individual consumer surplus* and to *total consumer surplus*.

cost (of seller) the lowest price at which a seller is willing to sell a good.

individual producer surplus the net gain to an individual seller from selling a good; equal to the difference between the price received and the seller's *cost*.

total producer surplus the sum of the *individual producer surpluses* of all the sellers of a good in a market.

producer surplus a term often used to refer both to *individual producer surplus* and to *total producer surplus*.

total surplus the total net gain to consumers and producers from trading in a market; the sum of the *producer surplus* and the *consumer surplus*.

▮ AFTER YOU READ THE CHAPTER

Tips

Tip #1. Students often struggle with the concept of comparative advantage and how it relates to the opportunity cost of producing the good. One fail-safe method for analyzing this type of problem is to follow these steps. (1) Identify the two individuals or the two countries (for the rest of this tip we assume that we are analyzing the comparative advantage with regard to two countries) that are involved in the problem. (2) Identify the two goods that are being produced. (3) For each country, draw a graph that illustrates the production possibility frontier for that country. Make sure you label the graph with the country's name and the two axes with the goods being produced. This labeling is very important since it helps ensure that you do not confuse the two countries or the two goods. (4) Find the slope of the production possibility frontier and then use this slope to calculate the opportunity cost of producing one more unit of the good measured along the x-axis. You can use the slope in this manner since the slope equals the "rise/run"—that is, the slope tells you the change in the y-variable divided by the change in the x-variable. So, for example, if one more unit of the x-variable was produced, the slope of the production possibility frontier would tell you how many units of the y-variable must be given up to produce this additional unit of the x-variable. (5) Under each country's graph, write a statement using this slope measure that says "OC of producing 1 good X is equal to |slope value| good Y." This statement just reminds you of what the opportunity cost of producing that additional unit of good X is. Below this statement write another statement that says "OC of producing 1 good Y is equal to |1/slope| good X." (6) Compare the opportunity cost of producing good X between the two countries, and decide which country can produce good X at the lowest opportunity cost. Circle the label on the x-axis for this country to identify the country that has the comparative advantage in producing good X. Then, on the other country's graph, circle the label on the y-axis to identify the country that has the comparative advantage in producing good Y. Figure 5.7 provides an example of this method. Note the labels, the OC statements, and the circling of the relevant labels as a means of identifying the country's comparative advantage. Faithful adherence to this method will certainly assure you of getting this concept right.

Figure 5.7

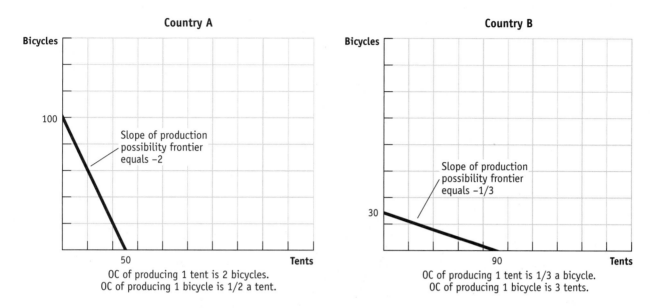

Country A

Bicycles

100

Slope of production
possibility frontier
equals –2

50   **Tents**

OC of producing 1 tent is 2 bicycles.
OC of producing 1 bicycle is 1/2 a tent.

Country B

Bicycles

Slope of production
possibility frontier
equals –1/3

30

90   **Tents**

OC of producing 1 tent is 1/3 a bicycle.
OC of producing 1 bicycle is 3 tents.

Tip #2. Students struggle with deciding what the relevant range of relative prices is for a good when countries specialize and then trade. Let's use the information in Figure 5.7 to work through a method for calculating this range of relative prices. Start with the good measured on the *x*-axis: tents. From the OC statements below the two graphs, we can see that the OC of producing 1 tent is between 1/3 a bicycle (country B's OC) and 2 bicycles (country A's OC). You can think about placing these two limits on a number line and noting that the relative price of 1 tent must fall somewhere between the lowest possible relative price of 1/3 a bicycle and the highest possible relative price of 2 bicycles. Figure 5.8 illustrates this number-line approach.

Figure 5.8

Country B is willing to trade 1 tent for bicycles provided that
country B gets at least 1/3 a bicycle. Country A is willing to
purchase a tent provided that it costs 2 bicycles or less.

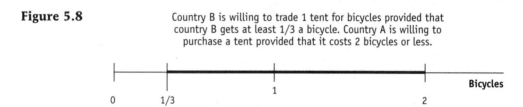

Bicycles

0   1/3   1   2

Tip #3. Working with quotas is often difficult for students: a quota is a legally established limit to the amount of imports a country allows during a given period. An alternative way of thinking about this legal limit is to recognize that the quota is the amount of imports that leads to the sum of the quantity supplied domestically plus the quota amount equaling the quantity demanded domestically. Thus, if you are told the quantity demanded domestically and the quantity supplied domestically at a given price, you can then calculate what the necessary quota would be in order for the total quantity supplied of the good (both the domestic production plus the world production) to equal the quantity demanded domestically. With this thought in mind, go back and revisit Figure 5.6 to see if you can apply this concept to the graph.

Tip #4   [from Appendix]. Figure 5.9 illustrates the concept of consumer surplus for a step-shaped demand curve. The area of consumer surplus consists of a series of rectangles that lie under the demand curve but above the market price. Each of these rectangles has been shaded separately in Figure 5.9, but the area of consumer surplus is the entire shaded area. Those consumers whose willingness to pay is equal to or greater than the market price will purchase the good for the market price, and their consumer surplus represents the net gain they receive from purchasing the good.

Figure 5.9

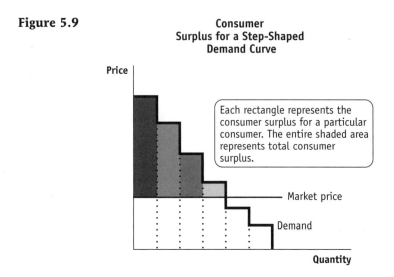

Tip #5   [from Appendix]. Figure 5.10 illustrates the concept of consumer surplus for a smooth demand curve. The area of consumer surplus consists of the area under the demand curve but above the market price. In Figure 5.10, the area of consumer surplus is shaded. The value of consumer surplus can be found by calculating the area of this shaded triangle. The consumer surplus represents the net gain consumers receive from purchasing the good.

Figure 5.10

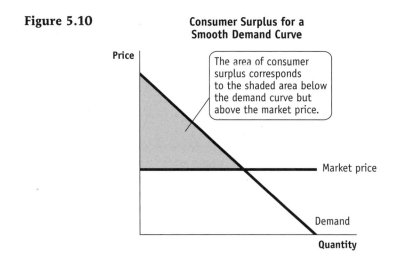

Tip #6 [from Appendix]. Figure 5.11 illustrates the concept of producer surplus for a step-shaped supply curve. The area of producer surplus consists of a series of rectangles that lie above the supply curve but below the market price. Each of these rectangles has been shaded as separate rectangles in Figure 5.11, but the area of producer surplus is the entire shaded area. Those producers whose willingness to sell is equal to or less than the market price, will sell the good for the market price, and their producer surplus represents the net gain they receive from selling the good.

Figure 5.11

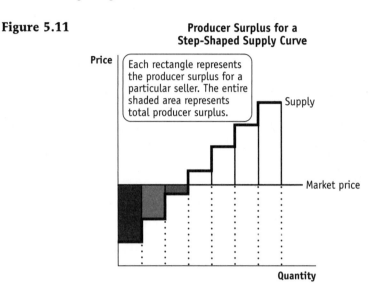

**Producer Surplus for a
Step-Shaped Supply Curve**

Tip #7 [from Appendix]. Figure 5.12 illustrates the concept of producer surplus for a smooth supply curve. The area of producer surplus is the shaded region above the supply curve but beneath the market price. The value of producer surplus can be found by calculating the area of this shaded triangle. The producer surplus represents the net gain producers receive from selling the good.

Figure 5.12

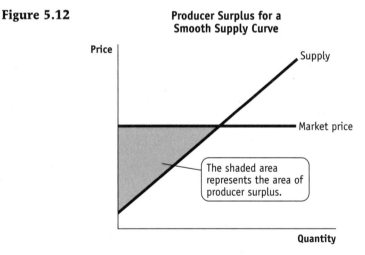

**Producer Surplus for a
Smooth Supply Curve**

Tip #8 **[from Appendix].** Figures 5.13 and 5.14 illustrate total surplus, which is the sum of consumer surplus and producer surplus. Figure 5.13 illustrates this concept for step-shaped demand and supply curves, and Figure 5.14 illustrates this concept for smooth demand and supply curves.

Figure 5.13   **Total Surplus for Step-Shaped Demand and Supply Curves**

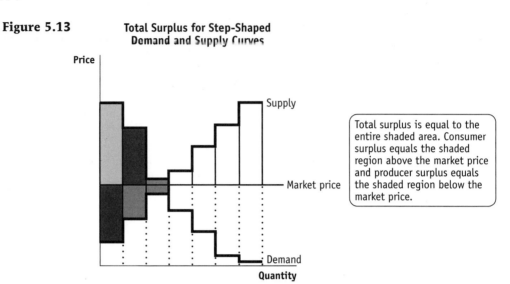

Total surplus is equal to the entire shaded area. Consumer surplus equals the shaded region above the market price and producer surplus equals the shaded region below the market price.

Figure 5.14   **Total Surplus for Smooth Demand and Supply Curves**

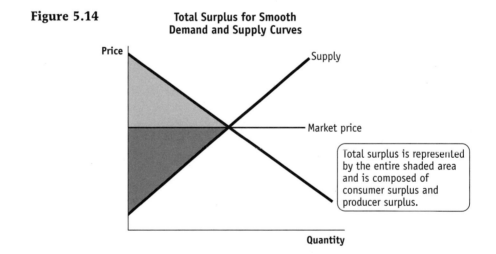

Total surplus is represented by the entire shaded area and is composed of consumer surplus and producer surplus.

1. Bob and Mary are the only inhabitants of Littleburg. Both Bob and Mary spend their time planting vegetables and looking for berries. They currently do not trade with each other. The following graph shows their production possibilities for a day. Assume that both goods are measured in terms of some type of unit measurement (e.g., rows of vegetables or pints of berries) and that Mary and Bob have equal amounts of resources and technology available to them.

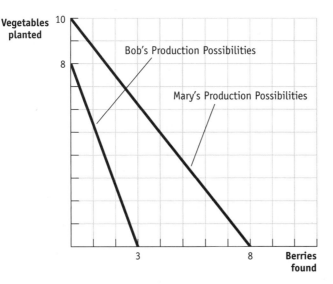

You are asked to determine who has the absolute advantage in planting vegetables and who has the absolute advantage in finding berries. You are also asked to identify who has the comparative advantage for each of these tasks. What is Mary's opportunity cost of finding berries? What is Bob's opportunity cost of finding berries? Finally, suppose that Bob and Mary decide to specialize according to their comparative advantages and then trade. What is the range of amounts of vegetables planted that both would agree to trade in exchange for one unit of berries found?

STEP 1: Review the definition of absolute advantage and then determine who has the absolute advantage in the production of each good.

Review the section "Comparative Advantage versus Absolute Advantage" on pages 132–134 (Econ pages 216–218).

From the available set of resources, Mary can produce more planted vegetables and found berries than can Bob: Mary has the absolute advantage in the production of both goods.

STEP 2: Review the definition of comparative advantage and then determine who has the comparative advantage in the production of each good.

Review the section "Comparative Advantage and International Trade" on pages 128–137 (Econ pages 212–221), Figure 5-2 and Tables 5-1 and 5-2.

The opportunity cost of producing a unit of berries is 8/3 units of planted vegetables for Bob and 10/8 units of berries for Mary. Mary has a lower opportunity cost of finding berries than does Bob: for each unit of berries that she finds, she gives up less than does Bob. Mary therefore has the comparative advantage in finding berries. Bob, in contrast, has the comparative advantage in planting vegetables: his opportunity cost of planting vegetables is 3/8 unit of found berries, while the opportunity cost of planting vegetables for Mary is 8/10 unit of found berries.

STEP 3: From the preceding graph determine the opportunity cost of finding berries for each of these individuals.

Review the section "Comparative Advantage and International Trade" on pages 128–137 (Econ pages 212–221), Figure 5-2 and Tables 5-1 and 5-2.

In Step 2, the opportunity cost of finding berries is given. Remember that you can find the opportunity cost of the good measured on the *x*-axis by using the slope measure if the production possibility frontier is linear. Thus, the slope of Mary's production possibilities curve is equal to –10/8: this indicates that for every unit of found berries she must give up 10/8 units of planted vegetables. The slope of Bob's production possibilities curve is equal to –8/3: this indicates that for every unit of found berries he must give up 8/3 units of planted vegetables. It is more costly for Bob to produce found berries than it is for Mary to produce found berries. Thus, Mary has the comparative advantage in finding berries, while Bob has the comparative advantage in planting vegetables.

STEP 4: Apply your knowledge of the opportunity cost of finding berries for each of these individuals to determine a range of amounts of vegetables planted that both would agree to trade for one unit of berries found.

Review the section "Comparative Advantage and International Trade" on pages 128–137 (Econ pages 212–221), Figure 5-2 and Tables 5-1 and 5-2.

Bob is willing to give up 8/3 units of planted vegetables for a unit of found berries, while Mary must receive 10/8 units of planted vegetables to be willing to give up a unit of found berries. Any time Mary can receive more than 10/8 units of planted vegetables for a unit of found berries, she is willing to trade; any time Bob pays less than 8/3 units of planted vegetables for a unit of found berries, he is willing to trade. The trading range for one unit of found berries is thus somewhere between 10/8 units of planted vegetables and 8/3 units of planted vegetables.

2. Suppose there are two individuals: Trent and Sue. Both Trent and Sue produce two different goods: clarinets and drums. Each of them has the same amount of resources, the same technology, and the same amount of time to spend producing clarinets and drums. If Trent devotes all of his time, resources, and technology to producing clarinets, he is able to produce 1,000 clarinets and 0 drums. When Trent devotes all of his time, resources, and technology to producing drums, he is able to produce 500 drums and 0 clarinets. If Sue devotes all of her time, resources, and technology to producing clarinets, she is able to produce 800 clarinets and 0 drums. When Sue devotes all of her time, resources, and technology to producing drums, she is able to produce 500 drums and 0 clarinets. Assume that the production possibility frontiers for both Trent and Sue are linear. You are asked to provide graphs of Trent's and Sue's production possibilities on which clarinets are measured on the vertical axis and drums are measured on the horizontal axis. After drawing this graph, you are asked to determine who has the absolute advantage in producing clarinets and drums. In addition, you are asked to determine who has the comparative advantage in the production of each of these goods. Suppose initially that Trent and Sue each devote half of their time and half of their resources to the production of clarinets. The rest of their time and resources goes toward producing drums. Currently Trent and Sue do not trade with each other. Fill in the following table given this information.

	Clarinets	Drums
Trent		
Sue		
Total Production		

Suppose that Trent increases his production of clarinets by one unit relative to his initial production level, while Sue decreases her production of clarinets by one unit relative to her initial production level. They both adjust their production of drums so that they stay on their respective production possibility frontiers. Complete the following table, based on these assumptions.

	Clarinets	Drums
Trent		
Sue		
Total Production		

Did total production increase or decrease when Trent and Sue altered their allocation of resources? Explain your answer. Suppose instead that Trent decreases his production of clarinets by one unit from the initial level, while Sue increases her production of clarinets by one unit from the initial level. They both adjust their production of drums so that they stay on their respective production possibility frontiers. Complete the following table, based on these assumptions.

	Clarinets	Drums
Trent		
Sue		
Total Production		

Did total production increase or decrease when Trent and Sue altered their allocation of resources? Explain your answer. When Trent and Sue adjust their production of these two goods, total production is affected: explain how their adjustments and their impact on total production are related to specialization, comparative advantage, and trade.

STEP 1: Draw graphs of Trent's and Sue's production possibilities on which clarinets are measured on the vertical axis and drums are measured on the horizontal axis.

Review the section "Production Possibilities and Comparative Advantage, Revisited" on pages 129–130 (Econ pages 213–214) and Figure 5-2.

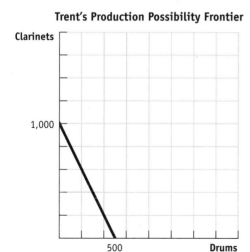

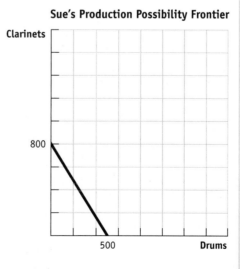

STEP 2: Determine who has the absolute advantage in the production of clarinets and who has the absolute advantage in the production of drums.

Review the section "Comparative Advantage versus Absolute Advantage" on pages 132–134 (Econ pages 216–218).

Trent can produce more clarinets than can Sue: Trent has the absolute advantage in the production of clarinets, since he is more productive than is Sue. Neither Sue nor Trent has an absolute advantage in producing drums, since each of them can produce an equivalent amount of drums from the same amount of resources.

STEP 3: Determine who has the comparative advantage in the production of clarinets and who has the comparative advantage in the production of drums.

Review the section "Production Possibilities and Comparative Advantage, Revisited" on pages 129–130 (Econ pages 213–214), Figures 5-2 and 5-3, and Tables 5-1 and 5-2.

To determine who has the comparative advantage in producing drums, you first need to determine the opportunity cost of producing a drum for both Trent and Sue. Trent's opportunity cost of producing a drum is equal to 2 clarinets, since each time he produces a drum he must give up the production of two clarinets. Sue's opportunity cost of producing a drum is equal to 8/5 clarinets, since each time she produces a drum she must give up the production of 8/5 clarinets. Trent's opportunity cost of producing a drum is greater than Sue's opportunity cost: Sue has the comparative advantage in producing drums.

To determine who has the comparative advantage in producing clarinets, you will need to determine the opportunity cost of producing a clarinet for both Trent and Sue. Trent's opportunity cost of producing a clarinet is equal to 1/2 drum, since each time he produces a clarinet he must give up the production of 1/2 drum. Sue's opportunity cost of producing a clarinet is equal to 5/8 drum, since each time she produces a clarinet she must give up the production of 5/8 drum. Sue's opportunity cost of producing a clarinet is greater than Trent's opportunity cost: Trent has the comparative advantage in producing clarinets.

STEP 4: Fill in the following table based on the assumption that Trent and Sue each devote half of their time and half of their resources to the production of clarinets. The rest of their time and resources goes toward the production of drums.

	Clarinets	Drums
Trent		
Sue		
Total Production		

Review the section "Production Possibilities and Comparative Advantage, Revisited" on pages 129–130 (Econ pages 213–214), Figures 5-2 and 5-3, and Tables 5-1 and 5-2.

To fill in the table you can consult the figures you drew in Step 1 and find the midpoints of each production possibility frontier. The results are given in the following table.

	Clarinets	Drums
Trent	500	250
Sue	400	250
Total Production	900	500

STEP 5: Fill in the following table based on the assumption that Trent decides to produce one more clarinet than he did initially, while Sue decides to produce one fewer clarinet than she did initially. Make sure that the new levels of production are on Trent's and Sue's respective production possibility frontiers.

	Clarinets	Drums
Trent		
Sue		
Total Production		

Review the section "Production Possibilities and Comparative Advantage, Revisited" on pages 129–130 (Econ pages 213–214), Figures 5-2 and 5-3, and Tables 5-1 and 5-2.

From the earlier discussion on comparative advantage (see step 3), you know what the opportunity cost of an additional clarinet is for Trent: to produce one more clarinet he must give up 1/2 drum. Thus, Trent can produce 501 clarinets and 249.5 drums. A similar calculation is performed for Sue: when she produces one fewer clarinet, she is able to increase her drum production by 5/8 (this is the same as 0.625) drum. The following table summarizes these results.

	Clarinets	Drums
Trent	501	249.5
Sue	399	250.625
Total Production	900	500.125

STEP 6: Determine the effect on total production of the change in resource allocation in Step 5. Explain your result.

Review the section "Production Possibilities and Comparative Advantage, Revisited" on pages 129–130 (Econ pages 213–214), Figures 5-2 and 5-3, Tables 5-1 and 5-2.

When Trent moves toward more clarinet production and less drum production, while Sue moves toward more drum production and less clarinet production, we see that total production increases. Notice that in this example both Trent and Sue are moving toward specializing in the production of the good for which they have comparative advantage, and this leads to greater overall production of the goods.

STEP 7: Fill in the following table based on the assumption that Trent decides to produce one fewer clarinet than he did initially, while Sue decides to produce one more clarinet than she did initially. Make sure that the new levels of production are on Trent's and Sue's respective production possibility frontiers.

	Clarinets	Drums
Trent		
Sue		
Total Production		

Review the section "Production Possibilities and Comparative Advantage, Revisited" on pages 129–130 (Econ pages 213–214), Figures 5-2 and 5-3, Tables 5-1 and 5-2.

Do the same type of analysis that you did for Step 5, but this time have Trent produce one fewer clarinet while Sue produces one more clarinet. Use the opportunity costs that you calculated in Step 3 to help you figure out what happens to drum production for both Trent and Sue. The following table summarizes these results.

	Clarinets	Drums
Trent	499	250.5
Sue	401	249.375
Total Production	900	499.875

STEP 8: **Determine the effect on total production of the change in resource allocation in Step 7. Explain your result.**

Review the section "Production Possibilities and Comparative Advantage, Revisited" on pages 129–130 (Econ pages 213–214), Figures 5-2 and 5-3, Tables 5-1 and 5-2.

This time total production decreases from its initial level: Trent and Sue are specializing, but they are not specializing according to their comparative advantage, and their decisions here result in less overall production than would be possible if they specialized according to their comparative advantage. It is best for overall production if Trent produces clarinets and Sue produces drums.

STEP 9: **Given your analysis in Steps 6 and 8, explain how these adjustments and their impact on total production are related to specialization, comparative advantage, and trade.**

Review the section "Production Possibilities and Comparative Advantage, Revisited" on pages 129–130 (Econ pages 213–214), Figures 5-2 and 5-3, Tables 5-1 and 5-2.

This example illustrates how specializing in the production of the good for which you have comparative advantage can result in greater overall production than is possible if there is no specialization. For specialization to be advantageous, two things must happen: you must specialize according to your comparative advantage, and you must engage in trade with others who are also specializing according to their comparative advantage.

3.   The small economy of Newville produces chocolate, and this market for chocolate is characterized by the following equations:

Domestic Demand for Chocolate: $P = 100 - Q$
Domestic Supply of Chocolate: $P = Q$

You are asked to determine the equilibrium price and quantity in this market if Newville continues to be a closed economy with regard to the chocolate market. You are also asked to provide a measure of the consumer and producer surplus when this market is closed to trade. Newville is considering opening this market to trade and imagines two possible scenarios: in the first scenario, the chocolate market is open to trade and the world price of chocolate is $80 per unit. Newville's government wants you to analyze the effect of opening this market to trade given this price: the government in particular wants to know the impact of opening the market on the level of imports or exports of chocolate it could anticipate as well as on the values of consumer and producer surplus when there is trade. In the second scenario, the chocolate market is open to trade, and the world price of chocolate is $20 per unit. You are also asked to provide an analysis of the impact of opening the market on the level of imports or exports of chocolate as well as on the values of consumer and producer surplus if the world price for chocolate is equal to $20 per unit. For both scenarios, you are asked to illustrate your answer with a graph to help the government officials understand the impact of opening the market to world trade. The government also wishes to understand if opening its market to trade is beneficial whether it is confronted by the first or the second scenario. Who (domestic consumers or domestic producers of chocolate) in Newville is more likely to favor opening the chocolate market to trade if the world price is anticipated to be $80 per unit?

STEP 1: Start by drawing a graph of the market for chocolate in Newville when its economy is closed to trade. Use this graph to calculate the levels of consumer and producer surplus if there is no trade.

Review the section "Supply, Demand, and International Trade" on pages 137–144 (Econ pages 221–228) and Figure 5-5.

Graph the two equations and then use these two equations to find the equilibrium price and equilibrium quantity in this market when the market is closed to world competition. Using the demand and supply equations—$P = 100 - Q$ and $P = Q$, respectively—we can solve for the equilibrium quantity and then use this quantity to find the equilibrium price. Thus, $100 - Q = Q$, or $2Q = 100$, and therefore $Q = 50$. Plugging $Q = 50$ back into either the demand or the supply equation, we can find that the equilibrium price is equal to $50.

The value of consumer surplus is equal to $(1/2)($100 per unit $- $50 per unit$)(50$ units$)$, or $1,250. The value of producer surplus is equal to $(1/2)($50 per unit $- $0 per unit$)(50$ units$)$, or $1,250. These areas are marked on the preceding graph.

STEP 2: Modify your graph from Step 1 by adding in a line that represents a world price for chocolate of $80 per unit.

Review the section "Supply, Demand, and International Trade" on pages 137–144 (Econ pages 221–228) and Figure 5-5.

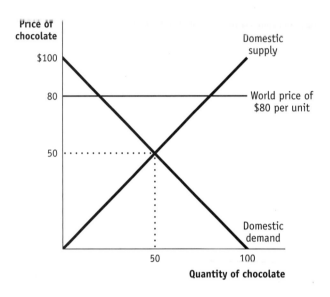

STEP 3: Analyze the impact on this market if the world price is equal to $80 and Newville opens its chocolate market. Be sure to identify whether Newville will export or import chocolate. In addition, determine the impact of this decision on consumer and producer surplus. Finally, analyze whether trade is beneficial if the world price of chocolate is equal to $80 per unit.

Review the section "Supply, Demand, and International Trade" on pages 137–144 (Econ pages 221–228), and Figures 5-8 and 5-9.

When Newville opens its chocolate market to international trade and the world price of chocolate is $80 per unit, domestic suppliers will be willing to supply 80 units of the good, while domestic demanders are willing to buy only 20 units of the good. This excess supply of 60 units will therefore be exported into the world market for chocolate.

To find the consumer surplus, first recognize that it is the area that is under the domestic demand curve but above the world price for chocolate. Then, calculate the value of this area: consumer surplus is equal to (1/2)($100 per unit – $80 per unit)(20 units), or $200.

To find the producer surplus, first recognize that it is the area that is under the world price for chocolate but above the domestic supply curve. Then, calculate the value of this area: producer surplus is equal to (1/2)($80 per unit – $0 per unit)(80 units), or $3,200.

The following figure illustrates the impact on consumer and producer surplus when the world price is equal to $80 per unit.

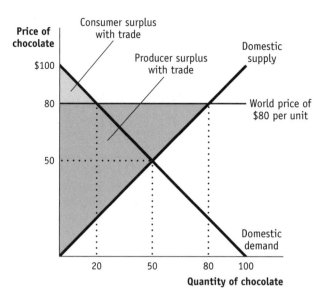

Trade is beneficial to Newville when the world price is $80 per unit since the value of total surplus, the sum of consumer and producer surplus in this case, is greater than the value of total surplus when Newville has a closed chocolate market.

STEP 4: Redraw your graph from Step 1 and revise it by adding in a line that represents a world price for chocolate of $20 per unit.

Review the section "Supply, Demand, and International Trade" on pages 137–144 (Econ pages 221–228) and Figure 5-6.

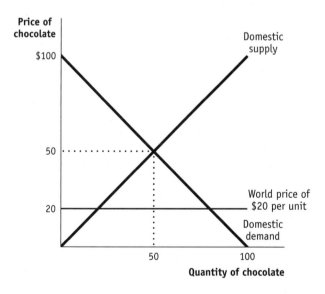

STEP 5: Analyze the impact on this market if the world price is equal to $20 and Newville opens its chocolate market. Be sure to identify whether Newville will export or import chocolate. In addition, determine the impact of this decision on consumer and producer surplus. Finally, analyze whether trade is beneficial if the world price of chocolate is equal to $20 per unit.

Review the section "Supply, Demand, and International Trade" on pages 137–144 (Econ pages 221–228) and Figures 5-6 and 5-7.

When Newville opens its chocolate market to international trade and the world price of chocolate is $20 per unit, domestic suppliers will only be willing to supply 20 units of the good, while domestic demanders want to buy 80 units of the good. This excess demand of 60 units will be met by Newville's importing 60 units of chocolate from the world market.

To find the consumer surplus, first recognize that it is the area that is under the domestic demand curve but above the world price for chocolate. Then, calculate the value of this area: consumer surplus is equal to (1/2)($100 per unit – $20 per unit)(80 units), or $3,200.

To find the producer surplus, first recognize that it is the area that is under the world price for chocolate but above the domestic supply curve. Then, calculate the value of this area: producer surplus is equal to (1/2)($20 per unit – $0 per unit)(20 units), or $200.

The following figure illustrates the impact on consumer and producer surplus when the world price is equal to $20 per unit.

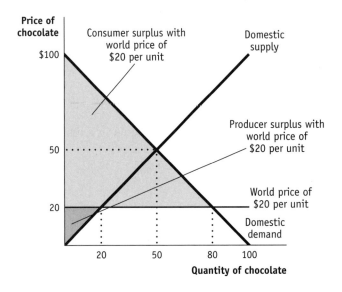

Trade is beneficial to Newville when the world price is $20 per unit since the value of total surplus, the sum of consumer and producer surplus in this case, is greater than the value of total surplus when Newville has a closed chocolate market.

STEP 6: Review your analysis in Step 3 to determine whether domestic demanders or domestic suppliers of chocolate will be more likely to favor opening the chocolate market to trade when the world price is $80 per unit.

Review the section "Supply, Demand, and International Trade" on pages 137–144 (Econ pages 221–228) and Figures 5-6 and 5-7.

Domestic producers will favor opening the chocolate market to trade when the world price is equal to $80 per unit, since they will be able to sell more units at a higher price. We can easily see the benefits to these producers by comparing the area of producer surplus when the economy is closed to trade (see Step 1) with the area of consumer surplus when the economy is open to trade and the world price is $80 (see Step 3). In contrast, domestic consumers of chocolate will be opposed to opening this market to trade, since their consumer surplus will shrink once the market is open to trade.

4. The small economy of Newville produces chocolate, and this market for chocolate is characterized by the following equations:

Domestic demand for chocolate: $P = 100 - Q$
Domestic supply of chocolate: $P = Q$

Furthermore, you know that the world price for chocolate is $20 per unit. Newville has decided to open its market for chocolate, and although recognizing that this will allow domestic consumers to consume more chocolate at lower prices, it has also determined that it will levy a tariff that raises the price of chocolate in Newville to $40 per unit. You are asked to compare the areas of consumer surplus with and without the tariff, the areas of producer surplus with and without the tariff, the amount of tax revenue the government of Newville will earn from this tariff, and the deadweight loss or efficiency cost of this tariff. The government of Newville has asked that you provide them with graphs that depict what happens if the market is opened to trade and what happens if this tariff is imposed.

STEP 1: Start by drawing a graph of the market for chocolate in Newville when its economy is closed to trade. Then, use the two equations to solve for the equilibrium price and quantity in this market. Once you have plotted the equilibrium price and quantity in your graph, you will then be able to use this graph to calculate the levels of consumer and producer surplus if there is no trade.

Review the section "Supply, Demand, and International Trade" on pages 137–144 (Econ pages 221–228) and Figure 5-7.

From Step 5 of problem 3, we can review the graph that represents this market if it opens to trade and the world price of chocolate is $20 per unit. In addition, we know from problem 3 that consumer surplus is equal to $3,200 and producer surplus is equal to $200.

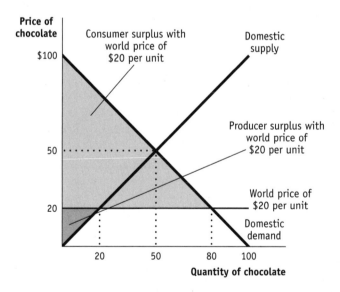

STEP 2: Draw a graph of the market for chocolate in Newville showing the effect of a tariff that raises the price of chocolate to $40 per unit. In this graph, indicate the areas that represent consumer surplus, producer surplus, tariff revenue for the government, and deadweight loss from the tariff. Calculate the values of these different areas.

Review the section "Supply, Demand, and International Trade" on pages 137–144 (Econ pages 221–228) and Figure 5-7, as well as the section "The Effects of a Tariff" on pages 144–146 (Econ pages 228–230) and Figure 5-10.

The tariff raises the price of chocolate to $40 per unit. This increase in price will reduce the quantity of chocolate demanded by domestic consumers while increasing the quantity of chocolate supplied by domestic producers. When the price of chocolate is

$40, domestic consumers demand 60 units while domestic producers are willing to provide 40 units. Newville will import that difference, or 20 units of chocolate. The government of Newville will collect $20 from every unit of chocolate that is imported and will therefore earn $400 in tariff revenue.

The deadweight loss for the tariff will equal $400. To find the area of deadweight loss, you first need to recognize that it is the sum of the areas of two triangles. Then, calculate the area of each triangle. From the following graph, we can see that the area of deadweight loss is equal to $(1/2)($40/unit − $20/unit)(20 units) + (1/2)($40/unit − $20/unit)(20 units)$, or $400.

The graph that follows depicts the impact of this tariff on the market for chocolate in Newville.

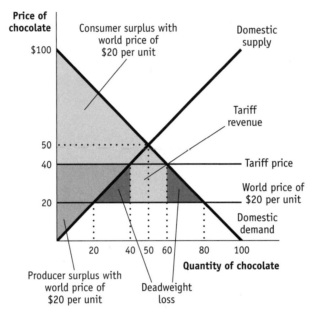

5. Suppose that Newville is still considering opening the market for chocolate that was described in problem 3, but is also now considering imposing a quota in the market once it is opened to trade. Suppose the government of Newville wishes to achieve the same outcome that it did with the tariff in problem 4, but now use a quota instead. What limit on imported chocolate would achieve the same outcome as the tariff described in problem 4, and what should the government of Newville charge the importer for the license to bring these imported chocolates into the Newville economy?

STEP 1: Review the graph in Step 2 of problem 4 to determine how many units of the chocolate are imported into Newville when there is a tariff that raises the price of chocolate to $40. This amount of imports is the amount that the quota must be set at in order to achieve the same outcome as under the proposed tariff.

Review the section "The Effects of Trade Protection" on pages 144-148 (Econ pages 228-232) and Figures 5-7 and 5-11.

From the graph we can see that Newville imports 20 units of chocolate when the price of chocolate is raised to $40 per unit. Thus, if the government of Newville limits imports to 20 units, this will cause the price of chocolate to rise to $40 per unit, since it is only at this price that the difference between the quantity demanded domestically (60 units) and the quantity supplied domestically (40 units) is exactly equal to the amount of allowed imports (20 units).

STEP 2: Determine the price of the license for importing the chocolates by looking at the tariff revenue.

Review the section "The Effects of Trade Protection" on pages 144–148 (Econ pages 228–232) and Figure 5-7.

The tariff revenue represents the revenue the government receives when it places a tax on the imported good. With the quota, the government places a limit on how many units of the good can be imported, and it limits these imports by selling the right to bring the imports into the market. By selling the rights for the same price as the tariff revenue, the government imposes a quota limit that has exactly the same impact as the proposed tariff. The government of Newville should sell the rights to import chocolate for $20 per unit, or a total of $400 for all the rights.

6.   **[from Appendix]** Mary is considering opening up a coffee shop and she has contacted three people who live and work near where she would like to open her shop. For each of these three people, she has gotten information about their willingness to buy coffee at her shop. Paul reports that he is willing to pay $4 for a daily cup of coffee. Justina reports that she is willing to pay $3 for a daily cup of coffee. Lee reports that he is willing to pay $5 for a daily cup of coffee. Given the data, evaluate who values coffee the least. In addition, if Mary decides to price her coffee at $3.50 a cup, how many cups will she sell on a daily basis if her market consists only of Paul, Justina, and Lee? In addition, what will be the value of consumer surplus in this market per day? Finally, construct a step-shaped demand curve illustrating the daily demand for coffee at Mary's coffee shop.

STEP 1: Determine who values coffee the least and provide an explanation for your answer.

Review the section "Consumer Surplus and the Demand Curve" on pages 159–161 (Econ pages 102–108).

The price people are willing to pay for the good tells you the value they place on the good: when individuals willing to pay a high price for the good, then they value the good more than when they are only willing to pay a low price. Given the data, we see that Justina places a lower value on the good than do Lee and Paul.

STEP 2: Draw the step-shaped daily demand curve for coffee at Mary's shop.

Review the section "Consumer Surplus and the Demand Curve" on pages 159–161 (Econ pages 102–108).

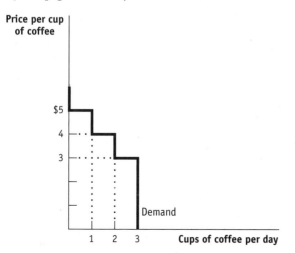

STEP 3: Determine how many cups of coffee Mary will sell daily at her coffee shop if the price of coffee is $3.50 a cup.

Review the section "Consumer Surplus and the Demand Curve" on pages 159–161 (Econ pages 102–108) and Figure 5A-1.

To determine how many cups of coffee Mary will sell daily at her coffee shop if the price of a cup of coffee is $3.50, see who is willing to pay at least that amount for a cup of coffee. Clearly Lee is willing to pay $3.50 per cup as is Paul. But Justina is unwilling to pay more than $3 per cup. Mary will be able to sell 2 cups of coffee per day.

STEP 4: Calculate the value of consumer surplus in this market per day if the price of coffee is $3.50 per cup.

Review the section "Consumer Surplus and the Demand Curve" on pages 159–161 (Econ pages 102–108) and Figure 5A-1.

First look at the step-shaped demand curve and determine where the area of consumer surplus is on the graph. Once you have found the area of consumer surplus, you can calculate its value. Alternatively, you can find consumer surplus for Lee as the difference between the price he is willing to pay and the price he does pay: in this case, Lee is willing to pay $5 per cup of coffee but he only pays $3.50 per cup, implying that his consumer surplus is equal to $1.50 per cup of coffee. Paul's consumer surplus per cup of coffee is the difference between the $4 per cup he is willing to pay and the $3.50 per cup that he pays: Paul's consumer surplus is equal to $.50 per cup of coffee. On a daily basis then, the consumer surplus when the price of a cup of coffee is $3.50 is equal to $2.00.

The shaded area in the following graph depicts the area of consumer surplus.

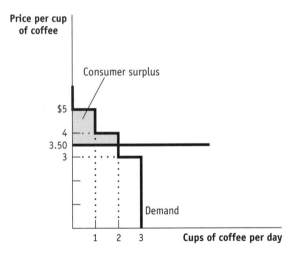

7. **[from Appendix]** Quench City has five beverage companies that provide a similar range of drink options to their customers. Suppose that you are given the following information about the five companies and the lowest prices they are each willing to accept for a case of their beverages in Quench City. Assume that each company has only one case of beverages available to be sold in this market.

Beverage Company	Lowest price the company is willing to accept for a case of beverages
The Sunny Cola	$6.00
Bubbling Bubbles	4.00
Cola Cola	7.00
Peppy Soda	5.00
Afternoon Delight	4.00

Create a step-shaped supply curve for this market and then evaluate how many cases of beverages will be sold if the price of a case of beverages is $5.50. In addition, provide a measure of producer surplus when the price of a case of beverages is $5.50. Finally, determine which companies will not sell a case of beverages if the price per case is set at $5.50.

STEP 1: Draw the step-shaped supply curve for the beverage market in Quench City.

Review the section "Producer Surplus and the Supply Curve" on pages 161–163 (Econ pages 109–113).

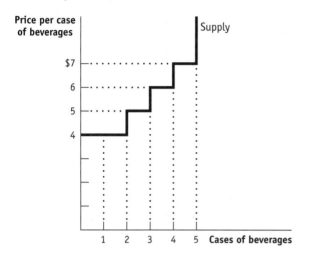

To draw the step-shaped supply curve, start with the lowest price that a company is willing to accept. In this example, both Bubbling Bubbles and Afternoon Delight are willing to sell a case of beverages for $4; the next step is occupied by Peppy Soda, which is willing to sell a case of beverages for $5; the next step is occupied by Sunny Cola, which is willing to sell a case of soda at $6; and the final step is occupied by Cola Cola, which is willing to sell a case of soda at $7.

STEP 2: Calculate the value of producer surplus when the price of a case of beverages is $5.50 in Quench City.

Review the section "Producer Surplus and the Supply Curve" on pages 161–163 (Econ pages 109–113) and Figure 5A-3.

If the price of a case of beverages is $5.50, Sunny Cola and Cola Cola will be unwilling to sell at this price. Thus, we can calculate producer surplus as the difference between the price of $5.50 and the lowest price that the sellers are willing to accept for a case of beverages. Thus, for Afternoon Delight and Bubbling Bubbles, the producer surplus is equal to the difference between $5.50 and the $4.00 they are willing to accept. Since there are two producers with the same price they are willing to accept, the producer surplus for each of them is $1.50, or a total of $3. The producer surplus for Peppy Soda is the difference between the price of $5 it is willing to accept and the $5.50 it receives when it sells the case of beverages: Peppy Soda has producer surplus of $.50. Total producer surplus is therefore equal to $3.50 when the price of a case of beverages is $5.50. The shaded area in the following graph depicts the area of producer surplus.

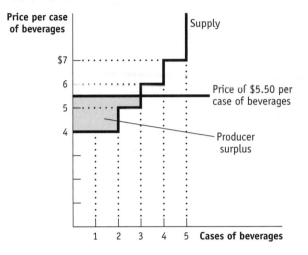

STEP 3: Determine who is willing to sell a case of beverages at $5.50 and who is not willing to sell a case of beverages at $5.50.

Review the section "Producer Surplus and the Supply Curve" on pages 161–163 (Econ pages 109–113) and Figure 5A-3.

When the price of a case of beverages is set at $5.50 per case, Sunny Cola and Cola Cola are unwilling to sell a case since both of these companies are only willing to accept a price that is greater than this. Sunny Cola must get a price of at least $6.00 per case to sell a case, and Cola Cola must get a price of $7.00 per case to sell a case.

8. **[from Appendix]** Metrocity employed a consulting firm to determine what the demand for and supply of mass transit were for their community. The consultants came back and provided Metrocity with the following graph of the monthly mass transit market in their community.

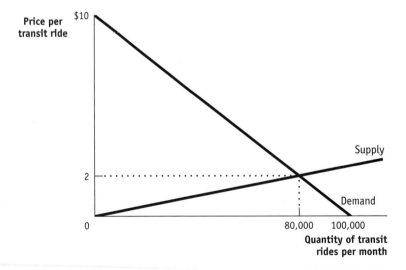

In the preceding graph, indicate the areas that correspond to consumer surplus and producer surplus and then calculate the numeric value of consumer surplus, producer surplus, and total surplus in this market. Metrocity is contemplating raising transit fares to $5. How would this policy change affect consumer surplus, producer surplus, and total surplus? Provide both a verbal explanation of the effect as well as numeric calculations. Would a fare increase increase or decrease efficiency in this market? Explain your answer. Does anyone benefit from a fare increase?

STEP 1: **First identify the areas of consumer and producer surplus on the graph. Then calculate the value of each of these areas.**

Review the sections "Consumer Surplus and the Demand Curve" on pages 159–161 (Econ pages 102–108) and "Producer Surplus and the Supply Curve" on pages 161–163 (Econ pages 109–113), along with Figures 5A-2 and 5A-4.

The following graph indicates the two areas that correspond to consumer surplus and producer surplus. The sum of these two areas is equal to total surplus.

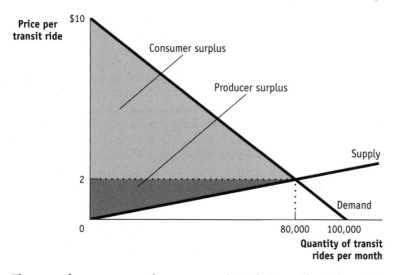

The area of consumer surplus corresponds to that area that is beneath the demand curve but above the price consumers pay for the good. In this case, consumers pay $2 per transit ride and they demand 80,000 transit rides per month. Consumer surplus is equal to $(1/2)(\$10 \text{ per ride} - \$2 \text{ per ride})(80{,}000 \text{ rides per month}) = \$320{,}000$ per month. The area of producer surplus corresponds to that area that is above the supply curve but beneath the price producers receive when they sell the good. In this case, producers sell each transit ride for $2 and they supply 80,000 transit rides per month. Producer surplus is equal to $(1/2)(\$2 \text{ per ride} - \$0 \text{ per ride})(80{,}000 \text{ rides per month}) = \$80{,}000$ per month. Total surplus is equal to the sum of consumer surplus and producer surplus in this example: total surplus = $320,000 + $80,000 = $400,000.

STEP 2: **Consider how a price increase will affect consumers and suppliers in this market. Provide a non-numerical analysis of the effect of this price increase.**

Review pages 159–163 (Econ pages 102–113).

In general, a price increase will decrease the area of consumer surplus and increase the area of producer surplus for a given demand curve and supply curve. To see this, let's consider what happens to these areas if the price was to change. In the following figure, we replicate the figure from Step 1 but raise the price.

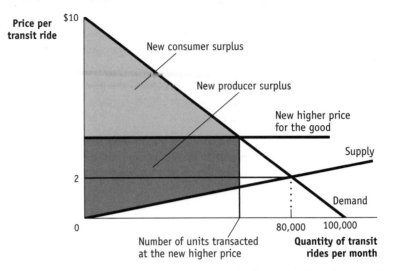

If we compare the figure from Step 1 with the preceding figure, what we see is the area of consumer surplus shrinks when the price in the market is increased: this is due to fewer transactions being made and each transaction occurring at a higher price. Consumers receive less consumer surplus. Comparing the two figures also reveals that producer surplus increases when the price is raised: producers capture some of the consumers' initial surplus. If you compare the two figures—you will note that there is an area that is shaded in the first figure but not shaded in the second figure: this area is composed of two parts—the loss in consumer surplus that occurs because consumers purchase fewer units and the loss in producer surplus that occurs because producers sell fewer units.

STEP 3: Calculate how many transit rides demanders will demand if the price of transit rides increases to $5 per transit ride. Calculate how many transit rides suppliers will supply if the price of transit rides increases to $5 per transit ride.

Review the sections "Consumer Surplus and the Demand Curve" on pages 159–161 (Econ pages 102–108) and "Producer Surplus and the Supply Curve" on pages 161–163 (Econ pages 109–113).

This step requires that you find the equations for the demand and supply curves and then use these equations to find the quantity demanded and supplied at a price of $5 per transit tickets.

Let's start with the demand equation. From the provided graph, we know that the y-intercept is $10 and that the point (100,000) sits on the line. Using this information and the slope intercept form, we can write the equation for the demand curve. The general slope intercept form is $Y = mX + b$. We know that b, the y-intercept, is equal to $10. Thus, $Y = mX + 10$. We also know that price (P) is the variable measured on the y-axis and quantity demanded (Q_d) is the variable measured on the x-axis. Thus, $P = mQ_d + 10$. Now, all we need is the slope, m. From the graph, we can measure the rise as 10 and the run as −100,000: thus, slope = rise/run = 10/(−100,000) = −1/10,000. The equation for the demand curve is $P = (−1/10,000)Q_d + 10$. When price is $5 per transit ticket that implies that $Q_d = 50,000$ transit tickets.

To find the supply equation, note that on the provided graph the supply curve is linear and goes through two points: $(Q_s, P) = (0, 0)$ and $(80,000, 2)$. Use this information and the general equation in slope intercept form to find the equation for the supply curve. Thus, $Y = mX + b$ can be rewritten as $P = mQ_s + 0$ since the *y*-intercept is 0 and the *x*-axis and *y*-axis are Q_s and P, respectively. Since we have two points on the linear supply curve, we can write the slope as the (change in *y*)/ (change in *x*) or $(0 - 2)/(0 - 80,000) = 1/40,000$. Thus, the supply equation is $P = (1/40,000)Q_s$. When price is $5 per transit ticket that implies that $Q_s = 200,000$ transit tickets.

Since the quantity demanded is less than the quantity supplied, at a price of $5 per transit ticket the market is not at its equilibrium. If the price is raised to $5 per transit ticket, 50,000 transit tickets will be sold and the remaining 150,000 transit tickets producers are willing to supply at that price will not be purchased.

STEP 4: Calculate the value of consumer surplus and producer surplus with the increase in the price of transit rides. Sum these two values to get the new total surplus value.

Review the sections "Consumer Surplus and the Demand Curve" on pages 159–161 (Econ pages 102–108) and "Producer Surplus and the Supply Curve" on pages 161–163 (Econ pages 109–113).

From our work in Step 3, we are ready to edit our graph from Step 2 by adding the numbers we calculated. Thus, our graph illustrating the new areas of producer and consumer surplus looks like the following graph.

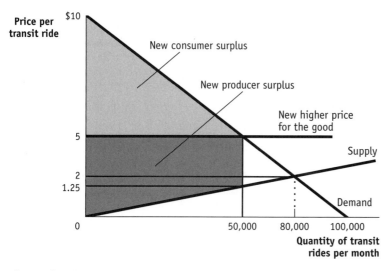

If you closely examine the preceding graph, you will realize that we need one more number: the price that corresponds to a quantity of 50,000 tickets on the supply curve. That is, we need to know the price that suppliers must receive to be willing to supply 50,000 tickets. Since we have the supply equation, it is a relatively simple matter to substitute 50,000 for Q_s and then solve for P. Thus, $P = (1/40,000)(50,000) = \$1.25$ per ticket.

Now that we have all the numbers we need, it is a relatively easy proposition to calculate the areas of the new consumer surplus and new producer surplus. The area of consumer surplus is equal to $(1/2)(\$10$ per ticket $- \$5$ per ticket$)(50,000$ tickets$) = \$125,000$. The area of producer surplus is more difficult to calculate: it is the sum of the area of a rectangle and the area of a triangle. Thus, producer surplus is equal to $(\$5$ per ticket $- \$1.25$ per ticket$)(50,000$ tickets$) + (1/2)(\$1.25$ per ticket$)(50,000)$ or $(\$3.75$ per ticket$)(50,000$ tickets$) + (\$1.25$ per ticket$)(25,000$ tickets$)$, which is equal to $\$187,500$ (the part of consumer surplus captured by producers) $+ \$31,250$ for a total of $\$218,750$.

STEP 5: Compare the initial total surplus when transit rides were $2 per ride to the value of total surplus when transit rides are $5 per ride. Relate this comparison to market efficiency.

Review pages 159–163 (Econ pages 102–113).

Total surplus when the price of transit tickets is equal to $2 per ticket is $400,000 (review Step 1 to see where we got this amount). Total surplus when the price of transit tickets is equal to $5 per ticket is equal to the sum of producer surplus and consumer surplus at that price; total surplus when the price of transit tickets is equal to $5 is equal to $343,750. Total surplus is smaller when the price is raised above the market-clearing price. This indicates a loss of efficiency: the loss of efficiency reflects how the increase in price prevents mutually beneficial trades from occurring. Rather than selling 80,000 tickets at a price of $2 per ticket, the increase in the price of tickets to $5 eliminates the purchase of 30,000 tickets.

Study the diagrams that have been provided in this discussion to see if you can see where the loss in consumer and producer surplus of $56,250 (the difference between the original total surplus of $400,000 and the new total surplus of $343,750) is in the graph.

STEP 6: Compare the initial level of consumer surplus and producer surplus to the new levels of consumer surplus and producer surplus to determine if consumers or producers benefit from an increase in mass transit fares.

Review the sections "Consumer Surplus and the Demand Curve" on pages 159–161 (Econ pages 102–108) and "Producer Surplus and the Supply Curve" on pages 161–163 (Econ pages 109–113).

The initial level of consumer surplus is equal to $320,000, while the level of consumer surplus after the increase in the price of transit tickets is equal to $125,000. Consumer surplus decreases when Metrocity raises the price of transit tickets, holding everything else constant.

The initial level of producer surplus is equal to $80,000, while the level of producer surplus after the increase in the price of transit tickets is equal to $218,750. Producer surplus increases when Metrocity raises the price of transit tickets, holding everything else constant.

Transit producers will be in favor of a fare increase, while transit consumers will be against a fare increase. Total surplus from the consumption of transit services is maximized at the market-clearing price of $2 per transit ticket.

Problems and Exercises

1. Paula and Harry both produce lawn care and window washing services, and they both have an equal number of hours available to them each week to engage in providing these services. Paula is able to clean 1/2 a window or care for 1 yard per hour, and Harry can clean 1 window or 1/2 yard per hour. Currently Paula and Harry divide their work time evenly between cleaning windows and doing yard work. Both Paula and Harry work 40 hours a week.

a. Suppose that Paula and Harry initially work independently of each other. Draw two graphs, with one graph illustrating Paula's production possibility frontier and the other graph illustrating Harry's production possibility frontier. Measure windows washed on the vertical axis and yards cared for on the horizontal axis.

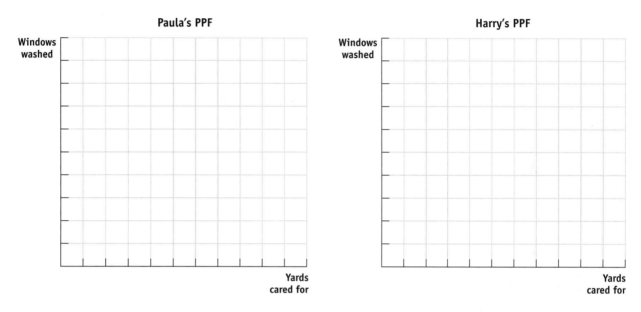

b. Who has the absolute advantage in performing yard care? Who has the absolute advantage in window washing?

c. Suppose both Paula and Harry divide their available time evenly between washing windows and doing yard care. Fill in the following table based on this assumption.

	Number of windows washed	Number of yards cared for
Paula		
Harry		
Total		

d. What is Paula's opportunity cost of washing a window? What is Paula's opportunity cost of caring for a yard?

e. What is Harry's opportunity cost of washing a window? What is Harry's opportunity cost of caring for a yard?

f. Who has the comparative advantage in washing windows? Who has the comparative advantage in caring for a yard? Explain your answers.

g. Assume that both Paula and Harry specialize according to comparative advantage and that both Paula and Harry produce only one type of good. Fill in the table that follows based on this specialization. What happens to total production of lawn care and window washing when Paula and Harry specialize according to their comparative advantage?

	Number of windows washed	Number of yards cared for
Paula		
Harry		
Total		

h. If both Harry and Paula specialize according to their comparative advantage and then trade with each other, what is the range of prices they will both accept for 1 washed window?

2. Titania and Phoenix are two countries that both produce steel and oats from their available resources. The production possibility frontiers for both countries are linear, and the following table provides information about the number of labor hours (the only resource either country uses in producing these two goods) it takes for each country to produce 1 unit of steel or 1 unit of oats. Assume that Titania and Phoenix both have 60 hours of labor available to produce either steel or oats or some combination of steel and oats.

	Number of labor hours needed to produce 1 unit of steel	Number of labor hours needed to produce 1 unit of oats
Titania	5	2
Phoenix	4	3

a. On two separate graphs, draw the production possibility frontiers for Titania and Phoenix. Place steel on the vertical axis and oats on the horizontal axis.

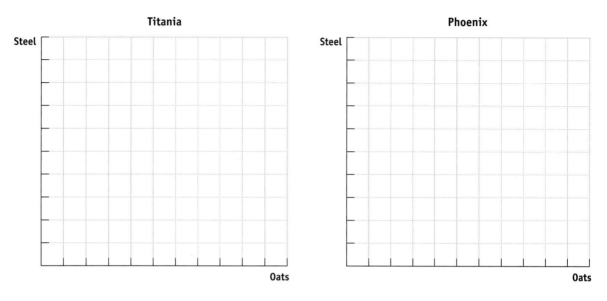

b. Which country has the absolute advantage in producing steel? Which country has the absolute advantage in producing oats?

c. What is the opportunity cost of producing 3 units of steel for Titania? What is the opportunity cost of producing 3 units of steel for Phoenix?

d. What is the opportunity cost of producing 5 units of oats for Titania? What is the opportunity cost of producing 5 units of oats for Phoenix?

e. Which country has the comparative advantage in producing steel? Which country has the comparative advantage in producing oats? Explain your answers.

f. Suppose that Titania and Phoenix both specialize according to their comparative advantage and then trade with each other. Furthermore, suppose that when they specialize these two countries only produce one type of good. What is the range of prices that steel will trade for once this specialization takes place? What is the range of prices that oats will trade for once this specialization takes place?

g. Titania proposes that Phoenix accept 1 unit of oats for 1 unit of steel. Will Phoenix agree to this trading price? Explain your answer.

3. Finlandia and Sweetland are two autarkies possessing equal resources. Both Finlandia and Sweetland produce two goods: food (*F*) and clothing (*C*). The following table provides information about the maximum amount of these two goods that these two countries can produce if they devote all of their resources to the production of just one good. Assume that the production possibility frontiers for both Finlandia and Sweetland are linear.

	Food	Clothing
Finlandia	1,000 units	2,000 units
Sweetland	600 units	1,800 units

a. On two separate graphs, draw Finlandia's and Sweetland's production possibility frontiers. Place units of food on the vertical axis and units of clothing on the horizontal axis.

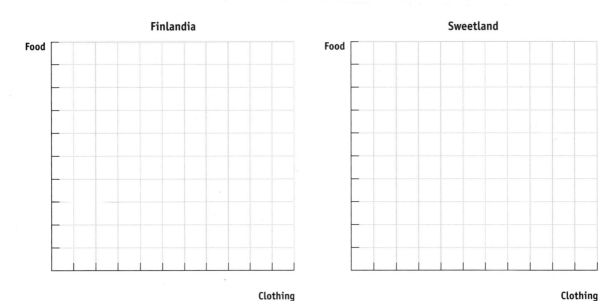

Finlandia

Food

Clothing

Sweetland

Food

Clothing

b. Both Finlandia and Sweetland currently produce at points that are located on their production possibility frontiers. Based on this information, fill in the following table. (Hint: you may find it helpful to write an equation for each country's production possibility frontier.)

	Food	Clothing
Finlandia	500 units	
Sweetland		900 units
Total production		

c. Suppose Finlandia and Sweetland open their economies to trade, but neither country fully understands the concept of comparative advantage. Suppose Finlandia and Sweetland adjust their production as given in the table that follows. Fill in the rest of the table assuming that both countries produce at points that are on their production possibility frontiers. Are Finlandia and Sweetland specializing according to their comparative advantage? Explain your answer.

	Food	Clothing
Finlandia	250 units	
Sweetland		390 units
Total production		

d. Finlandia and Sweetland alter their production once again in hopes of reaping the benefits of specialization and trade. Fill in the following table based on both countries producing on their production possibility frontiers.

	Food	Clothing
Finlandia		400 units
Sweetland		
Total production	892 units	

e. Given the production possibility choices Finlandia and Sweetland make in part (d), do these countries reap the advantages of specialization and trade?

4. Do you agree or disagree with the following statement: "Comparative advantage depends on the amount of resources used to produce a good." Explain your answer.

5. Do you agree or disagree with the following statement: "If two workers have different labor productivity, then their wage rates will usually differ from one another, with the worker with greater labor productivity earning a higher wage rate." Explain your answer.

6. What are the major sources of comparative advantage?

7. The Heckscher-Ohlin model predicts that countries have a comparative advantage in producing those goods whose production is intensive in the factors that are abundantly available in that country compared to other countries. What does the Heckscher-Ohlin model predict about factor prices for abundant resources versus less abundant resources? Explain your answer.

8. Use the following graph to answer this next set of questions. The graph depicts the domestic demand and domestic supply of bicycles in a small closed economy.

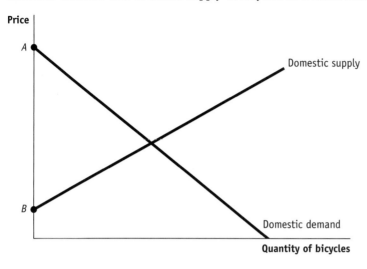

a. In the preceding graph, label the equilibrium price (P_e) and the equilibrium quantity (Q_e) for this autarky. Label the areas that correspond to producer surplus and consumer surplus.

b. Provide a mathematical expression for the areas of producer and consumer surplus based on the symbols and labels in the graph.

c. The same graph is replicated here, but this time the world price is also drawn on the graph. Suppose this autarky opens to trade. On the graph, indicate the quantity supplied domestically ($Q_{S_{dom}}$) and the quantity demanded domestically ($Q_{D_{dom}}$) when this country opens to trade. Identify how many bicycles this country will import or export when it opens its economy to trade.

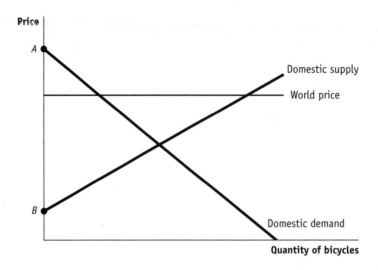

d. On the graph in part (c), label the areas that correspond to producer surplus with trade and consumer surplus with trade. Who benefits in this example from trade? Explain your answer.

e. The initial graph is replicated here, but this time the world price is also drawn on the graph. Suppose this autarky opens to trade. On the graph, indicate the quantity supplied domestically ($Q_{S_{dom}}$) and the quantity demanded domestically ($Q_{D_{dom}}$) when this country opens to trade. Identify how many bicycles this country will import or export when it opens its economy to trade.

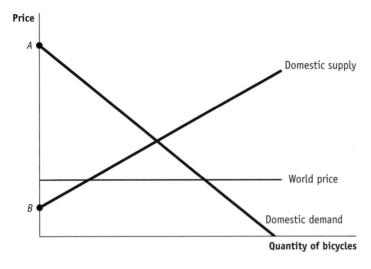

f. On the graph in part (e), label the areas that correspond to producer surplus with trade and consumer surplus with trade. Who benefits in this example from trade? Explain your answer.

9. Suppose the market for TVs in the small closed economy of Kennet can be described by the following domestic demand curve and domestic supply curve:

$$\text{Domestic demand: } Q = 1{,}000 - (1/2)P$$
$$\text{Domestic supply: } Q = (1/2)P$$

(Hint: for this question you will find it helpful to sketch graphs of the market.)

a. What is the equilibrium price and quantity in the market for TVs in Kennet? What is the value of consumer surplus, producer surplus, and total surplus?

b. Suppose Kennet opens to trade and the world price for TVs is $1,200. What is the quantity supplied domestically, the quantity demanded domestically, and the number of TVs imported into or exported out of Kennet given this world price? What happens to the value of consumer surplus, producer surplus, and total surplus when Kennet opens to trade?

c. Given the information and the analysis you did in part (b), who benefits from trade in the television market when Kennet opens its economy? Explain your answer.

d. Suppose Kennet's economy is still open to trade, but domestic demand in Kennet has significantly increased so that at every price domestic demand is now 500 units higher than it was initially. Although domestic demand in Kennet has increased, this has not impacted the world price for TVs since Kennet is a small economy. Given this change in demand, how many TVs will be domestically supplied and domestically demanded? Will Kennet import or export TVs? Calculate the numeric value of Kennet's imports or exports. What is the value of consumer surplus, producer surplus, and total surplus given this change in demand? (Hint: you will find it helpful to draw a sketch of these changes in the market for TVs and to calculate the new domestic demand equation.)

10. Pepperville is a small economy that currently operates as an autarky. In the market for green peppers, domestic demand and domestic supply can be represented as $P = 5,000 - 0.5Q$ and $P = 1.5Q$, respectively, where P is the price per ton of green peppers and Q is the quantity of green peppers measured in tons.

   a. Identify the equilibrium price and quantity of green peppers in Pepperville. What is the value of consumer surplus and producer surplus?

   b. The current world price of green peppers is $3,000 per ton, and domestic producers of green peppers are lobbying the government of Pepperville to remain an autarky. Explain why domestic producers of green peppers are not in favor of open trade in the green pepper market.

c. Domestic consumers of green peppers in Pepperville successfully lobby the Pepperville government to open trade in the green pepper market. How many tons of green peppers will be imported into or exported out of Pepperville, given the world price of $3,000 per ton when this market opens to trade? What is the value of consumer surplus and producer surplus with trade?

Domestic producers wage a successful campaign to enact a tariff in the market for green peppers. The tariff effectively raises the price of green peppers to $3,450 per ton. Answer questions (d) through (g) based on this tariff. Assume the world price for green peppers is unchanged and equal to $3,000 per ton.

d. How many tons of green peppers will be imported into Pepperville once this tariff is enacted?

e. What is the value of consumer surplus and producer surplus once this tariff is implemented?

f. What is the tariff revenue the government earns with this tariff?

g. What is the deadweight loss associated with this tariff?

h. Pepperville is considering replacing the tariff on green peppers with a quota. If consumer surplus and producer surplus are to remain the same under the quota as they are with the tariff, what must the amount of the quota equal?

i. From the domestic consumers' perspective, which trade policy—closed economy, open economy, or open economy with a tariff or quota—would they prefer? Explain your answer.

j. From the domestic producers' perspective, which trade policy—closed economy, open economy, or open economy with a tariff or quota—would they prefer? Explain your answer.

k. Given your answers in (i) and (j), why do governments frequently adopt tariffs or quotas in particular markets?

11. Evansville is a small closed economy. The domestic demand curve for shoes is given by the equation $P = 200 - Q$, where P is the price for a pair of shoes and Q is the quantity of pairs of shoes demanded. The domestic supply curve for shoes is given by the equation $P = 10 + Q$. Currently the world price of shoes is $40 a pair. Evansville is considering opening its economy to trade, and the government is debating three possible trade positions. Option I is to open the economy to trade with no trade protection intervention in the market. Option II is to open the economy to trade but limit the amount of pairs of shoes imported to a quota of 50 pairs of shoes. Option III is to open the economy to trade but impose a tariff on the shoe market that would increase the price of shoes to $80 a pair.

a. Analyze these three policies and enter your findings in the following table.

	Option I	Option II	Option III
Pairs of shoes imported			
Consumer surplus			
Producer surplus			
Tariff revenue or quota rent			
Deadweight loss			

b. From the perspective of domestic consumers, which is the best option?

c. From the perspective of domestic producers, which is the best option?

d. Which option results in the greatest efficiency cost? Explain your answer.

12. For each of the statements that follow, decide whether the statement reflects a desire for trade protection on the basis of national security, job creation, or the infant industry argument.

   a. Even though clothing can be produced more cheaply in other countries, clothing is a necessity, and if imports of clothing are disrupted by civil unrest in these foreign countries, our country will be ill prepared to provide for our citizens. The domestic clothing industry should therefore receive some form of trade protection.

   b. Since our economy is oil dependent and much of our oil comes from foreign economies, our economic well-being may be jeopardized by war or international disturbance. The domestic oil industry should therefore receive some form of trade protection from foreign oil producers.

   c. As call centers are opened in foreign countries, our country is losing many entry-level positions. The industries moving these call centers overseas should be discouraged from doing this via trade measures.

   d. The new product developed by corporation Z is a product that needs to be protected until corporation Z has had time to fully develop and market the idea.

   e. The country of Fantasia, until recently a provider of raw materials to the rest of the world, has begun to develop a manufacturing sector in its economy. People in Fantasia argue that these industries need to have trade protection during this early period of development.

13. **[from Appendix]** The following table expresses the amount people are willing to pay to buy a new music-playing device. Use this information to answer this series of questions.

Name of person	Price willing to pay
Joe	$100
Mary	200
Lucinda	150
Pete	50
Mario	300

a. Who places the highest value on this good? Explain your answer.

b. Who places the lowest value on this good? Explain your answer.

c. If the good is offered at a price of $100, who would buy it?

d. If the good is offered at a price of $50, who would buy it?

e. Construct a step-shaped demand curve illustrating the demand for a music-playing device for these five consumers.

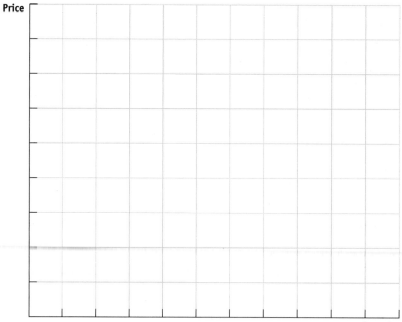

f. On the graph, shade in the area that represents Mary's consumer surplus if the good sells for $100. Label this area clearly. Calculate the value of Mary's consumer surplus.

g. On the graph, shade in the area that represents Mario's consumer surplus if the good sells for $100. Label this area clearly. Calculate the value of Mario's consumer surplus.

h. Create a new graph that is a duplicate of the one you drew for part (e) and shade in the entire area of consumer surplus if the good sells for a price of $100. Calculate the value of consumer surplus at this price.

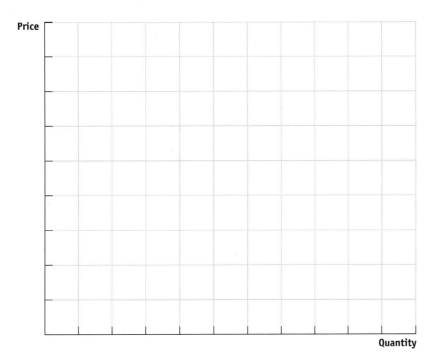

14. [from Appendix] The following table expresses the amount people are willing to pay to buy a new music-playing device. Use this information to answer this series of questions.

Name of person	Price willing to pay
Joe	$100
Mary	200
Lucinda	150
Pete	50
Mario	300

a. If the market price is $175, who will buy the good and what is the value of total consumer surplus?

b. Suppose the market price is $175, but a decision is made to allocate the two units of the good that are demanded at that price to Mario and Lucinda. What is the value of total consumer surplus in this case?

c. Why does the reallocation of the good in part (b) reduce the value of consumer surplus? What are the implications of the reduction in consumer surplus that occurs when the good is not allocated to those buyers who place the highest value on the good?

15. [from Appendix] Demand for widgets in Marksville is given by the equation $P = 100 - Q$.

a. If the market price of widgets in Marksville is $50, what is the value of consumer surplus in this market?

b. If the market price of widgets in Marksville is $40, what is the value of consumer surplus in this market?

c. For a linear downward sloping demand curve, what happens to consumer surplus when the market price rises?

d. Suppose the market price of widgets is $30 in Marksville. Will at least 80 widgets be demanded at this price? Explain your answer.

e. Suppose the market price of widgets is $30 in Marksville. Will at least 60 widgets be demanded at this price? Explain your answer.

16. [from Appendix] The following table provides a list of sellers of organic apples and the lowest price each seller is willing to accept for a bushel of apples. Assume that each seller will only offer a single bushel of apples for sale. Use this information to answer this series of questions.

Seller	Lowest price seller is willing to accept for a bushel of apples
Ski Top Orchards	$6.00
J. Appleseed's Finest	7.25
Red's Organic	5.80
Pure Apples	8.25
Nature's Medicine	8.00

a. Draw a diagram of this step-shaped supply curve.

Price

Bushels of apples

b. If only one bushel of apples is sold, which seller is most likely to make this sale? Explain your answer.

c. If the market price is $7.50, what is the value of the producer surplus received by J. Appleseed's Finest?

d. If the market price is $7.50, what is the value of the producer surplus received by Ski Top Orchards?

e. Redraw your sketch from part (a) and indicate the area of total producer surplus in this market if the market price is $7.50. What is the value of this producer surplus?

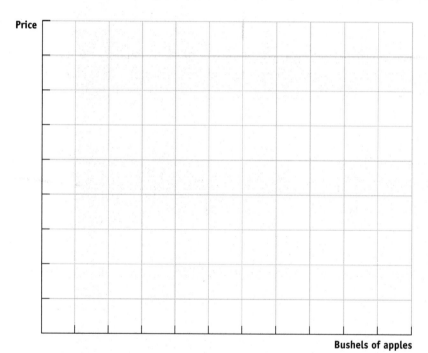

f. Which sellers will sell a bushel of apples in this market if the market price is $7.50?

17. **[from Appendix]** The following table provides a list of sellers of organic apples and the lowest price each seller is willing to accept for a bushel of apples. Assume that each seller will only offer a single bushel of apples for sale. Use this information to answer this series of questions.

Seller	Lowest price seller is willing to accept for a bushel of apples
Ski Top Orchards	$6.00
J. Appleseed's Finest	7.25
Red's Organic	5.80
Pure Apples	8.25
Nature's Medicine	8.00

a. Suppose the market price of apples is $7.00 a bushel. At this price, which of the potential sellers will agree to sell a bushel of apples? What is the value of producer surplus when the market price of apples is $7.00 a bushel?

b. Suppose the market price of apples is $7.00 a bushel and that J. Appleseed's Finest is forced to sell a bushel of apples while Ski Top Orchards is forced to not sell a bushel of apples. When we reallocate sales according to this plan, what happens to the value of producer surplus in this market?

c. How does reallocation of sales away from the market-provided allocation alter the value of producer surplus? What implications does this result have if your goal is to maximize producer surplus?

18. [from Appendix] Supply of widgets in Marksville is given by the equation $P = 1/3\ Q$.

a. Draw a sketch of this supply curve and then shade in the area of producer surplus if the market price is $10 per widget.

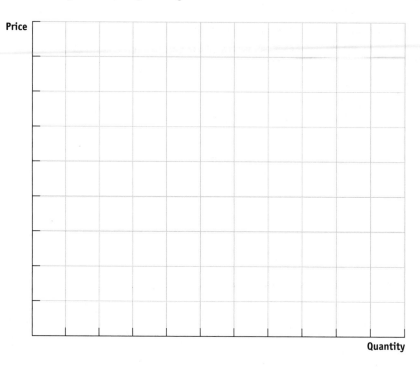

b. If the market price of widgets is $10, what is the value of producer surplus in this market?

c. If the market price of widgets is $20, what is the value of producer surplus in this market?

d. For a linear upward-sloping supply curve, what happens to producer surplus when the market price rises due to an increase in demand?

e. Suppose the market price is $30 per widget in Marksville. Will at least 80 widgets be supplied at this price? Explain your answer.

f. Suppose the market price is $30 per widget in Marksville. Will at least 60 widgets be supplied at this price? Explain your answer.

19. **[from Appendix]** Demand for widgets in Marksville is given by the equation $P = 100 - Q$, while the supply of widgets is given by the equation $P = 1/3\ Q$.

   a. Draw a sketch of the demand and supply curves and mark the equilibrium price and the equilibrium quantity. Solve the two equations for the specific equilibrium price and equilibrium quantity.

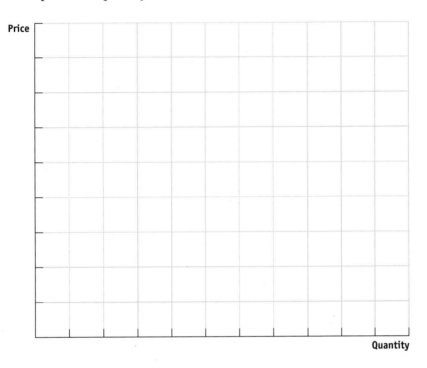

   b. On the graph, identify the areas of producer surplus and consumer surplus. Calculate a numeric value for each of these areas.

   c. What is the value of total surplus in the market for widgets?

20. **[from Appendix]** George is considering the purchase of some new shirts for work. He is willing to pay $35 for the first shirt, $25 for the second shirt, and $15 for the third. Oxford Clothiers, his favorite shirt manufacturer, currently is selling shirts for $28 a shirt. What is the efficient number of shirts for George to buy? What is George's consumer surplus in this situation? Explain your answers.

BEFORE YOU TAKE THE TEST

Chapter Review Questions

1. International trade based on comparative advantage is
   a. beneficial to some of the countries involved in the trade, but not beneficial to other countries.
   b. beneficial to all of the countries involved in the trade.
   c. rarely benefits any of the countries involved in the trade.
   d. only beneficial to relatively rich countries.

2. Sarah purchases wine from France, cheese from Italy, wheat crackers from Minnesota, potatoes from Idaho, and lamb from Australia. Sarah lives in New York.
   a. Sarah purchases imports of wine, cheese, and lamb.
   b. Sarah purchases only domestically produced goods, since she can purchase all of these goods at her local grocery store.
   c. The wine, cheese, and lamb represent exports from the perspective of the United States.
   d. Answers (a) and (c) are both true.

Use the following information to answer the next six questions. The table that follows gives information about the production possibility frontiers for two countries, Smallville and Gooseville, that each produce two types of goods, bicycles and cheese. Two possible production points on each country's production possibility frontier are given in the table. Both countries have linear production possibility frontiers.

	Bicycles	Tons of cheese
Smallville	1,000	0
Smallville	0	2,000
Gooseville	1,500	0
Gooseville	0	1,500

3. Suppose that Smallville and Gooseville have the same amount of resources and technology. Which of the following statements is true?
   a. Smallville has the absolute advantage in producing bicycles and Gooseville has the absolute advantage in producing cheese.
   b. Smallville has the absolute advantage in producing bicycles and cheese.
   c. Gooseville has the absolute advantage in producing bicycles and cheese.
   d. Smallville has the absolute advantage in producing cheese and Gooseville has the absolute advantage in producing bicycles.

4. The opportunity cost of producing one more bicycle in Smallville is
   a. greater than the opportunity cost of producing one more bicycle in Gooseville.
   b. less than the opportunity cost of producing one more bicycle in Gooseville.
   c. equal to 2 tons of cheese.
   d. Answers (a) and (c) are correct.
   e. Answers (b) and (c) are correct.

5. Suppose that both countries are in autarky and do not engage in trade. In autarky, both countries choose to produce at the midpoint of their production possibility frontiers. Total cheese production is equal to _____ and total bicycle production is equal to _____.
   a. 1,750 tons of cheese; 1,750 bicycles
   b. 1,750 tons of cheese; 1,250 bicycles
   c. 1,250 tons of cheese; 1,750 bicycles
   d. 1,250 tons of cheese; 1,250 bicycles

6. Suppose that both countries decide to specialize according to their comparative advantage and trade with each other. Then
   a. Smallville will produce cheese and Gooseville will produce bicycles.
   b. Smallville will produce bicycles and Goosevillle will produce cheese.

7. When the two countries specialize according to their comparative advantage and then trade with each other, the price of a bicycle measured in terms of cheese will be
   a. less than ½ ton of cheese.
   b. greater than 1 ton of cheese.
   c. between 1 ton of cheese and 2 tons of cheese.
   d. between ½ ton of cheese and 1 ton of cheese.

8. Suppose both countries specialize according to their comparative advantage and then trade. Which of the following represents the maximum possible amount of total production given this specialization?
   a. 3,500 tons of cheese and 2,500 bicycles
   b. 2,500 tons of cheese and 2,500 bicycles
   c. 2,000 tons of cheese and 1,500 bicycles
   d. 1,750 tons of cheese and 1,250 bicycles

9. When a production possibility frontier is linear, this implies that
    a. the opportunity cost of producing either of the two goods represented is constant and does not change.
    b. the country will have both a comparative and absolute advantage in producing both of the goods depicted relative to its trading partner.
    c. trade of either good to other countries will always be beneficial for this country.
    d. this country can not have a comparative advantage in the production of either good.

10. When a country does not engage in trade with other countries, this is referred to as
    a. independence.   c. Ricardian economics.
    b. autarky.   d. Heckscher-Ohlin economics.

11. Which of the following statements is true?
    I.   Gains from trade depend on absolute advantage.
    II. Comparative advantage depends on the amount of resources used to produce a good.
    III. A country's comparative advantage is translated into world markets through its wage rates: a country's wage rate typically reflects that country's labor productivity.
    a. Statement I is true.
    b. Statement II is true.
    c. Statement III is true.
    d. Statements I, II, and III are true.
    e. Statements II and III are true.

12. The pauper labor fallacy refers to the idea that
    a. importing goods from low-wage countries must hurt the standard of living of workers in the importing country.
    b. exporting goods from low-wage countries must hurt the standard of living of those workers in the exporting country.
    c. trade must be bad for workers in low-wage countries because they are paid such low wages by world standards.
    d. trade must be bad for workers in high-wage countries because they are paid such high wages by world standards.

13. The sweatshop labor fallacy refers to the idea that
    a. importing goods from low-wage countries must hurt the standard of living of workers in the importing country.
    b. exporting goods from low-wage countries must hurt the standard of living of those workers in the importing country.
    c. trade must be bad for workers in low-wage countries because they are paid such low wages by world standards.
    d. trade must be bad for workers in high-wage countries because they are paid such high wages by world standards.

14. Which of the following situations illustrate one of the three sources of comparative advantage?

a. A country produces olives that can only grow in a Mediterranean climate.

b. A country specializes in producing medical equipment whose production relies on the use of highly productive labor resources.

c. A country in the southern hemisphere specializes in providing grapes to the northern hemisphere during the winter season.

d. A country uses its extensive network of fiber-optic cable to produce information technology for countries located throughout the world.

e. All of the answers illustrate at least one of the sources of comparative advantage.

15. Which of the following statements is *not* supported by the Heckscher-Ohlin model?

a. Countries specialize in producing the good whose production is intensive in the factors that are abundantly available in that country compared with other countries.

b. After they specialize, countries find that those factors that are relatively scarce in their country compared to other countries command higher factor prices than those factors that are relatively abundant in their country.

c. Countries that are labor abundant produce goods that are labor intensive relative to countries that are less labor abundant.

d. Countries that are capital abundant produce goods that are capital intensive relative to countries that are less capital abundant.

16. Which of the following statements is true?

    I. Countries with highly skilled labor will tend to import goods whose production requires high levels of human capital.

    II. Countries whose exporting industries focus on using a higher ratio of highly educated workers to other workers are human capital intensive.

    III. Countries will find that their exporting industries utilize their relatively more abundant factors of production.

a. Statement I is true.   d. Statements I and II are true.

b. Statement II is true.   e. Statements II and III are true.

c. Statement III is true.   f. Statements I, II, and III are true.

Use the following graph to answer the next four questions. The graph shows the market for bicycles for the country of Pedalland. The demand curve indicates the domestic demand for bicycles and the supply curve indicates the domestic supply of bicycles.

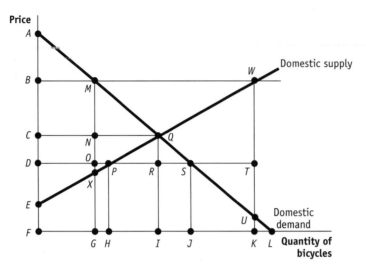

17. Suppose Pedalland is initially an autarky. In the graph, the area that corresponds to consumer surplus is equal to area _____, and the area that corresponds to producer surplus is equal to area _____.

    a. *ACQ; CQIF*   c. *ACQ; CQE*
    b. *ADS; DPE*   d. *BMNC; CNOD*

18. Suppose this country opens to trade and that the world price is equal to B in the preceding graph. Then we know that Pedalland will

    a. import the number of bicycles represented by the distance between points M and W.
    b. import the number of bicycles represented by the distance between points W and T.
    c. export the number of bicycles represented by the distance between points M and W.
    d. export the number of bicycles represented by the distance between points W and T.

19. Suppose this country opens to trade and that the world price is equal to D in the preceding graph. Then we know that Pedalland will import the number of bicycles represented by the distance between points

    a. R and S.   c. P and R.
    b. P and S.   d. P and T.

20. Suppose this country opens to trade and that the world price is equal to *B* in the preceding graph. Consumer surplus is equal to area _____, and producer surplus is equal to area _____.

a. *ABM; BWE*

b. *ABM; BMNE*

c. *ACNM; CNXE*

d. *ABM; BMQE*

Use the following graph to answer the next four questions. The graph shows the market for bicycles for the country of Pedalland. The demand curve indicates the domestic demand for bicycles and the supply curve indicates the domestic supply of bicycles.

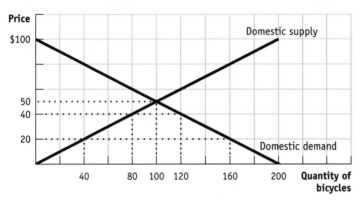

21. The world price in this market equals $20. If the market opens to trade,

a. Pedalland will import 120 bicycles, and the area of total surplus will increase by $6,800.

b. Pedalland will export 120 bicycles, and the area of total surplus will increase by $6,800.

c. Pedalland will import 120 bicycles, and the area of total surplus will increase by $1,800.

d. Pedalland will export 120 bicycles, and the area of total surplus will increase by $1,800.

22. Suppose the world price for bicycles is $20 and Pedalland opens its bicycle market to trade. Domestic producers successfully lobby the government of Pedalland, and the government imposes a quota on the number of bicycles that can be imported into Pedalland. Suppose license-holder revenue from the quota is equal to $800. Which of the following are possible quota limits that result in this license-holder revenue?

a. 20 bicycles

b. 40 bicycles

c. 60 bicycles

d. 80 bicycles

e. Answers (b) and (d) are both possible answers.

23. Suppose the world price of bicycles is $20 and Pedalland opens to trade. Domestic producers of bicycles in Pedalland successfully lobby for a tariff on imported bicycles, which results in the price of bicycles being $40. The deadweight loss associated with this tariff is equal to
    a. $400.
    b. $800.
    c. $1,600.
    d. $2,000.

24. The world price of bicycles is $20 and Pedalland opens its economy to trade. A quota of 60 bicycles is imposed in Pedalland. This will result in consumer surplus increasing by _____ relative to the level of consumer surplus when Pedalland was an autarky.
    a. $1,725
    b. $2,500
    c. $4,225
    d. $6,725

25. A country that engages in international trade will find that this international trade increases the demand for the factors used by the exporting industries and decreases the demand for the factors used in the import-competing industries.
    a. True
    b. False

26. Which of the following is *not* an argument used to defend trade protection?
    a. This domestic industry needs protection because it is a new industry and is not fully ready and able to compete against established companies located outside the domestic economy.
    b. This domestic industry needs protection because it would otherwise result in people elsewhere in the world being paid a wage rate that is substantially lower than the wage rate in this industry in this economy.
    c. This domestic industry needs protection because the good that is being produced is of vital national security for this economy.
    d. This domestic industry needs protection because it provides a substantial number of jobs for people who live in this country.

27. Which of the following is *not* an example of a trade agreement?
    a. NAFTA
    b. EU
    c. WTO

28. **[from Appendix]** To answer this question, use the following table that expresses the amount people are willing to pay for a dinner tonight at Fast Eddy's Grill.

Name of consumer	Price willing to pay
Matt	$20
Donovan	15
Savannah	8
Gertrude	12
Anna	7

If a dinner at Fast Eddy's tonight sells for $10, what is the value of Donovan's consumer surplus?

a. $20 c. $10
b. $15 d. $5

29. **[from Appendix]** To answer this question, use the following table that expresses the amount people are willing to pay for a dinner tonight at Fast Eddy's Grill.

Name of consumer	Price willing to pay
Matt	$20
Donovan	15
Savannah	8
Gertrude	12
Anna	7

If a dinner at Fast Eddy's tonight sells for $9, what is the value of the total consumer surplus?

a. $20 c. $10
b. $15 d. $5

30. **[from Appendix]** To answer this question, use the following table that expresses the amount people are willing to pay for a dinner tonight at Fast Eddy's Grill.

Name of consumer	Price willing to pay
Matt	$20
Donovan	15
Savannah	8
Gertrude	12
Anna	7

If a dinner at Fast Eddy's tonight sells for $11, who will not purchase a dinner at this restaurant?
a. Matt
b. Donovan
c. Savannah
d. Gertrude

31. **[from Appendix]** To answer this question, use the following table that expresses the amount people are willing to pay for a dinner tonight at Fast Eddy's Grill.

Name of consumer	Price willing to pay
Matt	$20
Donovan	15
Savannah	8
Gertrude	12
Anna	7

If a dinner at Fast Eddy's tonight costs $4, what is the value of the consumer surplus tonight?
a. $80
b. $42
c. $32
d. $12

32. **[from Appendix]** To answer this question, use the following table that expresses the amount people are willing to pay for a dinner tonight at Fast Eddy's Grill.

Name of consumer	Price willing to pay
Matt	$20
Donovan	15
Savannah	8
Gertrude	12
Anna	7

All five of these consumers want to go out to dinner together at Fast Eddy's tonight. Assuming each consumer pays for his or her own dinner, what is the maximum price that Fast Eddy can charge for each dinner if they all go out?
a. $5
b. $6
c. $7
d. $8

33. **[from Appendix]** The market demand curve for peanuts in Carterville is given by the equation $P = 1 - 0.001Q$, where price is measured in dollars and peanuts are sold by the bag. If the market price is $0.50 per bag, the quantity demanded will equal _____ and the value of consumer surplus will be _____.

a. 5 bags; $125

b. 50 bags; $125

c. 500 bags; $125

d. 5,000 bags; $125

34. **[from Appendix]** The market demand curve for peanuts in Carterville is given by the equation $P = 1 - 0.001Q$, where price is measured in dollars and peanuts are sold by the bag. If the market price is $0.20 per bag, the quantity demanded will equal _____ and the value of consumer surplus will be _____.

a. 80 bags; $640   c. 800 bags; $640

b. 80 bags; $320   d. 800 bags; $320

35. **[from Appendix]** For a given linear demand curve, the value of consumer surplus

a. decreases as the market price decreases.

b. decreases as the market price increases.

c. increases as the market price increases.

d. Answers (a) or (c) are possible.

36. **[from Appendix]** For a given linear demand curve, an increase in consumer surplus must be due to a(n)

a. decrease in the market price.

b. increase in the market price.

37. **[from Appendix]** To answer this question, use the following table that expresses the number of dinners Fast Eddy's Grill is willing to prepare tonight at different prices.

Total number of dinners prepared	Price per dinner
1	$ 3
2	6
3	10
4	12
5	15

If a dinner at Fast Eddy's tonight sells for $10, what is the value of Fast Eddy's producer surplus?

a. $11   c. $16

b. $9   d. $19

38. [from Appendix] To answer this question, use the following table that expresses the relationship between each dinner and the lowest price Fast Eddy's Grill is willing to accept to prepare that dinner.

	Lowest price Fast Eddy is willing to accept
First dinner	$ 3
Second dinner	6
Third dinner	10
Fourth dinner	12
Fifth dinner	15

If a dinner at Fast Eddy's tonight sells for $13, what is the value of Fast Eddy's producer surplus?

a. $10   c. $20
b. $17   d. $21

39. [from Appendix] To answer this question, use the following table that expresses the relationship between each dinner and the lowest price Fast Eddy's Grill is willing to accept to prepare that dinner.

	Lowest price Fast Eddy is willing to accept
First dinner	$ 3
Second dinner	6
Third dinner	10
Fourth dinner	12
Fifth dinner	15

If the price of a dinner at Fast Eddy's tonight is $9, how many dinners will Fast Eddy sell?

a. 1 dinner   c. 3 dinners
b. 2 dinners   d. 4 dinners

40. [from Appendix] To answer this question, use the following table that expresses the relationship between each dinner and the lowest price Fast Eddy's Grill is willing to accept to prepare that dinner.

	Lowest price Fast Eddy is willing to accept
First dinner	$ 3
Second dinner	6
Third dinner	10
Fourth dinner	12
Fifth dinner	15

If the price of a dinner at Fast Eddy's tonight is $13, how many dinners will Fast Eddy sell?

a. 1 dinner   c. 3 dinners
b. 2 dinners   d. 4 dinners

41. [from Appendix] To answer this question, use the following table that expresses the relationship between each dinner and the lowest price Fast Eddy's Grill is willing to accept to prepare that dinner.

	Lowest price Fast Eddy is willing to accept
First dinner	$ 3
Second dinner	6
Third dinner	10
Fourth dinner	12
Fifth dinner	15

Which of the following dinner prices will lead to Fast Eddy's highest value of producer surplus?
a. $9   c. $11
b. $10   d. $12

42. [from Appendix] Use the following graph to answer this question.

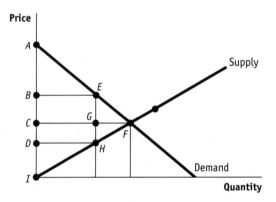

When this market is in equilibrium, consumer surplus is equal to area
a. AEB.   c. ACF.
b. EFG.   d. CFI.

43. [from Appendix] Use the graph in question 42 to answer this question. When this market is in equilibrium, producer surplus is equal to area
a. BEGC.   c. DHI.
b. GFH.   d. CFI.

44. [from Appendix] Use the graph in question 42 to answer this question. When this market is in equilibrium, total surplus is equal to area
a. AFI.   c. BEHD.
b. BEFHD.   d. EFH.

ANSWER KEY

Answers to Problems and Exercises

1. a.

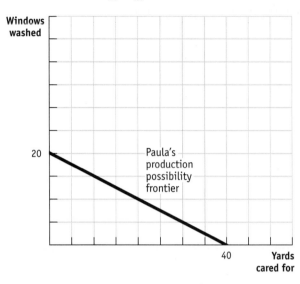

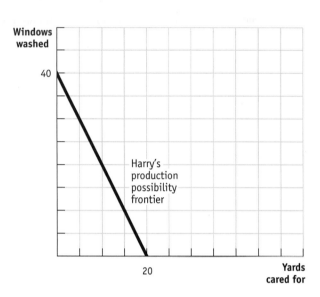

b. Paula has the absolute advantage in yard care since she can clean more yards than Harry with the same amount of resources (40 yards versus 20 yards), and Harry has the absolute advantage in window washing since he can wash more windows than Paula with the same amount of resources (40 windows versus 20 windows).

c.

	Number of windows washed	Number of yards cared for
Paula	10	20
Harry	20	10
Total	30	30

d. Paula's opportunity cost of washing a window is 2 yards cared for, since she must give up caring for 2 yards to free up enough resources to clean 1 window. Her opportunity cost of caring for a yard is ½ window washed since she must give up washing ½ a window to free up enough resources to care for a yard.

e. Harry's opportunity cost of washing a window is ½ yard cared for, since he must give up caring for ½ a yard to free up enough resources to clean 1 window. His opportunity cost of caring for a yard is 2 windows washed since he must give up washing 2 windows to free up enough resources to care for a yard.

f. Harry has the comparative advantage in washing windows, and Paula has the comparative advantage in caring for yards. Harry's opportunity cost of washing 1 window is only ½ a yard, and Paula's opportunity cost of washing 1 window is 2 yards, so Harry can produce a washed window at a lower opportunity cost than can Paula. Paula's opportunity cost of caring for 1 yard is ½ window washed, and Harry's opportunity cost of caring for 1 yard is 2 windows washed, so Paula can care for a yard at a lower opportunity cost than can Harry.

g.

	Number of windows washed	Number of yards cared for
Paula	0	40
Harry	40	0
Total	40	40

Through specialization according to comparative advantage, total production of both goods increases.

h. The range of prices for 1 window washed falls between ½ a yard cared for and 2 yards cared for. Paula is willing to trade up to 2 yards cared for to get a single window washed, while Harry is willing to wash a single window provided he is compensated by ½ a yard cared for.

2. a.

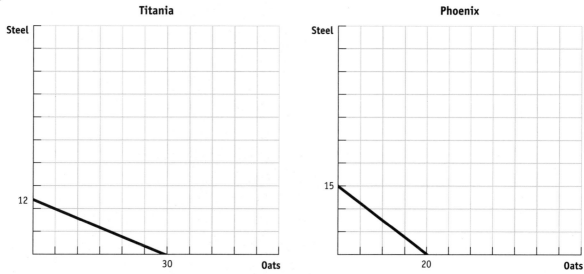

b. Phoenix has the absolute advantage in producing steel since, from the same amount of resources, Phoenix can absolutely produce more units of the good than can Titania. Titania has the absolute advantage in producing oats since, from the same amount of resources, Titania can absolutely produce more units of the good than can Phoenix.

c. The opportunity cost of producing 3 units of steel for Titania is equal to 7.5 units of oats. From the graph, the slope of the production possibility frontier for Titania is $-2/5$, which implies that the opportunity cost of Titania producing 1 unit of oats is $2/5$ units of steel. We can take the reciprocal of this measure and get the opportunity cost of 1 unit of steel is equal to $5/2$ units of oats. But since we want to know the opportunity cost of 3 units of steel, we need to multiply the $5/2$ units of oats by 3 to get $15/2$ units of oats, or 7.5 units of oats. The opportunity cost of producing 3 units of steel for Phoenix is equal to 4 units of oats. From the graph, the slope of the production possibility frontier for Phoenix is $-3/4$, which implies that the opportunity cost of Phoenix producing 1 unit of oats is $3/4$ units of steel. We can take the reciprocal of this measure and get the opportunity cost of 1 unit of steel is equal to $4/3$ units of oats. But since we want to know the opportunity cost of 3 units of steel, we need to multiply the $4/3$ units of oats by 3 to get $12/3$ units of oats, or 4 units of oats.

d. The opportunity cost of producing 5 units of oats for Titania is 2 units of steel, and the opportunity cost of producing 5 units of oats for Phoenix is 3.75 units of steel.

e. Titania has the comparative advantage in producing oats while Phoenix has the comparative advantage in producing steel. Titania's opportunity cost of producing 1 unit of oats is 2/5 units of steel, and Phoenix's opportunity cost of producing 1 unit of oats is ¾ units of steel, so Titania can produce oats at lower opportunity cost than can Phoenix. Titania's opportunity cost of producing 1 unit of steel is 5/2 units of oats, and Phoenix's opportunity cost of producing 1 unit of steel is 4/3 units of oats, so Phoenix can produce steel at lower opportunity cost than can Titania.

f. One unit of steel will trade for between 4/3 units of oats to 5/2 units of oats, and 1 unit of oats will trade for between 2/5 units of steel and 3/4 units of steel.

g. No, Phoenix is only willing to trade 1 unit of steel if the price is at least 4/3 units of oats.

3. a.

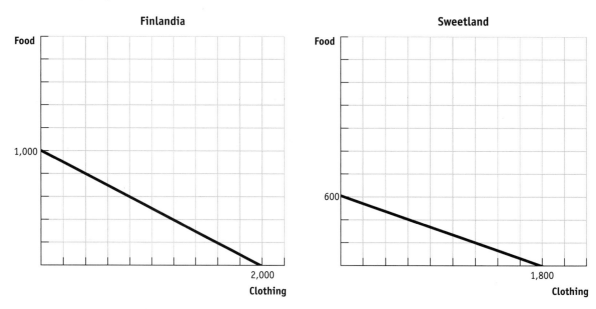

b. The equation for Finlandia's production possibility frontier is $F = 1{,}000 - (1/2)C$. When $F = 500$ units, then $C = 1{,}000$ units. The equation for Sweetland's production possibility frontier is $F = 600 - (1/3)C$. When $C = 900$ units, then $F = 300$ units.

	Food	Clothing
Finlandia	500 units	1,000 units
Sweetland	300 units	900 units
Total production	800 units	1,900 units

c. Use the equations you calculated in part (b) to fill in the table.

	Food	Clothing
Finlandia	250 units	1,500 units
Sweetland	470 units	390 units
Total production	720 units	1,890 units

Finlandia and Sweetland are not specializing according to their comparative advantage since their total production of the two goods has fallen as they altered their production.

d.

	Food	Clothing
Finlandia	800 units	400 units
Sweetland	92 units	1,524 units
Total production	892 units	1,924 units

e. Yes, by specializing according to their comparative advantage and then trading, the total level of production of the two goods increases.

4. Disagree. Comparative advantage depends on the opportunity cost of producing the good rather than the amount of resources used to produce the good.

5. Agree. Workers with lower labor productivity will earn a lower wage than workers with higher labor productivity since the competition for less-productive workers is less intense, resulting in a lower wage rate.

6. The major sources of comparative advantage are differences in climate, differences in factor endowments, and differences in technology between countries.

7. The Heckscher-Ohlin model predicts that factors of production that are abundant in a country that trades with other countries will command higher factor prices than factors of production that are less abundant. This is the result of the country's specialization in the production of the good whose production is intensive in the abundant factors of production. This specialization increases the demand for these factors and therefore increases the price of these factors.

8. a.

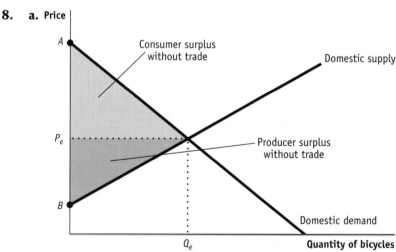

b. Consumer surplus $= (1/2)(A - P_e)(Q_e)$
Producer surplus $= (1/2)(P_e - B)(Q_e)$

c.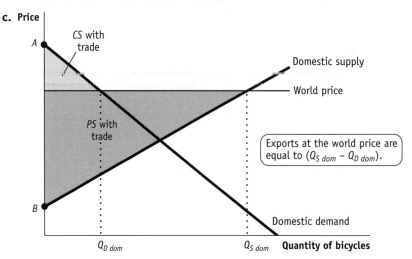

d. Domestic producers benefit from this trade because they can produce more units of the good and sell each unit at a higher price relative to the initial autarky equilibrium. Compare the graphs from part (a) and part (c) and note that the area of producer surplus is larger with trade than without trade.

e.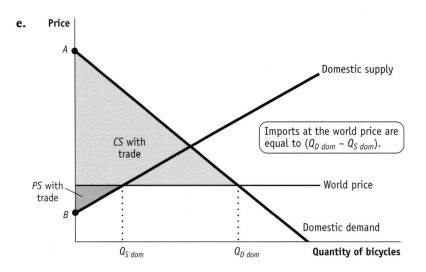

f. Domestic consumers benefit from this trade because they can consume more units of the good and purchase the good at a lower price relative to the initial autarky equilibrium. Compare the graphs from part (a) and part (e) and note that the area of consumer surplus is larger with trade than without trade.

9. a. Here is a sketch of Kennet's market for TVs.

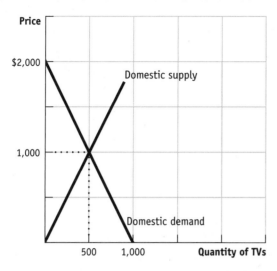

The equilibrium price is $1,000 and the equilibrium quantity is 500 TVs. Consumer surplus is equal to $250,000; producer surplus is equal to $250,000; and total surplus is equal to $500,000.

b. When Kennet opens to trade, it will buy and sell TVs at the world price since it is a small economy. Since $1,200 is greater than the domestic equilibrium price when Kennet is a closed economy, the quantity domestically demanded will fall and the quantity domestically supplied will increase. The quantity demanded domestically will equal 400 TVs, and the quantity supplied domestically will equal 600 TVs. Kennet will export the excess supply of 200 TVs. Consumer surplus with trade will decrease to $160,000 while producer surplus with trade will increase to $360,000; total surplus with trade will increase to $520,000. The following sketch illustrates this answer.

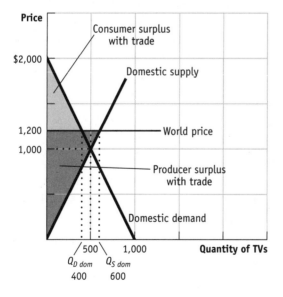

c. Domestic producers of TVs benefit from trade when Kennet opens its economy, because trade increases their producer surplus and decreases consumer surplus. The gain to producers is greater than the loss to consumers, so the net gain from trade is positive.

d. The following sketch provides a helpful guide to solving this problem.

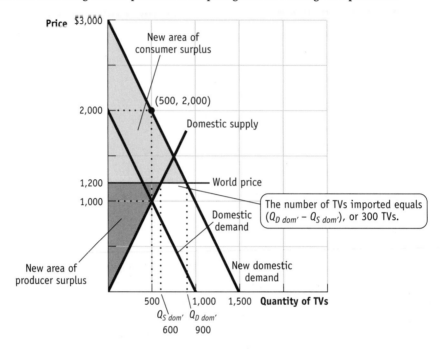

The equation for the new domestic demand curve is $Q = 1,500 - (1/2)P$. The domestic supply curve is still $Q = (1/2)P$. Use these two equations to analyze the effect on this market of the increase in domestic demand for TVs. At a world price of $1,200, the domestic demand for TVs is 900 while the domestic supply of TVs is 600. Kennet will import 300 TVs to meet this excess demand. Consumer surplus will now equal $810,000; producer surplus will equal $360,000; and total surplus will equal $1,170,000.

10. a. The equilibrium price of green peppers is $3,750 per ton, and the equilibrium quantity of green peppers in Pepperville is 2,500 tons. Consumer surplus is equal to $1,562,500 and producer surplus is equal to $4,687,500.

b. Domestic producers are currently selling 2,500 tons of green peppers at a price of $3,750 per ton. If the market opens to trade, each ton of peppers will sell for a lower price: domestic producers will sell fewer tons of peppers as the price falls (2,000 tons instead of 2,500 tons), and they will receive a lower price per ton than they do when the green pepper market is closed ($3,000 versus $3,750).

c. When the green pepper market is open to trade, the domestic demand for green peppers at $3,000 per ton is equal to 4,000 tons of green peppers. At a price of $3,000 per ton, the domestic quantity supplied is equal to 2,000 tons of green peppers. There is an excess demand for peppers when Pepperville opens to trade, and this excess demand will result in Pepperville importing green peppers to make up the difference between the amount domestically supplied and the amount domestically demanded. Pepperville will import 2,000 tons of green peppers. The value of consumer surplus with trade is equal to $4,000,000 and the value of producer surplus with trade is equal to $3,000,000.

d. At a price of $3,450, the quantity of green peppers demanded domestically is equal to 3,100 tons while the quantity supplied domestically is equal to 2,300 tons. Pepperville will import 800 tons of green peppers.

e. The value of consumer surplus is equal to $(1/2)(\$5,000 \text{ per ton} - \$3,450 \text{ per ton})(3,100 \text{ tons})$, or $2,402,500. The value of producer surplus is equal to $(1/2)(\$3,450 \text{ per ton})(2,300 \text{ tons})$, or $3,967,500.

f. The government earns the difference between the tariff price per ton of green peppers and the world price of green peppers on every ton of green peppers imported into Pepperville. The tariff revenue is equal to $(\$3,450 \text{ per ton} - \$3,000 \text{ per ton})(800 \text{ tons})$, or $360,000.

g. The deadweight loss is the difference between the total surplus with open trade and the sum of consumer surplus + producer surplus + tariff revenue, or $7,000,000 − ($2,402,500 + $3,967,500 + $360,000) = $270,000. Alternatively, the deadweight loss can be calculated as the sum of the areas of two triangles, which is equal to $(1/2)(\$3,450 \text{ per ton} - \$3,000 \text{ per ton})(2,300 \text{ tons} - 2,000 \text{ tons}) + (1/2)(\$3,450 \text{ per ton} - \$3,000 \text{ per ton})(4,000 \text{ tons} - 3,100 \text{ tons})$, or $270,000.

h. The quota has to equal the number of units Pepperville imports when the tariff raises the price of green peppers to $3,450 per ton. That is, the quota must be 800 tons of green peppers.

i. Consumer surplus is greatest when the trade policy is one of an open economy. Consumers rank these choices from best to worst in this order: open economy, open economy with a tariff or quota, closed economy. This ranking occurs whenever the world price is less than the closed economy price for the good.

j. Producer surplus is greatest when the trade policy is one of a closed economy. Producers rank these choices from best to worst in this order: closed economy, open economy with a tariff or quota, open economy. This ranking occurs whenever the world price is less than the closed economy price for the good.

k. Governments can successfully provide a benefit to both consumers and producers by choosing this option. If you review the consumer and producer surplus under each of these options, you will see that the middle option gives consumers a greater consumer surplus than they would get with a closed economy and it provides producers with a greater producer surplus than they would get with an open economy. It is a compromise position for the government to take between these two constituencies.

11. a.

	Option I	Option II	Option III
Pairs of shoes imported	130 pairs	50 pairs	50 pairs
Consumer surplus	$12,800	$7,200	$7,200
Producer surplus	450	2,450	2,450
Tariff revenue or quota rent	0	2,000	2,000
Deadweight loss	0	1,600	1,600

b. From the perspective of domestic consumers, the best option is the option that results in the greatest value for consumer surplus: option I, the open economy option.

   c. From the perspective of domestic producers, the best option is the option that results in the greatest value for producer surplus: option II and option III result in equivalent values for producer surplus, with the license holder earning a quota rent for option II and the government earning tariff revenue for option III. If the license holder is a domestic producer, then option II would be the best option from the perspective of domestic producers.

   d. Options II and III result in the largest, and equivalent, efficiency cost as measured by the deadweight loss that occurs with the imposition of these two trade protectionist policies.

12. a. This argument is based on national security and the belief that, should foreign supplies of clothing be disrupted, our country's national security will be compromised.

   b. This argument is based on national security and the belief that our economy will be compromised if there is a disruption in the supply of foreign-produced oil.

   c. This argument is based on the job creation argument: as jobs relocate overseas, this implies a decrease in jobs in the home economy. This argument does not consider that other jobs may be created in the home economy as jobs are sent overseas.

   d. This argument is based on the infant industry argument, which holds that new industries must be protected from foreign competition to give them time to get established.

   e. This argument is based on the infant industry argument, which holds that new industries must be protected from foreign competition to give them time to get established.

13. a. Mario places the highest value on this good since the $300 he is willing to pay is higher than the amount any other consumer in this market is willing to pay.

   b. Pete places the lowest value on this good since the $50 he is willing to pay is lower than the amount any other consumer in this market is willing to pay.

   c. If the good sells for $100, it will be purchased only by those consumers willing to pay $100 or more for the good. At this price Joe, Mary, Lucinda, and Mario will buy the good.

   d. All five consumers would buy the good at this price since their willingness to buy is equal to or greater than $50.

   e.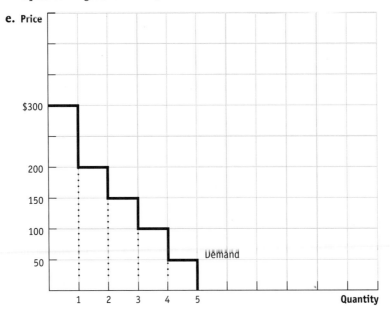

f. Mary's consumer surplus equals $200 − $100 = $100.

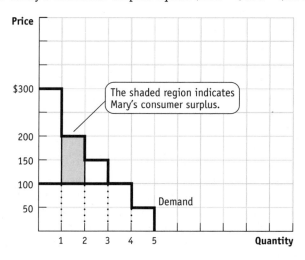

g. Mario's consumer surplus equals $300 − $100 = $200.

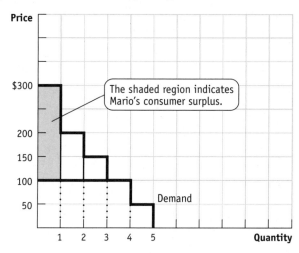

h. Total consumer surplus equals $350.

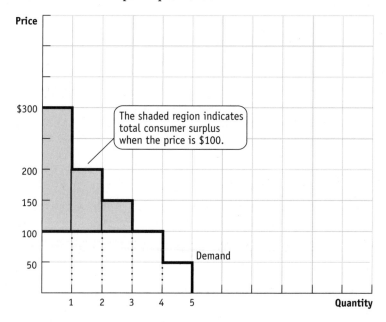

14. **a.** At a market price of $175, Mario and Mary will buy the good since they are the only potential consumers who are willing to pay a price that is equal to or greater than the market price. The value of consumer surplus is $150 (Mario receives consumer surplus of $125 while Mary receives consumer surplus of $25).

b. Mario has a consumer surplus of $300 − $175, or $125, while Lucinda's consumer surplus is equal to $150 − $175, or −$25. The total consumer surplus is therefore equal to $100 when the two units are allocated to Mario and Lucinda.

c. Consumer surplus is reduced when the good is reallocated, because the good goes to consumers who place a lower value on the good. This type of reallocation, away from the market's allocation, results in a failure to maximize consumer surplus.

15. **a.** When the price of widgets is $50, the value of consumer surplus is $1,250. To calculate the value of consumer surplus, you need to find the y-intercept of the demand curve ($100) and the quantity demanded (50 units) when the price is $50. Since the demand curve is smooth and linear, the value of consumer surplus is equal to the area under the demand curve and above the price: CS = (1/2)($100/widget − $50/widget)(50 widgets) = $1,250.

b. Use the process outlined in part (a) but with a price of $40 per widget instead of $50 per widget: CS = (1/2)($100/widget − $40/widget)(60 widgets) = $1,800.

c. When the market price rises, the consumer surplus decreases.

d. When the market price of widgets is $30, only 70 widgets will be demanded. At this price 80 widgets will not be sold.

e. Yes, when the market price is $30, the demand curve tells us 70 widgets will be demanded.

16. **a.**

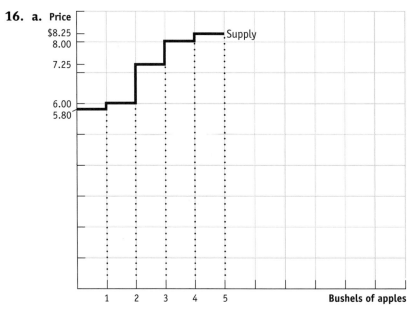

b. Red's Organic is the most likely seller at this quantity since they are willing to accept the lowest price for a bushel of apples.

c. At a price of $7.50 per bushel, the producer surplus for J. Appleseed's Finest is $0.25, or the difference between the market price and the seller's cost.

d. At a price of $7.50 per bushel, the producer surplus for Ski Top Orchards is $1.50, or the difference between the market price and the seller's cost.

e. The value of the producer surplus is $3.45 when the market price is $7.50.

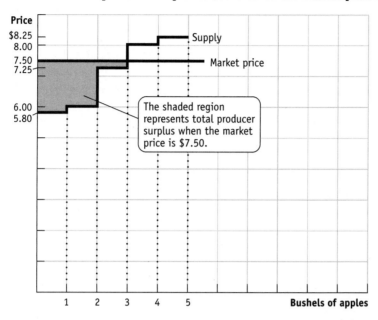

f. Ski Top Orchards, J. Appleseed's Finest, and Red's Organic will each sell a bushel of apples when the market price is $7.50.

17. a. At a price of $7.00 a bushel, Ski Top Orchards and Red's Organic will be willing to sell apples. The value of producer surplus is equal to $1.00 for Ski Top Orchards and $1.20 for Red's Organic, for a total producer surplus of $2.20.

b. When the sales in this market are reallocated away from the market-determined allocation, this reduces total producer surplus. Red's Organic's producer surplus is still equal to $1.20, while J. Appleseed's Finest's producer surplus is equal to $7.00 – $7.25, or –$0.25. Thus, total producer surplus under this reallocation plan equals $0.95.

c. Reallocation of sales away from the market-provided allocation reduces total producer surplus. Producer surplus is maximized when the market allocates sales of the good.

18. a.

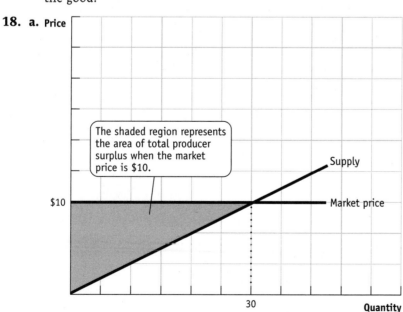

b. The value of producer surplus is equal to the area under the market price and above the supply curve. When the market price is $10, this area of producer surplus equals (1/2)($10/widget)(30 widgets) = $150.

c. When the market price is $20, the value of producer surplus equals (1/2)($20/widget)(60 widgets) = $600.

d. Holding everything else constant, for a linear upward-sloping supply curve, the value of producer surplus increases when the market price increases due to an increase in demand.

e. Yes, at a market price of $30 per widget, 90 widgets will be supplied.

f. Yes, at a market price of $30 per widget, 90 widgets will be supplied.

19. a.

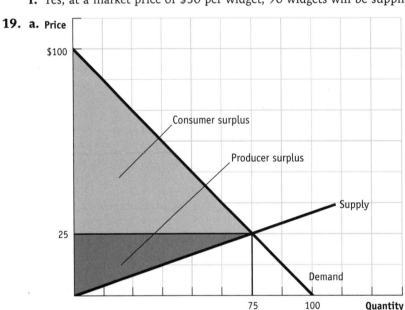

Since demand equals supply in equilibrium, we know 100 − Q = (1/3)Q. Solving for Q, we find that the equilibrium quantity equals 75 widgets and the equilibrium price is $25.

b. Consumer surplus equals (1/2)($100/widget − $25/widget)(75 widgets) = $2,812.50. Producer surplus equals (1/2)($25/widget − $0/widget)(75 widgets) = $937.50.

c. The value of total surplus in this market equals the sum of producer and consumer surplus, or $3,750.00. Alternatively, you can calculate this area as follows: TS = (1/2)($100/widget − $0/widget)(75 widgets) = $3,750.00.

20. George will purchase one shirt since the price he is willing to pay for that shirt ($35) is greater than or equal to the price Oxford Clothiers must receive ($28) to be willing to sell the shirt. George will receive a consumer surplus of $7 when he purchases this shirt. George will not purchase two shirts since the value of the second shirt from George's perspective ($25) is less than the seller's price ($28).

Answers to Chapter Review Questions

1. **Answer b.** International trade is a source of mutual benefit to the countries involved in the trade.

2. **Answer a.** The wine, cheese, and lamb are all imported goods into the American economy since these goods are produced elsewhere in the world and then brought into the American market. Exports refers to those goods produced in the domestic economy and sold in a foreign economy.

3. **Answer d.** Since Smallville can absolutely produce more cheese than can Gooseville, Smallville has the absolute advantage in producing cheese. Gooseville, on the other hand, can absolutely produce more bicycles than Smallville from the same resources, so Gooseville has the absolute advantage in producing bicycles.

4. **Answer d.** The opportunity cost of producing one more bicycle in Smallville is equal to the number of tons of cheese that must be given up to produce one more bicycle. In this case, 2 tons of cheese must be given up to produce one more bicycle in Smallville. The opportunity cost of producing a bicycle in Smallville is 2 tons of cheese, while the opportunity cost of producing a bicycle in Gooseville is equal to 1 ton of cheese.

5. **Answer b.** If Smallville produces at the midpoint of its production possibility frontier, it will produce 1,000 tons of cheese and 500 bicycles. If Gooseville produces at the midpoint of its production possibility frontier, it will produce 750 tons of cheese and 750 bicycles. Total cheese production will equal 1,750 tons and total bicycle production will equal 1,250 bicycles.

6. **Answer a.** Smallville will produce cheese since the opportunity cost of producing cheese for Smallville is ½ a bicycle while the opportunity cost of producing cheese for Gooseville is 1 bicycle. Smallville gives up fewer bicycles to produce a ton of cheese and therefore Smallville has the comparative advantage in producing cheese.

7. **Answer c.** The opportunity cost of producing a bicycle is 2 tons of cheese for Smallville and 1 ton of cheese for Gooseville. Smallville will be willing to pay up to 2 tons of cheese for 1 bicycle, while Gooseville is willing to trade 1 bicycle for any amount of cheese greater than 1 ton. The price of a bicycle will be in the range of 1 to 2 tons of cheese.

8. **Answer c.** If both countries fully specialize, then Smallville will produce only cheese (2,000 tons of cheese) and Gooseville will produce only bicycles (1,500 bicycles).

9. **Answer a.** A linear production function is a production function with a constant slope. This constant slope tells us that for a given change in the good measured on the *x*-axis there will be a given change in the good measured on the *y*-axis. Another way to express this idea is that the opportunity cost of producing either good is constant: for the good measured on the *x*-axis, the opportunity cost of producing one more unit of that good is equal to the absolute value of the slope of the production possibility frontier; for the good measured on the *y*-axis, the opportunity cost of producing one more unit of that good is equal to the absolute value of the reciprocal of the slope of the production possibility frontier. Provided that the slopes of the two countries' production possibility frontiers are not the same, then one of these countries cannot have the comparative advantage of producing both goods: one country must have the comparative advantage in producing one of the goods, while the other country must have the comparative advantage in producing the other good. Trade is beneficial, provided countries specialize in their comparative advantage. Trade without regard to comparative advantage results in lower total production.

10. **Answer b.** This is the definition of autarky. A country may be independent of other countries when it decides not to trade, but that is not the term used to describe this trade position. Answers (c) and (d) refer to models used to analyze international trade, but they are not direct references to the term describing a closed economy.

11. **Answer c.** Gains from trade stem from a country's comparative advantage and not its absolute advantage (statement I is false). Absolute advantage focuses on the amount of resources used to produce a good (for example, the number of hours of labor it takes to produce a shirt) while comparative advantage focuses on the opportunity cost of producing the good—that is, what must be given up to produce a unit of this good (statement II is false). When a country has a comparative advantage in producing a good, this means that its opportunity cost of producing the good is lower than the opportunity cost of producing the same good in some other country: this advantage in terms of opportunity cost is translated into wage rates. When a country has less-productive labor, then the wage rate for this labor is lower than it is for a country that has more-productive labor.

12. **Answer a.** The pauper labor fallacy focuses on the erroneous idea that trade with low-wage countries must necessarily reduce the standard of living of workers in high-wage countries. This idea stems from the belief that this trade "steals" jobs from the high-wage country and does not consider the consumption benefits to the high-wage country of access to the cheaper goods that are made available to the high-wage country by the low-wage country. Trade, willingly undertaken between two parties, must be beneficial to both parties.

13. **Answer c.** This is the definition of the sweatshop labor fallacy. Here the focus is on the idea that high-wage countries are exploiting labor in low-wage countries, since the wages in the latter countries are so much less than the wages in the high-wage countries. However, this argument fails to consider the relative productivity of the labor in these two types of countries, and it does not consider the other alternatives available to labor in the low-wage countries. Sometimes a job that looks terrible from the perspective of a person in a high-wage country is highly sought after in a low-wage country.

14. **Answer e.** The main sources of comparative advantage are differences in climate, differences in factor endowments, and differences in technology. Answers (a) and (c) illustrate a country's specialization based on climate differences, answer (b) illustrates a country's specialization based on factor endowments, and answer (d) illustrates a country's specialization based on differences in technology.

15. **Answer b.** According to the Heckscher-Ohlin model, countries have a comparative advantage in producing those goods and services whose production is intensive in the factors of production that are relatively abundant in that country compared with other countries. Thus, a country that has an abundance of labor relative to other countries tends to specialize in producing labor-intensive goods and services, while a country that is capital abundant specializes in producing capital-intensive goods and services. This specialization bids up the factor price of the factors that are abundant in a country due to the increased demand for these factors, and the factor price of the factors that are scarce in a country tends to fall due to decreased demand for these factors. Answer (b) is not true because the prices of the factors are moving in the wrong direction.

16. **Answer e.** Countries will tend to import those goods that are produced using factors of production which are relatively scarce in the importing country (statement I is therefore false). Countries that utilize a high ratio of highly skilled workers to less skilled workers are countries that tend to produce goods that are intensive in human capital (statement II is true). Countries will export goods whose production takes advantage of the relative abundance of the factor (statement III is true).

17. **Answer c.** The area of consumer surplus is the area beneath the demand curve but above the equilibrium price, or in this example, area ACQ. The area of producer surplus is the area above the supply curve but below the equilibrium price, or in this example, area CQE.

18. **Answer c.** When the world price of the good is greater than the autarky price and the country opens to trade, Pedalland will export the good to other countries in order to sell the good at the higher world price. In this case, domestic suppliers are willing to supply the amount represented as the distance between points B and W while domestic consumers are only willing to consume the number of bicycles represented by the distance between B and M. Thus, domestic producers will export the number of bicycles represented by the distance between points M and W.

19. **Answer b.** When the world price is below the domestic equilibrium price and the country opens to trade, the country will import goods. The country will import the number of goods that represents the difference between the amount domestically supplied at the world price and the amount domestically demanded at the world price. In this case, the country will import the number of goods represented by the distance between points P and S.

20. **Answer a.** The area of consumer surplus is the area beneath the demand curve and above the equilibrium price, while the area of producer surplus is the area above the supply curve and below the equilibrium price. When this country opens to trade and the world price is equal to B, the country will export the good, which benefits domestic producers who are able to sell more units of the good than they could when the country was closed to trade.

21. **Answer c.** When the world price of the good is less than the autarky price, the country will import the good if it opens its economy to trade. In this case, the country will import the difference between the quantity demanded domestically at a price of $20 and the quantity supplied domestically at a price of $20, or 120 bicycles. The area of total surplus is initially equal to $5,000, and when the country opens to trade, the area of total surplus has a value of $6,800, so the increase in total surplus is $6,800 − $5,000 or $1,800.

22. **Answer e.** To calculate the license-holder revenue from the quota you first need to rewrite the supply curve taking into account the quota. So, for example, if the supply equation is initially $P = (1/2)(Q)$, then with a quota of 40 units this supply equation will be $P = (1/2)q − 20$. Using this new supply equation and the demand equation, $P = 100 − (1/2)Q$, you can find the new price with a quota of 40 units. The price with this level of quota is $40 per bicycle. The license-holder revenue is equal to the difference between the price with the quota and the world price times the number of bicycles imported with the quota: ($40/bicycle − $20/bicycle), (40 bicycles) or $800. This argument, however, also works for a quota of 80 units: when the quota is 80 bicycles the supply curve can be written as $P = (1/2)Q − 30$ and the new price with this quota limit is $30 per bicycle. The license-holder revenue is equal to the difference between the price with the quota and the world price times the number of bicycles imported with the quota: (30/bicycle − $20/bicycle)(80 bicycles), or $800.

23. **Answer b.** The deadweight loss associated with this tariff is the result of two forces: (a) mutually beneficial trades do not take place because of the imposition of the tariff, and (b) the bicycles sold are produced at a price that exceeds the world price for bicycles. The area of deadweight loss can be calculated as the sum of the area of two triangles: $(1/2)(\$40 \text{ per bicycle} - \$20 \text{ per bicycle})(80 \text{ bicycles} - 40 \text{ bicycles}) + (1/2)(\$40 \text{ per bicycle} - \$20 \text{ per bicycle})(160 \text{ bicycles} - 120 \text{ bicycles}) = \$800$.

24. **Answer a.** This is a tough problem! You first need to figure out the price with the quota, the quantity supplied domestically with the quota, and the quantity demanded domestically with the quota. From the graph you know that if the quota price was $40, the quota would be equal to 40 units. From the graph you also know that, at the world price, 120 bicycles are imported into Pedalland. So, logically you know that the quota price must be lower than $40 and higher than $20. When the quota price is $35, the quantity demanded domestically is equal to 130 bicycles and the quantity supplied domestically is equal to 70 bicycles, for a difference of 60 bicycles. This difference is the same as the quota amount given in the question. Now you need only compute the original consumer surplus (equals $2,500) and the consumer surplus with the quota ($4,225) and subtract the original consumer surplus from the new consumer surplus to get the change in the value of consumer surplus that occurs with the imposition of the quota.

25. **Answer a.** When countries engage in trade, they produce those goods and services for which they have a comparative advantage. This specialization according to Heckscher-Ohlin advantage results in these countries producing those goods and services for which they have an abundant amount of resources. Thus, the exporting industries in the country will bid up the price of these resources as they increase their production of the good. The country will tend to import goods and services that are intensive in the factors that are scarce in its economy. This effectively decreases the demand for the relatively scarce factors and increases the demand for the relatively abundant factors. Trade will cause the factor price to increase for the relatively abundant factor and to decrease for the relatively scarce factor.

26. **Answer b.** The arguments used to defend trade protection fall into three broad categories: the infant industry argument given in answer (a), the job creation argument given in answer (d), and the national security argument given in answer (c). Answer (b) is not an argument used to defend trade protection, but it is an argument that accompanies the sweatshop labor fallacy described earlier in the chapter.

27. **Answer c.** The World Trade Organization (WTO) is an organization composed of many member nations who meet to discuss and decide on major international trade agreements, and it works to resolve trade disputes between its members. The North American Free Trade Agreement (NAFTA) is a trade agreement between Canada, the United States, and Mexico. The European Union (EU) is a trade agreement between many countries located in Europe.

28. **Answer d.** The value of Donovan's consumer surplus is the difference between the price Donovan is willing to pay ($15) and the market price ($10) of the good.

29. **Answer a.** When the price of a dinner is $9, Matt, Donovan, and Gertrude are willing to purchase a dinner, since the price they are willing to pay is greater than the $9 price. Matt's consumer surplus is equal to $20 – $9, or $11; Donovan's consumer surplus is equal to $15 – $9, or $6; and Gertrude's consumer surplus is equal to $12 – $9, or $3. Adding these three numbers together gives a total consumer surplus of $20.

30. Answer c. At a price of $11 per dinner, we know that Savannah and Anna are both unwilling to purchase a dinner since the prices they are willing to pay are less than the $11 price.

31. Answer b. The value of consumer surplus is the difference between the price each consumer is willing to pay and the market price for all those consumers who are willing to purchase a dinner at the current dinner price. Thus, the total value of consumer surplus is equal to $42.

32. Answer c. The maximum price Fast Eddy can charge per dinner is $7, since this is the highest price that Anna is willing to pay for a dinner. Any price greater than $7 would eliminate Anna from purchasing a dinner.

33. Answer c. To find the quantity demanded at a price of $0.50 a bag, simply plug $0.50 into the given demand equation for the price and then solve for the quantity. To find the consumer surplus, you need to calculate the area under the demand curve and above the price of $0.50. This area is equal to $(1/2)(\$1 - \$0.50)(500 - 0)$, or $125.

34. Answer d. To find the quantity demanded at a price of $0.20 a bag, simply plug $0.20 into the given demand equation for the price and then solve for the quantity. To find the consumer surplus, you need to calculate the area under the demand curve and above the price of $0.20. This area is equal to $(1/2)(\$1 - \$0.20)(800 - 0)$, or $320.

35. Answer b. Since the value of consumer surplus is equal to the area under the demand curve and above the given price, this implies that for any given demand curve an increase in the price will decrease the value of consumer surplus.

36. Answer a. This follows from the same reasoning as that given in the answer to question 8.

37. Answer a. When a dinner sells for $10, Fast Eddy will provide 3 dinners. Eddy would have been willing to sell the first dinner for $3, and thus his producer surplus is equal to $10 – $3, or $7. Fast Eddy would be willing to sell the second dinner for $6, and thus his producer surplus for this dinner is equal to $10 – $6, or $4. Fast Eddy is willing to sell the third dinner for $10, and thus his producer surplus on the third dinner is equal to $0. His total producer surplus is equal to $11.

38. Answer d. To answer this question, use the same reasoning as in question 10. The total producer surplus is equal to $21.

39. Answer b. Fast Eddy is only willing to sell 2 dinners at a price of $9 per dinner since the third, fourth, and fifth dinners must sell for more than this $9 price.

40. Answer d. Fast Eddy is willing to sell 4 dinners at a price of $13. He is unwilling to sell the fifth dinner since he must receive at least $15 to be willing to provide this dinner.

41. Answer d. Fast Eddy will have the greatest producer surplus at a dinner price of $12. When the price is $11, his producer surplus is equal to $14, and when the price is $12, his producer surplus is equal to $17.

42. Answer c. Consumer surplus is equal to the area under the demand curve and above the equilibrium price. Since the equilibrium price is equal to C in the graph, this implies that the area of consumer surplus is equal to area ACF.

43. Answer d. Producer surplus is equal to the area above the supply curve and below the equilibrium price, which is area CFI in the graph.

44. Answer a. Total surplus is the sum of consumer and producer surplus, which is equal to area AFI.

6 (21)

Macroeconomics: The Big Picture

▌ BEFORE YOU READ THE CHAPTER

Summary

This chapter provides an overview of macroeconomics and discusses how macroeconomics, the study of the economy as a whole, differs from microeconomics. The chapter introduces the concepts of business cycles, the management of business cycles through government policies, long-run growth, inflation, deflation, price stability, and the distinction between open economies, where countries trade with one another, and closed economies, where there is no international trade.

Chapter Objectives

Objective #1. Macroeconomics is the study of the aggregate economy or the economy as a whole. Macroeconomics considers how individual and firm behavior in the aggregate interact to produce a particular level of economic performance in the economy. Central topics in macroeconomics include the determination of the overall level of output, the overall level of prices, and the overall level of employment in the economy. Macroeconomics also considers the impact of the global economy on the behavior of the economy.

- Macroeconomics uses various economic aggregates to study the economy. Economic aggregates are measures of economic variables that summarize data collected from different markets for goods, services, workers, and assets. Examples of economic aggregates include unemployment, aggregate output, investment, and savings.

- Macroeconomics studies long-run economic growth and its causes. Long-run economic growth in the economy is measured as the economy's overall output per person. Long-run growth in an economy raises the level of aggregate income and results in a higher standard of living for people living in that economy. Long-run growth is more important than business cycles in determining a country's standard of living.

- In the short run, the combined effect of individual decisions may have a very different impact on the economy than what any one individual intended. For example, when individual households expect an economic downturn, they reduce their expenditures in order to prepare for this expected recession. This is known as the paradox of thrift since the effect of many households acting in a thrifty manner is to plunge the economy into a deeper recession. The macroeconomic result of individual decisions in the economy often proves to be greater than the sum of these individual decisions.

Objective #2.   In the short run, when the economy is in an economic expansion or boom, jobs are plentiful; when the economy is in an economic recession or bust, jobs are difficult to find. A business cycle consists of a period of short-run aggregate economic prosperity and a period of short-run aggregate economic hardship.

- Macroeconomics provides a rationale for government intervention to reduce short-run fluctuations in the economy. John Maynard Keynes argued that a government can help a depressed economy through fiscal and/or monetary policy. Fiscal policy refers to government spending and taxation policy, while monetary policy refers to the control of interest rates and the quantity of money in circulation. Both fiscal and monetary policy are useful tools for offsetting the economic effects of short-run fluctuations (recession or expansion) in the aggregate economy.

Objective #3.   Microeconomics focuses on the production and consumption of specific goods and the allocation of scarce resources among competing uses. Microeconomics analyzes how individuals and firms make decisions.

Objective #4.   Employment measures the total number of people working in the economy, while unemployment is the total number of people who are actively looking for work but currently not working. The unemployment rate is the most widely used indicator of conditions in the labor market. In a recession, the employment rate decreases while the unemployment rate increases. In an expansion, the employment rate increases while the unemployment rate decreases.

Objective #5.   The economy's real output level and unemployment rate move in opposite directions: as output increases, unemployment decreases and as real output decreases, unemployment increases. The economy's real aggregate output is the real value of the total production of final goods and services produced during a given time period and is referred to as real gross domestic product or real GDP.

Objective #6.   Long-run growth occurs when aggregate output per person increases. This growth in the economy occurs over several decades and does not refer to the short-run increase in aggregate output that occurs during an expansion. Long-run economic growth is essential in order for wages and the standard of living in an economy to increase.

Objective #7.   Inflation refers to a rise in the overall level of prices while deflation refers to a fall in the overall level of prices. In the short run, movements in inflation are closely related to the business cycle. In the long run, movements in inflation are primarily determined by changes in the money supply. Price stability is a desirable macroeconomic goal.

Objective #8.   Hyperinflation is always the result of governments printing money to pay their bills.

Objective #9.   An economy that does not engage in international trade is a closed economy. An economy that participates in international trade is an open economy. Countries engage in trade because this trade is mutually beneficial to them. Imports refers to the value of the goods and services a country buys from the rest of the world, and exports refers to the value of the goods and services a country sells to the rest of the world.

Objective #10. An open economy runs a trade deficit when the value of its imports is greater than the value of its exports. An open economy runs a trade surplus when the value of its imports is less than the value of its exports. A country's trade surplus or trade deficit ultimately depends on the saving and investment decisions made by that country.

Key Terms

self-regulating economy an *economy* in which problems such as *unemployment* are resolved without government intervention, through the working of the *invisible hand*, and in which government attempts to improve the economy's performance would be ineffective at best, and would probably make things worse.

Keynesian economics a school of thought emerging out of the works of John Maynard Keynes; according to Keynesian economics, a depressed *economy* is the result of inadequate spending and government intervention can help a depressed economy through *monetary policy* and *fiscal policy.*

monetary policy changes in the quantity of money in circulation designed to alter *interest rates* and affect the level of overall spending.

fiscal policy changes in government spending and taxes designed to affect overall spending.

recession a period of economic downturn when output and unemployment are falling; also referred to as a contraction.

expansion period of economic upturn in which output and employment are rising; most economic numbers are following their normal upward trend; also referred to as a recovery.

business cycle the short-run alternation between economic downturns, known as *recessions,* and economic upturns, known as *expansions.*

business-cycle peak the point in time at which the *economy* shifts from *expansion* to *recession.*

business-cycle trough the point in time at which the *economy* shifts from *recession* to *expansion.*

long-run economic growth the sustained rise in the quantity of goods and services the *economy* produces.

inflation a rise in the overall level of prices.

deflation a fall in the overall level of prices.

price stability a situation in which the overall cost of living is changing slowly or not at all.

open economy an *economy* that trades goods and services with other countries.

Key Terms *(continued)*

trade deficit when the value of the goods and services bought from foreigners is more than the value of the goods and services sold to consumers abroad.

trade surplus when the value of goods and services bought from foreigners is less than the value of the goods and services sold to them.

◼ AFTER YOU READ THE CHAPTER

Tips

Tip #1. Studying economics requires learning both new vocabulary and a new way of thinking. This chapter provides an overview of macroeconomics, the topics covered in the study of macroeconomics, and general definitions of macroeconomic variables. You will need to familiarize yourself with this information and vocabulary. You may find it helpful to make a set of flash cards for all the vocabulary you learn while studying macroeconomics. For each flash card you will find it helpful to write the term on one side of the card and its definition on the other side of the card. You might also find it helpful to identify on the first side of the card the chapter number where the term is first introduced. After you make a set of flash cards for the chapter, review these flash cards until you are thoroughly familiar and comfortable with each term.

Tip #2. Macroeconomics focuses on the economic behavior of the overall economy, while microeconomics focuses on the economic behavior of individuals, firms, and specific markets. Macroeconomics studies topics like the determination of the aggregate level of output, the aggregate price level, the level of employment, short-run economic fluctuations, and long-run economic growth. Microeconomics considers topics like supply and demand in particular markets, profit maximization by firms, and utility maximization by individuals.

Tip #3. Aggregation of data is at the heart of macroeconomics. This chapter briefly describes the meaning of aggregation and gives examples of aggregated measures like employment, real GDP, and the overall price level. The concept of aggregation is important to understand as you begin your study of macroeconomics.

Tip #4. In macroeconomics, the aggregate effect is often greater than the sum of the individual effects. In macroeconomics we find that the sum of many individual actions accumulates to produce outcomes that are larger than the simple sum of these individual actions. The combined effect of individual decisions can be much different from the intentions that any one individual had. The text provides an example of this with the paradox of thrift.

WORKED PROBLEMS

1. This chapter introduces the concepts of recession, fiscal and monetary policy, business cycles, unemployment, and trade deficits. Since 2007, many of these terms have been widely used in media reporting about the U.S. economy. For each term, think about what has been happening in the U.S. economy since 2007 and relate these real-life events to these terms.

STEP 1: In order to answer this question you will first want to make sure you know each of the terms and their definitions.

Review the section "Macroeconomics: Theory and Policy" on page 167 (Econ page 599), the section "The Business Cycle" on page 169 (Econ page 601), the section "International Imbalances" on page 179 (Econ page 611), and Figure 6-3 on page 171 (Econ page 603).

STEP 2: Once you have the definitions of these terms clearly in mind, then you will want to review what the economic situation in the United States has been since 2007. Then, apply these terms where appropriate.

Review the section "Macroeconomics: Theory and Policy" on page 167 (Econ page 599), the section "The Business Cycle" on page 169 (Econ page 601), the section "International Imbalances" on page 179 (Econ page 611), and Figure 6-3 on page 171 (Econ page 603).

Since 2007, the U.S. economy has experienced a serious recession that has resulted in high levels of unemployment. This recession represents a part of the business cycle, since a business cycle is composed of both periods of economic downturn and periods of economic expansion. At the same time that the U.S. economy experienced this recession, it was also running a large trade deficit: the U.S. economy was importing more goods than it was exporting.

2. The following table includes a number of potential research projects that a group of economists are considering working on during the next few years. Fill in the table to help them identify whether the topic is more likely a microeconomics topic or more likely a macroeconomics topic.

Research Topic	Macroeconomic or Microeconomic Topic?	Explanation for your answer
Impact of Gulf of Mexico oil spill on beach tourism in the Gulf States		
Impact of fiscal stimulus spending programs on employment and production in the United States		
The effect of a government program subsidizing investment on the level of aggregate production and aggregate employment in the economy		
Impact of China's allowing its exchange rates to be market-determined on the demand for Chinese textile goods		
Impact of recent monetary policy on inflation in the U.S. economy		

STEP 1: In order to answer this question, you will obviously need to read the chapter. But you will also find it helpful to think about what topics macroeconomics addresses and then try to relate these topics to the previous table.

Review the section "The Nature of Macroeconomics" on page 166 (Econ page 598) and Table 6-1 on page 166 (Econ page 598).

Here is the filled-in table:

Research topic	Macroeconomic or microeconomic topic?	Explanation for your answer
Impact of Gulf of Mexico oil spill on beach tourism in the Gulf States	Micro	This topic looks at the impact of an event on a specific market rather than on the aggregate economy
Impact of fiscal stimulus spending programs on employment and production in the United States	Macro	This topic looks at the impact of a policy on the entire, or aggregate, economy
The effect of a government program subsidizing investment on the level of aggregate production and aggregate employment in the economy	Macro	This topic looks at the impact of a policy on the entire, or aggregate, economy
Impact of China's allowing its exchange rates to be market-determined on the demand for Chinese textile goods	Micro	This topic looks at the impact of an event on a specific market rather than on the aggregate economy
Impact of recent monetary policy on inflation in the U.S. economy	Macro	This topic looks at the impact of a policy on the entire, or aggregate, economy

3. On page 174 (Econ page 606) of your text, the authors present Figure 6-5 as an illustration of long-run economic growth in America. To get a concrete sense of this economic growth, identify three people you can interview: these three people should be of different ages, and if possible, try to find someone who is at least seventy-five. Do a survey of these three people's memories of what items their family possessed and what items they can remember as new and original: for example, most college students today will list portable computers and cell phones, while someone in the fifty-year-old range may recall the family's first color television, while someone who is eighty may be able to remember the first family car. After completing this survey, decide whether or not it convinces you that there has been significant economic growth over the past eighty years.

STEP 1: In order to answer this question, you will first want to think about how you want to collect your data: that is, you will want to think about what questions you will ask the people you have chosen to interview.

Review the section "Long-Run Economic Growth" on page 174 (Econ page 606) and Figure 6-5 on page 174 (Econ page 606).

Since you are trying to get a sense of how people lived at different times, you will want to compose a set of questions that is designed to get this information. Thoughtful consideration before you start will help you get more and better information. You will want to make sure that some of your questions are specific, while other questions may be more open-ended.

STEP 2: Identify several people that you think will make good interview subjects. You might want to identify more than three people, since some of the people you have identified may be unavailable to interview. Contact these people to set up a time to come for the interview.

Review the section "Long-Run Economic Growth" on page 174 (Econ page 606) and Figure 6-5 on page 174 (Econ page 606).

Make sure you are prepared to take notes on what is said at the interview. As you collect your information, you will want to think about what things you can contrast or compare between the different individuals you are interviewing.

STEP 3: Create a summary statement comparing the information you received. Think about how this information helps support the argument that economic growth has occurred during this period.

Review the section "Long-Run Economic Growth" on page 174 (Econ page 606) and Figure 6-5 on page 174 (Econ page 606).

For example, you might decide to present your information in a table or graph. Review Figure 6-5 to see one example of a representation of changes that reflect economic growth over time. Think about and plan a method of presenting your data that makes a strong case in support of your argument.

The answers and presentations with respect to this question will vary with each student: underlying all of the presentations should be a sense of the economic growth and change that have occurred in the last seventy to eighty years.

4. Suppose Jerry's income was $40,000 last year and this year it is $50,000. But over the course of the year, the price of the food that he purchases has risen from $6,000 per year to $10,000 per year, and the price of the gasoline that he purchases has risen from $2,000 per year to $4,000 per year. All other prices that Jerry faces have remained constant over this period. Is Jerry better off now that his salary has increased to $50,000?

STEP 1: To answer this question, you will want to think about what is happening to Jerry's income and what is happening to the prices of gasoline and food. It would be helpful to calculate the percentage change in income, the percentage change in food prices, and the percentage change in gasoline prices in order to see how Jerry is doing.

Review the section "Inflation and Deflation" on page 177 (Econ page 609).

The percentage change in a variable can be found by calculating [(the new value – the previous value)/(the previous value)] × 100. Thus, the percentage change in Jerry's income is equal to [($50,000 – $40,000)/($40,000)] × 100 = 25%. The percentage change in the price of food and the percentage change in the price of gasoline can be calculated similarly. The percentage change in the price of food is equal to 67%, while the percentage change in the price of gasoline is 100%.

STEP 2: Once you have calculated the percentage changes, you will want to think about what this implies about how Jerry is doing.

Review the section "Inflation and Deflation" on page 177 (Econ page 609).

Jerry's income has increased, but so have the price of food and the price of gasoline; all other prices that Jerry faces have remained constant. Clearly, Jerry's income cannot purchase as much food or gasoline as it could when his income and the prices were at their initial level: Jerry is worse off than he was in the first year.

Problems and Exercises

1. For each of the following questions identify whether the question is more appropriate for the study of microeconomics or macroeconomics, and why.

   a. What will happen to the wages in our community if Corporation X, an employer of 1,000 people (that's 40% of our workforce), decides to relocate its plant to a different state?

   b. What will happen to the level of overall economic production in our economy if the federal government continues to run record levels of government deficit?

   c. If the government engages in monetary policy and increases the money supply, what will happen to the interest rate in our economy?

   d. How has the recent increase in the price of a barrel of oil affected the prices of bicycles, cars, and airplane fares?

   e. What will the effect of recent tropical storms be on the price of bananas?

2. Suppose that people anticipate an economic recession and decide to increase their rate of saving so they are better prepared financially for the recession. Explain why this response might actually make the recession worse.

3. This chapter distinguishes between an economic expansion as part of the business cycle and long-run economic growth. Concisely explain the difference between these two terms.

4. In the beginning of 2006, suppose the population in Neverland was 2 million people and the level of real GDP, or aggregate output, was $40 million. During 2006, population increased by 2%, while real GDP increased by 5%. During this same period, the aggregate price level was constant. Furthermore, suppose these growth rates continued into 2007 and 2008.

Fill in the following table using the given information. (Make all calculations to two places past the decimal.)

	Beginning of 2006	Beginning of 2007	Beginning of 2008	Beginning of 2009
Real GDP				
Population				
Real GDP/person				

5. In the beginning of 2006, suppose the population in Funland was 2 million people and the level of real GDP, or aggregate output, was $40 million. During 2006, population increased by 3% while real GDP increased by 3%. During 2007, population increased by 4% while real GDP increased by 3%. During 2008, population increased by 5% while real GDP increased by 3%.

a. Fill in the following table using the given information. (Make all calculations to two places past the decimal.)

	Beginning of 2006	Beginning of 2007	Beginning of 2008	Beginning of 2009
Real GDP				
Population				
Real GDP/person				

b. What do you know about this country's standard of living between the beginning of 2006 and the beginning of 2009? Explain your answer.

c. In comparing your answers in problem 4 to your answers in problem 5, what major concept do these problems illustrate?

6. China's economy is growing at a much faster annual rate than the U.S. economy. Does this mean that the standard of living in China is higher than the standard of living in the United States? Explain your answer.

BEFORE YOU TAKE THE TEST

Chapter Review Questions

1. Macroeconomics, unlike microeconomics,
    a. considers the behavior of individual firms and markets.
    b. focuses on the production and consumption of particular goods.
    c. tries to explain increases in living standards over time.
    d. finds that the behavior of individuals is more important in determining economic activity than is the aggregate summation of this behavior.

2. Which of the following statements is true?
    a. In macroeconomics, there is no role for government intervention in the economy.
    b. In microeconomics, the prices determined in economic models are aggregate price levels for the economy.
    c. Microeconomics studies business cycle fluctuations in the economy.
    d. Fiscal and monetary policy may be helpful in reducing short-term economic fluctuations in the economy due to adverse economic events.

3. Which of the following is NOT an aggregate macroeconomic variable?
    a. Savings: the sum of household, government, and business savings during a given year
    b. Investment: the addition to the economy's supply of productive physical capital
    c. Bicycle production: the total number of bicycles manufactured in an economy during a given year
    d. Capital account: the total net amount of assets sold to foreigners

4. In a recession,
    a. unemployment increases, aggregate output decreases and people enjoy higher living standards.
    b. unemployment increases while aggregate output and aggregate income decrease.
    c. aggregate output and aggregate income decrease, eventually leading, in all cases, to an economic depression.
    d. aggregate output must fall for at least three consecutive quarters.

5. Government intervention in the economy is
    a. called fiscal policy if it involves a policy change that alters the interest rate or the level of money in circulation in the economy.
    b. called fiscal policy if it involves changing government spending or taxing in order to offset the economic effects of short-run fluctuations in the macroeconomy.
    c. particularly useful in helping economies in the long run.
    d. only helpful during economic recessions.

6. Economic growth
    a. refers to increases in real GDP per capita over the long run.
    b. refers to short-term fluctuations in real GDP per capita.
    c. is best measured using the employment rate.
    d. is of little importance to economists.

7. Macroeconomics
   a. focuses on how the behavior of individuals and firms in the aggregate economy interact to produce a market price for each good and service offered in the economy.
   b. focuses on how the actions of individuals and firms in the economy interact to produce a particular economy-wide level of economic performance.
   c. considers how specific markets for goods and services determine their equilibrium prices and quantities.
   d. Answers (a), (b), and (c) are all correct.

8. Which of the following statements is true?
   a. An economy in a recession will have a lower unemployment rate than will the same economy operating in an expansion.
   b. In an economic expansion, the unemployment rate decreases while aggregate output increases.
   c. An economy's output level and employment rate move in opposite directions.
   d. Answers (b) and (c) are correct.

9. The paradox of thrift illustrates that
   a. in macroeconomics the combined effect of individual decisions can have effects that are very different from what any one individual intended.
   b. acting virtuously at the microeconomic level by spending less may result in an adverse macroeconomic outcome, since this behavior may result in a lower level of aggregate economic production.
   c. acting in a profligate manner at the microeconomic level by spending more may result in an expansion of the economy.
   d. Answers (a), (b), and (c) are all correct.

10. According to Keynesian economics, a depressed economy is the result of
    a. inadequate spending.
    b. irrational behavior on the part of individuals and firms operating in the economy.
    c. scarce resources.
    d. monetary and fiscal policy.

11. Inflation occurs when
    a. the aggregate level of output increases.
    b. the unemployment rate decreases.
    c. the aggregate price level rises over time.
    d. consumers' purchasing power increases over time.

12. A country that trades goods and services with another country is known as a(n)
    a. open economy.
    b. real economy.
    c. weak economy.
    d. closed economy.

13. Monetary policy refers to the changes in
    a. taxes and government spending designed to change the overall level of spending in an economy.
    b. interest rates and the money supply designed to change the overall level of spending in an economy.

14. The changes in taxes and government spending designed to change the overall level of spending in an economy is called
    a. monetary policy.
    b. fiscal policy.
    c. either monetary or fiscal policy depending upon what is happening to the interest rate.

15. Economic recessions and economic expansions are
    a. long-run in nature.
    b. short-run in nature.

16. An economic contraction is
    a. another term for an economic recession.
    b. indicates that the economy is experiencing a decrease in the level of employment.
    c. part of the business cycle.
    d. Answers (a), (b), and (c) are all correct.

17. An economic expansion is
    a. another term for an economic recovery.
    b. indicates that the economy is experiencing a decrease in the level of unemployment.
    c. is that part of the business cycle between the business-cycle trough and the business-cycle peak.
    d. Answers (a), (b), and (c) are all correct.
    e. Answers (a) and (c) are both correct.

18. Which of the following statements is true?
    I. The 2007–2009 recession in the United States hit the economy much harder than the 2001 recession did.
    II. The Great Depression in the United States was a 43-month-long economic downturn.
    III. The U.S. recession of 2001 lasted only eight months, while the recession of 2007–2009 lasted more than twice as long.
    a. Statements I, II, and III are all true.
    b. Statements II and III are true.
    c. Statements I and III are true.
    d. Statement II is true.

19. A sustained rise in the quantity of goods and services a country produces is referred to as
    a. an economic expansion or recovery.
    b. a period of employment.
    c. long-run economic growth.
    d. sound fiscal policy.

20. Long-run growth per capita is
   a. the key to higher wages and a rising standard of living.
   b. a situation that occurs when the economy's overall production grows at a faster rate than the economy's population.
   c. a sustained upward trend in output per person.
   d. Answers (a), (b), and (c) are all correct.

21. Deflation occurs when
   a. economic production increases in the aggregate economy.
   b. the overall price level decreases in an economy.
   c. the overall level of employment decreases in the aggregate economy.
   d. both the overall price level and the overall level of employment in an economy decrease.

22. When the economy is in a recession, jobs are
   a. hard to find and the overall level of prices in the economy tends to rise.
   b. easy to find and the overall level of prices in the economy tends to rise.
   c. hard to find and the overall level of prices in the economy tends to fall.
   d. easy to find and the overall level of prices in the economy tends to fall.

23. A country runs a trade deficit when
   a. its level of employment decreases.
   b. its overall price level is falling.
   c. the value of the goods and services it imports exceeds the value of the goods and services it exports.
   d. the value of the goods and services it exports exceeds the value of the goods and services it imports.

24. The value of a country's imports is equal to $1.2 billion this year while the value of the country's exports is equal to $1.3 billion this year. This country is running a
   a. trade surplus this year.
   b. trade deficit this year.

25. Whether a country runs a trade surplus or a trade deficit depends on
   a. what part of the business cycle the country is currently in.
   b. whether or not the country is experiencing deflation or inflation.
   c. whether the country is employing fiscal or monetary policy.
   d. decisions about saving and investment spending in the country.

26. A country's investment spending during the current year is equal to $400 million, while its level of saving for the current year is $350 million. Given this information, this country will likely run a trade
   a. surplus.
   b. deficit.

ANSWER KEY

Answers to Problems and Exercises

1. **a.** Microeconomics: this question is directed at understanding the local effect of this corporation's move instead of its total effect across the aggregate economy.

   b. Macroeconomics: this question focuses on the aggregate performance of the economy.

   c. Macroeconomics: this question considers the impact of monetary policy on the aggregate economy.

   d. Microeconomics: this question addresses the effect of a change in the price of a barrel of oil on specific markets like the market for bicycles, cars, or air travel service.

   e. Microeconomics: this question considers the price of a specific good rather than the overall price level in the economy.

2. Even though the individual's decision is a rational path to follow, the effect of many individuals making this decision is to reduce spending dramatically in the aggregate economy. As spending decreases, producers respond by decreasing their production and reducing their use of labor. This paradox of thrift has the effect of worsening the recessionary tendencies in the economy.

3. An economic expansion is a short-run increase in the level of aggregate output that may not be sustained indefinitely, while long-run economic growth reflects a sustainable increase in an economy's ability to produce more goods and services.

4.

	Beginning of 2006	Beginning of 2007	Beginning of 2008	Beginning of 2009
Real GDP	$40 million	$42 million	$44.1 million	$46.31 million
Population	2 million	2.04 million	2.08 million	2.12 million
Real GDP/person	$20	$20.59	$21.20	$21.84

5. **a.**

	Beginning of 2006	Beginning of 2007	Beginning of 2008	Beginning of 2009
Real GDP	$40 million	$41.20 million	$42.44 million	$43.71 million
Population	2 million	2.06 million	2.14 million	2.25 million
Real GDP/person	$20	$20	$19.31	$19.43

   b. The standard of living in Funland between the beginning of 2006 and the end of 2008 is decreasing, since the rate of population growth exceeds the rate of real GDP growth.

   c. Problems 4 and 5 illustrate the importance of the growth rates of population and real GDP in determining the standard of living. In problem 4, the standard of living increases, since real GDP grows at a faster rate than the rate of population increase, while in problem 5, the standard of living decreases since the population growth rate is greater than the rate of real GDP growth.

6. Although China's economy in recent years has grown at a much faster rate than the U.S. economy, this does not necessarily imply that China's standard of living is higher than the standard of living in the United States. Standard of living depends upon both the level of production in an economy and the population in the economy as well as the initial level of standard of living. Ten years ago the output per person in the United States was much larger than the output per person in China. Over the past ten years, even though China's rate of economic growth has surpassed the U.S. rate of economic growth, it has not been sufficiently long enough for the Chinese standard of living to catch up with the U.S. standard of living.

Answers to Chapter Review Questions

1. **Answer c.** Macroeconomics studies the aggregate economy, not individual action; in studying the aggregate economy, macroeconomics seeks to explain the factors that determine a country's standard of living. In macroeconomics we are reminded that the aggregation of individual behavior often has a larger impact than just the sum of these individual behaviors.

2. **Answer d.** In the aggregate economy, output and employment fluctuate in the short run. Macroeconomic theory analyzes the effect of fiscal and monetary policy on short-run economic fluctuations and provides a rationale for government intervention to lessen the economic impact of business cycles.

3. **Answer c.** Although each of these variables is aggregated to some extent, the bicycle production for the year only aggregates in a market for a single product rather than aggregating over multiple markets.

4. **Answer b.** A recession, by definition, occurs when aggregate output decreases and income decreases. As the economy produces a smaller level of output, employment of labor decreases since less labor is needed to produce the smaller level of output. Not all recessions turn into depressions, and there is no uniform agreement about the length of time aggregate output must decrease for the downturn in economic activity to be viewed as a recession.

5. **Answer b.** Government intervention in the economy is called fiscal policy if it involves a change in government spending and/or taxation implemented to reduce short-run business cycle fluctuation in the economy. Government intervention in the economy is called monetary policy if it involves a change in the interest rate or a change in the amount of money in circulation in the economy implemented in order to reduce short-run business cycle fluctuation in the economy.

6. **Answer a.** Economic growth is measured as an increase in the level of real GDP in the economy. This increase refers to an increase over the long run, rather than a short-run economic expansion.

7. **Answer b.** Macroeconomics is focused on the aggregate economy and its overall performance. Microeconomics focuses on specific markets and how the behavior of firms and individuals interact to determine the prices in those markets as well as the quantities in those markets.

8. **Answer b.** This question centers on the relationship between aggregate output and employment: as aggregate output increases, employment also increases and hence unemployment decreases. An economy can reduce its level of unemployment but cannot eliminate unemployment, since there will always be people newly entering the labor force and searching for their first jobs.

9. **Answer d.** The paradox of thrift refers to the situation that occurs when individuals, worried about the possibility of economic hard times, reduce their spending. This prudent behavior on the part of individuals results in less overall spending in the economy and therefore an even greater economic slowdown than would have happened if some of these individuals had not acted so prudently. Conversely, individuals can also elect to spend more when they are optimistic about the economy, and this spending will therefore result in an even greater expansion of the economy than individuals anticipate. Thus, the paradox of thrift is an illustration of how individual decisions can result in effects that are greater than what any one individual intended.

10. **Answer a.** Keynesian economics explains economic downturns as being the result of too little spending and suggests that monetary and/or fiscal policy can be used to stimulate the economy. Economics is about the allocation of scarce resources, but this scarcity of resources does not explain why business cycles occur in the economy.

11. **Answer c.** Inflation is defined as the increase in the aggregate price level over time.

12. **Answer a.** A country that engages in international trade is referred to as an open economy, while a country that does not trade is a closed economy.

13. **Answer b.** Monetary policy refers to the changes in interest rates that result from changes in the money supply: these interest rate changes result in a change in the overall level of spending in the economy.

14. **Answer b.** Changes in taxes and/or government spending that are designed to change the overall level of spending in the economy are referred to as fiscal policy. Monetary policy changes the overall level of spending in the economy by altering the level of interest rates in the economy through changes in the money supply.

15. **Answer b.** Business cycle fluctuations in the economy, whether recessions or expansions, are short-run fluctuations.

16. **Answer d.** An economic contraction or recession is that part of the business cycle where output and employment are falling.

17. **Answer d.** An economic expansion or recovery is that part of the business cycle when output and employment are increasing, and therefore unemployment is decreasing. The economic expansion occurs in that part of the business cycle between the business cycle trough and the business cycle peak, since this is the part of the business cycle when output and employment are increasing.

18. **Answer a.** All of these statements are factual statements that are discussed in this chapter.

19. **Answer c.** When the increase in the production of goods and services is sustained, this implies that the economy is experiencing economic growth; an economic expansion or recovery refers to a short-run increase (not sustained) in the level of production of goods and services in an economy.

20. **Answer d.** For wages and the standard of living to increase in the aggregate in an economy, it is necessary that production increases at a faster rate than the rate of population growth. Answer (b) is just an alternative way of stating long-run growth per capita.

21. **Answer b.** Deflation refers to a decrease in the overall level of prices in an economy and, although deflation may occur at the same time that employment in the economy decreases, the term only refers to the decrease in the overall price level.

22. **Answer c.** In a recession, production is falling, which implies that fewer units of labor will be employed. This, in turn, implies that jobs will be difficult to find. In addition, as the level of production falls in the economy there is less demand for goods and services, which leads to a general decrease in the overall level of prices in the economy.

23. **Answer c.** Answer (c) is the basic definition of a trade deficit.

24. **Answer a.** When the value of a country's exports is greater than the value of its imports for a given time period, then the country is running a trade surplus during that period of time.

25. **Answer d.** The saving and investment spending decisions made in a country ultimately determine whether or not that country will run a trade deficit or a trade surplus. When a country has high investment spending relative to its level of saving, it will run a trade deficit; when a country has low investment spending relative to its level of saving, it will run a trade surplus.

26. **Answer b.** When a country's level of investment spending is high relative to its saving, then the country will run a trade deficit. Since this country's investment spending exceeds its saving for the period under consideration, this implies that the country will run a trade deficit.

Tracking the
Macroeconomy

BEFORE YOU READ THE CHAPTER

Summary

This chapter focuses on the idea of economic aggregation and what aggregation means when measuring the level of aggregate production and the level of aggregate prices in an economy. In this chapter, a more complicated circular-flow diagram of the economy is presented. This diagram provides an illustration of different ways to calculate aggregate production or gross domestic product (GDP). The chapter then develops three ways of calculating GDP. The chapter also discusses the distinction between nominal and real GDP, the calculation of price indexes as measures of the aggregate price level, and how to calculate the inflation rate using a price index.

Chapter Objectives

Objective #1. Good macroeconomic policy depends on good measurement of key economic variables that provide information about how the aggregate economy is performing. These key variables include the level of aggregate income and aggregate output, the level of employment and unemployment, and the level and rate of change of prices in the economy.

Objective #2. The national income and product accounts, or the national accounts, provide a set of numbers that indicate the country's state of economic performance. The Bureau of Economic Analysis calculates the national accounts for the United States.

- An expanded circular-flow diagram of the economy, focusing on money flows, illustrates the key concepts underlying the national accounts. Note that the flow of money into each market or sector must be equal to the flow of money out of each market or sector. For instance, the value of household income, the sum of wages, dividends, interest, and rent, equals the sum of the values of household tax payments and government transfer payments, consumer spending, and private saving. Figure 7.1 illustrates the expanded circular-flow diagram.

Figure 7.1

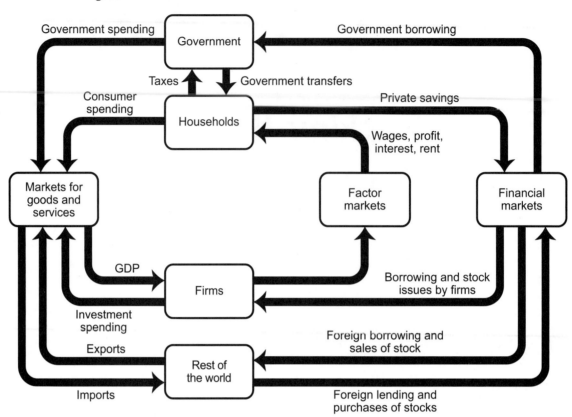

- The circular-flow diagram includes the output market, the factors of production market, and the financial market. The sectors represented in the more complicated circular-flow diagram in this chapter include households, firms, the government, and the rest of the world.

- Referring to Figure 7.1, note the following observations:

  - GDP is equal to the sum of wages, profit, interest, and rent.

  - GDP is equal to the sum of consumer spending, government spending, investment spending, and net exports (exports minus imports).

  - The flow of funds into the household sector is equal to wages, profits, interest, rent, and transfer payments, while the flow of funds out of the household sector is equal to consumer spending, taxes, and private saving. These two flows are equal to one another.

  - The flow of funds into the firm sector is equal to GDP plus the borrowing and stock issues by firms, while the flow of funds out of the firm sector is equal to investment spending plus wages, profit, interest, and rent. These two flows are equal to one another.

  - The flow of funds into the government sector is equal to taxes and government borrowing, while the flow of funds out of the government sector is equal to government spending and transfer payments. These two flows are equal to one another.

  - The flow of funds into the rest of the world is equal to spending on imports plus foreign borrowing and sales of stock, while the flow of funds out of the rest of the world is equal to spending on exports plus foreign borrowing and sales of stock. These two flows are equal to one another.

- Referring to Figure 7.1 and focusing on the three markets, note the following observations:

  - The flows into the market for goods and services are equal to the sum of consumer spending, investment spending, government spending, and net exports, and the flow out of the market for goods and services is equal to GDP. These two flows are equal to one another.

- The flows into the factor market are equal to the flows out of the factor market, and these flows are equal to the sum of wages, interest, profit, and rent.

- The flows into the financial market are equal to the flows out of the financial markets. The flows into the financial market are equal to the sum of foreign lending and purchases of stock plus private savings, while the flows out of the financial markets are equal to the sum of borrowing and stock issues by firms (domestic firms) plus foreign borrowing and the sales of stock.

Objective #3. The circular-flow diagram provides a simplified illustration of national income and national spending. Here is a brief summary of each sector's activity.

- Households receive income from selling factors of production to firms. Households receive income from wages earned by selling their labor; income, in the form of dividends and interest, from their indirect ownership (their stock and bond ownership) of physical capital used by firms; and income, in the form of rent, earned by selling the use of their land. Households gain the income they earn from selling factors of production and then use this income to purchase goods and services, to pay their taxes, and to provide private savings to financial markets. Household income net of taxes and government transfers is called disposable income. Private saving is that part of disposable income that is not spent on goods and services.

- The government collects tax revenue and then returns part of this money as transfer payments. Government transfer payments are payments made by the government to individuals for which no good or service is provided in return; for example, Social Security payments and unemployment insurance payments are government transfer payments. The sum of tax revenue net of transfer payments plus funds the government borrows from the financial markets is then used by the government to purchase goods and services.

- Firms hire factors of production to produce goods and services but they also expend funds to buy goods and services. This investment spending on productive physical capital and on inventories is included in the national accounts as part of total spending on goods and services. Investment spending includes expenditure on inventories, since these inventories will contribute to greater future sales of a firm. Construction of new homes is also included in investment spending, since a new home produces a future stream of housing services for the people who live in the house.

- The rest of the world participates in the domestic economy by purchasing goods and services produced in the domestic economy (the domestic economy's exports), by selling goods and services to the domestic economy (the domestic economy's imports), and by making transactions in the domestic economy's financial markets.

Objective #4. The financial markets receive funds from households, as well as from the rest of the world. These funds provide the basis for loans to the government, firms, and the rest of the world.

Objective #5. Gross domestic product, or GDP, is the sum of consumer spending on goods and services, investment spending, government spending, and the difference between spending on exports and imports. GDP is the total value of all final goods and services produced in an economy during a given time period. Final goods and services are goods and services sold to the final user. Intermediate goods and services are those items that are used as inputs for the production of final goods and services.

Objective #6. There are different ways to calculate GDP. One method is to add up the total value of final goods and services produced in an economy during a given time period. This method requires that the value of intermediate goods be excluded from the calculation in order to avoid double counting. An alternative method is to add up total spending on domestically produced final goods and services in an economy during a given time period. A third method of computing GDP is to sum the total value of factor income paid by firms in the economy to households. All three of these methods will yield identical values of GDP for an economy during a given time period.

- In calculating GDP, care must be taken to avoid double counting. For example, in measuring GDP as the value of total spending on final goods and services in an economy, we count only each producer's value added in the calculation. Or, if we calculate GDP as the value of total spending on final goods and services on domestically produced final goods and services, we avoid double counting by counting only the value of sales to final purchasers. When estimating GDP using spending data, we omit sales of inputs from one business to another, unless that spending represents investment spending by firms. Investment spending by firms represents a purchase that will last for a considerable time.

- GDP for an economy can be expressed as an equation: $GDP = C + I + G + X - IM$, where C is consumer spending, I is investment spending, G is government spending, X is spending on domestically produced goods and services by foreigners (the domestic economy's exports), and IM is spending on imports, or the spending on goods and services produced by foreign economies. The difference between exports and imports, or $X - IM$, is referred to as net exports.

- GDP can also be measured as the sum of all the income earned by factors of production in the economy: this is the sum of wages, interest, rent, and profit.

Objective #7.   Gross national product, or GNP, is the total factor income earned by citizens of a country irrespective of where they reside. GDP, in contrast, is the total factor income earned in a country without regard to the citizenship of the owners of those factors of production.

Objective #8.   GDP can change over time because the economy is producing more or because the prices of the goods and services it produces have increased. Real GDP calculates the value of aggregate production during a given time period, using prices from some given base year. In effect, real GDP uses constant prices. In contrast, nominal GDP is the calculation of GDP using current prices. Real GDP measures allow one to compare the growth in aggregate production in an economy over time.

Objective #9.   In comparing GDP across countries or over time, we can eliminate differences in population size by dividing each country's GDP by its population to get GDP per capita, or the average GDP per person. Real GDP per capita is one of many important determinants of human welfare: it measures what a country can do, but it does not address how that country uses that output to affect living standards.

Objective #10. Economists measure changes in the aggregate price level by tracking changes in the cost of buying a given market basket. A price index measures the cost of purchasing a given market basket in a given year, where that cost is normalized so that it is equal to 100 in the base year. To calculate the cost of the market basket, multiply the quantities of each good in the market basket times its price and then sum these products. Then use this information to calculate a price index by dividing the cost of the market basket for a particular time period by the cost of the market basket in the base year and then multiplying this ratio by 100. The price index for the base year is always equal to 100. An example of a price index is the consumer price index, or the CPI. The producer price index (also known as the wholesale price index), or the PPI, is another price index that measures the cost of a basket of goods typically purchased by producers. The inflation rate between two years can be calculated using this formula: Inflation rate = [(price index in year 2) − (price index in year 1)/(price index in year 1)] × 100.

CHAPTER 7(22) TRACKING THE MACROECONOMY **281**

Objective #11. Many payments are tied or "indexed" to the CPI: that is, many payments are adjusted up or down when the CPI rises or falls. For example, Social Security checks are indexed to the CPI as are income tax brackets and some wage settlements. Due to this indexing there is concern as to whether the CPI accurately reflects changes in the aggregate price level. Some economists believe that the CPI overstates the rate of inflation due to the fact that the CPI calculation uses a fixed market basket and does not allow for the fact that consumers substitute away from relatively more expensive goods and toward relatively cheaper goods when prices change. In addition, the CPI may be biased due to the presence of innovation. Innovation, by widening the range of consumer choice, makes a given amount of money worth more and this is like a fall in consumer prices.

Objective #12. The GDP deflator is not a price index, but it does provide a measure of prices. The GDP deflator is calculated as the ratio of nominal GDP for that year to real GDP for that year times 100: GDP deflator = [(nominal GDP for year n)/(real GDP for year n)] × 100. The value of the GDP deflator for the base year is always equal to 100.

Key Terms

Notes

national income and product accounts method of calculating and keeping track of *consumer spending*, sales of producers, business *investment spending*, government purchases, and a variety of other flows of money among different sectors of the *economy*; also referred to as *national accounts*.

consumer spending *household* spending on goods and services from domestic and foreign *firms*.

stock a share in the ownership of a company held by a shareholder.

bond a legal document based on borrowing in the form of an IOU that pays interest.

government transfers payments by the government to individuals for which no good or service is provided in return.

disposable income income plus *government transfers* minus taxes; the total amount of *household* income available to spend on consumption and saving.

private savings *disposable income* minus *consumer spending*; disposable income that is not spent on consumption but rather goes into *financial markets*.

financial markets the banking, *stock*, and *bond* markets, which channel *private savings* and foreign lending into *investment spending*, *government borrowing*, and foreign borrowing.

government borrowing the amount of funds borrowed by the government in *financial markets* to buy goods and services.

government purchases of goods and services total purchases by federal, state, and local governments on goods and services.

exports goods and services sold to other countries.

imports goods and services purchased from other countries.

Key Terms *(continued)*

inventories stocks of goods and raw materials held to satisfy future sales.

investment spending spending on productive *physical capital,* such as machinery and construction of structures, and on changes to *inventories.*

final goods and services goods and services sold to the final, or end, user.

intermediate goods and services goods and services, bought from one *firm* by another firm, that are inputs for production of *final goods and services.*

gross domestic product (GDP) the total value of all *final goods and services* produced in the *economy* during a given period, usually a year.

aggregate spending the total flow of funds into markets for domestically produced *final goods and services*; the sum of *consumer spending, investment spending, government purchases of goods and services,* and *exports* minus *imports.*

value added (of a producer) the value of a producer's sales minus the value of input purchases.

net exports the difference between the value of *exports* and the value of *imports.* A positive value for net exports indicates that a country is a net exporter of goods and services; a negative value indicates that a country is a net importer of goods and services.

aggregate output the total quantity of *final goods and services* the *economy* produces for a given time period, usually a year. *Real GDP* is the numerical measure of aggregate output typically used by economists.

real GDP the total value of all *final goods and services* produced in the *economy* during a given year, calculated using the prices of a selected base year.

nominal GDP the value of all *final goods and services* produced in the *economy* during a given year, calculated using the prices current in the year in which the output is produced.

chained dollars method of calculating *real GDP* that splits the difference between growth rates calculated using early base years and the growth rates calculated using late base years.

GDP per capita GDP divided by the size of the population; equivalent to the average GDP per person.

aggregate price level a single number that represents the overall price level for *final goods and services* in the *economy.*

market basket a hypothetical consumption bundle of consumer purchases of goods and services, used to measure changes in overall price level.

Key Terms *(continued)*

price index a measure of the cost of purchasing a given *market basket* in a given year, where that cost is normalized so that it is equal to 100 in the selected base year; a measure of overall price level.

inflation rate the annual percentage change in a price index—typically the *consumer price index*. The inflation rate is positive when the *aggregate price level* is rising (*inflation*) and negative when the aggregate price level is falling (*deflation*).

consumer price index (CPI) a measure of prices; calculated by surveying market prices for a *market basket* intended to represent the consumption of a typical urban American family of four. The CPI is the most commonly used measure of prices in the United States.

producer price index (PPI) a measure of the cost of a typical basket of goods and services purchased by producers. Because these commodity prices respond quickly to changes in demand, the PPI is often regarded as a leading indicator of changes in the *inflation rate*.

GDP deflator a price measure for a given year that is equal to 100 times the ratio of *nominal GDP* to *real GDP* in that year.

■ AFTER YOU READ THE CHAPTER

Tips

Tip #1. It is important that you understand thoroughly the concepts underlying the more complicated circular-flow diagram presented in this chapter. The circular-flow diagram tracks the flows of money into and out of different markets and sectors in the economy. The flows into a market or sector must equal the flows out of that market or sector. Review this material and practice working with some numerical examples until you are very comfortable with the concepts and relationships.

Tip #2. A primary focus of this chapter is the topic of economic aggregation. Discussion of macroeconomic issues requires the construction and development of different measures that can be used to describe the macroeconomy. Economic aggregation addresses this issue. In this chapter, you need to fully understand the process of economic aggregation and how it relates to the measurement of economic production and the overall price level.

Tip #3. The national income accounts provide measures about the aggregate or overall economy; understanding the concept of economic aggregation is essential in the study of macroeconomics. The national income accounts are data collected and provided by the government about aggregate economic performance. The national income accounts break down the components of total spending so the behavior of households, firms, the government, and the foreign sector can be studied. The national income accounts also break down national income into wages, interest, rent, and other factor payments so factor income can be analyzed.

Tip #4. There are three methods for calculating GDP, but each method yields the same measure of GDP for a given time period. These three methods of GDP calculation are: (1) multiply the price of final goods and services produced in an economy during a given time period by the quantities produced in that time period and then sum together these products; (2) add up the total expenditures in the domestic economy on final goods and services during a given time period by the sectors of the economy, or in other words, sum the total spending done by households, businesses, government, and the rest of the world on final goods and services during a particular time period; and (3) sum the value of factor payments in the domestic economy over the given time period. Each method yields the same value of GDP for a given time period. It is important for you to thoroughly understand the concepts underlying each of these approaches.

Tip #5. The distinction between real and nominal variables is important in macroeconomics. Prices are used to measure the relative value of goods and services, but because prices do not stay constant over time in an economy it is important to measure economic variables over time using methods that correct for these price changes. Real economic variables are variables measured using prices from a designated base year. In contrast, nominal economic variables are measured with current prices and therefore are measures that do not correct for price level fluctuations. It is important to realize that if there is inflation the national income and product accounts may indicate nominal GDP is increasing, even though real GDP may be decreasing, increasing, or staying constant.

WORKED PROBLEMS

1. You are given the following information about an economy that has three firms: Wisconsin Clothing Ltd., which produces clothing; Georgia Fabric Inc., which produces the various fabrics used in clothing production; and Texas Cotton Co., which grows the cotton needed for the production of fabric. From this set of information, you are asked to determine this economy's GDP. In addition, you are asked to identify what information you would need from the table to measure GDP using the factor payments approach. Finally, you are asked to fill in the missing values in the table.

	Wisconsin Clothing Ltd.	Georgia Fabric Inc.	Texas Cotton Co.	Total factor income
Value of sales	$3,200	$2,000	$750	
Intermediate goods	A	B	0	
Wages	500	1,000	400	C
Interest payments	200	25	50	D
Rent	400	150	200	E
Profit	100	75	100	F
Total expenditures by firm	3,200	2,000	750	
Value added per firm	G	H	I	

STEP 1: Start by reviewing the information in the table and thinking about the three ways of measuring GDP. Do you have enough information to measure GDP using one of these methods?

Review the section "The Circular-Flow Diagram, Revisited and Expanded" on page 188 (Econ page 620), the section "Gross Domestic Product" on page 191 (Econ page 623), the section "Calculating GDP" on page 192 (Econ page 624), and Figure 7-1 on page 189 (Econ page 621).

There are three ways to measure GDP: (1) survey firms and add up the total value of their production of final goods and services (the value-added approach); (2) add up aggregate spending on domestically produced final goods and services in the economy (the expenditure approach); and (3) sum the total factor income earned by households from firms in the economy (the factor payments approach). Surveying the table, we could measure GDP as the value of the final good being produced: the final good is the clothing that Wisconsin Clothing Ltd. produces. We could also measure GDP using the factor payments approach, since we know the value of payments to households in the form of wages, interest payments, rent, and profits. The value-added approach would take more work, since we would need to calculate the value added at each stage of production.

STEP 2: Provide a measure of this economy's GDP.

Review the section "The Circular-Flow Diagram, Revisited and Expanded" on page 188 (Econ page 620), the section "Gross Domestic Product" on page 191 (Econ page 623), the section "Calculating GDP" on page 192 (Econ page 624), and Figure 7-1 on page 189 (Econ page 621).

The value of GDP in this economy is equal to $3,200. We can see that this is the value of sales made by Wisconsin Clothing Ltd. Alternatively, we could sum the wages in this economy ($C = \$1,900$), the interest payments ($D = \$275$), rent ($E = \$750$), and profits ($F = \$275$) to get $3,200, the value of GDP for this economy.

STEP 3: Identify what information you would need in order to measure GDP using the factor payments approach.

Review the section "The Circular-Flow Diagram, Revisited and Expanded" on page 188 (Econ page 620), the section "Gross Domestic Product" on page 191 (Econ page 623), the section "Calculating GDP" on page 192 (Econ page 624), and Figure 7-1 on page 189 (Econ page 621).

The factor payments approach to measuring GDP says that the sum of wages, interest payments, rent, and profit is equal to GDP. We would need to have the values for C, D, E, and F in order to do this calculation. These values have already been found in Step 2.

STEP 4: Fill in the missing values in the table.

Review the section "The Circular-Flow Diagram, Revisited and Expanded" on page 188 (Econ page 620), the section "Gross Domestic Product" on page 191 (Econ page 623), the section "Calculating GDP" on page 192 (Econ page 624), and Figure 7-1 on page 189 (Econ page 621).

	Wisconsin Clothing Ltd.	Georgia Fabric Inc.	Texas Cotton Co.	Total factor income
Value of sales	$3,200	$2,000	$750	
Intermediate goods	A = 2,000	B = 750	0	
Wages	500	1,000	400	C = $1,900
Interest payments	200	25	50	D = 275
Rent	400	150	200	E = 750
Profit	100	75	100	F = 275
Total expenditures by firm	3,200	2,000	750	
Value added per firm	G = 1,200	H = 1,250	I = 750	

We already know the values for C, D, E, and F from Step 2. The value of B is $750, since this is the value of the cotton that Georgia Fabric Inc. purchases from Texas Cotton Co. The value of A is $2,000, since this is the value of the fabric that Wisconsin Clothing Ltd. purchases from Georgia Fabric Inc. To find the value for I, subtract the value of intermediate goods from the value of sales at Texas Cotton Co. The value of I is thus $750. The value of H is found in the same way: it is the difference between the value of sales and the cost of the intermediate goods at Georgia Fabric Inc. The value of H is $1,250. The value of G is found similarly: it is the difference between the value of sales and the cost of the intermediate goods at Wisconsin Clothing Ltd. The value of G is $1,200. Adding G + H + I together will give us a measure of GDP using the value-added approach: GDP is equal to $3,200, which is exactly the value we found using the other two approaches.

2. You are given the following information about an economy and you are asked to calculate nominal and real GDP for 2010 and 2011 in this economy. When calculating real GDP for this economy you are asked to use 2010 prices. In addition, you are asked to calculate the growth rate in nominal GDP and real GDP during this period. Finally, you are asked to provide guidance as to which growth rate is the more accurate one to use if you are trying to ascertain how much the economy is growing.

	2010	2011
Quantity of bicycles	20	22
Price of bicycle	$100	$110
Quantity of sweaters	10	9
Price of sweater	$20	$30
Quantity of hamburgers	100	140
Price of hamburger	$2	$3

STEP 1: Calculate nominal GDP for these two years.

Review the section "Real GDP: A Measure of Aggregate Output" on page 198 (Econ page 630), the section "Calculating Real GDP" on page 198 (Econ page 630), Table 7-1 on page 198 (Econ page 630), and Table 7-2 on page 199 (Econ page 631).

Nominal GDP is found by multiplying the price of the good in the current year times the quantity of the good in the current year and then summing these products for all the goods produced in the economy. Nominal GDP in 2010 is equal to (20 bicycles)($100 per bicycle) + (10 sweaters) ($20 per sweater) + (100 hamburgers)($2 per hamburger) = $2,400. Nominal GDP in 2011 is equal to (22 bicycles)($110 per bicycle) + (9 sweaters)($30 per sweater) + (140 hamburgers)($3 per hamburger) = $3,110.

STEP 2: Calculate real GDP for these two years.

Review the section "Real GDP: A Measure of Aggregate Output" on page 198 (Econ page 630), the section "Calculating Real GDP" on page 198 (Econ page 630), Table 7-1 on page 198 (Econ page 630), and Table 7-2 on page 199 (Econ page 631).

Real GDP is found by multiplying the price of the good in the base year times the quantity of the good in the current year and then summing these products for all the goods produced in the economy. Real GDP in 2010 is equal to nominal GDP in 2010, since both measures are using prices from 2010 and quantities from 2010. Real GDP in 2011 is equal to the price of the good in 2010 times the quantity of the good in 2011. Real GDP in 2011 is thus calculated as (22 bicycles)($100 per bicycle) + (9 sweaters)($20 per sweater) + (140 hamburgers)($2 per hamburger) = $2,660.

STEP 3: Calculate the growth rate of nominal GDP and real GDP during this period.

Review the section "Real GDP: A Measure of Aggregate Output" on page 198 (Econ page 630), the section "Calculating Real GDP" on page 198 (Econ page 630), Table 7-1 on page 198 (Econ page 630), and Table 7-2 on page 199 (Econ page 631).

To find the growth rate of a variable, use the following formula: [(value of the measure in the current period – value of the measure in the previous period)/(value of the measure in the previous period)] × 100. The rate of change in nominal GDP = [(3,110 – 2,400)/2,400] × 100 = 29.58%. The rate of change in real GDP = [(2,660 – 2,400)/(2,400)] × 100 = 10.83%.

STEP 4: Now, you need to provide guidance as to which growth rate measure is the better one if you are trying to decide how much the economy is growing. You will need to explain your answer.

Review the section "Real GDP: A Measure of Aggregate Output" on page 198 (Econ page 630), the section "Calculating Real GDP" on page 198 (Econ page 630), Table 7-1 on page 198 (Econ page 630), and Table 7-2 on page 199 (Econ page 631).

Given the goal of measuring the growth in the economy, the better measure is the growth rate of real GDP. This is because nominal GDP does not distinguish whether the change in nominal GDP is due to changes in production or changes in prices. In contrast, the growth rate of real GDP removes price fluctuation by holding prices constant and then looks at what is happening to aggregate production.

3. Belgium produces only three goods: chocolate, strawberries, and waffles. The following table gives you information about production and prices for these three goods for 2010 and 2011. You have been asked to calculate real GDP for Belgium using 2010 as the base year. In addition, you have been asked to calculate the growth rate of real GDP during this period and a measure of the GDP deflator for this period.

	Quantity in 2010	Price in 2010	Quantity in 2011	Price in 2011
Units of chocolate	20	$3	30	$4
Units of strawberries	75	4	150	2
Units of waffles	120	5	110	1

STEP 1: Calculate real GDP for 2010 and 2011 using 2010 as the base year.

Review the section "Real GDP: A Measure of Aggregate Output" on page 198 (Econ page 630), the section "Calculating Real GDP" on page 198 (Econ page 630), Table 7-1 on page 198 (Econ page 630), and Table 7-2 on page 199 (Econ page 631).

Since 2010 is the base year, we know that real GDP in 2010 is the same as nominal GDP in 2010. To find this value, multiply the price of the good in 2010 times the quantity of the good, then sum these products together for all the goods produced in Belgium. Thus, real GDP in 2010 = (price of chocolate in 2010)(quantity of chocolate in 2010) + (price of strawberries in 2010) (quantity of strawberries in 2010) + (price of waffles in 2010)(quantity of waffles in 2010) = $960. Real GDP in 2011 = (price of chocolate in 2010)(quantity of chocolate in 2011) + (price of strawberries in 2010)(quantity of strawberries in 2011) + (price of waffles in 2010)(quantity of waffles in 2011) = $1,240.

STEP 2: Calculate the growth rate of real GDP during this period of time.

Review the section "Real GDP: A Measure of Aggregate Output" on page 198 (Econ page 630), the section "Calculating Real GDP" on page 198 (Econ page 630), Table 7-1 on page 198 (Econ page 630), and Table 7-2 on page 199 (Econ page 631).

The growth rate of real GDP during this period = [(real GDP in 2011 – real GDP in 2010)/(real GDP in 2010)] × 100 = 29.17%.

STEP 3: Calculate the value of the GDP deflator for this period.

Review the section "Other Price Measures" on page 204 (Econ page 636).

The GDP deflator is equal to [(real GDP)/(nominal GDP)] × 100. With 2010, as the base year, this means that in 2010 real GDP is equivalent to nominal GDP and therefore the GDP deflator for 2010 is equal to 100. In 2011, we already know from Step 1 that real GDP is equal to $1,240. To calculate nominal GDP for 2011, multiply the quantities from 2011 by the prices from 2011: thus, nominal GDP in 2011 is equal to $530. Using this information, we can calculate the GDP deflator for 2011 as ($1,240/$530) × 100 = 2.34.

4. In Belgium the market basket is always equal to 4 units of chocolates, 5 units of strawberries, and 2 waffles. Using the information given in Worked Problem 3, calculate the consumer price index in Belgium for 2010 and 2011 using 2010 as your base year. Use this information to calculate the consumer price index for both years and then find the rate of inflation during this period. You are also asked to provide an interpretation of the inflation rate you calculate.

STEP 1: This first step in calculating the consumer price index is to calculate the cost of the market basket for each year.

Review the section "Price Indexes and the Aggregate Price Level" on page 202 (Econ page 634), the section "Market Baskets and Price Indexes" on page 202 (Econ page 634), the section "The Consumer Price Index" on page 203 (Econ page 635), and Table 7-3 on page 202 (Econ page 634).

The cost of the market basket is equal to the sum of the product of the price of each good in the current year times the market basket quantity of each good. The cost of the market basket in 2010 is equal to (price of chocolates in 2010)(4 units of chocolate)

+ (price of strawberries in 2010)(5 units of strawberries) + (price of waffles in 2010)(2 waffles) = $42. The cost of the market basket in 2011 is equal to (price of chocolates in 2011)(4 units of chocolate) + (price of strawberries in 2011)(5 units of strawberries) + (price of waffles in 2011)(2 waffles) = $28.

STEP 2: Now, use the cost of the market baskets you calculated in Step 1 to create the consumer price index.

Review the section "Price Indexes and the Aggregate Price Level" on page 202 (Econ page 634), the section "Market Baskets and Price Indexes" on page 202 (Econ page 634), the section "The Consumer Price Index" on page 203 (Econ page 635), and Table 7-3 on page 202 (Econ page 634).

The consumer price index in any year is calculated as [(cost of the market basket in the current year)/(cost of the market basket in the base year)] × 100. Since 2010 is the base year, the cost of the market basket in the current year is equal to the cost of the market basket in the base year: the consumer price index for 2010 has a value of 100. The consumer price index for 2011 is equal to ($28/$42) × 100 = 67.

STEP 3: Use the consumer price index you calculated in Step 2 to find the rate of inflation between 2010 and 2011. Provide an interpretation of the meaning of the inflation rate you calculate.

Review the section "Price Indexes and the Aggregate Price Level" on page 202 (Econ page 634), the section "Market Baskets and Price Indexes" on page 202 (Econ page 634), the section "The Consumer Price Index" on page 203 (Econ page 635), and Table 7-3 on page 202 (Econ page 634).

The inflation rate is calculated as [(price index in 2011 − price index in 2010)/(price index in 2010)] × 100 = −33%. The negative percentage tells us that using the consumer price index to measure the inflation rate indicates that the aggregate price level has fallen between 2010 and 2011 by 33%.

Problems and Exercises

1. You are given the following information about Macronesia. During 2011, the government of Macronesia spent $200 million on goods and services as well as $20 million on transfer payments, while collecting $150 million in taxes. During 2011, households paid $150 million in taxes, purchased goods and services worth $400 million, and received $800 million in the form of wages, dividends, interest, and rent. Firms in 2011 had $100 million of investment spending, and they borrowed or had stock issues of $100 million from the financial markets. In 2011, exports to this economy equaled $150 million, while imports to this economy equaled $50 million. In the financial markets, there was foreign borrowing of $120 million and foreign lending of $20 million.

   a. Sketch a circular-flow diagram of Macronesia's economy showing the quantitative flows.

    b. What is GDP in 2011 in Macronesia?

    c. What is the value of disposable income in Macronesia in 2011?

    d. What is the value of household saving in Macronesia in 2011?

    e. Is the government running a balanced budget during 2011? Explain your answer.

    f. Compute the flows of money into the financial markets and the flows of money out of the financial markets. Are they equal?

    g. Compute the flows of money into the market for goods and services and the flows of money out of the market for goods and services. Are they equal?

    h. Compute the flows of money into the factor markets and the flows of money out of the factor markets. Are they equal?

2. For the following list decide how the item affects the calculation of GDP for Macro States in 2011.

    a. A new house is constructed in Macro States during 2011.

    b. Bruce sells his house in Macro States without the help of a realtor in January 2011.

    c. The government purchases new textbooks for the schools of Macro States during 2011.

    d. Macro States sells 100,000 pounds of beet to Neverlandia during 2011.

e. Judy tutors Ellen's children in exchange for Ellen's driving the children's carpool three days a week throughout 2011.

f. A candlemaker produces 500 candles during 2011 but only sells 200 candles during 2011; the other 300 candles are added to the candlemaker's inventories.

3. Suppose you are told that Finlandia produces three goods: tennis shoes, basketballs, and lawn mowers. The following table provides information about the prices and output for these three goods for the years 2010, 2011, and 2012.

Year	Price of tennis shoes	Quantities of tennis shoes	Price of basketballs	Quantities of basketballs	Price of lawn mowers	Quantities of lawn mowers
2010	$50	100	$10	200	$100	10
2011	52	108	10	205	100	12
2012	54	115	10	212	110	12

a. Using the previous information, fill in the following table.

Year	Nominal GDP
2010	
2011	
2012	

b. What was the percentage change in nominal GDP from 2010 to 2011?

c. What was the percentage change in nominal GDP from 2011 to 2012?

d. Using 2010 as the base year, fill in the following table.

Year	Real GDP
2010	
2011	
2012	

e. What was the percentage change in real GDP from 2010 to 2011?

f. What was the percentage change in real GDP from 2011 to 2012?

g. Using 2010 as the base year, fill in the following table.

Year	GDP deflator
2010	
2011	
2012	

4. In Macro Space, the price index is based upon a market basket consisting of 10 apples, 2 pizzas, and 5 ice cream cones. You are given prices for these three items for 2010, 2011, and 2012 in the following table.

Year	Price of apples	Price of pizzas	Price of ice cream cones
2010	$0.50	$4.00	$1.00
2011	0.52	3.85	1.10
2012	0.49	3.90	1.30

a. Fill in the following table using year 2010 as your base year.

Year	Cost of market basket	Price index value
2010		
2011		
2012		

b. Using the information you computed in part (a), what was the rate of inflation between 2010 and 2011?

c. Using the information you computed in part (a), what was the rate of inflation between 2011 and 2012?

d. Fill in the following table using year 2011 as your base year.

Year	Cost of market basket	Price index value
2010		
2011		
2012		

e. Using the information you computed in part (d), what was the rate of inflation between 2010 and 2011?

f. Using the information you computed in part (d), what was the rate of inflation between 2011 and 2012?

g. Compare your answers in parts (b) and (c) to your answers in parts (e) and (f).

5. The following diagram provides a circular-flow diagram for the economy of Littleville.

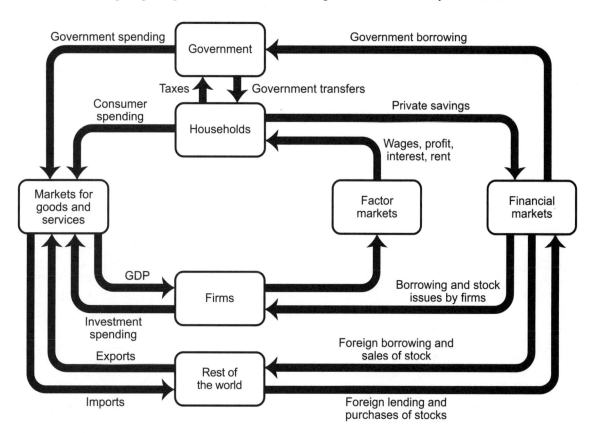

You are also told the following about the economy of Littleville:

Consumer spending (C) = $200 million
Investment spending (I) = $50 million
Spending on exports (X) = $20 million
Wages + profit + interest + rent = $320 million
Government borrowing = $60 million
Taxes = $20 million
Transfers = $10 million

a. What is the GDP in Littleville? Explain how you found this value given the preceding information.

b. What is the value of government spending (G) in Littleville's economy? Explain how you found this value.

c. What is the value of imports in Littleville's economy? Explain how you found this value.

d. What is the value of private savings in Littleville's economy? Explain how you found this value.

e. What is the level of firm borrowing and stock issues in this economy? Explain how you found this value.

f. Is the rest of the world a net borrower or a net lender, given the above information and your calculations in parts (a) through (e)? Explain your answer.

6. You are given the following information about the small economy of Hyattville.

Hyattville's economy is composed of three firms: Hyattville Forest, Inc., which harvests trees, which are used by Hyattville Lumber Products, Inc., to manufacture various lumber products, which are used by Hyattville Houses, Inc., to produce houses. Assume lumber is the only raw material used to produce the houses in Hyattville.

	Hyattville Forest, Inc.	Hyattville Lumber Products, Inc.	Hyattville Houses, Inc.	Total Factor Income
Value of sales	$15,000	A	$100,000	
Intermediate goods	B	$15,000	40,000	
Wages	6,000	15,000	35,000	G
Interest payments	1,000	3,000	6,000	H
Rent	3,000	D	3,000	I
Profit	5,000	4,000	F	J
Total expenditures by firm	15,000	40,000	100,000	
Value added per firm	C	E	60,000	

a. Fill in the missing entries [A–J] in the table recalling that GDP can be calculated in three different ways: (1) by measuring GDP as the value of the production of final goods and services in an economy as measured by the value added by each firm; (2) by measuring GDP as the sum of aggregate spending on domestically produced final goods and services in an economy; and (3) by measuring GDP as the sum of factor income earned from firms in the economy.

b. Using the value added approach, what is the value of GDP? Explain how you found this answer using the table as a reference.

c. Using the factor income approach, what is the value of GDP? Explain how you found this answer using the table as a reference.

d. Using the aggregate spending on domestically produced final goods and services approach, what is the value of GDP? Explain how you found this answer using the table as a reference.

■ BEFORE YOU TAKE THE TEST

Chapter Review Questions

1. Which of the following statements is true?
   a. In the circular flow diagram of the economy, the flow of money into each market or sector is not necessarily equal to the flow of money coming out of each market or sector.
   b. GDP in the United States includes income earned by American citizens living in foreign countries during a given time period.
   c. GNP in the United States measures the value of final goods and services produced within U.S. borders during a given time period.
   d. None of the above statements is true.

2. Households receive income from
   a. wages they earn from selling their labor.
   b. their indirect ownership of the physical capital used by firms.
   c. interest earned from bonds, dividends earned from stock ownership, and rent earned when they sell the use of their land to firms.
   d. All of the above are ways households earn income.

3. After the payment of taxes to the government, household income is referred to as
   a. transfer income.
   b. gross income.
   c. net income.
   d. disposable income.

4. Households, in the circular-flow diagram of the economy, can use their income to
   a. pay taxes, purchase goods and services, and engage in private saving.
   b. pay taxes and purchase goods and services only.
   c. purchase factors of production, pay taxes, or purchase goods and services.
   d. purchase factors of production, pay taxes, or engage in private saving.

5. Government raises funds through
   a. taxation and by borrowing in financial markets.
   b. taxation, purchases of goods and services, and by borrowing in financial markets.
   c. taxation, purchases of goods and services, and revenues received for intermediate goods produced by the government.
   d. taxation and transfer payments.

6. Suppose Country A sells $100 million worth of goods and services to Country B. Country B sells $50 million worth of goods and services to Country A. These are the only two countries in Macro World. Then, net exports in Country
   a. B equal –$50 million.
   b. A equal $150 million.
   c. A equal $150 million.
   d. B equal $50 million.

7. Investment spending includes
   a. expenditures on new residential housing.
   b. expenditures on new inventories by businesses.
   c. expenditures by businesses on productive physical capital.
   d. Answers (a), (b), and (c) are included in investment spending.

Use the information and the following table to answer the next three questions. The table represents data about an economy's performance during a year. Suppose in the economy represented in the table there are only three firms: American Racquet Co., which produces tennis racquets; American Metal Co., which produces the various metals that go into racquet production; and American Ore Co., which mines the ores needed for the manufacture of the metal. This economy produces 100 racquets that sell for $50 each.

	American Racquet Co.	American Metal Co.	American Ore Co.	Total factor income
Value of sales	$5,000	$3,000	$500	
Intermediate goods	A	B		
Wages	2,000	1,000	100	C
Interest payments	100	50	20	D
Rent	500	100	50	E
Profit	200	750	130	F
Total expenditures by firm	5,800	2,400	300	
Value added per firm	G	H	I	

8. GDP for this hypothetical economy is equal to
   a. $5,000 or the value of sales for American Racquet Co.
   b. $8,500 or the sum of the value added for the three firms.
   c. $3,500 or the value of the intermediate goods used by the American Racquet Co.
   d. $980 or the sum of the profits for the three firms.

9. GDP can be measured using different methods. If you were using the factor payments approach, which entries would you combine to get a measure of GDP?
   a. G, H and I
   b. A and B
   c. A, B, C, and D
   d. C, D, E, and F

10. GDP can be measured using the value added method. Using this method, which of the following values are correct for the missing entries in the table?
   a. A = $3,000, B = $3,000, G = $2,000, H = $0, I = $500
   b. A = $3,000, B = $500, G = $2,000, H = $2,500, I = $500
   c. A = $3,000, B = $3,000, G = $0, H = $4,500, I = $500
   d. A = $3,000, B = $500, G = $0, H = $4,500, I = $500

11. Double counting is
   a. the inclusion of the value of goods and services more than once when calculating GDP.
   b. the failure to include the value of intermediate goods in the final calculation of an economy's GDP.
   c. a process that artificially lowers the value of GDP.
   d. avoided if we do not use the value added method in calculating GDP.

Use the information in the following table to answer the next three questions.

	Price in 2011	Price in 2012
Oranges	$0.50	$0.40
Apples	0.25	0.40
Bananas	0.40	0.50

Suppose 2011 is the base year and the market basket for purposes of constructing a price index consists of 200 oranges, 100 apples, and 100 bananas.

12. What is the value of the price index in 2011?
   a. 1.15
   b. 100
   c. 165
   d. 190

13. What is the value of the price index in 2012, using 2011 as the base year?
   a. 0.97
   b. 1
   c. 100
   d. 103

14. What is the rate of inflation between 2011 and 2012 in this economy?
   a. 0%
   b. 3%
   c. 103%
   d. 67%, since two of the three prices increased between 2011 and 2012

15. In Macroland the GDP deflator for 2012 is 105, with 2011 the base year. Real GDP in 2012 equals $210 billion; therefore, nominal GDP in 2012 equals _____, while nominal GDP in 2011 equals _____.
   a. $220.5 billion; $200 billion
   b. $220.5 billion; $210 billion
   c. $200 billion; $210 billion
   d. $200 billion; $220.5 billion

16. Which of the following statements is true?

     I. In the circular-flow diagram, the flows into each market or sector must equal the outflow coming from that market or sector.

     II. The flow of money into the household sector includes the value of all the final goods and services that households purchase.

     III. The flow of money into the household sector does not include the value of government transfers.

    a. Statement I is true.

    b. Statements I and II are true.

    c. Statements I, II, and III are true.

    d. Statements I and III are true.

    e. Statements II and III are true.

17. From a household's perspective, a bond represents

    a. the indirect ownership of physical capital used by firms.

    b. a loan to the firm that will provide interest to the household.

18. From a household's perspective, a share of stock represents

    a. the indirect ownership of physical capital used by firms.

    b. a loan to the firm that will provide interest to the household.

19. When households receive income, they can pay taxes,

    a. pay transfer payments, purchase goods and services, and engage in private saving.

    b. receive transfer payments, purchase goods and services, and engage in private saving.

    c. purchase goods and services, and engage in private saving.

    d. and they can receive transfer payments.

20. Disposable income is equal to total income

    a. minus taxes.

    b. minus transfer payments.

    c. and transfer payments.

    d. minus taxes and plus government transfers.

21. The outflow of funds from the financial markets include

    a. funds for private savings to households.

    b. funds to finance government purchases of goods and services.

    c. funds to foreign borrowers.

    d. Answers (a), (b), and (c) are all correct.

    e. Answers (b) and (c) are both correct.

22. When inventories increase, this leads to a(n)
    a. increase in investment spending and an increase in GDP for the time period.
    b. increase in investment spending but no change in GDP since no one purchased the inventory items.
    c. decrease in investment spending and no change in GDP since no one purchased the inventory items.
    d. decrease in consumption spending since households could have bought these items, but instead the items were held as inventory.

23. $C + I + G + X - IM$ is
    a. equal to an economy's GDP for a given period of time.
    b. a measure of the overall market value of the goods and services the economy produces during a given period of time.
    c. the value of all final goods and services produced in an economy during a given time period.
    d. Answers (a), (b), and (c) are all correct.
    e. Answers (a) and (c) are both correct.
    f. Answers (a) and (b) are both correct.

24. Which of the following is NOT included in the calculation of GDP?
    a. Joey's Electronics manufactures CD players that individuals install in cars that do not have CD players.
    b. Susy's Leather Goods manufactures leather pieces that are sold to manufacturers that produce handbags and wallets from these leather pieces.
    c. Harry's Ice Cream Shoppe sells ice cream cones at the beach.
    d. Monica's Hair Salon sells haircuts and manicures to the residents of Marco Island.

25. To avoid double counting when computing GDP for an economy, it is important to
    a. count the total value of each producer's sales in an economy.
    b. only count each producer's value added in the calculation.
    c. include the cost of all inputs at each stage of production.
    d. exclude the cost of all inputs at each stage of production.

26. Income spent on imported goods
    a. represents income that has "leaked" across national borders.
    b. must be subtracted from spending data in order to calculate an accurate value for domestic production.
    c. is income that is not spent on domestically produced goods and services.
    d. Answers (a), (b), and (c) are all correct.

27. The difference between spending on inputs and spending on investment is
    a. spending on inputs is not included in the calculation of GDP.
    b. spending on investment goods is included in the calculation of GDP.
    c. inputs that are purchased by businesses are used up while capital goods that are purchased with business investment are not used up.
    d. Answers (a), (b), and (c) are all correct.
    e. Answers (a) and (c) are both correct.
    f. Answers (b) and (c) are both correct.

Use the information in the following table to answer the next three questions.

Smallville produces tractors and pizzas. You are given the following information about Smallville's production of these two goods and their prices for three years.

	Year 2010	Year 2011	Year 2012
Quantity of tractors	5	5	5
Price of tractors	$10,000	$12,000	$15,000
Quantity of pizzas	100	80	100
Price of pizzas	$10	$20	$20

28. Nominal GDP in 2011
   a. is greater than nominal GDP in 2010.
   b. is less than nominal GDP in 2012.
   c cannot be calculated until a base year is specified.
   d. Answers (a) and (b) are both correct.

29. Suppose the base year is 2010. Real GDP in 2011 using 2010 as the base year
   a. is greater than nominal GDP in 2011.
   b. is less than nominal GDP in 2011.
   c. is equal to nominal GDP in 2011.
   d. may be greater than, less than, or equal to nominal GDP in 2011.

30. Using 2011 as the base year, real GDP is greatest in
   a. 2010.
   b. 2011.
   c. 2012.
   d. 2010 and 2012 since real GDP using 2011 as the base year is the same for these two years.

Answer the next two questions based on the following information.

Littleville is a small economy whose current GDP in 2011 is $10,000 and whose population is 10 people.

31. GDP per capita in Littleville in 2011 is
   a. $10,000 per person.
   b. $1,000 per person.
   c. $100 per person.
   d. $100,000 per person.

32. Suppose GDP in Littleville in 2012 increases to $20,000 while the population increases by 50%. Then, GDP per capita in Littleville in 2012
   a. increases, since the percentage change in GDP is greater than the percentage change in population.
   b. equals approximately $1,333 per person.
   c. decreases due to the very large percentage increase in population.
   d. Answers (a) and (b) are correct.

■ ANSWER KEY

Answers to Problems and Exercises

1. a.

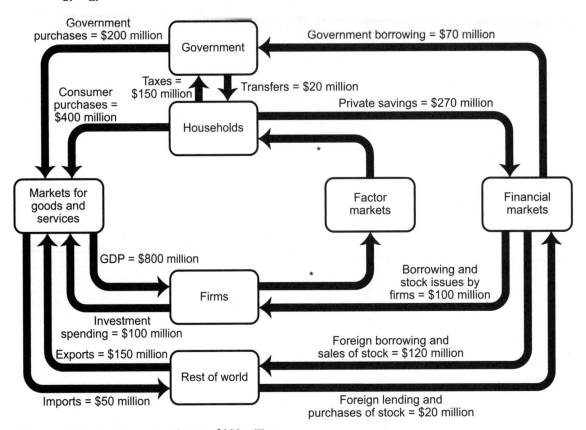

*Wages, dividends, interest, and rent = $800 million

b. The value of GDP in 2009 in Macronesia is $800 million: this is equivalent to the sum of factor payments to households in the form of wages, dividends, interest, and rent. It is also equivalent to the sum of consumer spending, government spending, investment spending, and net exports.

c. Disposable income is income received by households less taxes plus transfers. In this problem, disposable income equals $670 million.

d. Household saving equals household income minus taxes plus transfers minus consumption spending, or $270 million. Household saving is the amount households have left of their income once they pay their taxes and make their consumer purchases.

e. No. The government spends $200 million, and its net tax collections equal $130 million. To finance this level of spending without a change in taxes, the government will need to borrow $70 million from the financial markets.

f. The flow of money into the financial markets must equal the flow of money out of the financial markets in order for these markets to be in equilibrium. Borrowing in the financial markets equals the sum of government borrowing ($70 million) plus firm borrowing ($100 million) plus foreign borrowing ($120 million); lending in the financial market is equal to the sum of household saving ($270 million) plus foreign lending ($20 million).

g. The flow of money into the market for goods and services must equal the flow of money out of the market for goods and services. In this case, these flows equal $800 million. The flow of money into the market for goods and services includes government spending of $200 million, household purchases of $400 million, investment spending by firms of $100 million, and net exports of $100 million for a total of $800 million. The flow of money out of the market for goods and services equals GDP or the sum of wages, dividends, interest, and rent ($800 million).

h. The flow of money into the factor markets must equal the flow of money out of the factor markets. In this problem, these flows equal $800 million. The flow of money into the factor markets is equal to GDP ($800 million), while the flow of money out of the factor markets must equal the sum of wages, dividends, interest, and rent ($800 million).

2. **a.** New home construction is included in GDP as investment spending.

b. This is not included in GDP, since the value of the house was counted in GDP the year the house was built.

c. Textbook purchases by the government are included in GDP as government spending.

d. Macro States exports beef and the value of these exports are included in the GDP of Macro States.

e. Although there is production occurring, Ellen and Judy do not exchange money, therefore, this transaction does not get included in GDP.

f. The value of 200 candles sold is included in GDP as part of consumption. The increase in inventory of 300 candles is included in GDP as part of investment, since it represents new production in the economy of Macro States.

3. **a.**

Year	Nominal GDP
2010	$8,000
2011	8,866
2012	9,650

To calculate nominal GDP, multiply the price of each good times the quantity produced of that good and then sum together these products. For example, nominal GDP in 2010 = (price of tennis shoes)(quantity of tennis shoes) + (price of basketballs)(quantity of basketballs) + (price of lawn mowers)(quantity of lawn mowers) = $8,000.

b. The percentage change in nominal GDP from 2010 to 2011 was 10.83%: [(8,866 − 8,000)/8,000] × 10 × 0 = 10.83%.

c. The percentage change in nominal GDP from 2011 to 2012 was 8.84%: [(9,650 − 8,866)/8,866]100 = 8.84%.

d.

Year	Real GDP
2010	$8,000
2011	8,650
2012	9,070

To calculate real GDP, multiply the price of each good in the base year (2010) times the quantity produced of that good in a given year and then sum together these products. The value of real GDP will equal nominal GDP in the base year. In 2011, real GDP can be calculated as the following sum: ($50 per pair of tennis shoes)(108 pairs) + ($10 per basketball)(205 basketballs) + ($100 per lawn mower)(12 lawn mowers).

e. The percentage change in real GDP from 2010 to 2011 was 8.13%: [(8,650 − 8,000)/8,000] × 100.

f. The percentage change in real GDP from 2011 to 2012 was 4.86%: [(9,070 − 8,650)/8,650] × 100.

g.

Year	GDP deflator
2010	(8,000/8,000) × 100 = 100
2011	(8,866/8,650) × 100 = 102.50
2012	(9,650/9070) × 100 = 106.39

4. a.

Year	Cost of market basket	Price index value
2010	(10)(0.5) + (2)(4) + (5)(1) = $18	(18/18) × 100 = 100
2011	(10)(0.52) + (2)(3.85) + (5)(1.1) = $18.4	(18.4/18) × 100 = 102.22
2012	(10)(0.40) + (2)(3.9) + (5)(1.3) = $19.2	(19.2/18) × 100 = 106.67

b. The rate of inflation between 2010 and 2011 was 2.22%: [(102.22 − 100)/100] × 100 = 2.22%.

c. The rate of inflation between 2011 and 2012 was 4.35%: [(106.67 − 102.22)/102.22] × 100 = 4.35%.

d.

Year	Cost of market basket	Price index value
2010	(10)(0.5) + (2)(4) + (5)(1) = $18	(18/18.4) × 100 = 97.83
2011	(10)(0.52) + (2)(3.85) + (5)(1.1) = 18.4	(18.4/18.4) × 100 = 100
2012	(10)(0.40) + (2)(3.9) + (5)(1.3) = $19.2	(19.2/18.4) × 100 = 104.35

e. The rate of inflation between 2010 and 2011 was 2.22%: [(100 − 97.83)/97.83] × 100 = 2.22%.

f. The rate of inflation between 2011 and 2012 was 4.35%: [(104.35 − 100)/100] × 100 − 4.35%.

g. Answers (b) and (c) are the same as answers (e) and (f). This is not surprising since the choice of a base year will generate different values for the price index, but the rate of change in prices between years should be equivalent no matter what year is chosen as the base year.

5. a. GDP in Littleville is equal to $320 million and can be found by recognizing that GDP can be expressed in two ways given the above circular-flow diagram: (1) GDP is the sum of all the spending in Littleville's economy or *GDP = C + I + G + X − IM*; and (2) GDP is the sum of the value of factor payments in the economy or GDP = wages + profit + interest + rents. You are given the value of these factor payments in the above information.

b. To find government spending (*G*), we can focus on the government sector of the economy and recognize that the flow of funds into that sector must equal the flow of funds out of that sector. This idea can be expressed in equation form as Government borrowing + taxes = government spending + transfer payments. From the given information we know government borrowing, taxes, and transfers. Thus, $60 million + $20 million = G + $10 million or G = $70 million.

c. The value of imports (*IM*) in Littleville's economy is $20 million. To find this value, first recognize that $GDP = C + I + G + X - IM$. We know the value of GDP from answer (a), as well as the values of *C*, *I*, and *X* from the given information. In addition, answer (b) generated the value for *G*. So, $320 million = $200 million + $50 million + $70 million + $20 million − *IM* or *IM* = $20 million.

d. To find the value of private savings, remember that the inflow of funds into the household sector must equal the outflow of funds from this sector. Households receive funds from their selling of factors of production, and these funds are equal to the sum of wages, profit, interest, and rent or $320 million in this example. In addition, households receive funds from the government in the form of transfer payments; in this example, transfer payments are equal to $10 million. So, the total amount of funds flowing into the household sector is equal to $330 million. The flow of funds out of the household sector is equal to the sum of consumer spending, taxes, and private saving. Since consumer spending and taxes are given in the information ($220 million), this enables us to calculate private savings as $330 million − $220 million or private savings = $110 million.

e. Recall that the flow of funds into the firm sector must equal the flow of funds out of the firm sector, or GDP + (Borrowing and stock issues by firms) = (sum of wages, profits, interest, and rent) + investment spending. Since GDP is equal to the sum of wages, profits, interest, and rent, this implies that borrowing and stock issues by firms must equal investment spending, or $50 million.

f. To determine whether or not the rest of the world is a net borrower or a net lender, one needs to focus on the relationship between the flow of funds into and out of the rest of the world sector. The flow of funds into the rest of the world is equal to the sum of imports and foreign borrowing and sales of stock, while the flow of funds out of the rest of the world is equal to the sum of exports and foreign lending and purchases of stock. Or, $20 million + foreign borrowing and sales of stock = $20 million + foreign lending and purchases of stocks. This can be rewritten as $0 million = foreign lending and purchases of stocks − foreign borrowing and sales of stocks. This implies that the rest of the world in this example is neither a net lender nor a net borrower.

6.   a.

	Hyattville Forest, Inc.	Hyattville Lumber Products, Inc.	Hyattville Houses, Inc.	Total factor income
Value of sales	$15,000	$40,000	$100,000	
Intermediate goods	0	15,000	40,000	
Wages	6,000	15,000	35,000	$56,000
Interest payments	1,000	3,000	6,000	10,000
Rent	3,000	3,000	3,000	9,000
Profit	5,000	4,000	16,000	25,000
Total expenditures by firm	15,000	40,000	100,000	
Value added per firm	15,000	25,000	60,000	

b. To find GDP using the value added approach requires summing the horizontal entries that are found in the row labeled "Value added per firm" in the above table. From your answer in part (a), the sum of these entries is equal to $15,000 + $25,000 + $60,000, or $100,000.

c. To find GDP using the factor income approach requires first summing horizontally the entries of the amount of wages paid, the amount of interest payments, the amount of rent, and the amount of profit, (which corresponds to finding the values of *G*, *H*, *I*, and *J* in the table. Then, once these amounts have been calculated, these four values must be summed to find the total factor income in the economy; thus, from part (a) of this question we have $56,000 (the amount of total wages paid in the economy) + $10,000 (the total amount of interest payments in the economy) + $9,000 (the total amount of rent payments in this economy) + $25,000 (the total amount of profits in this economy) for a total of $100,000 (GDP using the factor payments approach).

d. To find GDP using the aggregate spending on domestically produced final goods and services approach, first recognize that Hyattville only produces one type of final good or service: houses. The value of the houses produced in Hyattville is equal to $100,000.

Answers to Chapter Review Questions

1. **Answer d.** An underlying principle of the circular-flow diagram is that the flow of money into a market or sector must equal the flow of money out of that market or sector. GDP measures the value of final production in an economy during a given time period, while GNP measures the value of final production in a country by its citizens no matter where they are located.

2. **Answer d.** All three answers describe different ways households can earn income through their selling of factors of production—land, labor, and capital—to businesses.

3. **Answer d.** By definition, household income less taxes is referred to as disposable income, since this is the income that households are left to "dispose of" once they have paid their tax obligations. Households use this disposable income to make purchases of goods and services and for private saving.

4. **Answer a.** Households use their income to pay taxes, to purchase goods and services, and to accumulate private saving.

5. **Answer a.** The sources of funding for the government are tax revenue and the funds the government borrows in the financial markets. Transfer payments are not a source of revenue for the government, since they represent a redistribution of purchasing power from one individual to another individual in the economy. The government purchases goods and services but does not actually manufacture intermediate or final goods.

6. **Answer a.** Net exports are defined as exports minus imports. Country A's net exports equal ($100 million – $50 million) or $50 million. Country B's net exports equal ($50 million – $100 million) or –$50 million.

7. **Answer d.** Investment spending, by definition, is the sum of expenditure on productive physical capital, inventories, and new residential housing.

8. **Answer a.** Since GDP is equal to the value of all final goods and services produced in an economy during a given time period, GDP for this economy can be found by multiplying the number of racquets produced during the given time period times their price. This yields $5,000. Alternatively, one could add up the total payments to factors of production: wages, interest payments, rent, and profit sum to $5,000.

9. **Answer d.** To get the value of GDP using the factor payments approach, you would need to add up the sum of factor payments. This would be the sum of wages, interest payments, rent, and profit, or cells *C*, *D*, *E*, and *F*.

10. **Answer b.** The cost of intermediate goods in entry *A* is equal to the value of metal sales from American Metal Co., or $3,000. The cost of intermediate goods in entry *B* is equal to the value of ore sales from American Ore Co., or $500. The value added by American

Racquet Co., or entry G, is equal to the value of sales by this company minus the value of intermediate goods used by this company ($5,000 – $3,000, or $2,000). The value added by American Metal Co., or entry H, is equal to the value of sales by this company minus the value of intermediate goods used by this company ($3,000 – $500, or $2,500); the value added by American Ore Co., or entry I, is equal to the value of sales by this company minus the value of intermediate goods used by this company ($500 – $0 or $500).

11. **Answer a.** Double counting is when you count the production of an item more than once when calculating the value of GDP. This can arise because the good is used as an intermediate good in the production of a final good. For this reason, intermediate goods are not counted as part of GDP because this would result in an overstatement of the level of production that has occurred in an economy.

12. **Answer b.** The value of a price index in the base year is always equal to 100. To calculate a price index in general, you need to calculate the ratio of the cost of the market basket in the current year to the cost of the market basket in the base year and then multiply this ratio by 100. In this question, the ratio is equal to 1 since the cost of the two market baskets is the same and thus the price index equals 100.

13. **Answer d.** Calculate the value of the market basket in the base year: (200 oranges)($0.5/orange) + (100 apples)($0.25/apple) + (100 bananas)($0.4/banana) = 165. Calculate the value of the market basket in 2009: (200 oranges)($0.4/orange) + (100 apples)($0.4/apple) + (100 bananas)($0.5/banana) = 170. Then put these two values into the following formula:

Price index = [(cost of market basket in current year)/(cost of market basket in base year)] × 100

Price index = [(170)/(165)] × 100 = 103

Note that the market basket stays fixed when calculating a price index.

14. **Answer b.** To calculate the inflation rate between two time periods, you need the price index for each time period. Then, use the following formula:

Inflation rate = [(price index in period 2 – price index in period 1)/(price index in period 1)] × 100

In this case,

Inflation rate = [(103 – 100)/100] × 100 = 3%

15. **Answer a.** To answer this question, it is helpful to first organize the information you are given in a table.

Year	GDP Deflator	Nominal GDP	Real GDP
2011	100		
2012	105		$210 billion

We know that in the base year nominal GDP equals real GDP, but we still need to calculate this value. We can calculate this value using the formula:

Price index in 2012 = [(real GDP in 2012)/(real GDP in base year)] × 100

Or, in this case

105 = [($210 billion)/(real GDP in base year)] × 100

or

Real GDP in base year = $200 billion

To calculate nominal GDP in 2012, we use the formula for the GDP deflator:

Price index in 2012 = [(nominal GDP in 2012)/(real GDP in 2012)] × 100

Rearranging the formula we have

Real GDP in 2012 = [(nominal GDP in 2012)/(price index in 2012)] × 100

or

$210 billion = [(nominal GDP in 2012)/105] × 100

or

Nominal GDP in 2012 = $220.5 billion

Our completed table is

Year	GDP Deflator	Nominal GDP	Real GDP
2011	100	$200 billion	$200 billion
2012	105	220.5 billion	210 billion

16. **Answer a.** The circular-flow diagram is based upon the principle that all the flows into each sector or market must equal all the outflows out of each sector or market. The flow of funds into the household sector includes the value of wages, interest, rent, and profit. In addition, the flow of funds into the household sector includes the value of government transfer payments. The value of all the final goods and services that households purchase is an outflow from the household sector.

17. **Answer b.** A bond from a household's perspective represents an IOU that the household has received from a firm. The firm borrows money from the household and provides the household with a bond, which symbolizes the money that the firm owes to the household. The household will receive interest from the firm as long as they hold the bond.

18. **Answer a.** A share of stock allows the firm to acquire funds to operate their business by selling a fractional ownership of the business to households. When a household purchases a share of stock, it provides funds to the business in exchange for part ownership in the business. This stock ownership therefore represents the household's indirect ownership of the physical capital that the firm uses since the firm uses the funds it acquires through the sale of stock to acquire the use of physical capital.

19. **Answer b.** Households use their income to pay taxes, purchase goods and services, and set aside funds as private savings. In addition, some households receive transfer payments from the government.

20. **Answer d.** Disposable income is equal to the income households have left over after paying taxes and receiving government transfers.

21. **Answer e.** The outflow of funds from the financial market to households is represented by the loans that households undertake. The flow of private savings is a flow of funds into the financial market and not an outflow of funds from this market. The financial market provides funds to the government through government borrowing to enable the government to purchase more goods and services than is possible from the government's tax revenue. The financial market also lends funds to foreign borrowers.

22. **Answer a.** When a firm increases its inventories, this is a form of investment spending and therefore this increase in inventories increases both investment spending and GDP for the economy during this time period.

23. **Answer d.** The sum of consumer spending, investment spending, government spending, and net exports is equal to GDP. GDP provides a measure of the market value of the goods and services produced in an economy: this is the value of all final goods and services produced in the economy.

24. **Answer b.** Answers (a), (c), and (d) are all included in GDP, since they each represent a final good or service. Answer (b) is not included in GDP, since the leather pieces are intermediate goods that are used to manufacture the final goods—handbags and wallets—that are included in GDP.

25. **Answer b.** To avoid double counting when calculating GDP, it is important to only count each producer's value added to GDP; alternatively, we can think about avoiding the double counting problem by subtracting out the cost of inputs—the intermediate goods—at each stage of production in order to arrive at the value added at that stage. Then, if the value added at each stage is summed, this will yield the economy's GDP without any double counting.

26. **Answer d.** Income spent on imported goods is by definition income that is not being spent on domestically produced goods and services; this income is leaking out of the domestic economy, since it is being spent in a foreign economy. In order to accurately calculate domestic production from spending data, it is necessary to subtract all the spending that occurs on foreign-produced final goods and services.

27. **Answer d.** All of these answers are correct. Spending on inputs represents expenditure by firms on resources that are used up. Spending on investment goods represents the purchase of capital that is not used up, but instead represents the purchase of equipment whose service life will last many years. Spending on inputs is not included in GDP, while investment spending is included: inputs get used up, while investment spending purchases maintain a useful life for the firm for many years.

28. **Answer d.** To answer this question, it is helpful to calculate the nominal GDP for each of these years. Nominal GDP in 2010 equals the sum of the product of the prices of the goods produced times the quantity of the goods produced or ($10,000/tractor)(5 tractors) + ($10/pizza)(100 pizzas), or $51,000. Using the same process, nominal GDP in 2011 equals $61,600 and nominal GDP in 2012 equals $77,000. Thus, nominal GDP in 2011 is greater than nominal GDP in 2010 and less than nominal GDP in 2012.

29. **Answer b.** To answer this question, first calculate real GDP in 2011 using 2010 as the base year. Real GDP in 2011 equals the sum of the product of the quantities produced in 2011 times the price of the product in the base year. Thus, real GDP in 2011 using 2010 as the base year equals ($10,000/tractor)(5 tractors) + ($10/pizza)(80 pizzas), or $50,800. Nominal GDP in 2011 equals $61,600 (see previous question), so real GDP in 2011 using 2010 as the base year is less than nominal GDP in 2011.

30. **Answer d.** To answer this question, first compute real GDP for each year using 2011 as the base year. Real GDP in 2011 will equal nominal GDP in 2011 since 2011 has been designated the base year. Thus, real GDP in 2011 equals $61,600. Real GDP in 2010 using 2011 as the base year equals ($12,000/tractor)(5 tractors) + ($20/pizza)(100 pizzas), or $62,000. Real GDP in 2012 using 2011 as the base year equals ($12,000/tractor)(5 tractors) + ($20/pizza)(100 pizzas), or $62,000.

31. **Answer b.** To find GDP per capita, divide the economy's GDP by its population. For Littleville, GDP per capita in 2011 is equal to ($10,000)/(10 people), or $1,000 per person.

32. **Answer d.** Littleville's GDP in 2012 increases by $10,000 (a 100% increase) from its GDP in 2011, while its population increases by 50%. Since the percentage increase in GDP is greater than the percentage increase in population, this implies that GDP per capita has risen in Littleville. To find GDP per person in 2012, we need to first find the level of population in 2012. Since population in 2012 is 50% larger than the population in 2011, this implies population in Littleville is now 15 people. GDP per capita in 2012 in Littleville is thus equal to ($20,000)/(15 people), or approximately $1,333 per person.

Unemployment and Inflation

BEFORE YOU READ THE CHAPTER

Summary

This chapter discusses how unemployment is measured and why the unemployment rate in an economy is significant. The chapter also explores the relationship between the unemployment rate and economic growth. The chapter develops the concept of the natural rate of unemployment. In addition, the chapter considers the costs of inflation and deflation and how inflation and deflation create winners and losers. Finally, the chapter discusses why policymakers want to avoid temporary rises in inflation.

Chapter Objectives

Objective #1. A person is considered to be employed if he or she has a job. To be considered unemployed, an individual must currently not have a job and, in addition, must have actively sought employment during the past four weeks. Individuals who are disabled or retired are not included in the number of unemployed in an economy. The economy's labor force is equal to the sum of the employed and the unemployed in that economy.

- The labor force participation rate is the percentage of the population over 16 years of age that is either employed or unemployed. The labor force participation rate is equal to [(labor force)/(population age 16 and older)] × 100.

- The unemployment rate is equal to [(number of unemployed workers)/(number of unemployed workers + number of employed workers)] × 100.

- Since the number of unemployed workers plus the number of employed workers is equal to the labor force, the unemployment rate is equal to [(number of unemployed workers)/(labor force)] × 100.

Objective #2.   The unemployment rate provides a good indicator of current conditions in the labor market, but it is not a perfect measure.

- The unemployment rate overstates the difficulty of finding a job since it includes those individuals who are looking for a job and are confident that they will be employed once they identify a suitable position.

- The unemployment rate understates the difficulty of finding a job since it does not include discouraged workers, those jobless individuals who have given up searching for a job because there are no jobs available where they live. The unemployment rate also does not include the marginally attached workers, a group of individuals who are out of work and have recently looked for work, but who are currently not seeking employment. Lastly, the unemployment rate does not include those individuals who are currently working part-time jobs but who want to work full-time; these underemployed workers are counted as employed rather than unemployed even though they are unable to find jobs that are full-time.

- The unemployment rate varies among demographic groups: younger workers and older workers typically experience higher rates of unemployment than do workers between the ages of 25 and 54.

Objective #3.   The unemployment rate rises during economic recession and generally falls during economic expansion. Economic data generally indicates that there is a negative relationship between economic growth and the rate of unemployment: when real GDP grows at a high rate, the unemployment rate falls; and when real GDP grows at a low or negative rate, the unemployment rate rises. A falling level of real GDP is always associated with increases in the unemployment rate and its resultant hardship on families.

Objective #4.   The unemployment rate never falls to zero. This is due to several reasons. First, jobs are constantly being created and eliminated. Jobs are created and eliminated due to structural changes in the economy: these changes reflect new technologies as well as changes in consumers' tastes. In addition, the process of locating a job or the job search can take time. *Frictional unemployment* is the term that describes unemployment that is due to job search whether this job search is due to the process of job creation and job destruction or the fact that new workers are constantly entering the labor force.

Objective #5.   Structural unemployment refers to unemployment that occurs when there are more people seeking jobs in a labor market than there are jobs. Structural unemployment may reflect a situation where there are more workers with a particular skill than there are available jobs using that skill, or where there are more workers in a particular geographic area than there are jobs in that area.

Objective #6.   In a labor market, the demand for labor indicates the amount of labor employers demand at different wage rates while the supply of labor indicates the amount of labor that individuals are willing to supply at different wage rates. The demand for labor is downward sloping: as the wage rate falls, firms demand more labor. The supply of labor is typically upward sloping: as the wage rate falls, individuals supply less labor. The equilibrium wage rate is that wage rate where the quantity demanded of labor is equal to the quantity supplied of labor. However, at that equilibrium wage rate there is still frictional unemployment, since there will always be some workers who are searching for a job even if the number of available jobs equals the number of available workers. But, at the equilibrium wage rate, structural unemployment is equal to zero. Whenever the wage rate exceeds the equilibrium wage rate, there is structural unemployment: the primary causes of this structural unemployment are the minimum wage, labor unions, efficiency wages, and the side effects of government policies.

- A minimum wage is a government-imposed floor on the price of labor and, when binding, the minimum wage can lead to structural unemployment since it artificially raises the wage rate above the equilibrium wage rate in the labor market. Although an effective minimum wage helps those who secure employment, it may also eliminate the opportunity to work for some workers who would have been willing to work for lower wages.

- Effective labor unions may also result in structural unemployment if the unions are successful in bargaining for wage contracts that are higher than the equilibrium market wage rate. Through successful collective bargaining, labor unions may raise the wage rate to a level where the number of people willing to work is greater than the number of jobs available at that wage rate.

- Firms that pay efficiency wages as an incentive for better worker performance may also create structural unemployment: the efficiency wage is a wage rate greater than the equilibrium wage rate.

- Public policy may generate unintended side effects that result in structural unemployment. For example, generous unemployment benefits may reduce the incentive of the unemployed to find new jobs.

Objective #7. The natural rate of unemployment is that rate of unemployment that the actual unemployment fluctuates around. This natural rate of unemployment takes into account frictional rate unemployment as well as structural rate unemployment. In contrast, cyclical unemployment is the difference between the actual rate of unemployment and the natural rate of unemployment: cyclical unemployment rate measures the amount of unemployment due to the business cycle fluctuations. Thus,

Natural unemployment = frictional unemployment + structural unemployment

Actual unemployment = natural unemployment + cyclical unemployment

Objective #8. The natural rate of unemployment is not constant over time and may be affected by economic policies. The natural rate of unemployment changes with changes in the characteristics of the labor force, changes in labor market institutions, changes in government policies, and changes in productivity.

- When the labor force has many inexperienced workers, this results in higher rates of frictional unemployment since these workers are apt to stay in a particular job for a shorter period of time than are experienced workers. In addition, older workers often have family responsibilities that provide a stronger incentive to find and keep jobs.

- Economies with strong labor unions tend to have higher rates of natural unemployment, since these labor unions may contribute to higher rates of structural unemployment. Temporary unemployment agencies and Internet Web sites listing jobs may reduce the level of frictional unemployment and therefore the natural rate of unemployment by helping match unemployed workers to jobs.

- Government policies such as a high minimum wage or generous unemployment benefits can cause structural unemployment and, thus, lead to a higher rate of natural unemployment. Government policies may also reduce the natural rate of unemployment. For example, job training works to provide unemployed workers with skills that will enable them to widen the range of jobs they can do, while employment subsidies provide payments to either workers or firms to create an incentive for these groups to accept or offer jobs.

Objective #9. The level of prices in an economy does not determine how well off people are, but the percentage increase in the overall level of prices per year, or the inflation rate, does matter since a high rate of inflation imposes significant economic costs. The inflation rate for a given year (for example, year 2) can be calculated using the following formula:

$$\text{Inflation rate for year 2} = \{[(\text{price index in year 2}) - (\text{price index in year 1})]/(\text{price index in year 1})\} \times 100$$

High rates of inflation result in shoe-leather costs, menu costs, and unit-of-account costs.

- Shoe-leather costs refer to the effort people expend to reduce their holdings of money during periods of high inflation. The high rate of inflation reduces the purchasing power of money and makes holding money less desirable since the money does not hold its value. The high rate of inflation significantly increases transactions costs, as individuals expend valuable resources to reduce their money holdings.

- Menu costs refer to the cost of changing the list price of items that are offered for sale. In periods of high inflation, firms are forced to alter prices often and this results in higher costs for the economy as a whole.

- Unit-of-account costs of inflation refer to the way inflation makes money a less reliable unit of measurement; in particular, in periods of high inflation, contracts that are stated in monetary terms are harder to evaluate due to the changing value of the monetary unit. Tax systems are subject to unit-of-account costs if these tax systems are not adjusted for inflation, since the inflation can distort the measures of income on which taxes are collected.

Objective #10. In addition to the three overall costs on the economy (shoe-leather costs, menu costs, and unit-of-account costs), inflation also produces winners and losers within the economy. This distributional effect of inflation primarily arises because many economic transactions involve contracts that extend over a period of time, and these contracts are normally specified in nominal, rather than real, terms. To understand this issue requires understanding the distinction between nominal and real interest rates: the nominal interest rate is the interest rate in dollar terms, while the real interest rate is the nominal interest rate minus the rate of inflation. When the actual inflation rate is greater than the expected inflation rate, borrowers gain at the expense of lenders: borrowers will repay their loans with funds that have a lower real value than had been expected. When the actual inflation rate is lower than the expected inflation rate, lenders gain at the expense of borrowers: borrowers will repay their loans with funds that have a higher real value than had been expected.

- Long-term contracts are adversely affected by uncertainty about the future inflation rate, since this uncertainty discourages people from entering into long-term contracts with one another. Thus, high rates of inflation and high levels of uncertainty about future rates of inflation reduce long-term investment in an economy.

- Deflation, an unexpected fall in the price level, also produces winners and losers. In periods of deflation, borrowers see a sharp increase in the real value of their debt: deflation redistributes wealth from borrowers to lenders.

Objective #11. Reducing the level of inflation in an economy, a process called disinflation, is difficult and costly once a high rate of inflation is established. To eliminate established inflation in an economy requires policies that temporarily depress the economy—and these policies lead to high levels of unemployment.

Key Terms

employment the total number of people currently employed for pay in the *economy,* either full-time or part-time.

unemployment the total number of people who are actively looking for work but aren't currently employed.

labor force the sum of *employment* and *unemployment*; that is, the number of people who are currently working plus the number of people who are currently looking for work.

labor force participation rate the percentage of the population age 16 or older who are in the *labor force.*

unemployment rate the percentage of the total number of people in the *labor force* who are unemployed, calculated as *unemployment/ (unemployment + employment).*

discouraged workers individuals who want to work but who have stated to government researchers that they aren't currently searching for a job because they see little prospect of finding one given the state of the job market.

marginally attached workers nonworking individuals who say they would like a job and have looked for work in the recent past but are not currently looking for work.

underemployment the number of people who work part-time because they cannot find full-time jobs.

job search when workers spend time looking for *employment.*

frictional unemployment *unemployment* due to time workers spend in *job search.*

structural unemployment *unemployment* that results when there are more people seeking jobs in a labor market than there are jobs available at the current wage rate.

efficiency wages wages that employers set above the *equilibrium* wage rate as an incentive for workers to deliver better performance.

natural rate of unemployment the normal *unemployment rate* around which the actual unemployment rate fluctuates; the unemployment rate that arises from the effects of *frictional* and *structural unemployment.*

cyclical unemployment the difference between the actual rate of *unemployment* and the *natural rate of unemployment.*

real wage the wage rate divided by the price level.

real income income divided by the price level.

shoe-leather costs (of inflation) the increased costs of transactions caused by *inflation.*

menu costs the real cost of changing a listed price.

Key Terms *(continued)*

unit-of-account costs (of inflation) costs arising from the way *inflation* makes money a less reliable unit of measurement.

nominal interest rate the *interest rate* in dollar terms.

real interest rate the *nominal interest rate* minus the *inflation rate.*

disinflation the process of bringing down *inflation* that has become embedded in expectations.

■ AFTER YOU READ THE CHAPTER

Tips

Tip #1. The distinction among frictional, structural, and cyclical unemployment is important. All economies experience frictional unemployment. Jobs are created and destroyed and new workers are constantly entering the labor market: these events make some unemployment inevitable. Structural unemployment occurs because there is a mismatch between the supply of labor and the demand for labor: this mismatch is the result of the current wage exceeding the wage rate that would equate the supply of labor to the demand for labor. Cyclical unemployment is the unemployment that occurs due to fluctuations in economic production due to the business cycle.

Tip #2. This chapter introduces new vocabulary and, as usual, you will want to make sure you learn and understand these new terms. In particular, you will want to be able to define and distinguish between real and nominal interest rates, and deflation and disinflation. The nominal interest rate is the interest rate expressed in money terms, while the real interest rate is the interest rate adjusted for inflation. The real interest rate is equal to the nominal interest rate minus the inflation rate. Deflation refers to a fall in the aggregate price level, and disinflation refers to a decrease in the inflation rate reflecting policymakers' decisions that the economy has built-in inflationary expectations that need to be reduced.

Tip #3. Students often find the concept of the natural rate of unemployment challenging. It is not possible for an economy to achieve and maintain zero unemployment due to the ongoing creation and destruction of jobs as well as the entry of new labor market participants. The natural rate of unemployment is that level of unemployment that the economy can achieve when it is producing with no cyclical unemployment: it is the rate of unemployment achieved when the economy produces at its potential output level.

1. Consider an economy that has 100,000 people who are 16 years old or older. Of this group, 2,000 are currently in the military, 1,000 are homemakers, 10,000 are retired, and 14,000 are full-time students who are not employed. Further, 10,000 people are currently not working and are actively seeking jobs, 5,000 people are temporarily laid off and anticipate that their jobs will resume within the next two months, and 5,000 people are currently not working and are not actively seeking jobs because they live in a community with a severely depressed economy (like Detroit today). All other adults in this economy can be assumed to be working: in this group, 80% are fully employed and 20% are underemployed. You are asked to identify what the civilian labor force is in this economy, what the number of unemployed people is in this economy, and what the number of employed people is in this economy. You are also asked to calculate the unemployment rate and the civilian labor force participation rate for this economy. The government of this economy is considering changing its definition of unemployed so that it includes discouraged workers. If this new policy is implemented, what will the new unemployment rate equal? Suppose the government changes its classification of discouraged workers and, in addition, decides to treat underemployed workers as unemployed workers since this group is not fully utilizing their labor resources. If both of these policy changes are implemented, what will happen to the unemployment rate?

STEP 1: Start by identifying all those individuals who would not be in the civilian labor force. Then identify all those who are considered employed and all those who are considered unemployed. Remember that the number of the employed plus the unemployed must sum to the civilian labor force. (Hint: your text refers to the labor force, but this is just the civilian labor force—in this example, we are emphasizing this since we want to make sure you do not include the military in your calculations of the employed and the unemployed.)

Review the section "The Unemployment Rate" on page 214 (Econ page 646), the section "Defining and Measuring Unemployment" on page 214 (Econ page 646), and the section "The Significance of the Unemployment Rate" on page 215 (Econ page 647).

The intent of the unemployment rate is to measure that fraction of the labor force that is not employed. The government does not want to include in this measurement individuals who are clearly not interested in working, individuals who clearly cannot work, or individuals who are not part of the adult population. The government also does not want to include military personnel since they are employed by the military. Thus, in this example, the civilian labor force excludes all those under 16, the military, homemakers who are not currently seeking work, the retired, and full-time students who are not currently seeking work. The civilian labor force is equal to 68,000. To find the civilian labor force, start with the initial population of 100,000 and then subtract out those in the military (2,000), full-time students (14,000), those not working and not looking for work (10,000), those that are discouraged workers (5,000), and those who are homemakers (1,000). The 5,000 who are laid off but who expect to be called back are treated as unemployed workers, since they are currently not working. The civilian labor force is equal to the sum of the employed plus the unemployed. We can find the number of unemployed workers: it is the sum of the unemployed plus the laid-off workers, or 10,000 plus 5,000, for a total of 15,000. To find the number of employed people, subtract the unemployed from the civilian labor force: 68,000 − 15,000 = 53,000.

STEP 2: Calculate the unemployment rate and the civilian labor force participation rate for this economy.

Review the section "The Unemployment Rate" on page 214 (Econ page 646), the section "Defining and Measuring Unemployment" on page 214 (Econ page 646), and the section "The Significance of the Unemployment Rate" on page 215 (Econ page 647).

The unemployment rate is equal to [(number of unemployed)/(civilian labor force)] × 100. Recall that the civilian labor force is just the sum of the unemployed plus the employed. In this example, the civilian labor force is equal to 68,000. The unemployment rate is [(15,000)/(68,000)] × 100, or 22%.

The civilian labor force participation rate is equal to [(civilian labor force)/(civilian population age 16 or older)] × 100 = [(68,000)/(98,000)] × 100, or 69.4%.

STEP 3: Recalculate the unemployment rate, but this time treat discouraged workers as part of the group of unemployed workers.

Review the section "The Unemployment Rate" on page 214 (Econ page 646), the section "Defining and Measuring Unemployment" on page 214 (Econ page 646), and the section "The Significance of the Unemployment Rate" on page 215 (Econ page 647).

This change in policy will change the number of unemployed from 15,000 to 20,000 and the number of the civilian labor force from 68,000 to 73,000. The new unemployment rate can be calculated as [(20,000)/(73,000)] × 100 = 27.4%. Notice that the treatment of discouraged workers can have a significant impact on the unemployment statistics. Current treatment makes the unemployment rate lower than it would be if discouraged workers were treated as unemployed workers.

STEP 4: Recalculate the unemployment rate, but this time treat both discouraged workers and underemployed workers as part of the group of unemployed workers.

Review the section "The Unemployment Rate" on page 214 (Econ page 646), the section "Defining and Measuring Unemployment" on page 214 (Econ page 646), and the section "The Significance of the Unemployment Rate" on page 215 (Econ page 647).

Initially, there are 53,000 employed people in this economy. Of that 53,000, we are told that 80% are fully employed and 20% are underemployed. The number of employed people is equal to 0.8(53,000), or 42,400, and the number of unemployed people is equal to 0.2(53,000), or 10,600. If the government changes its policy to include discouraged workers and underemployed workers in the category of unemployed workers, this means that the number of unemployed workers will increase from 15,000 to 30,600. In addition, the civilian labor force will now equal 73,000: the 30,600 who are unemployed and the 42,400 who are employed. To calculate the number of employed people, recall that initially there were 53,000 employed people but that this number included the underemployed. If we categorize the underemployed as unemployed, this will cause the unemployed number to increase by 10,600 and the employed number to decrease by 10,600. The new unemployment rate with these changes in policy will equal [(30,600)/(73,000)] × 100, or 41.92%. Notice that the treatment of discouraged workers and underemployed workers can have a significant impact on the unemployment statistics. Current treatment makes the unemployment rate lower than it would be if discouraged workers and underemployed workers were treated as unemployed workers.

2. In the library, you read the following newspaper headline from the 2008 archives: "Sharp rise in unemployment rate as global financial crisis hits jobs market." Based on this reading, what do you know about frictional, structural, and cyclical unemployment in this economy? What do you know about the relationship between this economy's current unemployment rate and its natural rate of unemployment?

STEP 1: Review the definitions of frictional, structural, and cyclical unemployment and then apply these definitions to this situation.

Review the section "The Natural Rate of Unemployment" on page 220 (Econ page 652), the section "Frictional Unemployment" on page 221 (Econ page 653), the section "Structural Unemployment" on page 222 (Econ page 654), and the section "The Natural Rate of Unemployment" on page 225 (Econ page 657).

The headline about the global financial crisis and the rise in unemployment suggests that the world economy is experiencing a deviation from the natural rate of unemployment, the level of unemployment that is the normal unemployment rate around which the actual unemployment rate fluctuates. This deviation is referred to as cyclical unemployment. So, in this economy not only is there frictional and structural unemployment, the kinds of unemployment that occur normally in an economy, but there is also the additional kind of unemployment that refers to the departure of the economy from its normal unemployment rate.

STEP 2: Review the definition of the natural unemployment rate and then consider how this economy's current unemployment rate differs from its natural unemployment rate.

Review the section "The Natural Rate of Unemployment" on page 220 (Econ page 652), the section "Frictional Unemployment" on page 221 (Econ page 653), the section "Structural Unemployment" on page 222 (Econ page 654), and the section "The Natural Rate of Unemployment" on page 225 (Econ page 657).

This economy is experiencing frictional, structural, and cyclical unemployment: this implies that its current unemployment rate is greater than its natural unemployment rate.

3. The following data on the labor market have been provided to you by the U.S. Bureau of Labor Statistics. You are asked to provide the overall unemployment rate for this economy, the unemployment rate for males, and the unemployment rate for females. Furthermore, you are asked to compute the labor force participation rate for this economy as well as the female labor force participation rate and the male labor force participation rate.

Adult Population	% Female
400	52%
Labor Force	% Female
310	40%
Employed	% Female
260	45%

STEP 1: It would be helpful to know the number of men and women in each of the above categories rather than just the percentages that have been provided.

Review the section "The Unemployment Rate" on page 214 (Econ page 646), the section "Defining and Measuring Unemployment" on page 214 (Econ page 646), and the section "The Significance of the Unemployment Rate" on page 215 (Econ page 647).

Take the time to construct a table that provides these data in a straightforward, easy-to-access manner. The following table provides this information.

Variable	Male	Female
Adult Population	192	208
Labor Force	186	124
Employed	143	117

STEP 2: **Find the unemployment rate in general and then find the unemployment rate for men and the unemployment rate for women.**

Review the section "The Unemployment Rate" on page 214 (Econ page 646), the section "Defining and Measuring Unemployment" on page 214 (Econ page 646), and the section "The Significance of the Unemployment Rate" on page 215 (Econ page 647).

Recall that the unemployment rate = [(number of unemployed)/(number of unemployed + number of employed)] × 100. To find the number of unemployed, you need to remember that the labor force is the sum of employed plus unemployed. Since the labor force is equal to 310 and the number of employed is equal to 260, the number of unemployed is equal to 50. The unemployment rate is [(50)/(310)] × 100, or approximately 16%.

To find the unemployment rate for males, you will need to find the number of unemployed men and the number of men in the labor force. From the preceding table, we know that there are 186 men in the labor force and 143 of them are employed. That implies that 43 are unemployed. The male unemployment rate is [(43)/(186)] × 100, or approximately 23%.

To find the unemployment rate for females, you will need to find the number of unemployed women and the number of women in the labor force. From the preceding table, we know that there are 124 women in the labor force and 117 of them are employed. That implies that 7 are unemployed. The female unemployment rate is [(7)/(124)] × 100, or approximately 5.6%.

STEP 3: **Compute the labor force participation rate for the entire economy and then compute the labor force participation rate for men and the labor force participation rate for women.**

Review the section "The Unemployment Rate" on page 214 (Econ page 646), the section "Defining and Measuring Unemployment" on page 214 (Econ page 646), and the section "The Significance of the Unemployment Rate" on page 215 (Econ page 647).

Recall that the labor force participation rate = [(labor force)/(population)] × 100. From the table, we know both the labor force and the population: the labor force participation rate is [(310)/(400)] × 100, or approximately 77.5%.

To find the labor force participation rate for men, you will need to know how many men there are in the labor force and how many men there are in the population. This information is in the table you created in Step 1. The labor force participation rate for men = [(number of men in the labor force)/(number of men in the population)] × 100. The labor force participation rate for men is [(186)/(192)] × 100, or approximately 97%.

To find the labor force participation rate for women, you will need to know how many women there are in the labor force and how many women there are in the population. This information is in the table you created in Step 1. The labor force participation rate for women = [(number of women in the labor force)/(number of women in the population)] × 100. The labor force participation rate for women is [(124)/(208)] × 100, or approximately 60%.

4. Answer the following set of questions using this CPI information for an economy.

Year	CPI with base year 2005
2008	100
2009	105
2010	110
2011	115

    a. Joe's nominal income in 2009 is $100,000. What must his nominal income be in 2011 in order for his real income to be unchanged?

STEP 1: **Examine the given data and determine what the base year is from the information that you are given.**

Review the section "Inflation and Deflation" on page 228 (Econ page 660). (Hint: you may find it helpful to return to Chapter 7 (Econ Chapter 22) and review the sections on the consumer price index in that chapter as well.)

Examination of the data indicates that 2008 is the base year, since the value of the consumer price index in the base year is always equal to 100.

STEP 2: **Now calculate the rate of inflation between each year.**

Review the section "Inflation and Deflation" on page 228 (Econ page 660).

The rate of inflation can be calculated from the CPI numbers that you are given. Thus, the rate of inflation between 2008 and 2009 is equal to {[(price index for 2009) – (price index for 2008)]/(price index for 2008)} × 100, or 5%. The rate of inflation for the other years can similarly be calculated. The following table provides the inflation rates.

Year	CPI with base year 2005	Rate of yearly inflation
2008	100	
2009	105	5%
2010	110	4.76%
2011	115	4.55%

STEP 3: **Calculate how much Joe's nominal income needs to change each year in order for him to have the same real purchasing power that he did in 2009.**

Review the section "Inflation and Deflation" on page 228 (Econ page 660).

If Joe earns $100,000 in 2009, then he will need to earn $100,000(1.0476) in 2010 to maintain the same purchasing power. Thus, in 2010, he needs to earn $104,760. If he earns $104,760 in 2010, then he will need to earn $104,760(1.0455) in 2011 to maintain the same purchasing power. Thus, in 2011, he needs to earn $109,526.

STEP 4: **Here's an alternative method for figuring out what nominal income Joe must earn in 2011 in order to maintain the same purchasing power that he had in 2009.**

Review the section "Inflation and Deflation" on page 228 (Econ page 660). (Hint: you might find it helpful to review the general formula for the GDP deflator, since we will be using a modified version of that relationship; you studied this in Chapter 7 [Econ Chapter 22].)

Use the following formula to calculate what nominal income Joe must receive in 2011 in order to have the same purchasing power as he has in 2009: the real value of the variable = [(nominal value of the variable)/(price index)] × 100. In this example, the price index is the CPI. So, in 2009, the nominal value of Joe's income is $100,000 and the CPI is 105. We can find the real value of this income for Joe measured in the base year or 2008 dollars as follows: the real value of Joe's income measured in 2008 dollars = [($100,000)/(105)] × 100, or $95,238.

    In 2011, Joe wants his real income to have the same purchasing power that he had in 2009. From our calculation, we know that this real income measured in 2008 dollars was equal to $95,238. So, let's use this information and our CPI information to solve for the nominal income Joe must get in 2011 in order to have the same command over goods and services. Thus, (real income in 2008 measured in 2008 dollars) = [(nominal income in 2011)/(CPI for 2011)] × 100, or $95,238 = [(nominal income in 2011)/(115)] × 100. Solving this equation, we get that Joe's nominal income in 2011 must equal $109,524. If you compare this nominal income with the nominal income you found in Step 3, you will see that they are very close to each other: the difference is due to rounding error.

> **b.** Mike borrows $1,000 in 2011 and repays this loan in 2009. Mike pays the lender $1,060 in 2009. What is the real value of this payment in 2009 using 2008 as the base year? What nominal interest rate is Mike paying for this loan? What real interest rate is Mike paying for the loan?

STEP 1: Start by calculating the nominal interest rate that Mike is paying for the loan.

Review the section "Inflation and Deflation" on page 228 (Econ page 660).

The nominal interest rate refers to the payment that a borrower makes in excess of the amount of the loan or principal that he or she borrowed. In this example, Mike borrowed $1,000, so he needs to repay this loan amount, or the principal amount. He also needs to compensate his lender for the use of the lender's money. So, when Mike pays the lender $1,060 a year after the loan, he is in effect making two payments: a payment of $1,000 representing the amount he borrowed, and a payment of $60 that represents the interest payment he is making. To find the nominal interest rate, you need to calculate what percentage of the loan amount the interest payment is: thus, the nominal interest rate is equal to [(the amount of money paid back – the principal)/(the principal)] × 100. The nominal interest rate is therefore equal to [(1,060 – 1,000)/1,000] × 100, or 6%.

STEP 2: Calculate what the real value of Mike's payment of $1,060 is, given the information you have about the CPI.

Review the section "Inflation and Deflation" on page 228 (Econ page 660).

Mike's payment of $1,060 is a nominal payment. To convert this payment to a real payment, you need to use the following formula: real payment = [(nominal payment)/(CPI)] × 100. Or, real payment = ($1,060/105) × 100 = $1,009.52.

STEP 3: Calculate the real interest rate that Mike is paying for the loan.

Review the section "Inflation and Deflation" on page 228 (Econ page 660).

The real interest rate is equal to [(the real payment made – the principal)/(the principal)] × 100. In this example, the real interest rate is equal to [(1,009.52 – 1,000)/1,000] × 100, or 0.952%. Alternatively, we can approximate the real interest rate by recalling that the real interest rate is equal to the nominal interest rate minus the rate of inflation. In this case, the rate of inflation is 5%, the nominal interest rate is 6%, and therefore the real interest rate is 1%. If you compare these two answers, you see that the approximation method provides a good estimate of the real interest rate.

Problems and Exercises

1. Use the following graph to answer this question.

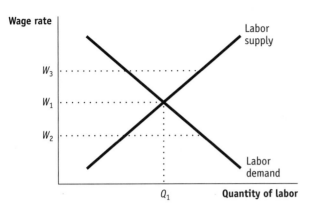

a. What is the equilibrium wage and quantity of labor in this labor market?

b. At the equilibrium wage rate, what is the structural unemployment rate? Explain your answer.

c. If the structural unemployment rate is a positive number, what do you know must be true about the current wage in this labor market? Explain your answer.

d. Suppose the government passes minimum wage legislation setting the minimum wage at W_2, where W_2 is less than W_1. Explain the effect of this legislation on this labor market.

e. Suppose the government passes minimum wage legislation setting the minimum wage at W_3, where W_3 is greater than W_1. Explain the effect of this legislation on this labor market.

2. Economists believe that the natural rate of unemployment is greater than zero. Assuming structural unemployment and cyclical unemployment are both zero, how do you explain this insistence that the natural rate of unemployment must still be a positive number? Explain your answer fully.

3. The text considers the effect of minimum wage legislation and union power on the workings of the labor market. Compare and contrast the effects of minimum wage legislation and union power on the labor market, noting how they are similar in their impact on the labor market as well as how they differ in their impact on the labor market.

4. Suppose there are 12,000 people living in Macroland. Of these 12,000 people, 1,000 are either too old to work or too young to work. Of the remaining individuals, 5,000 are employed with full-time jobs; 3,000 are employed part-time, but wish to work full time; 1,000 are underemployed, but working full-time jobs; 1,000 are currently not working, but are looking for work; and the remainder are discouraged workers.

a. What is the size of the labor force in Macroland?

b. What is the employment rate in Macroland?

c. What is the unemployment rate in Macroland?

d. What percentage of the population are discouraged workers?

e. Suppose you are told that 100 people find jobs for every $10,000 increase in the level of aggregate output in Macroland. If you wanted the unemployment rate to equal 8%, what would the change in output need to be? Assume no changes in the number of young and old in the population or in the number of discouraged workers.

f. Suppose the government department in Macroland responsible for compiling unemployment statistics redefines the employed as including only those with full time jobs. How does this change the unemployment rate, given the initial information?

5. Suppose that there are 10,000 adults in Finlandia and that 5,000 of these adults are employed, 2,000 are unemployed, 500 are discouraged workers, and the rest are not currently working and/or not seeking employment.

a. What is the labor force equal to in Finlandia?

b. What is the unemployment rate in Finlandia?

c. What would the unemployment rate equal in Finlandia if discouraged workers were counted as unemployed workers?

d. Currently the Bureau of Labor Statistics does not count discouraged workers as unemployed workers. How does this decision affect the calculated value of the unemployment rate?

e. Suppose that for every $10,000 increase in GDP in Finlandia, unemployment decreases by 100 people. If GDP increases by $20,000, what will Finlandia's unemployment rate equal? Assume there is no change in the number of discouraged workers and that discouraged workers are not counted as unemployed workers.

f. What is the relationship between GDP and unemployment?

6. Macroland decides to join the Central Union, which is a group of countries that have negotiated a trade zone. All members of the Central Union must adopt the CU dollar, the currency of the Central Union. Currently a Macroland dollar purchases 3 CU dollars.

a. Suppose you live in Macroland and have lent someone 50,000 Macroland dollars. Once Macroland joins the Central Union, how many CU dollars is your loan worth? Has the value of your loan changed with the change from Macroland dollars to CU dollars?

b. You have agreed to lend a friend of yours 10,000 Macroland dollars. Once Macroland joins the Central Union, how many CU dollars will your friend owe you?

c. When you made the loan described in part (b), you negotiated that you would be paid 10% of the value of the loan this year as compensation for the use of your funds. If this payment is made in Macroland dollars, how many Macroland dollars will you receive? If this payment is made in CU dollars, how many CU dollars will you receive? Are you better off being paid in Macroland dollars or CU dollars? Explain your answer.

7. Sarah currently works for a firm in which her union has negotiated a cost-of-living adjustment that automatically adjusts her income to whatever the annual rate of inflation is for her community. Bob works for a firm that routinely grants its employees a 5% annual income increase. Milt is retired and receives two payments: a pension payment from his former employer that is fixed at $2,000 per month and a government-provided retirement payment whose real value is equal to $1,000 per month in the base year. The government-provided retirement payment is indexed to the inflation rate in the community.

   a. Suppose the rate of inflation is 8% this year. Describe the effect of this inflation rate on Sarah, Bob, and Milt in terms of their real purchasing power. Who is left in worse shape with this inflation? Does anyone end up better off despite this inflation rate? Explain your answer.

   b. Suppose the rate of inflation is 20% this year. Describe the effect of this inflation rate on Sarah, Bob, and Milt.

▮ BEFORE YOU TAKE THE TEST

Chapter Review Questions

1. Which of the following statements is true?
   a. The natural rate of unemployment equals a country's unemployment rate during a recession.
   b. The natural rate of unemployment equals a country's unemployment rate during an expansion.
   c. The natural rate of unemployment is the sum of frictional and structural unemployment.
   d. The natural rate of unemployment is the sum of frictional and cyclical unemployment.

2. Job creation and job destruction are
   a. a natural occurrence in a labor market.
   b. only a problem during an economic expansion.
   c. a primary reason for why there is unemployment even when the economy is at full employment.
   d. Answers (a), (b), and (c) are all correct.
   e. Answers (a) and (c) are both correct.

3. Which of the following statements is true?
    a. Even small amounts of structural unemployment are harmful to an economy.
    b. There is always frictional unemployment since there are always new workers entering the job market.
    c. Even small amounts of frictional unemployment are harmful to an economy.
    d. Answers (a), (b), and (c) are all correct.
    e. Answers (a) and (b) are both correct.
    f. Answers (b) and (c) are both correct.

4. Which of the following statements is true?
    a. Structural unemployment refers to the unemployment that occurs when there are more employers demanding labor than there are employees supplying labor.
    b. Structural unemployment refers to a situation when the market wage rate is lower than the equilibrium wage rate.
    c. Structural unemployment occurs when there is a surplus of labor at the current wage rate.
    d. When there is structural unemployment, frictional unemployment equals zero.

5. In order to be binding, a minimum wage must be
    a. equal to or less than the equilibrium wage rate.
    b. greater than the equilibrium wage rate.
    c. set so that there is a persistent surplus in the labor market.
    d. set so that there is a persistent shortage in the labor market.
    e. Answers (a) and (d) are both correct.
    f. Answers (b) and (c) are both correct.

6. Which of the following statements is true?
    a. Strong labor unions and an effective minimum wage reduce the level of structural unemployment in an economy.
    b. Strong labor unions and an effective minimum wage benefit all workers equally.
    c. Workers acting collectively through a union may find that they have more power than if they act individually.
    d. Answers (a), (b), and (c) are all correct.
    e. Answers (b) and (c) are both correct.

7. Efficiency wages
    a. are wages negotiated by unions.
    b. are always less than the minimum wage.
    c. are wages paid by employers that exceed the equilibrium wage rate and that are offered as an incentive for better performance.
    d. are a means for employers to retain employees while providing incentives for greater work effort.
    e. Answers (b), (c), and (d) are all correct.
    f. Answers (c) and (d) are both correct.

8. The natural rate of unemployment is
   a. equal to 0% in every economy, since this is the level of unemployment that every economy should naturally want to achieve.
   b. the sum of frictional and cyclical unemployment.
   c. equal to cyclical unemployment when the economy is producing at the full employment level of aggregate output.
   d. Answers (b) and (c) are correct.
   e. None of the answers is correct.

9. The natural rate of unemployment
   a. is constant and does not change over time.
   b. changes when there are changes in labor force characteristics.
   c. may change due to changes in labor market institutions like unions, temporary employment agencies, and technological change.
   d. increases with increases in the minimum wage level.
   e. Answers (a), (b), (c), and (d) are all correct.
   f. Answers (b), (c), and (d) are correct.
   g. Answers (b) and (d) are both correct.

10. Which of the following statements is true?
    a. Most contracts that extend over a period of time are expressed in real terms so that borrowers and lenders can fully understand the consequences of their economic agreement.
    b. The nominal interest rate is equal to the real interest rate minus the inflation rate.
    c. When the actual inflation rate equals the anticipated inflation rate, borrowers are better off.
    d. Anticipated inflation can inflict real costs on the economy.

11. Mary expects the inflation rate to be 5%, and she is willing to pay a real interest rate of 3%. Joe expects the inflation rate to be 5%, and he is willing to lend money if he receives a real interest rate of 3%. If the actual inflation rate is 6% and the loan contract specifies a nominal interest rate of 8%, then
    a. Joe is glad he lent out funds even though his real interest rate has fallen.
    b. Joe is sorry he lent out funds since his real interest rate is now 9%.
    c. Mary is glad she borrowed the funds because her real interest rate has fallen.
    d. Mary is sorry she borrowed funds since her real interest rate is now 9%.

12. Disinflation in an economy, which has grown to expect inflation, is
    a. easy to achieve and does not affect actual output.
    b. difficult to accomplish and invariably results in an increase in the natural rate of unemployment.
    c. possible only if policymakers are willing to accept higher rates of unemployment and a lower level of aggregate output.
    d. Answers (a) and (c) are both correct.
    e. Answers (b) and (c) are both correct.

13. In a period of unexpected deflation,
    a. borrowers find that it is easier for them to make their loan payments, since prices are falling.
    b. lenders benefit, since there are more people eager to borrow money during a period of deflation.
    c. lenders benefit, since they are repaid dollars with greater real value than they anticipated when signing the loan contract.
    d. Answers (a), (b), and (c) are all correct.

Use the following information to answer the next two questions.

Suppose the adult population of Macronesia is 100,000 people. Of these 100,000 people, 20,000 are not in the labor force. Of the remaining 80,000 people, 16,000 have given up searching for a job and are not actively seeking work; 4,000 are unemployed and actively seeking work; 14,000 work part-time; and the remainder are fully employed.

14. What is the unemployment rate in Macronesia?
    a. 5%
    b. 6.25%
    c. 8.5%
    d. 10%

15. What would happen to Macronesia's unemployment rate, relative to your answer in the last question, if discouraged workers were counted as unemployed workers?
    a. The unemployment rate would be unchanged.
    b. The unemployment rate would decrease.
    c. The unemployment rate would increase.
    d. The unemployment rate could increase, decrease, or remain the same.

16. Which of the following statements is true?
    I. The two principal goals of macroeconomic policy are price stability and low frictional unemployment.
    II. The primary goals of macroeconomic policy are price stability and low unemployment.
    III. In order to achieve the two primary goals of macroeconomic policy of price stability and low unemployment, it is necessary for policymakers to reduce the level of frictional unemployment.
    a. Statements I, II, and III are all true.
    b. Statements I and II are true.
    c. Statements II and III are true.
    d. Statement I is true.
    e. Statement II is true.
    f. Statement III is true.

Answer the next three questions based on the following information about a small economy.

An economy is composed of five people: George, Sarah, Mason, Abbot, and Jin. George works for Plastics, Inc., 40 hours a week. Sarah works for Baker's United for 20 hours a week and would like to move from part-time work to full-time work. Mason has been looking for work for the past six months after he finished completing his high school education. Abbot worked for Baker's United for the first six months of the year before he was fired; for the next four months Abbot sought work, but finally gave up looking for work when he realized that it was unlikely he would be able to find work in this economy. Jin is 70 years old and enjoys reading, needlepoint, and watching movies.

17. In this economy, the employed include
  a. George, Sarah, and Mason.
  b. George and Sarah.
  c. George since he is the only person in this economy who is fully employed.
  d. George, Sarah, Mason, and Jin. (Jin is fully employed with a variety of activities that occupy all her waking moments.)

18. What is the labor force participation rate in this economy?
  a. 40%
  b. 60%
  c. 80%
  d. 100%

19. What is the unemployment rate in this economy?
  a. 20%
  b. 33%
  c. 40%
  d. 50%

20. Which of the following statements is true?
  I. To be considered unemployed, one must simply not have a job.
  II. To be considered unemployed, one must not have a job and must also not be looking for a job.
  III. To be considered unemployed, one must not have a job and must also be looking for a job.
  a. Statement I is true.
  b. Statement II is true.
  c. Statement III is true.
  d. Statements I, II, and III are all false.

21. When the unemployment rate is high, this usually implies that it is
  a. easy to find a job.
  b. difficult to find a job.

22. The Bureau of Labor Statistics' treatment of discouraged workers results in the unemployment rate
  a. overstating the true level of unemployment.
  b. understating the true level of unemployment.

23. Underemployed workers, those workers currently working part-time jobs but wishing to work full-time jobs, are
a. not included in the calculation of the employment rate.
b. included in the calculation of the employment rate.

24. Different age groups and different ethnic groups in the economy typically experience
a. the same unemployment rate.
b. different unemployment rates.

25. During an economic expansion, the unemployment rate typically
a. increases.
b. decreases.

26. Historically the relationship between the change in unemployment and the annual growth rate of real GDP is a
a. positive relationship.
b. negative relationship.

27. Job search refers to the time that workers spend looking for employment. Job search results in
a. cyclical unemployment.
b. structural unemployment.
c. frictional unemployment.
d. both structural and frictional unemployment.

28. Suppose the demand for labor is given by the equation $W = 15 - (1/200)L$ and the supply of labor is given by the equation $W = 5 + (1/200)L$, where W is the wage rate and L is the quantity of labor. What is the equilibrium wage and quantity of labor in this market?
a. The equilibrium wage is $15 while the equilibrium quantity of labor is 200 workers.
b. The equilibrium wage is $5 while the equilibrium quantity of labor is 100 workers.
c. The equilibrium wage is $10 while the equilibrium quantity of labor is 1,000 workers.
d. The equilibrium wage is $10 while the equilibrium quantity of labor is 200 workers.

29. Suppose the demand for labor is given by the equation $W = 15 - (1/200)L$ and the supply of labor is given by the equation $W = 5 + (1/200)L$, where W is the wage rate and L is the quantity of labor. Suppose the government imposes a minimum wage of $12 in this market. What will be the effect of this minimum wage in this market?
a. The minimum wage will not be binding since it is set below the equilibrium wage.
b. The minimum wage will create a situation of excess demand for labor since it is a binding minimum wage.
c. The minimum wage will create a situation of excess supply of labor since it is a binding minimum wage.
d. This minimum wage will benefit all workers in this labor market.

30. Binding minimum wages generally lead to
a. cyclical unemployment, since not everyone can find a job at the minimum wage rate.
b. frictional unemployment, since the binding minimum wage results in longer job search.
c. structural unemployment, since more people want to work than can find jobs at the minimum wage.
d. Answers (a), (b), and (c) are all correct.

31. Which of the following statements is true?

    I. An employer can encourage its workers to work hard by paying an efficiency wage.

    II. An efficiency wage is equal to the market wage rate.

    III. When many firms pay efficiency wages, this creates structural unemployment.

  a. Statement I is true.

  b. Statement II is true.

  c. Statement III is true.

  d. Statements I and II are true.

  e. Statements II and III are true.

  f. Statements I and III are true.

  g. Statements I, II, and III are all true.

32. Persistent high unemployment in Europe is thought to be primarily due to

  a. efficiency wages.

  b. generous unemployment benefits.

  c. government policies reducing the time of unemployment for most workers.

  d. strong union activity.

33. Utopia has recently experienced a high rate of inflation and proposes changing its currency from the Utopian dollar to the Utopian mark at an exchange rate of 5.0 Utopian dollars per Utopian mark. Suppose Joe currently has a debt of 100,000 Utopian dollars. Which of the following statements is true?

  a. The switch to Utopian marks will make Joe better off since the Utopian mark is replacing the Utopian dollar, whose purchasing power has fallen due to the presence of inflation in Utopia.

  b. The switch to Utopian marks will reduce the real value of Joe's debt.

  c. Joe's debt will now equal 20,000 Utopian marks.

  d. Joe's debt will now equal 500,000 Utopian marks.

34. The extra time and effort expended to make transactions during times of high rates of inflation impose

  a. shoe-leather costs.

  b. menu costs.

  c. unit-of-account costs.

■ ANSWER KEY

Answers to Problems and Exercises

1. **a.** The equilibrium wage rate is W_1 and the equilibrium quantity of labor is Q_1, where the quantity of labor supplied is equal to the quantity of labor demanded.

    b. At the equilibrium wage rate, the structural unemployment rate equals zero since the number of people seeking jobs in the labor market equals the number of jobs available at that equilibrium, or current, wage rate.

    c. If the structural unemployment rate is a positive number, then the wage rate must be greater than the equilibrium wage rate and the quantity supplied of labor must exceed the quantity demanded for labor, resulting in a surplus of labor.

    d. For a minimum wage to have any impact on the market, it must be set above the equilibrium wage rate. The minimum wage rate is just a specific example of a price floor, and price floors only impact markets when they are set above the equilibrium price.

    e. When the government sets the minimum wage above the equilibrium wage rate, it affects the market by preventing the wage rate from adjusting to that point where the quantity demanded for labor equals the quantity supplied of labor. Thus, an effective minimum wage will create a surplus of labor and, hence, a positive structural unemployment rate.

2. Even when the economy produces at its potential output and the unemployment rate equals the natural rate, there will be people entering the job market as well as workers moving between jobs. This frictional unemployment is a natural part of the working of the labor market; hence, even when the economy is at its natural rate of unemployment, there will still be positive frictional unemployment.

3. Labor unions and effective minimum wage legislation both affect the labor market by working to raise the current wage above the equilibrium wage rate and by creating barriers to prevent the wage from adjusting back to the equilibrium level. Both labor unions and minimum wage legislation have the potential to create structural unemployment through their ability to create a situation where the quantity supplied of labor is greater than the quantity demanded for labor. Labor unions, through collective bargaining, often result in workers securing higher wages than the market would have provided if workers bargained individually. Labor unions often negotiate for long-term contracts, and these contracts may lead to structural unemployment due to the wage rigidity they introduce into the labor market.

4. **a.** The labor force is defined as the number of employed workers plus the number of unemployed workers. The number of employed workers equals the sum of full-time workers, part-time workers, and underemployed workers, or, in this example, 9,000 workers. The number of unemployed workers is equal to the 1,000 workers who are currently not working, but who are actively looking for work. Thus, the labor force equals 10,000 workers.

    b. Employment rate = [employed/labor force] × 100 = (9,000/1,000) × 100 = 90%

    c. Unemployment rate = [unemployed/labor force] × 100 = (1,000/10,000) × 100 = 10%

    d. Percentage of discouraged workers in population = [(discouraged workers)/population] × 100 = (1,000/12,000) × 100 = 8.33%

    e. The current unemployment rate is 10%. To reduce the unemployment rate to 8% requires that 200 of the currently unemployed workers find jobs. If output increases by $10,000 for every 100 people who find jobs, then output must increase by $20,000 for 200 people to find employment.

f. Using the new definition of employment, the number of employed now equals 6,000, and the unemployed would increase by 3,000 for a total of 4,000 unemployed. This change in definition results in a much higher unemployment rate (40%) and a much lower employment rate (60%). The definitions underlying calculations do matter.

5. a. The labor force is equal to the sum of employed plus unemployed workers. In this case, the labor force is equal to 5,000 + 2,000, or 7,000.

b. To find the unemployment rate, use the formula Unemployment rate = (unemployed/labor force) × 100. In this case, the unemployment rate equals (2,000/7,000) × 100, or 28.57%.

c. If discouraged workers were counted as unemployed workers, the formula for calculating the unemployment rate would change to Unemployment rate = [(unemployed + discouraged workers)/(labor force)] × 100. The unemployment rate would equal (2,500/7,000) × 100, or 33%.

d. The decision by the Bureau of Labor Statistics to exclude discouraged workers from the calculation of the unemployment rate results in an understatement of the unemployment rate in the economy.

e. Since GDP increases by $20,000, we know that unemployment decreases by 200 people (2,000 − 200 = 1,800). Thus, the unemployment rate is now equal to (1,800/7,000) × 100, or 25.71%.

f. As GDP increases, unemployment decreases.

6. a. With the change to CU dollars, your loan will now be valued at 150,000 CU dollars. But, since 3 CU dollars trade for 1 Macroland dollar, the value of the loan has not changed with the switch to the new currency.

b. As in part (a), the change to CU dollars will make your loan value three times larger: your loan value will be 30,000 CU dollars. But, since 3 CU dollars trade for 1 Macroland dollar, the value of the loan has not changed with the switch to the new currency.

c. When the loan is 10,000 Macroland dollars, the interest payment the first year is equal to (0.1)(10,000 Macroland dollars) or 1,000 Macroland dollars. When the loan is denominated in CU dollars, the interest payment the first year is equal to (0.1)(30,000 CU dollars) or 3,000 CU dollars, which has the same value as 1,000 Macroland dollars when 1 Macroland dollar is exchanged for 3 CU dollars. The two payments are equivalent: the switch to the new currency does not change the value of the interest payment or the loan value.

7. a. With an inflation rate of 8% for the year, Sarah finds that her income is automatically adjusted upward by that 8%: Sarah's real income has not changed since prices rose by 8% as did her income. Bob's income will rise by 5% even though the inflation rate was 8%: Bob is worse off since his nominal income rose, but by an amount smaller than the amount needed to stay even with the inflation rate. Bob has less purchasing power than he did initially. Milt's situation is complicated: his pension from his former employer is fixed and does not adjust with the inflation rate: this implies that Milt will now have less purchasing power from his fixed pension of $2,000 per month than he did initially. Milt's government-provided retirement payment maintains its real value since it is adjusted with changes in the rate of inflation. Overall, Milt has less purchasing power than he did initially. No one in this example ends up better off despite this inflation rate.

b. Again, Sarah's purchasing power is not affected since her nominal income is adjusted each year based upon the rate of inflation. Bob is much worse off this year, since the overall price level rose 20% while his nominal income only rose 5%. Milt's fixed pension sees an even bigger erosion in its purchasing power than in part (a), while his government-provided retirement payment maintains its real value.

Answers to Chapter Review Questions

1. **Answer c.** The natural unemployment rate is defined as the sum of frictional and structural unemployment. It is the unemployment rate that occurs when there is no cyclical unemployment, which is the unemployment directly tied to economic business cycles.

2. **Answer e.** Job creation and job destruction naturally occur in an economy, and it is this natural process that leads to economies always having some unemployment even if the economy is producing at full employment. We can think about how there are always people in the economy who are entering the labor force and looking for work, and there are always people whose jobs are ending and are in need of finding new work. This process occurs during both economic expansions and recessions.

3. **Answer b.** All economies will experience some frictional and structural unemployment as a natural functioning of their labor market. Frictional unemployment occurs because of job creation and job destruction, and because there are always new workers entering the job market. Frictional unemployment can be beneficial to an economy, since the economy may be more productive if workers take the time to find jobs that are well matched to their skills. Structural unemployment occurs because of such factors as minimum wages, unions, efficiency wages, and government policies that are designed to help laid-off workers.

4. **Answer c.** Structural unemployment occurs when there is an excess supply of labor in a labor market. This occurs when the wage rate is greater than the equilibrium wage rate in the market. Every economy has frictional unemployment due to job creation and job destruction as well as the entry of new workers into the economy.

5. **Answer f.** To be effective and therefore binding, a minimum wage must be set at a level in excess of the equilibrium wage rate. This will result in the quantity supplied of labor exceeding the quantity demanded for labor and thus a surplus of labor.

6. **Answer c.** Strong labor unions and an effective minimum wage act to increase the level of structural unemployment in an economy, since they both tend to create a surplus of labor in the labor market. It is true, though, that workers acting collectively may possess greater negotiating power in an industry than would those workers acting individually. Strong unions and an effective minimum wage benefit those people who continue to work, but hurt those who become unemployed when the wage rate rises above the equilibrium wage rate in the labor market.

7. **Answer f.** Efficiency wages are those paid by employers in excess of the equilibrium wage rate. They are offered to improve employee work effort while also providing an incentive for workers to stay with their current employer. Efficiency wages may be equal to or greater than the minimum wage.

8. **Answer e.** The natural rate of unemployment is equal to the sum of frictional unemployment rate plus structural unemployment. It will always be greater than zero, since there will always be new workers entering the job market and workers moving from one job to another. The cyclical unemployment rate is equal to zero when the economy produces at the full employment level of aggregate output, but at this level of output there is still frictional unemployment.

9. **Answer f.** The natural rate of unemployment is affected by changes in labor force characteristics and by changes in labor market institutions. In addition, the natural rate of unemployment will increase whenever the government mandates more generous benefits for workers (for example, an increase in the minimum wage rate).

10. **Answer d.** Most contracts that extend over time are expressed in nominal terms and not real terms. The nominal interest rate equals the real interest rate plus the inflation rate. When the actual inflation rate equals the anticipated inflation rate, the inflation rate does not create winners or losers in loan contracts, since both parties to the contract

have used accurate expectations of inflation to anticipate the inflation rate, and they have both agreed to the real rate they actually receive when the contract is honored. Anticipated inflation diverts resources from productive uses to less productive uses: resources are used to avoid the inflation tax.

11. **Answer c.** Both Mary and Joe would like to negotiate a contract where the real interest rate is 3%, and they both anticipate the expected inflation rate will be 5%. Thus, the nominal rate in the contract will equal the desired real rate of interest plus the expected inflation rate, or 8%. When the actual rate of inflation is 6%, this means that the dollars paid back have less purchasing power than anticipated: Mary will find this beneficial to her as the borrower, while Joe will find this hurts him since the dollars he receives in payment for the loan have less purchasing power than the dollars he loaned out.

12. **Answer c.** Disinflation in an economy where inflationary expectations are embedded is possible only if policymakers are willing to push the economy into a recession and thereby reduce inflationary expectations. This will necessarily result in an increase in the unemployment rate and a decrease in the level of aggregate output the economy produces. This policy does not affect the natural rate of unemployment.

13. **Answer c.** In a period of unexpected deflation, borrowers will find that the real value of the loan payments they make have risen in value, so borrowers will be hurt by the unexpected deflation. Lenders will benefit because the loan payments they receive will have greater real value due to the deflation. Borrowers, due to the increased economic burden of their debt, will typically reduce their overall spending and will choose, therefore, to borrow less during a period of deflation.

14. **Answer b.** Calculate the unemployment rate using this formula: Unemployment rate = [(number of unemployed)/(labor force)] × 100, where the labor force is equal to the number of employed workers plus the number of unemployed workers. In this case, the unemployment rate = [(4,000)/(64,000)] × 100 = 6.25%. Note the labor force does not include discouraged workers (16,000) or the 20,000 people who are not currently in the labor force.

15. **Answer c.** The unemployment rate now equals [(20,000)/(80,000)] × 100, or 25%. The unemployment rate increases when discouraged workers are counted as unemployed workers.

16. **Answer e.** The two primary macroeconomic policy goals are low unemployment and price stability. In order to achieve low unemployment, the economy must produce at or near its potential output level: low unemployment necessitates reducing the level of cyclical unemployment. Economies always have some amount of frictional unemployment and although policymakers can adopt policies that will lower the level of frictional unemployment, they cannot eliminate it.

17. **Answer b.** To be considered employed, an individual must have a part-time or full-time job. Only George and Sarah satisfy this requirement in the described economy.

18. **Answer b.** The labor force participation rate is equal to the product of 100 times the sum of the employed plus the unemployed divided by the population over 16 years of age. In this example, the employed is equal to 2 (George and Sarah), the unemployed is equal to 1 (Mason), and the population over 16 years of age is equal to 5. Thus, (3/5) × 100 = 60%.

19. **Answer b.** The unemployment rate is equal to the product of 100 times the number of unemployed divided by the labor force. There is one unemployed person (Mason) and two employed people (George and Sarah); therefore, the labor force is equal to 3 while the number of unemployed is equal to 1. The unemployment rate equals (1/3) × 100 or 33%.

20. **Answer c.** To be considered unemployed, a person must not have a job and must, in addition, be actively seeking a job. For example, the retired neither have jobs nor are they seeking employment: they are not part of the unemployed and they are not part of the labor

force, since they do not intend to work. The discouraged worker, although not working, is not considered unemployed, since the discouraged worker has given up looking for a job.

21. **Answer b.** The unemployment rate is a good indicator of how easy or difficult it is to find a job in the economy. When the economy's unemployment rate is high, this implies that many people are out of work and it will therefore be difficult to find employment. When the economy's unemployment rate is low, this implies that it will be relatively easy to find a job.

22. **Answer b.** Currently the Bureau of Labor Statistics does not include discouraged workers in the number of unemployed even though these workers are currently not working. This exclusion results in a lower rate of unemployment than would be the case if these discouraged workers were included in the number of unemployed.

23. **Answer b.** Underemployed workers are included in the number of employed workers even though these workers would like to attain full-time employment.

24. **Answer b.** Unemployment rates in an economy vary widely depending upon the age group and ethnic group; for example, teenagers have much higher rates of unemployment than do adults between the ages of 25 and 54, while African Americans experience higher unemployment rates than the national average.

25. **Answer b.** When the economy is in an economic expansion, the unemployment rate usually falls as an increase in the level of aggregate output usually requires an increase in the level of aggregate employment in the economy.

26. **Answer b.** If the relationship between the change in unemployment and the annual growth rate of real GDP is graphed as a scatter diagram, these points indicate a negative relationship between these two measures.

27. **Answer c.** Frictional unemployment is unemployment due to the time workers spend in job search. Structural unemployment is the unemployment due to the number of people seeking work exceeding the number of available jobs at the current wage rate. Cyclical unemployment is unemployment due to economic recession; cyclical unemployment is a result of business cycle fluctuations.

28. **Answer c.** To find the equilibrium quantity of labor, set the demand equation equal to the supply equation and solve for L. L will equal 1,000 workers. Using either the demand equation or the supply equation, substitute 1,000 into the equation for L and then solve for W: the equilibrium wage will equal $10.

29. **Answer c.** To find out if $12 is a binding minimum wage requires first solving for the equilibrium wage in this market. From the previous question we know that the equilibrium wage is equal to $10, so $12 is a binding minimum wage. A binding minimum wage will create a situation of excess labor supply, since the wage is artificially raised above that level where the quantity demanded of labor equals the quantity supplied of labor. The minimum wage, when binding, does not benefit all workers since some workers would like to work at this higher minimum wage but cannot find jobs.

30. **Answer c.** A binding minimum wage results in the quantity supplied of labor exceeding the quantity demanded of labor; thus, more people want to work at the minimum wage rate than can find jobs. Thus, the binding minimum wage results in structural unemployment.

31. **Answer f.** An efficiency wage is one that is greater than the equilibrium wage rate in the labor market. A firm will pay an efficiency wage for a variety of reasons, including the hope that a wage exceeding the equilibrium wage rate will encourage its employees to put forth greater work effort, since the workers do not want to risk losing their relatively high-paying jobs. Payment of an efficiency wage results in excess supply of labor and, therefore, structural unemployment.

32. **Answer b.** Persistent high unemployment in Europe is thought to be primarily due to a public policy of generous unemployment benefits.

33. **Answer c.** To find Joe's debt measured in Utopian marks, multiply Joe's debt in Utopian dollars times the ratio (1 Utopian mark)/(5 Utopian dollars) or (100,000 Utopian dollars)(1 Utopian mark)/(5 Utopian dollars) to get 20,000 Utopian marks. Joe is not better off, since he is only changing the unit of measurement of his debt but not his real debt level.

34. **Answer a.** The transactions costs associated with high rates of inflation are referred to as shoe-leather costs. Menu costs refer to the cost associated with printing new menu and price lists due to the presence of inflation. Unit-of-account costs refer to the costs inflation imposes because of its effects on contracts that are stated in monetary, instead of real, terms.

Long-Run Economic Growth

BEFORE YOU READ THE CHAPTER

Summary

This chapter focuses on long-run economic growth and its sources. Long-run economic growth can be measured as the change in real GDP per capita over time. Comparison of real GDP per capita for different countries reveals different economic growth experiences: some countries have experienced rapid economic growth over time, while other countries have been much less fortunate. Long-run economic growth depends on productivity, which depends on physical capital, human capital, and technological progress. This chapter also discusses the convergence hypothesis: the theory states that relatively poor countries should have higher rates of growth of real GDP per capita than relatively rich countries. The chapter also discusses sustainability and the challenges to economic growth arising from natural resource scarcity and environmental damage.

Chapter Objectives

Objective #1. Real GDP per capita provides a measure of economic growth. This measure calculates the value of final goods and services produced in an economy in a given time period divided by the population of that economy.

Objective #2. When computing how long it takes real GDP per capita, or any other variable that grows slowly over time, to double, the rule of 70 is useful. This rule states that the number of years it takes a variable to double is approximately equal to 70 divided by the annual growth rate of the variable.

Objective #3. Long-run economic growth depends almost exclusively on increases in output per worker, or labor productivity. For the aggregate economy, we can measure labor productivity as real GDP divided by the number of people working. Increases in labor productivity are due to increases in physical capital, human capital, or changes in technology.

- Physical capital refers to man-made resources such as buildings and machines.

- Human capital refers to the improvement in labor created by education and knowledge.

- Technology refers to the technical means of producing goods and services.

Objective #4.   The aggregate production function is a mathematical equation describing the relationship between the level of output per worker (productivity) and the amount of human capital per worker, physical capital per worker, and the state of technology. The aggregate production function exhibits diminishing returns to physical capital: holding the level of human capital per worker and the state of technology constant, increases in physical capital per worker eventually increase output per worker by smaller and smaller amounts. That is, as the quantity of physical capital per worker increases, holding everything else constant, the growth rate of productivity will fall but remain positive. Figure 9.1 illustrates an aggregate production function. This function is drawn with a given amount of labor, human capital per worker, and technology, and it shows the relationship between physical capital per worker and real GDP per worker.

Figure 9.1

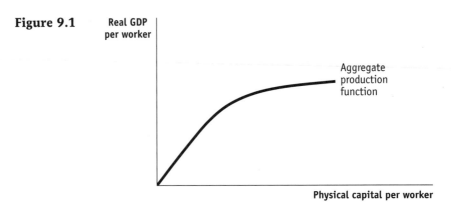

Notice that real GDP per worker eventually increases at a decreasing rate as physical capital per worker is increased. An increase in technology, the amount of labor, or the level of human capital will cause the aggregate production function to shift upward. Figure 9.2 illustrates the shift that occurs if there is an increase in one of these variables. The aggregate production function shifts upward whenever productivity is raised. This may be due to an increase in technology or an increase in human capital per worker.

Figure 9.2

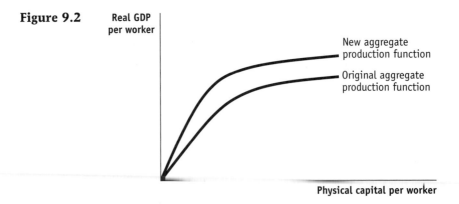

Objective #5.   Growth accounting estimates the contribution of each major factor-physical capital per worker, human capital per worker, and the state of technology-to-economic growth. Total factor productivity is the amount of output that can be produced from a given set of factor inputs. When total factor productivity increases, the economy can produce a high level of output from a given amount of physical capital, human capital, and labor. Technological change results in increases in total factor productivity: technological change is crucial for economic growth.

Objective #6. Growth rates differ across countries and across periods of time. Countries with rapid growth rates tend to be countries that increase their physical capital, human capital, and/or technology. Countries that pursue policies and support institutions that enhance these three factors experience greater economic growth.

- An economy increases its physical capital through investment spending. Investment spending can be funded by domestic savings or by borrowing funds from foreigners.

- A well-functioning banking system is very important for economic growth because this system is a primary means for directing savings into productive business investment. Financial regulation is necessary to ensure a well functioning banking system.

- A government can adversely affect economic growth if there is political instability, poor enforcement of property rights, government corruption, or excessive government intervention.

- A country's human capital is primarily enhanced through government spending on education. The quality of education in a country has a significant impact on a country's economic growth rate.

- A country's infrastructure, or that part of its physical capital that serves as a foundation of economic activity, is critical. Inadequate infrastructure slows the rate of economic growth. Government plays a critical role in building both physical capital and human capital infrastructure. For example, the government plays a vital role in ensuring clean water and disease control.

Objective #7. Technological improvement is a key force behind economic growth. Technological improvement depends upon scientific advance. Spending on research and development (R&D) enhances the development of new technologies and the practical uses of new technologies.

Objective #8. The convergence hypothesis says that economic differences between countries, measured as real GDP per capita, tend to narrow over time. That is, the convergence hypothesis suggests that differences in living standards between countries should narrow over time. Countries with relatively low real GDP per capita will tend to have higher growth rates than countries with relatively high real GDP per capita.

Objective #9. Conditional convergence states that countries with relatively low real GDP per capita will tend to have higher rates of growth than countries with relatively high real GDP per capita provided other things are equal. When there are differences in education, infrastructure, and political stability among countries, there is no clear tendency toward convergence in the world economy as a whole.

Objective #10. There is debate about the sustainability of economic growth due to the scarcity of natural resources and the impact of economic growth on the environment. Economists are optimistic about the ability of economies continuing to grow despite resource scarcity because they posit that increases in the price of these scarce resources will provide strong incentives to conserve these resources as well as find alternatives to these resources. Economists recognize that economic growth may be threatened by environmental damage and that the problem of addressing environmental damage is a difficult one, since it requires effective political action.

- Environmental damage from production often represents a negative externality, a situation where there are costs that individuals or firms impose on others without offering compensation for these costs. Without government intervention, these negative externalities will continue. Effective government intervention is necessary to eliminate or reduce negative externalities.

- In the case of climate change ,the government can implement a set of market-based incentives, like a "carbon tax" or a "cap and trade" system in order to provide incentives for firms to reduce the amount of greenhouse gases they emit into the environment.

Key Terms

Notes

rule of 70 a mathematical formula that states that the time it takes *real GDP* per capita, or any other variable that grows gradually over time, to double is approximately 70 divided by that variable's annual growth rate.

labor productivity output per worker; also referred to as simply *productivity*. Increases in labor productivity are the only source of *long-run economic growth*.

productivity output per worker; a shortened form of the term *labor productivity*.

physical capital manufactured resources, such as buildings and machines.

human capital the improvement in labor created by the education and knowledge embodied in the workforce.

technology the technical means for the production of goods and services.

aggregate production function a hypothetical function that shows how productivity (*real GDP* per worker) depends on the quantities of *physical capital* per worker and *human capital* per worker as well as the state of technology.

diminishing returns to physical capital in an *aggregate production function* when the amount of *human capital* per worker and the state of technology are held fixed, each successive increase in the amount of *physical capital* per worker leads to a smaller increase in productivity.

growth accounting estimates the contribution of each of the major factors (physical and human capital, labor, and technology) in the *aggregate production function*.

total factor productivity the amount of output that can be produced with a given amount of factor inputs.

research and development (R&D) spending to create new technologies and prepare them for practical use.

infrastructure *physical capital,* such as roads, power lines, ports, information networks, and other parts of an *economy,* that provides the underpinnings, or foundation, for economic activity.

Key Terms *(continued)*

convergence hypothesis a principle of economic growth that holds that international differences in *real GDP* per capita tend to narrow over time because countries that start with lower real GDP per capita tend to have higher growth rates.

sustainable describes continued *long-run economic growth* in the face of the limited supply of natural resources and the impact of growth on the environment.

▮ AFTER YOU READ THE CHAPTER

Tips

Tip #1. Real GDP per capita is a key statistic for measuring economic growth. Real GDP and not nominal GDP is used to measure economic growth, since real GDP focuses on the increase in the quantity of goods and services being produced and not on the effects of an increase in the aggregate price level. Real GDP per capita provides a measure of the average standard of living in a country.

Tip #2. Familiarize yourself with the rule of 70 and how to apply it. The rule of 70 provides a simple mathematical formula for estimating the amount of time it takes a variable that grows gradually over time to double. The rule of 70 states that the number of years it takes for a variable to approximately double is equal to 70 divided by the annual growth rate of the variable.

Tip #3. It is important to understand and know the sources of long-run economic growth. Economic growth arises because of increases in productivity, or output per worker. This increase in productivity is due to increases in human capital per worker, physical capital per worker, and/or technological advance. Economic growth is enhanced by high levels of saving and investment spending, a strong educational system, adequate infrastructure, well supported research and development, political stability, and appropriate levels of government intervention in the economy.

Tip #4. Productivity increases when physical capital per worker, human capital per worker, or technology increases. Increases in productivity are the primary source of economic growth over time. It is important to understand what productivity is and how an economy's productivity can be improved. You should make sure you understand what an aggregate production function is and how it illustrates the relationship between productivity and the variables that determine productivity.

Tip #5. The concept of diminishing returns to physical capital is important. Holding everything else constant, an increase in physical capital per worker will eventually lead to smaller increases in productivity. Adding additional physical capital to a fixed level of labor and technology initially increases output at an increasing rate, but eventually each successive addition to physical capital per worker produces a smaller increase in output per worker.

Tip #6. Investment spending determines the level of physical capital available to workers. Investment spending plays a vital role in determining an economy's rate of economic growth. Investment spending can be funded through domestic saving or through the borrowing of foreign saving.

WORKED PROBLEMS

1. Suppose that a country in 2010 has a GDP per capita that is equal to $20,000. Furthermore, suppose that GDP grows by 10% a year and that population holds steady at its current level. Using the rule of 70, in what year will this economy's GDP per capita quadruple? If the country's GDP grew by 5% a year, in what year would this economy's GDP quadruple? Does the growth rate of an economy's GDP matter?

STEP 1: Start by reviewing the rule of 70.

Review the section "Growth Rates" on page 224 (Econ page 656).

The rule of 70 states that the number of years it takes a variable to double is approximately equal to 70 divided by the annual growth rate of the variable. If the growth rate is 10% a year, then it will take approximately 7 years for the variable to double and 14 years for the variable to quadruple. Therefore, GDP per capita in this economy will be approximately $40,000 in 2017 and GDP per capita will be approximately $80,000 in 2024.

STEP 2: Complete a similar calculation, but this time assume that the growth rate of GDP per year is 5%.

Review the section "Growth Rates" on page 224 (Econ page 656).

When GDP grows by 5% a year, the rule of 70 predicts that it will take approximately 14 years for GDP to double. Thus, GDP per capita in this economy will be approximately $40,000 in 2024 and GDP per capita in this economy will be approximately $80,000 in 2038.

STEP 3: Discuss why the growth rate of GDP in an economy matters.

Review the section "Comparing Economies Across Time and Space" on page 242 (Econ page 674) and the section "Growth Rates" on page 224 (Econ page 656).

An economy's growth rate of GDP, considered along with its population growth rate, determines the rate of growth in GDP per capita. Holding everything else constant, when an economy grows at a faster rate, this implies that GDP per capita will increase by a faster rate: on average, living standards will improve.

2. The following graph depicts the aggregate production function for Macroland. This aggregate production function has been drawn holding the level of physical capital and technology in Macroland fixed. Currently, Macroland employs 200 units of labor per year. The graph indicates this level of labor usage and the level of real GDP that can be produced when 200 units of labor are employed. Holding everything else constant, what will happen to real GDP in Macroland if 400 units of labor are employed? What will happen to labor productivity when labor usage increases? Suppose that at the same time that Macroland increases its use of labor to 400 units, it simultaneously experiences a technological advance. How

will this alter the following graph, and how will it affect the level of real GDP produced in Macroland and labor productivity?

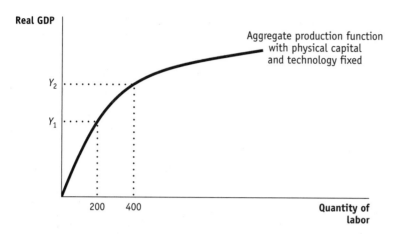

STEP 1: First describe the effect on real GDP of increasing the use of labor from 200 units to 400 units.

Review the section "The Sources of Long-Run Growth" on page 246 (Econ page 678).

When this economy increases its employment of labor from 200 units to 400 units, this leads to an increase in real GDP from Y_1 to Y_2. With more labor employed, the economy can produce more goods and services than it could when it employed a smaller amount of labor.

STEP 2: Now think about what happens to labor productivity as the level of labor usage increases, holding everything else constant.

Review the section "The Sources of Long-Run Growth" on page 246 (Econ page 678) and the section "Accounting for Growth: The Aggregate Production Function" on page 248 (Econ page 680).

Labor productivity is defined as output per worker. In the graph, we can see that as labor usage increases from 200 units to 400 units, output increases. But from the graph, we can also see that although as labor usage increases, output increases, it does so at a diminishing rate. This is due to the fact that capital and technology are being held constant: as more and more units of labor are employed, each additional unit of labor will be less productive due to the growing scarcity of capital for labor to use (since capital is fixed, the amount of capital available is not increasing as the amount of labor is increased). Thus, although both output and labor increase, output increases by a smaller proportion than does labor: labor productivity decreases.

STEP 3: Consider the effect of a change in technology holding the use of labor constant at 200 units and the effect of this change on real GDP and labor productivity. Now think about the effect of this change in technology on real GDP and labor productivity if labor simultaneously increases to 400 units.

Review the section "The Sources of Long-Run Growth" on page 246 (Econ page 678) and the section "Accounting for Growth: The Aggregate Production Function" on page 248 (Econ page 680).

If technology increases, this will cause the aggregate production function to shift upward at every level of labor usage, since this improvement in technology will allow the economy to produce a larger amount of goods and services (real GDP increases) from the available labor and capital. If technology changes and labor and capital are held constant, this will cause labor productivity to rise since each unit of labor can now produce more than it could before the technological change.

If technology improves and the amount of labor employed simultaneously increases to 400 units, real GDP will increase, but the effect of these two changes on labor productivity is impossible to calculate without quantitative information about the size of the shift in the aggregate production function due to the change in technology. Labor productivity may increase, decrease, or remain the same depending upon whether real GDP increases by a greater proportionate amount than does labor, real GDP increases by a smaller proportionate amount than does labor, or real GDP increases by the same proportionate amount as does labor.

STEP 4: Illustrate the changes in the above graph of this increase in technology and labor usage. Discuss the effect of these two changes on real GDP and labor productivity.

Review the section "The Sources of Long-Run Growth" on page 246 (Econ page 678) and the section "Accounting for Growth: The Aggregate Production Function" on page 248 (Econ page 680).

From Step 3 we know that an increase in technology will shift the aggregate production function upward. We also know from Step 3 that when technology improves and there is an increase in the amount of labor used, this leads to a situation where labor productivity may increase, decrease, or remain the same. The two graphs provided depict two possible scenarios: the first graph illustrates the case of increasing labor productivity, while the second graph illustrates the case of decreasing labor productivity.

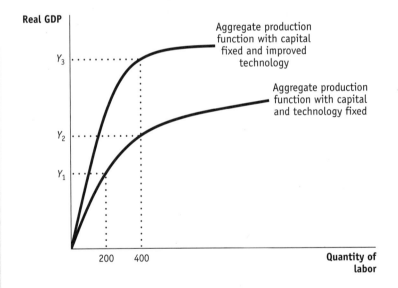

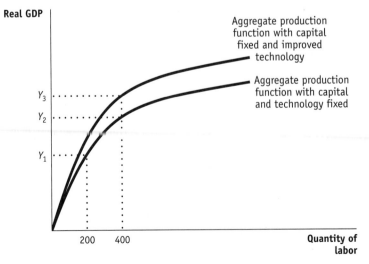

3. You recently went to a lecture on Economic Growth where the speaker, a noted expert, stressed the importance of increases in human capital, as well as increases in physical capital. The speaker then asserted that the most important factor determining the rate of economic growth is technological improvement. Comment on how changes in each of these factors improve an economy's ability to produce goods and services. With regard to growth accounting, order these three factors from the most important determinant of economic growth to the least important determinant.

STEP 1: Discuss what improvements in human capital mean and how an improvement in human capital affects an economy's growth rate.

Review the section "Explaining Growth in Productivity" on page 247 (Econ page 679) and the section "Accounting for Growth: The Aggregate Production Function" on page 248 (Econ page 680).

Improvements in human capital refer to changes in the labor force that reflect education and knowledge. The more educated and knowledgeable the workforce is, the greater the ability of this workforce to produce goods and services from a given amount of resources. As human capital increases, labor becomes more productive and real GDP increases.

STEP 2: Discuss what improvements in physical capital mean and how an improvement in physical capital affects an economy's growth rate.

Review the section "Explaining Growth in Productivity" on page 247 (Econ page 679) and the section "Accounting for Growth: The Aggregate Production Function" on page 248 (Econ page 680).

Improvements in physical capital refer to increases in manufactured resources such as buildings and machines. When there are improvements in physical capital, workers are more productive, and this enables a given amount of labor to produce a greater amount of output. As physical capital increases, this increases the rate of economic growth possible in an economy.

STEP 3: Discuss what improvements in technology mean and how an improvement in technology affects an economy's growth rate.

Review the section "Explaining Growth in Productivity" on page 247 (Econ page 679) and the section "Accounting for Growth: The Aggregate Production Function" on page 248 (Econ page 680).

Improvement in technology is broadly defined as improvement in the technical means for the production of goods and services. When technology improves, this implies that labor is more productive and that the economic growth rate in an economy increases.

STEP 4: Based on growth accounting, order improvements in human capital, physical capital, and technology in order of their importance in determining the rate of growth in an economy.

Review the section "Explaining Growth in Productivity" on page 247 (Econ page 679) and the section "Accounting for Growth: The Aggregate Production Function" on page 248 (Econ page 680).

According to growth accounting, technology is the primary driver of economic growth. This is followed by improvements in human capital and finally by increases in physical capital.

4. You are given the following information about Productiva and Macrostan. You are asked to compute and then compare labor productivity for both countries as well as GDP per capita for both countries.

Country	Population	Employment	Output (Real GDP)
Productiva	80 million	40 million	$ 300 billion
Macrostan	60 million	30 million	200 billion

STEP 1: Compute labor productivity for both countries.

Review the section "Comparing Economics Across Time and Space" on page 242 (Econ page 674) and the section "The Sources of Long-Run Growth" on page 246 (Econ page 678).

Labor productivity is defined as output per worker. For this example, output is measured as real GDP and the number of workers is given by the employment figures. Thus, labor productivity in Productiva is equal to ($300 billion)/(40 million workers), or $7,500 per worker. Labor productivity in Macrostan is equal to ($200 billion)/(30 million workers), or $6,667 per worker.

STEP 2: Compute GDP per capita for both countries.

Review the section "Comparing Economics Across Time and Space" on page 242 (Econ page 674) and the section "The Sources of Long-Run Growth" on page 246 (Econ page 678).

GDP per capita in a country is equal to the country's GDP divided by the country's population. Thus, GDP per capita in Productiva is equal to ($300 billion)/(80 million people), or $3,750 per person. GDP per capita in Macrostan is equal to ($200 billion)/(60 million people), or $3,333 per person.

STEP 3: Compare the labor productivity and GDP per capita for these two countries.

Review the section "Comparing Economics Across Time and Space" on page 242 (Econ page 674) and the section "The Sources of Long-Run Growth" on page 246 (Econ page 678).

Productiva has higher labor productivity and higher GDP per capita than does Macrostan.

Problems and Exercises

1. You are given the following information about the country of Macronesia.

Year	Nominal GDP	CPI	Real GDP	Population
2009	$10 billion	100		1.0 million
2010	10.5 billion	105		1.05 million
2011	11.0 billion	108		1.08 million

a. What is the base year for the economy represented in the table? How did you identify the base year?

b. Calculate the missing values in the table. Calculate the missing value and then round to the nearest thousand million: e.g., 14,829,000,000 would be rounded to 14.8 billion.

c. Use the completed table from part (b) to calculate the missing values in the following table. You will find it helpful to define real GDP in millions (for example, 14.8 billion is 14,800 million), since population is expressed in millions.

Year	Real GDP per capita
2009	
2010	
2011	

d. Let's compare the percentage changes in some of the variables we are working with in this problem. Use the following table to organize your calculations.

Year	Percentage change in nominal GDP	Percentage change in real GDP	Percentage change in population	Percentage change in real GDP per capita
2009				
2010				
2011				

e. In order for real GDP per capita to increase over time, what must be true about the relationship between the percentage change in real GDP and the percentage change in population?

f. Why do we focus on computing real GDP per capita instead of nominal GDP per capita?

2. Suppose real GDP per capita in Fun Land is $10,000 in 2009. Economists in Fun Land predict steady increases in real GDP in Fun Land of 7% a year for the foreseeable future.

a. According to the rule of 70, how many years will it take for Fun Land's real GDP per capita to double?

b. To verify your answer in part (a), compute the values for real GDP per capita in the following table.

Year	Real GDP per capita
2009	$10,000
2010	
2011	
2012	
2013	
2014	
2015	
2016	
2017	
2018	
2019	

c. Is your value for real GDP per capita for 2019 equal to $20,000? If it differs, does this surprise you? Explain your answer.

3. The economy of Macro States estimates its aggregate production function as

$$Y/L = 50(K/L)^{1/2}$$

when technology and human capital per worker are held constant. In the equation Y is real GDP, L is the number of workers, and K is the quantity of physical capital. Macro States has 500 workers.

a. Calculate real GDP per worker (Y/L) and physical capital per worker (K/L) for the given levels of physical capital in the following table. Round both (K/L) and (Y/L) to the nearest hundredth.

K	K/L	Y/L
0		
20		
40		
60		
80		
100		
200		
400		

b. Plot Macro States' aggregate production function on the following graph, where physical capital per worker is measured on the *x*-axis and real GDP per worker is measured on the *y*-axis.

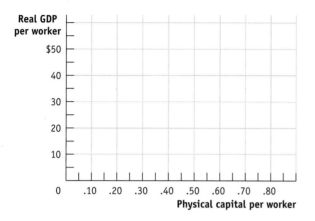

c. As physical capital per worker increases, what happens to real GDP per worker?

4. Suppose that Macro States increases its level of technology and human capital per worker relative to its economic condition in problem 3. Now, Macro States' economists estimate that the aggregate production function for Macro States is given by the equation

$$Y/L = 60(K/L)^{1/2}$$

a. Relative to the aggregate production function you plotted in problem 3b, what do you anticipate will happen to Macro States' aggregate production function because of this increase in human capital per worker and technology?

b. Compare productivity in Macro States in the initial situation to its new situation, assuming that Macro States has $100 worth of physical capital.

c. Why are increases in productivity important?

5. Suppose there are two countries, Macroland and Pacifica, that currently have real GDP per capita of $10,000 and $15,000, respectively. Furthermore, suppose Macroland's economy has an average annual growth rate of 2%, while Pacifica has an average annual growth rate of 1.4%.

a. Compute real GDP per capita for both Macroland and Pacifica 50 years from now.

   b. Compute real GDP per capita for both Macroland and Pacifica 100 years from now.

   c. Initially, Macroland's real GDP per capita is 67% of Pacifica's real GDP per capita. After 50 years, what will be the relationship of Macroland's real GDP per capita to Pacifica's real GDP per capita in percentage terms? What is this relationship after 100 years?

6. Many people worry that the world may run out of important resources like oil and that this depletion of a vital resource will bring an end to economic growth. Why do many economists *not* believe in this particular perspective?

7. Economists argue that the problems presented by widespread climate destruction can only be resolved through government intervention as well as cooperation among different governments. Why do they hold this view?

8. Paul Romer in his "new growth theory" emphasizes the importance of providing incentives in order to encourage research and development that will lead to technological innovation. Discuss how the presence of monopolies through patents or copyrights may encourage expenditures on research and development that can lead to technological innovation.

▮ BEFORE YOU TAKE THE TEST

Chapter Review Questions

1. Real GDP per capita is
    a. the value of real GDP divided by the number of units of capital in an economy in a given time period.
    b. always increasing over time for any given economy.
    c. the value of real GDP divided by population for a given country.
    d. Answers (b) and (c) are both correct.

2. Suppose real GDP for Macronesia is $200 million in 2010. Furthermore, suppose population in Macronesia is 100,000 in 2010. If population increases to 105,000 in 2011 while GDP increases by 5%, then it must be true that real GDP per capita in Macronesia in 2011
    a. increased.
    b. decreased.
    c. stayed constant.
    d. may have increased, decreased, or remained constant.

3. Which of the following statements is true?
    a. Other things being equal, an increase in population raises the average standard of living in an economy.
    b. In 1907, the U.S. economy produced only 16% as much per person as it did in 2007.
    c. The median American household income in the United States in 2007 was $50,000.
    d. Answers (a), (b), and (c) are all true.
    e. Answers (b) and (c) are both true.

4. Suppose that real GDP per capita grows at 2% per year. How many years will it take for real GDP per capita to approximately double? It will take:
    a. 70 years because of the rule of 70.
    b. 140 years, because the rule of 70 states that a variable will double in 70 years if the variable has an annual growth rate of 1%; therefore, a variable growing at 2% will take twice as long to double.
    c. 35 years, because the rule of 70 states that the number of years it takes for a variable to double is equal to 70 divided by the annual growth rate of the variable.
    d. 50 years, since at 2% per year it takes 50 years to reach 100% more than the initial real GDP per capita.

5. Which of the following has been most important in driving long-run economic growth?
    a. rising labor productivity or output per worker
    b. putting more people to work
    c. being a relatively rich country initially
    d. the availability of abundant natural resources

6. Productivity increases can be attributed to
   a. increases in physical capital or the amount of machinery and office space available to workers.
   b. increases in human capital or the level of workers' education.
   c. technological advances.
   d. Answers (a), (b), and (c) are all correct.

7. Which of the following statements is true?
   a. An aggregate production function indicates how output per worker depends on the level of physical capital per worker, human capital per worker, and the state of technology.
   b. Holding everything else constant, an increase in human capital per worker reduces the level of output per worker.
   c. Holding everything else constant, a decrease in physical capital per worker increases the level of output per worker.
   d. Answers (a), (b), and (c) are all true.

8. Suppose the amount of human capital per worker and the state of technology are held constant. As physical capital per worker increases, each additional increase in physical capital per worker leads to
   a. greater increases in output per worker.
   b. greater decreases in output per worker.
   c. smaller increases in output per worker.
   d. smaller decreases in output per worker.

9. Economists often use the other-things-equal expression. This expression indicates that
   a. a group of variables is held constant while we examine how changing one variable affects our economic model.
   b. an individual views two possible outcomes as being equivalent in their impact.
   c. the distribution of income is equal among all members of an economy.
   d. equal amounts of all factors of production are used in the economy under study.

Use the following information to answer the next two questions.

An economy initially has 100 units of physical capital per worker. Each year it increases the amount of physical capital by 5%. According to the aggregate production function for this economy, each 1% increase in physical capital per worker, holding human capital and technology constant, increases output per worker by 1/5th of 1%, or 0.20%.

10. In two years time, what is the level of physical capital per worker in this economy?
    a. 110 units of physical capital per worker
    b. 105 units of physical capital per worker
    c. 110.25 units of physical capital per worker
    d. 210 units of physical capital per worker

11. Suppose output per worker is initially $1,000. After one year, what does estimated output per worker equal? Assume there is no inflation in this economy: real GDP equals nominal GDP.
a. $1,000
b. $1,001
c. $1,010
d. $1,100

12. An economy increases its level of physical capital per worker by increasing the level of investment spending. This can be achieved by
a. having domestic residents spend more of their income on consumption spending.
b. having domestic residents spend less of their income on consumption spending while increasing their domestic saving.
c. borrowing foreign savings from residents of other countries.
d. Answers (a) and (c) are both correct.
e. Answers (b) and (c) are both correct.

13. Which of the following statements is true?
a. Between 1907 and 2007, U.S. real GDP per capita increased by approximately 620%.
b. Despite dramatic economic growth in China and India over the past 30 years, as of 2007 China and India were still poorer than the United States was in 1907.
c. Today more than 50% of the world's population live in countries that are poorer than the United States was a century ago.
d. Answers (a), (b), and (c) are all true.

14. Suppose real GDP in Macroland was $400 billion in 2010 and $450 billion in 2011. Then the growth rate of real GDP in Macroland between 2010 and 2011 was
a. 50%.
b. 5%.
c. 125%.
d. 12.5%.

15. Which of the following statements is true?
a. Countries with low levels of infrastructure typically experience low rates of economic growth.
b. Infrastructure is primarily provided by private companies.
c. Basic public health measures, like clean water, are not considered part of an economy's infrastructure.
d. Answers (a), (b), and (c) are all true.

16. Long-run economic growth requires
a. the imposition of bureaucratic restrictions on business and household activity.
b. political stability and respect for property rights.
c. extensive government intervention in markets in the form of import restrictions, government subsidies, and protection of firms from competitive economic pressures.
d. Answers (a), (b), and (c) are all correct.

17. Economic growth can be especially fast

    a. for countries playing catch-up with countries that already have high real GDP per capita.

    b. for relatively poorer countries, if the convergence hypothesis holds true.

    c. if the country is able to benefit from adopting the technological advances already utilized in advanced countries.

    d. Answers (a), (b), and (c) are all true.

18. Suppose that real GDP per capita in an economy doubles in 10 years. Using the rule of 70, the average growth rate of real GDP for this economy is approximately

    a. 70%.

    b. 0.7%.

    c. 7%.

    d. 1.43%.

19. Which of the following statements is true?

    a. Today there is approximately $130,000 worth of physical capital per average U.S. private-sector worker.

    b. The American population today is more highly educated than it was 50 years ago.

    c. Modest innovations can result in large technological gains for an economy.

    d. Answers (a), (b), and (c) are all true.

    e. Answers (a) and (b) are both true.

20. Holding human capital per worker, the number of workers, and the level of technology constant, suppose an economy increases the amount of physical capital per worker. In this economy, output per worker will

    a. initially increase at a diminishing rate but will eventually increase at an increasing rate as the economy uses greater amounts of physical capital per worker.

    b. eventually lead to output per worker increasing at a diminishing rate.

    c. eventually lead to output per worker increasing at an increasing rate.

    d. eventually lead to output per worker staying constant at the potential output level for the economy.

21. Growth accounting estimates the

    a. effect of a change in physical capital per worker on real GDP per worker.

    b. effect of a change in human capital per worker on real GDP per worker.

    c. effect of a change in the growth rate of real GDP per worker on a country's average standard of living.

    d. contribution of each major factor in the aggregate production function to economic growth.

22. Suppose that the amount of human capital per worker grows by 6% a year in Myland. Furthermore, suppose that estimates of the aggregate production function in Myland show that for each 1% increase in human capital per worker, holding physical capital per worker and technology constant, output per worker increases by 0.5 of 1%. What is your estimate of the effect of this growing human capital per worker on the productivity growth per year in Myland? The growth in human capital per worker in Myland accounts for approximately

    a. 6% of productivity growth per year.

    b. 0.5% of productivity growth per year.

    c. 3% of productivity growth per year.

    d. 30% of productivity growth per year.

23. When total factor productivity increases, this implies that

    a. the economy can produce the same amount of output with a greater quantity of physical capital, human capital, and labor.

    b. the economy can produce the same amount of output with a smaller quantity of physical capital, human capital, and labor.

    c. the economy can produce a greater amount of output with a greater quantity of physical capital, human capital, and labor.

    d. each factor's productivity increases by the same amount.

24. Natural resources in the modern world are

    a. less important in determining productivity than human or physical capital for the majority of countries.

    b. more important in determining productivity than human or physical capital for the majority of countries.

25. Sometimes the development of a new technology does not immediately translate into a large increase in productivity because

    a. the new technology provides a new means of producing the good, but the new means may not necessarily enable greater production from a given set of resources.

    b. it may take time for firms to learn how to effectively use the new technology.

26. Which of the following statements is true?

    a. In 1820, Mexico and Japan had equal real GDP per capita.

    b. In 2007, Japan had higher real GDP per capita than most European nations.

    c. Over the long run, Japan's economy grew faster than Mexico's economy.

    d. Answers (a), (b), and (c) are all true.

    e. Answers (b) and (c) are both true.

27. Fast growing economies typically spend a

    a. very small share of their GDP on investment goods.

    b. large share of their GDP on government-provided goods and services.

    c. very large share of their GDP on investment goods.

    d. very large share of their GDP on consumer goods.

28. Which of the following statements is true?
    I. In 2007, China saved a higher percentage of its GDP than it invested in China and therefore was able to invest these extra savings in other economies, including the U.S. economy.
    II. In 2007, investment spending in China was 41 percent of China's GDP, while in the United States, investment spending was only 15% of the U.S. GDP.
    III. In 2007, the economic growth rate in China was greater than the economic growth rate in the United States.
    a. Statement I is true.
    b. Statement II is true.
    c. Statement III is true.
    d. Statements I and II are true.
    e. Statements II and III are true.
    f. Statements I and III are true.
    g. Statements I, II, and III are all true.

29. Resource scarcity
    a. is inevitable and will lead to reduced economic growth.
    b. will result in price increases for those scarce resources, and these price increases will provide incentives to conserve scarce resources and to find alternatives to these scarce resources.

30. Environmental damage from economic growth
    a. is of no great consequence and can easily be remedied through market forces.
    b. may lead to climate change, and this environmental damage can only be reduced by concerted government intervention to provide incentives for businesses and individuals to reduce environmentally degrading activities.
    c. can be remedied through the appropriate use of "carbon taxes" or "cap and trade" systems for carbon emissions.
    d. Answers (b) and (c) are both correct.

31. Which of the following statements is true about "new growth theory"?
    a. This theory recognizes that spending on research and development by businesses is different than spending on equipment and factories.
    b. This theory recognizes that spending on research and development may result in improvements in our knowledge for how to work with our available resources.
    c. This theory recognizes that once new knowledge has been discovered, it can be used by other people at no or very low cost.
    d. This theory recognizes the importance of innovators' ability to establish monopolies if there is an incentive for engaging in research and development.
    e. Answers (a), (b), (c), (d), and (e) are all correct answers.

▮ **ANSWER KEY** ▮

Answers to Problems and Exercises

1. **a.** 2009. The base year is that year with the CPI value of 100.

b.

Year	Nominal GDP	CPI	Real GDP	Population
2009	$10 billion	100	$10 billion	1.0 million
2010	10.5 billion	105	10 billion	1.05 million
2011	11 billion	108	10.19 billion	1.08 million

c.

Year	Real GDP per capita
2009	$10,000
2010	9,524
2011	9,435

d.

Year	Percentage change in nominal GDP	Percentage change in real GDP	Percentage change in population	Percentage change in real GDP per capita
2009	—	—	—	—
2010	5%	0%	5%	−4.8%
2011	4.8	1.9	2.9	−0.93

e. The percentage change in real GDP must be greater than the percentage change in population for real GDP per capita to increase over time.

f. Real GDP per capita allows us to track the increase in the quantity of goods and services available in our economy rather than just the effects of a rising price level.

2.   a. Ten years, since the rule of 70 says the number of years it takes for a variable to double is approximately equal to 70 divided by the annual growth rate of the variable.

b.

Year	Real GDP per capita
2009	$10,000
2010	10,700
2011	11,449
2012	12,250
2013	13,108
2014	14,026
2015	15,007
2016	16,058
2017	17,182
2018	18,385
2019	19,672

c. The value of real GDP per capita for 2019 is $19,672, which is less than the estimated $20,000. This is not surprising, since the rule of 70 is an estimation of the number of years it takes a variable to double rather than a numerically precise calculation.

3.   a.

K	K/L	Y/L
0	0	0
20	0.04	10.00
40	0.08	14.14
60	0.12	17.32
80	0.16	20.00
100	0.20	22.36
200	0.40	31.62
400	0.80	44.72

b.

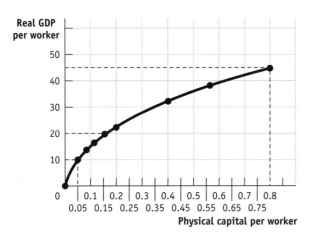

c. Real GDP per worker increases as physical capital per worker increases, but it increases at a diminishing rate. For example, if we hold the number of workers and all other variables constant, real GDP per worker increases by $4.14 when physical capital increases from $20 to $40, but real GDP per worker increases by $3.18 when physical capital increases from $40 to $60.

4.   a. Macro States' aggregate production function will shift up relative to its initial position for every level of physical capital per worker. We can see this by recalculating output per worker given the new aggregate production function.

K	K/L	Y/L
0	0	0
20	0.04	12.00
40	0.08	16.97
60	0.12	20.78
80	0.16	24.00
100	0.20	26.83

b. Productivity is defined as output per worker. When physical capital equals $100, output per worker is initially $22.50, while, after the increase in human capital per worker and technology, output per worker increases to $27.00.

c. Increases in productivity are important because they indicate that each worker on average is now producing a greater level of output. This, in turn, makes it possible for people on average to experience higher standards of living.

5.   a. Real GDP per capita in Macroland in 50 years will equal ($10,000)(1 + 0.02)^{50}, or $26,916. Real GDP per capita in Pacifica in 50 years will equal ($15,000)(1 + 0.014)^{50}, or $30,060.

b. Real GDP per capita in Macroland in 100 years will equal ($10,000)(1 + 0.02)^{100}, or $72,446. Real GDP per capita in Pacifica in 100 years will equal ($15,000)(1 + 0.014)^{100}, or $60,240.

c. In 50 years, Macroland's real GDP per capita to Pacifica's real GDP per capita in percentage terms will be 89.5%, while in 100 years it will be 120.3%.

6. Economists argue that vital resources, as they grow scarce, will command increasing higher prices and that these high prices will cause people to conserve these resources and in addition spur the development of alternatives to replace the scarce, but vital, resources.

7. Climate destruction arises from widespread economic growth, and this destruction is an example of a negative externality. Negative externalities arise when a market fails to include all the costs of producing a good in the calculation of the good's price. Many goods produced today also produce significant pollution, and the market does not internalize these costs of pollution. Without government intervention, firms and individuals do not have any incentive to reduce negative externalities. Reducing pollution and the climate destruction that accompany this pollution will require the cooperation of governments in the imposition of some form of market-based incentives: for example, a "carbon tax" or a "cap and trade" system both would reduce the amount of carbon emitted into the air.

8. Paul Romer in his research on economic growth notes the importance of technological innovation that basically results in a "new set of instructions" for how to use resources. However, he also notes that this kind of technological innovation, once discovered, can be copied at either no cost or very low cost by competitors. Businesses will have little incentive to engage in this kind of research and development if their ideas can be quickly copied by those who have not invested in this research. Government, by providing monopoly power to the business that creates this information via patents or copyrights, effectively creates an incentive for businesses to engage in research and development that may lead to technological innovation.

Answers to Chapter Review Questions

1. **Answer c.** Real GDP per capita is defined as the value of real GDP in a country divided by that country's population. Real GDP per capita may increase, decrease, or remain steady over time.

2. **Answer c.** In 2012, the population in Macronesia increased by 5% as did real GDP. Since both population and real GDP increased by the same percentage amount, real GDP per capita is unaffected.

3. **Answer e.** Answers (b) and (c) are factual statements that are in the chapter text. Answer (a) is not true: an increase in population, other things equal, will reduce the average standard of living since the average standard of living is calculated as real GDP per capita. The increase in population increases the size of the denominator in this ratio, while the numerator, or real GDP, stays constant.

4. **Answer c.** This is a straightforward use of the definition of the rule of 70: this rule states that an estimation of the number of years it takes for a variable to double is equal to 70 divided by the annual growth rate of the variable.

5. **Answer a.** Sustained economic growth occurs only when an economy steadily increases the amount of output each worker produces; in other words, long-run economic growth depends upon rising labor productivity. Putting more people to work can increase output in the short run, but it does not result in sustained economic growth. Long-run economic growth is possible in relatively poor countries (for example, South Korea before 1970) and countries endowed with low levels of resources (for example, Japan).

6. **Answer d.** Each of these reasons—physical capital, human capital, and technological advances—contributes to increases in productivity, or the ability to produce more output per worker.

7. **Answer a.** Answer (a) provides a definition of the aggregate production function. In answers (b) and (c), we know there is a relationship between output per worker and the amount of human capital per worker or physical capital per worker: in both cases, an increase in either human or physical capital, holding everything else constant, will lead to an increase in output per worker.

8. **Answer c.** This question focuses on the concept of diminishing returns to physical capital: given an aggregate production function with a constant level of human capital per worker and state of technology, an increase in the quantity of physical capital per worker will lead the rate of productivity to fall while remaining positive. Thus, output per worker will increase but by smaller and smaller amounts.

9. **Answer a.** The other-things-equal expression is used when economists want to single out the effect of a change in one variable on their economic model. To see this effect, all other variables that might affect the model are held constant, or equal to their initial value, while the single variable is allowed to change.

10. **Answer c.** Physical capital per worker in the first year increases by 5%, or $(100)(1.05) =$ 105 units. In the second year, physical capital per worker increases another 5%, or $(105)(1.05) = 110.25$ units.

11. **Answer c.** Using growth accounting, we can estimate output per worker as being equal to the percentage change in physical capital per worker times the impact on output per worker. In this case, a 5% increase in physical capital per worker will lead to a 1% increase in output per worker. Since output is initially $1,000, a 1% increase in output will equal $1,010.

12. **Answer e.** Investment spending depends upon the availability of savings. An increase in investment spending is possible either by increasing the level of domestic savings or by borrowing foreign savings.

13. **Answer d.** All of these statements are factual statements found in the text of the chapter.

14. **Answer d.** To find the growth rate of real GDP in Macroland between 2010 and 2011, use the following formula:

    Growth rate of real GDP between 2010 and 2011 = {[(real GDP in 2011) − (real GDP in 2010)]/(real GDP in 2010)} × 100 = [(450 − 400)/(400)] × 100 = 12.5%

15. **Answer a.** Infrastructure includes roads, power lines, ports, information networks, and basic public health measures. Countries lacking this infrastructure find it hard to maintain high rates of economic growth. Infrastructure is primarily provided by government, not private enterprise.

16. **Answer b.** Long-run economic growth requires political stability and well-defined property rights. Long-run economic growth is hindered by bureaucratic restrictions and excessive government intervention in markets.

17. **Answer d.** The convergence hypothesis says that differences in real GDP per capita among countries tend to narrow over time because countries that start with lower GDP per capita tend to grow at faster rates than countries that start with higher GDP per capita. Answers (a) and (b) express comparable ideas. Relatively poor countries may experience fast economic growth if they implement existing technological advances.

18. **Answer c.** The rule of 70 says that the number of years for a variable to double is approximately equal to 70 divided by the annual growth rate of that variable. Hence, if the real GDP per capita in an economy doubles in 10 years, then the annual growth rate of that variable must equal 70/10, or 7%.

19. **Answer d.** All of the statements are true: answers (a) and (b) are in the text. Answer (c) refers to the idea that technological innovation can result from relatively modest innovations and not just major innovations: the text provides the examples of flat-bottomed paper bags and Post-it® notes.

20. **Answer b.** With fixed technology, labor, and human capital, an increase in physical capital per worker will eventually result in output per worker increasing at a decreasing rate due to diminishing returns to physical capital. The economy, despite its increased physical capital per worker, finds that each additional unit of this physical capital per worker results in smaller and smaller increases to output per worker, since the fixed amount of labor cannot fully utilize the increases in physical capital per worker.

21. **Answer d.** This answer is the definition of growth accounting. Growth accounting seeks to assign the contribution of each major factor—physical capital per worker, human capital per worker, and technology—in the aggregate production function to economic growth.

22. **Answer c.** To find the productivity growth per year from this growth in human capital per worker, multiply the growth rate of human capital per worker times the effect of a 1 percent change in the human capital per worker on output per worker, or 6%(0.5). The growth in human capital per worker is responsible for 3 percentage points of productivity growth per year.

23. **Answer b.** When total factor productivity increases, this enables an economy to produce more output from a given set of resources or to produce the same amount of output from fewer resources.

24. **Answer a.** In the world today, human and physical capital are far more important in determining a country's productivity than are natural resources.

25. **Answer b.** New technology takes time to fully incorporate at the firm level: the new technology may require reconfiguring the physical setup of the firm, or the training of labor in the new technology. In addition, it may take time for firms to learn how to best use the new technology.

26. **Answer e.** In 1820, Mexico had higher real GDP per capita than Japan. But, in 2007, Japan's real GDP per capita was greater than most European nations; in addition, in 2007, Japan had a far greater average standard of living than did Mexico. This higher average standard of living was due to real GDP per capita growing faster in Japan than in Mexico over the long run.

27. **Answer c.** Fast-growing economies grow fast because their capital stock is increasing rapidly. This increase in capital stock can only occur if there is a high level of investment spending. Thus, the share of GDP that reflects investment goods tends to be very large in comparison to countries that have lower economic growth rates.

28. **Answer g.** All of these statements are true. See the text for coverage of these statements.

29. **Answer b.** Economists believe that resource scarcity will lead to higher prices for those resources. As the prices of these resources rise, people will move to conserve the scarce resources and, in addition, new alternatives to replace these scarce resources will be developed.

30. **Answer d.** Environmental damage from economic growth and, in particular, the use of fossil fuels contributes to climate change and can be remedied by the government imposing "carbon taxes" or "cap and trade" systems for carbon emissions. Government intervention is necessary, since the negative externality of the pollution created by firms and individuals will not be eliminated without government intervention to limit these activities through the appropriate incentive system.

31. **Answer e.** All of these statements are true. "New growth theory" recognizes that technological innovation, which consists of new knowledge, provides information on how to better use existent resources. Once this knowledge has been discovered, it can be used by many people at no or very low additional cost. However, if everyone can use this knowledge once it has been discovered, then there is little incentive for businesses to engage in activities to find this knowledge. Paul Romer discusses the need to provide innovators with monopoly power at least initially so that the innovators who discover new knowledge can profit from their effort before the information is made available to other producers.

chapter 10(25)

Savings, Investment Spending, and the Financial System

BEFORE YOU READ THE CHAPTER

Summary

This chapter examines the relationship between saving and investment and how financial markets facilitate economic growth. The chapter also discusses four principal types of assets: stocks, bonds, loans, and bank deposits. It examines the role of financial intermediation in the economy and how financial intermediation enables investors to diversify while simultaneously reducing their exposure to risk and the costs of their transactions, while increasing their access to liquidity. The chapter discusses the determination of stock prices and the effect of stock market fluctuations on the macroeconomy. The appendix discusses present value and provides a discussion of how to evaluate the relationship between costs and benefits of a project when these costs and benefits arrive at different times.

Chapter Objectives

Objective #1. Long-run economic growth depends on a well functioning financial system that can link savers with excess funds to borrowers in need of funds to finance productive investment activities. The financial system provides the mechanism for increasing physical capital, a critical source of productivity growth.

Objective #2. Investment spending refers to spending on physical capital, while investment refers to the purchase of financial assets like stocks, bonds, or existing real estate.

Objective #3. Human capital is primarily provided by the government through its support of education, while physical capital, excluding infrastructure, is provided through private investment spending.

Objective #4. Domestic savings and foreign savings are the two sources of savings in an economy.

Objective #5. The saving–investment spending identity states that saving is always equal to investment whether the economy is a closed economy with no international trade or an open economy with trade.

- In a closed economy, investment spending (I) can be written as $I = GDP - C - G$.

- Private savings ($S_{Private}$) in a closed economy can be expressed as total income plus government transfers minus taxes and consumption, or $S_{Private} = GDP + TR - T - C$.

- When the government spends more than it collects in tax revenue, it runs a budget deficit; and when the government spends less than it collects in tax revenue, it runs a budget surplus. A budget surplus is equivalent to savings by the government. The budget balance ($S_{Government}$) is equal to taxes minus government transfers and government spending, or $S_{Government} = T - TR - G$. A positive budget balance indicates the government is saving, while a negative budget balance indicates the government is dissaving.

- National savings (NS) is the sum of private savings plus government savings, or $NS = GDP - C - G$.

Objective #6. In an open economy, savings need not be spent on physical capital in the same country where the savings occurred. Countries can receive inflows of savings from other countries, and countries can generate outflows of savings to other countries. We call the net effect of international inflows and outflows of funds on the total savings available for investment spending in a country its capital inflow, or KI symbolically.

- Capital inflow can be positive or negative. When capital inflow is positive, the inflow of funds into a country exceeds the outflow of funds; and when capital inflow is negative, the inflow of funds into a country is less than the outflow of funds.

- A positive capital inflow represents funds borrowed from foreigners, while a negative capital inflow represents funds lent to foreigners. Capital inflow is related to a country's exports and imports: a country that spends more on imports than it earns from exports must borrow the difference from foreigners. That borrowing is equal to the country's capital inflow. This implies that a country's capital inflow is equal to the difference between imports and exports, or $KI = IM - X$.

- In an open economy, investment spending equals the sum of national savings and capital inflows, or $I = S_{Private} + S_{Government} + KI = NS + KI$.

- We can restate our findings: investment spending equals savings, where savings is defined as national savings plus capital inflow. In an open economy, some of the funds supporting investment spending may be the savings of foreigners.

Objective #7. The loanable funds market is a hypothetical market where savers, or those individuals supplying funds, interact with borrowers, or those individuals demanding funds. The loanable funds market maximizes the gains from trade between lenders and borrowers.

- The equilibrium price or interest rate equates the quantity demanded of funds with the quantity supplied of funds. This interest rate is the return a lender receives for allowing borrowers the use of a dollar for one year.

- The real interest rate is the interest rate adjusted for changes in prices over the length of the loan, while the nominal interest rate is the interest rate unadjusted for changes in prices.

- The relationship between the nominal interest rate and the real interest rate can be expressed as "the real interest rate is equal to the nominal interest rate minus the inflation rate." When there is no inflation, the nominal and real interest rates are equivalent.

- The Fisher effect asserts that the expected real interest rate is unaffected by the change in expected inflation. As long as inflation is expected, the inflation does not affect the equilibrium quantity of loanable funds or the expected real interest rate; the expected inflation only affects the equilibrium nominal interest rate.

Objective #8. A business will borrow money to finance a project provided that the rate of return on the project exceeds the cost of borrowing for the project; that is, a project will be undertaken by a business only if the rate of return is equal to or greater than the interest rate levied on the loan.

Objective #9. Crowding out refers to the negative effect on private investment spending from government budget deficits. If the government's budget deficit results in crowding out, less physical capital is accumulated each year in the economy. Holding everything else constant, this can result in lower long-run economic growth.

Objective #10. Some government spending is essential for long-run economic growth. For example, government expenditure on infrastructure is critical for long-run economic growth. The negative impact of crowding out is based on the other-things-equal assumption that all government spending necessary for the economy's infrastructure has occurred and that any additional government expenditure resulting in a government deficit will reduce the level of private investment spending and therefore the level of economic growth in the economy.

Objective #11. Households invest their savings and wealth, or accumulated savings, by purchasing financial assets in financial markets. Financial assets are paper claims that provide the buyer of the claim future income from the seller of the claim. Financial assets represent an asset to the purchaser of the claim and a liability to the seller of the claim. For example, if you borrow funds from a bank, the loan represents an asset to the bank because the bank will receive income in the future from the loan. And the loan represents a liability to you, since you must repay the funds you have borrowed at some point in the future.

Objective #12. The financial system provides borrowers and lenders a cost-effective way to reduce transactions costs and risk while enhancing their liquidity.

- Transactions costs are the expenses suppliers and demanders incur when they negotiate and execute a transaction.

- Financial risk refers to the uncertainty about future outcomes that involve financial losses and gains. A risk-averse person views potential losses and gains in an asymmetrical way: the total decrease in the person's welfare from losing a given amount of money is greater than the total increase in the person's welfare from gaining an equivalent amount of money. The risk-averse person is willing to expend a greater amount of resources to avoid losing a dollar than he or she is willing to expend to gain a dollar.

- Diversification, or the holding of different types of financial and physical assets, reduces the level of financial risk an individual faces. Investing in several assets with unrelated risks lowers the total risk of loss for the individual.

- Liquidity refers to the ease with which an asset can be converted into cash. A liquid asset is easily converted into cash, while an illiquid asset cannot be easily converted into cash.

Objective #13. The four primary types of financial assets are loans, bonds, stocks, and bank deposits.

- A loan is an agreement between a particular lender and a particular borrower. Loans are typically tailored to the needs of the borrower. Loans have high transactions costs.

- A bond is a promise to repay the owner of the bond a specific amount at some point in the future plus yearly interest for the life of the bond. Information about the bond issuer is freely available from bond-rating agencies that assess the creditworthiness of the bond issuer. Bonds are easy to resell, which enhances their liquidity.

- A stock is a share in the ownership of a company. Owning a share of stock in a given company is riskier than owning a bond from this same company; stock ownership generally results in a higher return for the investor than a bond, but it also carries higher risk.

Objective #14. Financial intermediaries are institutions that transform funds gathered from many individuals into financial assets. Four important financial intermediaries are mutual funds, pension funds, life insurance companies, and banks.

- A mutual fund creates a diversified stock portfolio and then resells shares of the stock portfolio to individual investors. This enables investors with a small amount of money to indirectly invest in a diversified portfolio that yields a better return for any given level of risk than would otherwise be available to the investor.

- Pension funds are nonprofit institutions that collect savings from their members and then invest these funds in a wide variety of assets in order to provide retirement income for their members.

- Life insurance companies collect funds from policyholders in order to guarantee payments to the policyholders' beneficiaries when the policyholders die. Life insurance companies increase individual welfare by reducing risk.

- Banks are institutions that gather funds from depositors and then use these funds to make loans. Banks enhance financial liquidity while serving the financing needs of those borrowers who do not want to use the stock or bond markets.

  - A bank deposit is an asset for the individuals depositing their funds at the bank and a liability for the bank.

  - A bank loan is an asset for the bank and a liability for the individuals who borrow the funds.

  - Bank deposits provide liquid assets to the owners of these deposits while simultaneously providing a source of funds to finance the illiquid investments of borrowers.

Objective #15. Stock market indexes are numbers intended as a summary of average prices in the stock market. Three examples of stock market indexes are the Dow Jones Industrial Average, the S&P 500, and the NASDAQ.

Objective #16. Financial fluctuations in the financial system can be a source of macroeconomic instability.

Objective #17. The value of an asset comes from its ability to generate higher future consumption of goods and services. This future income can be earned as interest or dividends, or it can be earned from selling the asset in the future at a profit. Therefore, the value of an asset today depends upon investors' beliefs about the future value of the asset. For example, stock prices will change in response to changes in investors' expectations about future stock prices.

Objective #18. There are two principal competing viewpoints about how stock price expectations are determined. The efficient markets hypothesis says that asset prices always include all publicly available information: this implies that stock prices are fairly valued and are neither overpriced nor underpriced. A contrasting view holds that markets often behave irrationally, leading to the possibility that some stocks are underpriced and represent potential profit-making opportunities for the investor.

Objective #19. There is no reason to assume stock prices will be stable. Stock price fluctuations can have major macroeconomic effects, requiring policymaker intervention.

Objective #20 [from Appendix]. The present value calculation is a method for evaluating the value today of a payment to be received or made at some point in the future. This calculation is useful when comparing the benefits and costs from an activity when these benefits and costs arrive at different points in time. By using present values in evaluating a project, you can evaluate the project as if all the costs and benefits from the project were occurring today rather than at different times.

- The present value calculation recognizes that a dollar held today is worth more than a dollar held a year from now. You can use the interest rate to compare the value of a dollar today to a dollar received at some point in the future: the interest rate measures the cost to you of delaying the receipt of a dollar of benefit, or the benefit to you of delaying the payment of a dollar of cost.

- Suppose you lend out $x today with the expectation that you will be repaid a dollar a year from now. The dollar you receive a year from now should be equal to $x plus the interest you receive from the borrower. If interest rate is represented as r, then we can express this idea as follows: the payment you receive a year from now ($1) equals $x(1 + r)$. Thus $x is the present value of the $1 you receive a year from now, and the present value of a payment of $1 made a year from now is $x = 1/(1 + r)$. This method converts future dollars into their present values so that the time factor issue can be eliminated when making decisions. The present value concept can be expanded to a number of years. For example, the present value of a payment made N years from now is (future value)$/(1 + r)N$.

- The net present value is the present value of current and future benefits minus the present value of current and future costs. When comparing potential projects, the project with the highest net present value is financially the most attractive project to undertake.

Key Terms

savings–investment spending identity an accounting fact that states that savings and *investment spending* are always equal for the *economy* as a whole.

budget surplus the difference between tax revenue and government spending when tax revenue exceeds government spending; saving by the government in the form of a budget surplus is a positive contribution to *national savings*.

budget deficit the difference between tax revenue and government spending when government spending exceeds tax revenue; dissaving by the government in the form of a budget deficit is a negative contribution to *national savings*.

budget balance the difference between tax revenue and government spending. A positive budget balance is referred to as a *budget surplus*; a negative budget balance is referred to as a *budget deficit*.

national savings the sum of *private savings* and the government's *budget balance*; the total amount of savings generated within the economy.

Key Terms *(continued)*

capital inflow the net inflow of funds into a country; the difference between the total inflow of foreign funds to the home country and the total outflow of domestic funds to other countries. A positive net capital inflow represents funds borrowed from foreigners to finance domestic investment; a negative net capital inflow represents funds lent to foreigners to finance foreign investment.

loanable funds market a hypothetical market that brings together those who want to lend money (savers) and those who want to borrow (*firms* with *investment spending* projects).

interest rate the price, calculated as a percentage of the amount borrowed, charged by lenders to borrowers for the use of their savings for one year.

present value the number of dollars today that are equivalent to a dollar at that future date.

crowding out the negative effect of *budget deficits* on private investment, which occurs because government borrowing drives up *interest rates*.

Fisher effect the principle by which an increase in expected future *inflation* drives up the *nominal interest rate*, leaving the expected real interest rate unchanged.

wealth (of a *household*) the value of accumulated savings.

financial asset a paper claim that entitles the buyer to future income from the seller. *Loans, stocks, bonds,* and *bank deposits* are types of financial assets.

physical asset a claim on a tangible object that gives the owner the right to dispose of the object as he or she wishes.

liability a requirement to pay income in the future.

transaction costs the expenses of negotiating and executing a deal.

financial risk uncertainty about future outcomes that involve financial losses and gains.

diversification investment in several different assets with unrelated, or independent, risks, so that the possible losses are independent events.

liquid describes an asset that can be quickly converted into cash without much loss of value.

illiquid describes an asset that cannot be quickly converted into cash without much loss of value.

loan a lending agreement between an individual lender and an individual borrower. Loans are usually tailored to the individual borrower's needs and ability to pay but carry relatively high transaction costs.

default the risk that the bond issuer fails to make payments as specified by the bond contract.

loan-backed securities assets created by pooling individual *loans* and selling shares in that pool.

Key Terms *(continued)*

financial intermediary an institution, such as a *mutual fund, pension fund, life insurance company*, or *bank*, that transforms the funds it gathers from many individuals into *financial assets*.

mutual fund a *financial intermediary* that creates a *stock* portfolio by buying and holding shares in companies and then selling shares of this portfolio to individual investors.

pension fund a type of *mutual fund* that holds assets in order to provide retirement income to its members.

life insurance company a *financial intermediary* that sells policies guaranteeing a payment to a policyholder's beneficiaries when the policyholder dies.

bank deposit a claim on a *bank* that obliges the bank to give the depositor his or her cash when demanded.

bank a *financial intermediary* that provides *liquid* assets in the form of *bank deposits* to lenders and uses those funds to finance the *illiquid* investments or *investment spending* needs of borrowers.

efficient markets hypothesis a principle of asset price determination that holds that asset prices embody all publicly available information. The hypothesis implies that *stock* prices should be unpredictable, or follow a *random walk*, since changes should occur only in response to new information about fundamentals.

random walk the movement over time of an unpredictable *variable*.

▮ AFTER YOU READ THE CHAPTER

Tips

Tip #1. It is important to understand that savings and investment spending are always equal whether the economy is open or closed. This is an accounting fact and is referred to as the savings–investment spending identity.

Tip #2. It is important to know and understand the formulas and definitions of investment spending, private savings, the budget balance, national savings, and capital inflow. This chapter includes a number of equations that provide a mathematical expression of important relationships among variables. Make sure you familiarize yourself thoroughly with these formulas:

$I = GDP - C - G$ in a closed economy

$S_{Private} = GDP + TR - T - C$

$S_{Government} = T - TR - G$

$NS = S_{Private} + S_{Government} = GDP - C - G$ in a closed economy

$KI = IM - X$ in an open economy

$I = S_{Private} + S_{Government} + (IM - X)$ in an open economy

$I = NS + KI$

Tip #3. It is important to understand that some government spending is essential for a well functioning economy. An economy cannot function without a basic infrastructure that includes a well functioning system of law and order including a court system, a public health system to prevent the spread of disease, and systems of transportation, communication, and education. When economists discuss the crowding out of private investment spending because of government budget deficits, they are assuming that this additional government spending is spending that is in excess of this basic infrastructure.

Tip #4 **[from Appendix].** The calculation of present value is a calculation that allows you to compare a stream of payments occurring over time to another stream of payments occurring over some other period of time. This calculation is highly useful, and you should practice using it until you are comfortable with the concept as well as the technique.

WORKED PROBLEMS

1. Suppose that consumption spending in an economy is given by the equation $C = 100 + .8(Y - T)$ where C is consumption spending, Y is real GDP (or aggregate spending), and T is net taxes. In this economy, T is a constant $20 per year. Furthermore, suppose that investment spending, I, is also constant and equal to $40 per year. The government in this economy spends a constant $20 per year. This economy is a closed economy. You have been asked to prove to government officials that saving in this economy is equal to investment spending. You have also been asked to identify the level of total income for this economy given the above information.

STEP 1: Write an expression that depicts the relationship between total income and total spending in this economy.

Review the section "Matching Up Savings and Investment Spending" on page 276 (Econ page 708).

Recall that the circular flow diagram of the economy tells us that total spending in an economy must equal total income in the economy: that is, one person's spending on goods and services is someone else's income. Thus, if total income is equal to total spending, we can rewrite this as total income is equal to the consumption spending plus investment spending plus government spending, since in this economy spending can only come from households, businesses, and government. Symbolically, we have

$$\text{Total Income} = C + I + G$$

STEP 2: Use the expression you found in Step 1 to calculate the value of total spending, or real GDP, for this economy.

Review the section "Matching Up Savings and Investment Spending" on page 276 (Econ page 708).

We can rewrite the expression in Step 1 using the data that was provided as

$$Y = 100 + .8(Y - T) + 40 + 20$$
$$Y = 160 + .8(Y - 20)$$
$$Y = 144 + .8Y$$
$$.2Y = 144$$
$$Y = 720$$

Real GDP in this economy is equal to $720 per year.

STEP 3: Given your work in Steps 1 and 2, determine the level of consumption spending in this economy.

Review the section "Matching Up Savings and Investment Spending" on page 276 (Econ page 708).

Consumption spending is given as $C = 100 + .8(Y - T)$. Since we now know the value of Y as well as T it is a simple matter to calculate the value of C. Thus, $C = 100 + .8(720 - 20) = \$660$.

STEP 4: Calculate the value of national savings for this economy.

Review the section "Matching Up Savings and Investment Spending" on page 276 (Econ page 708).

National savings is equal to the sum of private savings and the budget balance, where private savings is disposable income (income after taxes) minus consumption. The budget balance is the difference between tax revenues and government spending. In this example private savings is equal to $(720 - 20) - 660$ or $\$40$ while the budget balance is equal to $20 - 20$ or $\$0$. National savings is therefore equal to $\$40 + \$0$ or $\$40$ per year.

STEP 5: Compare the value of national savings to investment spending in this economy. Are the two equal?

Review the section "Matching Up Savings and Investment Spending" on page 276 (Econ page 708).

National savings and investment spending are both equal to $\$40$. The savings-investment identity is true for this economy.

2.   Suppose that all of the information you were given in problem 1 is true except that taxes have fallen to $\$10$ per year. You have been asked by the government officials to evaluate the effect of this tax decrease on this economy. In particular you have been asked to calculate the value of real GDP and the value of the budget balance. You have also been asked to explain the significance of the number you have calculated for the budget balance. Finally you have been asked to verify that the savings-investment spending identity is still true for this economy.

STEP 1: To address the issues raised by this question you will first want to calculate the value of total spending in this economy for the year.

Review the section "Matching Up Savings and Investment Spending" on page 276 (Econ page 708).

Total spending for this economy will equal total income in the economy (review Step 1 from the previous question if you are still struggling with this concept). Total spending in this closed economy is equal to $C + I + G$. Or,

$$\text{Total spending} = 100 + .8(Y - T) + 40 + 20$$
$$Y = 160 + .8(Y - 10)$$
$$Y = 152 + .8Y$$
$$.2Y = 152$$
$$Y = \$760$$

Total income (and total spending or real GDP) in this economy will equal $\$760$ per year given the reduction in net taxes and holding everything else constant.

STEP 2: Calculate the value of the budget balance for this economy and explain whether the budget balance indicates a budget surplus or a budget deficit.

Review the section "Matching Up Savings and Investment Spending" on page 276 (Econ page 708).

The budget balance is equal to taxes minus government spending or 10 – 20 in this example. The budget balance is therefore equal to –$10. A negative budget balance indicates that the government is running a budget deficit: the government is spending more than it is receiving in tax revenues. The government will need to borrow in order to finance this expenditure that exceeds its tax revenue.

STEP 3: Determine the level of consumption spending in this economy.

Review the section "Matching Up Savings and Investment Spending" on page 276 (Econ page 708).

Consumption spending is given as $C = 100 + .8(Y - T)$. Since we now know the value of Y as well as T, it is a simple matter to calculate the value of C. Thus, $C = 100 + .8(760 - 10) = \$700$.

STEP 4: Calculate the value of national savings for this economy.

Review the section "Matching Up Savings and Investment Spending" on page 276 (Econ page 708).

National savings is equal to the sum of private savings and the budget balance, where private savings is disposable income (income after taxes) minus consumption. The budget balance is the difference between tax revenues and government spending. In this example private savings is equal to $(760 - 10) - 700$ or $50, while the budget balance is equal to 10 – 20 or –$10. National savings is therefore equal to $50 + –$10, or $40 per year.

STEP 5: Compare the value of national savings to investment spending in this economy. Are the two equal?

Review the section "Matching Up Savings and Investment Spending" on page 276 (Econ page 708).

National savings and investment spending are both equal to $40. The savings-investment identity is true for this economy.

3. The demand for loanable funds from businesses in an economy is a downward sloping line: as the interest rate decreases, the quantity of loanable funds demanded by businesses increases. In addition, in this economy the government also demands a constant amount of loanable funds due to the government operating with a persistent, but constant, deficit. The supply of loanable funds curve in this economy is upward sloping: as the interest rate increases, the quantity of loanable funds supplied in this economy increases. Initially the level of capital inflows in this economy is equal to zero. Given this information, you have been asked to provide a graph of the loanable funds market that depicts business demand for loanable funds, total demand for loanable funds (this is business demand as well as the government's demand), and the total supply of loanable funds. In this graph you are asked to identify the equilibrium level of loanable funds as well as the equilibrium interest rate. You are also asked to identify the level of investment spending (I_1) by businesses. In a second graph you are asked to analyze how an increase in government spending to a new, but constant, level will affect the level of investment spending (I_2) by businesses. In this second graph you are also asked to identify the new equilibrium interest rate as well as the new equilibrium level of loanable funds. Indicate the amount of business investment spending that is crowded out due to the increase in the government spending. Finally, suppose that this second graph is modified one more time. In your third graph analyze the effect of an increase in capital inflows on the interest rate, the level of

investment spending by businesses, and the equilibrium level of loanable funds. In this analysis compare your results with the results you had in the second graph.

STEP 1: Draw the initial loanable funds situation presented in this question. In your graph note the business demand for loanable funds curve (I), the total demand for loanable funds curve (D_{LF}), which includes the business demand as well as the government demand for loanable funds, and the total supply of loanable funds curve (S_{LF}).In this graph label the equilibrium interest rate as r_1, the equilibrium level of loanable funds as LF_1, and the initial level of business investment spending as I_1.

Review the section "Matching Up Savings and Investment Spending" on page 276 (Econ page 708) and the section "The Market for Loanable Funds" on page 281 (Econ page 713).

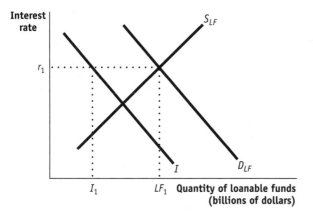

STEP 2: Draw a new graph of the loanable funds market illustrating the effect of an increase in the government deficit in this market. In this graph note the business demand for loanable funds curve (I), the total demand for loanable funds curve (D_{LF_2}), which includes the business demand as well as the new, higher level of government demand for loanable funds, and the total supply of loanable funds curve (S_{LF}). In this graph label the equilibrium interest rate as r_2, the equilibrium level of loanable funds as LF_2, and the new level of business investment spending as I_2. Indicate on this graph as well as verbally the amount of business investment spending that is crowded out due to the increase in government spending holding everything else constant.

Review the section "Matching Up Savings and Investment Spending" on page 276 (Econ page 708) and the section "The Market for Loanable Funds" on page 281 (Econ page 713).

The demand for loanable funds curve will shift to the right when the government increases its level of spending while holding constant its level of taxation. In the following graph, this shift is illustrated as D_{LF_2}. When the demand for loanable funds curve shifts to the right, holding everything else constant, this causes the equilibrium interest rate to increase and the equilibrium quantity of loanable funds to increase. However, the increase in the interest rate will cause the level of business investment spending to fall: note how as the interest rate rises from r_1 to r_2 there is a movement along the curve labeled I in the following graph. The increase in government expenditure results in crowding out of business investment of $I_1 - I_2$.

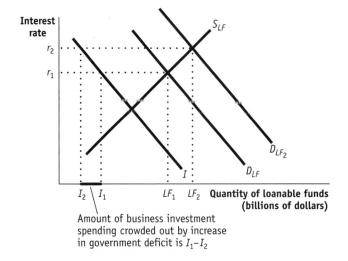

Amount of business investment
spending crowded out by increase
in government deficit is I_1-I_2

STEP 3: Draw a third graph of the loanable funds market illustrating the effect of an increase in capital inflows on this market. In this graph note the business demand for loanable funds curve (I), the total demand for loanable funds curve (D_{LF_2}), which includes the business demand as well as the new, higher level of government demand for loanable funds, and the new total supply of loanable funds curve (S_{LF_2}), which includes the increase in capital inflows. In this graph label the equilibrium interest rate as r_3, the equilibrium level of loanable funds as LF_3, and the new level of business investment spending as I_3.

Review the section "Matching Up Savings and Investment Spending" on page 276 (Econ page 708) and the section "The Market for Loanable Funds" on page 281 (Econ page 713).

When capital inflows increase, holding everything else constant, this causes the supply of loanable funds curve to shift to the right. At every interest rate there is a greater quantity of loanable funds supplied in this market due to the increase in capital inflows. In the following graph, two potential supply of loanable funds curves have been drawn. Look closely at each of these. Relative to r_2 and LF_2, we can see that the equilibrium interest rate will decrease and the equilibrium quantity of loanable funds will increase with this increase in capital inflows. But, relative to r_1 and LF_1, we see that the equilibrium interest rate may increase, decrease or equal r_1 depending upon the size of the rightward shift in the supply of loanable funds curve. Relative to LF_1 we see that the equilibrium level of loanable funds has increased. Thus, this change relative to r_1 and LF_1 results in the equilibrium interest rate being indeterminate, while the equilibrium quantity of loanable funds increases.

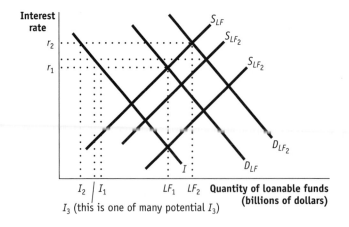

I_3 (this is one of many potential I_3)

4.   **[from Appendix]** Joel starts the year with $0. Each year Joel is able to earn $5,000 during the year so that at the beginning of the next year he has another $5,000. For example, at the beginning of the first year Joel has $0, and at the end of the first year (or the beginning of the second year) he has $5,000 to add to his first $0. Joel is contemplating two options for this money: in the first option, Joel simply places the money in a box under his bed; and in the second option, Joel places the money at the beginning of each year in the bank and earns 5% interest on that money during that year. He does not remove the money, and whatever interest he earns in the first year gets added to his initial deposit for that year. With this second option, he plans to keep the money in for five years. Joel has asked you to provide a numerical calculation of the value of these two options to him at the end of five years.

STEP 1: Calculate the value of the first option for Joel.

It is helpful when calculating the value to Joel to think about a number line with each mark on the number line signifying a year. For Joel, we start at the initial point (Year 0) and note that he has $0. At the end of the first year, Joel has this $0 plus an additional $5,000. Look at the following sketch to see how we can illustrate the first option.

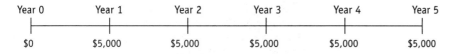

From the sketch, we can see that Joel has a total of $25,000 if he earns $5,000 per year and saves this amount of money for five years.

STEP 2: Calculate the value of the second option for Joel.

In the second option, Joel places the first $5,000 in the bank at the beginning of the second year and earns interest of 5% on this deposit for the year. At the end of the year, Joel will have his initial $5,000 plus his interest payment: we can write this amount as $(5,000)(1 + .05)$. Joel plans to keep all of this in the bank and earn interest of 5% on this total amount for the next year. Thus, for the first $5,000 he deposited, he will earn $(5,000)(1 + .05)(1 + .05)$ after it has been deposited at the bank for two years. Joel will be able to keep this first deposit in the bank for four years, so this first deposit will have a value of $(5,000)(1 + .05)^4$ after five years. But, Joel plans to deposit a second $5,000 at the end of year 2: this second $5,000 will earn interest for three years, and its value to Joel after five years can be written as $(5,000)(1 + .05)^3$. This same reasoning can be used for the $5,000 Joel will deposit at the end of year 3: its value will be $(5,000)(1 + .05)^2$. The $5,000 Joel will deposit at the end of year 4 will have a value of $(5,000)(1 + .05)$. The value of the $5,000 Joel will deposit at the end of year 5 will simply be $5,000. Total value of option 2 for Joel can be written as

Total Value $= (5,000)(1 + .05)^4 + (5,000)(1 + .05)^3 + (5,000)(1 + .05)^2 + (5,000)(1 + .05) + 5,000 = \$27,628.16$

STEP 3: Compare the values of the two options for Joel and make a recommendation.

Clearly, option 2 results in Joel having a larger amount of savings after five years.

Problems and Exercises

1. You are given the following information about the open economy of Macroland for 2009.

GDP	$100 billion
C	70 billion
T	15 billion
TR	8 billion
G	20 billion
X	10 billion
IM	12 billion

In 2009:

a. What is the level of investment spending in Macroland?

b. What is the level of capital inflow for Macroland? Is Macroland borrowing from foreigners or lending to foreigners? Explain your answer.

c. What is private savings equal to in Macroland?

d. What is the budget balance equal to in Macroland?

e. Does national savings plus capital inflow equal investment spending for this economy?

f. Is the government of Macroland saving or borrowing funds? Explain your answer.

2. Use the following information about the three economies, Funland, Upland, and Downland, to answer the following questions.

	Funland	Upland	Downland
GDP	$1,000	$5,000	$4,000
C	800	3,500	3,000
I			
G	100	800	300
X	50	400	400
IM	30	500	500
T	50	600	600
TR	20	200	200

a. Fill in the missing information in this table.

b. From the information you are given and your calculations in part (a), fill in the following table.

	Funland	Upland	Downland
$S_{Private}$			
$S_{Government}$			
KI			

c. Now, calculate capital inflow, private savings, and investment spending as a percentage of GDP for each economy. Report your calculations in an organized table.

d. What is the budget balance as a percentage of GDP for Funland, Upland, and Downland?

e. Are Funland, Upland, and Downland running a budget deficit or a budget surplus? How does your answer relate to the capital inflow each economy experiences?

3. Suppose in a closed economy, the demand for loanable funds can be expressed as $r = 0.1 - .00005Q$ and the supply of loanable funds can be expressed as $r = 0.00005Q$, where r is the real interest rate expressed as a decimal (for example, 8% is expressed as 0.08 in the equation) and Q is the quantity of loanable funds. Assume the government initially has a budget balance of zero.

a. What is the equilibrium real interest rate and the equilibrium quantity in the loanable funds market?

b. Suppose the government's budget balance decreases to −$100 at every real interest rate. What will happen to the demand and supply of loanable funds with this change? What do you predict will happen to the equilibrium interest rate and the equilibrium quantity in the loanable funds market?

c. Does crowding out occur in this economy when the budget balance is −$100? Explain your answer.

4. For each of the following, decide whether they represent investment in physical assets, investment in financial assets, or investment in human capital. For each example also decide whether they represent investment spending.

a. The government increases expenditures on education for children and training for post–high school graduates.

b. Michael purchases a $100 bond issued by a local company that provides technical support for computer users.

c. Susan purchases $1,000 worth of filing cabinets and office desks for her business office.

d. A neighboring country purchases $10 million in U.S. government bonds.

e. Mary purchases a newly constructed factory that manufactures auto parts.

5. Briefly identify critical areas of government spending that are necessary if an economy is to experience economic growth.

6. Briefly describe three important problems that lenders and borrowers face and how the financial system addresses these three problems.

7. Suppose that in Macroland the expected inflation rate is 5% for the coming year. Suppose that the nominal interest rate in the loanable funds market is currently 10%.

a. What do you predict is the value of the real interest rate given this information?

b. According to the Fisher effect, what would happen to the nominal interest rate if the expected inflation rate for Macroland increased to 7% for the coming year?

8.   Suppose the demand for loanable funds from firms is given by the equation $r = 10 - (1/100) \times I$, where r is the interest rate in the loanable funds market (expressed as a percentage and not a decimal) and I is the amount of investment spending. Furthermore, suppose that the supply of loanable funds is given by the equation $r = 2 + (3/500) \times S_{Private}$. Assume initially that there are no capital inflows and that the government has a budget balance.

   a.   What is the equilibrium interest rate given the above information and what is the equilibrium amount of investment spending in this market?

   b.   Suppose that the government runs a budget deficit and that at every interest rate the government now finds that it needs to borrow $200 in loanable funds. How will this budget deficit affect the demand for loanable funds curve and the supply of loanable funds curve? What do you predict will happen to the equilibrium interest rate in this market? (Do not make a calculation here; just simply give an intuitive answer.)

   c.   Given the information in part (b), calculate what the equilibrium interest rate will be with the government running a deficit. In addition, identify the amount of private investment spending that will occur when the government runs a deficit. How does the government deficit affect the level of private investment spending?

9.   For each of the following situations, state the effect on the equilibrium interest rate and the equilibrium quantity of loanable funds. In your answer make reference to how the demand and supply curves in the loanable funds market are affected. Holding everything else constant:

   a.   There is an increase in capital inflows into a country.

   b.   The government reduces the government deficit.

c. There is an increase in the expected inflation rate. Comment on the real interest rate as well as the nominal interest rate in your answer to this question.

d. There is an increase in private savings.

e. There is a decrease in perceived business opportunities.

10. **[from Appendix]** Mary offers to pay Joe $1,000 a year from now if he will loan her money today. Suppose Joe wants to earn 10% interest and there is no inflation over this period. What is the maximum amount Joe will lend Mary, given her offer?

11. **[from Appendix]** Sarah borrows $1,000 from Joe at the beginning of the year and promises to repay him at the end of five years. She also agrees to pay him an annual interest rate of 12%. What is the total amount Joe will receive at the end of the fifth year?

12. [from Appendix] Joe can't decide between two financial options: he can loan Sarah $1,000 as outlined in problem 11, or he can invest the $1,000 in a new venture. He estimates that during the first year the venture will earn 5% interest, during the second and third years it will earn 10% interest, and during the fourth and fifth years it will earn 18% interest. Evaluate these two options for Joe and then make a recommendation based on this evaluation.

13. [from Appendix] You have won the lottery and you can either receive your winnings as a single payment of $2 million in cash now, or you can receive a payment of $500,000 a year for five years starting now. The interest rate is constant and equal to 10% per year. Which payment plan do you prefer?

14. [from Appendix] Does your decision in problem 13 change if the interest rate is constant and equal to 8% instead of 10%?

15. [from Appendix] Does your decision in problem 13 change if the interest rate is constant and equal to 15% instead of 10%?

▮ BEFORE YOU TAKE THE TEST

Chapter Review Questions

1. Financial markets are beneficial
   a. to savers, since they provide interest payments for the use of savers' funds.
   b. to borrowers, since they provide a source of funds for productive investments.
   c. to the government, since they provide both a use for surplus government funds and a source of funds should the government run a deficit.
   d. Answers (a), (b), and (c) are all correct.

2. Investment spending includes all of the following *except* the
   a. construction of a new residence during the current year.
   b. purchase of a new piece of equipment at a factory during the current year.
   c. purchase of a home, built 20 years ago, during the current year.
   d. acquisition of new computers for a business during the current year.

3. Sources of funds for investment spending include
   a. domestic savings.
   b. foreign savings.
   c. the Federal Reserve Bank.
   d. Answers (a), (b), and (c) are all correct.
   e. Answers (a) and (b) are both correct.

4. Which of the following statements is true?
   a. In an open economy, the only source of funds for investment spending is domestic savings.
   b. In a closed economy, the only use of savings is to provide funds to finance government deficits.
   c. In a closed economy, the only source of funds for investment spending is domestic savings.
   d. Answers (a) and (b) are both true.
   e. Answers (b) and (c) are both true.

5. Which of the following statements is true?
   a. $I = GDP - C - G$ in a closed economy
   b. $GDP = C + I + G + X - IM$ in an open economy
   c. $GDP = S_{Private} + T + C - TR$
   d. $S_{Government} = T - TR - G$
   e. Answers (a), (b), (c), and (d) are all true.

6. When government spending is greater than net taxes,
   a. government savings is positive.
   b. there is a budget surplus.
   c. there is a positive surplus.
   d. there is a budget deficit.

7. The term "budget balance" can be abbreviated as $S_{Government}$. The value of $S_{Government}$ is
    a. positive when the government is running a budget surplus.
    b. positive when the government is running a budget deficit.
    c. negative when the government is running a budget deficit.
    d. zero when the government's expenditure equals its net taxes.
    e. Answers (a), (c), and (d) are all correct.
    f. Answers (b) and (d) are both correct.

8. Which of the following statements is true about national savings in a closed economy?
    a. National savings is the sum of private savings plus the budget balance.
    b. National savings is GDP minus consumption spending minus government spending.
    c. National savings is always equal to investment spending.
    d. Answers (a), (b), and (c) are all correct.

9. Capital inflow is the
    a. net inflow of foreign funds plus domestic savings into an economy.
    b. net inflow of funds into a country, or the total inflow of foreign funds into a country minus the total outflow of domestic funds to other countries.
    c. total outflow of domestic funds to other countries minus the net inflow of foreign funds into a country.
    d. total outflow of domestic funds to other countries plus the net inflow of foreign funds into a country.

10. Economists differentiate between these types of capital: physical capital, human capital, and financial capital. Which of the following statements is false?
    a. Human capital includes changes in the level of education or training workers possess.
    b. Physical capital includes changes in inventories.
    c. Financial capital refers to the funds available in an economy for investment spending.
    d. Financial capital refers to expenditures on manufacturing equipment.

11. Suppose a country exports $50 million worth of goods and services, while it imports $60 million worth of goods and services. This country
    a. has a positive capital inflow.
    b. lends funds to foreigners.
    c. has a negative capital inflow.
    d. Answers (a) and (b) are both correct.
    e. Answers (b) and (c) are both correct.

12. In an open economy, investment spending equals
    a. domestic savings.
    b. private savings plus the budget balance.
    c. the sum of private savings, the budget balance, and the difference between imports and exports.
    d. private savings plus capital inflows.

13. The loanable funds market

    a. provides a market where savers and borrowers can make mutually beneficial transactions.

    b. uses supply and demand to determine an equilibrium price or interest rate.

    c. interest rate is the return a lender receives for allowing borrowers the use of a dollar for one year.

    d. Answers (a), (b), and (c) are all correct.

Use the following information to answer the next two questions.

Suppose Joe lends Maxine $100 for the year. At the end of the year, Maxine repays Joe the $100 plus an additional payment of $15 for the use of Joe's money during the year.

14. Assuming there is no inflation during the year, what is the interest rate Maxine pays Joe?

    a. 0.15%

    b. 1.5%

    c. 15%

    d. 115%

15. Maxine, when borrowing the funds from Joe, anticipates the inflation rate for the year will be 10%, while Joe expects it to be 7%. Inflation is actually 8% for the year. Which of the following statements is true?

    a. Joe benefits unexpectedly from this higher-than-expected inflation rate.

    b. Maxine benefits unexpectedly from this lower-than-expected inflation rate.

    c. The nominal interest rate for this loan is 7%.

    d. The real interest rate for this loan is 7%.

16. When the government runs a deficit, this shifts the

    a. supply of loanable funds curve to the right.

    b. supply of loanable funds curve to the left.

    c. demand for loanable funds curve to the right.

    d. demand for loanable funds curve to the left.

17. Which of the following is an asset from a bank's perspective?

    a. Joe's checking account deposit of $500 at the bank

    b. Mike's car loan of $2,000 that he borrowed from the bank

    c. Mary's savings account balance of $325 at the bank

    d. From the bank's perspective, answers (a), (b), and (c) are all assets.

18. Financial markets provide a means for

    a. reducing risk for borrowers and lenders.

    b. reducing transaction costs for borrowers and lenders.

    c. enhancing liquidity for borrowers and lenders.

    d. Answers (a), (b), and (c) are all correct.

19. A person who is willing to spend more resources to avoid losing a fixed sum of money than is willing to expend on gaining the same sum of money is
   a. a risk lover.
   b. risk averse.
   c. displaying diminishing returns to risk.
   d. irrational.

20. Which of the following assets is most liquid?
   a. a home with a market value of $200,000
   b. a checking account balance of $1,000
   c. a three-carat diamond engagement ring
   d. a rare edition of an out-of-print book

21. Financial intermediaries
   a. transform funds gathered from many individuals into financial assets.
   b. provide a means of increasing risk for investors as well as business owners.
   c. only invest in bonds.
   d. only invest in stocks.

22. Banks
   a. provide liquidity to lenders.
   b. serve the financing needs of borrowers who do not use or cannot be served by the stock and bond markets.
   c. accept deposits from individuals who have excess funds.
   d. Answers (a), (b), and (c) are all correct.

23. Stock market prices are neither overvalued or undervalued according to
   a. irrational exuberance.
   b. the theory of stock market "bubbles."
   c. the efficient markets hypothesis.
   d. Answers (a), (b), and (c) are all correct.

24. In most economies, human capital is largely provided by the
   a. private sector.
   b. government.

25. When the government runs a budget surplus in an open economy, this implies
   a. that the government is spending more than its tax revenue.
   b. that net exports are positive.
   c. that net exports are negative.
   d. that the government is saving.
   e. Answers (b) and (d) are both correct.
   f. Answers (c) and (d) are both correct.

26. Which of the following statements is true?

    I. A dollar of investment spending financed by a capital inflow results in interest being paid to a foreigner for the use of that dollar.

    II. A dollar of investment spending, no matter how it is financed, results in interest being paid to the lender for the use of that dollar.

    III. No matter the source, a dollar of investment spending results in exactly the same outcome.

    a. Statement I is true.

    b. Statement II is true.

    c. Statement III is true.

    d. Statements I and II are true.

    e. Statements II and III are true.

    f. Statements I and III are true.

    g. Statements I, II, and III are all true.

27. Which of the following statements is true?

    a. Since the 1980s, the United States has had consistently low levels of savings when compared to other wealthy countries.

    b. Over the past 30 years, the difference in the U.S. savings level relative to other wealthy countries is attributable to the large government deficits the U.S. government has run during much of this time period.

    c. Investment spending in the United States during 2007 was financed through a combination of private savings and capital inflows while U.S. government savings were negative.

    d. Answers (a), (b), and (c) are all true.

    e. Answers (a) and (b) are both true.

    f. Answers (b) and (c) are both true.

    g. Answers (a) and (c) are both true.

28. In the loanable funds market, which of the following statements is true?

    a. Savers are best represented by the demand for loanable funds curve.

    b. Borrowers are best represented by the demand for loanable funds curve.

    c. The equilibrium interest rate equates the quantity of loanable funds supplied to the quantity of loanable funds demanded.

    d. Answers (a), (b), and (c) are all true.

    e. Answers (a) and (b) are both true.

    f. Answers (b) and (c) are both true.

    g. Answers (a) and (c) are both true.

29. Suppose an investment project is projected to provide $100,000 in revenues this year if the project is undertaken. The investment project will cost the company $90,000 and the current interest rate for funds is 10%. Given this information, the firm should

    a. commit to the investment project since its rate of return is greater than the prevailing interest rate.

    b. not commit to the investment project since its rate of return is less than the prevailing interest rate.

30. The loanable funds market enhances efficiency because
   a. only those investment projects with rates of return greater than the equilibrium interest rate are undertaken.
   b. the funds that are lent out are provided by those savers who are willing to lend out these funds at lower interest rates than other potential lenders.
   c. the richest people get all the investment funds that they need to undertake any investment project they have in mind.
   d. Answers (a), (b), and (c) are all correct.
   e. Answers (a) and (b) are both correct.

31. Holding everything else constant, when the government runs a deficit this results in
   a. the equilibrium interest rate in the loanable funds market increasing.
   b. the level of private investment spending in the loanable funds market decreasing.
   c. a decrease in capital inflows into this economy.
   d. Answers (a), (b), and (c) are all correct.
   e. Answers (a) and (b) are both correct.

Use the following information to answer the next two questions.

Marty borrows $1,000 from Harry on January 1, 2009, and promises to repay Harry on December 31, 2014, a payment that will result in Harry earning an annual rate of interest of 10%.

32. [from Appendix] Which of the following expressions correctly states the value of Marty's payment on December 31, 2014?
   a. $(\$1,000)(1 + 10)$
   b. $(\$1,000)/(1 + 0.10)^5$
   c. $(\$1,000)(1 + 0.10) + (\$1,000)(1 + 0.10)^2 + (\$1,000)(1 + 0.10)^3 + (\$1,000)$
      $(1 + 0.10)^4 + (\$1,000)(1 + 0.10)^5$
   d. $(\$1,000)(1 + 0.10)^5$

33. [from Appendix] Suppose Harry tells Marty he will lend him the money if he earns an annual rate of interest of 12%. This will result in Marty paying Harry a
   a. smaller amount than if the interest rate were 10%.
   b. larger amount than if the interest rate were 10%.

34. [from Appendix] Holding everything else constant, the present value of a future payment increases when the interest rate rises.
   a. True
   b. False

Use the following information to answer the next three questions.

Courtney's Computers is thinking about whether it should invest in a new software program. Development of this program will require an initial expenditure of $4 million now, but will result in annual profits of $2 million for three years.

35. [from Appendix] No matter what the interest rate, Courtney's Computers should invest in this new software since the profits from this new software far outweigh the costs of developing this software.
   a. True
   b. False

36. **[from Appendix]** Given the information provided, and an interest rate of 20%, Courtney's Computers should
    a. invest in the development of this new software.
    b. not invest in the development of this new software.

37. **[from Appendix]** Given the information provided, and an interest rate of 20%, the net present value of this new software for Courtney's Computers is equal to
    a. −$2 million.
    b. $2 million.
    c. $0.21 million.
    d. −$0.21 million.

38. **[from Appendix]** When considering a new investment project, companies
    a. do not care if the net present value is positive or negative provided the interest rate is at least 10%.
    b. are only willing to undertake investment projects when the interest rate is 5% or lower.
    c. ignore the interest rate.
    d. None of the statements is correct.

ANSWER KEY

Answers to Problems and Exercises

1. **a.** The level of investment spending can be calculated using the formula $GDP = C + I + G + (X - IM)$. Using the information in the table and solving for I we find investment spending is equal to $12 billion.

    b. Capital inflow equals imports minus exports or $2 billion. Since capital inflow for Macroland in 2009 is a positive number we know capital is flowing into Macroland from other countries and therefore Macroland is borrowing funds from foreigners.

    c. We can calculate private savings, $S_{Private}$, using this formula:

    $$S_{Private} = GDP + TR - T - C$$

    Using the information from the table, $S_{Private}$ equals $23 billion.

    d. We can calculate the budget balance, $S_{Government}$, using the following formula:

    $$S_{Government} = T - TR - G$$

    Using the information from the table, $S_{Government}$ equals –$13 billion.

    e. Yes, national savings plus capital inflow is equivalent to private savings plus the budget balance plus capital inflow. For Macroland in 2009 this sums to $12 billion, which is equivalent to the level of investment spending.

    f. The government of Macroland has a negative budget balance in 2009. This indicates that the government is running a budget deficit and is therefore borrowing funds.

2. **a.** To find investment spending for any of the economies use the formula $GDP = C + I + G + X - IM$. For Funland investment spending equals $80, in Upland investment spending equals $800, and in Downland investment spending equals $800.

    b. To find $S_{Private}$, use the formula $S_{Private} = GDP + TR - T - C$. To find $S_{Government}$, use the formula $S_{Government} = T - TR - G$. To find KI use the formula $KI = IM - X$. using the formulas and the given information you can complete the table as follows:

	Funland	Upland	Downland
$S_{Private}$	170	1,100	600
$S_{Government}$	−70	−400	100
KI	−20	100	100

    c. Capital inflows as a percentage of GDP can be calculated as $[KI/GDP] \times 100$. This formula can be modified for all the other percentage calculations by replacing KI in the numerator with the relevant variable. Here are the calculations organized in a table.

	Funland	Upland	Downland
Capital inflow as a percentage of GDP	−2%	2%	2.5%
Private savings as a percentage of GDP	17	22	15
Investment spending as a percentage of GDP	8	16	20

d. We can answer this question using the information we calculated in part (b) or we can use the formula $I = S_{Private} + S_{Government} + KI$ and solve for $S_{Government}$ while measuring all terms as a percentage of GDP. The first method calculates the budget balance as a percentage of GDP for Funland as $[-70/1,000] \times 100$, or -7%; for Upland as $[-400/5,000] \times 100$, or -8%; and for Downland as $[100/4,000] \times 100$, or 2.5%. Using the equation we get $S_{Government}$ for Funland as -7% (since $S_{Government} = 8\% - 17\% - (-2\%)$); $S_{Government}$ for Upland as -8% (since $S_{Government} = 16\% - 22\% - 2\%$); and $S_{Government}$ for Downland as 2.5% (since $S_{Government} = 20\% - 15\% - 2.5\%$).

e. Funland is running a government deficit of $70, since Funland collects $50 in taxes and expends $20 on transfers and $100 on government spending. This implies Funland's government is borrowing funds: since private savings in Funland equals $170 and the capital inflow equals $-$20, this indicates that Funland is lending funds to foreigners because their level of private savings is sufficient to cover the government's budget deficit as well as its level of investment spending.

Upland is running a government deficit of $400, since Upland collects $600 in taxes and expends $200 on transfers and $800 on government spending. When we look at the relationship among I, $S_{Private}$, $S_{Government}$, and KI, we find that Upland's capital inflow is a positive $100; so Upland is borrowing from foreigners. Private savings is equal to $1,100, government savings is $-$400, and capital inflow is $100, resulting in investment spending in Upland of $800.

Downland is running a government surplus of $100, since Downland collects $600 in taxes and expends $200 on transfers and $300 on government spending. When we look at the relationship among I, $S_{Private}$, $S_{Government}$, and KI, we find that Downland's capital inflow is a positive $100; so Downland is borrowing from foreigners. Private savings is equal to $600, government savings is $100, and capital inflows is $100, resulting in investment spending in Downland of $800.

3. a. To find the equilibrium quantity in the loanable funds market set demand equal to supply or $0.1 - 0.00005Q = 0.00005Q$. Solving for Q, we get Q equals $1,000. The equilibrium interest rate equals $0.00005Q$, using the supply equation, or $0.1 - 0.00005Q$, using the demand equation. Substituting 1,000 for Q, we get the equilibrium real interest rate, r, which equals 5%.

b. The government is now running a deficit and must demand funds in the loanable funds market. At every real interest rate, demand for loanable funds has now increased by $100. Thus, the demand curve shifts to the right. There is no shift in the supply of loanable funds with this change. When the demand curve shifts, there is a movement along the supply curve: we anticipate that the equilibrium real interest rate and quantity of loanable funds will increase when the government runs a negative budget balance.

c. In this economy, there is partial crowding out when the budget balance is $-$100. Investment spending decreases when the government's budget balance is $-$100.

4. a. Increases in expenditures on education and training represent investment in human capital.

b. Michael's purchase of the bond represents an investment in a financial asset, since Michael will receive a payment in the future as compensation for the use of his money today.

c. Susan's purchases represent investment spending, since they are investments in physical capital.

d. The purchase of government bonds by a country or by an individual represents an investment in a financial asset.

e. Mary's purchase represents investment spending, since it is an investment in physical capital.

5. Answers to this question will vary but will include expenditures on public health, on systems of law and order including the court system, education systems, communication systems, and transportation systems. Economies that lack basic health, fail to educate their population, support corrupt legal systems, or do not provide basic infrastructure will lack the core supports necessary for economic growth.

6. Lenders and borrowers face three broad categories of problems: the problem of transaction costs, the problem of risk, and the problem of achieving the desired level of liquidity.

Transaction costs refer to the costs of making transactions: both borrowers and lenders face transaction costs when they commit to borrowing or lending funds. The financial system reduces transaction costs by making the arrangements between lenders and borrowers more efficient. For example, a business can borrow funds from a bank much more efficiently than it can borrow the same amount of funds from 1,000 potential lenders.

Financial risk, or risk, refers to the uncertainty people face with regard to future outcomes that involve financial gains and losses. The financial system helps borrowers and lenders share the risk they are exposed to through diversification, since this diversification, or investing in assets with unrelated risks, reduces the total risk of loss the individual faces.

The financial system also addresses the need for liquidity for investors. Stocks and bonds as well as banks provide a mechanism for individuals to have liquid assets while also enabling the financing of illiquid investments.

7. a. The real interest rate is equal to the nominal interest rate minus the inflation rate. In this case, the real interest rate is equal to 10% – 5%, or 5%.

b. The nominal interest rate would increase by the amount of the increase in the inflation rate. Thus, if the expected inflation rate increases from 5% to 7%, this implies that the nominal interest rate will need to increase by 2% in order to maintain the same real interest rate of 5%.

8. a. In equilibrium in the loanable funds framework we know that investment spending must equal saving at the equilibrium interest rate. Thus, $2 - (1/100) \times I = 2 + (3/500) \times S$, where $I = S$ since the government is running a balanced budget and there are no capital inflows. Solving this equation yields $I = S = 500$ and plugging this value back into either the demand for loanable funds equation or the supply of loanable funds equation, we have that $r = 5\%$.

b. When the government runs a budget deficit, this causes the demand for loanable funds curve to shift to the right since at every interest rate there is now greater demand for loanable funds. This will cause a movement along the supply of loanable funds curve. The new loanable funds demand curve can be written as $r = 12 - (1/100) \times I$. When the loanable funds demand curve shifts to the right for a given loanable funds supply curve, this should result in the equilibrium interest rate increasing.

c. The new equilibrium interest rate equals 5.75%. To find this equilibrium interest rate, first solve for the equilibrium quantity of loanable funds: $12 - (1/100) \times I = 2 + (3/500) \times S$ since in equilibrium the level of investment spending equals the level of savings. Solving this equation yields $I = S = 625$ and plugging this value back into either the demand for loanable funds equation or the supply of loanable funds equation, we have that $r = 5.75\%$. But remember that now 200 of the investment spending represents the government's demand for loanable funds: this implies that private investment spending is now equal to 625 – 200, or 425. The government deficit results in less private investment spending occurring due to the crowding out effect.

9. a. An increase in capital inflows into a country will shift the supply of loanable funds curve to the right, which will cause the equilibrium interest rate to decrease and the equilibrium quantity of loanable funds to increase.

b. When the government reduces the level of the government deficit, this implies that the demand for loanable funds from the government has diminished. This will cause the demand for loanable funds curve to shift to the left and result in a decrease in the equilibrium interest rate and a decrease in the total equilibrium quantity of loanable funds. But, since the interest rate is now lower, this will cause the quantity of funds for private investment spending to increase.

c. Both the demand and the supply curves for loanable funds will shift due to the change in expected inflation. The demand curve will shift to the right reflecting the fact that borrowers are willing to borrow just as much as they did at the original nominal interest rate as they are now willing to borrow at the now higher nominal interest rate (remember that the real interest rate is equal to the nominal interest rate minus the inflation rate). The supply curve will shift to the left since lenders now are willing to lend the same amount of funds only if the nominal interest rate they receive reflects the new higher expected inflation rate. Both curves shift resulting in the nominal interest rate rising by the amount of the change in the expected inflation rate; there is no change in the equilibrium quantity of loanable funds.

d. An increase in private savings will cause the supply of loanable funds curve to shift to the right resulting in a decrease in the equilibrium interest rate and an increase in the equilibrium quantity of loanable funds.

e. When there is a decrease in perceived business opportunities, this causes the demand for loanable funds curve to shift to the left, which will result in both the equilibrium interest rate and the equilibrium quantity of loanable funds decreasing.

10.   **[from Appendix]** To calculate this value, use the present value formula: $PV = $ (future value)$/(1 + r)$. Thus, $PV = (\$1,000)/(1 + 0.10) = \$909.09$. Joe will be willing to lend Mary $909.09 today, given her offer.

11.   **[from Appendix]** The future value Joe will receive equals $(\$1,000)(1 + 0.12)^5$, or $1,762.34.

12.   **[from Appendix]** From Problem 11, we know Joe will earn a total of $762.34 if he loans Sarah $1,000 for five years. To evaluate what Joe should do requires a calculation of the value of the second option. This second option is a bit more complicated to calculate than the loan to Sarah. At the end of the first year, this option is worth $(\$1,000)(1 + 0.05)$, or $1,050. This amount remains with the venture, and at the end of the second year the value of this option will equal $(\$1,050)(1 + 0.10)$. At the end of the third year the value of this option will equal $(\$1,050)(1 + 0.10)(1 + 0.10)$, or $1,270.50. At the end of the fourth year the value of this option is $(\$1,270.50)(1 + 0.18)$, and at the end of the fifth year the value of this option is $(\$1,270.50)(1 + 0.18)(1 + 0.18)$, or $1,769.04. Subtracting out Joe's initial investment of $1,000 yields Joe a net income of $769.04. Since this amount is greater than what he receives from Sarah, Joe should invest in the new venture.

13.   **[from Appendix]** To compare these payments requires calculating the present value of the future payments you would receive if you opted for five payments over time instead of a single payment now. The present value of these payments is $500,000 + $(\$500,000)/(1.1) + (\$500,000)/(1.1)^2 + (\$500,000)/(1.1)^3 + (\$500,000)/(1.1)^4$, or $2,084,933. You will receive a larger total payment if you choose to receive the lottery winnings over a five-year period.

14.   **[from Appendix]** No, the decision does not change, although this change in the interest rate does change the present value of the stream of payments received over five years. The present value of this stream of payments is now equal to $500,000 + $(\$500,000)/(1.08) + (\$500,000)/(1.08)^2 + (\$500,000)/(1.08)^3 + (\$500,000)/(1.08)^4$, or $2,156,063. A decrease in the interest rate makes the stream of payments over five years even more attractive to you.

15.   **[from Appendix]** Yes, when the interest rate increases to 15%, this makes the single payment option more valuable than the stream of five payments. To see this, compare the single payment of $2 million to the present value of the stream of payments. The present value of the payments over five years is equal to $500,000 + ($500,000)/(1.15) + ($500,000)/(1.15)^2 + ($500,000)/(1.15)^3 + ($500,000)/(1.15)^4, or $1,927,489, which is less than $2 million.

Answers to Chapter Review Questions

1.   **Answer d.** Financial markets provide funds for those who need to borrow funds, as well as a means of earning interest for those with surplus funds.

2.   **Answer c.** Investment spending refers to spending on the economy's stock of physical capital. It includes spending on physical equipment, inventories and new construction. It does not include the selling of a preexisting structure since this represents a change of ownership rather than new productive capacity.

3.   **Answer: e.** The Federal Reserve Bank is not a source of funds for investment spending, while domestic and foreign savings do provide funds for investment spending.

4.   **Answer c.** A closed economy does not have any economic interaction with the rest of the world while an open economy does. A closed economy finances its investment spending solely through domestic savings, while an open economy funds its investment spending through both domestic and foreign savings.

5.   **Answer e.** We know that GDP is equal to total spending on goods and services in an open economy (answer b); in a closed economy there are no imports or exports, so GDP is equal to total domestic spending on goods and services (answer a). Private savings plus consumption plus net transfers equals GDP (answer c), and government savings is equal to net taxes minus the level of government spending (answer d).

6.   **Answer d.** If the government spends more than its net revenue, it runs a budget deficit or a negative surplus. This implies that government saving is negative.

7.   **Answer e.** By definition $S_{Government}$ is equal to government net taxes (taxes minus transfers) minus government spending. When $S_{Government}$ is greater than zero this indicates that net taxes exceed government spending: this is a budget surplus. When $S_{Government}$ is less than zero this indicates that government spending exceeds net taxes: this is a budget deficit.

8.   **Answer d.** All of these statements are true by definition.

9.   **Answer b.** Capital inflow measures the total level of funds available in a country to finance investment spending. It consists of the inflow of foreign funds into the economy minus the outflow of domestic funds to other economies, or the net inflow of funds into an economy.

10.   **Answer d.** Expenditures on manufacturing equipment are considered physical capital and not financial capital.

11.   **Answer a.** Capital inflow is defined as imports minus exports: in this case, capital inflow is positive. When capital inflow is positive the country spends more on imports than it earns from exports and must therefore borrow the difference from foreigners.

12.   **Answer c.** In any economy, investment spending equals savings. In an open economy, savings is equal to the sum of private saving, the budget balance, and capital inflows. Capital inflow is defined as the difference between imports and exports.

13.   **Answer d.** The loanable funds market is a hypothetical market where savers can lend money or supply funds to borrowers, the demanders of funds. The price for borrowing funds is the interest rate, or the return the lender of funds receives for loaning out a dollar for a year.

14. **Answer c.** To calculate the interest rate Maxine pays, use the following formula:

Interest rate = [(total payment at end of year − amount of loan)/(amount of loan)] × 100

which yields the following:

Interest rate = [(115−100)/(100)] × 100 = 15%

15 **Answer d.** When making the loan, Joe, with his expected inflation rate of 7%, anticipates a real interest rate of 8%; when the actual inflation rate is 8% rather than 7%, Joe's real interest rate on the loan falls to 7% and he is worse off than he anticipated. When making the loan, Maxine, with her expected inflation rate of 10%, anticipates a real interest rate of 5%; when the actual inflation rate is 8% rather than 5%, Maxine's real interest rate on the loan rises to 7% and she is worse off than she anticipated. The nominal interest rate is 15%, while the real interest rate is the nominal interest rate minus the inflation rate, or 7%.

16. **Answer c.** When the government runs a deficit, it becomes a borrower in the loanable funds market and this implies that the demand curve for loanable funds shifts to the right at any given interest rate.

17. **Answer b.** Joe's checking account balance is an asset from Joe's perspective and a liability from the bank's perspective. Mary's saving account balance is similarly an asset from her perspective and a liability from the bank's perspective. Mike's car loan represents an asset for the bank since Mike is legally obligated to repay the funds he has borrowed; the car loan represents a liability from Mike's perspective.

18. **Answer d.** Answers (a), (b), and (c) focus on three problems that financial markets address for borrowers and lenders.

19. **Answer b.** This statement is the definition of a risk-averse person.

20. **Answer b.** The checking account balance is the most liquid asset in this list, since it can be effectively used as cash at most business locations. The other three assets must be sold to a buyer in order to convert them into cash: this transaction takes time and reduces the liquidity of these assets.

21. **Answer a.** Financial intermediaries provide a means for reducing risk for investors and business owners when they gather funds from many individuals and then invest these funds in a diversified portfolio of financial assets that can include stocks as well as bonds.

22. **Answer d.** Banks do provide liquidity for lenders in the form of deposits that can be accessed easily, while at the same time banks provide funds to finance the illiquid investments of borrowers.

23. **Answer c.** The efficient markets hypothesis says that all publicly available information about a stock is already included in the stock's price. Thus, all stocks are fairly valued: they are neither underpriced nor overpriced.

24. **Answer b.** In most economies, human capital is primarily provided by the government through public education.

25. **Answer d.** When the government runs a budget surplus, this means that tax revenue is greater than government spending: the government is saving. It is not possible with the information given to determine whether or not net exports are positive or negative.

26. **Answer d.** A dollar of investment spending financed by national savings or capital inflow results in an additional dollar of investment spending; however, the dollar of investment spending financed by national savings results in interest being paid to someone domestically while a dollar of investment spending financed by capital inflow results in interest being paid to a foreigner. No matter the source of the financing, interest is paid, but the recipient of that interest varies depending upon the source of the financing.

27. **Answer g.** These are statements discussed in the text. The statement in answer (b) is incorrect since the disparity in savings level between the United States and other wealthy countries over the past 30 years is primarily due to low U.S. private savings over this period rather than large budget deficits.

28. **Answer f.** The demand for loanable funds curve represents borrowers who enter this market in order to demand funds for investment spending. The supply of loanable funds curve represents savers who provide excess funds to this market in order to supply these excess funds to those individuals who want to borrow funds. The equilibrium interest rate equates the quantity of loanable funds supplied with the quantity of loanable funds demanded.

29. **Answer a.** Since the rate of return on this investment project is equal to 11.1% and this is greater than the prevailing interest rate, it is in the firm's interest to invest in the project. To find the rate of return, recall that this is equal to the [(revenue from the project) − (cost of project)/(cost of project)] × 100 or [($100,000 − $90,000)/($90,000)] × 100.

30. **Answer e.** The loanable funds market is efficient since it results in funds being made available to the most profitable investment opportunities (those investment opportunities where the rate of return is highest) while securing these funds from savers who are willing to lend at the lowest possible interest rate (the equilibrium interest rate). The savers who are willing to lend at lower rates than other savers are the savers who provide the funds for these investment projects.

31. **Answer e.** When the government runs a deficit, this implies that the government is spending more than its tax revenue. This requires the government to borrow funds to finance the deficit, which results in the demand for loanable funds curve shifting out to the right. Holding everything else constant, this causes the equilibrium interest rate in the loanable funds market to increase. At a higher interest rate, less private investment spending will occur: the government deficit will crowd out private investment spending. There is not enough information to know with certainty what will happen to capital inflows when the government runs a deficit.

32. **[from Appendix] Answer d.** This is a simple illustration of the present value formula.

33. **[from Appendix] Answer b.** When the interest rate increases, this means the cost of borrowing money has risen and therefore the amount of money to be paid back will rise.

34. **[from Appendix] Answer b.** The present value of a future payment decreases when the interest rate rises, since the higher interest rate means that a smaller amount today will accumulate to a larger amount in the future.

35. **[from Appendix] Answer b.** Whether an investment project should be undertaken depends on the benefits as well as the costs associated with the investment project. It is possible that even though this project has positive projected profits, the cost of borrowing funds to undertake the project will exceed these projected profits.

36. **[from Appendix] Answer a.** If you compute the net present value for the project, the value is a positive number and, therefore, the project should be undertaken. This computation is done in the answer to question 37.

37. **[from Appendix] Answer c.** To compute the net present value entails calculating the present value of the benefits and the present value of the costs and then subtracting the present value of the costs from the present value of the benefits. The present value of the benefits is equal to $(2)/(1 + 0.2) + (2)/(1 + 0.2)^2 + (2)/(1 + 0.2)^3$, or approximately $4.21 million, and the present value of the costs is equal to $4 million. The difference between these two present values is approximately $0.21 million.

38. **[from Appendix] Answer d.** None of the answers is true. Companies decide to undertake investment projects when the net present value is a positive number for the given interest rate.

Income and Expenditure

BEFORE YOU READ THE CHAPTER

Summary

This chapter develops the aggregate consumption function and uses it to explain the relationship between disposable income and consumer spending. The chapter explores the effect of expected future income and aggregate wealth on consumer spending. In addition, the determinants of investment spending and the distinction between planned investment spending and unplanned inventory investment are discussed. The chapter explores the significance of the level of investment spending as an indicator of the future state of the economy. The chapter illustrates how the inventory adjustment process enables the economy to regain its equilibrium after a demand shock. The chapter uses the multiplier process to quantify the effect of a change in the consumption function or a change in planned investment on the income–expenditure equilibrium real GDP. The appendix explains the process for deriving the multiplier from the simple model presented in the chapter.

Chapter Objectives

Objective #1. This chapter makes four simplifying assumptions in building a model of income and expenditure. These assumptions are:

- Producer prices are fixed and therefore any change in aggregate spending results in a change in aggregate output or real GDP. Given this assumption, real GDP and nominal GDP are equivalent since the aggregate price level is fixed and does not change.

- The interest rate is given in this simple model.

- Government spending and taxes are equal to zero.

- Exports and imports are equal to zero.

Objective #2. The marginal propensity to consume, or the *MPC*, measures the increase in consumer spending that occurs if current disposable income increases by $1. The *MPC* can be calculated as the change in consumer spending divided by the change in disposable income. The *MPC* is a number between 0 and 1. The marginal propensity to save, or the *MPS*, is the fraction of an additional dollar of disposable income that is saved. The *MPS* is equal to $(1 - MPC)$.

Objective #3. An initial rise or fall in aggregate spending at a given level of GDP is an autonomous change in aggregate spending. This change in aggregate spending will result in a multiplier process where the total change in real GDP caused by the initial change in autonomous spending is equal to the multiplier times the initial change in autonomous aggregate spending. The simple multiplier developed in this chapter is equal to $[1/(1 - MPC)]$. Thus, the change in real GDP = $[1/(1 - MPC)] \times$ (change in autonomous aggregate spending).

Objective #4. The consumption function is an equation that shows the relationship between a household's current disposable income and its level of consumer spending. We can write a simple version of the consumption function for an individual household as $c = a + MPC \times yd$, where *c* is individual household consumer spending, *a* is individual autonomous consumer spending or the level of consumer spending a household would do if its disposable income equaled zero, and *yd* is individual household current disposable income. In this equation individual autonomous consumption and *yd* are assumed to be constant. A graph of the individual household consumption function with disposable income on the horizontal axis and consumer spending on the vertical axis would have a slope equal to the *MPC* and a y-intercept equal to *a*. Figure 11.1 illustrates an example of an individual household consumption function. Consumer spending and disposable income are positively related to each other: as disposable income increases, consumer spending increases.

Figure 11.1

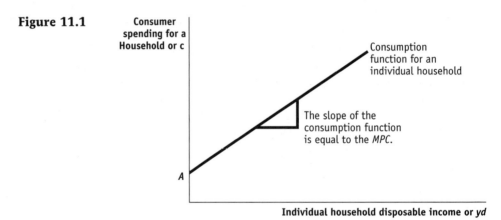

Objective #5. The aggregate consumption function illustrates the relationship between the aggregate disposable income in an economy and the level of aggregate consumer spending. This relationship is similar to the one depicted in the individual household consumption function. The aggregate consumption function is written as $C = A + MPC \times YD$, where *C* is aggregate consumer spending, *A* is aggregate autonomous consumer spending, and *YD* is aggregate disposable income. The aggregate consumption function, *C*, indicates a positive relationship between the level of aggregate consumer spending and the level of aggregate disposable income. Figure 11.2 provides an example of an aggregate consumption function.

Figure 11.2

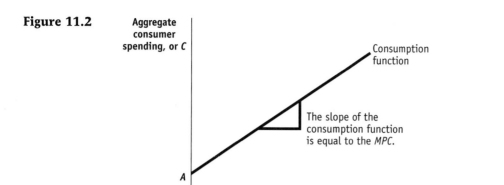

Aggregate consumer spending, or C

Consumption function

The slope of the consumption function is equal to the *MPC*.

A

Aggregate disposable income, or *YD*

Objective #6. The two principal causes of shifts in the aggregate consumption function are changes in expected future disposable income and wealth. The life-cycle hypothesis theorizes that consumers plan their spending over a lifetime, and as a result try to smooth, or even out, their consumption spending over the course of their entire lives. The permanent income hypothesis holds that consumer spending is ultimately dependent on the income people expect to have over the long term rather than on their current income.

- An increase in expected future disposable income or wealth causes the vertical intercept A, aggregate autonomous consumer spending, to increase, and this results in an upward shift of the aggregate consumption function. Similarly, a decrease in expected future disposable income or wealth causes the aggregate consumption function to shift down.

Objective #7. Econometrics is the use of statistical techniques to analyze the fit between economic models and empirical data.

Objective #8. The level of investment spending is a critical determinant of economic performance: most recessions result from a decrease in investment spending. In addition, declines in consumer spending are usually the result of a reaction to a fall in investment spending and the accompanying multiplier process.

- The two most important factors determining the level of investment spending are interest rates and expected future real GDP.
- The level of investment spending that businesses actually engage in is not always the level of investment spending that they have planned.
  - Planned investment spending refers to the investment spending firms plan to make during a given time period and is dependent primarily on the interest rate, the expected future level of real GDP, and the current level of productive capacity.
  - The level of interest rates determines whether or not a firm will undertake a particular investment project. Investment projects with a rate of return equal to or greater than the equilibrium interest rate will be funded, while those investment projects with a rate of return less than the equilibrium interest rate will not be funded.
- Retained earnings refer to past profits that are used to finance investment spending. Even if the firm finances its investment spending using retained earnings, the firm still compares the rate of return for the investment project to the equilibrium interest rate. This interest rate reflects the opportunity cost of using the firm's retained earnings to fund the investment project rather than lending out the retained earnings and earning interest.
- An increase in the market interest rate makes any given investment project less profitable, while a decrease in the market interest rate makes any given investment project more profitable. Therefore, planned investment spending is inversely related to the interest rate.

Objective #9. The accelerator principle is the idea that a higher rate of growth in real GDP leads to higher planned investment spending. The higher rate of growth in real GDP typically indicates rapid growth in sales, leading businesses to quickly use up any excess productive capacity and resulting in higher planned investment spending.

Objective #10. Inventories are the stock of goods that firms hold in anticipation of future sales and the stock of inputs firms hold in order to have a reliable, and at hand, supply of raw materials and spare parts. Inventory investment refers to the change in total inventories held in the economy during a given period of time. Inventory investment may be positive, negative, or equal to zero. Positive inventory investment indicates that the economy has added to its stock of inventories, while negative inventory investment indicates that the level of inventories in the economy has decreased.

- Inventories fluctuate over time. Unintended changes in inventories, due to unpredicted fluctuations in sales, are referred to as unplanned inventory investment.

- Thus, actual investment spending in an economy in any given period of time is comprised of two parts: planned investment spending, $I_{Planned}$, and unplanned inventory investment, $I_{Unplanned}$. Positive unplanned inventory investment typically occurs in a slowing economy where actual expenditure on goods and services is less than forecasted expenditure. Negative unplanned inventory investment occurs in a growing economy where actual expenditure exceeds forecasted expenditure on goods and services.

- Inventories play a key role in short-run macroeconomic models, and the behavior of firms' inventories often signals the future state of the economy.

Objective #11. In a closed economy with no government and a fixed aggregate price level, there are only two sources of aggregate demand (AD): consumer spending and investment spending. In this type of economy, aggregate disposable income, YD, equals GDP. Figure 11.3 illustrates a simple economy and the following points about that simple economy.

Figure 11.3

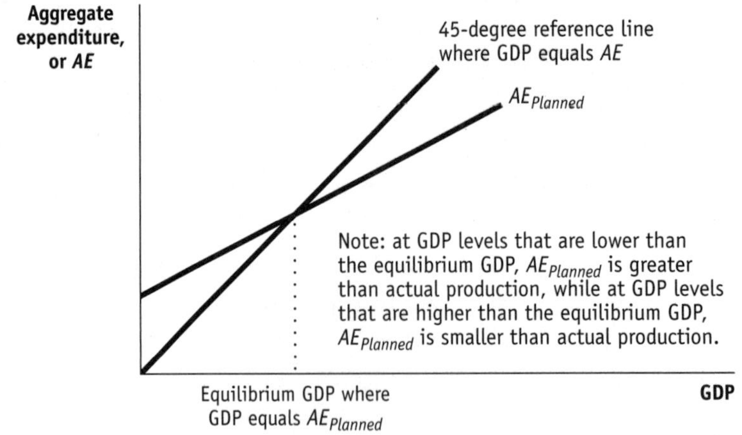

- In this economy planned aggregate spending, $AE_{Planned}$, or the total amount of planned spending in the economy, is comprised of consumption spending, C, and planned investment, $I_{Planned}$.

- The slope of the $AE_{Planned}$ line equals the MPC.

- $AE_{Planned}$ may differ from GDP because of the influence of unplanned aggregate spending in the form of unplanned inventory investment, $I_{Unplanned}$.

- Over time the economy moves to that point where $AE_{Planned}$ equals GDP, or the income–expenditure equilibrium.

Objective #12. The ideas in objective #11 can be expressed using equations. In this simple economy with no government sector, a fixed aggregate price level, and a given interest rate, $GDP = C + I$. Furthermore, investment spending, I, can be written as the sum of planned investment plus unplanned inventory investment or $I = I_{Planned} + I_{Unplanned}$. Thus, $GDP = C + I_{Planned} + I_{Unplanned}$. Planned aggregate spending, $AE_{Planned}$, is the sum of consumption spending plus planned investment or $AE_{Planned} = C + I_{Planned}$. Thus, $GDP = AE + I_{Unplanned}$.

- When GDP is greater than $AE_{Planned}$, this implies that $I_{Unplanned}$ is positive: the inventories of firms increase, and this acts as a signal to firms to decrease their production. Over time the economy moves back to the income–expenditure equilibrium.

- When GDP is less than $AE_{Planned}$, this implies that $I_{Unplanned}$ is negative: the inventories of firms decrease, and this acts as a signal to firms to increase their production. Over time the economy moves back to the income–expenditure equilibrium.

- When GDP equals $AE_{Planned}$, then the economy is at the income–expenditure equilibrium. At this equilibrium, $I_{Unplanned}$ equals zero and firms have no incentive to change their levels of production in the next period. We refer to this level of GDP as the income–expenditure equilibrium GDP. A 45-degree reference line helps identify the income–expenditure equilibrium GDP. When $AE_{Planned}$ is graphed on the vertical axis and GDP is graphed on the horizontal axis, the income–expenditure equilibrium GDP is that level of GDP where the AE line intersects the 45-degree line. This diagram identifying the income–expenditure equilibrium GDP where $AE_{Planned}$ equals GDP is called the Keynesian cross diagram. Figure 11.3 illustrates the Keynesian cross diagram.

- The macroeconomy self-corrects when GDP is not equal to $AE_{Planned}$ through inventory adjustment.

Objective #13. The AE line, or $AE_{Planned}$, shifts in this simple model if there is a change in planned investment spending, $I_{Planned}$, or if there is a shift in the consumption function, C. Either shift triggers the multiplier process, so for a change in either variable there will be an even bigger change in the equilibrium level of GDP. This idea can be expressed as the change in the income–expenditure equilibrium GDP equals the multiplier times the change in planned aggregate spending. Recall that the multiplier in this simple model equals $1/(1 - MPC)$.

Objective #14. The paradox of thrift refers to how individuals concerned about a potential economic downturn may worsen that economic downturn when they choose to act prudently and increase their level of saving. It is a paradox, since what is "good," households saving their money, produces a "bad," an economy with a more severe recession.

Key Terms

marginal propensity to consume (MPC) the increase in *consumer spending* when *disposable income* rises by $1. Because consumers normally spend part but not all of an additional dollar of disposable income, *MPC* is between 0 and 1.

marginal propensity to save (MPS) the fraction of an additional dollar of *disposable income* that is saved; *MPS* is equal to $1 - MPC$.

autonomous change in aggregate spending an initial rise or fall in *aggregate spending* at a given level of *real GDP*.

Notes

Key Terms *(continued)*

multiplier the ratio of total change in *real GDP* caused by an *autonomous change in aggregate spending* to the size of that autonomous change.

consumption function an equation showing how an individual *household's consumer spending* varies with the household's current *disposable income.*

aggregate consumption function the relationship for the *economy* as a whole between aggregate current *disposable income* and aggregate *consumer spending.*

planned investment spending the *investment spending* that *firms* intend to undertake during a given period. Planned investment spending may differ from actual investment spending due to *unplanned inventory investment.*

accelerator principle the proposition that a higher rate of growth in *real GDP* results in a higher level of *investment spending,* and a lower growth rate in real GDP leads to lower planned investment spending.

inventories stocks of goods and raw materials held to satisfy future sales.

inventory investment the value of the change in total *inventories* held in the *economy* during a given period. Unlike other types of *investment spending,* inventory investment can be negative, if inventories fall.

unplanned inventory investment unplanned changes in *inventories,* which occur when actual sales are more or less than businesses expected.

actual investment spending the sum of *planned investment spending* and *unplanned inventory investment.*

planned aggregate spending the total amount of planned spending in the *economy;* includes *consumer spending* and *planned investment spending.*

income–expenditure equilibrium a situation in which *aggregate output,* measured by *real GDP,* is equal to *planned aggregate spending* and *firms* have no incentive to change output.

income–expenditure equilibrium GDP the level of *real GDP* at which real GDP equals *planned aggregate spending.*

Keynesian cross a diagram that identifies *income-expenditure equilibrium* as the point where the *planned aggregate spending* line crosses the 45-degree line.

Notes

AFTER YOU READ THE CHAPTER

Tips

Tip #1. A thorough understanding of the aggregate consumption function and the variables that shift the aggregate consumption function is essential. Make sure you review the aggregate consumption function and understand the relationship between consumer spending and autonomous consumer spending, the marginal propensity to consume, and disposable income. The consumption function will shift upward with increases in wealth or expected future disposable income. Figure 11.4 is a representation of an aggregate consumption function: the slope of this function equals the MPC, and the y-intercept equals autonomous consumption spending, or A.

Figure 11.4

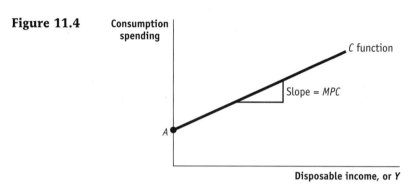

Tip #2. The 45-degree line in the Keynesian cross diagram provides a helpful visual tool for identifying the income–expenditure equilibrium GDP. The Keynesian cross diagram illustrates the relationship between $AE_{Planned}$ and GDP: to the left of the point of intersection in the Keynesian cross, we know that AE is greater than GDP, inventories are falling, and firms will respond by increasing their production; to the right of the point of intersection in the Keynesian cross, we know that AE is less than GDP, inventories are rising, and firms will respond by decreasing their production. Figure 11.5, which follows, illustrates these points.

Figure 11.5

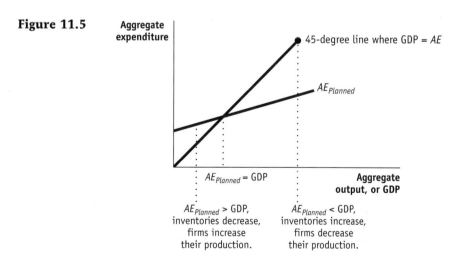

Tip #3. An understanding of investment spending and its components is a critical aspect of this chapter. Make sure you can distinguish between planned investment spending and unplanned inventory investment. In the macroeconomic model presented in this chapter, the mechanism that ensures the attainment of equilibrium is unplanned inventory adjustment. This concept is essential for understanding how this short-run model of the economy works. Figure 11.5 illustrates this inventory adjustment.

Tip #4. This chapter develops the concept of the multiplier and it considers the impact of the multiplier on the macroeconomic model presented in this chapter. The text starts with a relatively simple economic model to develop important economic concepts like the multiplier. Review the definition of the multiplier, its calculation, and then practice using this concept in questions provided in the text and the study guide. Figure 11.6 illustrates this multiplier effect. The economy is initially producing Y_1. When there is an increase in autonomous spending, this causes $AE_{Planned}$ to shift up by an amount equal to this change in spending. This leads to a higher equilibrium level of output, Y_2. The multiplier equals the ratio of this change in aggregate output divided by the change in autonomous spending.

Figure 11.6

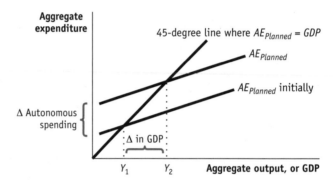

WORKED PROBLEMS

1. Suppose that the marginal propensity to save in an economy is equal to 0.2. Furthermore, suppose that you are told that the level of investment spending increases by $200 during this year. Trace out the total increase in real GDP showing the increase in consumer spending for at least the second, third, and fourth round of spending. Provide the numeric value of the increase in consumer spending for each of these rounds as well as the total increase in real GDP. Assume that in this economy there is no government sector, no taxes, no transfers, and that the aggregate price level and the interest rate are fixed.

   STEP 1: Find the marginal propensity to consume from the given information.

   Review the section "The Multiplier: An Informal Introduction" on page 312 (Econ page 744).

   We are given information about the marginal propensity to save (*MPS*) but are not given the information about the marginal propensity to consume (*MPC*). Since the *MPS* is equal to 1 – *MPC*, we can easily compute the *MPC* as equal to 0.8. To see why this is true, recall that disposable income is income minus net taxes. So, if disposable income is equal to consumption spending plus savings, then a change in disposable income must be equal to the change in consumption spending plus the change in savings. Or, symbolically, Δ(Disposable Income) = Δ*C* + Δ*S*, where *C* is consumption spending and S is savings. Dividing both sides of this equation by Δ(Disposable Income) we get $1 = MPC + MPS$, since the $MPC = \Delta C/\Delta$(Disposable Income) and the $MPS = \Delta S/\Delta$(Disposable Income).

STEP 2: Create a table to record the change in spending for each round as well as the initial impact of the change in investment spending.

Review the section "The Multiplier: An Informal Introduction" on page 312 (Econ page 744).

In the table, we will want a column that identifies the change and a column to record its numeric value. Thus,

Increase in investment spending	$200
+Second-round increase in consumer spending	$= (MPC \times \$200) = \$160$
+Third-round increase in consumer spending	$= (MPC)(MPC \times \$200) = \$128$
+Fourth-round increase in consumer spending	$= (MPC)[(MPC)(MPC \times \$200)] = \$102.40$
...Total Increase in real GDP	$= [1/(1 - MPC)] \times (\$200) = \$1,000$

STEP 3: Calculate the total increase in real GDP.

Review the section "The Multiplier: An Informal Introduction" on page 312 (Econ page 744).

Our table in Step 2 already provides the answer to this question, but let's review the process. To find the total increase in real GDP recall, that the change in real GDP will equal the product of $[1/(1 - MPC)] \times$ (the initial change in spending). In this case since the MPC is equal to .8, we can calculate the value of $[1/(1 - MPC)]$, or the multiplier, as 5. Since the initial change in spending is equal to $200, we can therefore calculate that the change in real GDP will be equal to $5 \times (\$200)$, or $1,000.

2. Suppose that the marginal propensity to consume in an economy is equal to 0.75 and that you are told that investment spending decreases this year by –$50. You are asked to calculate the change in consumer spending for the second-round, third-round, and fourth-round, and in addition, you are asked to calculate the change in real income due to this change in investment spending. Assume that in this economy there is no government sector, no taxes, no transfers, and that the aggregate price level and the interest rate are fixed.

STEP 1: Create a table to record the change in spending for each round as well as the initial impact of the change in investment spending.

Review the section "The Multiplier: An Informal Introduction" on page 312 (Econ page 744).

In the table, we will want a column that identifies the change and a column to record its numeric value. Thus,

Increase in investment spending	–$50
+Second-round increase in consumer spending	$= [MPC \times (-\$50)] = -\$37.50$
+Third-round increase in consumer spending	$= (MPC)[(MPC) \times (-\$50)] = -\$28.125$
+Fourth-round increase in consumer spending	$= MPC(MPC)[(MPC) \times (-\$50)] = -\$21.094$
...Total Increase in real GDP	$= [1/(1 - MPC)] \times (-\$50) = -\$200$

STEP 2: Calculate the total increase in real GDP.

Review the section "The Multiplier: An Informal Introduction" on page 312 (Econ page 744).

The table in Step 2 already provides this answer for us, but let's take a moment to review the process. Since we know the *MPC*, it is easy to calculate the value of the multiplier: the multiplier is equal to $1/(1 - MPC)$, or 4 in this example. Since investment spending has decreased by $50, then we know the overall change in real GDP must be a decrease of $4 \times (-\$50)$ or $-\$200$.

3. You are told that the consumption function in an economy is a linear relationship. Furthermore, you are told that when disposable income is equal to $200, consumption spending is equal to $184 and when disposable income is equal to $500, consumption spending is equal to $385. You are asked to compute autonomous consumer spending for this economy, the value of the marginal propensity to consume for this economy, the consumption function for this economy, and finally the impact on real GDP in this economy if autonomous consumption increases by $50 from its initial level. Assume that in this economy there is no government sector, no taxes, no transfers, and that the aggregate price level and the interest rate are fixed.

STEP 1: Use the given information to find the marginal propensity to consume (*MPC*) for this economy.

Review the section "Consumer Spending" on page 315 (Econ page 747) and Figure 11-2 on page 317 (Econ page 749).

In the information we are provided, there are two relationships between disposable income and consumption spending: (disposable income, consumption spending) = (200, 184) and (500, 385). From this information we can calculate the change in consumer spending as $385 - 184$, or 201, and the change in disposable income as $500 - 200 = 300$. Using this information and recalling that the marginal propensity to consume is defined as the change in consumer spending divided by the change in disposable income, the $MPC = 201/300 = .67$.

STEP 2: Use the *MPC* and one of the given consumption points to find the value of autonomous consumer spending for this economy.

Review the section "Consumer Spending" on page 315 (Econ page 747) and Figure 11-2 on page 317 (Econ page 749).

From the discussion in the text, we know that a linear consumption function can be written as $C = A + MPC \times$ (disposable income). From Step 1, we know that the *MPC* has a value of 0.67. Thus, $C = A + 0.67 \times$ (disposable income). Replacing *C* and disposable income with one of the given points, we can find the value of autonomous consumer spending. Thus, $385 = A + 0.67(500)$, or $184 = A + 0.67(200)$. Using either of these equations, we find that the value of *A* is 50.

STEP 3: Write the equation for the consumption function for this economy.

Review the section "Consumer Spending" on page 315 (Econ page 747) and Figure 11-2 on page 317 (Econ page 749).

The consumption function for this economy can be written in general as $C = A + MPC \times$ (disposable income), or given the values we calculated in Steps 1 and 2, as $C = 50 + 0.67$(disposable income).

STEP 4: Calculate the value of the multiplier for this economy.

Review the section "The Multiplier: An Informal Introduction" on page 312 (Econ page 744) and the section "Consumer Spending" on page 315 (Econ page 747) and Figure 11-2 on page 317 (Econ page 749).

Recall that the multiplier in this model is defined as $1/(1 - MPC)$. From Step 1, we know that the MPC is equal to 0.67. Using this information, we can calculate the value of the multiplier as 3.03.

4. Consider a simple economy in which there is only consumption spending by households and investment spending by businesses. Furthermore, assume that the consumption function in this economy is linear and that the level of taxes in this economy is equal to zero. You are told that when consumption spending is equal to $150, disposable income is equal to $100 and that when consumption spending is equal to $350, disposable income is equal to $500. Planned investment spending in this economy is equal to $100 no matter what the level of disposable income. You are asked to find the consumption function, to identify the equilibrium level of real GDP in this economy, to depict the equilibrium level of real GDP as well as the aggregate expenditure function and consumption function in a graph, and to describe what is happening in this economy when real GDP is equal to $200. Assume that in this economy there is no government sector, no taxes, no transfers, and that the aggregate price level and the interest rate are fixed.

STEP 1: Find the value of the marginal propensity to consume (*MPC*) for this economy from the given information.

Review the section "The Multiplier: An Informal Introduction" on page 312 (Econ page 744).

Recall that the multiplier is equal to the change in consumer spending divided by the change in disposable income. From the given information, we know two points on the consumption function: (disposable income, consumption) = (100, 150) and (500, 350). Thus, the change in consumption spending is equal to $350 - 150$, or 200, while the change in disposable income is equal to $500 - 100$, or 400. Thus, the MPC is equal to 200/400, or 0.5.

STEP 2: Find the consumption function for this economy given the above information.

Review the section "Consumer Spending" on page 315 (Econ page 747).

From Step 1, we know that the MPC is equal to 0.5. We also know that the consumption function can be written as $C = A + MPC \times$ (disposable income). Using one of the points that we are given from the consumption function, we can solve this equation for the value of A, the autonomous consumer spending. Thus, $150 = A + 0.5(100)$, or $A = 100$, or $350 = A + 0.5(500)$, or $A = 100$. The consumption function can be written as $C = 100 + 0.5 \times$ (disposable income).

STEP 3: Calculate the equilibrium value of real GDP for this economy.

Review the section "The Income-Expenditure Model" on page 326 (Econ page 758) and Figure 11-9 on page 300 (Econ page 762).

In this simple economy, planned aggregate expenditure is equal to consumption spending plus investment spending. Thus, $AE_{Planned} = C + I$. Or, $AE_{Planned} = 100 + 0.5 \times$ (disposable income) $+ 100$. Simplifying this we get $AE_{Planned} = 200 + 0.5 \times$ (disposable income). In equilibrium the level of real GDP produced is equal to $AE_{Planned}$. Thus, $Y = 200 + 0.5 \times Y$, since there are no taxes and that implies that disposable income is equal to real GDP or Y. We can solve for the equilibrium value of Y and we will find that equilibrium Y, or equilibrium real GDP, is 400. When this economy's real GDP is equal to $400, then planned aggregate expenditure is equal to this level of production.

STEP 4: Provide a graph illustrating the equilibrium level of real GDP for this economy as well as the aggregate expenditure function.

Review the section "The Income-Expenditure Model" on page 326 (Econ page 758) and Figure 11-9 on page 330 (Econ page 762).

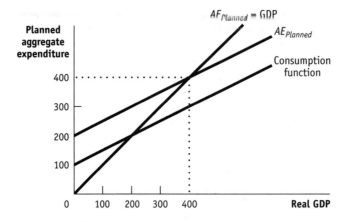

STEP 5: Describe what is happening in this economy when the level of real GDP is equal to $200. Illustrate this idea by referencing the graph you created in Step 4.

Review the section "The Income-Expenditure Model" on page 326 (Econ page 758) and Figure 11-9 on page 330 (Econ page 762).

When real GDP is equal to 200, consumption is equal to 200, and planned aggregate expenditure is equal to 300 (since C is equal to 200 and planned investment spending is equal to 100, for a total planned expenditure of 300). That implies that the level of production (200) is less than the level of expenditure (300) and therefore, holding everything else constant, that there are unplanned changes in inventories of 100. That is, since spending is greater than production, there is unplanned investment in the form of inventory changes in order to meet the demand for goods and services. As unplanned inventories fall, this decrease acts as a signal for producers to produce a higher level of output, and the economy will naturally move toward the equilibrium level of real GDP that we found to be equal to 400 in Step 4.

Problems and Exercises

1. Econoland analyzes its aggregate consumer spending and aggregate disposable income and finds the following data. All numbers in the table are dollar amounts.

YD	C
$ 0	$100
100	180
200	260
300	340
500	500

Assume Econoland is a closed economy with no government spending, no taxes, and no transfers. Furthermore, assume the aggregate price level and interest rate are fixed in Econoland.

a. What does autonomous consumer spending equal in this economy?

b. What is the value of the *MPC* for Econoland?

c. Use the following graph to graph the data given in the previous table. Label the consumption function you construct with a *C*.

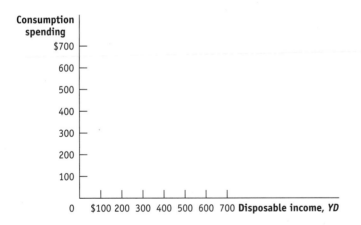

d. What is the slope of the consumption function you graphed in part (c)?

e. What is the relationship between the slope of the consumption function and the *MPC*? Explain your answer.

f. Suppose future expected disposable income increases in Econoland. How will this affect autonomous consumer spending, the *MPC*, and the consumption function?

2. Use the following data to answer this question for Funland, a closed economy with no government sector, a fixed aggregate price level, and a fixed interest rate. All numbers in the table are dollar amounts.

GDP	YD	C	$I_{Planned}$	$AE_{Planned}$	$I_{Unplanned}$
	$20	$22	$20		
	50		20		−$10
$ 80			20		2
100		70	20		

a. Fill in the missing values in the previous table.

b. What is the value of autonomous consumer spending?

c. What is the *MPC* for Funland?

d. Graph the above information using a Keynesian cross diagram. Label the income-expenditure equilibrium GDP.

e. What is the income–expenditure equilibrium real GDP for Funland? (Hint: the table does not include the income-expenditure equilibrium GDP, but the table does provide the information necessary to find this equilibrium.)

f. Suppose $I_{Planned}$ increases by 20, holding everything else constant. Fill in the following table given this change.

GDP′	YD′	C′	I′_{Planned}	AE′_{Planned}	I′_{Unplanned}
	$20	$22	$40		
	50		40	$80	
$ 80			40	98	
100		70	20		

g. Given the change in part (f), what is the new equilibrium level of real GDP for Funland?

h. Explain the relationship between the multiplier and the answer you gave for part (f).

3. Outlandia's planned aggregate expenditure line is depicted in the following graph, where the vertical axis measures planned aggregate expenditure and the horizontal axis measures real GDP.

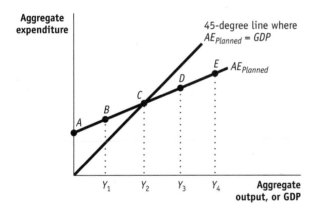

a. The previous graph is referred to as a Keynesian cross diagram. Interpret the information provided in the graph.

Suppose Outlandia's economy currently is operating at point B.

b. Is this an income–expenditure equilibrium for Outlandia? Explain your answer.

c. At point B, describe what is happening to inventories and production in Outlandia.

d. What level of GDP will this economy produce once it is at an income–expenditure equilibrium?

e. At what levels of labeled GDP on the previous graph is unplanned inventory investment positive? Explain your answer.

f. At what levels of labeled GDP on the previous graph is planned aggregate expenditure greater than income? Explain your answer.

g. Explain the significance of point C in the previous graph.

4. Suppose Inlandia's autonomous consumer spending equals 500 and that consumer spending increases by $50 for every $100 increase in aggregate disposable income. Assume Inlandia is a closed economy with no government sector, a fixed aggregate price level, and fixed interest rates.

a. Use the following graph to plot Inlandia's consumption function.

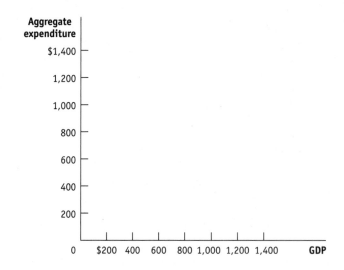

b. Suppose you are told that planned investment spending equals $100, no matter what the level of income in the economy. Graph this information in the previous graph and label the line you draw $I_{Planned}$.

c. On the previous graph, graph the $AE_{Planned}$ line and label it $AE_{Planned}$.

d. What is the income–expenditure equilibrium real GDP for Inlandia?

e. Sketch a diagram showing the relationship between $AE_{Planned}$, $I_{Planned}$, the consumption function, and the 45-degree line.

f. What is the value of the multiplier for this economy?

g. What will be the change in the income–expenditure equilibrium level of real GDP if autonomous consumption decreases by $50?

5. In Mainland, a small closed economy with no government sector, when disposable income is equal to $800, consumer spending is equal to $800 and when disposable income is equal to $1,800, consumer spending is equal to $1,600. Assume that the aggregate price level and the interest rate are fixed in Mainland.

a. What is the value of autonomous consumer spending in Mainland?

b. What is the value of the *MPC* in Mainland?

c. What is the consumption function in Mainland?

d. Suppose that planned investment spending is equal to $500 in Mainland and this level of planned investment spending does not change, no matter what the level of income is in Mainland. Suppose the current level of aggregate expenditure is equal to $3,000. Describe how this economy will respond to this level of aggregate expenditure given the model developed in this chapter. In your answer comment on what is happening to unplanned investment spending, inventories, and the level of real GDP. Explain your answer fully.

e. Suppose that planned investment spending is equal to $500 in Mainland and this level of planned investment spending does not change, no matter what the level of income is in Mainland. Suppose the current level of aggregate expenditure is equal to $4,000. Describe how this economy will respond to this level of aggregate expenditure given the model developed in this chapter. In your answer comment on what is happening to unplanned investment spending, inventories, and the level of real GDP. Explain your answer fully.

f. What is the income–expenditure equilibrium in Mainland if planned investment spending is equal to $500 and this level of planned investment spending does not change, no matter what the level of income is in Mainland?

6. Suppose the economy described in problem 5 is currently in income–expenditure equilibrium. For each of the following situations, describe the effect of the described change on the consumption function and the planned aggregate expenditure function, and then identify the new income–expenditure equilibrium given the consumption function and the initial level of planned investment identified in problem 5.

a. The level of autonomous consumer spending increases by $200.

b. The level of planned investment spending falls to $400.

c. The level of planned investment spending increases to $700.

d. The level of wealth in the economy increases, which leads to an increase in autonomous consumer spending of $100.

BEFORE YOU TAKE THE TEST

Chapter Review Questions

1. Which of the following statements is true?
   a. Investment spending during the Great Depression fell by more than 80%.
   b. Automatic stabilizers, like taxes and some government programs, reduce the size of the multiplier.
   c. The marginal propensity to consume in an economy is a positive number.
   d. Answers (a), (b), and (c) are all true.
   e. Answers (a) and (b) are both true.

2. Consumer spending
   a. usually accounts for two-thirds of total spending on goods and services in the U.S. economy.
   b. holding everything else constant, will cause the *AE* function to shift if there is a change in consumer spending.
   c. has a powerful impact on the economy's aggregate output and aggregate price level according to the simple model developed in this chapter.
   d. Answers (a), (b), and (c) are all correct.
   e. Answers (a) and (b) are both correct.

3. Consumer spending is affected by changes in
   a. current disposable income.
   b. expected future disposable income.
   c. wealth.
   d. All of these factors affect consumer spending.

Use the following information to answer the next two questions.

Suppose aggregate consumer spending equals $5,000 when aggregate disposable income is zero. Furthermore, suppose that when disposable income increases from $300 to $400, consumer spending increases by $70 and that this relationship between a change in disposable income and its affect on consumer spending is predictable and constant.

4. What is the equation for the aggregate consumption function, given the previous information?
   a. $C = 5,000 + 70YD$
   b. $C = 500 + 0.7YD$
   c. $C = 5,000 + 0.7YD$
   d. $C = 5,000 + 7YD$

5. If aggregate disposable income equals $2,000, then what is the value of aggregate consumer spending?
   a. $7,000
   b. $19,000
   c. $6,400
   d. $5,140

6. Suppose aggregate wealth decreases in the economy due to the bursting of a housing price bubble. This will, holding everything else constant,
   a. reduce wealth and result in a decrease in autonomous consumer spending.
   b. cause the aggregate expenditure function to shift down.
   c. result in a lower level of consumer spending for any given level of disposable income.
   d. Answers (a), (b), and (c) are all correct.
   e. Answers (a) and (b) are both correct.

7. Which of the following statements is true?
   a. Holding everything else constant, an increase in planned investment spending shifts the *AE* function downward, leading to a higher level of GDP.
   b. Most recessions start with a decrease in investment spending.
   c. Economists think that decreases in consumer spending often follow decreases in investment spending.
   d. Answers (a), (b), and (c) are all true.
   e. Answers (b) and (c) are both true.

8. An increase in the market interest rate
   a. will make any given investment project less profitable.
   b. will cause companies to rely more heavily on financing their investment projects through retained earnings rather than borrowing.
   c. will reduce the rate of return for any given investment project.
   d. Answers (a), (b), and (c) are all correct.

9. The accelerator principle

   a. helps to explain investment booms.

   b. refers to an increase in planned investment spending due to a higher rate of growth in real GDP.

   c. refers to an increase in government spending intended to stimulate the economy.

   d. Answers (a), (b), and (c) are all correct.

   e. Answers (a) and (b) are both correct.

10. Which of the following is *not* an assumption underlying the multiplier process for this chapter?

   a. Since this is a short-run process, the aggregate price level is sticky but not fixed.

   b. The interest rate is assumed to be fixed and unaffected by the factors analyzed in our model of the multiplier process.

   c. The multiplier process assumes a closed economy where government spending, taxes, and transfers equal zero.

   d. In the short run, the economy always produces at the full-employment level of output.

Use the following information to answer the next five questions.

Suppose Macroland is a closed economy with no government sector and therefore no government expenditure, taxes, or transfers. Furthermore, assume the aggregate price level and interest rate in Macroland is fixed. You are also told that the *MPC* in Macroland is constant. You are provided the following information about Macroland. (All numbers in the following table are dollar amounts.)

GDP	YD	C	$I_{Planned}$	$I_{Unplanned}$
$100	$100	$150	$50	−$100
200			50	
400		300	50	

11. What is the consumption function for this economy?

   a. $C = 150 + 0.5YD$

   b. $C = 250 + 0.5YD$

   c. $C = 100 + 0.5YD$

   d. $C = 50 + 0.5YD$

12. When GDP equals 400, which of the following statements is true?

   a. Unplanned inventory investment is negative.

   b. Planned aggregate expenditure equals 400.

   c. Unplanned inventory investment is positive.

   d. The economy is in income–expenditure equilibrium when GDP equals 400.

13. What is the income–expenditure equilibrium GDP for Macroland?

   a. 200

   b. 300

   c. 500

   d. 600

14. Holding everything else constant, suppose aggregate wealth in an economy increases by $100. Which of the following statements is true?
    a. The *AE* curve shifts upward.
    b. The income–expenditure equilibrium real GDP increases by more than $100.
    c. The multiplier effect on real GDP is a positive number that is greater than $0 and less than $100.
    d. Statements (a), (b), and (c) are all true.
    e. Statements (a) and (b) are both true.

15. Given the change in wealth in question 14, the equilibrium level of GDP
    a. increases relative to its initial level.
    b. decreases relative to its initial level.
    c. is unaffected.
    d. may increase, decrease, or stay the same relative to its initial level.

16. Holding everything else constant in an economy, the larger the *MPS*, the
    a. smaller the value of the multiplier.
    b. larger the value of the multiplier.

17. Suppose the *MPC* is equal to 0.5. In the simple model presented in this chapter, a $100 increase in investment spending will lead to a
    a. $100 increase in spending in the first round, and a total increase in spending of $500.
    b. $50 increase in spending in the first round, and a total increase in spending of $100.
    c. $100 increase in spending in the first round, and a total increase in spending of $200.
    d. total increase in spending of $100 since an increase in investment spending does not create a multiplier effect.

18. The marginal propensity to consume
    a. is the increase in disposable income from a $1 increase in consumer spending.
    b. is the increase in consumer spending from a $1 increase in disposable income.
    c. is usually a number between zero and one, but occasionally is a number greater than one.
    d. can be written as the change in consumer spending divided by the change in disposable income.
    e. Answers (a), (c), and (d) are all correct.
    f. Answers (b), (c), and (d) are all correct.
    g. Answers (b) and (d) are both correct.

19. Joe's disposable income increases by $500, and he finds that he spends $400 of this increase in disposable income. Joe
    a. saves $100 and his *MPS* is equal to 0.8.
    b. saves $100 and his *MPC* is 0.8.
    c. saves 20% of any increase in his disposable income.
    d. Answers (a) and (c) are both correct.
    e. Answers (b) and (c) are both correct.

20. During the multiplier process, the final change in real GDP is limited because
   a. with each round of spending, some disposable income leaks out of the income–expenditure stream as households choose to save some portion of any increase in disposable income.
   b. people reach a point where they have all the goods and services they need and so they stop spending the additional increases in disposable income they receive.

21. The relationship between consumer spending and current disposable income is a
   a. positive relationship.
   b. negative relationship.

22. Suppose when Sue's disposable income is $10,000 she spends $8,000 and when her disposable income is $20,000 she spends $14,000. Sue's autonomous consumer spending is equal to _____ and her *MPS* is equal to _____.
   a. $0; 0.2
   b. $2,000; 0.2
   c. $0; 0.4
   d. $2,000; 0.4

23. Which of the following statements is true?
   a. The slope of the consumption function is the change in consumption divided by the change in disposable income.
   b. The slope of the consumption function is equal to (1 − *MPS*).
   c. A change in autonomous consumer spending will cause the slope of the consumption function to change.
   d. Statements (a), (b), and (c) are all true.
   e. Statements (a) and (b) are both true.

24. The argument that consumer spending depends primarily on the income people expect to have over the long term rather than on their current income is referred to as the
   a. life-cycle hypothesis.
   b. permanent income hypothesis.

25. The argument that consumers smooth their spending over a lifetime rather than adjusting their consumer spending in response to their current disposable income is referred to as the
   a. life-cycle hypothesis.
   b. permanent income hypothesis.

26. Planned investment spending depends on the
   a. interest rate.
   b. expected future level of real GDP.
   c. current level of production capacity.
   d. Answers (a), (b), and (c) are all correct.
   e. Answers (a) and (c) are both correct.

27. Holding everything else constant, when interest rates rise, this
    a. does not affect the profitability of investment projects financed through retained earnings.
    b. makes any given investment project less profitable.
    c. does not affect the opportunity cost of an investment project financed through retained earnings.
    d. leads to a lower level of planned investment spending, holding everything else constant.

28. Suppose the level of planned aggregate expenditure in an economy is $500 while the level of real GDP is $600. According to the simple model developed in this chapter, where the aggregate price level is assumed to be constant, we can expect
    a. inventories will increase.
    b. inventories will decrease.
    c. inventories will be unaffected and will remain at the planned inventory level.
    d. this situation of excess production to continue since there is no mechanism to restore the level of production to the level of spending.

29. Suppose an economy expects its future growth rate of real GDP to be high. This will
    a. have no effect on investment spending, but will lead to an increase in the growth rate of real GDP due to the accelerator principle.
    b. cause investment spending to increase in the economy, which will lead to an increase in the growth rate of real GDP due to the accelerator principle.
    c. cause investment spending to slow in anticipation of the increase in the future growth rate of real GDP, which will lead to a decrease in the current growth rate of real GDP due to the accelerator principle.
    d. cause investment spending to increase in anticipation of the increase in the future growth rate of real GDP, which will lead to a decrease in the current growth rate of real GDP due to the accelerator principle.

30. In the model presented in this chapter, the role of inventories is to
    a. ensure that aggregate expenditure is equal to aggregate production.
    b. provide a signal to producers to increase or decrease their prices.

ANSWER KEY

Answers to Problems and Exercises

1. **a.** Autonomous consumer spending refers to the level of consumer spending that occurs when disposable income equals zero. In the data given, when disposable income equals zero, consumer spending equals 100: autonomous consumer spending therefore equals 100.

    b. The *MPC* equals the change in consumption divided by the change in disposable income. For any two data points (consumption and disposable income combinations), the *MPC* = 0.8.

    c.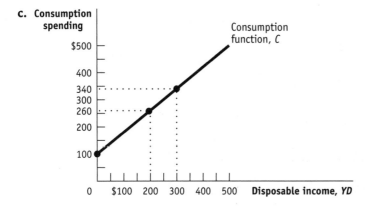

    d. The slope of the consumption function equals the *MPC*, or 0.8.

    e. They are equal. It indicates there is a positive relationship between changes in disposable income and changes in consumption. The *MPC* tells us the change in consumer spending for a dollar increase in disposable income. In this problem, the *MPC* equals 0.8, so we know that when disposable income increases by $1, then consumer spending will increase by $0.80.

    f. An increase in future expected disposable income will increase autonomous consumption, according to the life-cycle hypothesis. This will cause the consumption function to shift upward by the amount of the change in autonomous consumer spending. There will be no change in the *MPC*.

2. **a.**

GDP	YD	C	$I_{Planned}$	$AE_{Planned}$	$I_{Unplanned}$
$ 20	$ 20	$22	$20	$42	−$22
50	50	40	20	60	−10
80	80	58	20	78	2
100	100	70	20	90	10

    b. We know $C = A + MPC \times YD$. We can calculate the *MPC* as the change in consumer spending divided by the change in disposable income: for example, the *MPC* equals $(40 − 22)/(50 − 20) = 0.6$. Plugging this value for the *MPC* back into our equation for the consumption function yields $C = A + 0.6YD$. We can choose a consumption spending and disposable income level like (22, 20), substitute these values into this equation, and solve for A. Doing this, we find A equals 10.

c. The *MPC* equals the change in consumption divided by the change in disposable income, or in this case, 0.6. See explanation in part (b).

d.

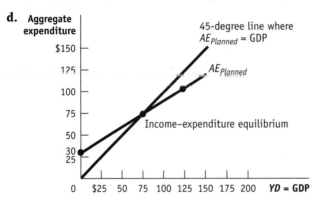

e. To find the income–expenditure equilibrium real GDP in Funland, set $AE_{Planned}$ equal to GDP, since at the income-expenditure equilibrium these two variables are equal. $AE_{Planned}$ equals consumption spending plus planned investment spending. So, GDP = $C + I_{Planned}$ or GDP = 10 + 0.6YD + 20. Recall that GDP equals *YD* in this simple model with no government sector, so we can rewrite this equation as GDP = 10 + 0.6GDP + 20 and then solve for GDP to get 75 for our equilibrium real GDP.

f.

GDP′	YD′	C′	I′$_{Planned}$	AE′$_{Planned}$	I′$_{Unplanned}$
$ 20	$ 20	$22	$40	$ 62	−$42
50	50	40	40	80	−30
80	80	58	40	98	−18
100	100	70	40	110	−10

g. The old equilibrium level of real GDP from part (d) was 75. We have a change in investment spending of 20, and this change will be magnified by the multiplier process. The multiplier in this example equals 2.5, so the change in real GDP equals 2.5 times the $20 change in investment spending. The new equilibrium is the original 75 plus the 2.5(20) or 50, for a total new equilibrium of 125. We could also find the equilibrium by equating $GDP' = AE'_{Planned}$ where $AE'_{Planned} = 10 + 0.6YD + 40$. Recalling that GDP equals *YD* in this simple model, we can rewrite this relationship as *GDP* = 50 + 0.6GDP. Solving for GDP, we get 125 as the new equilibrium GDP. The following graph illustrates this.

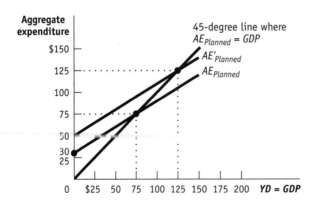

h. We can use the multiplier to see the effect of a change in investment spending on the change in the equilibrium level of real GDP.

3. a. This is a graph of the Keynesian cross, which depicts the planned aggregate expenditure line: this line illustrates the positive relationship between GDP and the level of planned expenditure in the economy. The cross is made by this line and the 45-degree reference line. The point of intersection of these two lines identifies the income–expenditure equilibrium where GDP equals $AE_{Planned}$. When Y is less than Y_2, planned aggregate expenditure is greater than GDP, inventories are falling, and this change in inventories acts as a signal to producers to increase their production. When Y is greater than Y_2, planned aggregate expenditure is less than GDP, inventories are rising, and this change in inventories acts as a signal to producers to decrease their production.

b. No, the income–expenditure equilibrium is at point C on the graph. At point B, $AE_{Planned}$ is greater than GDP, or income. This causes inventories to fall, and firms view this as a signal that they should increase their production from Y_1 toward Y_2, the income-expenditure equilibrium real GDP.

c. See the answer in part (b).

d. This economy, holding everything else constant, will produce GDP equal to Y_2 when it is in income-expenditure equilibrium.

e. Unplanned inventory investment is positive wherever GDP is greater than $AE_{Planned}$: GDP output levels Y_3 and Y_4 represent two output levels where unplanned inventory investment is positive. So, at any output level greater than Y_2, unplanned inventory investment is positive.

f. This is true for any level of GDP less than Y_2. For example, at points A and B, $AE_{Planned}$ exceeds GDP.

g. Point C represents the income–expenditure equilibrium level of real GDP where $AE_{Planned}$ equals GDP.

4. a. See answer at part (c).

b. See answer at part (c).

c.
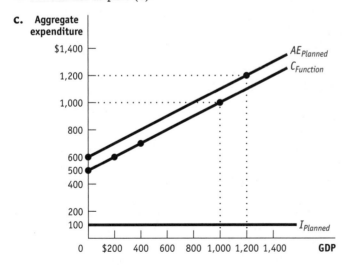

d. Solving for the income-expenditure requires us to know the consumption function (C = 500 + 0.5YD) and the level of planned investment spending (100). We know $AE_{Planned}$ equals GDP in equilibrium and that $AE_{Planned}$ is the sum of consumption spending plus planned investment spending. So, GDP = $AE_{Planned}$ = C + $I_{Planned}$ = 500 + 0.5YD + 100. We also know in our simple model that GDP equals YD. So, GDP = 600 + 0.5GDP, and solving for GDP we find it is equal to 1,200.

e.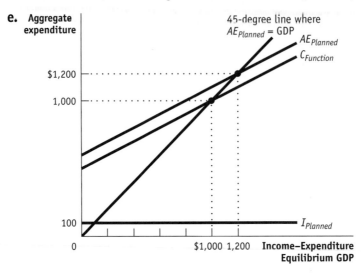

f. We calculate the multiplier as $1/(1 - MPC)$: if the MPC equals 0.5, then the multiplier equals 2.

g. The change in equilibrium real GDP equals the multiplier times the change in autonomous consumption or $(2)(-50)$ or -100. Equilibrium real GDP will fall by 100 with this change in autonomous consumption.

5. a. The value of autonomous consumer spending in Mainland is equal to $160. To find this value first recall that the consumption function can be written as $C = A + MPC \times YD$. Then find the MPC, which is the change in consumer spending divided by the change in disposable income, or $800/1,000 = 0.8$. Then substitute one of the consumer spending and disposable income combinations into the consumption function to find the value of autonomous consumer spending: thus, $C = A + 0.8 \times YD$ and 800 = A + $(0.8) \times (800)$ or A = $160.

b. The MPC is equal to 0.8. See the explanation in part (a) of this problem.

c. The consumption function is $C = 160 + 0.8 \times YD$. See the explanation in part (a) of this problem.

d. When the level of planned aggregate expenditure is $3,000, the level of real GDP is equal to $2,925: this economy is not in equilibrium since the level of planned aggregate expenditure is greater than the level of real GDP. To find the level of real GDP, start with the aggregate expenditure function, $AE = 160 + 0.8 \times YD + 500$ and substitute $3,000 for AE. Then solve for YD. When AE is equal to $3,000, YD is equal to $2,925. When spending exceeds production, this causes a change in unplanned investment as inventories fall due to the fact that spending is greater than production. Firms increase their level of production in response to their falling inventories, moving the economy toward the income-expenditure equilibrium.

e. When the level of planned aggregate expenditure is $4,000, the level of real GDP is equal to $4,175: this economy is not in equilibrium since the level of planned aggregate expenditure is less than the level of real GDP. To find the level of real GDP, start with the aggregate expenditure function, $AE = 160 + 0.8 \times YD + 500$ and substitute $4,000 for AE. Then solve for YD. When AE is equal to $4,000, YD is equal to $4,175. When spending is less than production, this causes a change in unplanned investment as inventories rise due to the fact that spending is less than production. Firms decrease their level of production in response to their rising inventories, moving the economy toward the income–expenditure equilibrium.

f. The income-expenditure equilibrium in Mainland is $3,300. To find this equilibrium recall that in equilibrium planned aggregate expenditure is equal to real GDP. Or, in the model presented in this chapter, $YD = AE$ since disposable income and real GDP are equal to one another when there is no government sector. AE is equal to $660 + 0.8 \times YD$. So, $YD = 660 + 0.8 \times YD$, or YD is equal to $3,300.

6.   **a.** The consumption function will change to $C = 360 + 0.8 \times YD$, the planned aggregate expenditure function will shift upward and the new income-expenditure equilibrium will be $4,300.

b. The level of investment spending will now equal $400, so the planned aggregate expenditure function will be $AE = 160 + 0.8 \times YD + 400$. There will be no change in the consumption function, but the planned aggregate expenditure function will shift down. This will lead to a decrease in the income-expenditure equilibrium: the new income-expenditure equilibrium will be $4,300.

c. The level of investment spending will now equal $700, so the planned aggregate expenditure function will be $AE = 160 + 0.8 \times YD + 700$. There will be no change in the consumption function, but the planned aggregate expenditure function will shift up. This will lead to an increase in the income-expenditure equilibrium: the new income-expenditure equilibrium will be $4,300.

d. The consumption function will change to $C = 260 + 0.8 \times YD$, the planned aggregate expenditure function will shift upward, and the new income-expenditure equilibrium will be $3,800.

Answers to Chapter Review Questions

1.   **Answer d.** Answers (a) and (c) are factual statements. Automatic stabilizers, like taxes and some government programs, reduce the size of the multiplier. For example, in a recession as people's incomes fall, their tax obligations also decrease: this decrease in taxes moderates or lessens the overall fall in aggregate income from the recession.

2.   **Answer e.** Answer (a) is a factual answer. Consumer spending affects the level of AE on goods and services and will therefore cause the AE function to shift if there is a change in the level of consumer spending. Consumer spending in the model developed in this chapter has a powerful impact on the level of aggregate output, but it does not affect the aggregate price level since the model assumes that the aggregate price level is fixed.

3.   **Answer d.** All three of these variables affect the level of consumer spending.

4.   **Answer c.** The basic equation for the aggregate consumption function is $C = A + MPC \times YD$, and from the information we know, A, the aggregate autonomous consumer spending, equals $5,000 and the MPC can be calculated as the change in consumer spending divided by the change in aggregate disposable income, or $70/100$, which equals 0.7. So, $C = 5,000 + 0.7YD$.

5. **Answer c.** Using the equation from question 4, substitute $2,000 for *YD* and solve for *C*. In this case, *C* equals $5,000 + 0.7($2,000), or $6,400.

6. **Answer d.** When the housing price bubble bursts, this reduces households' wealth and causes them to reduce their level of consumption spending, including autonomous consumption spending, at every level of disposable income. This downward shift in the consumption function results in a downward shift of the aggregate expenditure function and a decrease in the value of autonomous consumer spending.

7. **Answer e.** An increase in planned investment spending increases *AE* for goods and services and causes the *AE* function to shift upward (and not downward) leading to a higher level of GDP. Studies of recessions indicate that most recessions follow a drop in investment spending, and this drop in investment spending results in a fall in consumer spending.

8. **Answer a.** A change in the market interest rate does not affect the rate of return for any given investment project. It does, however, affect the opportunity cost of borrowing and as the market interest rate increases, this makes any given investment project less profitable due to the relationship between the market interest rate and the project's rate of return. Firms, whether they use retained earnings or borrow, recognize that the market interest rate reflects the opportunity cost of using or acquiring funds.

9. **Answer e.** The accelerator principle states that a higher rate of growth in real GDP leads to higher planned investment spending. This results in a boom in investment spending. Government spending intended to stimulate the economy is expansionary fiscal policy.

10. **Answer a.** Both answers (b) and (c) are assumptions in our model of the multiplier process in this chapter. This model allows the level of aggregate output to vary in the short run (answer d). Answer (a) is not true.

11. **Answer c.** We know the general equation for the consumption function is $C = A + MPC \times YD$. We need to find the values for *A* and the *MPC*. From the table and the assumptions underlying Macroland's economy, we know *GDP* equals *YD*. The *MPC* is the change in consumption divided by the change in disposable income: from the table, we can calculate that the change in consumption from 150 to 300 equals 150 and that the change in *YD* from 100 to 400 equals 300: thus, the *MPC* equals 0.5. We can now write $C = A + 0.5YD$ and use one of the combinations of consumption and disposable income from the table to solve for *A*; for example, when consumption equals 150, *YD* equals 100 and *A* can be computed as 100.

12. **Answer c.** When GDP equals 400, we can calculate $AE_{Planned}$ by summing *C* plus $I_{Planned}$. $AE_{Planned}$ equals 350, so income (GDP) is greater than expenditure, and therefore unplanned inventory investment is positive.

13. **Answer b.** To find the income–expenditure equilibrium level of real GDP, we need to identify where $AE_{Planned}$ equals GDP. Recall that $AE_{Planned} = C + I_{Planned} = 100 + 0.5YD + 50 = 150 + 0.5YD$. Since GDP equals *YD* for Macroland, this gives us GDP = $150 + 0.5YD$ = $150 + 0.5GDP$. Solving for GDP we get 300. When *YD* equals GDP at 300, $AE_{Planned}$ also equals 300.

14. **Answer e.** An increase in wealth, holding everything else constant, leads to an increase in consumption spending, which causes the *AE* curve to shift upward. When the *AE* curve shifts upward, this leads to a higher income–expenditure equilibrium and, because of the multiplier effect, the increase in the income–expenditure equilibrium will be greater than the initial change in wealth: real GDP will increase by more than $100.

15. **Answer a.** A change in wealth of 100 will cause the equilibrium level of real GDP to increase, since the increase in wealth causes the planned aggregate expenditure line to shift up.

16. **Answer a.** The multiplier in the simple model presented in this chapter is equal to $1/(1 - MPC)$. In addition, the sum of the MPC and the MPS is equal to one. Thus, a given level of the MPC implies a particular MPS (for example, if the MPC is equal to 0.8, then the MPS is equal to 0.2). Using this information, the greater the MPC, the larger the multiplier: the intuition for this is straightforward since a large MPC implies that consumers spend a greater proportion of an increase in their income and this spending leads to the multiplier process. Hence, the multiplier is larger when the MPS is low, and smaller when the MPS is high.

17. **Answer c.** If the MPC is equal to 0.5, then the multiplier is equal to 2. In the first round of spending, expenditure will increase by the $100 of additional investment spending. But this spending is income for people in the economy and in the second round $(0.5)(\$100)$ or $50 will be spent. In the third round $(0.5)(\$50)$ will be spent. This process will continue until the total amount of new spending converges to $200 or the change in real GDP is equal to $[1/(1 - MPC)] \times$ (the initial change in investment spending).

18. **Answer g.** Answers (b) and (d) are the definition of the MPC with one expressed verbally and the other expressed as a mathematical relationship. Answer (c) is incorrect since the MPC must always be a number that is greater than zero but less than one since people cannot consume more than 100% of their disposable income.

19. **Answer e.** To calculate Joe's MPC, look at the ratio of the change in consumer spending divided by the change in disposable income: $\$400/\$500 = 0.8$. If Joe's MPC is equal to 0.8, then his MPS is equal to 0.2. When Joe's MPS is 0.2, this implies that he saves 20% of any increase in this disposable income since 0.2 is equal to 20% when expressed as a percentage rather than a decimal.

20. **Answer a.** The multiplier process describes the effect of a change in autonomous aggregate expenditure on the level of aggregate income. When there is a change in autonomous aggregate expenditure, this leads to an increase in aggregate income: part of this increase in aggregate income is spent and part is saved. The increase in aggregate income leads to more spending and more saving. Each successive round of increases in income is smaller than the preceding round since individuals save a portion of the increase in income.

21. **Answer a.** As the level of current disposable income increases, this leads to a higher level of consumer spending: the two variables are positively related to one another.

22. **Answer d.** To find Sue's autonomous consumer spending, it is helpful to write Sue's consumption function, $C = MPC \times YD + A$. You know two points on Sue's consumption function are ($10,000, $8,000) and ($20,000, $14,000) where the variable measured on the x-axis is disposable income and the variable measured on the y-axis is consumer spending. The MPC can be calculated as (the change in consumer spending)/(the change in disposable income) or $(\$6,000)/(\$10,000) = 0.6$. Thus, the MPS is equal to 0.4. Using this information, Sue's consumption function can be written as $C = 0.6 \times YD + A$. Using one of the two known points from Sue's consumption function you can solve for the value of A, Sue's autonomous consumer spending, as $2,000.

23. **Answer e.** The slope of the consumption function is given by the MPC, which is equal to the change in consumer spending divided by the change in disposable income. When autonomous consumer spending changes, this causes the consumption function to shift: it shifts up if there is an increase in autonomous consumer spending, and it shifts down if there is a decrease in autonomous consumer spending.

24. **Answer b.** This is a definitional statement: see the text for the definition as well as an example illustrating this hypothesis.

25. **Answer a.** The life-cycle hypothesis emphasizes the effect of wealth on spending and hypothesizes that consumers plan their spending over their lifetime rather than planning their consumer spending on the basis of their current income.

26. **Answer d.** Investment spending primarily depends on these three factors.

27. **Answer d.** When interest rates rise, this makes any given investment project less profitable since the firm is either going to find that borrowed funds are now more expensive or that retained earnings used to finance the project will not be available to be invested in order to earn the higher rate of interest. When a firm finances an investment project through retained earnings, there is still an opportunity cost to using these funds for the project since the firm cannot invest the funds and earn the higher interest rate. Interest rates and the level of investment are inversely related to each other.

28. **Answer a.** When real GDP exceeds the level of planned aggregate expenditure, this implies that the level of spending in the economy is too low to absorb all the goods and services being produced. This situation will lead to an increase in inventories if the aggregate price level is assumed to be constant since the level of spending is less than the level of aggregate production.

29. **Answer b.** The accelerator principle is a proposition about the relationship between the future growth rate of real GDP and the level of investment spending: when the future growth rate of real GDP is expected to be high, this leads to an increase in investment spending and this increase in investment spending leads to a higher growth rate of real GDP. Conversely, when the future growth rate of real GDP is expected to be low, this leads to lower planned investment spending; this, in turn, does affect the growth rate of future real GDP.

30. **Answer a.** In the model presented in this chapter, the prices of goods and services are assumed to be constant. The role of inventories is to adjust the level of output to the level of aggregate expenditure: when aggregate expenditure exceeds aggregate production, the level of inventories fall; and when aggregate expenditure is less than aggregate production, the level of inventories rises.

Aggregate Demand and Aggregate Supply

![BEFORE YOU READ THE CHAPTER]

Summary

This chapter develops the basic model of aggregate supply (*AS*) and aggregate demand (*AD*) that describes the relationship between the level of aggregate output and the aggregate price level. A distinction is made between the short-run *AS* curve, where the aggregate price level is positively related to the aggregate output level, and the long-run *AS* curve, a vertical curve where aggregate output is at the economy's potential output and independent of the aggregate price level. This model enables us to find both the short-run and the long-run macroeconomic equilibrium. The chapter further explores the economic changes that result in the *AD* or *AS* curve shifting and the effect of these shifts on economic fluctuations. The chapter introduces the multiplier and its relationship to autonomous spending. The chapter also explores how monetary and fiscal policies can stabilize the economy.

Chapter Objectives

Objective #1. Deflation refers to the fall in the aggregate price level, while inflation refers to an increase in the aggregate price level. Stagflation refers to the combination of inflation coupled with a decrease in the level of aggregate output and an increase in unemployment.

Objective #2. The model of aggregate supply (*AS*) and aggregate demand (*AD*) can help us understand economic fluctuations and the use of macroeconomic policy to reduce these fluctuations.

Objective #3.   The *AD* curve depicts the inverse relationship between the aggregate price level (P) and the total quantity of aggregate output demanded by households, businesses, government, and the foreign sector. A higher aggregate price level, other things equal, reduces the quantity of aggregate output demanded; a lower aggregate price level, other things equal, increases the quantity of aggregate output demanded.

- A movement up or down the *AD* curve is due to changes in the prices of all final goods and services. In contrast, a movement up and down the demand curve for any individual good is due to a change in the price of that good while all other prices are held constant.

- *AD* curves are downward sloping because of the wealth effect and the interest rate effect.

  - When the aggregate price level changes, this affects the purchasing power of consumers' assets and hence consumers' wealth. This effect on purchasing power is called the wealth effect. For example, a decrease in the aggregate price level increases the purchasing power of many assets and therefore leads to an increase in the quantity of aggregate output demanded.

  - When the aggregate price level changes, this affects the purchasing power of a given amount of money; for example, as the price level increases, people find they need more money to purchase the same basket of goods and services. Consumers bid up interest rates with their increased demand for money. As interest rates increase, this results in less investment spending and therefore a reduction in the quantity of aggregate output demanded. This effect is referred to as the interest rate effect.

Objective #4.   The AD curve can be derived from the income–expenditure model. In the income–expenditure model presented in the previous chapter, the aggregate price level was assumed to be constant. Consider what happens to the planned aggregate expenditure curve if the aggregate price level is allowed to change. When the aggregate price level decreases, this increases the level of planned spending at every level of real GDP: the planned aggregate expenditure curve shifts upward. When the aggregate price level increases, this decreases the level of planned spending at every level of real GDP: the planned aggregate expenditure curve shifts downward. Thus, as the aggregate price level increases, the level of spending, or aggregate demand, will decrease: the *AD* curve is thus downward sloping, indicating an inverse relationship between the level of real GDP and the aggregate price level. Figure 12.1 illustrates this relationship: in the first graph the income–expenditure model is depicted showing two planned aggregate expenditure lines with AE_1 drawn with the aggregate price level P_1, and AE_2 drawn with the aggregate price level P_2 where P_1 is greater than P_2. In the second graph in this figure, the *AD* curve is illustrated indicating the relationship between the income–expenditure equilibrium and the price level: Y_1 is the income–expenditure equilibrium when the aggregate price level is P_1 and Y_2 is the income–expenditure equilibrium when the aggregate price level is P_2.

Figure 12.1

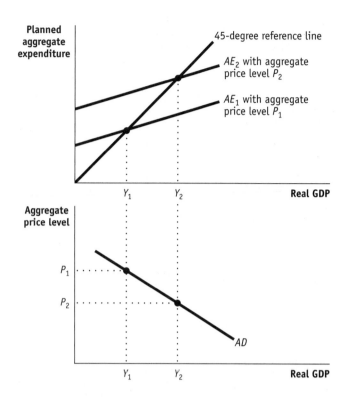

Objective #5. The AD curve shifts, holding everything else constant, when there are changes in expectations, wealth, or physical capital, or when there are changes in government fiscal or monetary policy.

- When consumers and firms become more optimistic, spending increases and the AD curve shifts to the right. A negative change in consumer or firm expectations shifts the AD curve to the left.

- When the value of household assets increases, consumer spending increases. AD shifts to the right with an increase in household wealth and to the left with a decrease in household wealth, other things held constant.

- Firms' incentives to engage in investment spending depend on many things, including how much physical capital they already have. If firms already have a high level of physical capital, the incentive to engage in investment spending is low: AD, holding everything else constant, shifts to the left when firms experience higher levels of physical capital. If firms have a low level of physical capital, the incentive to engage in investment spending is high: AD, holding everything else constant, shifts to the right when firms experience low levels of physical capital.

- Fiscal policy, or government spending and taxing policy, can cause the AD curve to shift to the right or to the left. An increase in government spending or a decrease in taxes, holding everything else constant, shifts AD to the right. A decrease in government spending or an increase in taxes, holding everything else constant, shifts AD to the left.

- An increase in the money supply reduces interest rates and increases investment spending. Thus, an increase in money shifts the AD curve to the right, while a decrease in money shifts the AD curve to the left.

Objective #6. The aggregate supply (*AS*) curve illustrates the relationship between the aggregate price level and the total quantity of final goods and services, or aggregate output, producers are willing to supply. In the short run there is a positive relationship between the amount of aggregate output or real GDP producers are willing to supply and the aggregate price level. That is, holding everything else constant, in the short run as the aggregate price level increases, the level of aggregate production increases. Figure 12.2 illustrates a short-run *AS* curve (*SRAS*): notice the positive relationship between the aggregate price level and the level of aggregate output or real GDP.

Figure 12.2

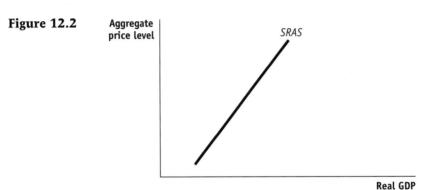

- In the short run, producers decide on their level of production by comparing the price they receive from selling a unit of output to their costs of producing that unit of output. Since some production costs are fixed in the short run, an increase in the aggregate price level increases profit per unit and therefore leads producers to increase their level of production. Hence, the short-run *AS* curve is upward sloping.

- In the short run, nominal wages are sticky due to the existence of both formal and informal agreements. This means that nominal wages decrease slowly even in the presence of high unemployment and increase slowly in the presence of low unemployment. In the long run, nominal wages are completely flexible.

- The short-run *AS* curve shifts due to changes in commodity prices, nominal wages, and productivity. An increase in commodity prices or nominal wages results in a shift to the left of the short-run *AS* curve, while a decrease in commodity prices or nominal wages results in a shift to the right of the short-run *AS* curve. An increase in productivity shifts the short-run *AS* curve to the right. There will be a movement along the *AS* curve with a change in the aggregate price level.

Objective #7. In the long run, nominal wages and prices are flexible and therefore in the long run, the aggregate price level has no effect on the quantity of aggregate output supplied. The *AS* curve in the long run is vertical, where the level of aggregate output equals potential output, or the level of real GDP the economy would produce if all prices and wages were completely flexible. Figure 12.3 illustrates a long-run *AS* curve (*LRAS*): notice that this curve is vertical and that no matter what the aggregate price level, the level of real GDP is constant and equal to potential GDP.

Figure 12.3

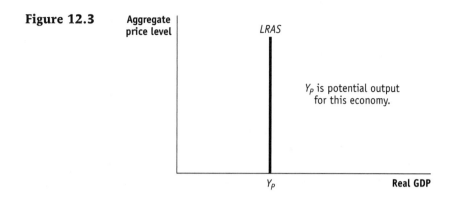

- Over time if the level of potential output for an economy increases, then this implies that the long-run *AS* curve is shifting to the right. These shifts represent economic growth and are due to increases in the labor force and increases in the productivity of labor.

Objective #8.   The economy is always in only one of two states with respect to the short-run and long-run *AS* curves: (1) it can be on both curves simultaneously by being at a point where the two curves cross; or (2) it can be on the short-run *AS* curve but not on the long-run *AS* curve. Figure 12.4 illustrates these two possibilities. In the graph on the left, the *SRAS* and the *LRAS* curves intersect at the potential output level Y_P and the aggregate price level *P*. In the graph on the right, the economy is producing at Y_1 with the aggregate price level *P*: this level of production is not equal to potential output. In the short run, the economy can produce at a level of aggregate output that is less than potential output (as illustrated in the right graph in Figure 12.4), or it can produce at a level of aggregate output that is greater than potential output (you might want to practice drawing this situation).

Figure 12.4

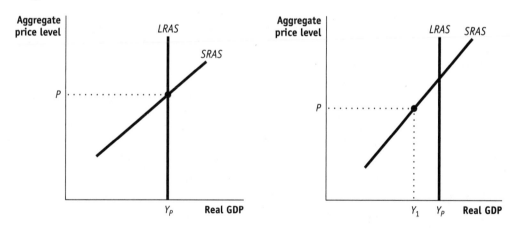

- When the level of aggregate production is less than potential output, this implies that unemployment is high. Jobs are scarce and workers are abundant, which causes nominal wages to fall over time; the short-run *AS* curve will shift to the right, moving the short-run level of aggregate production closer to potential output. Figure 12.5 illustrates this situation.

Figure 12.5

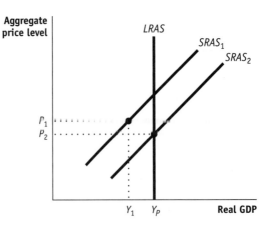

- When the level of aggregate production is greater than potential output, this implies that unemployment is low. Jobs are abundant and workers are scarce, which causes nominal wages to rise over time; the short-run *AS* curve will shift to the left, moving the short-run level of aggregate production closer to potential output. Figure 12.6 illustrates this situation.

Figure 12.6

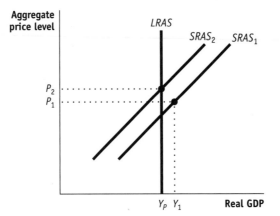

Objective #9. The *AD-AS* model is the basic model we use to understand economic fluctuations. In the *AD-AS* model there are two states of equilibrium the economy can be in: (1) the economy can be in short-run equilibrium where *AD* equals short-run *AS*; or (2) the economy can be in long-run equilibrium where *AD* equals long-run *AS* (as well as short-run *AS*) and aggregate output equals potential output. If the economy is in the first state, over time the short-run *AS* curve will shift eventually, bringing the economy into long-run equilibrium.

- In short-run equilibrium, aggregate output may be less than, equal to, or greater than potential output. If aggregate output is less than potential output, this implies unemployment is relatively high: since jobs are scarce and workers are abundant, nominal wages will respond by falling over time and this will shift the short-run *AS* to the right, leading output to expand toward the level of potential output. Figure 12.7 illustrates this situation. The economy moves from the short-run equilibrium where real GDP equals Y_1 and the aggregate price level equals P_1, to the long-run equilibrium where real GDP equals Y_2 or the potential output level Y_P and the aggregate price level equals P_2.

Figure 12.7

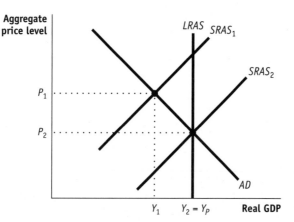

- If aggregate output is greater than potential output, this implies unemployment is relatively low. Since jobs are plentiful and workers are scarce, nominal wages will respond by rising over time and this will shift the short-run *AS* to the left, leading output to contract toward the level of potential output. Figure 12.8 illustrates this situation. The economy moves from the short-run equilibrium where real GDP equals Y_1 and the aggregate price level equals P_1, to the long-run equilibrium where real GDP equals Y_2 or the potential output level Y_p and the aggregate price level equals P_2.

Figure 12.8

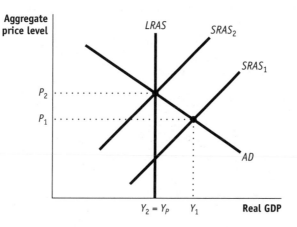

Objective #10. In the *AD–AS* model the short-run macroeconomic equilibrium occurs at the intersection of the *AD* curve with the short-run *AS* curve.

- An event that shifts the short-run *AS* curve is called a supply shock. Negative supply shocks shift the short-run *AS* curve to the left, while positive supply shocks shift the short-run *AS* curve to the right.

  - A negative supply shock leads to stagflation, where falling aggregate output and rising unemployment combine with an increasing price level.

  - A positive supply shock leads to rising aggregate output, falling unemployment, and a decrease in the aggregate price level.

  - Supply shocks cause aggregate output and the aggregate price level to move in the opposite directions.

- An event that shifts the *AD* curve is called a demand shock.

    - A positive demand shock shifts the *AD* curve to the right, resulting in higher aggregate output and a higher aggregate price level.

    - A negative demand shock shifts the *AD* curve to the left, resulting in lower aggregate output and a lower aggregate price level.

    - Demand shocks cause aggregate output and the aggregate price level to move in the same direction.

- Short-run macroeconomic equilibrium aggregate output may be less than, equal to, or greater than potential output. Thus, the short-run macroeconomic equilibrium can represent an economy in an economic recession or an economy in an economic expansion.

Objective #11. Long-run macroeconomic equilibrium occurs when the short-run macroeconomic equilibrium is also a point on the long-run *AS* curve. Long-run macroeconomic equilibrium aggregate output is always equal to potential output.

- A recessionary gap occurs when the short-run macroeconomic equilibrium is below potential output. Recessionary gaps are hurtful due to the high levels of unemployment and low levels of production associated with them. Eventually, high unemployment causes nominal wages to fall and this shifts the short-run *AS* to the right leading to higher levels of production and lower unemployment as the economy reaches long-run macroeconomic equilibrium. Figure 12.7 represents a recessionary gap since the equilibrium level of short-run production (Y_1) is less than the long-run equilibrium level of production (Y_2 or Y_P): the recessionary gap is the difference between potential output and actual short-run output, or $Y_P - Y_1$.

- An inflationary gap occurs when the short-run macroeconomic equilibrium is above potential output. In an inflationary gap, unemployment is low and this leads to increases in nominal wages that shift the short-run AS to the left, leading to lower levels of production and higher unemployment as the economy reaches long-run macroeconomic equilibrium. Figure 12.8 represents an inflationary gap since the equilibrium level of short-run production (Y_1) is greater than the long-run equilibrium level of production (Y_2 or Y_P): the inflationary gap is the difference between actual short-run output and potential output, or $Y_1 - Y_P$.

- In both the recessionary gap and inflationary gap, the economy is self-correcting: given enough time the economy will adjust to economic shocks so that these shocks affect aggregate output in the short run but have no effect on aggregate output in the long run, provided the government does not intervene with activist policy.

Objective #12. Active stabilization policy by the government can be used to offset demand shocks to the economy: active stabilization policy can reduce the severity of recessions that are due to negative demand shocks.

- Figure 12.9 illustrates a negative demand shock and the use of active stabilization policy to reduce the severity of the recession created by the demand shock. Initially the economy is in long-run equilibrium where *LRAS* intersects *SRAS* and AD_1: the economy produces $Y_1 - Y_P$ and the aggregate price level is P_1. Then there is a negative demand shock that shifts the *AD* curve from AD_1 to AD_2. The new short-run equilibrium is where *SRAS* and AD_2 intersect and the level of aggregate output is Y_2 and the aggregate price level is P_2: the economy operates with a recessionary gap equal to $Y_P - Y_2$. If the government engages in active stabilization policy, by either increasing the money supply, increasing the level of government spending, or decreasing taxes, this will cause the *AD* curve to shift from AD_2 to AD_3 (the same as AD_1): the economy will return to its initial long-run equilibrium aggregate output level Y_P and its initial aggregate price level P_1.

Figure 12.9   Aggregate price level

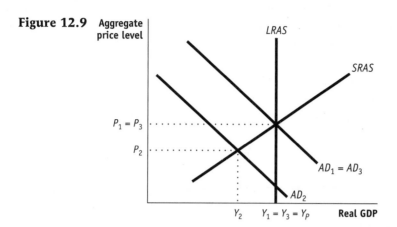

- Figure 12.10 illustrates a positive demand shock and the use of active stabilization policy to reduce the economic expansion created by the demand shock. Initially the economy is in long-run equilibrium where $LRAS$ intersects $SRAS$ and AD_1: the economy produces $Y_1 = Y_P$ and the aggregate price level is P_1. Then there is a positive demand shock that shifts the AD curve from AD_1 to AD_2. The new short-run equilibrium is where $SRAS$ and AD_2 intersect and the level of aggregate output is Y_2 and the aggregate price level is P_2: the economy operates with an inflationary gap equal to $Y_2 - Y_P$. If the government engages in active stabilization policy, by either decreasing the money supply, decreasing the level of government spending, or increasing taxes, this will cause the AD curve to shift from AD_2 to AD_3 (the same as AD_1): the economy will return to its initial long-run equilibrium aggregate output level Y_P and its initial aggregate price level P_1.

Figure 12.10   Aggregate price level

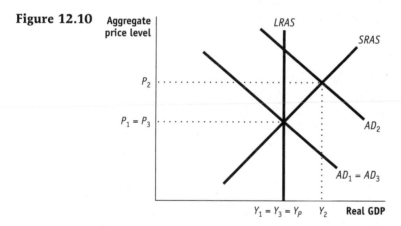

Objective #13. There are no easy stabilization policies available to offset negative supply shocks. When policymakers try to offset negative supply shocks, they face a difficult trade-off: one can increase aggregate output only by increasing the aggregate price level, or one can decrease the aggregate price level only by decreasing aggregate output.

- Figure 12.11 illustrates a negative supply shock. The economy is initially in long-run equilibrium with aggregate output equal to Y_P and the aggregate price level equal to P_1. Then the $SRAS$ shifts to the left due to a negative supply shock: the aggregate output level falls to Y_2 and the aggregate price level rises to P_2. If the government engages in active stabilization policy, it can either (1) shift AD to the right through increases in the money supply, increases in government spending, or decreases in taxes; or it can (2) shift AD to the left through decreases in the money supply, decreases in government spending, or increases in taxes. With the first option, the equilibrium level of aggregate output will increase as will the aggregate price level; with the second option, the equilibrium level of aggregate output will decrease as will the aggregate price level. In the case of active stabilization policy for a negative supply shock, it is not possible to simultaneously increase the level of aggregate output while decreasing the aggregate price level.

Figure 12.11

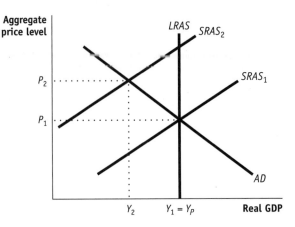

Key Terms

aggregate demand curve a graphical representation that shows the relationship between the *aggregate price level* and the quantity of *aggregate output* demanded by *households, firms,* the government, and the rest of the world. The aggregate demand curve has a negative slope due to the *wealth effect of a change in the aggregate price level* and the *interest rate effect of a change in the aggregate price level*.

wealth effect of a change in the aggregate price level the effect on *consumer spending* caused by the change in the purchasing power of consumers' assets when the *aggregate price level* changes. A rise in the aggregate price level decreases the purchasing power of consumers' assets, so consumers decrease their consumption; a fall in the aggregate price level increases the purchasing power of consumers' assets, so consumers increase their consumption.

interest rate effect of a change in the aggregate price level the effect on *consumer spending* and *investment spending* caused by a change in the purchasing power of consumers' money holdings when the *aggregate price level* changes. A rise (fall) in the aggregate price level decreases (increases) the purchasing power of consumers' money holdings. In response, consumers try to increase (decrease) their money holdings, which drives up (down) interest rates, thereby decreasing (increasing) consumption and investment.

aggregate supply curve a graphical representation that shows the relationship between the *aggregate price level* and the total quantity of *aggregate output* supplied.

nominal wage the dollar amount of any given wage paid.

sticky wages *nominal wages* that are slow to fall even in the face of high *unemployment* and slow to rise even in the face of labor shortages.

Notes

Key Terms *(continued)*

short-run aggregate supply curve a graphical representation that shows the positive relationship between the *aggregate price level* and the quantity of *aggregate output* supplied that exists in the short run, the time period when many production costs, particularly *nominal wages,* can be taken as fixed. The short-run aggregate supply curve has a positive slope because a rise in the aggregate price level leads to a rise in profits, and therefore output, when production costs are fixed.

long-run aggregate supply curve a graphical representation that shows the relationship between the *aggregate price level* and the quantity of *aggregate output* supplied that would exist if all prices, including *nominal wages,* were fully flexible. The long-run aggregate supply curve is vertical because the aggregate price level has no effect on aggregate output in the long run; in the long run, aggregate output is determined by the *economy's potential output.*

potential output the level of *real GDP* the *economy* would produce if all prices, including *nominal wages,* were fully flexible.

AD-AS model the basic model used to understand fluctuations in *aggregate output* and the *aggregate price level*. It uses the *aggregate supply curve* and the *aggregate demand curve* together to analyze the behavior of the *economy* in response to shocks or government policy.

short-run macroeconomic equilibrium the point at which the quantity of *aggregate output* supplied is equal to the *quantity demanded.*

short-run equilibrium aggregate price level the *aggregate price level* in *short-run macroeconomic equilibrium.*

short-run equilibrium aggregate output the quantity of *aggregate output* produced in *short-run macroeconomic equilibrium.*

demand shock an event that shifts the *aggregate demand curve*. A positive demand shock is associated with higher demand for *aggregate output* at any price level and shifts the curve to the right. A negative demand shock is associated with lower demand for aggregate output at any price level and shifts the curve to the left.

supply shock an event that shifts the *short-run aggregate supply curve*. A negative supply shock raises production costs and reduces the *quantity supplied* at any *aggregate price level,* shifting the curve leftward. A positive supply shock decreases production costs and increases the quantity supplied at any aggregate price level, shifting the curve rightward.

stagflation the combination of *inflation* and falling *aggregate output.*

long-run macroeconomic equilibrium the point at which the *short-run macroeconomic equilibrium* is on the *long-run aggregate supply curve;* so *short-run equilibrium aggregate output* is equal to *potential output.*

recessionary gap exists when *aggregate output* is below *potential output.*

Key Terms (continued)

inflationary gap exists when *aggregate output* is above *potential output*.

output gap the percentage difference between the actual level of *real GDP* and *potential output*.

self-correcting describes an *economy* in which shocks to *aggregate demand* affect *aggregate output* in the short run but not in the long run.

stabilization policy the use of government policy to reduce the severity of *recessions* and to rein in excessively strong *expansions*. There are two main tools of stabilization policy: *monetary policy* and *fiscal policy*.

■ AFTER YOU READ THE CHAPTER

Tips

Tip #1. It is important to distinguish between short-run and long-run *AS*. In the short run, wages are sticky: this stickiness results in a short-run *AS* curve (*SRAS*) that is upward sloping. In the long run, wages are fully flexible, leading the economy to always produce its long-run equilibrium at the potential output level of real GDP. This is the output level the economy produces when all wages and prices are fully flexible. In Figure 12.12, the short-run aggregate supply curve is *SRAS*, the aggregate demand curve is *AD*, the long-run aggregate supply curve is *LRAS*, and the potential output level, which represents the long-run equilibrium level of output, is Y_P. The economy in the short run may produce an aggregate output level that is greater than or less than the potential level of output Y_P. Figure 12.12 represents an economy where the short-run level of aggregate output Y_1 is less than the long-run level of output, labeled Y_P.

Figure 12.12

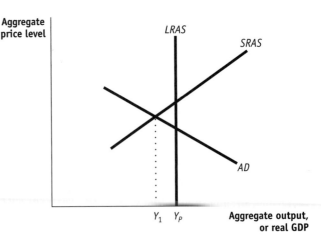

Tip #2. It is important to distinguish between a movement along the *AD* or *SRAS* curve and a shift of the *AD* or *SRAS* curve. A change in the aggregate price level causes a movement along either curve (see Figures 12.13a and 12.13b), while a change in commodity prices, nominal wages, or productivity shifts the *SRAS* curve, and a change in expectations, wealth, physical capital, fiscal policy, or monetary policy shifts the *AD* curve (see Figures 12.13c and 12.13d).

Figure 12.13a

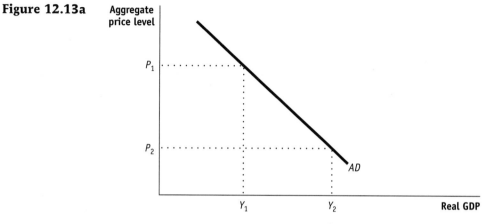

Figure 12.13b

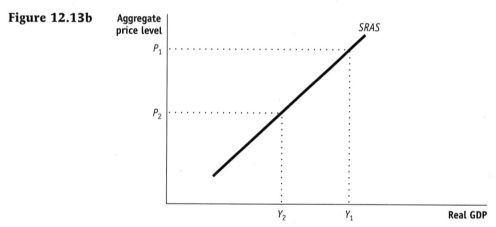

Figure 12.13c

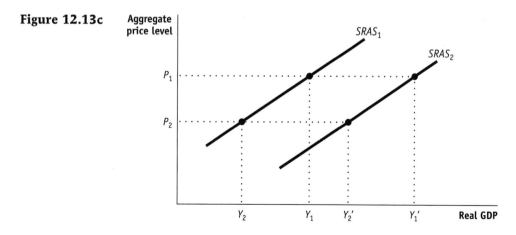

Figure 12.13d

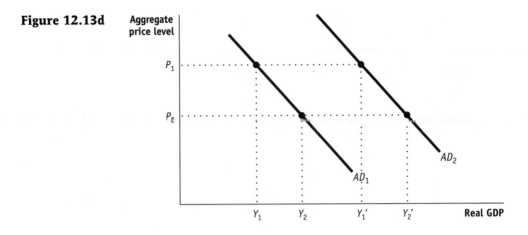

Tip #3. It is important to know the variables that shift *SRAS* and *AD* curves. The text provides a list and an explanation for the variables that cause either the *SRAS* or the *AD* curves to shift. It is crucial that you know these variables and that you understand the direction the curves shift with changes in these variables. (See the previous tip for a quick review of these variables.)

Tip #4. Changes in commodity prices have large impacts on production costs. Understanding the impact of commodity prices on the *SRAS* curve will enhance your understanding of the impact of supply shocks on the *AD-AS* model.

Tip #5. The long-run *AS* curve (*LRAS*) is vertical, and its position represents the economy's potential output when all resources are fully employed. It is important to understand why the *LRAS* curve is vertical as well as the relevance of its position on the horizontal axis. Over time if an economy experiences economic growth the *LRAS* curve shifts to the right, indicating the economy's potential output has increased.

Tip #6. It is important to understand why the *AD* curve is downward sloping. Note that the inverse relationship between the aggregate price level and aggregate output are explained by the wealth and interest rate effects.

Tip #7. It is important to understand the difference between short-run and long-run macroeconomic equilibria and the relationship between these equilibria. In long-run macroeconomic equilibrium, aggregate output equals potential output and the economy's *AD* equals both its short-run and long-run *AS* (see Figure 12.14a). In short-run macroeconomic equilibrium aggregate, output need not equal potential output, but the economy's *AD* must equal the short–run *AS*. Figure 12.14b illustrates a short-run equilibrium for an economy that is operating with an inflationary gap. Figure 12.14c illustrates a short-run equilibrium for an economy that is operating with a recessionary gap.

Figure 12.14a

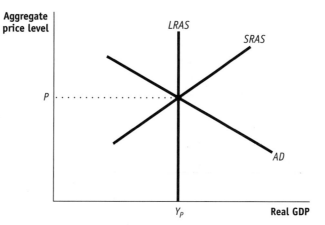

Figure 12.14b

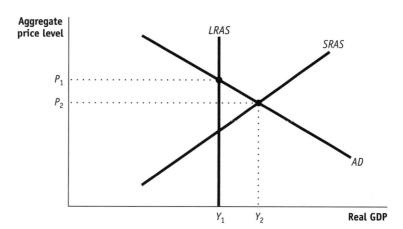

Figure 12.14c

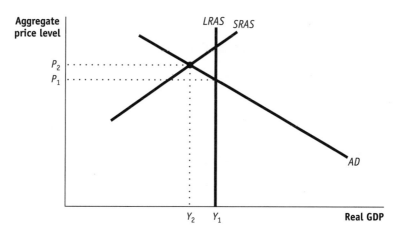

WORKED PROBLEMS

1. For each of the following changes, determine the effect on the aggregate demand curve and the short-run aggregate supply curve, as well as the effect on the aggregate price level and aggregate level of output.

Description of change	Effect on aggregate demand	Effect on short-run aggregate supply	Effect on the aggregate price level	Effect on the aggregate level of production
World oil prices increase				
The central bank increases the money supply				
The government reduces taxes				
The government reduces taxes at the same time that nominal wages increase				
The country goes to war at the same time that world oil prices increase				
People's real wealth decreases				

STEP 1: Review the factors that shift the aggregate demand curve and the aggregate supply curve. In addition, think about sketching a graph that will help guide your answer to this question.

Review the section "Shifts of the Aggregate Demand Curve" on page 346 (Econ page 778), the section "Shifts of the Short-Run Aggregate Supply Curve" on page 350 (Econ page 782), Table 12-1 on page 342 (Econ page 774), and Table 12-2 on page 344 (Econ page 776).

Before you can begin to answer this question, you must have a firm grasp of the factors that shift the aggregate demand curve and the factors that shift the short-run aggregate supply curve. Then, for each description determine which curve or curves are shifting and sketch a diagram to guide your thinking.

STEP 2: There is a challenge in this question when both the aggregate demand curve and the short-run aggregate supply curve shift simultaneously.

Review the section "Shifts of the Aggregate Demand Curve" on page 346 (Econ page 778), the section "Shifts of the Short-Run Aggregate Supply Curve" on page 350 (Econ page 782), Table 12-1 on page 342 (Econ page 774), and Table 12-2 on page 344 (Econ page 776).

When both curves shift and there is no quantitative information about the size of the shift, this results in either the change in the equilibrium aggregate price level or the change in the equilibrium aggregate output level being ambiguous. Be particularly careful in your analysis when you see that both curves are shifting.

STEP 3: Fill in the table.

Review the section "Shifts of the Aggregate Demand Curve" on page 346 (Econ page 778), the section "Shifts of the Short-Run Aggregate Supply Curve" on page 350 (Econ page 782), Table 12-1 on page 342 (Econ page 774), and Table 12-2 on page 344 (Econ page 776).

Description of change	Effect on aggregate demand	Effect on short-run aggregate supply	Effect on the aggregate price level	Effect on the aggregate level of production
World oil prices increase	This event causes a movement along the *AD* curve.	This event causes the *SRAS* curve to shift to the left.	The aggregate price level increases.	The aggregate level of production decreases.
The central bank increases the money supply	This event causes the *AD* curve to shift to the right.	This event causes a movement along the *SRAS* curve.	The aggregate price level increases.	The aggregate level of production increases.
The government reduces taxes	This event causes the *AD* curve to shift to the right.	This event causes a movement along the *SRAS* curve.	The aggregate price level increases.	The aggregate level of production increases.
The government reduces taxes at the same time that nominal wages increase	The reduction in taxes causes the *AD* curve to shift to the right.	The increase in nominal wages causes the *SRAS* curve to shift to the left.	The aggregate price level will increase.	The aggregate level of production may increase, decrease, or remain the same.
The country goes to war at the same time that world oil prices increase	The country's entry into war causes the *AD* curve to shift to the right.	The rise in world oil prices causes the *SRAS* curve to shift to the left.	The aggregate price level will increase.	The aggregate level of production may increase, decrease, or remain the same.
People's real wealth decreases	This event causes the *AD* curve to shift to the left.	This event causes a movement along the *SRAS* curve.	The aggregate price level will decrease.	The aggregate level of production will decrease.

2. Today on a radio talk show you heard the commentator say that aggregate demand expresses an inverse relationship between the level of aggregate production and the aggregate price level. The commentator said this was due to the wealth effect and the interest rate effect. A friend listening to the show with you doesn't understand what this means, and she has asked you to explain the ideas behind these two effects and how they are related to the inverse relationship between the aggregate price level and the aggregate level of production.

STEP 1: Review the definitions of the wealth effect and the interest rate effect.

Review the section "Why Is the Aggregate Demand Curve Downward Sloping?" on page 343 (Econ page 775).

The wealth effect focuses on the effect of a change in the aggregate price level on the purchasing power or real income of consumers. When the aggregate price level increases, this reduces the real income that consumers have: for any given level of nominal income, a rise in the aggregate price level will lower consumers' ability to purchase goods and services. As the aggregate price level rises, consumption spending will therefore fall. Thus, as the aggregate price level increases, the level of aggregate output demanded will fall.

The interest rate effect focuses on the effect of a change in the aggregate price level on the interest rate in the economy. When the aggregate price level increases, people will demand more money since they will need more money in order to purchase the same basket of goods and services. As the demand for money increases, this causes the interest rate to rise, and this rise in interest rates means that it will cost more for businesses to borrow to finance their investment spending. Thus, as the interest rate rises, investment spending falls. This fall in investment spending results in a decrease in aggregate demand as the aggregate price level rises.

STEP 2: Explain why these two effects suggest that there is an inverse relationship between the aggregate price level and the aggregate level of production.

Review the section "Why Is the Aggregate Demand Curve Downward Sloping?" on page 343 (Econ page 775).

Both effects, the wealth effect and the interest rate effect, indicate that when the aggregate price level rises, this will cause aggregate demand to decrease. The aggregate demand curve is downward sloping: there is an inverse relationship between the level of real GDP and the aggregate price level.

3.   Suppose that you know the following information about an economy.

Long-run aggregate supply:	$Y = 8$
Short-run aggregate supply:	$P = 100Y$
Aggregate demand:	$P = 1{,}000 - 100Y$

As shown here, P refers to aggregate prices and Y refers to the aggregate level of production. You are asked to determine the short-run equilibrium aggregate price level and aggregate output level. You are also asked to identify if there is a short-run recessionary gap or a short-run inflationary gap. Comment on the implications of this gap on the level of unemployment in this economy in the short run. In addition, you are asked to provide a graph that depicts this short-run equilibrium as well as the long-run aggregate supply curve for this economy. Finally, you are asked to propose several policy options for the government of this country if it wishes to return to the long-run equilibrium. You are also asked to discuss the implications of not implementing any active policy to return the economy to long-run equilibrium.

STEP 1: Use the short-run aggregate supply curve and aggregate demand curve to determine the short-run equilibrium level of aggregate prices and the short-run equilibrium level of aggregate output.

Review the section "The AD-AS Model" on page 360 (Econ page 792), the section "Macroeconomic Policy" on page 368 (Econ page 800), and Figure 12-13 on page 363 (Econ page 795).

Since you are given equations for the three curves, you can solve for the equilibrium values of P and Y. To find the short-run equilibrium aggregate price level and the short-run equilibrium aggregate output level, use the short-run aggregate supply curve and the aggregate demand curve. Thus, $100Y = 1{,}000 - 100Y$, and therefore $P = 500$ and $Y = 5$.

STEP 2: Determine whether there is a recessionary gap or an inflationary gap by comparing the short-run equilibrium level of aggregate output to the long-run level of aggregate output. Then consider the implications of this gap on this economy's unemployment rate.

Review the section "The AD-AS Model" on page 360 (Econ page 792), the section "Macroeconomic Policy" on page 368 (Econ page 800), and Figure 12-13 on page 363 (Econ page 795).

A recessionary gap occurs when the short-run level of aggregate output is less than the long-run level of aggregate output. An inflationary gap occurs when the short-run level of aggregate output is greater than the long-run level of aggregate output. In this case, the short-run level of aggregate output is equal to 5 and the long-run level of aggregate output is equal to 8: this economy has a recessionary gap. It is currently producing a level of aggregate output that is lower than its potential or long-run level of output: the economy is in a recession and unemployment is relatively high.

STEP 3: Draw a graph that depicts the short-run aggregate supply curve, the long-run aggregate supply curve, and the aggregate demand curve. On your graph, mark the short-run equilibrium aggregate price level and the short-run equilibrium level of aggregate output. Also, mark the long-run level of aggregate output.

Review the section "The AD–AS Model" on page 360 (Econ page 792), the section "Macroeconomic Policy" on page 368 (Econ page 800), and Figure 12-13 on page 363 (Econ page 795).

Here is the graph of this economy's short-run equilibrium as well as its long-run level of aggregate output.

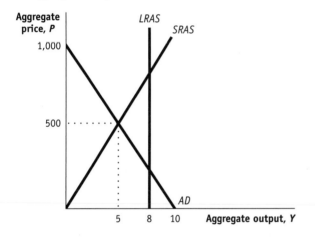

STEP 4: Determine what type of activist policy, monetary or fiscal, will move this economy to the long-run level of aggregate output.

Review the section "The AD–AS Model" on page 360 (Econ page 792), the section "Macroeconomic Policy" on page 368 (Econ page 800), and Figure 12-13 on page 363 (Econ page 795).

Since short-run aggregate output is less than long-run aggregate output, activist policy should stimulate the economy. The government could implement activist fiscal policy: this could involve an increase in government spending, a decrease in taxes, or a combination of these two policies. The effect of this government intervention in the economy would be to shift the aggregate demand curve to the right, restoring the economy to its long-run equilibrium level of aggregate output. This policy would also raise the aggregate price level.

   Alternatively, the government could pursue activist monetary policy: the central bank could increase the money supply in order to shift the aggregate demand curve to the right. As with fiscal policy, activist monetary policy in this example will cause aggregate output to increase to the long-run level while also causing the aggregate price level to rise.

STEP 5: Discuss what would happen in this economy if no activist policy is implemented.

Review the section "The AD–AS Model" on page 360 (Econ page 792), the section "Macroeconomic Policy" on page 368 (Econ page 800), and Figure 12-13 on page 363 (Econ page 795).

If there is no activist policy implemented, this economy will return to the long-run level of aggregate output eventually. With the recessionary gap, the economy finds that its unemployment rate is relatively high and over time this will cause nominal wages to decrease. As nominal wages decrease, this will cause the short-run aggregate supply curve to shift to the right. The short-run aggregate supply curve will shift to the right until the economy's production returns to the potential or long-run level of aggregate output. Notice that this adjustment to the long-run equilibrium results in a higher level of aggregate output than was present in the short run and a lower aggregate price level than the short-run aggregate price level.

4.   For this question, continue with the information you were given in Worked Problem 3 about the economy's short-run aggregate supply curve, the economy's long-run aggregate supply curve, and the economy's aggregate demand curve. You are told that simultaneously this economy experiences three shocks. These three shocks are as follows:

- The price of every unit produced in this economy increases by $100 due to a change in the price of inputs. This shock only affects the short-run aggregate supply curve.

- There is an increase in the wealth of individuals that increases the y-intercept of the aggregate demand curve by 30%. This change in wealth does not alter the slope of the aggregate demand curve.

- A hurricane destroys a significant amount of capital in this economy, and the long-run aggregate supply curve is now $Y = 5$.

Given these three shocks to the economy you are asked to determine the short-run equilibrium aggregate price level and the short-run equilibrium level of aggregate output. You are also asked to identify if there is a short-run recessionary gap or a short-run inflationary gap. Comment on the implications of this gap on the level of unemployment in this economy in the short run. In addition, you are asked to provide a graph that depicts this short-run equilibrium as well as the long-run aggregate supply curve for this economy. Finally, you are asked to propose several policy options for the government of this country if it wishes to return to the long-run equilibrium. You are also asked to discuss the implications of not implementing any active policy to return the economy to long-run equilibrium.

STEP 1: Determine what the new short-run aggregate supply curve is, given the above information. Then determine what the aggregate demand curve is, given this information. Finally, determine what the long-run aggregate supply curve is, given the above information.

Review the section "The AD-AS Model" on page 360 (Econ page 792), the section "Macroeconomic Policy" on page 368 (Econ page 800), and Figure 12-13 on page 363 (Econ page 795).

To answer this set of questions, you will first need to determine how these three shocks affect the three equations that you have been given.

We know that the short-run aggregate supply curve has shifted to the left due to the increase in the price of inputs. The y-intercept of the short-run aggregate supply curve has shifted up by $100. We can write this as $P = 100 + 100Y$.

The aggregate demand curve has shifted to the right due to the increase in wealth. The y-intercept of the aggregate demand curve is initially 1,000 and now it will be 30% greater. 30% of 1,000 is 300, so the new y-intercept for the aggregate demand curve is 1,300. Since the slope of the aggregate demand curve is unaffected, we can write the new aggregate demand curve as $P = 1,300 - 100Y$.

The long-run aggregate supply curve has shifted to the left due to the loss in the capital stock. The new long-run aggregate supply curve can be written as $Y = 5$.

STEP 2: Use the short-run aggregate supply curve and aggregate demand curve to determine the short-run equilibrium level of aggregate prices and the short-run equilibrium level of aggregate output.

Review the section "The AD–AS Model" on page 360 (Econ page 792), the section "Macroeconomic Policy" on page 368 (Econ page 800), and Figure 12-13 on page 363 (Econ page 795).

From the short-run aggregate supply, we have $P = 100 + 100Y$ and from the aggregate demand, we have $P = 1,300 - 100Y$. Setting these two equations equal to one another, we find that $Y = 6$ and that $P = 700$.

STEP 3: Determine whether there is a recessionary gap or an inflationary gap by comparing the short-run equilibrium level of aggregate output to the long-run level of aggregate output. Then consider the implications of this gap on this economy's unemployment rate.

Review the section "The AD–AS Model" on page 360 (Econ page 792), the section "Macroeconomic Policy" on page 368 (Econ page 800), and Figure 12-13 on page 363 (Econ page 795).

A recessionary gap occurs when the short-run level of aggregate output is less than the long-run level of aggregate output. An inflationary gap occurs when the short-run level of aggregate output is greater than the long-run level of aggregate output. In this case, the short-run level of aggregate output is equal to 6 and the long-run level of aggregate output is equal to 5: this economy has an inflationary gap. It is currently producing a level of aggregate output that is greater than its potential or long-run level of output: the economy currently has an unemployment rate that is lower than its natural rate of unemployment.

STEP 4: Draw a graph that depicts the short-run aggregate supply curve, the long-run aggregate supply curve, and the aggregate demand curve. On your graph, mark the short-run equilibrium aggregate price level and the short-run equilibrium level of aggregate output. Also, mark the long-run level of aggregate output.

Review the section "The AD–AS Model" on page 360 (Econ page 792), the section "Macroeconomic Policy" on page 368 (Econ page 800), and Figure 12-13 on page 363 (Econ page 795).

Here is the graph of this economy's short-run equilibrium as well as its long-run level of aggregate output.

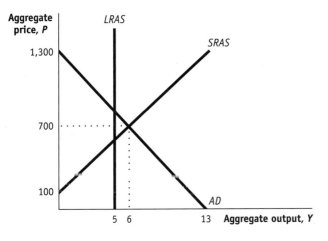

STEP 5: **Determine what type of activist policy, monetary or fiscal, will move this economy to the long-run level of aggregate output.**

Review the section "The AD–AS Model" on page 360 (Econ page 792), the section "Macroeconomic Policy" on page 368 (Econ page 800), and Figure 12-13 on page 363 (Econ page 795).

Since short-run aggregate output is greater than long-run aggregate output, activist policy should contract the economy. The government could implement activist fiscal policy: this could involve a decrease in government spending, an increase in taxes, or a combination of these two policies. The effect of this government intervention in the economy would be to shift the aggregate demand curve to the left, restoring the economy to its long-run equilibrium level of aggregate output. This policy would also the decrease the aggregate price level.

Alternatively, the government could pursue activist monetary policy: the central bank could decrease the money supply in order to shift the aggregate demand curve to the left. As with fiscal policy, activist monetary policy in this example will cause aggregate output to decrease to the long-run level while causing the aggregate price level to fall.

STEP 6: **Discuss what will happen in this economy if no activist policy is implemented.**

Review the section "The AD–AS Model" on page 360 (Econ page 792), the section "Macroeconomic Policy" on page 368 (Econ page 800), and Figure 12-13 on page 363 (Econ page 795).

If no activist policy is implemented, this economy will eventually return to the long-run level of aggregate output. With the inflationary gap, the economy finds that its unemployment rate is relatively low, and over time this will cause nominal wages to increase. As nominal wages increase, this will cause the short-run aggregate supply curve to shift to the left. The short-run aggregate supply curve will shift to the left until the economy's production returns to the potential or long-run level of aggregate output. Notice that this adjustment to the long-run equilibrium results in a lower level of aggregate output than was present in the short run and a higher aggregate price level than the short-run aggregate price level.

5. Suppose that an economy is initially in long-run equilibrium and is producing a level of aggregate output that is equal to its potential output level. What will the short-run consequences be in this economy if there is an increase in the price of oil? Make sure that your answer addresses the effect of this price increase on both the level of aggregate output and the aggregate price level. In the short run, will this economy experience an inflationary gap or a recessionary gap?

STEP 1: **Analyze the short-run effect of a change in the price of oil on the short-run aggregate supply curve and the aggregate demand curve.**

Review the section "The AD–AS Model" on page 360 (Econ page 792), the section "Macroeconomic Policy" on page 368 (Econ page 800), and Figure 12-13 on page 363 (Econ page 795).

When the price of oil rises, this is a change in a commodity price or an input price, which will cause the short-run aggregate supply curve to shift to the left. The change in the oil price will not cause a shift in the aggregate demand curve.

STEP 2: **Having determined in Step 1 what the impact of this change in the price of oil was on the short-run curves in the aggregate demand and aggregate supply model, now predict the impact of this change on the aggregate price level and the aggregate output level.**

Review the section "The AD–AS Model" on page 360 (Econ page 792), the section "Macroeconomic Policy" on page 368 (Econ page 800), and Figure 12-13 on page 363 (Econ page 795).

If the short-run aggregate supply curve shifts to the left, this will cause a movement along the aggregate demand curve: the aggregate price level will increase while the aggregate output level will decrease.

STEP 3: **Determine whether this economy experiences an inflationary gap or a recessionary gap in the short run.**

Review the section "The AD–AS Model" on page 360 (Econ page 792), the section "Macroeconomic Policy" on page 368 (Econ page 800), and Figure 12-13 on page 363 (Econ page 795).

Since the level of aggregate output has decreased, which implies that the economy is now producing at a level of output that is lower than the potential or full employment level of output. The economy is experiencing a recessionary gap. Notice that this economy has both higher prices and lower output: this is an example of stagflation.

Problems and Exercises

1. Consider an economy that is initially in long-run equilibrium as drawn in the following graph where *LRAS* is the long-run *AS* curve, AD_1 is the aggregate demand curve, $SRAS_1$ is the short-run *AS* curve, Y_1 is potential output, and P_1 is the equilibrium aggregate price level.

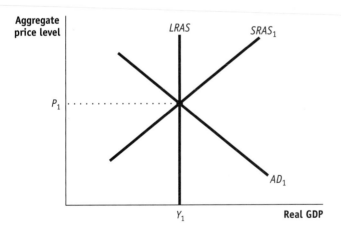

a. Draw a graph using the *AD-AS* model to illustrate the effect of each of the following separate changes to the model in the short run.

(1) The economy's central bank decreases the money supply.

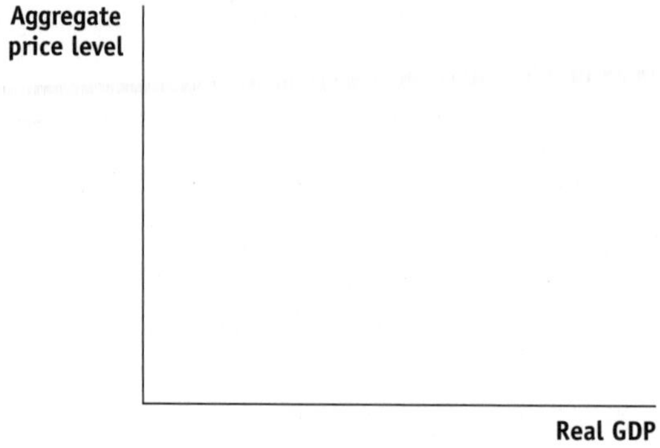

Aggregate price level

Real GDP

(2) Productivity decreases in the economy.

Aggregate price level

Real GDP

(3) Consumer confidence in the economy increases.

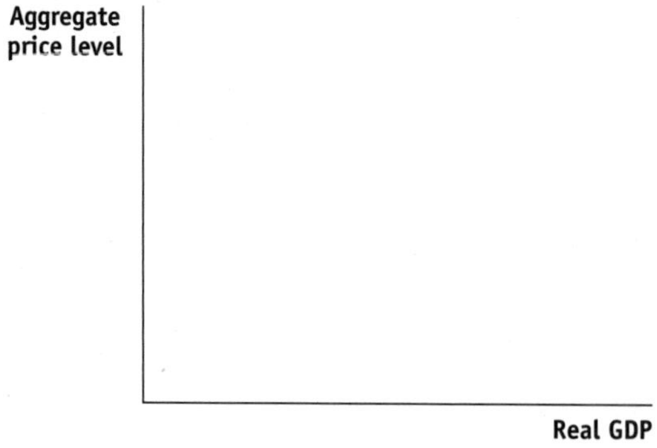

Aggregate price level

Real GDP

(4) Commodity prices fall dramatically.

Aggregate
price level

Real GDP

b. Identify verbally what happens to aggregate output and the aggregate price level relative to the initial long-run equilibrium for each of the scenarios.

c. For each of the scenarios determine whether the economy faces a short-run recessionary gap or an inflationary gap.

d. For each of the scenarios determine if there is an active stabilization policy that will offset the particular shock. If so, discuss what this active stabilization policy is. You may find it helpful to draw a graph illustrating the effects of your active policy prescription on the aggregate economy.

e. For each of the scenarios identify what happens in the long run to the aggregate price level and the aggregate output level if there is no active stabilization policy.

2. Consider an economy operating with an inflationary gap in the short run. Briefly describe what this short-run equilibrium looks like, making specific reference to potential output and then describe the process by which this economy moves from short-run to long-run macroeconomic equilibrium. Use a graph to illustrate your description.

Aggregate price level

Real GDP

3. Consider an economy operating with a recessionary gap in the short-run.

   a. Why does this represent a problem for this economy? Draw a graph illustrating your answer.

Aggregate price level

Real GDP

   b. What policies are available to policymakers to address this problem? Draw a graph illustrating possible policies.

Aggregate price level

Real GDP

c. If policymakers do nothing, describe the mechanism by which this economy will return to long-run macroeconomic equilibrium. Draw a graph illustrating this long-run adjustment.

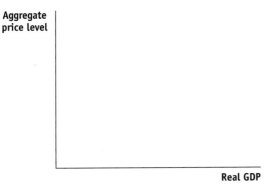

4. Suppose you are given the following information about Macroland, a small, closed economy where Y is real GDP, T is taxes, C is consumption spending, and I is planned investment spending. Assume that government spending is currently equal to $0, taxes are constant at $50, and the aggregate price level is originally fixed and has a value of 100.

Year	Y	T	C	I
1	$100	$50	$ 40	$50
2	150	50	80	50
3	300	50	200	50

a. Fill in the following table using the information given above.

Year	Disposable income
1	
2	
3	

b. What is the MPC for this economy?

c. What is the MPS for this economy?

d. What is the value of the multiplier for this economy?

    e. What is the consumption function for this economy?

    f. Given the information, what is the equilibrium output level for this economy?

    g. Suppose that the price level decreases to $50 and that with this decrease in the price level, consumption spending rises to $60 when aggregate income is $100, to $100 when aggregate income is $150, and to $220 when aggregate income is $300. Furthermore, suppose that businesses increase their investment spending due to the higher aggregate price level and investment spending rises to a constant $60. Assume that taxes and government spending remain fixed at their initial levels. Given this information, what is the new equilibrium output level for this economy?

    h. Graph this economy's *AD* curve and illustrate the relationship between the aggregate price level (measured on the vertical axis) and the level of real GDP (measured on the horizontal axis).

        Aggregate price level

                  Real GDP

5. The *AD-AS* model is said to have a self-correcting mechanism. Explain what this means and how this self-correcting mechanism works. Use a graph to illustrate your answer.

        Aggregate price level

                  Real GDP

6. Use a graph of the *AD–AS* model to illustrate long-run economic growth in an economy. Explain your graph and how it illustrates economic growth. Assume in your answer that *AD* does *not* change over time.

Aggregate price level

Real GDP

7. Macroland is a small, closed economy that is currently operating at the long-run equilibrium level of output. It is therefore producing Y_P where Y_P is potential output. Its aggregate price level is P_1.

    a. Draw a graph of this long-run equilibrium for Macroland depicting the *AD* curve, the *SRAS* curve, and the *LRAS* curve. Label both axes and identify Y_P and P_1 on your graph.

b. Suppose that Macroland experiences a negative demand shock. Draw a new graph depicting the short-run changes in the original equilibrium that will occur because of this demand shock. On your graph identify the new short-run equilibrium level of output Y_2 and the new short-run equilibrium aggregate price level P_2. Label any shifts in *AD* or *AS* clearly.

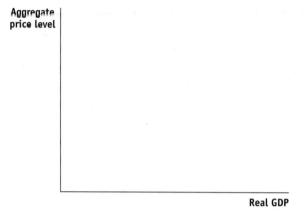

c. Given the change in part (b), draw a third graph illustrating the long-run adjustment to the negative demand shock. Label any shifting curves clearly and identify the new long-run equilibrium level of aggregate output Y_3 and the new long-run aggregate price level P_3.

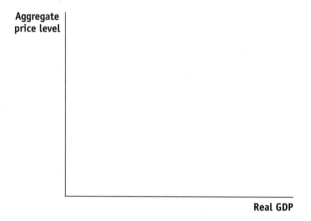

d. Given the change in part (b), suppose the government wishes to engage in activist monetary policy in order to restore the economy to its initial equilibrium. What monetary policy would you advise in order to reach this goal?

e. Given the change in part (b), suppose the government wishes to engage in activist fiscal policy in order to restore the economy to its initial equilibrium. Provide two policy approaches that would enable this economy to return to its initial equilibrium.

8.   For each of the following scenarios, describe the effect on the *AD* curve, the *SRAS* curve, and the *LRAS* curve. Identify whether the effect causes a shift of the curve or a movement along the curve and identify the direction of the shift or the movement.

   a.   An increase in the money supply causes interest rates to fall.

   b.   The price of commodities increases by 10% this year.

   c.   The price of oil falls.

   d.   Labor unions successfully negotiate an increase in nominal wages for their workers.

   e.   The supply of unsold houses in an economy increases by 20%.

   f.   There is an increase in labor productivity due to increases in human capital.

   g.   The government increases spending in order to finance the war against terrorists.

BEFORE YOU TAKE THE TEST

Chapter Review Questions

1.   In the short run, a situation where the aggregate price level increases while the aggregate output level decreases is
   a.   best explained as the result of a positive demand shock.
   b.   stagflation.
   c.   best explained as the result of a negative demand shock.
   d.   Answers (a) and (b) are both correct.
   e.   Answers (b) and (c) are both correct.

2. In the short run, an increase in the aggregate price level due to a shift in *AD* first results in
    a. a rightward shift in the *SRAS* curve.
    b. a movement along the *SRAS* curve.
    c. no change in the level of aggregate production.
    d. a leftward shift in the *SRAS* curve.

3. Suppose the *AD-AS* model is initially in long-run equilibrium. Suppose there is an increase in wealth, holding everything else constant. Then, in the short run,
    a. there will be a movement along the *AD* curve.
    b. the economy will produce at its potential level of output.
    c. there will be a rightward shift in the *AD* curve.
    d. the aggregate level of production will increase while the aggregate price level will fall.

4. Nominal wages
    a. are often determined by contracts that were signed at some previous point in time.
    b. are slow to decrease in times of high unemployment, since employers may be reluctant to alter wages as a response to economic conditions.
    c. are fully flexible in both the short run and the long run.
    d. Answers (a) and (b) are both correct.
    e. Answers (a), (b), (c), and (d) are all correct.

5. Which of the following statements is true? In the short run, holding everything else constant,
    a. as production costs increase, profit per unit decreases, and this causes suppliers to increase their production.
    b. as production costs increase, profit per unit decreases, and this causes suppliers to reduce their production.
    c. as production costs decrease, profit per unit increases, and this causes suppliers to reduce their production.
    d. the *AS* curve is unaffected by changes in production costs.

6. Suppose there is an increase in the price of a commodity, holding everything else constant. In the short run,
    a. the producer will increase production since commodity prices have risen.
    b. the producer's profit per unit of output will decrease.
    c. the producer's price per unit of output will decrease.
    d. there will be a movement along the *AS* curve.
    e. Answers (a) and (b) are both correct.

7. Which of the following will *not* make the *AS* curve shift to the left?
    a. an increase in the aggregate price level
    b. a decrease in commodity prices
    c. an increase in nominal wages
    d. None of the above causes the *AS* curve to shift to the left.
    e. Answers (a) and (b) are both correct.
    f. Answers (b) and (c) are both correct.

8. In comparing the short run with the long run, which of the following statements is true?
  a. In both the short run and the long run, the aggregate price level and the aggregate output level are positively related.
  b. In the short run, the economy never produces at the potential output level, while in the long run, the economy always produces at the potential output level.
  c. In the short run, nominal wages are slow to fully adjust to economic changes, while in the long run, nominal wages are completely flexible and make full adjustment to economic changes.
  d. All these are correct.
  e. Statements (a) and (c) are both true.
  f. Statements (b) and (c) are both true.

9. In the long run, the aggregate price level increases. This
  a. is due to the short-run *AS* curve shifting to the right and the economy producing a level of aggregate output that is not equal to its potential output.
  b. is due to the *AD* curve shifting to the right.
  c. has no effect on the level of aggregate production in the economy.
  d. results in the economy moving to the level of production where aggregate output excceds potential output.
  e. Answers (a) and (c) are both correct.
  f. Answers (b) and (c) are both correct.
  g. Answers (c) and (d) are both correct.

10. Suppose the economy is in short-run equilibrium and the level of aggregate output is less than potential output. Then, it must be true that
  a. unemployment in this economy is relatively low.
  b. over time the short-run *AS* curve will shift to the left.
  c. over time nominal wages will fall.
  d. the economy is also in long-run equilibrium.

11. *AD*
  a. depicts the relationship between the aggregate price level and the quantity of aggregate output demanded.
  b. is a positive relationship between the aggregate price level and the quantity of aggregate output demanded.
  c. is always equal to potential output, no matter what the aggregate price level is.
  d. increases, other things equal, as the aggregate price level increases.

12. As the aggregate price level increases, holding everything else constant,
  a. this reduces the purchasing power of many assets.
  b. this reduces the purchasing power of a given amount of money.
  c. the wealth and interest rate effects lead to a reduction in the quantity of aggregate output demanded.
  d. Answers (a), (b), and (c) are all correct.

13. Holding everything else constant, the *AD* curve will shift to the right when
   a. the central bank decreases the money supply.
   b. household wealth increases.
   c. the government increases taxes paid by households.
   d. Answers (a), (b), and (c) are all correct.
   e. Answers (a) and (b) are both correct.
   f. Answers (b) and (c) are both correct.

14. Which of the following statements is true?
   a. Stagflation refers to the economic situation where aggregate output is falling and the aggregate price level is rising.
   b. Stagflation is most easily explained as the economic outcome that occurs due to a negative supply shock.
   c. Stagflation is most easily explained as the economic outcome that occurs due to a negative demand shock.
   d. Stagflation is most easily explained as the economic outcome that occurs due to either a negative supply shock or a negative demand shock.
   e. Statements (a) and (b) are both true.
   f. Statements (a) and (c) are both true.
   g. Statements (a) and (d) are both true.

15. The economic slump of the 1970s was largely due to events in the Middle East that caused oil prices to
   a. increase and lead to a leftward shift in aggregate demand.
   b. decrease and lead to a rightward shift in short-run aggregate supply.
   c. increase and lead to a rightward shift in aggregate demand.
   d. increase and lead to a leftward shift in short-run aggregate supply.

Answer the next two questions using the following information:

Suppose Macroland is initially in long-run equilibrium. Then, suppose the central bank of Macroland increases the money supply.

16. In the short run, we know that this policy action
   a. will reduce interest rates and therefore stimulate investment spending.
   b. will lead to a reduction in unemployment and an increase in aggregate production.
   c. will lead to the short-run *AS* curve shifting to the right.
   d. Answers (a), (b), and (c) are all correct.
   e. Answers (a) and (b) are both correct.
   f. Answers (b) and (c) are both correct.
   g. Answers (a) and (c) are both correct.

17. In the long run, Macroland will produce at
   a. the potential output level.
   b. a level of aggregate output greater than potential output.
   c. a level of aggregate output less than potential output.
   d. the same level of aggregate output as it did initially before the central bank increased the money supply, but with a lower aggregate price level than its initial level.

18. Which of the following statements is true?

a. In a recessionary gap, aggregate output exceeds potential output.

b. In an inflationary gap, aggregate output exceeds potential output.

c. A recessionary gap is a long-run phenomenon that requires government policy action to eliminate.

d. Recessionary gaps and inflationary gaps, if they exist, will be eliminated in the short run by the natural workings of the economy.

19. Suppose Funland is initially in long-run macroeconomic equilibrium. Then, there is a supply shock due to a severe increase in commodity prices. If Funland's policymakers use active stabilization policy to offset this supply shock,

a. they can effectively eliminate the economic effects of the supply shock.

b. they can either reduce the aggregate price level down to its initial equilibrium level, or they can increase aggregate output to its initial level.

c. they can either increase the aggregate price level to its initial equilibrium level, or they can decrease aggregate output to its initial level.

d. this will greatly reduce the economic fluctuations Funland experiences from this supply shock.

20. Which of the following statements is true?

I. One reason the aggregate demand curve slopes downward is the wealth effect, which states that as the aggregate price level increases, holding everything else constant, the purchasing power of people's assets decline, leading people to decrease the quantity of aggregate production they demand at every price.

II. One reason the aggregate demand curve slopes downward is the interest rate effect, which states that as the aggregate price level increases, holding everything else constant, people demand more money and this causes interest rates to rise. This increase in interest rates causes the level of investment spending in the economy to decline.

III. One reason the aggregate demand curve slopes downward is that as the aggregate price level decreases, people decide to buy more units of relatively inexpensive goods and fewer units of relatively expensive goods.

a. Statements (I), (II), and (III) are all true.

b. Statements (I) and (II) are both true.

c. Statements (I) and (III) are both true.

d. Statements (II) and (III) are both true.

21. An increase in the interest rate, holding everything else constant,

a. reduces investment spending since the cost of borrowing is now higher.

b. reduces consumer spending since households will respond to the higher interest rate by saving more.

c. leads to a reduction in the level of aggregate demand for final goods and services.

d. Answers (a), (b), and (c) are all correct.

22. Suppose that the aggregate price level increases. Holding everything else constant, this will cause the planned aggregate expenditure line to shift

a. upward.

b. downward.

23. A change in the aggregate price level in an economy, holding everything else constant, will cause
    a. both the aggregate planned expenditure line and the aggregate demand curve to shift.
    b. the aggregate planned expenditure line to shift while there is a movement along the aggregate demand curve.
    c. a movement along the aggregate planned expenditure line while there is a shift in the aggregate demand curve.
    d. a movement along both the aggregate planned expenditure line as well as the aggregate demand curve.

24. Which of the following will *not* cause a shift in the *AD* curve?
    a. an increase in the level of wealth in the economy
    b. a reduction in government spending
    c. the decision by the central bank in an economy to expand the money supply
    d. the increase in the price of a commodity

25. Suppose the aggregate price level in the economy falls. Holding everything else constant, this will result in the wealth effect,
    a. which will cause the *AD* curve to shift to the right.
    b. because the fall in the aggregate price level increases consumers' purchasing power and this increase in purchasing power will result in a downward movement along the *AD* curve.
    c. which will cause the *AD* curve to shift to the left.
    d. because the fall in the aggregate price level increases consumers' purchasing power and this increase in purchasing power will result in an upward movement along the *AD* curve.

26. Which of the following policies will shift the *AD* curve to the right?
    a. The government increases its level of taxation in the economy.
    b. The government decreases the money supply in the economy.
    c. The government decreases its level of taxation in the economy.
    d. The government decreases its level of spending in the economy.
    e. Answers (a) and (d) will both shift the *AD* curve to the right.
    f. Answers (c) and (d) will both shift the *AD* curve to the right.

27. An increase in the aggregate price level, holding everything else constant, causes
    a. movement along the *AS* curve.
    b. a shift to the right of the *AD* curve due to the wealth effect and the interest rate effect.
    c. a shift to the left of the *AD* curve due to the wealth effect and the interest rate effect.
    d. a shift to the right of the *AS* curve since producers will be willing to supply more goods and services at every price than they were initially.
    e. a shift to the left of the *AS* curve since producers will supply fewer goods and services at every price than they did initially.

28. Suppose an economy is currently in short-run equilibrium where the level of real GDP is less than potential output. Which of the following statements is true?

    a. In the long run, nominal wages will fall and the *SRAS* curve will shift to the left, restoring the economy to potential output.

    b. In the long run, nominal wages will fall and the *SRAS* curve will shift to the right, restoring the economy to potential output.

    c. In the long run, nominal wages will fall and the *AD* curve will shift to the left, restoring the economy to potential output.

    d. In the long run, nominal wages will fall and the *AD* curve will shift to the right restoring the economy to potential output.

29. In the *AD–AS* model, a key feature that distinguishes the long run from the short run is wages and prices are sticky in the

    a. long run.

    b. short run.

30. Suppose that short-run equilibrium real GDP for an economy is currently greater than potential output. This implies that

    a. nominal wages will need to adjust upward as the economy moves from the short run to the long run.

    b. the level of unemployment is very low for this economy.

    c. jobs are plentiful in this economy.

    d. to reach long-run equilibrium, the *SRAS* curve will shift to the left resulting in a higher aggregate price level.

    e. Answers (a), (b), (c), and (d) are all correct.

    f. Answers (a), (b), and (c) are correct.

    g. Answers (a) and (d) are both correct.

31. A positive demand shock shifts *AD* to the

    a. right and results in a higher aggregate price level and a higher level of real GDP in the short run, holding everything else constant.

    b. left and results in a higher aggregate price level and a higher level of real GDP in the short run, holding everything else constant.

32. Suppose an economy is initially in long-run equilibrium. Then, holding everything else constant, there is an increase in people's wealth in this economy. If the government wishes to maintain the same aggregate price level and aggregate level of real GDP as it had initially, it should increase

    a. government spending.

    b. the money supply.

    c. the level of investment spending.

    d. the level of taxes.

▮ ANSWER KEY

Answers to Problems and Exercises

1. a.

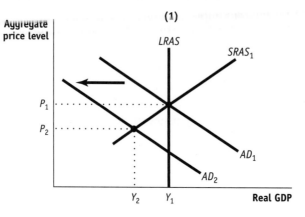

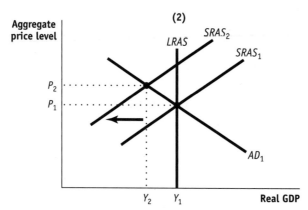

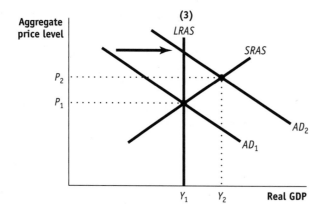

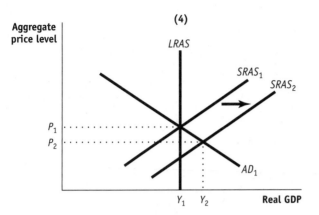

b. In scenario (1), the aggregate price level and the aggregate level of output both decrease relative to their initial levels. In scenario (2), the aggregate price level increases, while the aggregate level of output decreases relative to their initial levels. In scenario (3), the aggregate price level and the aggregate level of output both increase relative to their initial levels. In scenario (4), the aggregate price level falls, while the aggregate level of output increases relative to their initial levels.

c. A short-run recessionary gap is defined as a situation where the economy produces at a level of output that is less than potential output: scenarios (1) and (2) illustrate this situation. Scenarios (3) and (4) represent inflationary gaps since the level of aggregate output is greater than potential output.

d. For scenario (1), active stabilization policy can be used to bring the economy back to its initial aggregate price level and aggregate output level. This policy would need to shift AD to the right (back to its initial position) and could be accomplished by increasing government spending, decreasing taxes, or increasing the money supply.

For scenario (2), active stabilization policy cannot restore the economy to its initial equilibrium. A policy that shifts AD to the right would result in an increase in the aggregate price level relative to its initial level (P_3 versus P_1), and a return to the initial level of production, Y_1, for aggregate output. The following graph illustrates the implementation of an active stabilization policy that shifts AD to the right.

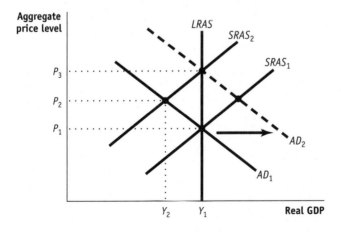

A policy that shifts AD to the left would result in a return to the initial aggregate price level of P_1, and a decrease in the level of aggregate output relative to its initial position (Y_3 versus Y_1). The following graph illustrates this.

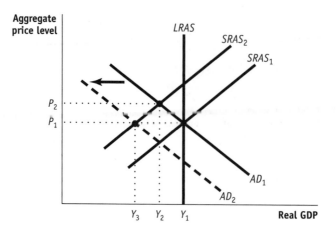

In scenario (3), active stabilization policy can be used to bring the economy back to its initial equilibrium. This policy would shift *AD* to the left and could be accomplished by decreasing government spending, increasing taxes, or decreasing the money supply.

In scenario (4), active stabilization policy cannot restore the economy to its initial equilibrium: shifting *AD* to the right restores the original price level to P_1, but increases the level of output above the initial level (Y_3 versus Y_1), thus creating an inflationary gap. The following graph illustrates this.

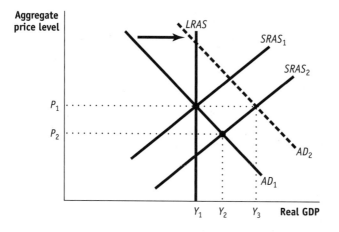

Shifting *AD* to the left restores output to its initial level Y_1, but the aggregate price level falls relative to its initial level (P_3 versus P_1). The following graph illustrates this.

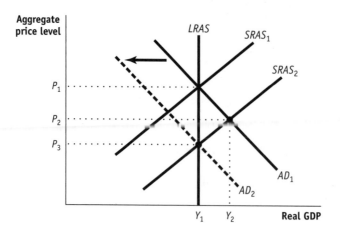

e. If there is no active stabilization policy implemented, then in scenario (1) the short-run *AS* curve will shift to the right as the nominal wage decreases in response to the recessionary gap. As the short-run *AS* curve shifts out, the economy will eventually reach long-run equilibrium where the aggregate output level returns to potential output, Y_1, while the aggregate price level falls to a lower long-run aggregate price level than the initial long-run P_1. In scenario (2), if there is no active stabilization policy implemented, the short-run *AS* curve will shift to the right, returning the economy back to its initial long-run macroeconomic equilibrium. In scenario (3), if there is no active stabilization policy implemented, the short-run *AS* curve will shift to the left, restoring the economy to the original level of aggregate output but a higher aggregate price level than the initial long-run P_1. In scenario (4), if there is no active stabilization policy implemented, the short-run *AS* curve will shift to the left, returning the economy to its initial equilibrium position.

2. An economy operating in the short run with an inflationary gap is producing a level of aggregate output, Y_1, that is greater than potential output, Y. This is illustrated in the following diagram.

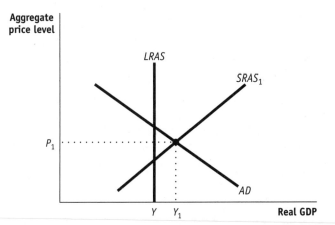

This implies that unemployment is relatively low and, therefore, workers are scarce and jobs are abundant. Over time this situation puts pressure on nominal wages to rise and this causes the short-run *AS* curve to shift to the left. As short-run *AS* shifts to the left ($SRAS_2$), the level of aggregate production in the economy falls and this brings aggregate output closer to potential output. The nominal wage will continue to adjust until the short-run *AS* curve intersects the *AD* curve and the long-run *AS* curve at the same point. Then the economy will be in long-run macroeconomic equilibrium, where aggregate output equals potential output while the aggregate price level has risen to P_2 from P_1. This is illustrated in the following graph.

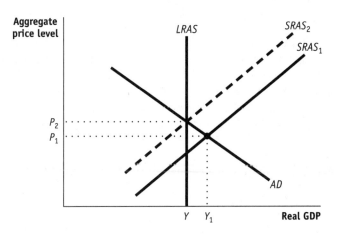

3.   **a.** A recessionary gap for an economy is problematic, since it indicates that the economy is producing a lower level of aggregate output (Y_1) than its potential (Y): this lower output also signals that the economy faces higher unemployment than necessary. This is illustrated in the following graph.

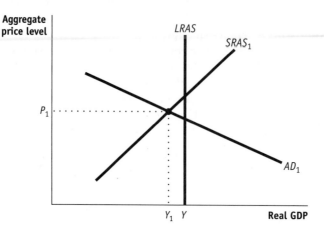

   b. To offset a recessionary gap, active stabilization policy can be implemented that will return the economy to potential output. A recessionary gap caused by a leftward shift in AD is easily offset by using fiscal policy or monetary policy to shift AD to the right and returning the aggregate output to the level of potential output (Y). A recessionary gap caused by a leftward shift in short-run AS is a more difficult problem: active stabilization policy that shifts AD to the right can bring the aggregate level of production back to potential output but only by raising the aggregate price level to a higher level (P_2 versus P_0). This is illustrated in the following graph.

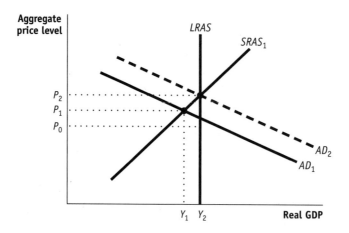

   c. If policymakers do nothing, the economy will return to a long-run macroeconomic equilibrium over time through changes in the nominal wage and accompanying shifts in the short-run AS curve. If the recessionary gap is due to a leftward shift in AD, over time we can expect short-run AS to shift to the right, bringing the economy back to potential output and a lower aggregate price level than experienced during the recessionary gap. If the recessionary gap is due to a leftward shift in short-run AS, over time we can expect short-run AS to shift back to the right, returning the economy to its potential output and a lower aggregate price level than it experienced during the recessionary gap. Both of these possibilities are illustrated in the following graph.

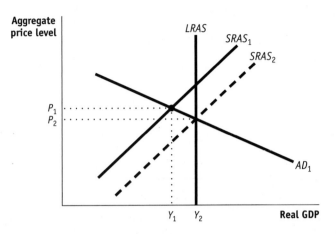

4. a.

Year	Disposable income
1	$ 50
2	100
3	250

b. The *MPC* is defined as the change in consumption spending divided by the change in disposable income. Using the information given to you and your calculations in part (a), you can calculate the *MPC* as 0.8 (since the change in consumption from year 1 to year 2 is 40 and the change in disposable income from year 1 to year 2 is 50).

c. The *MPS* plus the *MPC* equals one. Since the *MPC* equals 0.8, this implies that the *MPS* equals 0.2.

d. The value of the multiplier for this economy equals $[1/(1 - MPC)]$, or 5.

e. The consumption function for this economy can be written as $C = A + MPC \times (Y - T)$. But, from part (b) you know the *MPC* is equal to 0.8, and the taxes are constant and equal to $50. Thus, $C = A + 0.8 (Y - 50)$. Using one of the real GDP and consumption pairs from the table, you can solve this equation for the value of A, the autonomous level of consumption spending. Thus, $40 = A + 0.8 (100 - 50)$, or $A = 0$. The consumption function is therefore $C = 0.8 \times (Y - T)$.

f. The equilibrium level of output is where planned aggregate expenditure equals production, or where planned *AE* equals *Y*. Planned *AE* is the sum of consumption spending and investment spending since there is no government spending and there is no foreign trade. Thus, $AE = 0.8 \times (Y - T) + 50$. Substituting 50 for taxes we get $AE = 0.8 \times (Y - 50) + 50$ or $AE = 0.8Y + 10$. Recall that in equilibrium planned *AE* equals *Y* so $Y = AE = 0.8Y + 10$. Solving for *Y*, the equilibrium level of real GDP, we get *Y* equals 50.

g. Given the change in consumption spending at each level of real GDP, this means that you need to recalculate the consumption function for this economy. Now, when real GDP is 100, consumption spending is 60. The *MPC* does not change, but the value of A, the autonomous consumption spending measure, does change. Thus, $C = 20 + 0.8(Y - T) = 20 + 0.8(Y - 50) = -20 + 0.8Y$. Use this consumption function and the new level of investment spending to find where planned *AE* equals *Y*. Thus, $Y = AE$ and $AE = -20 + 0.8Y + 60$. Therefore, $Y = -20 + 0.8Y + 60$, or $Y = 200$.

h.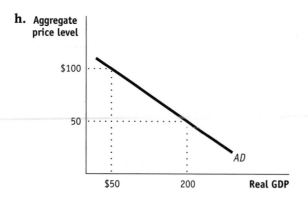

5. The *AD-AS* model is self-correcting, since it will always return to long-run macroeconomic equilibrium if given a sufficient amount of time for the short-run *AS* curve to adjust to economic changes through changes in the nominal wage. This adjustment process has been reviewed in several earlier problems: essentially, it is the idea that the short-run *AS* curve shifts due to changes in the nominal wage until that point where *AD* intersects both the short-run and the long-run *AS* curves at potential output. If this is still unclear to you, review questions 1 and 2 and the diagrams illustrating their answers.

6. Long-run economic growth is depicted in the *AD-AS* model as the long-run *AS* shifting to the right. Thus, your graph should depict several vertical *AS* curves, with each one farther to the right on the horizontal axis representing the ability of the economy to reach even higher levels of potential output. For a given *AD* curve, the level of aggregate output increases as the *LRAS* curve shifts to the right. The following graph illustrates this idea.

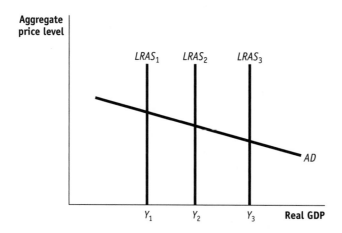

7. **a.**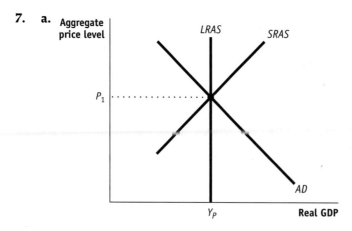

b. Aggregate price level

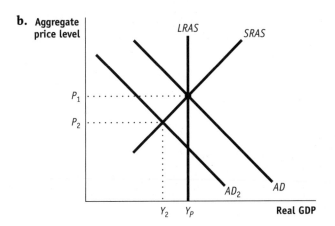

c. Aggregate price level

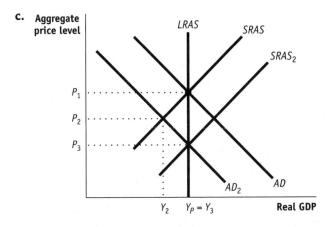

d. To offset a negative demand shock, the government needs to shift the *AD* curve to the right. Monetary policy that increases the money supply will shift the *AD* curve to the right and return the economy to P_1 and Y_P.

e. To offset a negative demand shock, the government needs to shift the *AD* curve to the right. Fiscal policy offers two approaches to shifting the *AD* curve to the right: the government can increase the level of government spending or it can decrease the level of taxes.

8. a. An increase in the money supply is an example of monetary policy: the *AD* curve will shift to the right and there will be a movement upward along the *SRAS* curve. There will be no change in the *LRAS* curve.

b. When the price of commodities increases, this causes the *SRAS* curve to shift to the left. There will be a movement upward along the *AD* curve and no change in the *LRAS* curve.

c. When the price of oil decreases, this causes the *SRAS* curve to shift to the right and results in a downward movement along the *AD* curve. There is no change in the *LRAS* curve.

d. The result of the successful labor union negotiation is higher wages, which leads to a leftward shift in the *SRAS* curve and an upward movement along the *AD* curve. There is no change in the *LRAS* curve.

e. When the inventory of unsold houses increases in an economy, this implies that the level of investment is high and there is therefore less incentive for firms to invest in this economy. As investment spending falls, this causes the *AD* curve to shift to the left, resulting in a downward movement along the *SRAS* curve. There is no change in the *LRAS* curve.

f. When labor productivity increases, this causes the *SRAS* curve to shift to the right, but it also causes the *LRAS* curve to shift to the right since the economy can now produce at a higher potential output level. There is a downward movement along the *AD* curve.

g. When the government increases spending to finance a war, this causes the *AD* curve to shift to the right, resulting in a movement upward along the *SRAS* curve. There is no change in the *LRAS* curve.

Answers to Chapter Review Questions

1. **Answer b.** Stagflation refers to the combination of rising inflation and decreasing aggregate production. When the *SRAS* curve shifts to the left (a negative supply shock), this causes the aggregate price level to increase and the aggregate level of output to decrease.

2. **Answer b.** A change in the aggregate price level due to a shift in *AD* results in a movement along the *SRAS* curve. In the short run the *SRAS* curve is upward sloping, so an increase in the aggregate price level results in a higher level of aggregate production.

3. **Answer c.** The economy produces at its potential level of output if it is at a long-run equilibrium. The increase in wealth will cause the *AD* curve to shift to the right, causing a movement along the *SRAS* curve, and an increase in aggregate production and the aggregate price level.

4. **Answer d.** In the short run, nominal wages are sticky and take time to adjust to changes in economic conditions due to pre-existing contracts and employer reluctance to frequently alter wages. In the long run, nominal wages are fully flexible.

5. **Answer b.** Production costs affect the level of aggregate production: as production costs increase, holding everything else constant, profit per unit decreases. Producers respond to this decrease in profit per unit by decreasing the quantity of goods and services they are willing to supply.

6. **Answer b.** An increase in the price of a commodity, holding everything else constant, will cause the *AS* curve to shift to the left as aggregate production decreases at any given aggregate price level. Aggregate production decreases due to the decrease in producers' profit per unit, arising from the higher commodity price they must now pay.

7. **Answer e.** An increase in the aggregate price level results in a movement along the *AS* curve and not a shift of the curve. A decrease in commodity prices results in a rightward shift of the *AS* curve. An increase in nominal wages causes the *AS* curve to shift to the left.

8. **Answer c.** In the long run, the *AS* is vertical and not upward sloping as it is in the short run. It is possible for an economy to be in both long-run and short-run equilibrium simultaneously so that the economy is producing its potential level of output. In the short run, we assume nominal wages are constrained from full adjustment and are therefore sticky, while in the long run, nominal wages are assumed to be fully flexible.

9. **Answer f.** In the long run, the economy by definition is already producing at the level of aggregate output we refer to as potential output. An increase in the aggregate price level in the long run can only be explained by a shift in the *AD* curve, and this shift will not affect aggregate output since the long-run *AS* curve is vertical.

10. **Answer c.** Since the economy is producing at a level of aggregate output smaller than the level of potential output, the economy cannot be in long-run equilibrium. Since output is below potential output, we know that not all workers are being fully utilized: if all workers were fully employed this would result in higher levels of production. Therefore, unemployment must be relatively high, and this will lead to decreases in the nominal wage over time since jobs are scarce and workers are abundant.

11. **Answer a.** The aggregate price level and the quantity of aggregate output demanded is the relationship captured by the *AD* curve. It is an inverse relationship: as the aggregate price level increases, other things equal, there is a decrease in the quantity of aggregate output demanded.

12. **Answer d.** An increase in the aggregate price level, holding everything else constant, leads to a decrease in aggregate demand for goods and services. This is due to the wealth effect and the interest rate effect. Answer (a) expresses how an increase in the aggregate price level affects people's wealth, while answer (b) expresses how this price change affects their purchasing power (via the interest rate effect).

13. **Answer b.** The *AD* curve will shift to the left if the central bank decreases the money supply, since this policy action will increase interest rates, reduce investment spending, and therefore lead to a reduction in the quantity of aggregate goods and services demanded at every aggregate price level. An increase in taxes reduces the disposable income households have and will therefore lead to a reduction in the quantity of aggregate goods and services demanded at every aggregate price level (the *AD* curve will shift left). An increase in household wealth will shift the *AD* curve to the right, since households will increase their spending due to their increased wealth.

14. **Answer e.** Stagflation refers to a falling aggregate output level accompanied by a rising aggregate price level. In the *AD-AS* model this is most easily explained as a negative supply shock since this shift in the short-run *AS* curve causes economic output to fall while the aggregate price level increases.

15. **Answer d.** During the 1970s, events in the Middle East caused oil prices to rise. This increase in commodity prices caused the short-run aggregate supply curve to shift to the left, resulting in lower levels of aggregate output and a higher aggregate price level.

16. **Answer e.** Since the economy is initially in long-run macroeconomic equilibrium, we know aggregate output is initially equal to potential output. The central bank's policy action will cause interest rates to fall and investment spending to increase. This will cause the *AD* curve to shift to the right, resulting in short-run aggregate output exceeding potential output. This increase in output will result in a decrease in unemployment. Over time this will lead nominal wages to increase, which will result in the short-run *AS* curve shifting to the left.

17. **Answer a.** In the long run, macroeconomic equilibrium requires that the economy produce at that point where *AD* equals long-run *AS* as well as short-run *AS*. Short-run *AS* adjusts though changes in nominal wages to bring the equilibrium to this long-run equilibrium. When the central bank increases the money supply, this shifts the *AD* curve to the right. For a given long-run *AS* curve and this central bank action, it is possible to return to long-run macroeconomic equilibrium only if the short-run *AS* curve shifts to the left, resulting in a higher aggregate price level.

18. **Answer b.** A recessionary gap is a situation in the short run where aggregate output is less than potential output. A recessionary gap is eliminated in the long run as the short-run *AS* curve adjusts to return the economy to potential output and long-run equilibrium. An inflationary gap is a situation in the short run where aggregate output is greater than potential output. As the economy moves to a long-run equilibrium, this inflationary gap will be eliminated and aggregate output will return to potential output.

19. **Answer b.** Policymakers face a difficult trade-off when they try to offset a supply shock. In this case, the supply shock reduces aggregate output and increases the aggregate price level. Active stabilization policy can shift *AD* to the right or to the left: if *AD* shifts to the right, this will stimulate aggregate output while simultaneously increasing the aggregate price level to even higher levels; and if *AD* shifts to the left, this will reduce the aggregate price level while simultaneously decreasing the aggregate output level to even lower levels.

20. **Answer b.** The aggregate demand curve slopes downward due to the wealth and interest rate effects. Answer (c) is true for the demand for a particular good or service, but is not true for the aggregate demand for all final goods and services.

21. **Answer d.** When the interest rate rises, this makes borrowing more expensive for firms and leads firms to reduce their level of investment spending. At the same time, a higher interest rate will provide households with an incentive to save more. Both of these effects will lead to the quantity of aggregate output demanded to fall when there is a rise in the interest rate: this is referred to as the interest rate effect on aggregate demand.

22. **Answer b.** When the aggregate price level increases, this causes planned aggregate expenditure to decrease at every level of real GDP. This results in the planned aggregate expenditure line shifting downward in the Keynesian cross diagram.

23. **Answer b.** A change in the aggregate price level will cause the aggregate planned expenditure line to shift due to the interest rate and wealth effects; this shift in the aggregate planned expenditure line will result in a different income–expenditure equilibrium given the new aggregate price level. In graphing the aggregate demand curve, a change in the aggregate price level, holding everything else constant, will cause a movement along the aggregate demand curve.

24. **Answer d.** An increase in the price of a commodity will shift the AS curve to the left, which will result in a movement along the AD curve. Changes in wealth, the level of government spending, or the money supply will shift the AD curve.

25. **Answer b.** A fall in the aggregate price level changes the purchasing power of consumers' existing wealth and this wealth effect, due to the fall in the aggregate price level, will result in a movement down the AD curve. At the new lower aggregate price level, the quantity of aggregate output demanded for the economy increases.

26. **Answer c.** When the AD curve shifts to the right, this implies that the level of aggregate output demanded is greater at any given aggregate price level than it was initially. When the government increases government spending, decreases taxes, or increases the money supply, this results in greater aggregate output demanded at every price level. When the government decreases government spending, increases taxes, or decreases the money supply, this results in less aggregate output demanded at every price level.

27. **Answer a.** A change in the aggregate price level, holding everything else constant, causes a movement along the SRAS curve. It is important to realize that a change in the aggregate price level, holding everything else constant, causes a movement along the AD and the SRAS curves. For instance, suppose the aggregate price level is currently greater than the equilibrium aggregate price level: in the AD-AS model this will result in a situation of excess aggregate supply and over time as the aggregate price level falls the level of aggregate output demanded will increase while the level of aggregate output supplied will decrease until the aggregate price level falls to that level where the AD cuts the SRAS.

28. **Answer b.** In the short run this economy is producing a level of real GDP that is less than potential GDP. This implies that jobs are scarce and unemployment high: over time workers will accept lower nominal wages in order to find employment. As the level of nominal wages falls, this causes the SRAS curve to shift to the right causing the level of real GDP to increase toward the potential output level.

29. **Answer b.** In the short run, wages and prices are not perfectly flexible because of informal and formal agreements that limit the short-run flexibility of wages and prices. Ultimately, formal contracts and informal agreements can be renegotiated to take into account changed economic circumstances. In the long run, wages and prices are fully flexible.

30. **Answer e.** When the economy in the short run produces a level of real GDP that is greater than potential output, this implies that unemployment is very low (since output is greater than the long-run potential level of output) and jobs very plentiful. In order to reach long-run equilibrium at the potential output, this economy's *SRAS* curve must shift to the left, which will cause the aggregate price level to rise. This shift of the *SRAS* curve will be due to the increase in nominal wages that occurs over time due to the tension between very low levels of unemployment and the abundance of jobs.

31. **Answer a.** A positive demand shock implies that the quantity of goods and services demanded at any given aggregate price level has increased: *AD* shifts to the right. As *AD* shifts to the right for a given *SRAS* curve, the aggregate price level and the aggregate level of real GDP increases.

32. **Answer d.** An increase in wealth causes the *AD* curve to shift to the right, resulting in a higher aggregate price level and a higher level of real GDP. If the government wishes to restore the economy to the original aggregate price level and aggregate output level, it can accomplish this goal by reducing government spending, raising taxes, or decreasing the money supply.

Fiscal Policy

| **BEFORE YOU READ THE CHAPTER** |

Summary

This chapter focuses on fiscal policy—government spending and taxation—and its use as an economic tool for managing economic fluctuations. The chapter discusses expansionary fiscal policy, or the use of government spending and/or taxation policy to stimulate the economy, as well as contractionary fiscal policy, or the use of government spending and/or taxation policy to slow down the economy. In addition, the chapter explores the multiplier effect of fiscal policy as well as the effect of automatic stabilizers on the size of the multiplier. The chapter continues with the development of the budget balance and how economic fluctuations affect this budget balance. The chapter also discusses the long-run consequences of public debt and the significance of the government's implicit liabilities.

Chapter Objectives

Objective #1.   Discretionary fiscal policy refers to the use of government spending or tax policy to manage aggregate demand (*AD*). Discretionary fiscal policy may be used to stimulate or contract *AD*.

Objective #2.   Government collects funds in the form of taxes and government borrowing and then uses these funds to make government purchases of goods and services and government transfers to individuals. Total government spending includes government expenditure on goods and services as well as government expenditure on transfer payments.

- The three most expensive transfer programs in the United States are Social Security, Medicare, and Medicaid.

- Social insurance refers to government programs aimed at protecting families against economic hardship.

Objective #3.   The basic equation of national income accounting, $GDP = C + I + G + X - IM$, reminds us that government purchases of goods and services (G) has a direct impact on total spending in the economy. The government also affects C through changes in taxes and transfers, and it may affect I through government policy.

- Increases in taxes, holding everything else constant, reduce disposable income and consumer spending. Decreases in taxes, holding everything else constant, increase disposable income and consumer spending.

- Increases in government transfer payments, holding everything else constant, increase disposable income and consumer spending. Decreases in government transfer payments, holding everything else constant, decrease disposable income and consumer spending.

- Government can impact the incentives to engage in investment spending through changes in tax policy.

- The government can use changes in taxes or government spending to shift the *AD* curve. Holding everything else constant, *AD* shifts to the right with increases in government spending, decreases in taxes, or increases in government transfers; *AD* shifts to the left with decreases in government spending, increases in taxes, or decreases in government transfers.

- When the country faces a recessionary gap, aggregate output is less than potential output: use of expansionary fiscal policy will shift *AD* to the right to help eliminate the gap between actual and potential GDP.

- When an economy faces an inflationary gap, aggregate output is greater than potential output: use of contractionary fiscal policy will shift *AD* to the left to help eliminate the gap between actual and potential GDP.

Objective #4. Important lags exist in the use of fiscal or monetary policy. These lags include the time necessary for the government to realize the need for policy intervention, the time necessary for the government to develop policy, and the time necessary for the government to implement the policy and have the policy take effect. The existence of lags makes the use of fiscal policy and monetary policy to correct economic fluctuations more challenging than our simple analysis suggests.

Objective #5. A change in government spending is an example of an autonomous change in aggregate spending. Holding the price level constant, this change in autonomous aggregate spending will change GDP by an amount equal to the multiplier times the change in autonomous aggregate spending. Recall that the multiplier in our simple model equals $1/(1 - MPC)$.

Objective #6. A change in taxes or government transfers of a given size shifts the *AD* curve by less than an equal-sized change in government purchases. A decrease in taxes or increase in transfers will increase GDP by $MPC/(1 - MPC)$ times the change in taxes (measured in absolute value terms) or the change in transfers; an increase in taxes or a decrease in transfers will decrease GDP by $MPC/(1 - MPC)$ times the change in taxes or the change in transfers (measured in absolute value terms).

Objective #7. Holding everything else constant, when GDP increases, government tax revenue automatically increases. The effect of this automatic increase in government tax revenue when GDP rises is to reduce the size of the multiplier.

- When the economy slows down and GDP falls, the automatic fall in government tax revenue acts like an automatic expansionary fiscal policy implemented in the face of the recession.

- When the economy expands, the automatic increase in government tax revenue acts like an automatic contractionary fiscal policy implemented in the face of the expansion.

- Government spending and taxation rules that cause fiscal policy to be automatically expansionary when the economy contracts and automatically contractionary when the economy expands are referred to as automatic stabilizers since they act to automatically stabilize the economy.

- Examples of automatic stabilizers include taxes, unemployment insurance benefits, Medicaid, and food stamps. Transfer programs as well as taxes can act as automatic stabilizers.

Objective #8. Discretionary fiscal policy refers to fiscal policy that is the direct result of policy action by policymakers. It does not refer to automatic adjustment in the economy that occurs because of automatic stabilizers.

Objective #9. Recall that the budget balance equals tax revenue minus government spending on both goods and services as well as government transfers. We can write the budget balance, $S_{Government}$, symbolically as $S_{Government} = T - G - TR$.

- A positive budget balance indicates a budget surplus, while a negative budget balance indicates a budget deficit.

- Holding everything else constant, discretionary expansionary fiscal policy reduces the budget balance, while discretionary contractionary policy increases the budget balance.

- Equal-sized changes in government spending or taxes impact the budget balance equally, but have very different impacts on *AD* due to the multiplier effect of a change in government spending being greater than the multiplier effect of an equal-sized change in government taxes or transfers.

- Changes in the budget balance often are the result of economic fluctuations.

Objective #10. The cyclically adjusted budget balance estimates the size of the budget balance if real GDP was exactly equal to potential output. It effectively eliminates the impact of recessionary or inflationary gaps on tax revenue and government transfers.

Objective #11. Most economists do not endorse legislation requiring that the government maintain a balanced budget, since this type of rule would undermine the role of taxes and transfers as automatic stabilizers.

Objective #12. When governments spend more than their tax revenue, they usually borrow the extra funds needed. Governments that run persistent deficits find that they have a rising government debt.

- A government deficit is the difference between the amount of money a government spends and the amount of money the government receives in taxes over a given period of time.

- A government debt is the sum of money a government owes at a particular point in time.

- The public debt refers to the government debt held by individuals and institutions outside the government at a particular point in time.

- When the government runs persistent budget deficits, it competes with firms that plan to borrow funds for investment spending. The government borrowing may crowd out private investment spending and lead to a reduction in the economy's long-run growth rate.

- When the government runs persistent budget deficits, this leads to financial pressure on future budgets due to the increasing size of the interest payments on the accumulated debt. Holding everything else constant, a government that owes large amounts in interest must raise more revenue from taxes or spend less.

- Governments that print money to pay their bills find that this leads to inflation.

- The long-run effects of persistent budget deficits suggest that governments should run a budget that is approximately balanced over time.

Objective #13. In the United States, government budget totals are kept for the fiscal year that starts on October 1 and runs through September 30. For example, fiscal 2010 began on October 1, 2009, and ended on September 30, 2010.

Objective #14. The debt–GDP ratio is a measure used to assess the ability of governments to pay their debt. The debt–GDP ratio measures government debt as a percentage of GDP. This measure recognizes that the size of the economy as a whole, as measured by GDP, provides information about the amount of potential taxes a government can collect. When GDP grows at a faster rate than the rate of growth of the government's debt, then the burden of paying the debt is falling relative to the government's ability to collect tax revenue.

- The debt–GDP ratio can fall even when debt is rising provided that GDP grows faster than debt.

- The debt–GDP ratio will rise when debt is rising if GDP grows more slowly than debt.

Objective #15. Implicit liabilities are promises made by governments that represent debt not included in the government's debt statistics. In the United States, the largest implicit liabilities are Social Security, Medicare, and Medicaid.

- Spending on Social Security is projected to rise dramatically over the next few decades due to demographic issues related to the retirement of the baby boomer generation.

- Spending on Medicare and Medicaid is also projected to rise dramatically primarily because long-run health care spending increases faster than overall spending.

- Both Social Security and Medicare are funded from dedicated taxes, a special tax levied on wages. At the time of this writing, there is a surplus of tax revenue from these dedicated taxes. For example, the surplus funds of Social Security are held in a Social Security Trust Fund. The funds in these trust funds are owed to the Social Security system and other trust funds by another part of the government; this debt is referred to as the United States government debt held by Social Security and other trust funds. The gross debt for the U.S. government thus consists of two parts: first, the public debt, and second, the United States government debt held by Social Security and other trust funds.

Objective #16. [From Appendix] Taxing income at a tax rate t allows us to model a macroeconomy where taxes increase as the level of aggregate output increases. The inclusion of this tax rate alters the multiplier for a change in autonomous spending from $1/(1 - MPC)$ to $1/[1 - MPC(1 - t)]$. This new multiplier will have a smaller value than the original multiplier for a given MPC.

Key Terms

social insurance government programs—like Social Security, Medicare, unemployment insurance, and food stamps—intended to protect families against economic hardship.

expansionary fiscal policy *fiscal policy* that increases aggregate demand by increasing government purchases, decreasing taxes, or increasing transfers.

Notes

Key Terms *(continued)*

contractionary fiscal policy *fiscal policy* that reduces aggregate demand by decreasing government purchases, increasing taxes, or decreasing transfers.

lump-sum taxes taxes that don't depend on the taxpayer's income.

automatic stabilizers government spending and taxation rules that cause *fiscal policy* to be automatically expansionary when the *economy* contracts and automatically contractionary when the economy expands without requiring any deliberate actions by policymakers. Taxes that depend on *disposable income* are the most important example of automatic stabilizers.

discretionary fiscal policy *fiscal policy* that is the direct result of deliberate actions by policymakers rather than rules.

cyclically adjusted budget balance an estimate of what the *budget balance* would be if *real GDP* were exactly equal to *potential output.*

fiscal year the time period used for much of government accounting, running from October 1 to September 30. Fiscal years arc labeled by the calendar year in which they end.

public debt government debt held by individuals and institutions outside the government.

debt–GDP ratio government debt as a percentage of GDP, frequently used as a measure of a government's ability to pay its debts.

implicit liabilities spending promises made by governments that are effectively a debt despite the fact that they are not included in the usual debt statistics. In the United States, the largest implicit liabilities arise from Social Security and Medicare, which promise transfer payments to current and future retirees (Social Security) and to the elderly (Medicare).

■ AFTER YOU READ THE CHAPTER

Tips

Tip #1. This chapter contains some new vocabulary. You need to be familiar with these concepts, including the government deficit, government debt, implicit liabilities, and the debt–GDP ratio. As in the other chapters it is essential that you learn and understand any new terms that are introduced. Many of the terms in this chapter represent complicated concepts or relationships.

Tip #2.   Two multipliers are presented and used in this chapter: the multiplier for a change in government spending and the multiplier for a change in taxes. The multiplier for a change in government spending equals $1/(1 - MPC)$, while the multiplier for a change in taxes equals $[-MPC/(1 - MPC)]$. For example if the MPC equals 0.8, then the multiplier for a change in government spending is equal to 5, while the multiplier for a change in taxes is equal to -4. A \$1 increase in government spending will increase aggregate output by \$5, holding everything else constant, while a \$1 increase in taxes will decrease aggregate output by \$4, holding everything else constant. Make sure you work some problems using these multipliers and that you understand why they do not have equivalent values. Also, spend time thinking about why the multiplier for government spending is positive while the multiplier for a change in taxes is negative. An increase in government spending represents an increase in the level of spending in the economy and will stimulate aggregate production, while an increase in taxes reduces the level of spending in the economy and will therefore contract aggregate production.

Tip #3.   Review the distinction between fiscal policy that is discretionary versus fiscal policy that reflects the impact of automatic stabilizers.

Tip #4.   The use of the multiplier thus far in our models presumes a horizontal $SRAS$. If the $SRAS$ is upward sloping, then the impact on aggregate output will be smaller than that predicted by the multiplier. Essentially this tip should remind you that a horizontal $SRAS$ implies a fixed price level, while an upward-sloping $SRAS$ implies that the aggregate price level is not fixed. A shift in AD due to a change in autonomous spending or taxes will cause a larger change in aggregate output (and a change equal to the amount predicted by the multiplier effect) if the aggregate price level is constant than if the aggregate price level is allowed to change. Let's look at a diagram of this represented in Figure 13.1.

Figure 13.1

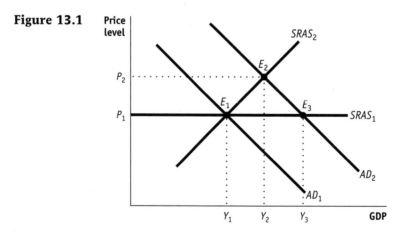

AD_1 is our initial AD curve; $SRAS_1$ is the short-run aggregate supply curve if the aggregate price level is held constant, and $SRAS_2$ is the short-run aggregate supply curve if the aggregate price level is allowed to vary in the short run. Initially the economy is at point E_1, producing Y_1 at an aggregate price level P_1. When autonomous aggregate spending increases, this shifts AD_1 to AD_2, and the horizontal distance Y_1 to Y_3 measures the multiplier effect on aggregate output (moving from the initial equilibrium E_1 to the new equilibrium E_3). However, given $SRAS_2$ a rightward shift in AD from AD_1 to AD_2 increases output from Y_1 to Y_2 while simultaneously increasing the aggregate price level from P_1 to P_2 (moving from the initial equilibrium E_1 to the new equilibrium E_2).

Tip #5. You will want to understand what the cyclically adjusted budget balance is and how it relates to the budget balance and to potential GDP. The cyclically adjusted budget balance is an estimate of what the budget balance would be if real GDP were exactly equal to potential GDP. This measure takes into account the extra tax revenue the government would receive and the smaller level of transfer payments the government would make if the recessionary gap were eliminated or the tax revenue the government would lose and the extra transfer payments the government would make if the inflationary gap were eliminated. The cyclically adjusted budget balance fluctuates less than the actual budget deficit, because years with a large budget deficit are typically associated with large recessionary gaps.

WORKED PROBLEMS

1. Suppose you are an economic advisor for a country with a closed economy. You estimate that this country's potential level of output is $1,000 in year 1 and that this level of potential output will grow 10% a year for the next four years. Your government employers ask you to complete the following table for them based on this information.

Year	Potential output
Year 1	$1,000
Year 2	
Year 3	
Year 4	
Year 5	

You are also given the following information (all numbers in the table are in dollars) about projected spending over the next five years and are asked to provide the government with an equation that expresses this country's consumption function based on the information you have received. In the table, T is net taxes, YD is disposable income, C is consumption spending, I is investment spending, and G is government spending. Besides providing an equation for the country's consumption function, you are also asked to fill in the missing information in the table.

Year	Potential output	Actual output	T	YD	C	I	G
Year 1	$1,000		$50	$950	$770	$200	$30
Year 2		$1,200	50			200	110
Year 3		1,300	50			200	150
Year 4			50	1,100		200	90
Year 5			50	1,200	920	200	80

You are also asked to provide this country with guidance about the projected state of its economy in each of the next five years. From your previous work, fill in the following table for this economy.

Year	Recessionary gap	Inflationary gap	Actual output equals potential output
Year 1			
Year 2			
Year 3			
Year 4			
Year 5			

Finally, suppose this economy wishes to pursue fiscal policy that will ensure that actual output equals potential output every year. For each year, describe whether the government should pursue contractionary fiscal policy, expansionary fiscal policy, or no fiscal policy. Summarize your findings in the following table.

Year	Discretionary fiscal policy
Year 1	
Year 2	
Year 3	
Year 4	
Year 5	

STEP 1: **Start by calculating potential output, or GDP, based on an annual growth rate of 10%.**

Review the section "Fiscal Policy: The Basics" on page 378 (Econ page 810) and the section "Fiscal Policy and the Multiplier" on page 385 (Econ page 817).

You will want to enter your calculations in the summary table. To find year 2's potential GDP, multiply year 1's GDP by 1.10 since year 2's GDP will be 10% greater than year 1's GDP. Continue the same calculation for the next three years.

Year	Potential output
Year 1	$1,000
Year 2	1,100
Year 3	1,210
Year 4	1,331
Year 5	1,464

STEP 2: From the information that you have been given, find this economy's consumption equation.

Review the section "Fiscal Policy: The Basics" on page 378 (Econ page 810) and the section "Fiscal Policy and the Multiplier" on page 385 (Econ page 817).

Inspecting the table, you see that there are two rows that provide you with information about consumption and disposable income: in year 1, when disposable income is $950, consumption is $770; and in year 5, when disposable income is $1,200, consumption is $920. You know that in general the relationship between consumption and disposable income can be written as $C = a + b(Y - T)$, where a is autonomous consumption, b is the marginal propensity to consume, and $(Y - T)$ is disposable income. From the information in the table, you can write two consumption relationships: $770 = a + b(950)$ and $920 = a + b(1,200)$. Use these two equations to find the values for autonomous consumption and the marginal propensity to consume. The consumption equation for this economy can be written as $C = 200 + 0.6(Y - T)$.

Now, you are ready to complete the table. Recall that actual output is equal to the sum of spending in the economy: thus, actual output = $C + I + G$. In year 1, actual output = $770 + 200 + 30 = 1,000$. In year 2 and year 3, you need first to calculate disposable income and then to use this disposable income and the consumption equation to find consumption. In year 4 and year 5, you are given disposable income and net taxes, and with this information you can find actual output.

The following table summarizes this work.

Year	Potential output	Actual output	T	YD	C	I	G
Year 1	$1,000	$1,000	$50	$ 950	$770	$200	$30
Year 2	1,100	1,200	50	1,150	890	200	110
Year 3	1,210	1,300	50	1,250	950	200	150
Year 4	1,331	1,150	50	1,100	860	200	90
Year 5	1,464	1,250	50	1,200	920	200	80

STEP 3: From the information you are given and the work you did in Steps 1 and 3, determine whether this economy is projected to operate with a recessionary gap, an inflationary gap, or at potential output for each of the five years.

Review the section "Fiscal Policy: The Basics" on page 378 (Econ page 810) and the section "Fiscal Policy and the Multiplier" on page 385 (Econ page 817).

Remember that when actual output is less than potential output, the economy is operating with a recessionary gap; when actual output is greater than potential output, the economy is operating with an inflationary gap. Use this information and the table you completed in Step 2 to ascertain the projected state of the economy for the next five years. The following table summarizes this work.

Year	Recessionary gap	Inflationary gap	Actual output equals potential output
Year 1	No	No	Yes
Year 2	No	Yes	No
Year 3	No	Yes	No
Year 4	Yes	No	No
Year 5	Yes	No	No

STEP 4: Determine the type of activist fiscal policy the government of this economy will need to implement in each of the five years if the economy is going to produce at the level of aggregate output at which actual output equals potential output. Base your advice on the projections you have calculated in the previous steps of this problem.

Review the section "Fiscal Policy: The Basics" on page 378 (Econ page 810) and the section "Fiscal Policy and the Multiplier" on page 385 (Econ page 817).

Expansionary fiscal policy acts to increase the level of actual output: activist expansionary fiscal policy is the appropriate fiscal policy response if the desire of the government is to increase the level of actual output. Contractionary fiscal policy acts to decrease the level of actual output: activist contractionary fiscal policy can slow the economy and bring actual output down to the level of potential output.

Year	Fiscal policy
Year 1	None needed since actual output equals potential output
Year 2	Contractionary fiscal policy needed since actual output exceeds potential output
Year 3	Contractionary fiscal policy needed since actual output exceeds potential output
Year 4	Discretionary fiscal policy needed since actual output is less than potential output
Year 5	Discretionary fiscal policy needed since actual output is less than potential output

2. The current short-run economic situation in Urbana is depicted in the following graph: *SRAS* is the short-run aggregate supply curve, *LRAS* is the long-run aggregate supply curve, and *AD* is the aggregate demand curve. You are asked to describe the current short-run economic situation with regard to the relationship between current production and potential production. In addition, you are asked to compare the current level of unemployment to the natural rate of unemployment. Is Urbana operating with a recessionary gap or an inflationary gap? Finally, you are asked to comment on the effect of three possible government policies on both the short-run and the long-run economy in Urbana. The first government policy is a policy that would provide incentives to increase private investment spending. The second government policy is a decision to attack a neighboring country and engage in a large-scale war effort. The third government policy is a decision to increase the level of taxes in this economy. Consider each of these policy choices as independent of one another: that is, assume the government in Urbana will only implement one of these policies at a time.

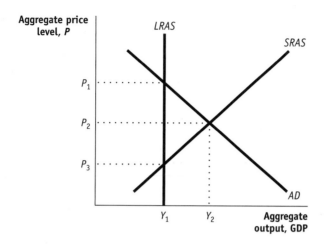

STEP 1: Describe the current state of the economy in Urbana, making sure to identify whether the economy is operating with a recessionary gap or an inflationary gap. In your description, describe the state of the labor market as well as the relationship between actual output and potential output.

Review the section "Fiscal Policy: The Basics" on page 378 (Econ page 810), the section "Fiscal Policy and the Multiplier" on page 385 (Econ page 817), and Figure 13-5 on page 381 (Econ page 813).

In the previous graph, you can see that the long-run level of aggregate output, or the potential output level, is at Y_1. Since the economy is currently operating at the short-run equilibrium where *SRAS* intersects *AD*, we know that actual output is at Y_2. Thus, actual output is greater than potential output, and therefore this economy is operating with an inflationary gap. Since actual output exceeds potential output, this tells us that unemployment is relatively low and is below the natural rate of unemployment.

STEP 2: Evaluate the short-run and long-run implications of the government of Urbana implementing a policy to encourage greater private investment spending.

Review the section "Fiscal Policy: The Basics" on page 378 (Econ page 810), the section "Fiscal Policy and the Multiplier" on page 385 (Econ page 817), and Figure 13-5 on page 381 (Econ page 813).

If the government implements a policy that encourages increased private investment spending, this will cause the aggregate demand curve to shift to the right. Holding everything else constant, in the short run this will cause the level of actual output to increase to an even higher level and the aggregate price level to increase as well. In the long run, the low unemployment rate will cause nominal wages to increase, and this will shift the *SRAS* curve to the left. In the long-run equilibrium, aggregate output will return to potential output, while the aggregate price level may increase, decrease, or remain unchanged. To see why the aggregate price level in the long run is ambiguous, consider the effect of increased private investment spending on the level of capital in this economy. Increases in private investment spending will increase the capital stock in this economy, leading to greater economic growth. This, in turn, will shift the long-run aggregate supply curve to the right. Since we do not know how big this shift is, we cannot with certainty predict what will happen to the aggregate price level in the long run.

STEP 3: Evaluate the short-run and long-run implications of the government of Urbana implementing a policy to go to war.

Review the section "Fiscal Policy: The Basics" on page 378 (Econ page 810), the section "Fiscal Policy and the Multiplier" on page 385 (Econ page 817), and Figure 13-5 on page 381 (Econ page 813).

A decision to go to war will shift the aggregate demand curve to the right, as the government increases its spending in order to fight the war. In the short run, this will cause the level of aggregate output to increase, which will lead to an even greater inflationary gap. In the short run, there will be an increase in the aggregate price level as well. In the long run, the very low levels of unemployment will cause nominal wages to rise. As these nominal wages rise, the short-run aggregate supply curve will shift back to the left, returning the economy to potential output but at a higher level of aggregate prices.

STEP 4: Evaluate the short-run and long-run implications of the government of Urbana increasing the level of taxes in the economy.

Review the section "Fiscal Policy: The Basics" on page 378 (Econ page 810), the section "Fiscal Policy and the Multiplier" on page 385 (Econ page 817), and Figure 13-5 on page 381 (Econ page 813).

A decision to increase the level of taxes will shift the aggregate demand curve to the left, since the increase in taxes will reduce disposable income and therefore lead to decreases in consumption spending. In the short run, this will cause the level of aggregate output to fall relative to its initial short-run level. The aggregate price level will also fall. In the long run, the economy will return to potential output as the short-run aggregate supply curve adjusts. Since we do not know the magnitude of the tax increase, it is impossible to tell whether the short-run aggregate supply curve will need to shift to the left or to the right to bring the economy back to the natural level of output.

3.   Grandview is a closed economy where the level of planned investment spending is constant and equal to $50. In Grandview, people always spend 80% of any increase in disposable income and their autonomous consumption is equal to $10. Grandview currently has a zero budget balance and the level of net taxes is equal to $20. Grandview also is assumed to have fixed prices in the short run. Long-run potential output in Grandview is equal to $400. You are asked to find the short-run level of production in Grandview and determine whether Grandview is currently operating with a recessionary gap or an inflationary gap. In addition, you are asked to provide three possible fiscal policies for returning Grandview to its long-run potential output: a tax policy using lump-sum taxes, a government spending policy, and a tax and government-spending policy that requires that the government budget balance remain zero (continue to assume that the tax change is a change in lump-sum taxes). For each of these three policies, you are asked to provide numerical values for the size of the policy to be implemented. In addition, you should calculate what happens to the government budget balance if there are no other changes.

STEP 1: Before you can find the short-run equilibrium level of output in Grandview, you will first need to find the consumption function for this economy.

Review the section "Fiscal Policy: The Basics" on page 378 (Econ page 810), the section "Fiscal Policy and the Multiplier" on page 385 (Econ page 817), and the section "The Budget Balance" on page 389 (Econ page 821).

Recall that the consumption function is written as $C = a + b(Y - T)$, where a is autonomous consumption and b is the marginal propensity to consume. In the provided information, we are told the value of autonomous consumption, and we are also told that consumers spend 80% of any increase in disposable income. The marginal propensity to consume is defined as the change in consumption divided by the change in disposable income: in this example, the marginal propensity to consume would equal 0.8. Thus, the consumption function is $C = 10 + 0.8(Y - T)$.

STEP 2: Recall that actual output is equal to the sum of expenditure in the economy. Use this information to find the short-run equilibrium level of output in Grandview.

Review the section "Fiscal Policy: The Basics" on page 378 (Econ page 810), the section "Fiscal Policy and the Multiplier" on page 385 (Econ page 817), and the section "The Budget Balance" on page 389 (Econ page 821).

Since Grandview is a closed economy, spending will only come from three sectors: households, businesses, and the government. We can find total expenditure by summing $C + I + G$. In equilibrium, total expenditure will equal production, Y. Thus, $Y = C + I + G$. By substituting the consumption function into this equation along with the given values for I and G, we can solve for the short-run equilibrium level of output. $Y = 10 + 0.8(Y - T) + 50 + 20$, or the short-run equilibrium level of output, Y, is equal to $320.

STEP 3: Compare the short-run equilibrium level of output with the long-run potential level of output to decide whether Grandview is currently operating with a recessionary gap or an inflationary gap.

Review the section "Fiscal Policy: The Basics" on page 378 (Econ page 810), the section "Fiscal Policy and the Multiplier" on page 385 (Econ page 817), and the section "The Budget Balance" on page 389 (Econ page 821).

The short-run equilibrium level of output is $320, which is smaller than the long-run or potential level of output. Grandview is currently operating with a recessionary gap since its actual level of output is less than its potential level of output.

STEP 4: Grandview wishes to use activist fiscal policy to restore the economy to the potential level of aggregate output. Calculate the change in lump-sum taxes that would be necessary for Grandview to achieve this goal by changing current tax policy. Once you have calculated the change in lump-sum taxes, then calculate the change in the government budget balance.

Review the section "Fiscal Policy: The Basics" on page 378 (Econ page 810), the section "Fiscal Policy and the Multiplier" on page 385 (Econ page 817), and the section "The Budget Balance" on page 389 (Econ page 821).

The government of Grandview wishes to stimulate the economy through a change in lump-sum taxes so that output in the economy increases from $320 to $400. The tax expenditure multiplier is equal to $[(-b)/(1 - b)]$, and in this case the value of this multiplier is −4. In order to increase output by $80, lump-sum taxes will need to be reduced by $20 since $(-4)(-20)$ is equal to $80, the desired increase in aggregate production. If government spending is constant at $20 and taxes decrease by $20, then the government budget balance will become negative since the government will be spending more than the amount of tax revenue that it is collecting.

STEP 5: Grandview wishes to use activist fiscal policy to restore the economy to the potential level of aggregate output. Calculate the change in government spending that would be necessary for Grandview to achieve this goal by changing current government spending. Once you have calculated the change in government spending, then calculate the change in the government budget balance.

Review the section "Fiscal Policy: The Basics" on page 378 (Econ page 810), the section "Fiscal Policy and the Multiplier" on page 385 (Econ page 817), and the section "The Budget Balance" on page 389 (Econ page 821).

The government of Grandview wishes to stimulate the economy through a change in government spending so that output in the economy increases from \$320 to \$400. The multiplier for a change in government spending is equal to $[1/(1 - b)]$, and in this case the value of the multiplier is 5. In order to increase output by \$80, government spending would need to be increased by \$16 since (5)(16) is equal to \$80, the desired increase in aggregate production. If taxes are constant and equal to \$20, then this increase in government spending will result in total government spending of \$36. The government budget balance will be negative and equal to –\$16, since the government is spending more than it is collecting in tax revenue.

STEP 6: Grandview wishes to use activist fiscal policy to restore the economy to the potential level of aggregate output while at the same time maintaining a government budget balance of zero. Calculate what the change in government spending and lump-sum taxes must be to achieve this goal.

Review the section "Fiscal Policy: The Basics" on page 378 (Econ page 810), the section "Fiscal Policy and the Multiplier" on page 385 (Econ page 817), and the section "The Budget Balance" on page 389 (Econ page 821).

We know that the desired increase in aggregate output is \$80, and the government of Grandview would like to achieve this level of output by increasing government spending and lump-sum taxes by an equivalent amount so that the government budget balance will remain equal to zero. This implies that the change in government spending should be exactly equal to the change in lump-sum taxes. The change in output will equal the government spending multiplier times the change in government spending, plus the tax expenditure multiplier times the change in lump-sum taxes. Symbolically we can write this as $\Delta Y = [1/(1 - b)]\Delta G + [(-b)/(1 - b)]\Delta T$. Since $\Delta G = \Delta T$, we can rewrite this equation as $\Delta Y = [1/(1 - b)]\Delta G + [(-b)/(1 - b)]\Delta G$, or $\Delta Y = \Delta G$. This means that if the government of Grandview wishes to increase output by \$80 while maintaining a budget balance of zero, it will need to increase government spending and lump-sum taxes by \$80.

4.   Zinfindel is a closed economy that is concerned about its debt–GDP ratio and the projections about this ratio for the next five years. The government of Zinfindel anticipates that real GDP will grow by 10% a year over the next five years, while the level of government deficit is expected to grow by 5% a year over the next five years. The following table provides information about Zinfindel this year. You are asked to complete the table, giving Zinfindel some projections about what it can expect over the next five years. For this problem assume that government debt in the next year is equal to the debt from the year before plus the deficit for that year: for example, in year 2, the debt would be equal to \$25 million plus the additional \$10 million in deficit spending for a total debt of \$35 million. Round all numbers to the nearest hundredth.

Year	Real GDP (millions of dollars)	Debt (millions of dollars)	Budget deficit (millions of dollars)	Debt (percentage of real GDP)	Budget deficit (percentage of real GDP)
Year 1	\$100	\$25	\$10	25%	10%
Year 2					
Year 3					
Year 4					
Year 5					

STEP 1: Start by calculating the value of real GDP for each of the next four years given the assumption that real GDP is growing by 10% a year.

Review the section "The Budget Balance" on page 389 (Econ page 821) and the section "Long-Run Implications of Fiscal Policy" on page 394 (Econ page 826).

To find real GDP for year 2, you will multiply real GDP in year 1 by 1.1. To find real GDP for year 3, you will multiply real GDP in year 2 by 1.1. The results of these calculations are provided in the table at the end of this problem.

STEP 2: Calculate the value of the government deficit for each year given the assumption that this deficit will grow by 5% a year.

Review the section "The Budget Balance" on page 389 (Econ page 821) and the section "Long-Run Implications of Fiscal Policy" on page 394 (Econ page 826).

To find the government deficit for year 2, you will multiply the government deficit for year 1 by 1.05. To find the government deficit for year 3, you will multiply the government deficit for year 2 by 1.05. The results of these calculations are provided in the table at the end of this problem.

STEP 3: Calculate the value of the debt using the budget deficit figures that you calculated in step 2.

Review the section "The Budget Balance" on page 389 (Econ page 821) and the section "Long-Run Implications of Fiscal Policy" on page 394 (Econ page 826).

Remember that the value of the debt in a particular year is equal to the sum of the debt and the budget deficit from the previous year. The results of these calculations are provided in the table at the end of this problem.

STEP 4: Calculate the debt as a percentage of GDP and the budget deficit as a percentage of GDP.

Review the section "The Budget Balance" on page 389 (Econ page 821) and the section "Long-Run Implications of Fiscal Policy" on page 394 (Econ page 826).

To find the debt as a percentage of GDP, divide the debt by real GDP and then multiply your answer by 100 to make it a percentage.

To find the budget deficit as a percentage of GDP, divide the budget deficit by real GDP and then multiply your answer by 100 to make it a percentage. The results of these calculations are provided in the table at the end of this problem.

Year	Real GDP (millions of dollars)	Debt (millions of dollars)	Budget deficit (millions of dollars)	Debt (percentage of real GDP)	Budget deficit (percentage of real GDP)
Year 1	$100	$25	$10	25%	10%
Year 2	110	35	10.5	31.82	9.55
Year 3	121	45.5	11.03	37.60	9.12
Year 4	133.1	56.53	11.58	42.47	8.70
Year 5	146.41	68.10	12.16	46.51	8.31

Problems and Exercises

1. For each of the following situations identify whether it is an example of expansionary discretionary fiscal policy, contractionary discretionary fiscal policy, or fiscal policy in the form of an automatic stabilizer.

   a. During 2009, tax revenue for Macrovia falls as the economy enters a recession.

   b. During 2009, in light of projected deficiencies in *AD*, Macrovia's legislature authorizes an expenditure of $200 million in order to build a new hydroelectric dam.

   c. In 2012, fearing a too rapidly expanding economy, Macrovia adopts a budget that calls for 10% spending cuts in all government departments for the following fiscal year.

   d. In 2011, unemployment benefits rise 5% in response to rising unemployment in Macrovia.

2. The following graph depicts the economy of Macroland's short-run aggregate supply curve (*SRAS*), its long-run aggregate supply curve (*LRAS*), and its aggregate demand curve (*AD*). Macroland is currently producing at point *E*.

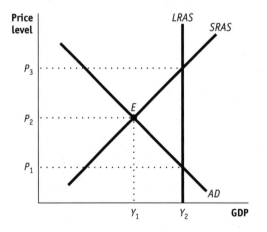

   a. Is potential GDP for Macroland equal to Y_1 or Y_2? Describe Macroland's current production relative to its potential production.

b. Does Macroland have a recessionary gap or an inflationary gap? Explain your answer.

c. Suppose Macroland wishes to produce at its potential output level. Holding everything else constant, identify which of the following policy initiatives might help it reach this goal and how these policy initiatives would help.

   i. The government initiates policies that encourage private investment spending.

   ii. The government increases the amount of money it borrows in the loanable funds market in order to increase its level of government spending in the economy.

   iii. The government increases taxes on consumers and corporations.

   iv. The government authorizes new spending programs.

d. What is the current price level in Macroland? If Macroland successfully engages in expansionary fiscal policy so that *AD* shifts and actual output equals potential output, what will happen to the price level?

3. Funlandia's economists estimate that its potential level of output is $100 in year 1 and this level of potential output grows 5% per year. Assume Funlandia is a closed economy.

a. Fill in the following table for Funlandia given the information.

Year	Potential output
Year 1	$100
Year 2	
Year 3	
Year 4	

Suppose Funlandia's economists provide you with the following table of data. All numbers in the table are in dollars.

Year	Potential output	Actual output	T	YD	C	I	G
Year 1	$100		$10	$ 90	$55	$30	$15
Year 2		$104	10			30	17
Year 3		115	10			30	22.5
Year 4			10	108	64	30	24

b. What is the consumption function for this economy?

c. Fill in the missing values for the same table using the information you have been given or that you computed in parts (a) and (b).

d. Fill in the following table for Funlandia.

Year	Recessionary gap	Inflationary gap	Actual output equals potential output
Year 1	No	No	Yes
Year 2			
Year 3			
Year 4			

e. Suppose Funlandia maintains a policy of using discretionary fiscal policy to ensure that actual output equals potential output. Summarize the recommended discretionary fiscal policy necessary to achieve this goal in the following table.

Year	Discretionary fiscal policy
Year 1	
Year 2	
Year 3	
Year 4	

4. Suppose Uplandia is a closed economy where the level of planned investment spending equals $100 and is unaffected by the level of aggregate spending. Furthermore, suppose consumers consume 60% of any increase in their disposable income and autonomous consumer spending equals $20. Uplandia currently has a zero budget balance, with taxes equal to $50, transfers equal to $0, and government spending on goods and services equal to $50. Furthermore, assume the price level is fixed in Uplandia in the short run.

a. What is Uplandia's consumption function?

b. What is the income–expenditure equilibrium for Uplandia?

c. Suppose Uplandia wants output to equal $400, the potential level of output. Does Uplandia have an inflationary gap or a recessionary gap? Explain your answer.

d. What is the change in government spending needed to enable this economy to reach its potential output, holding everything else constant?

e. Instead of a change in government spending, Uplandia decides to pursue a change in taxes in order to reach its potential output. Holding everything else constant, what is the change in taxes needed to enable this economy to reach its potential output?

f. Suppose the government decides it wants to maintain a zero budget balance. This implies that any increase in government spending, G, must be accompanied by an equivalent increase in taxes, T. Suppose Uplandia chooses to reach its potential output level while maintaining a zero budget balance. What will the change in G and T need to be in order to accomplish this goal?

g. In your answers to parts (d), (e) and (f), you use different multipliers to reach potential output in Uplandia. If your only criterion for choosing policy is getting the most "bang for the buck" or, in other words, getting the largest change in aggregate output for a given dollar change in government spending or taxation, which is the best policy? Explain your answer.

h. Relate your answer in part (g) to the debate over the wisdom of a balanced-budget rule for the federal government.

5. Uplandia is concerned about its debt–GDP ratio and the projections about this ratio over the next five years. The following table gives data about Uplandia's real GDP for this year (year 1) and its projected real GDP for the next five years. Real GDP is projected to grow 3% per year over the next five years as is the government deficit.

    a. Fill in the missing cells in the table.

Year	Real GDP (millions of dollars)	Debt (millions of dollars)	Budget deficit (millions of dollars)	Debt (percentage of real GDP)	Budget deficit (percentage of real GDP)
Year 1	$800	$200	$20	25%	2.5%
Year 2					
Year 3					
Year 4					
Year 5					
Year 6					

    b. Describe in words what is happening to the government's debt–GDP ratio and deficit–GDP ratio when real GDP and the government deficit grow at the same rate.

    Suppose Uplandia decides to reduce government spending over the next five years. This results in the government deficit growing 1% per year over the next five years while real GDP continues to grow 3% per year.
    c. Fill in the table based on these projections.

Year	Real GDP (millions of dollars)	Debt (millions of dollars)	Budget deficit (millions of dollars)	Debt (percentage of real GDP)	Budget deficit (percentage of real GDP)
Year 1	$800	$200	$20	25%	2.5%
Year 2					
Year 3					
Year 4					
Year 5					
Year 6					

    d. Describe in words what is happening to the government's debt–GDP ratio and deficit–GDP ratio when real GDP grows at 3% per year while the deficit grows at 1% per year.

Suppose Uplandia, buoyed by its projected real GDP growth rate, passes legislation reducing its taxes while simultaneously deciding to go to war. Its economists project real GDP will continue to grow at 3% per year but now, due to these policy decisions, the government deficit is projected to grow at 10% per year. The results of these changes is shown in the following table.

Year	Real GDP (millions of dollars)	Debt (millions of dollars)	Budget deficit (millions of dollars)	Debt (percentage of real GDP)	Budget deficit (percentage of real GDP)
Year 1	$800	$200	$20	25%	2.5%
Year 2	824	222	22	26.94	2.67
Year 3	848.72	246.2	24.2	29.01	2.85
Year 4	874.18	272.82	26.62	31.21	3.05
Year 5	900.41	302.10	29.38	33.55	3.25
Year 6	927.42	334.30	32.2	36.05	3.47

e. Describe in words what is happening to the government's debt–GDP ratio and deficit–GDP ratio when real GDP grows at 3% per year while the deficit grows at 10% per year.

f. Can you generalize your findings from this exercise? What general principles does this exercise present?

6. Explain why automatic stabilizers reduce the size of the multiplier. Provide several examples of automatic stabilizers and their effect on the economy during economic fluctuations.

7. Suppose that the government currently operates with a deficit and that this deficit grows by 4% a year. Furthermore, suppose that this economy initially had zero debt until the government started operating with a deficit. The economy's annual economic growth rate is 5% a year. What will happen to this economy's debt–GDP ratio over time given this information? Explain your answer fully.

8. **[from Appendix]** Suppose you are given the following set of equations to describe the closed economy of Fantasia.

$C = A + MPC \, (Y - T)$

$T = tY$, where t is the tax rate

Furthermore, suppose the price level in Fantasia is fixed in the short run.

a. Using the information provided, derive an expression for the multiplier for this economy.

You are given some additional information about Fantasia's economy. You are told

$C = 10 + 0.5 \, (Y - T)$

$T = 0.1Y$

$I_{Planned} = \$50$ million

$G = \$50$ million

b. What is the income–expenditure equilibrium in Fantasia?

c. What is the value of the multiplier for changes in autonomous spending in Fantasia?

Suppose you are told that the potential output level in Fantasia is $180 million.

d. Given your answer in part (b), is Fantasia operating with a recessionary or an inflationary gap?

e. The government in Fantasia decides to engage in discretionary fiscal policy to make Fantasia's level of aggregate output equal to its potential output. As Fantasia's chief economist, what change in the level of government spending is necessary to restore the economy to potential output?

BEFORE YOU TAKE THE TEST

Chapter Review Questions

1. Which of the following statements is true?
   a. Personal income taxes, corporate profits taxes, and social insurance taxes are the primary taxes at the federal level of government in the United States.
   b. State and local governments in the United States rely on sales taxes, property taxes, income taxes, and fees for their sources of revenues.
   c. In 2007, 48% of government revenue in the United States came from taxes on personal income and corporate profits.
   d. All of the above statements are true statements.
   e. Statements (a) and (b) are both true.
   f. Statements (b) and (c) are both true.

2. Total government spending differs from government expenditure because it
   a. refers to the purchase of goods and services and does not include transfers since this represents a transfer of income from one individual to another.
   b. refers to the purchase of goods and services as well as expenditures on transfers.
   c. includes, in the United States, transfers such as spending on Social Security, Medicare, and Medicaid.
   d. Answers (a) and (c) are both correct.
   e. Answers (b) and (c) are both correct.

3. Contractionary fiscal policy
   a. is most helpful for restoring an economy to the potential output level of production when there is a recessionary gap.
   b. shifts the *AD* curve to the right, restoring the equilibrium level of output to the potential output level for the economy.
   c. often causes inflation or an increase in the aggregate price level.
   d. if effective, shifts *AD* to the left, resulting in a reduction in the aggregate output and the aggregate price level for a given short-run aggregate supply curve (*SRAS*).

4. Which of the following statements is true? Holding everything else constant,
   a. an economy can eliminate an inflationary gap by increasing government spending.
   b. expansionary fiscal policy refers to an increase in taxes.
   c. when potential output is greater than actual aggregate output, the economy faces a recessionary gap.
   d. when *SRAS* intersects *AD* to the right of the long-run aggregate supply (*LRAS*) curve, the economy faces a recessionary gap.

5. Monetary and fiscal policy
   a. affect the economy in predictable ways and with relatively short time lags.
   b. involve significant time lags with regard to their implementation and effect on the economy.
   c. take so long to implement in the economy that they prove to be useless policies.
   d. when implemented always worsen economic fluctuations because of the lags involved in their implementation.

6. The Social Security program in the United States
   a. is a "pay-as-you-go" system where current workers pay payroll taxes that fund the benefits of current retirees.
   b. had 34 retirees receiving benefits for every 10 workers in 2010, while projections suggest that in 2030 there will be 46 retirees receiving benefits for every 100 workers.
   c. had accumulated a Social Security trust fund of $2.9 trillion at the end of fiscal 2011.
   d. Answers (a), (b) and (c) are all correct.

7. Holding everything else constant, the multiplier effect for taxes or transfers
   a. is the same as the multiplier effect for changes in autonomous aggregate spending.
   b. is smaller than the multiplier effect for changes in autonomous aggregate spending.
   c. is larger than the multiplier effect for changes in autonomous aggregate spending.
   d. may be smaller than, larger than, or equal to the multiplier effect for changes in autonomous aggregate spending.

8. Which of the following statements is true?
   a. Automatic stabilizers act like automatic expansionary fiscal policy when the economy is in a recession.
   b. Automatic stabilizers refer to government spending and taxation rules that cause fiscal policy to be expansionary when the economy expands and contractionary when the economy contracts.
   c. Automatic stabilizers reduce the size of the multiplier.
   d. Statements (a), (b), and (c) are all true.
   e. Statements (a) and (c) are both true.

9. Discretionary fiscal policy refers to
   a. the effect of automatic stabilizers on the economy.
   b. a situation in which citizens can choose to participate or not participate in government programs.
   c. fiscal policy that is the direct result of deliberate decisions made by policymakers.
   d. fiscal policy that is either the direct result of deliberate decisions made by policymakers or the result of the impact of automatic stabilizers on the economy.

10. Holding everything else constant, the government's budget balance
   a. tends to increase during a recession.
   b. tends to increase during an expansion.
   c. will increase if the government pursues expansionary fiscal policy.
   d. Answers (a) and (c) are both correct.
   e. Answers (b) and (c) are both correct.

11. Which of the following statements is true?
   a. Two different changes in fiscal policy that have equal effects on the budget balance will always have equal effects on *AD*.
   b. A change in taxes or transfers will have a larger effect on *AD* than an equal-sized change in government purchases of goods and services.
   c. The budget deficit almost always falls when unemployment rises.
   d. The cyclically adjusted budget balance provides an estimate of the budget balance assuming real GDP is equal to potential output.

12. When a government decides to spend more than it collects in tax revenue,
   a. it usually borrows the necessary funds.
   b. the budget balance increases.
   c. it runs a budget deficit but reduces its overall level of government debt.
   d. it is forced to sell valuable assets to finance its spending.

13. Which of the following statements is true?
   a. The fiscal year 2001 runs from October 1, 2001 through September 30, 2002.
   b. Public debt is that amount of government debt held by individuals and institutions outside the government.
   c. The government's total debt includes the public debt as well as the debt owed by one part of the government to another part of the government (for example, the Social Security trust funds).
   d. Statements (a), (b), and (c) are all true.
   e. Statements (b) and (c) are both true.

14. In the United States, at the end of fiscal year 2007, the
   a. total government debt equaled 37% of GDP.
   b. government's public debt at the federal level equaled 37% of GDP.
   c. government's public debt equaled $7.4 trillion.
   d. level of government debt as measured by the public debt–GDP ratio was far higher than that of comparable economies.

15. The government debt is
   a. an alternative but equivalent term for the government deficit.
   b. the difference between the amount of money government spends and the amount of tax revenue the government collects during a given period of time.
   c. the amount of money the government owes at a particular point in time.
   d. best measured over a given period of time.

16. Suppose the government of Macroland repeatedly finds itself running a deficit. This may
   a. result in less private investment spending as government borrowing crowds out this spending.
   b. result in lower long-run economic growth if the deficit reduces private investment spending.
   c. cause the government of Macroland to have less budgetary flexibility in the future due to the diversion of tax revenue to pay interest on the debt.
   d. Answers (a), (b), and (c) are all possible effects of repeatedly running a deficit.

17. The debt–GDP ratio
   a. provides a measure of government debt as a percentage of GDP.
   b. provides a measure of government debt relative to the potential ability of the government to collect taxes to cover that debt.
   c. can fall, even if the level of government debt is rising, provided that GDP grows faster than the debt.
   d. Answers (a), (b), and (c) are all correct.

18. Implicit liabilities
   a. are not included in the calculation of the debt–GDP ratio in the United States.
   b. are promises made by the government that represent a debt that must be paid by the government at some future point in time.
   c. are usually included in debt statistics.
   d. Answers (a), (b), and (c) are all correct.
   e. Answers (a) and (b) are both correct.

19. Which of the following statements is true?
   a. The demographic issues underlying Social Security will lessen with the passage of time in the United States as the baby boom generation moves into retirement.
   b. Health costs tend to rise at approximately the same rate as other costs in wealthy economies like the United States.
   c. Social Security and Medicare are funded by dedicated taxes: any excess funds collected from these dedicated taxes accumulate in trust funds that other parts of the government may borrow from to fund other spending. When this type of borrowing occurs an implicit liability is created.
   d. The sum of public debt and the United States government debt held by Social Security and other trust funds overstates the seriousness of the government's fiscal health.

20. When an economy is operating with a recessionary gap, the decision to increase government spending in order to stimulate the economy is an example of
   a. discretionary fiscal policy.
   b. monetary policy, since it will lead to everyone having more money than they did prior to the increase in government spending.
   c. automatic stabilizers acting to stabilize the economy.
   d. Answers (a) and (c) are both correct.

21. Revenue for the operation of state and local governments come primarily from
   a. personal income taxes.
   b. corporate taxes.
   c. a mix of sales taxes, property taxes, income taxes, and fees of various kinds.
   d. payroll taxes.

22. Government transfers are payments from the government
   a. to households as compensation for taxes that the household has paid.
   b. to households for which no good or service is provided in return.
   c. that redistribute purchasing power from one group of households to another group of households.
   d. Answers (a) and (c) are both correct.
   e. Answers (b) and (c) are both correct.

23. Government programs that are designed to protect individuals or families from economic hardship are described as
   a. fiscal policy.
   b. discretionary fiscal policy.
   c. monetary policy.
   d. social insurance.

24. Which of the following will cause the *AD* curve to shift to the left?

    a. Government increases the amount of transfer payments it makes.

    b. Government increases the amount of taxes it collects from households.

    c. Government increases its level of defense spending after declaring war on a nearby country.

    d. Government institutes an investment tax credit that effectively reduces the cost of investment purchases made by firms.

25. Suppose an economy currently is operating with an inflationary gap. If the government wishes to return the economy to potential output, which of the following initiatives is most likely to achieve this goal?

    a. The government implements an investment tax credit.

    b. The government passes more generous social insurance programs for the retired and disabled in the economy.

    c. The government increases taxes.

    d. The government increases spending on national defense.

26. Which of the following situations describes the use of contractionary fiscal policy?

    a. Recovery Rebate and Stimulus for the American People Act of 2008

    b. Investment Tax Credit of 2002

    c. Argentina's reductions in government spending and increases in taxes during the period 1997 to 2001

    d. President Lyndon Johnson's surcharge on income taxes in 1968

    e. Answers (c) and (d) are both examples of contractionary fiscal policy.

27. Economists caution that

    a. recessionary gaps are so threatening that the government ought to be always ready to enact discretionary fiscal policy to counteract the recessionary gap.

    b. there are important time lags in the use of fiscal policy and that discretionary fiscal policy must be carefully employed if it is to result in less economic fluctuation rather than more economic fluctuation.

    c. recessionary gaps are often over before discretionary fiscal policy has any impact and, thus, the discretionary policy has no impact on the economy.

    d. the existence of lags makes the implementation of fiscal policy easier than it would be without the lags.

28. Assume an economy is initially in long-run income–expenditure equilibrium. In addition, assume that this economy's short-run aggregate supply curve is upward sloping. Holding everything else constant, an increase in government spending causes the planned aggregate expenditure line to shift up, the *AD* curve to shift to the

    a. right, the aggregate price level to increase, and the total change in output to equal the multiplier effect.

    b. left, the aggregate price level to increase, and the total change in output to be less than the amount calculated as the multiplier effect.

    c. right, the aggregate price level to increase, and the total change in output to be less than the amount calculated as the multiplier effect.

29. The government is considering two proposals: one would increase government spending by $100 while the other would decrease the level of taxes collected by the government by $100. Suppose the government's goal is to stimulate the economy as much as possible for a given level of expenditure. Which of the following statements is true?

a. The government will stimulate the economy more when it increases government spending.

b. The government will stimulate the economy more when it decreases taxes.

c. The stimulus to the economy from these two proposals is the same: it does not matter which proposal the government implements.

30. Which of the following statements is true?

   I. The *MPC* for unemployed people is usually higher than the *MPC* for people who own stocks.

   II. The macroeconomic effects of an increase in unemployment benefits will be greater than the macroeconomic effects of a decrease in taxes on profits distributed as dividends to shareholders.

   III. Automatic stabilizers reduce the size of the multiplier.

a. Statement I is true.

b. Statement II is true.

c. Statement III is true.

d. Statements I and II are both true.

e. Statements I and III are both true.

f. Statements II and III are both true.

g. Statements I, II, and III are all true.

31. Suppose the government spends $500 billion during the fiscal year 2007 on goods and services. In addition, the government collects tax revenues of $480 billion and makes transfer payments equal to $150 billion. Assume the economy is producing at the potential output level. The budget balance for this economy is equal to _____ and the government is running a _____.

a. $170 billion; surplus

b. −$170 billion; deficit

c. $130 billion; surplus

d. −$130 billion; deficit

32. Economists generally do not believe that the government should balance its budget every year. Instead, economists advocate that governments run a surplus during economic

a. recessions and a deficit during economic expansions.

b. expansions and a deficit during economic recessions.

33. When a government runs a deficit persistently year after year, this may

a. place financial pressure on future budgets.

b. result in higher taxes over time since the government will need to collect tax revenue to cover its interest payments on the government debt.

c. reduce the level of private investment spending as the government's borrowing crowds out over investment spending.

d. Answers (a), (b), and (c) are all correct.

e. Answers (a) and (b) are both correct.

34. **[from Appendix]** Suppose the *MPC* equals 0.5 and the tax rate is 0.1 for an economy. Holding everything else constant, when government spending increases by $10 billion, what is the total change in aggregate output?
    a. $10 billion
    b. $20 billion
    c. $18.2 billion
    d. $10.5 billion

35. **[from Appendix]** Which of the following statements is true?
    a. When the government "captures" a fraction *t* of any increase in GDP in the form of taxes, this produces a larger multiplier effect.
    b. If the tax rate is 0.05 and the *MPC* is 0.4, then the multiplier for a change in autonomous spending equals 1.61.
    c. If the tax rate is 0.1 and GDP increases by $1.2 billion, then the government will collect an additional $0.12 billion during the given time period.
    d. Statements (a), (b), and (c) are all true.
    e. Statements (b) and (c) are both true.

■ ANSWER KEY

Answers to Problems and Exercises

1. **a.** This is an example of an automatic stabilizer: as GDP in Macrovia falls, this leads automatically to smaller tax collections for a given tax rate.

   b. This is an example of expansionary discretionary fiscal policy: the additional government expenditure will stimulate *AD*.

   c. This is an example of contractionary discretionary fiscal policy: Macrovia moves to cut government spending, which will reduce *AD* and slow down the economic expansion.

   d. This is an example of an automatic stabilizer: as unemployment rises, this leads to less *AD*. But the payment of unemployment benefits lessens this fall in aggregate spending and results in a smaller overall impact on *AD*.

2. **a.** The potential output level for Macroland is Y_2 where *LRAS* equals *SRAS* equals *AD*. Currently, Macroland is producing Y_1 at price level P_2: this represents a recessionary situation, or a recessionary gap, since Macroland has the potential to produce a higher level of output than it is currently producing.

   b. Macroland has a recessionary gap since their current level of production, Y_1, is less than their potential level of production, Y_2.

   c. Any policy initiative that shifts *AD* to the right will help Macroland move toward its potential output level. Items (i) and (iv) will both shift *AD* to the right: government policies that stimulate private investment spending lead to higher levels of aggregate spending and a rightward shift in *AD*; and new spending by government will also lead to higher levels of aggregate spending and a rightward shift in *AD*. Item (ii) will cause the *AD* to shift to the right unless the increase in government borrowing crowds out private investment to that point where private investment decreases by an amount equal to the increase in government spending. In that case item (ii) would result in no shift in the *AD* curve. Item (iii) will reduce disposable income and lead to lower levels of aggregate spending: *AD* may shift to the left if the decrease in spending is greater than the increase in government spending, or *AD* may shift to the right if the increase in government spending is greater than the decrease in spending

   d. The current price level in Macroland is P_2. If the government engages in fiscal policy that results in the economy's returning to the potential level of output, this will lead to increases in the price level from P_2 to P_3.

3. **a.**

Year	Potential output
Year 1	$100
Year 2	105
Year 3	110.25
Year 4	115.76

   b. The consumption function can be written as $C = A + MPC(Y - T)$. From the table we can compute the MPC as the change in consumption divided by the change in disposable income, or 9/18, which equals 0.5. To find *A*, we need to use one of the consumption and disposable income combinations from the table. For example, when disposable income equals 90, consumption equals 55. So, $C = A + 0.5 (Y - T)$ can be rewritten as $55 = A + 0.5(90)$ and solving for *A*, we find *A* equals 10. Thus, the consumption function for this economy is $C = 10 + 0.5 (Y - T)$.

c.

Year	Potential output	Actual output	T	YD	C	I	G
Year 1	100	100	10	90	55	30	15
Year 2	105	104	10	94	57	30	17
Year 3	110.25	115	10	105	62.5	30	22.5
Year 4	115.76	118	10	108	64	30	24

d.

Year	Recessionary gap	Inflationary gap	Actual output equals potential output
Year 1	No	No	Yes
Year 2	Yes	No	No
Year 3	No	Yes	No
Year 4	No	Yes	No

e.

Year	Discretionary fiscal policy
Year 1	No policy necessary
Year 2	Increase government spending or decrease taxation
Year 3	Decrease government spending or increase taxation
Year 4	Decrease government spending or increase taxation

4. **a.** To find the consumption function first recall the general form: $C = A + MPC(Y - T)$. From the given information we know A equals \$20 and the MPC equals 0.6. Thus, $C = 20 + 0.6(Y - T)$.

   b. To find the income–expenditure equilibrium, solve the equation $Y = C + I + G$. We know C can be written as $20 + 0.6(Y - T)$; I equals \$100; and G equals \$50. We also know T, taxes, equals \$50. So, $Y = 20 + 0.6(Y - 50) + 100 + 50$, or Y equals \$350.

   c. Uplandia is currently producing with a recessionary gap, since its current output of \$350 is less than its potential output of \$400.

   d. The multiplier for a change in aggregate spending equals $1/(1 - MPC)$. We know that the change in aggregate production equals the multiplier times the change (in this case) in government spending. In this problem, we want output to increase by \$50, our multiplier value is 2.5, and thus government spending must increase by \$20 in order for this economy to produce its potential output of \$400.

   e. The multiplier for a change in taxes equals $-MPC/(1 - MPC)$, or in this case -1.5, since the MPC equals 0.6. Recall that the change in aggregate output equals the multiplier times the change in the level of taxes. We want output to increase by \$50, the multiplier's value is -1.5, and, thus, taxes must decrease by \$33.33. Here you need to remember that aggregate output increases as taxes fall, holding everything else constant, and aggregate output decreases as taxes increase, holding everything else constant.

f. We can find our answer by recognizing that we have two multiplier effects occurring simultaneously it the government chooses to maintain a zero budget balance. We could write this as the change in aggregate output equals the multiplier effect from the change in government spending plus the multiplier effect from the change in taxes. Note, though, that the change in government spending equals the change in taxes. Thus, the change in aggregate output equals $1/(1 - MPC)$ times the change in government spending plus $[-MPC/(1 - MPC)]$ times the change in government spending. Since the desired change in aggregate output equals $50, we can solve this equation and find that the change in government spending and in taxes must both equal $50.

g. The most "bang for the buck" comes from a change in government spending since the multiplier has a value of 2.5. A change in taxes is multiplied by the smaller (in absolute value) multiplier of 1.5 and the balanced budget scenario has an even smaller multiplier value of 1.

h. A balanced budget rule for the federal government would restrict the government's ability to engage in discretionary fiscal policy in times of economic need. It would also prove costly, since for any given change in aggregate output, a balanced-budget rule forces the federal government to spend more than it would if the government were free to pursue discretionary fiscal policy without regard to its budgetary consequences.

5. **a.**

Year	Real GDP (millions of dollars)	Debt (millions of dollars)	Budget deficit (millions of dollars)	Debt (percentage of real GDP)	Budget deficit (percentage of real GDP)
Year 1	$800.00	$200.00	$20.00	25%	2.5%
Year 2	824.00	220.60	20.60	26.77	2.5
Year 3	848.72	241.82	21.22	28.49	2.5
Year 4	874.18	263.68	21.85	30.16	2.5
Year 5	900.41	286.18	22.51	31.79	2.5
Year 6	927.42	309.37	23.19	33.36	2.5

b. When the real GDP and the government deficit grow at the same rate, the deficit–GDP ratio stays constant at 2.5%, while the debt–GDP ratio increases from 25% to 33.36% in five years.

c.

Year	Real GDP (millions of dollars)	Debt (millions of dollars)	Budget deficit (millions of dollars)	Debt (percentage of real GDP)	Budget deficit (percentage of real GDP)
Year 1	$800.00	$200.00	$20.00	25%	2.5%
Year 2	824.00	220.20	20.20	26.72	2.45
Year 3	848.72	240.60	20.40	28.35	2.40
Year 4	874.18	261.21	20.61	29.88	2.36
Year 5	900.41	282.02	20.81	31.32	2.31
Year 6	927.42	303.04	21.02	32.67	2.27

d. When the real GDP grows at 3% per year and the government deficit grows at 1% per year, the deficit–GDP ratio falls from 2.5% to 2.27% in five years, while the debt–GDP ratio increases from 25% to 32.68% in five years.

e. When real GDP grows at 3% per year and the deficit grows at 10% per year, the deficit–GDP ratio increases from 2.5% to 3.47% over five years while the debt–GDP ratio increases from 25% to 36.05% over five years.

f. The rate of growth of both real GDP and the deficit each year are important when considering what happens to the debt–GDP ratio and the deficit–GDP ratio. If GDP grows at a faster rate than the deficit, the deficit–GDP ratio will decline while the debt–GDP ratio may continue to increase, but at a slower rate than would occur if the deficit and GDP grew at the same rate.

6. Automatic stabilizers act to moderate the effects of economic recessions or economic expansions. In the case of economic recessions, the automatic stabilizers provide a source of additional spending that occurs as the economy goes into the recession. For example, as production and spending slow in the economy, the amount of taxes people pay naturally decrease as their income levels decrease, and this moderates the fall in consumer spending. Or, as unemployment rates increase, the number of people receiving unemployment compensation rises, and this enables people to spend more than they would otherwise be able to spend. In the case of economic expansions, the automatic stabilizers slow down spending: as people's incomes rise, their taxes also rise reducing the overall increase in consumer income, and this moderates the economic expansion. (Students may provide different examples of automatic stabilizers.)

7. The government will operate with a deficit each year and, therefore, the government debt will grow over time. But, because the economy is growing at a faster rate than the growth rate of the deficit, this means that the debt–GDP ratio will fall over time.

8. **a.** **[from Appendix]** To find the multiplier, start by recalling the equilibrium condition where aggregate expenditure equals aggregate income. We can write this as $Y = C + I + G$ for the closed economy of Fantasia. We can substitute A for C and get $Y = A + MPC (Y - T) + I + G$. We can also substitute tY for T and have $Y = A + MPC (Y - tY) + I + G$. Rearranging terms we have $Y - MPC(1 - t)Y = A + I + G$ or $Y[1 - MPC (1 - t)] = A + I + G$. We can solve this equation for Y and have $Y = \{1/[1 - MPC (1 - t)]\}(A + I + G)$. The multiplier is $\{1/[1 - MPC (1 - t)]\}$.

b. Use the equation $Y = C + I + G$ and substitute in the data you have to get $Y = 10 + 0.5 (Y - 0.1Y) + 100$. Solving for Y, the income–expenditure equilibrium equals $200.

c. The value of the multiplier, $\{1/[1 - MPC (1 - t)]\}$, equals 1.818, or approximately 1.82.

d. Fantasia is operating with an inflationary gap since actual output of $200 exceeds potential output of $180 million.

e. Since aggregate output needs to fall by $20 million and the multiplier equals 1.82, that implies that government spending must decrease by $10.99 million.

Answers to Chapter Review Questions

1. **Answer d.** This question is a review of facts presented in the chapter. Each statement is factual.

2. **Answer a.** Total government spending includes the government's purchases of goods and services as well as the expenditures the government makes in the form of transfer payments. The three primary transfer programs in terms of dollar cost in the United States are Social Security, Medicare, and Medicaid.

3. **Answer d.** Contractionary fiscal policy is a reduction in government spending or an increase in taxes aimed at shifting *AD* to the left. For a given *SRAS,* this leftward shift in *AD* will lead to a lower level of equilibrium aggregate output and a reduction in the aggregate price level. Contractionary fiscal policy is implemented when the economy produces a level of output in excess of potential output: contractionary fiscal policy is used to offset an inflationary gap.

4. **Answer c.** When *SRAS* intersects *AD* to the right of *LRAS,* the economy faces an inflationary gap. This inflationary gap can be eliminated through a decrease in government spending or an increase in taxes, since either policy will cause *AD* to shift to the left holding everything else equal. A decrease in government spending and an increase in taxes are examples of contractionary fiscal policy. By definition, when potential output is greater than actual aggregate output, the economy is operating with a recessionary gap.

5. **Answer b.** There are significant lags involved in the implementation of fiscal and monetary policy. These lags can result in a situation where the implemented policy actually worsens the economic situation (for example, using expansionary fiscal policy to counteract a recessionary gap that has turned into an inflationary gap by the time the fiscal policy takes effect).

6. **Answer d.** Answers (a), (b), and (c) are all factual statements about the Social Security program in the United States. These statements are all discussed in the text.

7. **Answer b.** In our simple model, the multiplier effect for changes in taxes or transfers equals (in absolute value) $MPC/(1 - MPC)$, while the multiplier effect for changes in autonomous aggregate spending equals $1/(1 - MPC)$. The multiplier effect of changes in taxes and transfers is smaller than the multiplier effect of changes in autonomous aggregate spending.

8. **Answer e.** Automatic stabilizers act to automatically lessen the economic consequences of recessions and expansions. They do this by providing an automatic fiscal policy response that stimulates a contractionary economy and slows down, or contracts, an expansionary economy. This activity effectively lessens the multiplier process and therefore reduces the size of the multiplier.

9. **Answer c.** Discretionary fiscal policy refers to fiscal policy that is implemented at the discretion of policymakers. It is therefore the direct result of deliberate actions taken by policymakers.

10. **Answer b.** The budget balance, $S_{Government}$, is defined by the equation $S_{Government} = T - G - TR$. In an expansion, tax revenue increases and transfers decrease (both of these changes are the result of automatic stabilizers): for a given level of government spending, the budget balance increases. If the government pursues expansionary fiscal policy while holding everything else constant, this will decrease the budget balance.

11. **Answer d.** Answers (a), (b), and (c) are all incorrect. The multiplier effect from a change in taxes and transfers is smaller than the multiplier effect from a change in government spending and therefore the effect of a change in taxes and transfers on *AD* will be smaller than an equal change in government spending. When unemployment rises, this leads to lower tax revenue (as income falls in the economy, tax revenue also decreases) and higher expenditures on transfer programs like unemployment compensation: thus, the budget deficit almost always rises when unemployment rises. Answer (d) provides a straightforward definition of the cyclically adjusted budget balance.

12. **Answer a.** When the government spends more than it collects in tax revenue, the government runs a deficit and must acquire additional funds: typically it does this by borrowing the necessary funds. When the government's deficit increases, this adds to the value of the government debt. It is unusual for governments to sell valuable assets to finance their spending programs. When the government spends more than it collects in tax revenue, this causes the budget balance to decrease (recall the budget balance is defined in equation form as $S_{Government} = T - G - TR$).

13. **Answer e.** The fiscal year runs from October 1 through September 30th: so, for example, if the fiscal year runs from October 1, 2002 through September 30, 2002, it is considered fiscal year 2002 (and *not* fiscal year 2001). Public debt is defined as given in answer (b), and the total government debt includes not only the public debt but also the debt that one part of government owes to another part of government.

14. **Answer b.** At the end of fiscal year 2007, the United States' total government debt equaled $8.95 trillion. The public debt for fiscal year 2007 equaled $5 trillion, which represented 37% of GDP. The public debt–GDP ratio for the United States and other wealthy countries was more or less the same.

15. **Answer c.** The government debt is not the same as the government deficit. The government deficit is the difference between the amount of money a government spends and the amount of money it collects in tax revenue during a given period of time. The government debt, in contrast, is the total amount of money a government owes at a particular point in time.

16. **Answer d.** Answers (a), (b), and (c) are all possibilities. When the government runs a deficit, it will typically borrow funds. When the government borrows funds, it competes with firms in the financial markets for those funds. This competition may crowd out private investment spending and therefore lead to lower long-run rates of economic growth. In addition, as the deficits persist the government will find that increasing amounts of its tax revenue must be dedicated to paying the interest expense of the debt, and this means the government must either reduce its spending in other areas or raise more revenue from taxes.

17. **Answer d.** The debt–GDP ratio provides a measure of the size of the government debt relative to the size of the economy: this is a helpful comparison, since the size of the economy provides a measure of the potential tax revenue that can be raised by the government. If the government debt is increasing at the same time that GDP is also increasing, it is possible that the debt–GDP ratio is actually falling, provided that GDP is growing at a faster rate than debt.

18. **Answer e.** Implicit liabilities are promises made by governments that represent future payments that must be made by the governments. Examples in the United States would include transfer programs like Social Security and Medicare. Implicit liabilities are not included in debt statistics typically, nor are they included in the calculation of the debt–GDP ratio.

19. **Answer c.** The demographic issues of the retirement of the baby boom generation will only worsen as this group reaches retirement age and begins drawing on Social Security and Medicare. In addition to these demographic issues related to an aging population, we also need to recognize that health care costs rise faster than other costs in wealthy economies: this will place additional financial pressures on the cost of Medicare and Medicaid. Social Security and Medicare are funded by dedicated taxes: when the taxes generated exceed the level of spending, the excess funds are set aside in trust funds. These funds may then be borrowed by other parts of the government: this borrowing creates an implicit liability where the borrowing by one part of the government reflects a responsibility to repay these dollars back to the trust funds where they originated. Often the focus is just on the United States debt owed to the public; such a focus understates the true nature of the government debt, since it does not include the implicit liabilities that represent borrowing within the government. Including both public debt and the United States government debt held by trust funds gives a full accounting of the level of debt the government faces.

20. **Answer a.** A change in government spending is an example of fiscal policy. An increase in government spending, holding everything else constant, will stimulate the economy in the short-run while a decrease in government spending, holding everything else constant, will contract the economy in the short-run.

21. **Answer c.** State and local governments rely on revenue that comes from sales taxes, property taxes, income taxes, and various fees.

22. **Answer e.** Government transfers are payments that the government makes to households even though the government has not received a good or a service from the household. These transfer payments effectively redistribute purchasing power in the economy: the household receiving the transfer payment can now command more goods and services than they could before the transfer.

23. **Answer d.** This is just a definitional question. See the text for a description of these programs. For example, social insurance programs include Social Security, Medicare, and Medicaid.

24. **Answer b.** When the government increases the amount of taxes it collects from households, this reduces disposable income and leads households to reduce their level of consumption spending. This decrease in consumption spending leads to further reductions in spending in the economy due to the multiplier effect: the *AD* curve shifts to the left. Answers (a), (c), and (d) would all shift the *AD* curve to the right.

25. **Answer c.** If the economy is currently operating with an inflationary gap, that implies that the level of actual output in this economy is greater than potential output. To return the economy to its potential output level, the government will need to shift the *AD* curve to the left. Only answer (c) causes a leftward shift in *AD*; the other answers all cause the *AD* curve to shift to the right.

26. **Answer e.** Argentina's reduction in government spending and increase in taxes in the period 1997–2001 were designed to contract the economy as was the Lyndon Johnson surcharge on income taxes enacted in 1968. This was a temporary increase of 10% on income taxes designed to reduce consumer spending and thereby contract the economy. Answers (a) and (b) are both examples of expansionary fiscal policy; in each example, the policy was enacted with the hope that it would spur greater spending and hence higher levels of aggregate output.

27. **Answer b.** Discretionary fiscal policy is difficult to use due to significant time lags: there is the lag in recognizing that there is an economic problem, there is a legislative lag, and there is an implementation lag. These lags result in a situation where the discretionary fiscal policy may not actually be felt in an economy until after the recessionary gap is eliminated; in this case, the discretionary fiscal policy may cause economic fluctuations to be greater than they would have been absent the discretionary fiscal policy.

28. **Answer c.** With an upward-sloping aggregate supply curve, an increase in government spending will cause the *AD* curve to shift to the right (as the planned aggregate expenditure line shifts up) while causing a movement along the short-run aggregate supply curve. In the short run the level of real GDP will increase in this economy but by an amount less than that predicted by the multiplier, while the aggregate price level increases.

29. **Answer a.** The multiplier effect for a change in government spending is greater than the multiplier effect for a change in taxes: the government will stimulate the economy more if it increases government spending.

30. **Answer g.** Unemployed people tend to be less wealthy than people who own stocks: this leads them to spend more of their disposable income. Since unemployed people tend to have a higher *MPC* than people who own stocks, this leads to a larger multiplier effect on the level of aggregate output from an increase in unemployment benefits than from a decrease in taxes on profits. The effect of automatic stabilizers is to reduce economic fluctuations. For example, when income increases, this causes tax revenue to increase automatically, and this increase in tax revenue results in the increase in aggregate output being less than it would have been had there been no taxes. Thus, automatic stabilizers reduce the size of the multiplier.

31. Answer b. To find the budget balance, recall that this is the same as government saving, or $S_{Government}$, which can be written as $S_{Government} = T - G - TR$. In this example, the budget balance is therefore equal to −$170 billion. When the budget balance is negative, this indicates that the government is running a deficit since the sum of spending plus transfer payments exceed the value of tax revenue.

32. Answer b. The government should run a deficit during a recession: in a recession there is too little spending and the government can augment the level of spending by operating with a deficit during the recession. The government should run a surplus during an expansion: in an expansion there is the potential for too much spending and the government can moderate this tendency toward overspending by operating with a surplus during the expansion.

33. Answer d. All of the answers are correct. See the text for the discussion of how persistent deficit spending can place financial pressure on future budgets, crowd out investment spending due to government borrowing, and result in the need for higher taxes in order to pay the interest payments on the government debt

34. Answer c. [from Appendix] To find this answer we need to use the multiplier presented in the appendix: $1/[1 - MPC(1 - t)]$. In this example this multiplier equals 1.82, so the $10 billion increase in government spending leads to aggregate output increasing by (1.82)($10 billion), or $18.2 billion.

35. Answer e. [from Appendix] We know that the inclusion of a tax rate in our model, holding everything else constant, reduces the size of the multiplier. Using the formula for this multiplier, $1/[1 - MPC(1 - t)]$, and substituting in the given information, we find that answer (b) is correct. Answer (c) is a simple, and an accurate, mathematical computation and also a correct answer.

chapter **14(29)**

Money, Banking, and the Federal Reserve System

■ BEFORE YOU READ THE CHAPTER

Summary

This chapter explores the topic of money. It considers the role of money and different forms of money in an economy, the impact of private banks and the Federal Reserve on the money supply, and the use of open-market operations by the Federal Reserve to change the monetary base.

Chapter Objectives

Objective #1.   Money is an asset that can easily be used to make purchases of goods and services. Money includes cash, which is liquid, plus other assets that are highly liquid.

- Currency in circulation consists of cash in the hands of the public. Checkable bank deposits are bank accounts that provide check-writing privileges to the owners of these accounts.

- The money supply is the total value of financial assets in the economy that are considered money. There are multiple definitions of the money supply based on the degree of liquidity of the assets included in the particular measure of the money supply.

- Debit cards automatically transfer funds from the buyer's bank account, while credit cards access funds that can be borrowed by the user of the credit card. Debit cards allow the user to access part of the money supply while credit cards create a liability for the user and therefore are not part of the money supply.

Objective #2.   Money enhances gains from trade by making indirect exchange possible. In a barter economy, exchange can only occur when there is a double coincidence of wants: you must want the good or service I offer and I must want the good or service you offer. Money, by increasing gains from trade, increases welfare.

521

Objective #3.   Money acts as a medium of exchange, a store of value, and a unit of account.

- An asset that is used to make purchases of goods and services serves as a medium of exchange. Over time many different kinds of assets have served in this role.

- Money acts as a store of value due to its ability to maintain its purchasing power over time, provided there is little inflation.

- Money is a measure people use to set prices and make economic calculations. We refer to this role for money as the unit of account.

Objective #4.   The types of money fall into three broad categories.

- Commodity money refers to the use of an asset as a medium of exchange that has useful value independent of its role as a medium of exchange.

- Commodity-backed money refers to items used as medium of exchange that have no intrinsic value (for example, paper currency) but whose ultimate value rests on the promise that they could be exchanged for valuable goods.

- Fiat money refers to money whose value derives strictly from the government's decree that it be accepted as a means of payment.

Objective #5.   The Federal Reserve (the Fed) provides two measures of the money supply. These monetary aggregates—M1 and M2—measure the money supply using different definitions. M1 defines money most narrowly as the sum of currency in circulation, travelers' checks, and checkable bank deposits. M2 is comprised of M1 plus other near-monies, which are financial assets that are easily converted into cash or checkable bank deposits. M1 measures the money supply from a liquidity perspective: all items included in M1 are highly liquid. M2 includes the liquid assets of M1 as well as a group of less liquid assets.

Objective #6.   A T-account is a type of financial spreadsheet that displays an institution's financial position. On the left-hand side of the T-account, the institution's assets and their value are listed; on the right-hand side of the T-account, the institution's liabilities and their values are listed. Banks hold reserves in order to meet the demand for funds from their depositors. Bank reserves are composed of the currency in the banks' vaults and the bank deposits held by the Fed in each bank's own account. The reserve ratio is the fraction of bank deposits a bank holds as reserves: in the United States the reserve ratio is regulated by the Fed.

Objective #7.   Banks receive deposits of funds from their customers and then use these funds to make interest-earning financial transactions. For example, banks make loans to customers and purchase Treasury bills: both financial transactions provide income in the form of interest to the bank.

Objective #8.   Bank runs occur when many depositors at a bank, fearing a bank failure, simultaneously decide to withdraw their funds. Banks can find themselves in a situation where they lack the liquidity to satisfy these depositor demands since many of the deposited funds are used to finance relatively illiquid bank loans.

Objective #9.   Bank regulation reduces the probability of bank runs.

- The Federal Deposit Insurance Corporation (FDIC) provides deposit insurance, a guarantee by the federal government that depositors will be paid up to a designated maximum amount per account (currently $250,000 per depositor at any given bank) even if the bank fails. When there is deposit insurance depositors have no incentive to remove their funds from a bank, even if there are rumors that the bank is in financial trouble.

- The existence of deposit insurance creates an incentive problem: banks, knowing they are insured, are apt to engage in overly risky behavior while depositors, knowing they are insured, are inclined to not monitor bank behavior. Capital requirements address this incentive problem by requiring owners of banks to hold more assets than the value of their bank deposits. Should some loans prove bad, the bank will still have assets larger than their deposits: the bank owners, rather than the government, can absorb the loss from the bad loans.

- Bank runs are also prevented by requiring banks to hold a higher reserve ratio than the banks would otherwise choose to hold.

- Banks that are in financial trouble can borrow money from the Fed through an arrangement referred to as the discount window. This enables banks to get funds instead of being forced to sell their assets at prices below their value when confronted by a sudden demand for funds from depositors.

Objective #10. Banks affect the money supply in two ways. First, they remove some money out of circulation by holding currency in their bank vaults and in their reserve accounts at the Fed. Second, banks create money when they accept deposits and make loans.

Objective #11. Excess reserves are those reserves held by a bank that exceed the level of reserves required by the Fed.

- In a simplified model, where banks lend out all their excess reserves and borrowers hold their loans as bank deposits and not currency, the increase in bank deposits from lending out the excess reserves equals the excess reserves divided by the required reserve ratio. We can write this money multiplier as $1/rr$, where rr is the required reserve ratio.

- In the real world, the money multiplier is smaller than the money multiplier in our simplified model. The monetary base equals the sum of currency in circulation and reserves held by the bank. The monetary base is controlled by the monetary authorities. The money supply equals currency in circulation plus bank deposits. The money multiplier is the ratio of the money supply to the monetary base. The actual money multiplier is smaller than our simple model predicted because a dollar of currency in circulation, unlike a dollar in reserves, does not support multiple dollars of the money supply.

Objective #12. Central banks oversee and regulate the banking system and they control the monetary base. In the United States the central bank is the Federal Reserve. The Federal Reserve consists of a Board of Governors and 12 regional Federal Reserve Banks. The Board of Governors has seven members including the Chairman of the Federal Reserve.

- The Federal Reserve Bank of New York carries out open-market operations in which the Fed buys or sells some of the existing stock of U.S. Treasury bills.

- Monetary policy decisions are made by the Federal Open Market Committee (FOMC), whose members include the Board of Governors and five of the regional bank presidents. The president of the Federal Reserve Bank of New York is always a member of the FOMC while the other 11 presidents rotate on and off the FOMC.

- The Fed's organizational structure creates an organization that is accountable to the voting public while simultaneously insulated from short-term political pressures.

Objective #13. The Fed possesses three monetary policy tools: the reserve requirement, the discount rate, and open-market operations.

- The reserve requirement sets the minimum level of reserves each bank must hold. Penalties are assessed on banks that fail to meet the required reserve ratio on average over a two-week period. The Fed seldom changes the required reserve ratio.

- The discount rate is the interest rate banks must pay the Fed if they borrow additional reserves from the Fed. Banks that are in need of additional reserves usually borrow these reserves from other banks in the federal funds market. The federal funds market interest rate, the federal funds rate, is determined by supply and demand. The Fed typically sets the discount rate above the federal funds rate to discourage bank borrowing from the Fed. Normally the discount rate is set one percentage point above the federal funds rate, but starting in the fall of 2007 the Fed, in response to the financial crisis, reduced the spread between the discount rate and the federal funds rate.

- Open-market operations are the Fed's most important monetary policy tool. The Fed possesses both assets and liabilities: its liabilities consist of bank reserves, both deposited at the Fed and in bank vaults, and currency in circulation. In other words, the Fed's liabilities are equal to the monetary base.

  - When the FOMC directs the Federal Reserve Bank of New York to purchase Treasury bills, it effectively increases the amount of reserves in the banking system by crediting the commercial banks that sell the Treasury bills with additional reserves. These additional reserves start the money multiplier process, which leads these additional reserves to support a higher level of bank deposits. The money supply increases.

  - When the FOMC directs the Federal Reserve Bank of New York to sell Treasury bills, it effectively decreases the amount of reserves in the banking system: commercial banks that purchase these Treasury bills pay for them when the Fed debits their reserve accounts at the Fed. This reduction in reserves starts the money multiplier process, which results in these reduced reserves supporting a lower level of bank deposits. The money supply decreases.

  - The Fed can create the funds it needs to purchase Treasury bills. Thus, the Fed can create monetary base at its own discretion. In addition, the Fed earns interest from the Treasury bills its holds: this interest is returned to the Treasury and provides a source of revenue to the Treasury.

Objective #14. There are many different central banks in the world today. The European Central Bank is the central bank for the members of the European Union. Like the Federal Reserve its organization is answerable to voters while protected from short-term political pressures.

Objective #15. Financial crises over the course of U.S. history have resulted in legislation as well as awareness of policy issues with regard to financial markets and institutions.

- After the financial crisis of 1907, legislation was passed creating the Federal Reserve. The Fed was given responsibility for centralizing the holding of reserves, inspecting banks, and providing a sufficiently elastic money supply in response to changing economic conditions.

- During the Great Depression in the early 1930s, bank runs were a problem and legislation was passed creating federal deposit insurance to help eliminate these bank runs. In addition, during this time period the federal government recapitalized banks by lending to them and purchasing shares of banks. In 1933, banks were separated into two classes of banks: commercial banks and investment banks.

- In the 1980s, the S&L Crisis revealed tendencies for banking institutions to engage in overly speculative transactions and pointed out the need not only for federal deposit insurance, but also regulation with regard to capital requirements and reserve requirements.

- In the 1990s, some firms—using huge amounts of leverage—speculated in global markets, and this speculation led to financial crises in Asia and Russia. During this crises there were particular problems associated with deleveraging where large firms (in particular LTCM) sold their assets to cover their losses and this selling of assets created balance sheet problems for other firms around the world. These problems led to the failure of various credit markets and required intervention by the New York Fed to get these world credit markets functioning.

- In the mid-2000s, the housing bubble in the United States—accompanied by the securitization of subprime lending—led to massive losses by banks and other nonbank financial institutions once the housing bubble burst. This financial crisis required intervention by the U.S. government to expand its lending to bank and nonbank institutions as well as the provision of bank capital through government purchase of bank shares. By 2008, it was clear that this latest financial crisis would result in the creation of a wider safety net and broader regulation of the financial sector.

Key Terms

Notes

money any asset that can easily be used to purchase goods and services.

currency in circulation actual cash held by the public.

checkable bank deposits *bank* accounts on which people can write checks.

money supply the total value of *financial assets* in the *economy* that are considered *money*.

medium of exchange an asset that individuals acquire for the purpose of trading for goods and services rather than for their own consumption.

store of value an asset that is a means of holding purchasing power over time.

unit of account a measure used to set prices and make economic calculations.

commodity money a *medium of exchange* that is a good, normally gold or silver, that has intrinsic value in other uses.

commodity-backed money a *medium of exchange* that has no intrinsic value whose ultimate value is guaranteed by a promise that it can be converted into valuable goods on demand.

fiat money a *medium of exchange* whose value derives entirely from its official status as a means of payment.

monetary aggregate an overall measure of the *money supply*. The most common monetary aggregates in the United States are M1, which includes *currency in circulation*, travelers' checks, and *checkable bank deposits*, and M2, which includes M1 as well as *near-monies*.

near-money a *financial asset* that cannot be directly used as a *medium of exchange* but can be readily converted into cash or *checkable bank deposits*.

Key Terms *(continued)*

bank reserves currency held by *banks* in their vaults plus their deposits at the Federal Reserve.

T-account a simple tool that summarizes a business's financial position by showing, in a single table, the business's assets and liabilities, with assets on the left and liabilities on the right.

reserve ratio the fraction of *bank deposits* that a *bank* holds as reserves. In the United States, the minimum required reserve ratio is set by the Federal Reserve.

bank run a phenomenon in which many of a *bank*'s depositors try to withdraw their funds due to fears of a bank failure.

deposit insurance a guarantee that a *bank*'s depositors will be paid even if the bank can't come up with the funds, up to a maximum amount per account.

reserve requirements rules set by the Federal Reserve that set the minimum *reserve ratio* for banks. For *checkable bank deposits* in the United States, the minimum reserve ratio is set at 10%.

discount window a protection against *bank runs* in which the Federal Reserve stands ready to lend money to *banks* in trouble.

excess reserves a *bank*'s *reserves* over and above the reserves required by law or regulation.

monetary base the sum of *currency in circulation* and *bank reserves*.

money multiplier the ratio of the *money supply* to the *monetary base*.

central bank an institution that oversees and regulates the banking system and controls the *monetary base*.

federal funds market the *financial market* that allows *banks* that fall short of *reserve requirements* to borrow funds from banks with *excess reserves*.

federal funds rate the *interest rate* at which funds are borrowed and lent in the *federal funds market*.

discount rate the rate of interest the Federal Reserve charges on loans to *banks* that fall short of *reserve requirements*.

open-market operation a purchase or sale of U.S. Treasury bills by the Federal Reserve, normally through a transaction with a *commercial bank*.

commercial bank a *bank* that accepts deposits and is covered by *deposit insurance*.

investment bank a *bank* that trades in *financial assets* and is not covered by *deposit insurance*.

Key Terms *(continued)*

savings and loans (thrifts) deposit-taking *banks,* usually specialized in issuing home loans.

leverage the degree to which a financial institution is financing its investments with borrowed funds.

balance sheet effects the reduction in a firm's net worth from falling asset prices.

vicious cycle of deleveraging the sequence of events that takes place when a *firm's* asset sales to cover losses produce negative *balance sheet effects* on other firms and force creditors to call in their *loans,* forcing sales of more assets and causing further declines in asset prices.

subprime lending lending to home buyers who don't meet the usual criteria for borrowing.

securitization the pooling of loans and mortgages made by a financial institution and the sale of shares in such a pool to other investors.

▐ AFTER YOU READ THE CHAPTER

Tips

Tip #1.   It is important to understand the definition and the distinction between the monetary base, the money supply, and reserves. The money supply is the value of financial assets in the economy that are considered money: this would include cash in the hands of the public, checkable bank deposits, and traveler's checks, using the narrow definition of the money supply given by the monetary aggregate M1. Bank reserves are composed of the currency banks hold in their vaults plus their deposits at the Federal Reserve. The monetary base is the sum of currency in circulation and bank reserves. The monetary base is not equal to the money supply: the money supply is larger than the monetary base.

Tip #2.   It is important to understand the distinction between assets and liabilities. Make sure you clearly understand what an asset and a liability are and then recognize that any financial instrument represents both an asset and a liability. For example, a mortgage represents a liability for the borrower and an asset for the lender; a checking account deposit represents a liability for the bank providing the check service and an asset to the individual depositing the funds.

Tip #3.   For any T-account, clearly identify whose perspective is represented in the T-account. T-accounts represent the assets and liabilities of an institution or an individual. When making a T-account, consider whose T-account it represents: this will help you more clearly identify whether the financial instruments you include are assets or liabilities. For example, bank reserves are a liability in the Fed's T-account and an asset in a bank's T-account.

Tip #4. Each T-account must always balance: that is, total assets must equal total liabilities where total liabilities include capital. If your T-account does not balance, check your entries to find your error.

Tip #5. Remember that when the Fed purchases Treasury bills it injects reserves into the banking system and this increases the money supply. When the Fed sells Treasury bills, it removes reserves from the banking system and this decreases the money supply.

WORKED PROBLEMS

1. Your professor instructs you to create a T-account of your financial situation. In this T-account, you should list your assets and your liabilities and then you should compute your net worth. Your professor explains that net worth is simply total assets minus total liabilities. Your professor also instructs you to interview someone who is at least 20 years older than you are and create a T-account that lists this person's assets, liabilities, and net worth. How might your T-account differ from the T-account of this older person? Why do you anticipate this difference?

STEP 1: Review the definition of a T-account as well as the definitions of assets, liabilities, and net worth. Create a T-account form that you will be able to use both for yourself and when you interview the other person.

Review the section "The Monetary Role of Banks" on page 418 (Econ page 850) and Figure 14-2 on page 418 (Econ page 850).

A T-account provides a summary of the financial position of an individual or firm. On the left side, assets are listed: these are all the items that the individual or firm owns that are valuable. The value of these assets is listed along with the name of the asset. On the right side, liabilities are listed: these are all the items that the individual or firm owes. The value of these liabilities is listed along with the name of the liability. Net worth, the difference between assets and liabilities, is listed on the right side of the T-account: the sum of the value of total liabilities and net worth always equals the value of total assets.

Here is a T-account form that you can use when constructing your own T-account or the T-account of the individual you have chosen to interview.

Assets	Liabilities
	Net worth
Value of total assets	Value of total liabilities + net worth

STEP 2: Make a list of all of those items, both physical and financial, that you own that are valuable. Make a list of all of those items, both physical and financial, that you owe to others or that represent a debt.

Review the section "The Monetary Role of Banks" on page 418 (Econ page 850) and Figure 14-2 on page 418 (Econ page 850).

Enter the items that you own on the left side of your T-account along with their value. Sum the values together to get the value of total assets.

Enter the items that you owe or the debt that you have on the right-hand side of your T-account along with their value. Sum the values together to get the value of total liabilities.

Now compare the value of your total assets to the value of your total liabilities to get a measure of your net worth. It is possible that you have a negative net worth: if you have not had a chance to work full-time and you have taken out student loans, your liabilities may well exceed your assets.

Here is an example of a possible T-account for a mythical student, Joe. Joe is 20 years old and is a full-time student. He owns a car that is worth $2,000, he has $500 in a checking account, and he has student loans equal to $10,000. This is his T-account:

Assets		Liabilities	
Car	$2,000	Student loan	$10,000
Checking account	$500		
		Net worth	−$7,500
Total value of assets	$2,500	Total liabilities + net worth	$2,500

STEP 3: **Find a person to interview who will be comfortable discussing his or her financial position.**

Review the section "The Monetary Role of Banks" on page 418 (Econ page 850) and Figure 14-2 on page 418 (Econ page 850).

Make a list of the person's assets and liabilities and the dollar value of each item. Construct the person's T-account and calculate his or her net worth.

Answers in Step 3 will vary for each person since each person's financial situation is unique to him or her.

STEP 4: **Compare and contrast the two T-accounts.**

Review the section "The Monetary Role of Banks" on page 418 (Econ page 850) and Figure 14-2 on page 418 (Econ page 850).

It is likely that the older individual has a positive and greater net worth than does the student. This is due to the fact that older people have had more time to accumulate assets, have likely saved for retirement, have had a full-time job for a longer period of time than the student, and have likely had time to pay off some of their debt, particularly educational debt.

2.   Suppose that there is only one bank, First National Bank, in your economy. First National Bank maintains its required reserves but never holds excess reserves. The required reserve ratio in this economy is 10% of checkable deposits. Furthermore, suppose that everyone in this community banks at this bank and that all of their transactions are made using checks or their debit cards. No one carries currency in this economy. The following tables provide the initial T-accounts of the central bank of this economy as well as of First National Bank. Suppose that the central bank in this economy purchases $50,000 worth of Treasury bills from First National Bank. How will this affect the money supply in this economy? Make sure you indicate what the initial money supply is before the central bank makes this purchase and what the final money supply is once all adjustments to this purchase have occurred. What is the value of the money multiplier in this economy? For this example, assume that the difference between First National Bank's assets and its liabilities stays constant.

Initial situation at the central bank:

Assets		Liabilities	
Treasury bills	$20,000	Reserves of First National Bank	$20,000

Initial situation at First National Bank:

Assets		Liabilities	
Reserves at the central bank	$20,000	Checkable deposits	$200,000
Treasury bills and other loans	$180,000		

STEP 1: Start by thinking about how the T-accounts for the central bank and First National Bank will change when the central bank purchases $50,000 worth of Treasury bills. Do not try to analyze more than just the initial change in the T-accounts.

Review the section "The Monetary Role of Banks" on page 418 (Econ page 850), the section "Open-Market Operations" on page 429 (Econ page 861), and Figure 14-8 on page 430 (Econ page 862).

When the central bank purchases Treasury bills, its assets will increase. But the central bank must pay for these new assets, and the simplest way to do this is for the central bank to simply credit the reserve account of First National Bank with the value of the purchase. The central bank's T-account looks like the following:

Assets		Liabilities	
Treasury bills	$70,000	Reserves of First National Bank	$70,000

Notice that the central bank's purchase of Treasury bills alters both the asset and the liability entries for its T-account.

First National Bank's T-account is also altered by this transaction. First National Bank has $50,000 less in Treasury bills but $50,000 more in its reserve account. The T-account for First National bank follows.

Assets		Liabilities	
Reserves at the central bank	$70,000	Checkable deposits	$200,000
Treasury bills and other loans	$130,000		

Notice that First National Bank now has excess reserves. First National Bank has $70,000 in reserves, but it needs only $20,000 to meet its required reserve. First National Bank will want to lend out these excess reserves in order to earn interest.

STEP 2: Calculate the level of checkable deposits that First National Bank can support if it holds $70,000 in reserves. Once you have calculated this, provide a new T-account showing First National Bank's financial position once all adjustments to the central bank's purchase have occurred.

Review the section "The Monetary Role of Banks" on page 418 (Econ page 850), the section "Open-Market Operations" on page 429 (Econ page 861), and Figure 14-8 on page 430 (Econ page 862).

A simple way to think about this is to realize that required reserves equal the product of the required reserve ratio and the level of checkable deposits. In this example, you know the level of reserves and the required reserve ratio, but you do not know the level of checkable deposits. Thus, $70,000 = (0.10)(checkable deposits), or checkable deposits equal $700,000.

Assets		Liabilities	
Reserves at the central bank	$70,000	Checkable deposits	$700,000
Treasury bills and other loans	$630,000		

STEP 3: Compare the level of the initial money supply to the level of the money supply after all adjustments to the central bank's purchase of $50,000 in Treasury bills have occurred.

Review the section "The Monetary Role of Banks" on page 418 (Econ page 850), the section "Open-Market Operations" on page 429 (Econ page 861), and Figure 14-8 on page 430 (Econ page 862).

The money supply is defined as currency in circulation plus checkable deposits. In this example, there is no currency in circulation since all transactions are made with checks or with debit cards. The money supply initially is $200,000, and the money supply after the full adjustment to the central bank's purchase is $700,000. The money supply increases by $500,000.

STEP 4: Calculate the value of the money multiplier in this example.

Review the section "The Monetary Role of Banks" on page 418 (Econ page 850), the section "Open-Market Operations" on page 429 (Econ page 861), and Figure 14-8 on page 430 (Econ page 862).

The money multiplier is equal to [1/(required reserve ratio)], or in this example, 1/0.1, which is equal to 10. In this example, the central bank increased the amount of reserves in the banking system by $50,000 when it purchased the Treasury bills. This led to the money supply increasing by $500,000: the change in the money supply equals the product of the money multiplier and the change in reserves. That is, $500,000 = (10)($50,000).

3.   The government's provision of deposit insurance for checkable deposits is often cited as an example of government intervention that helps stabilize the financial system by eliminating or at least vastly reducing the probability of bank runs. Is there any incentive problem associated with the provision of deposit insurance? Discuss how deposit insurance reduces the risk of bank runs but creates a different kind of problem. How does regulation address the incentive problem created by deposit insurance?

STEP 1: Discuss what a bank run is and why provision of deposit insurance by the government eliminates bank runs.

Review the section "The Problem of Bank Runs" on page 419 (Econ page 851) and the section "Bank Regulation" on page 420 (Econ page 862).

A bank run is when bank depositors try to withdraw their funds due to fears that the bank may fail. If a sufficient number of depositors seek their funds, the bank will fail since the bank will not have adequate funds on hand to meet all of these demands. In addition, the failure of one bank may lead to other banks failing as depositors at these other banks lose faith in their own bank's solvency.

When the government provides deposit insurance this means that even if the bank fails, the depositor will not lose his or her deposit. Deposit insurance thus protects the banking system from bank runs.

STEP 2: Discuss the incentive problem that is created by banks once deposit insurance is in effect. In your answer, provide one method used by regulators to deal with this incentive problem.

Review the section "The Problem of Bank Runs" on page 419 (Econ page 851) and the section "Bank Regulation" on page 420 (Econ page 862).

Deposit insurance creates an incentive problem, since once people's deposits are insured, they have little incentive to actually monitor what their bank does. Banks will often take riskier positions than would be considered optimal from the perspective of the taxpayers who will have to cover the deposits should the bank fail. One way to reduce this incentive problem is to require banks to provide a minimum level of capital that provides a buffer against bad loans.

4.   The Federal Reserve has three monetary policy tools: the required reserve ratio, the discount rate, and open-market operations. Briefly describe each of these tools and then comment on each tool's usefulness in controlling the money supply in the economy.

STEP 1: Review what the required reserve ratio is and how it can affect the money supply. Then explain why the Federal Reserve does not rely on this monetary policy tool to change the money supply.

Review the section "What the Fed Does: Reserve Requirements and the Discount Rate" on page 428 (Econ page 860) and the section "Open-Market Operations" on page 429 (Econ page 861).

The required reserve ratio refers to the percentage of checkable deposits that a bank must hold in its reserve account. The higher the required reserve ratio, the smaller will be the money multiplier. If the Federal Reserve wanted to alter the money supply using the required reserve ratio, it could either raise this ratio to reduce the money supply or lower this ratio to increase the money supply. However, changing the required reserve ratio is administratively costly to banks because they must adjust their balance sheets to meet the new required reserve levels. The Federal Reserve rarely changes the required reserve ratio.

STEP 2: Review what the discount rate is and how it can affect the money supply. Then explain why the Federal Reserve does not rely on this monetary policy tool to change the money supply.

Review the section "What the Fed Does: Reserve Requirements and the Discount Rate" on page 428 (Econ page 860) and the section "Open-Market Operations" on page 429 (Econ page 861).

The discount rate refers to the interest rate that the Federal Reserve charges banks that borrow funds from the Federal Reserve. Typically the Federal Reserve sets the discount rate above the federal funds rate: banks will find it cheaper to borrow funds from other banks than to borrow funds from the Federal Reserve at the discount window. If the Federal Reserve wanted to change the money supply via the discount rate, it could lower the spread between the discount rate and the federal funds rate: this would effectively reduce the cost of being short on reserves, and banks would therefore increase their borrowing. This action by banks to the reduced spread will cause the money supply to increase. In contrast, an increase in the spread between the discount rate and the federal funds rate will cause the money supply to decrease. The Federal Reserve does not try to manage the level of the money supply via the discount rate, however, because this method is not very flexible, nor is it easy to fine-tune this method to ensure that the appropriate level of the money supply is achieved.

STEP 3: **Review what open-market operations are and how they can affect the money supply. Then explain why the Federal Reserve relies on this monetary policy tool to change the money supply.**

Review the section "What the Fed Does: Reserve Requirements and the Discount Rate" on page 428 (Econ page 860) and the section "Open-Market Operations" on page 429 (Econ page 861).

Open-market operations refer to the buying and selling of Treasury bills by the Federal Reserve in the open market. This is the Federal Reserve's primary monetary policy tool because it is flexible, can easily be fine-tuned to get precisely the effect the Federal Reserve desires, and can be implemented at relatively low administrative cost. When the Federal Reserve purchases Treasury bills it injects new reserves into the financial system, and via the money multiplier process these new reserves lead to a higher level of the money supply. When the Federal Reserve sells Treasury bills it removes reserves from the financial system, and via the money multiplier process this reduction in reserves leads to an even greater reduction in the money supply.

Problems and Exercises

1. Consider the following three lists of assets.

List A	List B	List C
$50 in cash	A car	A boat
A six-month CD worth $50,000, redeemable without penalty six months from today's date	A checking account deposit	The coins you collect in a jar
A share of stock	A Treasury bond issued by the government of the United States	A savings account deposit
A savings account deposit		

a. Rank each of these lists of assets from the most liquid asset to the least liquid asset.

b. For each list, identify any item that is included in M1.

c. For each list, identify any item that is included in M2.

d. Why is money *not* equivalent to wealth?

2.   Suppose Fantasia has a single bank that initially has $10,000 of deposits, reserves of $2,000, and loans of $8,000. To simplify our example, we will assume that bank capital equals zero. Furthermore, Fantasia's central bank has a required reserve of 10% of deposits. All monetary transactions are made by check: no one in Fantasia uses currency.

a. Construct a T-account depicting the initial situation in Fantasia. In your T-account, make sure you differentiate between required and excess reserves and that your T-account's assets equal its liabilities.

b. Explain how you calculated the level of excess reserves in Fantasia.

c. Suppose the bank in Fantasia lends these excess reserves [the amount of excess reserves you calculated in part (b)] until it reaches the point where its excess reserves equal zero. How does this change the T-account?

d. Did the money supply in Fantasia change when the bank loaned out the excess reserves? Explain your answer.

e. What is the value of the money multiplier in Fantasia? Using the money multiplier, compute the change in deposits.

3. You are provided the following T-accounts for the central bank of Economia and the only commercial bank in Economia. In Economia, all financial transactions occur within the banking system: no one holds currency. The required reserve ratio imposed by the central bank is 20% of deposits.

Central bank of Economia

Assets		Liabilities	
Treasury bills	$20,000	Reserves	$20,000
Total assets	$20,000	Total liabilities	$20,000

Commercial bank of Economia

Assets		Liabilities	
Required reserves	$20,000	Deposits	$100,000
		Capital	$20,000
Loans	$70,000		
Treasury bills	$30,000		
Total assets	$120,000	Total liabilities and capital	$120,000

Suppose the central bank in Economia purchases $2,000 of Treasury bills from the commercial bank.

a. Provide a T-account for both the central bank and the commercial bank showing the immediate effect of this transaction. Be sure to differentiate between required and excess reserves for the commercial bank.

b. Provide a T-account for the commercial bank once the commercial bank lends out its excess reserves and all adjustments have been made through the money multiplier process.

c. What happens to the money supply when the central bank purchases $2,000 of Treasury bills from the commercial bank?

d. Relate the change in the money supply to the money multiplier.

e. What was the monetary base initially?

f. What is the monetary base after all adjustments to the central bank's monetary policy have taken effect?

4. The following T-accounts are for the central bank of Macropedia and its sole commercial bank. In Macropedia, citizens always hold $1,000 in currency and the reserve requirement equals 10%. The commercial bank adheres to a strict policy of always lending out its excess reserves.

Central bank of Macropedia			
Assets		**Liabilities**	
Treasury bills	$11,000	Reserves	$10,000
		Currency in circulation	$1,000
Total assets	$11,000	Total liabilities	$11,000

Commercial bank of Macropedia			
Assets		**Liabilities**	
Reserves	$10,000	Deposits	$100,000
Loans	$80,000	Capital	$0
Treasury bills	$10,000		
Total assets	$100,000	Total liabilities and capital	$100,000

a. Does the commercial bank initially satisfy the required reserve? Explain your answer.

Suppose the central bank sells $5,000 in Treasury bills to the commercial bank.

b. Provide T-accounts for both the central bank and the commercial bank showing the immediate effect of this transaction.

c. Given your answer in part (b), describe the commercial bank's problem. Be specific in your answer and identify what options the commercial bank has for resolving its problem.

d. Provide a T-account for the commercial bank after it fully adjusts to the central bank's selling of $5,000 in Treasury bills.

e. What happens to the monetary base in this problem?

f. What happens to the money supply?

5. Use the following information about Macroland to answer this question.

Bank deposits at the central bank	$100 million
Currency in bank vaults	$ 50 million
Currency held by the public	75 million
Checkable deposits	600 million
Traveler's checks	5 million

a. What are bank reserves equal to in Macroland?

b. Suppose banks hold no excess reserves in Macroland. What is the required reserve ratio given the information in this table?

c. If the public does not change its currency holdings, what will happen to the level of checkable deposits in Macroland, relative to their initial level, if the central bank of Macroland purchases $10 million worth of Treasury bills in the open market? Explain your answer and provide a numerical answer.

d. If the public does not change its currency holdings, what will happen to the level of checkable deposits in Macroland, relative to their initial level, if the central bank of Macroland sells $5 million in Treasury bills in the open market? Explain your answer and provide a numerical answer.

6. Explain how the use of money increases the gains from trade.

7. For each of the following situations, determine what kind of money—commodity money, commodity-backed money, or fiat money—is being described.

    a. Prisoners of war use cigarettes as the monetary unit.

    b. When they babysit for other families, young families in Anytown receive paper coupons that can be redeemed for babysitting services. These coupons serve as a monetary unit for these transactions.

    c. Two tribes use corn as the monetary unit when trading with one another.

    d. In Midtown the central bank issues paper currency that is fully redeemable in gold or silver.

    e. In Uptown the central bank issues paper currency that the government of Uptown accepts as payment for taxes.

8. Currently in the United States the money supply is large enough that people on average hold over $3,000 in their wallets. Yet, clearly most individuals do not carry that large an amount of money in their wallets. Explain how the money supply could be so large and yet we do not on average hold this amount of dollars per person.

9. Bank deposit insurance provides insurance for depositors so that they do not have to worry about losing money they have deposited into insured banks. This seems like a really good protection to have. Is there a downside to this protection? Explain your answer fully.

10. How does a requirement that banks hold more assets than liabilities help to reduce the banks' tendency to engage in riskier investment behavior than is optimal from the government's point of view?

11. Financial panics have been a relatively common occurrence in U.S. history. Based upon the information provided in the text on financial crises, answer the following questions.

    a. During the panic of 1907, why did the failure of Knickerbocker Trust lead to bank runs among other trusts?

    b. As a result of the panic of 1907, the Federal Reserve Act was passed in 1913 creating the Federal Reserve. What did the legislature hope to accomplish with the creation of the Federal Reserve?

c. Why were there more bank runs during the Great Depression?

d. The text includes a discussion of the S&L Crisis of the 1980s and, in this discussion, the text mentions "new freedom did not bring with it increased oversight." Explain what the text meant by this statement and then explain how this statement helps us understand the S&L Crisis of the 1980s.

e. How was the financial crisis of 2007 similar to other financial crises experienced in the United States?

▌ BEFORE YOU TAKE THE TEST

Chapter Review Questions

1. Which of the following statements is true?
   a. The definition of money includes all forms of wealth.
   b. Money is an asset that can be easily used to purchase goods and services.
   c. Money consists of cash, which is liquid, plus other assets that are relatively illiquid.
   d. All of the above are true.
   e. Statements (a) and (b) are both true.
   f. Statements (b) and (c) are both true.

2. Credit cards
   a. are just another name for debit cards that allow users to access funds in their bank account.
   b. create an asset for users since the use of credit cards enables people to purchase goods and services.
   c. provide a means of borrowing funds, thus creating a liability, in order to make purchases of goods and services.
   d. Answers (a) and (b) are both correct.
   e. Answers (a) and (c) are both correct.

3. Money

    a. increases welfare since it increases gains from trade.

    b. eliminates the need for a "double coincidence of wants" between trading partners.

    c. includes currency in circulation plus checkable deposits.

    d. Answers (a), (b), and (c) are all correct.

    e. Answers (b) and (c) are both correct.

4. Use the following statements to answer the question.

    I. The price of bananas is quoted in dollars rather than in units of apples, and the price of apples is quoted in dollars rather than in units of bananas.

    II. The $100 Sue saved this year will have $100 worth of purchasing power five years from now, provided there is no inflation.

    III. The building contractor said the new roof for our house would cost $6,000.

Money has three roles in an economy. Statement _____ illustrates the use of money as a medium of exchange; statement _____ illustrates the use of money as a unit of account; and statement _____ illustrates the use of money as a store of value.

    a. III; I; II   c. III; II; I

    b. I; III; II   d. II; III; I

5. Which of the following statements is true?

    a. Fiat money is paper currency issued by the government and redeemable in a valuable asset like gold.

    b. Fiat money is money issued by a ruler and thus is found only in countries with a monarchy.

    c. Commodity money is poor type of money, since it cannot be used in trade even though it is a valuable commodity.

    d. None of these statements is true.

6. M1 includes currency in circulation,

    a. savings account deposits, and checkable bank deposits.

    b. travelers' checks, other near-monies, and checkable bank deposits.

    c. travelers' checks, and checkable bank deposits.

    d. travelers' checks, checkable bank deposits, and saving account deposits.

7. In a bank's T-account,

    a. Joe's checking account deposit is treated as an asset.

    b. Ellen's car loan is counted as a liability.

    c. bank deposits at the Fed are an asset for the bank.

    d. assets exactly equal liabilities when there are positive capital requirements.

Use the following T-account for a bank to answer the next three questions. T-bill refers to Treasury bills.

Assets		Liabilities	
Required reserves	$100	Deposits	$1,000
Loans	$400		
Treasury bills	$800		

8. Given this T-account and assuming the bank holds no excess reserves, what is the required reserve ratio?
   a. 10%   c. 80%
   b. 40%   d. 1%

9. Given this T-account, how much capital does this bank currently hold?
   a. zero
   b. $300
   c. $400
   d. $500
   e. $1,300

10. Suppose this is the only bank in the banking system. Furthermore, suppose all money is held in this bank and the bank holds no excess reserves. If the Fed makes an open-market sale of $50 worth of T-bills to this bank, what will happen to the money supply after all adjustments are made?
    a. The money supply will increase by $50.
    b. The money supply will decrease by $50.
    c. The money supply will increase by $500.
    d. The money supply will decrease by $500.

11. Bank runs
    a. can be reduced by providing deposit insurance, requiring banks to hold significant amounts of capital, and mandating required reserves.
    b. are often caused by rumor and the fear that other people will withdraw their funds.
    c. when rumored, may significantly impact the prices banks receive when they sell assets to increase their liquidity.
    d. Answers (a), (b), and (c) are all correct.

12. Banks affect the money supply
    a. when they take deposited currency out of circulation and deposit it into their bank vaults.
    b. when they lend their excess reserves to their customers.
    c. when a customer from one bank writes a check to a customer of another bank who deposits that check into his or her checking account.
    d. All of the above are true.
    e. Answers (a) and (b) are correct.

13. The monetary base consists of

    a. currency in circulation plus bank deposits.

    b. bank deposits plus bank reserves.

    c. bank deposits, bank reserves, and currency in circulation.

    d. currency in circulation plus bank reserves.

14. In a simple banking system, where banks hold no excess reserves and all funds are kept as bank deposits, then

    a. the money multiplier equals 1 divided by the required reserve ratio.

    b. total deposits will equal reserves multiplied by the reciprocal of the required reserve ratio.

    c. $1 increase in excess reserves will increase deposits by an amount equal to 1 divided by the required reserve ratio.

    d. Answers (a), (b), and (c) are all correct.

15. Holding everything else constant, in the simple banking model presented in the text, the greater the numeric value of the required reserve ratio the

    a. higher the discount rate the Federal Reserve Bank charges for loans from the Federal Reserve Bank.

    b. greater the money multiplier.

    c. smaller the money multiplier.

    d. Answers (a) and (b) are both correct.

    e. Answers (a) and (c) are both correct.

16. Suppose the required reserve ratio initially is 10% of bank deposits and is increased by the Fed to 20% of bank deposits. Holding everything else constant, this will

    a. reduce the size of the money multiplier.

    b. cause the banking system to contract the level of bank deposits in the banking system.

    c. change the value of the money multiplier from 10 to 5.

    d. Answers (a), (b), and (c) are all correct.

17. Which of the following statements is true?

    a. Americans increased their holdings of currency between 1929 and 1933.

    b. As Americans withdrew currency from the banking system between 1929 and 1933, this led to increases in bank deposits as banks lent funds to customers who lacked adequate funding.

    c. M1 fell sharply between 1929 and 1933, as the decline in currency holding by the public was much greater than the decline in bank deposits.

    d. All of the above are true.

    e. Statements (a) and (b) are both true.

    f. Statements (a) and (c) are both true.

18. Which of the following statements is true?

    I. Provided that no one knows that counterfeit dollars are being used, the use of these counterfeit dollars does not hurt anyone in an economy.

    II. The use of counterfeit dollars in an economy reduces the revenues available to pay for the operations of that economy's government.

    III. Counterfeit money is not an issue when the government uses fiat money and not commodity-backed money.

    a. Statement I is true.

    b. Statement II is true.

    c. Statement III is true.

    d. Statements I, II, and III are all true.

    e. Statements II and III are both true.

19. To be included in the measure of M1, the asset must be

    a. a near-money.

    b. highly liquid.

    c. money.

    d. either money or some other form of wealth.

20. Commodity-backed money

    a. restricts the use of fewer resources than does commodity money.

    b. is money that has no intrinsic value but whose value is guaranteed by a promise that the commodity-backed money can be converted into valuable goods on demand.

    c. is a way for society to provide the functions of money without tying up valuable resources.

    d. Answers (a), (b), and (c) are all correct.

21. Stocks and bonds are

    a. part of M1.

    b. part of M2, but not M1.

    c. not part of M1 or M2 because they are not sufficiently liquid.

22. Bank reserves include

    a. the currency banks hold in their vaults.

    b. bank deposits held at the Federal Reserve.

    c. outstanding loans that the bank has made to borrowers.

    d. the bank capital that the owners of the bank provide.

    e. Answers (a), (b), (c), and (d) are all correct.

    f. Answers (a) and (b) are both correct.

    g. Answers (a), (b), and (d) are correct.

23. Bank regulation is helpful in reducing bank runs since bank regulation typically

a. requires banks to keep a minimum required reserve ratio.

b. provides deposit insurance so that depositors have little incentive to remove their money from a bank even when there are rumors about the bank's soundness.

c. sets capital requirements to help align the incentive problem for banks so that they will have a lower tendency to engage in overly risky investment behavior.

d. Answers (a), (b), and (c) are all correct.

e. Answers (a) and (b) are both correct.

f. Answers (a) and (c) are both correct.

g. Answers (b) and (c) are both correct.

24. When banks find that they must borrow money, and they can only borrow from the Federal Reserve, this is referred to as using

a. open-market operations.

b. the discount window.

c. the FDIC.

d. the required reserve ratio.

25. Which of the following statements is true?

  I. Banks decrease the money supply because they remove some currency from circulation when they place currency in their bank vaults or deposit currency at the Federal Reserve.

  II. Banks increase the money supply when they accept deposits and then make loans with some of the money that has been deposited.

a. Statement I is true.   c. Statements I and II are true.

b. Statement II is true.   d. Neither statement I nor II is true.

26. The three primary policy tools available to the Federal Reserve include

a. reserve requirements, the ability to tax banks, and the discount rate.

b. reserve requirements, the discount rate, and open-market operations.

c. reserve requirements, the ability to tax banks, and open-market operations.

d. the ability to tax banks, the discount rate, and open-market operations.

27. When banks borrow from one another, the rate of interest they pay for this loan is called the

a. discount rate.

b. federal funds rate.

28. Suppose a hypothetical economy that uses a checkable-deposits-only monetary system has a required reserve ratio of 20%. When the central bank in this economy purchases $100 million worth of Treasury bills, this will increase the money supply by

a. 20%.

b. $100 million.

c. $500 million.

d. $5 million.

29. Suppose a hypothetical economy that uses a checkable-deposits-only monetary system has a required reserve ratio of 10%. When the central bank in this economy sells $10 million worth of Treasury bills, this will decrease the money supply by
   a. 10%.
   b. $10 million.
   c. $100 million.
   d. $1 million.

30. Which of the following statements is true?
   I. Regarding the United States and its economic history, the financial crisis of 2008 is an event that is unlike any other event in U.S. history.
   II. The U.S. economy is never subject to financial crisis.
   III. Financial crisis in a country usually results in legislation providing for greater financial regulation.
   a. Statement I is true.
   b. Statement II is true.
   c. Statement III is true.
   d. Statements I and II are true.

31. The financial crisis of 2008 can be characterized as a financial crisis with
   a. excessive speculation particularly in the housing market.
   b. a failure to regulate some of the involved institutions.
   c. inadequate intervention by the government when the crisis first appeared.
   d. excessive amounts of leverage in use by some of the involved firms.
   e. Answers (a), (b), (c), and (d) are all correct.

ANSWER KEY

Answers to Problems and Exercises

1. **a**. List A: $50 in cash, a savings account deposit, a share of stock, a six-month CD redeemable without penalty six months from today's date

    List B: The checking account deposit, a Treasury bond issued by the government of the United States, a car

    List C: The coins you collect in a jar, a savings account deposit, a boat

    b. In List A, the $50 in cash is included in M1; in List B, the checking account deposit is included in M1; and in List C, the coins in a jar are included in M1.

    c. M2 includes any item in M1 plus the savings account deposit (List A) and (List C), and the six-month CD (List A).

    d. Wealth includes all assets, physical or financial, that an individual owns at a particular point in time. Although these assets may be quite valuable, they may not all possess the characteristic of liquidity. Money possesses this characteristic, and thus includes only those items that can easily be used to purchase goods and services. In this question, the bonds, stock, car and boat are assets and therefore part of the owner's wealth, but they are not considered money.

2. **a.**

Assets		Liabilities	
Required reserves	$1,000	Deposits	$10,000
Excess reserves	$1,000		
Loans	$8,000		
Total assets	$10,000	Total liabilities	$10,000

    b. Excess reserves are equal to total reserves minus required reserves, or $1,000. To find required reserves, multiply deposits by the required reserve ratio [($10,000)(0.1) = $1,000].

    c.

Assets		Liabilities	
Required reserves	$2,000	Deposits	$20,000
Excess reserves	$0		
Loans	$18,000		
Total assets	$20,000	Total liabilities	$20,000

    d. Yes, since the money supply is defined as bank deposits plus currency in circulation. Since Fantasia has no currency in circulation, we need only consider what happens to bank deposits. Initially, bank deposits equaled $10,000 and after the lending out of all the excess reserves, bank deposits equal $20,000. Thus, the money supply increased by $10,000.

e. The money multiplier equals $1/rr$, or 10 in this example, since no one holds currency and the bank does not hold excess reserves. The change in deposits equals the money multiplier times the change in reserves or, in this case, the change in deposits equals $(1/0.1)(\$1,000)$ or $10,000$.

3. a.

Central bank of Economia			
Assets		**Liabilities**	
Treasury bills	$22,000	Reserves	$22,000
Total assets	$22,000	Total liabilities	$22,000

Commercial bank of Economia			
Assets		**Liabilities**	
Required reserves	$20,000	Deposits	$100,000
		Capital	$20,000
Excess reserves	$2,000		
Loans	$70,000		
Treasury bills	$28,000		
Total assets	$120,000	Total liabilities and capital	$120,000

b.

Commercial bank of Economia			
Assets		**Liabilities**	
Required reserves	$22,000	Deposits	$110,000
		Capital	$20,000
Loans	$80,000		
Treasury bills	$28,000		
Total assets	$130,000	Total liabilities and capital	$130,000

c. The money supply increases from $100,000 to $110,000. Recall that the money supply equals checkable deposits plus currency in circulation: since Economia has no currency in circulation, the money supply equals the level of deposits.

d. The change in the money supply equals the money multiplier times the change in the monetary base. In this problem, the money multiplier equals 5, and the change in the monetary base is the $2,000 increase in reserves that occurs when the central bank purchases the Treasury bills.

e. The monetary base equals reserves plus currency in circulation. In Economia, currency in circulation equals zero, so the monetary base is equivalent to reserves. Initially the monetary base is $20,000.

f. The monetary base increases to $22,000.

4. a. Yes, the commercial bank has reserves of $10,000 and deposits of $100,000: reserves equal 10% of deposits, which satisfies the required reserve ratio.

b.

Central bank of Macropedia

Assets		Liabilities	
Treasury bills	$6,000	Reserves	$5,000
		Currency in circulation	$1,000
Total assets	$6,000	Total liabilities	$6,000

Commercial bank of Macropedia

Assets		Liabilities	
Reserves	$5,000	Deposits	$100,000
Loans	$80,000	Capital	$0
Treasury bills	$15,000		
Total assets	$100,000	Total liabilities	$100,000

c. The commercial bank has insufficient reserves to meet the required reserve ratio: when its deposits equal $100,000, it needs $10,000 in required reserves. With reserves of $5,000, it can only support $50,000 of deposits. In the short term, it can borrow reserves from the central bank of Macropedia. Since there is only one commercial bank in Macropedia, it cannot borrow from the federal funds market since there is no federal funds market. Over time the commercial bank will find it needs to decrease its outstanding loans and therefore deposits until its reserves are sufficient to meet the required reserve ratio.

d.

Commercial bank of Macropedia

Assets		Liabilities	
Reserves	$5,000	Deposits	$50,000
Loans	$30,000	Capital	$0
Treasury bills	$15,000		
Total assets	$50,000	Total liabilities	$50,000

e. The monetary base is initially equal to $11,000 ($10,000 in reserves plus $1,000 in currency in circulation). After the central bank's activity, the monetary base is $6,000 ($5,000 in reserves plus $1,000 in currency in circulation).

f. The money supply is initially $101,000 ($100,000 in checkable bank deposits plus $1,000 in currency in circulation). After the central bank's actions and full adjustment, the money supply is $51,000 ($50,000 in checkable bank deposits plus $1,000 in currency in circulation). The money supply decreases by $50,000, or the amount predicted by the money multiplier process.

5. a. Bank reserves equal currency in bank vaults plus bank deposits at the central bank, or $150 million.

b. We can calculate the required reserve ratio, rr, as the ratio of required reserves to checkable deposits. Since there are no excess reserves in Macroland, the bank reserves calculated in part (a) equal the required reserves: thus, $150 million/$600 million equals a required reserve ratio of 0.25.

c. When the central bank of Macroland purchases $10 million in Treasury bills, this increases the level of reserves in the banking system by $10 million. This increase in reserves starts the multiplier process: the change in the money supply is calculated as the increase in reserves times the money multiplier or ($10 million)(4) = $40 million. Thus, the money supply increases by $40 million when the Central Bank purchases Treasury bills on the open market.

d. Using the concept explained in part (c), this sale of Treasury bills by the central bank will decrease the money supply by $20 million. We can see this by recalling that the change in the money supply equals the change in reserves times the money multiplier or (−$5 million)(4), or −$20 million.

6. Money makes indirect exchange possible, which enhances the possible gains from trade since it eliminates the need for a double coincidence of wants between two trading individuals. Money enables people to trade for what they have to offer and then use the money they receive from selling these goods and services to then purchase the goods and services they want.

7.   **a.** Cigarettes are an example of commodity money since the unit of exchange is a commodity that has intrinsic value in other uses.

b. The paper coupons are an example of commodity-backed money since these paper coupons can be redeemed for a particular commodity: a certain number of hours of babysitting.

c. Corn is an example of commodity money since the unit of exchange is a commodity that has intrinsic value in other uses.

d. This is an example of commodity-backed money since the paper currency can be exchanged for a commodity: gold or silver.

e. This is an example of fiat money since it is not backed by anything other than the government's guarantee: if the government were no longer willing to accept this currency in payment for taxes, it would lose its value as a monetary unit.

8. Although the money supply divided by the U.S. population suggests that individuals on average hold a very high level of dollars, the reality is that most people carry a considerably smaller amount of dollars. The other dollars are held in business cash registers and by people not living in the United States since dollars are used by many foreigners, particularly in places where the stability of the national currency is questionable over time.

9. Although deposit insurance protects individual depositors so that they do not have to fear losing the dollars they deposit in insured institutions, it does create a moral hazard problem. Depositors, once they are insured, do not need to monitor the actions their banking institution engages in, which may lead to a situation where the institutions engage in riskier investment activities than is optimal. The banks have an incentive to engage in risky investments since the owners of the bank will benefit if the investment proves profitable and can pass on the loss to the government if the investment proves unprofitable.

10. When a bank holds more assets than liabilities, this means that the bank faces a potential loss for any investment that proves unprofitable. Another way of thinking about this is to realize that if some of the banks' loans prove to be bad and the banks take a loss, the banks will still have assets larger than their deposits. This reduces the probability that the government will need to step in and provide funds to cover depositors' funds.

11.   **a.** The failure of Knickerbocker Trust led to bank runs among other trusts because of rumors about these other institutions. Trusts during this period were less regulated and, in addition, opted not to join the New York Clearinghouse. Over time the trusts speculated in real estate and the stock market until 1907 when Knickerbocker Trust was the first trust to suffer massive losses in unsuccessful stock market speculation.

b. The Federal Reserve was meant to create a financial system where all deposit-taking institutions would be forced to hold adequate reserves. In addition, the legislative act made provision for all deposit-taking institutions covered by the Federal Reserve to undergo inspection by regulators.

c. Even with the creation of the Federal Reserve, there were still problems with bank runs since it was possible for banks to hold fewer reserves than the value of their total deposits. The Glass-Steagall Act of 1932 created federal deposit insurance and increased the ability of banks to borrow from the Federal Reserve. The creation of federal deposit insurance effectively ended the problem of bank runs since depositors no longer had to fear losing their deposits.

d. Prior to the S&L Crisis of the 1980s, the S&Ls were covered by federal deposit insurance and tightly regulated. During the 1970s, high inflation meant that S&Ls found it increasingly difficult to maintain the level of deposits they needed in order to make long-term mortgages. In addition, the high inflation rates eroded the value of the S&L assets. Congress passed legislation designed to help S&Ls respond to the problem of insufficient deposits and eroding asset values: this legislation enabled S&Ls to undertake riskier investments. Unfortunately, the legislation gave the S&Ls greater investment freedom but failed to consider what the appropriate level of oversight would be for this increased freedom. This meant that some S&Ls engaged in riskier investment than was optimal from the government's point of view since the government ultimately had to cover any losses to depositors.

e. The financial crisis of 2007 shared many commonalities with other financial crises from other periods of time. Like the Panic of 1907, the financial crisis of 2007 involved excessive speculation as well as institutions that were not as strictly regulated as depository institutions. As in the Great Depression, the financial crisis of 2007 involved a federal government that was reluctant to take action until the level of financial loss was very large.

Answers to Chapter Review Questions

1. **Answer b.** Answer (b) provides a straightforward definition of money. Money includes cash plus other assets that are highly liquid like checking accounts. Money does not include all forms of wealth since some forms of wealth are highly illiquid.

2. **Answer c.** Credit cards and debit cards are not equivalent: credit cards allow the user to borrow funds, and this borrowing represents a liability for the user since the funds must be repaid.

3. **Answer d.** Answers (a), (b), and (c) are factual statements about money that are all discussed in the text.

4. **Answer a.** Statement I is an example of money used as a unit of account since it provides a standard measure for the prices of all goods and services in an economy. Statement II is an example of money's role as a store of value: we value money because of its ability to represent purchasing power over time. Statement III provides an example of money as a medium of exchange: the building contractor gives us a price for a particular item.

5. **Answer d.** Each of these statements is incorrect. Fiat money is money whose value derives entirely from its official status as a means of exchange: this is not limited to countries with monarchies. Fiat money is not redeemable in some other commodity. Commodity money is a more limited form of money than commodity-backed money or fiat money, since it ties up more of an economy's resources to facilitate making transactions rather than using those resources for more productive uses.

6. **Answer c.** M1 is the narrowest definition of money and includes only currency in circulation, travelers' checks, and checkable bank deposits.

7. **Answer c.** Joe's checking account balance is an asset from Joe's perspective but a liability from the bank's perspective since the bank is liable, or owes money, to Joe. Ellen's car loan is a liability for Ellen since it represents something she owes to someone else, while it represents an asset to the bank since it represents a promise to pay the bank a certain amount of money. When the bank deposits funds at the Federal Reserve, this deposit is an asset for the bank and a liability for the Federal Reserve. If there are positive capital requirements, then assets are greater than liabilities.

8. **Answer a.** The required reserve ratio is equal to required reserves divided by checkable deposits: in this example, this bank holds 10% of its checkable deposits as required reserves.

9. **Answer b.** The bank's capital is the difference between its total assets and total liabilities. In this case, the bank's assets sum to $1,300 while the liabilities total $1,000. The difference, $300, is the bank's capital.

10. **Answer d.** When the Fed sells $50 worth of T-bills, it debits the reserve account of the bank that sells the T-bills to the Fed. This results in the bank having insufficient reserves to support their current level of deposits. The bank will contract the loans it holds until the deposits in the bank are the amount that can be supported by the new level of reserves. The new reserves in this problem equal $50 (the initial $100 minus the $50 spent on the T-bills): $50 in reserves can support $500 in deposits when the required reserve ratio equals 10. So the money supply will decrease from $1,000 to $500, or a decrease of $500.

11. **Answer d.** Even the rumor of a potential bank run can result in dramatic decreases in the value of a bank's assets. Rumor and fear can combine to create a self-fulfilling prophecy: depositors fear that the behavior of other depositors will drive even a financially stable bank into instability. The potential for bank runs can be eliminated through effective regulation that provides deposit insurance while requiring bank capital and a designated reserve ratio.

12. **Answer e.** Banks affect the money supply, or the sum of currency in circulation plus bank deposits, when they hold currency in their bank vaults, thus reducing the total amount of currency in circulation. Banks also affect the money supply when they lend out their excess reserves and create additional bank deposits. Check writing and check cashing do not affect the money supply since they do not change the overall level of currency in circulation plus bank deposits.

13. **Answer d.** The monetary base consists of currency in circulation and bank reserves, while the money supply equals currency in circulation plus bank deposits.

14. **Answer d.** All of the statements restate the relationship between excess reserves and the required reserve ratio and their impact on the level of bank deposits. We can write this relationship as the change in bank deposits equals excess reserves times $(1/rr)$. Recall that $1/rr$ is simply the reciprocal of the required reserve ratio.

15. **Answer c.** Since the money multiplier is defined as $1/rr$, when the required reserve ratio increases, the money multiplier decreases, holding everything else constant. The required reserve ratio has no impact on the discount rate, the interest rate that the Federal Reserve charges banks that borrow funds from the Federal Reserve.

16. **Answer d.** When the required reserve ratio increases, the money multiplier, defined as $1/rr$, must necessarily decrease. If the required reserve ratio equals 10%, the money multiplier equals 10; and if the required reserve ratio equals 20%, the money multiplier equals 5. When the reserve requirement increases, banks find that their reserves' ability to support bank deposits decreases, and this leads banks to contract the level of bank deposits in the banking system.

17. **Answer a.** As banks failed in the period 1929 to 1933, many Americans withdrew their bank deposits from the banking system due to their fear that more banks would fail. As bank deposits were withdrawn, this led to lower bank reserves, which reduced the capacity of the banking system to support bank deposits: bank deposits fell sharply. M1 did fall during this period due to the decrease in bank deposits being much greater than the increase in currency in circulation.

18. **Answer b.** The use of counterfeit money in an economy hurts the ability of that economy's government to generate revenues to pay for government services even if no one in the economy recognizes that counterfeit dollars are being used to make exchanges. Governments cover a small amount of their expenses by issuing new currency to meet the growing demand for this currency. Counterfeit money exacts this cost of the government no matter if the government endorses fiat money or commodity-backed money.

19. **Answer b.** To be included in the measure of M1, the asset must be highly liquid since M1 is defined very narrowly to include only currency in circulation, travelers' checks, and checkable bank deposits. M2, a broader defined monetary aggregate, includes near-monies. Wealth is not the same as money and may include assets that are highly illiquid.

20. **Answer d.** Commodity-backed money is something that is used as a medium of exchange that has no intrinsic worth itself (e.g., paper money) but that can be converted into a valuable good on demand. Commodity-backed money reduces the amount of resources used to provide the functions of money since it does not require the circulation and direct use of the commodity in order to serve its various monetary roles. So, for example, if the commodity-backed money is backed by gold and silver, only enough gold and silver must be kept on hand in order to satisfy the demands for those individuals wishing to redeem their commodity-backed money.

21. **Answer c.** M1 is just checkable deposits, travelers' checks, and currency in circulation. M2 includes all of M1 plus other near-monies. Near-monies do not include stocks or bonds because neither of these two types of financial assets are sufficiently liquid.

22. **Answer f.** Bank reserves are composed of the currency in bank vaults and the bank deposits held at the Federal Reserve. Bank reserves are not part of currency in circulation.

23. **Answer d.** The text provides a description of these three components of bank regulation: deposit insurance, capital requirements, and reserve requirements. All three of these aspects of bank regulation help to reduce the probability of a bank run.

24. **Answer b.** When banks borrow from the Federal Reserve, this is referred to as using the discount window. The FDIC is the Federal Deposit Insurance Corporation, and it refers to the group that provides and oversees deposit insurance for the banking industry. Open market operations refers to the buying and selling of Treasury bills by the Federal Open Market Committee (FOMC). The required reserve ratio is set by the Federal Reserve and is the percentage of deposits that the Fed requires banks to hold either in their vaults or in their account at the Federal Reserve.

25. **Answer c.** Both of these statements are true. On the one hand, banks decrease the money supply when they remove currency from circulation and place that currency in their vaults or deposit it at the Federal Reserve; on the other hand, banks increase the money supply by accepting deposits and then lending out a portion of these deposited dollars to borrowers.

26. **Answer b.** The Federal Reserve can affect the money supply by engaging in open market operations where the Federal Reserve either purchases Treasury bills or sells Treasury bills. The Fed can also affect the money supply by changing the reserve requirements: when the reserve requirement increases, this reduces the money supply, and when the Fed reduces the reserve requirement, this increases the money supply. Finally, the Fed can affect the money supply by changing the discount rate. When the discount rate falls relative to the federal funds rate, this means that it is now relatively cheaper to borrow from the Fed, which leads to increases in the money supply.

27. **Answer b.** The interest rate charged for loans from one bank to another is called the federal funds rate. The interest rate charged for a loan to a bank from the Fed is called the discount rate.

28. **Answer c.** In a checkable-deposits-only monetary system, the money multiplier is equal to $1/rr$, where rr is the required reserve ratio. Thus, for this economy the money multiplier is equal to 5 and a $100 million purchase of Treasury bills by the central bank will result in an increase in the money supply of $500 million.

29. **Answer c.** When the required reserve ratio is 10%, this implies that the money multiplier is equal to 10 in a checkable-deposits-only monetary system. Thus, an open market sale of $10 million worth of Treasury bills will result in a $100 million decrease in the money supply.

30. **Answer c.** Over the course of its history, the United States has experienced numerous financial crises, with each crisis typically resulting in a mandate for greater regulation of the financial market.

31. **Answer e.** All of these statements are true, and they are discussed in the text. As you read this section, notice the similarities and comparisons that the authors make among various financial crises.

chapter 15(30)

Monetary Policy

BEFORE YOU READ THE CHAPTER

Summary

This chapter explains money demand and then uses this concept to develop the liquidity preference model of short-run interest rate determination. The chapter considers the Fed's ability to move interest rates and explores the effect of monetary policy on short-run economic performance. The chapter also explores why monetary policy is the primary tool used by the central bank to stabilize the economy. The chapter also discusses monetary neutrality, or the idea that monetary policy in the long run does not affect real aggregate output but does affect the price level.

Chapter Objectives

Objective #1. Money is held by individuals and firms in order to facilitate making transactions. There is an opportunity cost to holding money: money normally yields a lower rate of return than nonmonetary assets. The opportunity cost of holding money is the difference between the interest rate on assets that are not money and the interest rate on assets that are money. The higher the short-term interest rate, the higher the opportunity cost of holding money: people reduce their holding of money as the short-term interest rate increases. This implies that the demand curve for money slopes downward: as the interest rate decreases, the quantity of money demanded increases. Figure 15.1 illustrates the relationship between the quantity of money demanded and the interest rate.

Figure 15.1

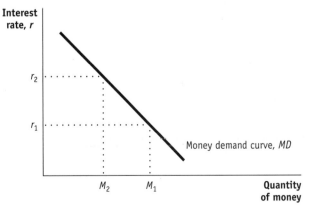

555

- Short-term interest rates are interest rates on financial assets that mature in less than a year. Short-term interest rates tend to move together since they are in effect competing for the same business. A short-term asset that offers a lower-than-average interest rate will be sold by investors. When these assets are sold, this forces the interest rate on these assets to increase since new buyers must be rewarded with a higher rate in order to be willing to buy the asset. This reasoning implies that short-term interest rates will tend to equalize across the financial assets found in the short-term interest rate market.

- Long-term interest rates are interest rates paid on financial assets that mature a number of years into the future. Long-term interest rates may differ from short-term interest rates. In this chapter's discussion of interest rates, we will simplify our discussion and assume that there is only one interest rate.

Objective #2. The money demand curve illustrates the relationship between the nominal quantity of money demanded and the interest rate. It is a downward-sloping curve. For a given interest rate, an increase in the aggregate price level causes the demand curve for money to shift to the right, while a decrease in the aggregate price level causes the demand curve for money to shift to the left. Figure 15.2 illustrates the effect of a change in the aggregate price level on the demand for money.

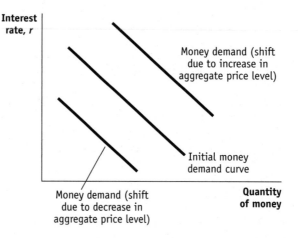

Figure 15.2

- The quantity of money, M, is proportional to the aggregate price level. Holding everything else constant, if the aggregate price level doubles, then the nominal quantity of money will double. In other words, holding everything else constant, the real quantity of money demanded after an aggregate price level change (M_2/P_2) is the same as the real quantity of money demanded before the aggregate price level change (M_1/P_1).

- There are a number of factors that shift the real money demand curve, including changes in the level of real aggregate spending, changes in banking technology, and changes in banking institutions that alter people's real demand for money.

  - Holding everything else constant, an increase in real aggregate spending will shift the real money demand curve to the right, while a decrease in real aggregate spending will shift the real money demand curve to the left.

  - Holding everything else constant, advances in information technology tend to shift the real money demand curve to the left since these advances make it easier for the public to make transactions while holding smaller amounts of money.

  - Changes in institutions can increase or decrease the demand for money by changing the opportunity cost of holding money.

Objective #3. In the United States, the Federal Open Market Committee (FOMC) sets a target interest rate for the federal funds rate and then uses open-market operations to achieve that target interest rate.

- The liquidity preference model of the interest rate illustrates how the Fed can control the interest rate through its open-market operations. The liquidity preference model says that the interest rate is determined by the intersection of the supply and demand for money in the market for money.

- In the liquidity preference model, the money supply is a vertical line whose location is controlled by the Fed through its open-market operations. The intersection of this vertical money supply curve with the downward-sloping money demand curve determines the equilibrium interest rate. Figure 15.3 illustrates this relationship.

Figure 15.3

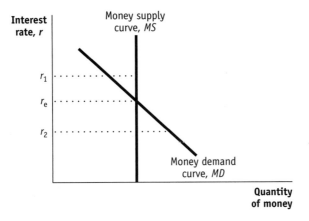

- If the nominal interest rate is lower than the equilibrium level, then the quantity of money demanded will be greater than the quantity of money supplied. People will want to increase their money holdings, and they will sell other financial assets to achieve this goal: in order to sell these financial assets, they will have to offer a higher interest rate to attract buyers. This will lead the nominal interest rate in the market for money to increase, bringing about equilibrium between the demand and supply of money.

- If the nominal interest rate is higher than the equilibrium level, then the quantity of money demanded will be less than the quantity of money supplied. People will want to decrease their money holdings and they will do so by buying other financial assets. Due to the increased demand for these interest-bearing financial assets, sellers of these assets will find that they can offer them at a lower nominal interest rate and still find willing buyers. Thus, the nominal interest rate will decrease, thereby restoring the money market to equilibrium, where the supply of money equals the demand for money.

- When the Fed purchases Treasury bills in the open market, this increases the money supply, causing the money supply curve to shift to the right. For a given money demand curve, this increase in the supply of money will result in interest rates decreasing. Thus, if the FOMC sets a target interest rate lower than the prevailing interest rate, it can reach this target by engaging in open-market purchases. Figure 15.4 illustrates an open-market purchase by the Fed.

Figure 15.4

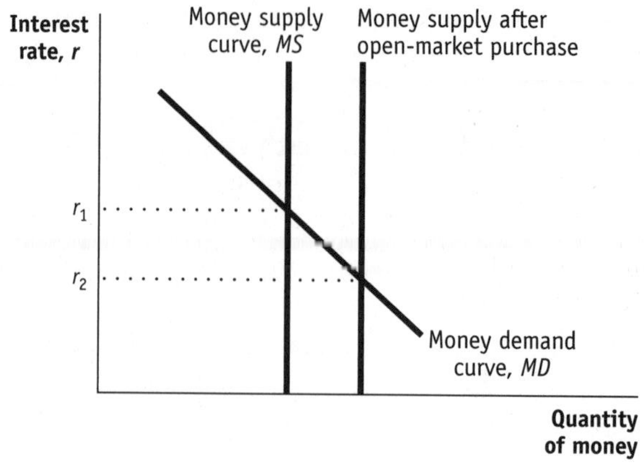

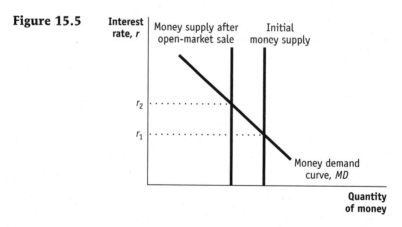

- When the Fed sells Treasury bills in the open market, this decreases the money supply, causing the money supply curve to shift to the left. For a given money demand curve, this decrease in the supply of money will result in interest rates increasing. Thus, if the FOMC sets a target interest rate higher than the prevailing interest rate, it can reach this target by engaging in open-market sales. Figure 15.5 illustrates an open-market sale.

Figure 15.5

Objective #4. Changes in the money supply cause the short-run level of real GDP to change.

- Monetary expansion in the short run reduces the interest rate and leads to higher investment spending and higher consumer spending, holding everything else constant. This higher investment spending results in higher GDP through the multiplier process. Thus, an increase in the money supply causes the *AD* curve to shift to the right and is referred to as expansionary monetary policy. The Federal Reserve and other central banks tend to engage in expansionary monetary policy when real GDP is below potential real GDP.

- Monetary contraction in the short run increases the interest rate and leads to lower investment spending and lower consumer spending, holding everything else constant. This lower investment spending results in lower GDP through the multiplier process. Thus, a decrease in the money supply causes the *AD* curve to shift to the left and is referred to as contractionary monetary policy. The Federal Reserve and other central banks tend to engage in contractionary monetary policy when real GDP is above potential real GDP.

- The Taylor rule for monetary policy is a rule for setting the federal funds rate that takes into account both the inflation rate and the output gap. The Taylor rule for the period from 1988 to 2008 can be summarized as: Federal funds rate = 2.07 + (1.28 × inflation) − (1.95 × unemployment gap).

Objective #5. The Federal Reserve bank does not set an explicit inflation target, but pursues monetary policy that will keep inflation low but positive. Other central banks do set inflation targets: central banks with inflation targets announce the inflation rate that they are trying to achieve and then set policies in an attempt to hit the stated target. Inflation targeting is based on forecasts of future inflation while the Taylor rule adjusts monetary policy in response to past inflation: the former is forward looking while the latter is backward looking.

- Inflation targeting proponents argue that this type of policy is both transparent and accountable.

- Inflation targeting opponents argue that this type of policy is too restrictive.

Objective #6. Monetary expansion in the short run can increase aggregate output beyond the potential output level, but in the long run this monetary expansion does not result in an increase in aggregate output since aggregate output in the long run always equals potential output due to adjustments in the level of nominal wages. Thus, a monetary expansion in the long run raises the aggregate price level while having no effect on real GDP.

- A change in the money supply leads to a proportional change in the aggregate price level in the long run. That is, if an economy is initially in long-run equilibrium and the nominal money supply increases, long-run equilibrium can only be restored when all real values return to their original levels. Since the nominal money supply increased, the real money supply can only return to its initial level with a proportionate increase in the aggregate price level.

- Money neutrality refers to the idea that changes in the money supply have no real effects on the economy. An increase in the money supply results in the money supply curve shifting to the right. It also results in the money demand curve shifting to the right. In the long run, these two shifts result in the interest rate returning to its initial level and the money supply increasing from its initial level. Monetary policy, in the long run, has no effect on the interest rate.

- Monetary policy does have powerful real effects in the short run and can be used to ward off recessions or slow an expanding economy.

Key Terms

Notes

short-term interest rate the *interest rate* on *financial assets* that mature within less than a year.

long-term interest rate the *interest rate* on *financial assets* that mature a number of years into the future.

money demand curve a graphical representation of the relationship between the *interest rate* and the quantity of money demanded. The money demand curve slopes downward because, other things equal, a higher interest rate increases the *opportunity cost* of holding money.

liquidity preference model of the interest rate a model of the market for money in which the *interest rate* is determined by the supply and demand for money.

money supply curve a graphical representation of the relationship between the quantity of money supplied by the Federal Reserve and the *interest rate*.

Key Terms *(continued)*

target federal funds rate the Federal Reserve's desired level for the *federal funds rate*. The Federal Reserve adjusts the *money supply* through the purchase and sale of Treasury bills until the actual rate equals the desired rate.

expansionary monetary policy *monetary policy* that, through the lowering of the *interest rate*, increases aggregate demand and therefore output.

contractionary monetary policy *monetary policy* that, through the raising of the *interest rate*, reduces aggregate demand and therefore output.

Taylor rule for monetary policy a rule for setting the *federal funds rate* that takes into account both the *inflation rate* and the *output gap*.

inflation targeting an approach to *monetary policy* that requires the *central bank* try to keep the *inflation rate* near a predetermined target rate.

monetary neutrality the concept that changes in the *money supply* have no real effects on the *economy* in the long run and only result in a proportional change in the price level.

Notes

AFTER YOU READ THE CHAPTER

Tips

Tip #1. The interest rate is the price of money, because the interest rate provides a measure of the opportunity cost of holding money. As the interest rate increases, the quantity of money demanded decreases since the opportunity cost of holding money rises with increases in the interest rate. This relationship implies that the demand for money is downward sloping: the quantity of money demanded is inversely related to the interest rate. This relationship is illustrated in Figure 15.6: when the interest rate is r_1, the quantity of money demanded is M_1; when the interest rate rises to r_2, the quantity of money demanded decreases to M_2.

Figure 15.6

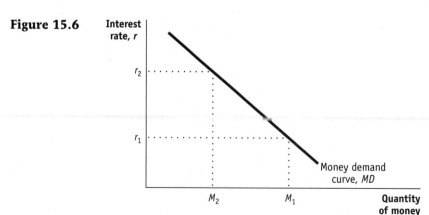

Tip #2. It is important to understand what causes a movement along the money demand curve and what factors cause a shift in the money demand curve. As with other demand curves, a change in the price of money—the interest rate—causes a movement along the demand curve (see Figure 15.6). A change in the aggregate price level shifts the nominal money demand curve: when the aggregate price level increases, the nominal money demand curve shifts to the right since people will now demand a greater amount of nominal money at every interest rate due to the higher aggregate price level; when the aggregate price level decreases, the nominal money demand curve shifts to the left since people will now demand a smaller amount of nominal money at every interest rate due to the lower aggregate price level. Money demand (real or nominal) also shifts with changes in real aggregate spending, changes in banking technology, and changes in banking institutions. We can summarize these changes in the following table.

Change	Effect on money demand
Increase in interest rate	Movement along money demand curve and decrease in quantity of money demanded
Decrease in interest rate	Movement along money demand curve and increase in quantity of money demanded
Increase in aggregate price level	Money demand shifts to the right
Decrease in aggregate price level	Money demand shifts to the left
Increase in real aggregate spending	Money demand shifts to the right
Decrease in real aggregate spending	Money demand shifts to the left
Advance in bank technology	Money demand shifts to the left
Changes in institutions	Money demand shifts to the left or right, depending on the institutional change

Tip #3. Equilibrium in the money market equates the quantity of money demanded with the quantity of money supplied at the equilibrium interest rate. Figure 15.7 illustrates the money market.

Figure 15.7

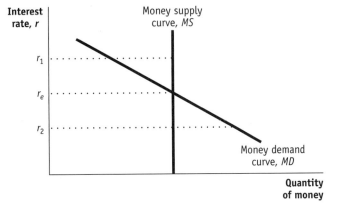

If the interest rate (r_1 in Figure 15.7) is greater than the equilibrium interest rate (r_e), the quantity of money supplied is greater than the quantity of money demanded at that interest rate. Investors will drive the interest rate down to the equilibrium level r_e by shifting their assets out of money holdings and into nonmonetary interest-bearing financial assets. This will cause the interest rate to decrease toward r_e.

If the interest rate (r_2 in Figure 15.7) is less than the equilibrium interest rate (r_e), the quantity of money supplied is less than the quantity of money demanded at that interest rate. Investors will drive the interest rate up to the equilibrium level r_e by shifting their assets out of nonmonetary interest-bearing financial assets and into money holdings. This will cause the interest rate to increase toward r_e.

Tip #4. It is important to understand how the Federal Open Market Committee (FOMC) through its open-market operations effectively controls interest rates in the economy. Figure 15.8 illustrates the effect of an open-market purchase on the interest rate. When the FOMC purchases Treasury bills in the open market, this injects new reserves into the banking system and leads to an expansion in the money supply from MS_1 to MS_2. For a given money demand curve MD, this results in a decrease in the interest rate from r_1 to r_2.

Figure 15.8

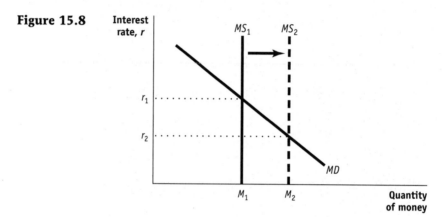

When the FOMC sells Treasury bills in the open market, this removes reserves from the banking system and effectively shifts the money supply curve to the left. For a given money demand curve, this action by the FOMC results in an increase in the interest rate.

Tip #5. It is important to distinguish between the short-run and long-run effects of monetary policy. In the short run, monetary policy can be used to stimulate AD and shift it to the right, resulting in an increase in aggregate real output, or monetary policy can be used to contract AD, thereby shifting it to the left and leading to a decrease in the level of aggregate real output. In the long run, monetary policy has no effect on aggregate real output since aggregate real output in the long run will always equal potential output. Economists refer to this as monetary neutrality: money is neutral in its effect on aggregate real output in the long run, since it cannot affect the level of aggregate real output.

1. The following table provides different situations. For each situation, determine whether the money demand curve or the money supply curve shifts and, if so, the direction of the shift. Then, determine what happens to the equilibrium interest rate and the equilibrium quantity of money.

Situation	Shift in the demand for money (provide direction of shift)	Shift in the supply of money (provide direction of shift)	Effect on the equilibrium interest rate	Effect on the equilibrium quantity of money
The information technology for making transactions improves				
The Federal Reserve makes an open-market purchase of Treasury bills				
Real GDP increases in the economy				
Real GDP decreases in the economy, and the Federal Reserve makes an open-market purchase of Treasury bills				
The aggregate price level increases				

STEP 1: Before you fill out the table, you will want to review the factors that shift the money demand curve. You may also find it helpful to review the effect of open-market operations by the Federal Reserve on the money supply curve.

Review the section "Shifts of the Money Demand Curve" on page 451 (Econ page 883).

The money demand curve will shift to the right with increases in the aggregate price level and increases in real income. The money demand curve will also shift with changes in institutions (the shift may be to the right or the left depending upon the nature of the change) or changes in technology (again, the shift can be to the right or the left depending upon the nature of the change).

The money supply curve will shift to the right when the Federal Reserve makes an open-market purchase of bonds, since the Federal Reserve will be injecting new reserves into the banking system with this purchase. The money supply curve will shift to the left when the Federal Reserve makes an open-market sale of bonds, since the Federal Reserve will be removing reserves from the banking system when it makes this sale.

STEP 2: Now that you have reviewed the factors that shift the two curves, you are ready to fill in the table.

Review the section "Shifts of the Money Demand Curve" on page 451 (Econ page 883).

Here is the completed table.

Situation	Shift in the demand for money (provide direction of shift)	Shift in the supply of money (provide direction of shift)	Effect on the equilibrium interest rate	Effect on the equilibrium quantity of money
The information technology for making transactions improves	Demand for money shifts left, since at every interest rate people will wish to hold less money	There is a movement along the supply of money curve due to the shift in the demand for money	The equilibrium interest rate will decrease	The equilibrium quantity of money will be unchanged
The Federal Reserve makes an open-market purchase of Treasury bills	There is a movement along the demand for money curve due to the shift in the supply of money	Supply of money will shift to the right, as the Federal Reserve injects new reserves into the banking system	The equilibrium interest rate will decrease	The equilibrium quantity of money will increase
Real GDP increases in the economy	Demand for money will shift to the right when real GDP increases	There is a movement along the supply of money curve due to the shift in the demand for money	The equilibrium interest rate will increase	The equilibrium quantity of money will be unchanged
Real GDP decreases in the economy, and the Federal Reserve makes an open-market purchase of Treasury bills	Demand for money will shift to the left when real GDP decreases	Supply of money will shift to the right when the Federal Reserve makes an open-market purchase	The equilibrium interest rate will decrease	The equilibrium quantity of money will increase
The aggregate price level increases	Demand for money shifts to the right when the aggregate price level increases	There will be a movement along the supply of money curve due to the shift in the demand for money	The equilibrium interest rate will increase	The equilibrium quantity of money will be unchanged

2. Suppose there are two kinds of assets that an individual can choose between as a means of holding wealth: money, which does not provide any interest payment, and bonds, which provide the owner of the bond with an interest payment. Suppose that the money market is currently not in equilibrium and that the interest rate is lower than the equilibrium interest rate. First, describe the money market and whether there is a shortage or a surplus of money. Then, using these two types of assets, explain how the money market adjusts in order to ensure that the quantity of money demanded is equal to the quantity of money supplied.

STEP 1: Determine whether there is a shortage or a surplus of money when the interest rate is lower than the equilibrium interest rate in the market for money.

Review the section "The Equilibrium Interest Rate" on page 453 (Econ page 885) and Figure 15-3 on page 454 (Econ page 886).

In general when price is lower than the equilibrium price this results in a situation of excess demand for the good. This is no different in the market for money: when the interest rate, the price of money, is lower than the equilibrium level, then we know that the quantity of money demanded will be greater than the quantity of money supplied.

STEP 2: Explain how the money market returns to equilibrium when the quantity of money demanded is greater than the quantity of money supplied.

Review the section "The Equilibrium Interest Rate" on page 453 (Econ page 885) and Figure 15-3 on page 454 (Econ page 886).

When the quantity of money demanded exceeds the quantity of money supplied this means that people want to shift some of their wealth out of interest-bearing assets and into money. When there is excess quantity of money demanded this implies that there is excess supply of interest-bearing assets like bonds: to induce people to purchase bonds, the owners of these bonds will have to offer higher interest rates. Interest rates will rise until the bond market clears and the money market clears: when the interest rate rises sufficiently, then the quantity of money demanded will equal the quantity of money supplied.

3. Suppose there are two kinds of assets that an individual can choose between as a way of holding wealth: money, which does not provide any interest payment, and bonds, which provides the owner of the bond with an interest payment. Suppose that the money market is currently not in equilibrium and that the interest rate is higher than the equilibrium interest rate. First, describe the money market and whether there is a shortage or a surplus of money. Then, using these two types of assets, explain how the money market adjusts in order to ensure that the quantity of money demanded is equal to the quantity of money supplied.

STEP 1: Determine whether there is a shortage or a surplus of money when the interest rate is higher than the equilibrium interest rate in the market for money.

Review the section "The Equilibrium Interest Rate" on page 453 (Econ page 885) and Figure 15-3 on page 454 (Econ page 886).

In general when price is higher than the equilibrium price this results in a situation of excess supply of the good. This is no different in the market for money: when the interest rate, the price of money, is higher than the equilibrium level, then we know that the quantity of money demanded will be less than the quantity of money supplied.

STEP 2: Explain how the money market returns to equilibrium when the quantity of money demanded is less than the quantity of money supplied.

Review the section "The Equilibrium Interest Rate" on page 453 (Econ page 885) and Figure 15-3 on page 454 (Econ page 886).

When the quantity of money demanded is less than the quantity of money supplied this means that people want to shift some of their wealth into interest-bearing assets and out of money. When there is excess quantity of money supplied this implies that there is excess demand for interest-bearing assets like bonds: people desire bonds and the interest rate on bonds can fall since there is excess demand for these bonds. Interest rates will fall until the bond market clears and the money market clears: when the interest rate falls sufficiently, then the quantity of money demanded will equal the quantity of money supplied.

4. Suppose the economy in the short run is currently operating with an inflationary gap in which actual output is greater than potential output. If the government wishes to address this issue with activist monetary policy in order to restore the economy to potential output, what monetary policy should the central bank pursue? How will the implementation of this monetary policy work to return the economy to potential output?

STEP 1: **First think about the implications of operating in the short run with an inflationary gap.**

Review your notes on inflationary gaps and consult the preceding chapter on this topic if you need further review.

It is important that you can visualize this economic situation in terms of the AD-AS model. The following graph depicts the initial situation for this economy.

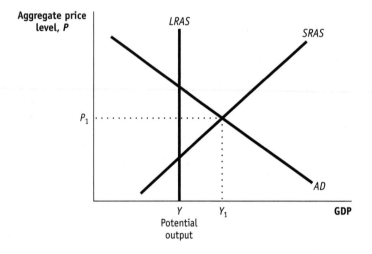

This economy is producing Y_1 in the short run: it is operating with an inflationary gap since actual output exceeds potential output. This implies that the economy has very low unemployment.

STEP 2: **Consider the effect of a change in the money supply and how this will impact the level of aggregate production. Make a decision about the optimal activist monetary policy to pursue.**

Review the section "Monetary Policy and Aggregate Demand" on page 458 (Econ page 890) and Figure 15-7 on page 459 (Econ page 891).

When the Federal Reserve engages in an open-market purchase, this increases the level of reserves in the banking system, expands the money supply through the money multiplier process, and reduces interest rates. These in turn cause aggregate demand to shift to the right at every aggregate price level.

When the Federal Reserve engages in open-market sales, this decreases the level of reserves in the banking system, reduces the money supply through the money multiplier process, and increases interest rates. These in turn cause aggregate demand to shift to the left at every aggregate price level.

If you examine the preceding graph, you can see that to return to the potential output level using an aggregate demand curve shift, the aggregate demand curve must shift to the left. The Federal Reserve will need to make open-market sales in order to shift the aggregate demand curve to the left.

STEP 3: Discuss how this activist monetary policy returns this economy to potential output.

Review the section "Monetary Policy and Aggregate Demand" on page 458 (Econ page 890) and Figure 15-7 on page 459 (Econ page 891).

When the Fed contracts the money supply this leads to a higher interest rate. The higher interest rate leads investment spending to fall, and therefore the level of aggregate expenditure will fall. As aggregate expenditure falls, this results in a decrease in real GDP. With the fall in the total quantity of goods and services demanded, the *AD* curve shifts to the left, restoring the economy to potential output *Y*.

5.   Suppose the economy is initially in long-run equilibrium as depicted in the *AD-AS* model. Suppose politicians view the current level of output as too low, and they encourage the central bank to engage in expansionary monetary policy. Describe the effects of this expansionary monetary policy on this economy in the short run, and then discuss what will happen in this economy in the long run if there are no further shocks to the economy. How does this example illustrate monetary neutrality?

STEP 1: Start by drawing a graph of this economy in long-run equilibrium using the *AD–AS* model.

Review the section "Money, Output, and Prices in the Long Run" on page 463 (Econ page 895) and Figure 15-10 on page 463 (Econ page 895).

In the *AD-AS* model, long-run equilibrium occurs at that output level at which *SRAS*, *AD*, and *LRAS* all intersect. This will occur at the potential output level of real GDP. The following figure illustrates this long-run equilibrium.

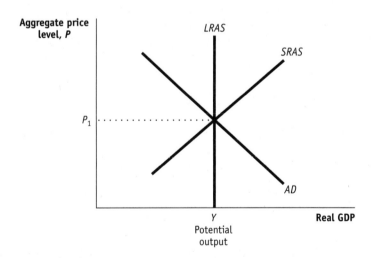

STEP 2: Alter your graph to illustrate the short-run effects of the expansionary monetary policy on this economy, making sure to note what happens to real GDP in the short run.

Review the section "Money, Output, and Prices in the Long Run" on page page 463 (Econ page 895) and Figure 15-10 on page page 463 (Econ page 895).

When the Fed engages in expansionary monetary policy this means that the Fed is purchasing Treasury bills in the open market. This will cause *AD* to shift to the right. The following graph illustrates the short-run effects of this policy: notice that real GDP increases to Y_2 and the aggregate price level increases to P_2. Y_2 is greater than potential output, which indicates that the economy is operating with an inflationary gap and that unemployment is unusually low.

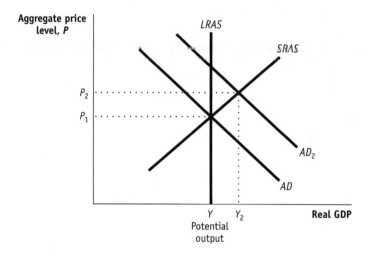

STEP 3: Discuss the adjustment process in this economy to the long-run equilibrium, making sure to note what happens to real GDP in the long run.

Review the section "Money, Output, and Prices in the Long Run" on page 463 (Econ page 895) and Figure 15-10 on page 463 (Econ page 895).

Since unemployment is unusually low, this indicates that over time there will be pressure for nominal wages to increase. As nominal wages increase, this will cause the SRAS curve to shift to the left. This curve will continue to shift until it intersects AD_2 at the potential output level. The following figure represents this shift. Notice that the economy returns to a real GDP level that is equal to potential output and that the aggregate price level has increased to P_3.

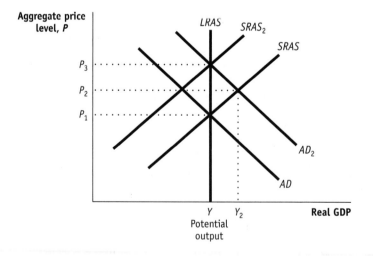

STEP 4: Discuss monetary neutrality and how it relates to your findings in Step 3.

Review the section "Money, Output, and Prices in the Long Run" on page 463 (Econ page 895) and Figure 15-10 on page 463 (Econ page 895).

In the preceding graph, we see the economy return to long-run equilibrium after the full adjustment to the expansionary monetary policy. Although the expansionary monetary policy altered real GDP in the short run to Y_2, in the long run this expansionary monetary policy had no effect on real GDP. The expansionary monetary policy does have a long-run impact on our model: this policy causes the aggregate price level to increase.

This idea that changes in the money supply have no long-run impact on the level of real GDP is an illustration of the concept of monetary neutrality. Money is neutral in the long run since it does not impact the level of real GDP; the impact of money in the long run is to alter the aggregate price level.

Problems and Exercises

1. The following figure illustrates the relationship between the nominal quantity of money, M, and the interest rate, r.

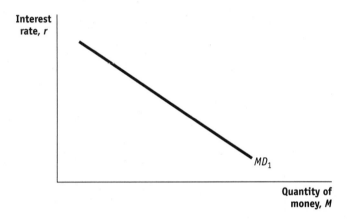

For each of the following situations, use the graph provided for reference.

a. Holding everything else constant, the interest rate increases from r_1 to r_2. Graph this in the following figure.

b. Holding everything else constant, the level of aggregate real income decreases. Graph this in the following figure.

Interest
rate, *r*

Quantity of
money, *M*

c. Holding everything else constant, there is an increase in the aggregate price level. Graph this in the following figure.

Interest
rate, *r*

Quantity of
money, *M*

d. Holding everything else constant, individuals in a community arc now able to use Internet banking for their money and financial assets accounts. Graph this in the following figure.

Interest
rate, *r*

Quantity of
money, *M*

2. Consider two assets: both Asset A and Asset B are one-month bonds issued by different companies that have the same amount of risk. Asset A initially earns a higher interest rate for its holder than does Asset B. Explain why you would expect this interest rate differential to disappear. Explain the process that leads Assets A and B to have approximately the same interest rate.

3. Use the following table to answer this question.

Change	Effect on nominal money demand	Effect on real money demand
Decrease in aggregate price level		
Increase in interest rate		
Change in regulation so that interest is now allowed on checking accounts		

a. In the table, enter how each scenario will affect nominal money demand and real money demand.

b. Explain why a change in the aggregate price level affects the nominal demand curve differently than it does the real money demand curve.

4. Use the following figure of the money demand and money supply curves to answer this question. Assume this market is initially in equilibrium with the quantity of money equal to M_1 and the interest rate equal to r_1.

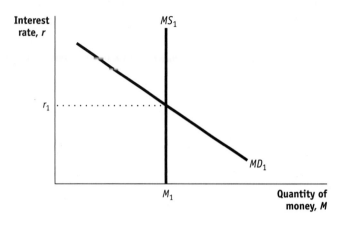

a. Suppose the FOMC engages in an open-market purchase of Treasury bills. Holding everything else constant, what happens to the equilibrium quantity of money and the equilibrium interest rate? Sketch a graph illustrating these changes.

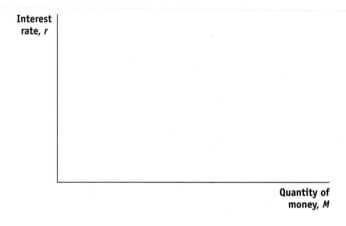

b. Suppose the FOMC engages in an open-market sale of Treasury bills. Holding everything else constant, what happens to the equilibrium quantity of money and the equilibrium interest rate? Sketch a graph illustrating these changes.

c. Suppose the aggregate price level increases. Holding everything else constant, what happens to the equilibrium quantity of money and the equilibrium interest rate? Sketch a graph illustrating these changes.

Interest
rate, *r*

Quantity of
money, *M*

5. Use the *AD–AS* model to answer this question.
(i) Scenario I

The economy of Macroland is initially in long-run equilibrium. Then the FOMC of Macroland decides to reduce interest rates through an open-market operation.

a. Draw a graph representing the initial situation in Macroland. In your graph, be sure to include the short-run aggregate supply curve (*SRAS*), the long-run aggregate supply curve (*LRAS*), and the aggregate demand curve (*AD*). On your graph mark the equilibrium aggregate price level and the aggregate output level as well as potential output.

Aggregate
price
level, *P*

Real GDP

b. Draw a graph of the money market depicting Macroland's initial situation before the FOMC engages in expansionary monetary policy as well as the effect of the FOMC's monetary policy actions. Be sure to indicate the initial equilibrium as well as the equilibrium after the monetary policy action.

c. How does this monetary policy action affect the aggregate economy in the short run? Explain your answer verbally while also including a graph of the *AD–AS* model to illustrate your answer.

d. How does this monetary policy action affect the aggregate economy in the long run?

(ii) Scenario II

Econoland is currently operating with a recessionary gap.

e. Draw a graph representing Econoland's economic situation using an *AD–AS* model. Be sure to indicate in your graph *SRAS, LRAS, AD*, the short-run equilibrium aggregate price level (P_1), the short-run equilibrium aggregate output level (Y_1), and the potential output level (Y_E).

f. What monetary policy would you suggest the FOMC of Econoland pursue if its only goal is to restore production in Econoland to the potential output level? Explain how this monetary policy would achieve this goal.

g. Is there a potential drawback to the implementation of this particular monetary policy? Explain your answer.

(iii) Scenario III

Upland is currently operating with an inflationary gap.

h. Draw a graph representing Upland's economic situation using an *AD–AS* model. Be sure to indicate in your graph *SRAS, LRAS, AD*, the short-run equilibrium aggregate price level (P_1), the short-run equilibrium aggregate output level (Y_1), and the potential output level (Y_E).

Aggregate
price
level, *P*

Real GDP

    i. What monetary policy would you suggest the FOMC of Upland pursue if its only goal is to restore production in Upland to the potential output level? Explain how this monetary policy would achieve this goal.

    j. Is there a potential drawback to the implementation of this particular monetary policy? Explain your answer.

6. Suppose that when the FOMC reduces the interest rate by 1 percentage point it increases the level of investment spending by $500 million in Macroland. If the marginal propensity to save equals 0.25, what will be the total rise in real GDP, assuming the aggregate price level is held constant? Explain your answer.

7. In your own words, explain how the Fed's actions can affect the economy. Be sure to include an explanation about how the Fed can affect the economy when the economy is in recession or when the economy is producing at an aggregate output level that is greater than the potential output level.

8. Why is the quantity of money people want to hold inversely related to the interest rate? Explain your answer fully.

9. Suppose the aggregate price level increases by 25%. What does this increase imply about the percentage increase in the quantity of money demanded in the long run? Explain your answer fully.

10. For each of the following situations, determine the appropriate central bank monetary response.

    a. The central bank adopts an interest rate target of 5%. Currently the interest rate in the economy is at 8%.

    b. The central bank adopts an inflation target of 3%. Currently the inflation rate is 4%.

    c. The central bank adopts an inflation target of 4%. Current inflation is 4%. However, this quarter the central bank expects data to reveal that the economy is entering a recession and has a projected negative output gap.

    d. Current unemployment is greater than the natural rate of unemployment.

BEFORE YOU TAKE THE TEST

Chapter Review Questions

1. People choose to hold money because
   a. it has little or no opportunity cost since money does not earn interest.
   b. it facilitates making transactions.
   c. it yields a lower rate of return than nonmonetary assets.
   d. Answers (b) and (c) are both correct.

2. The opportunity cost of holding money is
   a. always greater than the short-term interest rate.
   b. equal to the difference between the interest rate on assets that are not money and the interest rate on assets that are money.
   c. equal to the long-term interest rate.
   d. always equal to zero since it costs you nothing to hold money.

3. Which of the following statements is true?
   a. The nominal demand for money is proportional to the real demand for money.
   b. All short-term interest rates tend to move together.
   c. The higher the short-term interest rate, the lower the opportunity cost of holding money.
   d. The quantity of money demanded is positively related to the interest rate.

4. Which of the following statements is true?
   a. The real quantity of money is equal to the nominal amount of money divided by the aggregate price level.
   b. The real quantity of money measures the purchasing power of the nominal quantity of money.
   c. The real quantity of money is proportional to the nominal quantity of money for any given interest rate.
   d. All of these statements are true.
   e. Statements (a) and (b) are both true.
   f. Statements (a) and (c) are both true.
   g. Statements (b) and (c) are both true.

5. If the price level doubles, holding everything else constant, we know that
   a. the nominal quantity of money demanded also doubled.
   b. the real quantity of money demanded also doubled.
   c. the interest rate also doubled.
   d. Answers (a) and (b) are both correct.

6. For a given interest rate, when the quantity of money demanded is greater than the quantity of money supplied, then
   a. interest rates will increase.
   b. interest rates will decrease.
   c. people will sell nonmonetary assets.
   d. people will buy nonmonetary assets.
   e. Answers (a) and (c) are both correct.
   f. Answers (b) and (d) are both correct.
   g. Answers (a) and (d) are both correct.

7. The Federal Open Market Committee sets a target interest rate and can achieve that interest rate through
   a. open-market purchases, if the federal funds rate is initially less than the target rate.
   b. open-market sales, if the federal funds rate is initially less than the target rate.
   c. legislative action by Congress that decrees the level of the discount rate and thus the federal funds rate.
   d. stimulating the demand for money, if the initial interest rate is less than the target rate.

8. The liquidity preference model of interest rate determination states that
   a. interest rates are determined solely by the Federal Open Market Committee.
   b. interest rates are determined by the supply of and demand for money.
   c. people always prefer liquidity and do not consider the opportunity cost of holding money when they decide how much money they wish to hold at any given point in time.
   d. interest rates are determined in the market for nonmonetary assets and not the market for money.

9. The money supply curve in the liquidity preference model is drawn as a vertical line, since
   a. there is only one level of money supply that will enable an economy to produce at the full employment level of output and the appropriate aggregate price level.
   b. Congress sets by law the level of the money supply in the economy.
   c. the Fed can control the level of the money supply through its open-market operations.
   d. the money supply curve is unimportant in determining the equilibrium level of interest rates in the liquidity preference model.

10. When people offering to sell nonmonetary financial assets find that they must increase the interest rate these assets pay in order to sell them, this tells us that
    a. the quantity of money demanded is less than the quantity of money supplied.
    b. the quantity of money supplied equals the quantity of money demanded.
    c. the quantity of money demanded is greater than the quantity of money supplied.
    d. we cannot know anything about the relationship between the quantity of money demanded and the quantity of money supplied from this information.

11. Which of the following statements is true?
    a. Short-term interest rates tend to move independently of one another.
    b. Long-term interest rates tend to move together, and they tend to mimic short-term interest rates.
    c. Open-market purchases by the FOMC result in the interest rate decreasing.
    d. Open-market sales by the FOMC increase the money supply and cause a movement along the money demand curve.

Use the following graph to answer the next two questions.

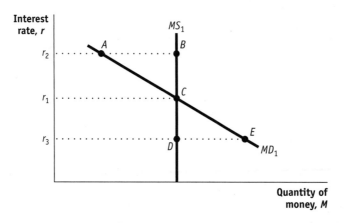

12. The economy is currently operating at its potential output level. Which point in the graph is most likely to represent this long-run situation in the money market? Point
    a. *A*, since high interest rates encourage people to save more leading to higher levels of investment
    b. *B*, since the FOMC controls the money supply we know we must be on the money supply curve in the long run
    c. *C*, since at this point the money market is in equilibrium
    d. *D*, since low interest rates encourage business investment, which leads to higher economic growth
    e. *E*, since low interest rates reduce inflationary pressures in the economy

13. In the graph, which point *most* likely represents a possible new short-run equilibrium if the FOMC conducts an open-market sale? Point
    a. *A*
    b. *B*
    c. *C*
    d. *D*
    e. *E*

14. Which of the following statements is true?
    a. In the long run, an increase in the nominal money supply increases the potential output level.
    b. In the long run, an increase in the nominal money supply will have no effect on real variables, including the aggregate price level.
    c. In the long run, an increase in the nominal money supply will lead to a proportionate increase in the aggregate price level.
    d. Answers (a) and (b) are both true.
    e. Answers (a), (b), and (c) are all true.

15. Suppose that an economy experiences an increase in the aggregate output level. Assuming that the central bank does not engage in monetary policy, which of the following statements is true?

    a. The interest rate in this economy will increase.

    b. The interest rate in this economy will decrease.

    c. The interest rate in this economy will be unaffected by this change in aggregate output.

    d. This change in aggregate output will cause a movement along the money demand curve.

16. The money supply curve shifts to the left. The most likely cause for this shift is the FOMC's open-market

    a. purchase of Treasury bills.

    b. sale of Treasury bills.

17. The money demand curve shifts to the right. The most likely cause for this shift among the following explanations is

    a. an increase in the interest rate.

    b. a decrease in the interest rate.

    c. a change in bank institutions that allows banks to pay even higher rates of interest on checking account funds.

    d. Answers (b) and (c) are both correct.

18. When the quantity of money demanded is greater than the quantity of money supplied, this implies that the interest rate is too low and people will decide to

    a. sell interest-bearing assets, resulting in the price of these assets falling while the interest rate paid on these assets rises.

    b. buy interest-bearing assets, resulting in the price of these assets rising while the interest rate paid on these assets rises.

19. When the Fed targets the federal funds rate, this means that the FOMC changes the money supply through open-market operations until the

    a. rate of inflation in the economy matches their target.

    b. actual federal funds rate equals the target rate.

20. Expansionary monetary policy will, holding everything else constant,

    a. lower the interest rate and cause *AD* to shift to the right.

    b. lower the interest rate and cause *AD* to shift to the left.

    c. raise the interest rate and cause *AD* to shift to the right.

    d. raise the interest rate and cause *AD* to shift to the left.

21. Suppose in the short run the level of aggregate output in an economy decreases at the same time the aggregate price level decreases. This is most likely due to a

    a. leftward shift in the short-run aggregate supply curve, holding everything else constant.

    b. rightward shift in the short-run aggregate supply curve, holding everything else constant.

    c. leftward shift in the aggregate demand curve, holding everything else constant.

    d. rightward shift in the aggregate demand curve, holding everything else constant.

22. When the economy is currently producing at a short-run level of aggregate output that is less than potential output, it is most likely that the Fed will engage in open-market
   a. purchases of Treasury bills.
   b. sales of Treasury bills.

23. The Taylor rule for monetary policy for the period from 1988 through 2008 provided guidance for setting the federal funds rate and stated that this rate should be set by considering
   a. both the inflation rate and the output gap.
   b. both the inflation rate and the level of unemployment.
   c. both the output gap and the level of unemployment.
   d. the inflation rate, the output gap, and the level of unemployment.

24. Inflation targeting means that
   a. the central bank adheres to maintaining a very strict interest rate target.
   b. the central bank announces the inflation rate that it is trying to achieve and then uses monetary policy to achieve this inflation rate.
   c. there may be a range of acceptable inflation rates or a specific inflation rate that the central bank hopes to achieve through monetary policy.
   d. Answers (a), (b), and (c) are all correct.
   e. Answers (b) and (c) are both correct.

25. Suppose the aggregate economy in the short run is operating at an aggregate output level that is greater than the potential output level. Holding everything else constant, what do you anticipate will happen to nominal wages in the long run given this information?
   a. Nominal wages will decrease.
   b. Nominal wages will remain constant.
   c. Nominal wages will increase.

26. In the short run, money is
   a. neutral since it can have no effect on real aggregate output.
   b. not neutral since changes in the money supply can cause real aggregate output to change.

27. After 2008, the Taylor rule
   a. resulted in a negative interest rate due to the combination of high unemployment and low inflation.
   b. did not predict Federal Reserve policy well since it is impossible to have a negative interest rate.

28. The zero lower bound refers to
   a. an upper limit for the interest rate where no matter what happens in the economy the interest rate cannot rise above this limit.
   b. the idea that interest rates cannot be less than zero since no one would be willing to accept a negative interest rate as the interest rate they would receive for lending out funds.

29. When an economy faces a zero lower bound, this implies that the central bank in this economy will be able to stimulate the economy
   a. by engaging in open market purchases.
   b. by engaging in open market sales.
   c. by engaging in open market purchases since interest rates cannot fall any further than their current level.
   d. at very low cost since the interest rate is so low.

30. The Federal Reserve Bank engaged in "quantitative easing" in November of 2010 because
   a. the Fed no longer believed, no matter what the situation, in open market operations as a monetary policy tool.
   b. the Fed recognized the zero lower bound problem and thought that "quantitative easing" might be a method of stimulating the economy given that open market purchases were ineffective.
   c. the Fed hoped this would drive interest rates on long-term debt down and that this would lead to economic expansion.
   d. Answers (a), (b), and (c) are all correct.
   e. Answers (b) and (c) are both correct.
   f. Answers (a) and (c) are both correct.

◼ ANSWER KEY

Answers to Problems and Exercises

1. **a.** An increase in the interest rate causes a movement along the money demand curve as illustrated in the following figure.

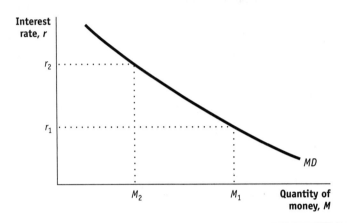

b. As the level of aggregate real income decreases, this causes the money demand curve to shift to the left as individuals demand less money at every interest rate. This is illustrated in the following figure.

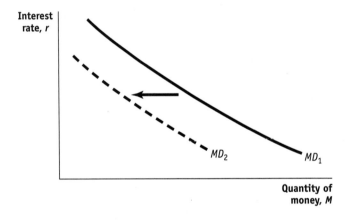

c. An increase in the aggregate price level causes the money demand curve to shift to the right, as individuals demand more money at every interest rate to facilitate making their transactions at the new higher price levels. This is illustrated in the following figure.

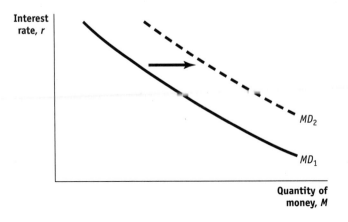

d. With new technology for managing money and financial assets, people will decrease their demand for money at every interest rate. This will cause money demand to shift to the left, as illustrated in the figure from part (b) of this answer.

2. Since both Asset A and Asset B are short-term financial assets, we anticipate that the interest rate paid on both assets should be roughly equivalent. If the returns differ, investors will sell the asset offering the lower return: to find a buyer for this asset, they must offer a higher rate on it. This buying and selling of assets will lead the returns on these short-term financial assets to move toward approximately the same return.

3. a.

Change	Effect on nominal money demand	Effect on real money demand
Decrease in aggregate price level	Shifts the nominal money demand curve to the left	Has no effect
Increase in interest rate	Causes a movement along the nominal money demand curve	Causes a movement along the real money demand curve
Change in regulation so that interest is now allowed on checking accounts	Shifts the nominal money demand curve to the right	Shifts the real money demand curve to the right

b. When the aggregate price level changes, the nominal money demand curve does not automatically take into account the effect of this change in prices on the nominal demand for money. For example, as the aggregate price level rises, people will find that, due to the increase in the aggregate price level, they need to hold greater amounts of money in order to make their transactions. This causes the nominal money demand curve to shift to the right: people demand a greater quantity of nominal money at every interest rate. In contrast, the real money demand curve automatically takes into account any change in the aggregate price level: a change in the aggregate price level requires a proportionately equal change in the nominal quantity of money in order that the real quantity of money is unchanged.

4. a. When the Fed increases the money supply through an open-market purchase of Treasury bills, this shifts the money supply curve from MS_1 to MS_2 and results in a decrease in the equilibrium interest rate from r_1 to r_2 and an increase in the equilibrium quantity of money from M_1 to M_2. The following figure illustrates these changes.

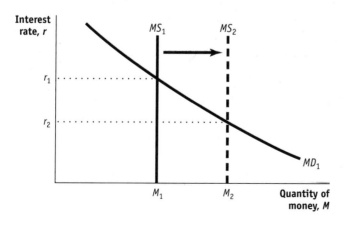

b. When the FOMC decreases the money supply through an open-market sale of Treasury bills, the money supply curve shifts from MS_1 to MS_2. This causes the equilibrium interest rate to increase from r_1 to r_2, while the equilibrium quantity of money decreases from M_1 to M_2. These changes are illustrated in the following figure.

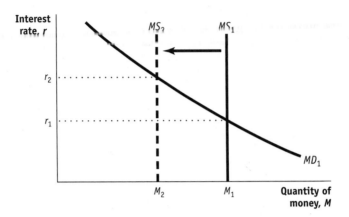

c. An increase in the aggregate price level shifts the money demand curve to the right from MD_1 to MD_2. This causes the equilibrium interest rate to increase from r_1 to r_2, while the equilibrium quantity of money is unchanged. The following figure illustrates this situation.

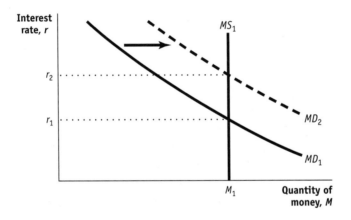

5.   a.

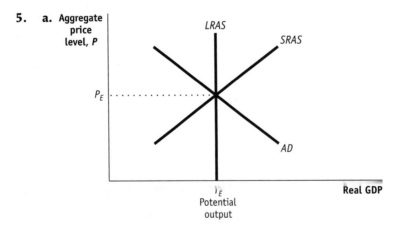

b.

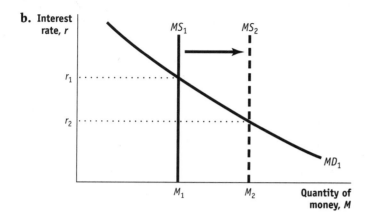

c. When the FOMC reduces interest rates through an open-market purchase of Treasury bills, this increases aggregate demand and causes the *AD* curve to shift to the right to AD_2. In the short run, this causes aggregate real output to increase to Y_2 and the aggregate price level to increase to P_2. This is illustrated in the following figure.

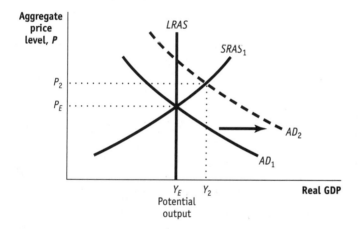

d. In the long run, the economy must return to producing its potential output, Y_E. This economic adjustment will occur as the *SRAS* curve shifts to the left as nominal wages rise. As the *SRAS* curve shifts back to $SRAS_3$, this will eliminate the inflationary gap, restore the economy to its potential output level, and lead to an even higher aggregate price level, P_3. The following figure illustrates this long-run adjustment.

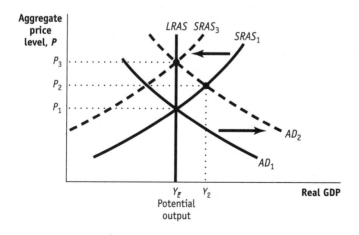

e. Aggregate price level, *P*

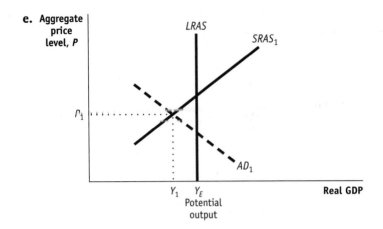

f. If the FOMC expands the money supply through open-market purchases, this will reduce interest rates and stimulate investment spending and, therefore, aggregate demand. As *AD* shifts to the right from AD_1 to AD_2, this will cause real GDP to increase to Y_E and prices to rise to P_2. The following figure illustrates this situation.

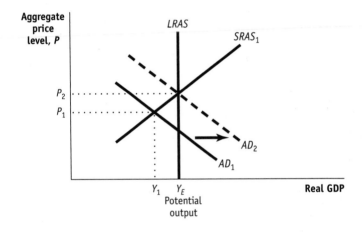

g. If the FOMC engages in activist monetary policy, this will cause the aggregate price level to increase. Alternatively, policymakers could do nothing and wait for the *SRAS* to shift to the right as nominal wages fall. In the long run, aggregate output would return to Y_E and the aggregate price level would fall below its initial level of P_1.

h. Aggregate price level, *P*

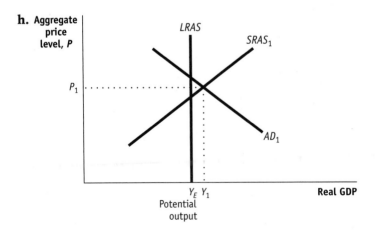

i. The FOMC should decrease the money supply and thereby increase the interest rate through open-market sales of Treasury bills. This action by the FOMC will cause the *AD* to shift to the left, restoring the economy to its potential output level at a lower aggregate price level than P_1.

j. No, this policy restores the economy to its long-run position without raising the aggregate price level.

6. The action by the FOMC effectively creates a change in autonomous investment spending of $500 million. This change in autonomous investment spending will cause real GDP to increase by a larger, multiplied amount due to the multiplier process. Since the multiplier equals $1/(1 - MPC)$ or, in this case, 4, we can compute the total change in real GDP as 4 ($500 million), or $2 billion.

7. The Fed can affect the economy through its open-market operations. When the Fed expands the money supply by purchasing Treasury bills, this causes the interest rate to fall, holding everything else constant. As the interest rate declines, this acts as a stimulus to investment and consumer spending and, therefore, as a stimulus to aggregate demand. Thus, open-market purchases typically are used to stimulate the economy: when the economy is producing below the potential output level (i.e., the economy is in a recession), the Fed has the potential to alter this output level via active monetary policy. Conversely, when the economy is producing at a level greater than the potential output level, the Fed can engage in open-market sales that will effectively lead to higher interest rates and lower investment and consumer spending, thereby causing the level of aggregate demand to fall, holding everything else constant.

8. Holding money has an opportunity cost since the money could have been used to purchase a financial item that could have yielded the holder an interest return. Thus, when the interest rate increases, this implies that the opportunity cost of holding money has risen: people will want to hold less money as the opportunity cost of holding that money increases. Thus, the interest rate and the quantity of money that people want to hold (that is, the quantity of money they demand) are inversely related to one another.

9. When the aggregate price level increases by 25%, this means on average prices in the economy have risen by 25%. This in turn implies that people will need 25% more money to make the same purchases; thus, the demand for money at any given interest rate will need to shift to the right and by an amount that is 25% greater than the original money demand. The idea here is that the demand for money will be proportional to the price level in the long run.

10. a. The central bank will want to decrease the interest rate. It can accomplish this goal by engaging in open-market purchases of Treasury bills.

b. The central bank wants to reduce the inflation rate. It can do this by increasing the interest rate since this will slow the economy and result in a smaller output gap, which will help to pull the interest rate and, therefore, the rate of inflation down in the economy. The central bank should engage in open-market sales of Treasury bills.

c. Since the central bank anticipates a slowdown in the economy, they also anticipate that there will be downward pressure on the aggregate price level as the level of spending in the economy falls. The central bank can stabilize the aggregate price level by engaging in expansionary monetary policy: the central bank should engage in open-market purchases of Treasury bills.

d. Since the current rate of unemployment is greater than the potential rate of unemployment, the economy is in a recession. The central bank will want to engage in expansionary monetary policy unless it is actively seeking to reduce the targeted rate of inflation and the actual rate of inflation in the economy.

Answers to Chapter Review Questions

1. **Answer b.** Although money typically does yield a lower rate of return than nonmonetary assets, this is not the reason people choose to hold money. Rather, they choose to hold money because money facilitates making transactions. There is an opportunity cost of holding money: when holding money you forego the higher rate of return you could earn by holding nonmonetary assets.

2. **Answer b.** The opportunity cost of holding money is measured by what is lost when holding money: this is calculated as the difference between the rate of return you could earn by holding nonmonetary assets minus the rate of return on monetary assets.

3. **Answer b.** The nominal demand for money is proportional to the aggregate price level. The higher the short-term interest rate, the greater the opportunity cost of holding money since you could be earning this higher short-term interest rate if you chose to hold nonmonetary assets. The quantity of money demanded is inversely, or negatively, related to the interest rate: as the interest rate increases, the quantity of money demanded decreases. Short-term interest rates do move together since if there is a difference in the rate of return on short-term financial assets, there will be movement toward the asset that pays the higher return and away from the asset that pays the lower return. As the market adjusts to this movement, there will be a tendency for the rate of returns for both assets to move toward one another: short-term interest rates will therefore tend to move together.

4. **Answer e.** The first two statements are factual statements that are true by definition. The real quantity of money is not proportional to the nominal quantity of money. However, the nominal quantity of money demanded is proportional to the aggregate price level.

5. **Answer a.** To maintain the same level of purchasing power as was initially had, when the aggregate price level doubles, the nominal quantity of money demanded will also double. However, a doubling of prices will have no effect on the real quantity of money demanded since this real money demand is, by definition, the amount of money that holds purchasing power constant. Holding everything else constant, assumes that a doubling of the price level will have no impact on the interest rate.

6. **Answer e.** When the quantity of money demanded is greater than the quantity of money supplied, people wish to increase their money holdings. This will cause them to sell their nonmonetary assets: as the supply of these nonmonetary assets increases, people will find they must offer higher interest rates on these assets in order to sell them. Thus, interest rates will increase.

7. **Answer b.** If the target interest rate is greater than the federal funds rate, then the Fed needs to engage in monetary policy that will shift the money supply curve to the left, resulting in an increase in interest rates for a given money demand curve. The FOMC, therefore, will engage in open-market sales of Treasury bills. Congress does not set the discount rate, and the Fed's monetary policy affects the money supply curve and not the money demand curve.

8. **Answer b.** The liquidity preference model uses the interaction between the quantity of money demanded and the quantity of money supplied to analyze the determination of interest rates. Interest rates are impacted by Federal Reserve policy and its effect on the money supply curve. People consider the opportunity cost of holding money when making their decisions about the level of money they wish to hold. One can model interest rate determination in either the framework of money demand and supply or the framework of demand and supply of loanable funds.

9. **Answer c.** The Fed controls the money supply through open-market operations. We know that the determination of interest rates depends not only on the quantity of money demanded but also on the quantity of money supplied. Congress does not have the authority to determine the country's money supply. Different levels of money supply are compatible with the full-employment level of output, since interest rate determination depends on both the money supply and the money demand.

10. **Answer c.** When interest rates must rise, this implies they are initially too low: in the money market, this would imply that the interest rate is initially below the equilibrium interest rate or where the quantity of money demanded is greater than the quantity of money supplied.

11. **Answer c.** Short-term interest rates tend to move together, while long-term interest rates may or may not mimic short-term interest rates. When the FOMC makes an open-market purchase, this increases the level of reserves in the banking system, which leads to an expansion in the money supply and a decrease in the interest rate.

12. **Answer c.** In the long run, the economy is in equilibrium, including the money market where the quantity of money demanded must equal the quantity of money supplied. This is only true at point C in the graph.

13. **Answer a.** When the FOMC conducts an open-market sale, this causes the money supply to shift to the left and, for a given demand curve, results in the interest rate increasing. Only point A illustrates this scenario.

14. **Answer c.** In the long run, the economy will operate at the potential output level: any increase in the money supply will not affect the real value of aggregate output, but will lead to a proportionate increase in the aggregate price level.

15. **Answer a.** When aggregate real output increases in an economy, this causes the demand for money to shift to the right. For a given money supply curve (remember the central bank is not engaging in monetary policy), this will cause the interest rate to increase.

16. **Answer b.** When the FOMC engages in open-market sales of Treasury bills, it sells Treasury bills to the public and receive dollars for those Treasury bills. The FOMC effectively removes reserves from the banking system with the sale of Treasury bills, which reduces the quantity of money supplied at every interest rate: the supply of money curve shifts to the left.

17. **Answer c.** A change in the interest rate, whether an increase or a decrease, causes a movement along the money demand curve. An increase in the amount of interest banks can pay on checking account funds reduces the opportunity cost of holding funds in a checking account rather than in an interest-bearing asset: people will increase the quantity of money they demand at every interest rate with this change, which will result in the money demand curve shifting to the right.

18. **Answer a.** When quantity of money demanded is greater than quantity of money supplied, this implies that the interest rate is too low: the opportunity cost of holding money is relatively low and, therefore, people choose to hold more money. This causes people to sell interest-bearing assets (like bonds) and as the supply of these interest-bearing assets increases, this leads to a decrease in the price of these interest-bearing assets. As the price of these assets decreases, this implies that the interest rate paid on these assets is increasing.

19. **Answer b.** Targeting the federal funds rate means that the Fed is using open-market operations to alter the interest rate banks charge one another for loans (the federal funds rate) so that it reaches a desired, or targeted, level.

20. **Answer a.** Expansionary monetary policy is an increase in the money supply: when the money supply increases, this means that the supply of money curve shifts to the right causing the interest rate to fall. A fall in the interest rate results in higher investment spending and consumption spending: this causes the AD curve to shift to the right.

21. **Answer c.** If there is only one shift in either the short-run AS curve or the AD curve, then a fall in both the aggregate output level and the aggregate price level is only possible with a leftward shift of the AD curve.

22. **Answer a.** When the current level of aggregate output is less than potential output, the Fed will likely engage in expansionary monetary policy to stimulate the economy to return to the potential output level. Expansionary monetary policy implies that the Fed is increasing the money supply; hence, the Fed is purchasing Treasury bills in the open market.

23. **Answer b.** The original Taylor rule for setting the Federal funds rate for the period 1988 through 2008 is given by the following equation: Federal funds rate = 2.07 + 1.28 × inflation − 1.95 × unemployment gap. Although there is a relationship between the level of output and the unemployment rate, the Taylor rule for this time period does not explicitly include the output gap.

24. **Answer e.** Inflation targeting involves having the central bank announce the inflation rate or range for the inflation rate it is trying to achieve and then use its monetary policy to achieve this announced goal. Monetary policy to achieve a stated inflation goal will necessarily imply the loss of interest rate control since the interest rate will need to vary in order for the central bank to achieve its inflation target.

25. **Answer c.** When the economy operates in the short run at an aggregate output level greater than the potential level of output, this implies that unemployment is below the natural rate of unemployment. As the economy moves to the long run, nominal wages will increase due to labor market pressures arising from this lower-than-natural level of unemployment. The nominal wage will continue to increase until the short-run *AS* curve shifts far enough to the left to return this economy to its potential output level.

26. **Answer b.** Money in the short run is not neutral: when the central bank changes the money supply, this causes the *AD* curve to shift and in the short run this shift will cause the economy to either contract or expand. In the long run, the short-run aggregate supply curve shifts, returning the aggregate economy to its potential output level: in the long run, money is neutral since it cannot alter the level of aggregate real output.

27. **Answer b.** Application of the Taylor rule after 2008 predicted that interest rates would be negative. But it is impossible for interest rates to be negative, so the Taylor rule was not very insightful after 2008 due to the combination of high unemployment and low inflation creating a prediction that simply could not come true.

28. **Answer b.** Interest rates must be positive or equal to zero because no one would willingly accept a negative return since they can always earn an interest rate of zero if they choose to hold cash. The zero lower bound refers to the idea that interest rates cannot fall below zero.

29. **Answer c.** Open market purchases are used by central banks to stimulate the economy because these open market purchases typically result in the interest rate decreasing when the money supply increases. When an economy is operating at its zero lower bound, this implies that interest rates in the economy are as low as they can go and that any open market purchase will have little impact since the interest rate will not drop any further.

30. **Answer e.** In November 2010, the Fed wanted to pursue an expansionary economic policy due to the state of the economy. However, the interest rate at that time was at or near zero and open market purchases would have been ineffective since the interest rate could not be lowered any further. The Fed engaged in "quantitative easing" so that it would lead to lower interest rates on long-term debt, which, the Fed hoped, would lead to an expansionary effect on the economy,

Inflation, Disinflation, and Deflation

▌ BEFORE YOU READ THE CHAPTER

Summary

This chapter analyzes the underlying causes of inflation as well as the costs of inflation. The chapter explores the relationship between the rate of growth of the money supply and the inflation rate: economies that collect an inflation tax by printing money find that this practice can lead to high rates of inflation. The chapter also discusses the relationship between high inflation and hyperinflation. In the chapter, the costs of inflation as well as the costs of disinflation are discussed along with the debate about the optimal rate of inflation. In addition, the chapter discusses why even moderate rates of inflation may be difficult to eliminate and why deflation presents a problem for economic policy. The chapter also develops the concept of the short-run Phillips curve to illustrate the short-run relationship between inflation and unemployment. In addition, the chapter discusses the relationship between the short-run Phillips curve and the long-run Phillips curve. Finally, the chapter discusses the difficulty of ending even moderate inflation and why periods of deflation create significant economic problems.

Chapter Objectives

Objective #1. Economists define hyperinflation as a very high rate of inflation. Hyperinflation is always associated with rapid increases in the money supply.

Objective #2. In the long run, any given percentage increase in the money supply does not change the level of real GDP, but it does result in an equal percentage rise in the overall price level. Thus, an increase in the nominal money supply, M, leads to a long-run increase in the aggregate price level, P, that leaves the real money supply, M/P, at its original level.

Objective #3. The classical model of the price level is a simplified model that equates the short run as equivalent to the long run. In this model, the real quantity of money, M/P, is always at its long-run equilibrium level. This model assumes the neutrality of money in the long run: that is, in the long run, the level of the nominal money supply does not affect the level of real GDP. The classical model of the price level assumes that the economy moves from one long-run equilibrium to another because wages and prices are flexible: in this model, the economy always produces at a point on its *LRAS* curve. This assumption is a poor assumption during periods of low inflation, but seems to work well as a model in periods of high inflation since in periods of high inflation wage and price stickiness seems to disappear.

- In countries with high inflation, changes in the money supply are quickly translated into changes in the inflation rate.

- Fiat money is money that has no intrinsic value, and in modern economies this reliance on the use of fiat money means that governments can choose to pay for some of their expenditures by simply printing money and using this printed money to pay some of their bills. In the United States, the U.S. Treasury finances the government's spending: the Fed monetizes this debt by creating money when it buys the debt back from the public through open-market purchases of Treasury bills.

- Sources of revenue for the government include the right to print money, or seigniorage. When governments run large deficits and are unwilling to increase taxes or decrease spending, they often turn to printing money to finance their deficit and this leads to large increases in the aggregate price level. This action imposes an inflation tax on those people who currently hold money. When inflation is high, people will try to avoid holding money and will instead substitute real goods as well as interest-bearing assets for money.

- The revenue created by printing money in real terms is the real seignorage. Real seignorage is calculated as the change in the money supply divided by the price level, or real seignorage is equal to the rate of growth of the money supply times the real money supply.

- Over time for a given amount of real seignorage, the government must impose an ever higher rate of inflation. Thus, governments that pay for goods and services by printing money may end up creating higher and higher rates of inflation leading eventually to hyperinflation.

Objective #4. In the face of high inflation, the public will reduce the level of real money it holds. This reduction in real money holding forces the government to generate a higher rate of inflation in order to collect the same amount of real inflation tax: this action causes the inflation rate to accelerate and can easily lead to the inflation rate spiraling out of control.

Objective #5. Economies will experience moderate inflation if they pursue economic policies that target an unemployment rate that is below the natural rate of unemployment. Governments may purposefully pursue such targets prior to an election in order to achieve low rates of unemployment at the time of the election. The government may choose too low a target for the natural rate of unemployment: the pursuit of this overly optimistic target will lead to moderate inflation.

- Disinflation refers to the process of bringing down inflation when the inflation has become embedded in expectations. An economy trying to reduce inflation that is built into expectations will find this a difficult task: policymakers will need to keep the unemployment rate above the natural rate for an extended period of time in order to bring down this kind of inflation.

- Moderate inflation may also be the result of supply shocks to the economy. If the short-run *AS* curve shifts to the left, this brings a higher level of aggregate prices while reducing the level of real GDP. Policymakers find it difficult to pursue anti-inflationary policy when there is a negative supply shock, since this will produce even higher levels of unemployment. The great disinflation of the 1980s in the United States illustrates this problem: disinflation was achieved by pushing the economy into the worst recession since the Great Depression.

Objective # 6. In an economy, actual output fluctuates around potential output in the short run: a recessionary gap occurs when actual output is less than potential output, and an inflationary gap occurs when actual output is greater than potential output. The percentage difference between the actual level of real GDP and the potential output is called the output gap. A negative output gap is associated with an unusually high unemployment rate, while a positive output gap is associated with an unusually low unemployment rate.

- Okun's law provides an estimate of the negative relationship between the output gap and the unemployment rate. According to Okun's law, each additional percentage point of output gap reduces the unemployment rate by less than one percentage point. A modern estimate of Okun's law is that the unemployment rate in the United States is equal to the natural rate of unemployment minus half the output gap or in equation form: unemployment rate = natural rate of unemployment – (0.5 × output gap).

  - The relationship between the output gap and the unemployment rate is less than one to one for several reasons. First, firms meet changes in demand for their products by changing the number of hours their existing workers work rather than changing the number of workers they hire. Second, the number of workers looking for work is affected by the availability of jobs: as the number of jobs fall, some workers will become discouraged and stop looking for work, and this will cause the unemployment rate to rise less than it would if these workers were to continue their job search.

Objective #7. Economic data suggests that when the unemployment rate is high, the wage rate tends to fall, and when the unemployment rate is low, the wage rate tends to rise. There is a similar pattern between the unemployment rate and the rate of inflation: in the short run, the rate of inflation is negatively related to the unemployment rate. The short-run Phillips curve (*SRPC*) represents this negative relationship between the unemployment rate and the inflation rate. The *SRPC* says that at any given point in time, there is a trade-off between unemployment and inflation: lower unemployment is possible only with higher inflation.

- In the short run, an increase in the aggregate price level due to shifts in the *AD* result in increases in real GDP, which in turn lead to lower unemployment rates. Thus, aggregate price increases occur as unemployment decreases. That is, a low rate of unemployment corresponds to an economy in which there are shortages of labor and other resources, leading to rising prices.

- The most important factor affecting inflation rates other than the unemployment rate is the expected inflation rate. The expected inflation rate is that rate of inflation that employers and workers expect in the near future.

- The expected inflation rate affects the *SRPC*. When the expected inflation rate increases, this causes the *SRPC* to shift up by the amount of the expected inflation at every unemployment rate.

- In general people base their expectations about inflation on experience. If the inflation rate has been 5%, then people will expect the inflation rate to continue to be around 5%; if the inflation rate rises to 10%, then people will expect the inflation rate to be around 10%.

- The *SRPC* worked in the 1960s but seemed to break down in the 1970s as the economy experienced both high unemployment and high inflation. This stagflation is believed to be the result of supply shocks and a buildup of expectations about inflation.

- The long-run Phillips curve (*LRPC*) is a vertical line at an unemployment level high enough that the actual inflation rate equals the expected inflation rate. This unemployment rate is called the nonaccelerating inflation rate of unemployment, or the NAIRU, since it is the level of unemployment that equates the actual rate of inflation with the expected inflation rate. An economy operating at levels of unemployment below the

NAIRU will experience accelerating inflation; that is, an unemployment rate below NAIRU cannot be maintained in the long run. The NAIRU is just another name for the natural rate of unemployment, or the sum of frictional and structural unemployment.

Objective #8.   Deflation refers to a falling aggregate price level. Unexpected deflation benefits lenders who are owed money, because the real value of the payments they receive from borrowers increases during deflation; unexpected deflation hurts borrowers who owe money, because the real value of the payments they make to lenders increases during deflation.

- During a period of deflation, borrowers must cut their spending when the burden of their debt increases due to the deflation: this leads to a sharp decrease in aggregate demand which worsens the economic slump. The effect of deflation in reducing aggregate demand is known as debt deflation.

- During a period of deflation, people will expect inflation to fall: these expectations will lead to a reduction in the aggregate price level. There is a limit, however, to how far the nominal interest rate can fall: this is called the zero bound, a situation where the nominal interest rate cannot fall below 0%. This zero bound means that the central bank can find itself in a situation where it cannot effectively use monetary policy to stimulate the economy: if the nominal interest rate is already zero, the central bank cannot cut the nominal interest rate any further. This situation is called the liquidity trap where monetary policy is useless as a means of stimulating aggregate demand because the nominal interest rate simply cannot fall any further.

Key Terms

classical model of the price level a simplified financial model of the price level in which the real quantity of money, M/P, is always at its long-run *equilibrium* level. This model ignores the distinction between the short run and the long run but is useful for analyzing the case of high *inflation*.

inflation tax the reduction in the value of money held by the public caused by *inflation*.

Okun's law the negative relationship between the *output gap* and the *unemployment rate*, whereby each additional percentage point of output gap reduces the unemployment rate by about one-half of a percentage point.

short-run Phillips curve (SRPC) a graphical representation of the negative short-run relationship between the *unemployment rate* and the *inflation rate*.

nonaccelerating inflation rate of unemployment (NAIRU) the *unemployment rate* at which, other things equal, *inflation* does not change over time.

long-run Phillips curve (LRPC) a graphical representation of the relationship between *unemployment* and *inflation* in the long run after expectations of inflation have had time to adjust to experience.

disinflation the process of bringing down *inflation* that has become embedded in expectations.

Key Terms *(continued)*

debt deflation the reduction in aggregate demand arising from the increase in the real burden of outstanding debt caused by *deflation;* occurs because borrowers, whose real debt rises as a result of deflation, are likely to cut spending sharply, and lenders, whose real assets are now more valuable, are less likely to increase spending.

zero bound the lower bound of zero on the *nominal interest rate.*

liquidity trap a situation in which *monetary policy* is ineffective because *nominal interest rates* are up against the *zero bound.*

■ AFTER YOU READ THE CHAPTER

Tips

Tip #1. The chapter introduces new vocabulary that you will want to learn and understand. In particular, you will want to be able to define and distinguish between deflation and disinflation. You will also want to understand the concept of debt deflation. Deflation refers to a fall in the aggregate price level, and disinflation refers to a decrease in the inflation rate reflecting policymakers' decisions that the economy has built-in inflationary expectations that need to be reduced. Debt deflation refers to a situation where deflation makes existent loan contracts more costly for borrowers: as the real burden of their debt increases, borrowers will decrease their spending. This reduction in aggregate spending is referred to as debt deflation.

Tip #2. It is important to understand the distinction between inflation and hyperinflation and their causes. Inflation refers to an increase in the general price level in the economy and may be due to positive demand shocks or negative supply shocks. Figure 16.1 illustrates a positive demand shock, while Figure 16.2 illustrates a negative supply shock: both types of shocks lead to higher aggregate price levels.

Figure 16.1

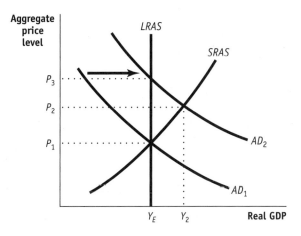

Figure 16.2

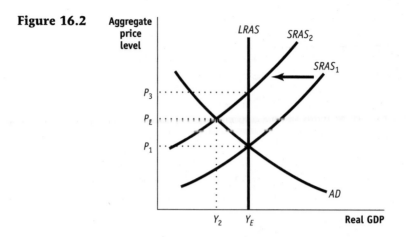

Hyperinflation refers to very high rates of inflation: hyperinflation in an economy is caused by the government printing money to finance its government deficits.

Tip #3. You will want to review the concept of the liquidity trap and the zero bound for nominal interest rates. The zero bound refers to the lower limit for the nominal interest rate: nominal interest rates cannot fall below zero percent. When an economy finds that its nominal interest rate has fallen to zero, it will no longer be able to use monetary policy to stimulate the economy: monetary policy will be unable to stimulate aggregate spending through decreases in the nominal interest rate. This situation is referred to as a liquidity trap: increasing the money supply, an increase in liquidity, does nothing for the economy since the economy is "trapped" by the inability of the nominal interest rate to fall further.

Tip #4. It is important to fully understand the concept of the natural rate of unemployment, or the NAIRU. The NAIRU provides a measure of the unemployment rate that corresponds to the economy operating at its potential output level without any inflationary pressures. Economies that adopt policies in order to reduce their unemployment rate below this natural rate will experience inflation: persistent adoption of these policies will generate accelerating inflation.

Tip #5. It is important to understand the short-run Phillips curve (SRPC) and how the expected inflation rate affects it as well as why the long-run Phillips curve (LRPC) is a vertical line at the NAIRU. The SRPC illustrates the negative relationship between the inflation rate and the unemployment rate. The SRPC is drawn with a given level of expected inflation. If expected inflation increases, this will shift the SRPC upward by the change in the expected inflation rate. In the long run, the economy—no matter what the expected inflation rate—will settle at an unemployment rate equal to the NAIRU. Figure 16.3 depicts three SRPC: $SRPC_0$ is drawn with expected inflation equal to 0%; $SRPC_1$ is drawn with expected inflation equal to 1%; and $SRPC_2$ is drawn with expected inflation equal to 3%. On the graph we see that this economy operates at its natural rate of unemployment (point A) when the unemployment rate equals 4%, the inflation rate equals 0%, and the expected inflation rate equals 0%. If the expected inflation rate increases to 1%, then the natural rate of unemployment of 4% is only possible with an inflation rate of 1% (point B on the graph). If the expected inflation rate rises to 3%, this shifts the SRPC to $SRPC_2$ and the natural rate of unemployment of 4% is only possible with an inflation rate of 3% (point C). The economy in the long run will gravitate back to the vertical line representing the natural rate of unemployment and its independence in the long run from the inflation rate.

Figure 16.3

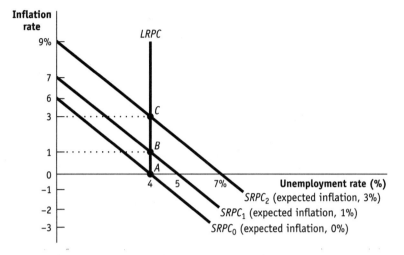

Tip #6.   It is important to understand how Okun's law works and the relationship between the natural rate of unemployment, the level of aggregate production in the economy, and the actual rate of unemployment expressed by Okun's law. A modern version of Okun's law for the United States can be stated as unemployment rate = natural rate of unemployment − (0.5 × output gap). This equation depicts the relationship between the output gap (the difference between actual output and potential output measured in percentage terms) and the unemployment rate. When the output gap equals zero, this implies actual output equals potential output and, therefore, the unemployment rate equals the natural rate of unemployment. When an economy has a negative output gap, this implies actual output is less than potential output and the economy faces a recessionary gap. Okun's law indicates that this negative output gap will result in the unemployment rate exceeding the natural rate of unemployment. When an economy has a positive output gap, this implies actual output is greater than potential output and the economy faces an inflationary gap. Okun's law indicates that this positive output gap will result in the unemployment rate falling below the natural rate of unemployment.

WORKED PROBLEMS

1.   In Zerbia, the aggregate price level has been changing quite rapidly. Your friend, Zorba, owns a restaurant where he charges a fixed price of $10 per dinner. He has come to you for advice on what price he should charge for dinner, given the changes in the aggregate price level. You tell him you will provide him guidance after you look into the situation. Upon consulting the available economic data, you find that the aggregate price level in Zerbia is increasing 50% per month. Using this information, provide Zorba with his menu prices for the next year using the following table to organize your response. Finally,

calculate the percentage increase in the price of dinner from the beginning of the year to the end of the year.

Month	Price of dinner
January	$10.00
February	
March	
April	
May	
June	
July	
August	
September	
October	
November	
December	

STEP 1: Analyze the data you have been given and determine how to use that data to answer Zorba's question.

Review the section "Money and Inflation" on page 476 (Econ page 908).

The aggregate price level in Zerbia is increasing by 50% per month. That means that if Zorba wants to price his dinners at a nominal price that maintains the real price of the dinner at $10, he will need to increase his dinner price by 50% each month. For February, the price of dinner will be equal to (the price of the dinner in January)(1 + the inflation rate as a decimal) or (the price of the dinner in January)(1 + .5). For March, we will use this basic formula but replace the price of the dinner in January with the price of the dinner in February. This process will continue for each of the months for which we want to compute the price of dinner.

STEP 2: Use the given monthly inflation rate to calculate the needed adjustment in the price of dinner. Fill in the table for Zorba.

Review the section "Money and Inflation" on page 476 (Econ page 908).

Month	Price of dinner
January	$10.00
February	15.00
March	22.50
April	33.75
May	50.63
June	75.94
July	113.91
August	170.86
September	256.29
October	384.43
November	576.65
December	864.98

STEP 3: Finally, calculate the percentage increase in the price of dinner from the beginning of the year to the end of the year.

Review the section "Money and Inflation" on page 476 (Econ page 908).

To find the percentage increase in the price of dinner from the beginning of the year to the end of the year, we use the prices in the preceding table and the simple percentage change formula. Thus, [($864.98 − $10.00)/($10.00)](100) = 8,549.80%.

2. Joe's Used Cars negotiates a loan from First Bank of $500,000 for its business operations for the coming year. Joe's Used Cars and First Bank agree on the terms of the loan: First Bank will loan Joe's Used Cars the $500,000 for the year, and Joe's Used Cars will repay the full amount of the loan at the end of the year plus $50,000. At the time the loan is made, both Joe's Used Cars and First Bank anticipate that the rate of inflation for the year will be 5%. The actual rate of inflation during the year is 2%. Given this information, identify the nominal interest rate on the loan, the expected real interest rate on the loan, and the actual real interest rate on the loan. In addition, determine who is made better off when the actual rate of inflation is less than the expected rate of inflation, and then explain your answer.

STEP 1: Calculate the nominal rate of interest given the information.

Review the section "Deflation" on page 494 (Econ page 926).

The nominal rate of interest on this loan is found by using the following formula:

Loan repayment = Principal (1 + nominal interest rate)

We know that the loan repayment is $550,000 and we know that the principal, or the amount borrowed, is $500,000. Thus, the given formula can be written as 550,000 = 500,000(1 + nominal interest rate). Simplifying this formula we get (50,000)/(500,000) = nominal interest rate or the nominal interest rate is equal to 10%. An alternative way to see this is to recognize that $50,000, the interest payment, is 10% of the total amount borrowed.

STEP 2: Calculate the expected real rate of interest.

Review the section "Deflation" on page 494 (Econ page 926).

The expected real rate of interest can be found by using the formula

Expected real interest rate = nominal interest rate − expected inflation rate

From Step 1 we know that the nominal interest rate is 10%, and from the given information we know that the expected inflation rate is 5%: thus, the expected real interest rate is 5%.

STEP 3: Calculate the actual real rate of interest.

Review the section "Deflation" on page 494 (Econ page 926).

The actual real rate of interest can be found by using the formula

Actual real interest rate = nominal interest rate − actual inflation rate

From Step 1 we know that the nominal interest rate is 10%, and from the given information we know that the actual rate of inflation was 2%: thus, the actual real interest rate is 8%.

STEP 4: Determine who benefits when the actual rate of inflation is greater than the expected rate of inflation.

Review the section "Deflation" on page 494 (Econ page 926).

First Bank benefits since it made the loan anticipating that it would earn a real rate of interest of 5%, and instead it actually earned a real rate of interest of 8%. Joe's Used Cars is hurt because it agreed to pay a real interest rate of 5% for the loan, and it is instead paying a real interest rate of 8% for this loan.

3. Pedro bought a house in 2004 and his monthly mortgage payments for this house are equal to $1,200 a month. In 2004, when he bought the house, Pedro's annual income was $57,600. Unfortunately, Pedro lost his job during the financial crisis of 2008. He was lucky to find new employment, but his employer is only willing to pay him $48,000 a year. This loss in income reflects an overall decrease in the aggregate price level that occurred as a result of the financial crisis of 2008. Pedro knows that he is earning a lower nominal income, but he is also recognizing that his debt on the house is creating additional stress. What was the ratio of annual mortgage payments to income when Pedro took out the loan, and what is this ratio now? Using these two ratios calculate what the percentage change in Pedro's mortgage payment to income ratio has been. What do you anticipate Pedro will do if you assume that he continues to make his mortgage payment each month and if his income does not change? Finally, how will Pedro's behavior (along with the behavior of other homeowners in a similar position) affect the aggregate economy? In your answer be sure to incorporate the concept of debt deflation.

STEP 1: Calculate Pedro's yearly mortgage payments.

Review the section "Deflation" on page 494 (Econ page 926).

This is a simple mathematical calculation: Pedro pays $1,200 per month and there are 12 months in a year, so his yearly mortgage payment is equal to ($1,200/month)(12 months), or $14,400.

STEP 2: Calculate the ratio of Pedro's yearly mortgage payment to his initial income.

Review the section "Deflation" on page 494 (Econ page 926).

We know that Pedro's initial income is $57,600 and his yearly mortgage payment is $14,400. So the ratio of Pedro's yearly mortgage payment to his initial annual income is $14,400/$57,600, or .25. This ratio indicates that Pedro initially spent 25% of his annual income on his house payments.

STEP 3: Calculate the ratio of Pedro's yearly mortgage payment to his new income.

Review the section "Deflation" on page 494 (Econ page 926).

We know that Pedro's new income is $48,000 and his yearly mortgage payment is $14,400. So the ratio of Pedro's yearly mortgage payment to his new annual income is $14,400/$48,000, or .3. This ratio indicates that Pedro is now spending 30% of his annual income on his house payments.

STEP 4: Calculate the percentage change in Pedro's yearly mortgage payment to income ratio.

Review the section "Deflation" on page 494 (Econ page 926).

The percentage change in Pedro's yearly mortgage payment to income ratio is equal to [(.3 −.25)/(.25)](100), or 20%.

STEP 5: Comment on why this change in the ratio of yearly mortgage payment to income adversely affects Pedro and why this kind of change might also affect the aggregate economy if many homeowners were experiencing this kind of change in their incomes. In your answer include the concept of debt deflation and how it relates to this scenario.

Review the section "Deflation" on page 494 (Econ page 926).

Fisher in discussing debt deflation focused on how deflation would take away resources from borrowers and redistribute these resources to lenders, and as this happens it worsens the economic slump. In this story, Pedro has experienced a loss of income due to the economic slump and the accompanying decrease in the aggregate price level. This loss of income effectively means that a greater percentage of his income is now devoted to his house payments. As Pedro continues to make these house payments, he is apt to find that he is short of cash and must curtail other spending that he might otherwise undertake. If others are in a similar situation, the overall level of aggregate spending will fall making the economic slump worse. This effect of deflation (in this case, a decrease in Pedro's annual income) in reducing aggregate demand is known as debt deflation.

4. The following graph illustrates the short-run Phillips curve for an economy when expected inflation is 0%. You are asked to advise the leaders of the government of this economy as to what the natural rate of unemployment is in the economy. Currently, the economy is producing at 5% unemployment, and you are asked to explain to the government officials what the level of expected inflation is in this economy when unemployment is 5% as well as discuss how this economy will adjust if unemployment is kept at 5%. You are also asked what will happen to expected inflation and the short-run Phillips curve if the government decides to pursue an unemployment rate of 2%. Finally, the government would like to know what the long-run Phillips curve looks like for this economy, given the graph that follows. The government officials hope that you will explain your findings with graphs as well as words. Assume that the short-run Phillips curve is linear for this question.

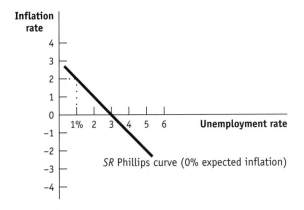

STEP 1: Identify the natural rate of unemployment.

Review the section "Moderate Inflation and Disinflation" on page 481 (Econ page 913) and Figure 16-12 on page 493 (Econ page 925).

The natural rate of unemployment for this economy is 3% because when the unemployment rate is at 3%, the actual rate of inflation (0%) is equal to the expected rate of inflation (0%). When the economy deviates from this unemployment rate the actual inflation rate will either rise (as the unemployment rate decreases), or the actual inflation rate will fall (as the unemployment rate increases). This deviation of actual inflation rate from expected inflation rate will cause the short-run Phillips curve to shift as these changes in actual inflation are incorporated into expectations about inflation.

STEP 2: Evaluate the effect of producing at 5% unemployment on this economy's expected inflation.

Review the section "Moderate Inflation and Disinflation" on page 481 (Econ page 913) and Figure 16-12 on page 493 (Econ page 925).

From the given graph, we can see that the unemployment rate and the inflation rate are negatively related to one another. When the unemployment rate is 5%, then the actual inflation rate is equal to −2% (deflation). This lower inflation rate will result in the short-run Phillips curve shifting downward as expectations about inflation get incorporated in this new short-run Phillips curve. If policy makers act to keep the unemployment rate at 5%, this will result in further revisions of the expected inflation rate with further downward shifts in the short-run Phillips curve. An unemployment rate above the natural rate of unemployment results in ever-accelerating deflation. The following graph illustrates the first shift in the short-run Phillips curve as people adjust to the deviation of the actual inflation rate from the expected inflation rate.

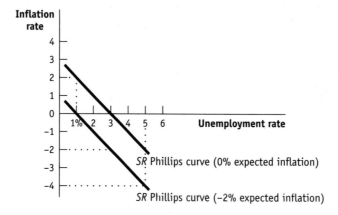

STEP 3: Discuss how the change in expected inflation alters the short-run Phillips Curve.

Review the section "Moderate Inflation and Disinflation" on page 481 (Econ page 913) and Figure 16-12 on page 493 (Econ page 925).

This is illustrated in the graph given in Step 2. When there is a change in expected inflation the short-run Phillips curve shifts: it shifts upward if the change in expected inflation represents an increase in the expected rate of inflation, and it shifts downward if the change in expected inflation represents a decrease in the expected rate of inflation.

STEP 4: What happens to the expected inflation and the graph if the government decides to pursue policy that will result in an unemployment rate of 2%?

Review the section "Moderate Inflation and Disinflation" on page 481 (Econ page 913) and Figure 16-12 on page 493 (Econ page 925).

From the initial graph we can see that the rate of inflation associated with an unemployment rate of 2% is 1%. Since an actual inflation rate of 1% is different from the expected rate of inflation of 0%, this will cause the short-run Phillips Curve to shift upward as people revised their inflationary expectations. If the government persists in pursuing policy that results in an unemployment rate of 2%, the short-run Phillips curve will continue to shift upward resulting in ever-accelerating inflation. The following graph illustrates this idea.

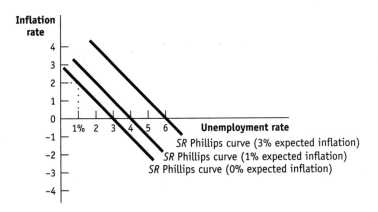

STEP 5: **Identify the long-run Phillips Curve given the initial graph.**

Review the section "Moderate Inflation and Disinflation" on page 481 (Econ page 913) and Figure 16-12 on page 493 (Econ page 925).

The long-run Phillips curve is a vertical line at 3% unemployment. When unemployment is 3% and the expected inflation is 0%, the actual rate of inflation is equal to the expected rate of inflation. When the expected inflation increases to 1%, then the short-run Phillips curve shifts upward, and we see that at an unemployment rate of 3% the actual rate of inflation of 1% is equal to the expected inflation of 1%. As expectations of inflation change the short-run Phillips curve shifts, but the long-run Phillips curve remains a vertical line where unemployment is equal to 3%. The following graph illustrates this idea.

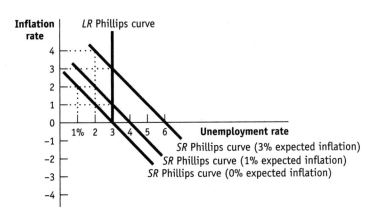

Problems and Exercises

1. Use the following table to answer this question.

Real inflation tax	Inflation rate	Real money supply
$ 5 million	5%	$100 million
	5	120 million
12.80 million		160 million
14 million	7	
20 million		200 million

a. We know that the real inflation tax is equal to the inflation rate times the real money supply. Use this information to fill in the missing entries in the table.

b. For a given level of the real money supply, what happens to the real inflation tax if the inflation rate increases?

c. For a given level of the real money supply, if the real inflation tax is decreasing, what must be true about the inflation rate?

d. For a given real inflation tax, what happens to the real money supply if the inflation rate increases?

2. Suppose you live in an economy that is currently experiencing hyperinflation. At the start of the year, the cost of a loaf of bread is $2.

a. If the inflation rate is 100% a month, what will be the price of the loaf of bread in 12 months? You might find it helpful to organize your answer in a table giving the month of the year and the price of the bread for that month.

b. What is the total price increase in percentage terms for the year?

3. Joe lends Mary $1,000 for the year. They agree that Mary will repay the full $1,000 at the end of the year and in addition, they agree that Mary will pay Joe $50 in interest payments.

    a. What is the nominal interest rate that Mary and Joe have agreed to in this contract?

    b. If Joe and Mary both anticipate that inflation will be 3% for the year, what real interest rate are each of them trying to achieve in their loan contract?

    c. Suppose the actual inflation rate for the year is 2%. Who benefits more from this inflation rate, and why do you think they benefit more? Explain your answer.

    d. Suppose the actual inflation rate for the year is 4%. Who benefits more from this inflation rate, and why do you think they benefit more? Explain your answer.

    e. If the actual inflation rate equals the nominal interest rate, how does this affect the outcome of this loan contract?

    f. If you knew what the actual inflation rate was going to be, and it happened to equal the nominal interest rate, would you be willing to be a lender? Why or why not? Explain your answer.

4. Suppose that both borrowers and lenders anticipate correctly that the inflation rate will increase by 5 percentage points over the next year.

    a. What do you know will happen to the real interest rate?

    b. What do you know will happen to the nominal interest rate?

c. Describe the effects of this anticipated inflation on the demand for loanable funds curve and the supply of loanable funds curve. Use the following graph to illustrate your answer.

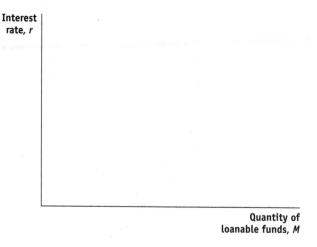

5. This chapter describes both disinflation and deflation: write a brief essay contrasting and comparing these two terms. How are these terms similar and how are they dissimilar?

6. Expansionary monetary policy typically reduces the nominal interest rate, and this in turn acts as a stimulus for aggregate demand. Why does this not work in the case of a liquidity trap? In your answer, make sure you identify what a liquidity trap is and why it prevents monetary policy from stimulating the economy. Use the following graph to illustrate your answer.

7. Explain why during a period of deflation the debt burden increases and how this relates to debt deflation.

8. Use the following graph to answer this question.

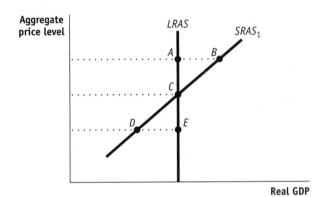

a. On the graph, which point best represents a recessionary gap for this economy in the short run? Explain your answer.

b. Given the graph, how would you explain this economy's recessionary gap? Using Okun's law, what are the consequences of a recessionary gap on a country's unemployment rate?

c. What is the level of actual unemployment relative to the natural rate of unemployment when this economy operates in the short run with a recessionary gap? Explain your answer and be sure to indicate what type of unemployment would cause these two rates to be different from one another.

d. At what point(s) on the graph is the actual unemployment rate equal to the natural rate of unemployment? Explain your answer.

e. On the graph, which point best represents an inflationary gap for this economy in the short run? Explain your answer.

f. Given the graph, how would you explain this economy's inflationary gap? Using Okun's law, what are the consequences of an inflationary gap on a country's unemployment rate?

g. What is the level of actual unemployment relative to the natural rate of unemployment when this economy operates in the short run with an inflationary gap? Explain your answer.

9. Suppose the natural rate of unemployment in Macroland equals 5% and the economy of Macroland is currently producing at its potential output level of real GDP.

a. If the level of real GDP increases by 2% from its potential output level, then what happens to the unemployment rate in Macroland according to Okun's law?

b. If the level of real GDP decreases by 3% from its potential output level, then what happens to the unemployment rate in Macroland according to Okun's law?

c. Suppose that the level of real GDP initially in Macroland equals $100 million. If real GDP increases to $105 million, what will the new unemployment rate equal according to Okun's law?

10. Suppose you are given the following information about the economy of Funland.

Unemployment rate	Inflation rate	Expected inflation rate
1%	6%	2%
2	5	2
3	4	2
4	3	2

a. Draw a graph with the unemployment rate on the horizontal axis and the inflation rate on the vertical axis. On this graph, represent the above short-run Phillips curve (*SRPC*) based on expected inflation of 2%. Label this *SRPC*$_1$. Assume this curve is linear.

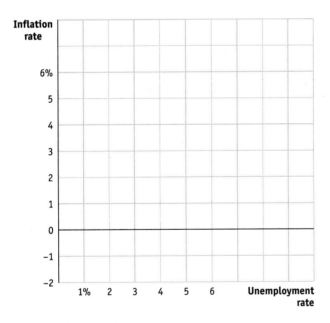

b. Given $SRPC_1$, at what rate of unemployment will inflation equal 0% for this economy? If expected inflation is 2%, then how will this economy adjust over time to this expected inflation rate? Illustrate this short-run adjustment on a graph and then explain your answer.

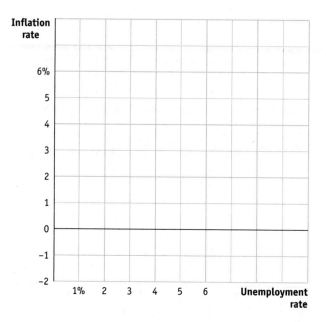

c. If policymakers could effectively change inflationary expectations to where people expected inflation to be 0%, then what would be this country's NAIRU? Illustrate this on a graph labeling all new information clearly on your graph. Explain your answer.

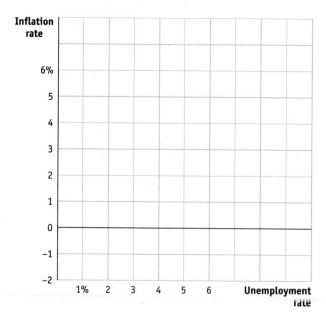

d. For the economy of Funland, what will the long-run Phillips curve (*LRPC*) look like and where will it be located? Explain your answer using a graph to illustrate this answer.

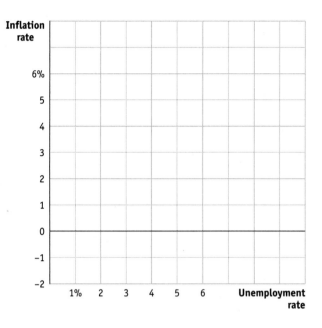

▮ BEFORE YOU TAKE THE TEST

Chapter Review Questions

1. Which of the following statements is true?
   a. Hyperinflation refers to a very high rate of inflation.
   b. During periods of high inflation, people are eager to hold large sums of money since these sums of money grow in value, the higher the inflation rate.
   c. In the long run, an increase in the money supply does not change real GDP.
   d. All of the statements are true.
   e. Statements (a) and (b) are both true.
   f. Statements (a) and (c) are both true.

2. The classical model of the price level
   a. reflects the work of John Maynard Keynes.
   b. ignores the short-run movements of the economy in response to a change in the money supply.
   c. works well particularly for periods in which inflation is low.
   d. All of the statements are true.
   e. Answers (a) and (b) are both correct.
   f. Answers (a) and (c) are both correct.
   g. Answers (b) and (c) are both correct.

3. In periods of high inflation, the short-run *AS* curve
    a. adjusts quickly by shifting to the right.
    b. adjusts slowly, if at all, and will eventually shift to the left.
    c. is insensitive to the high inflation and is therefore unaffected by the high inflation.
    d. adjusts swiftly and shifts to the left due to rising nominal wages.
    e. None of the statements is true.

4. The Fed monetizes the government's debt when it
    a. sells U.S. Treasury bills on the open market.
    b. purchases U.S. Treasury bills on the open market.
    c. mandates the use of fiat money as a medium of exchange.
    d. Answers (a) and (c) are both correct.
    e. Answers (b) and (c) are both correct.

5. *Seigniorage* is the term
    a. used to describe open-market operations.
    b. that dates back to the Middle Ages and refers to the government's right to issue coins and to charge, and therefore, collect a fee for issuing these coins.
    c. that economists use to refer to the government's right to print money.
    d. Answers (a), (b), and (c) are all correct.
    e. Answers (a) and (b) are both correct.
    f. Answers (a) and (c) are both correct.
    g. Answers (b) and (c) are both correct.

6. An inflation tax
    a. is a tax that is levied on the Fed when it increases the money supply.
    b. is a tax on those who hold money that occurs when the inflation erodes the purchasing power of their money.
    c. occurs when the government prints money to cover its budget deficit.
    d. Answers (a), (b), and (c) are all correct.
    e. Answers (a) and (b) are both correct.
    f. Answers (a) and (c) are both correct.
    g. Answers (b) and (c) are both correct.

7. For a given inflation rate, an increase in the real money supply
    a. does not affect the real inflation tax.
    b. increases the real inflation tax.
    c. decreases the real inflation tax.
    d. may increase, decrease, or have no effect on the real inflation tax.

8. When there is unexpected inflation in an economy, then
    a. real GDP will decrease in the economy in the long run.
    b. real income will decrease in the economy in the long run.
    c. borrowers benefit while lenders lose.
    d. lenders benefit while borrowers lose.
    e. Answers (a), (b), and (c) are all correct.
    f. Answers (a), (b), and (d) are all correct.

9. Which of the following statements is true?

a. When actual output is equal to potential output, the natural rate of unemployment equals the actual rate of employment.

b. During an inflationary gap, the unemployment rate is greater than the natural rate of unemployment.

c. During a recessionary gap, the unemployment rate is greater than the natural rate of unemployment.

d. Actual output fluctuates around potential output in the long run.

10. Cyclical unemployment and the output gap

a. move together, but cyclical unemployment fluctuates more than the output gap.

b. have a relationship with one another that can be quantified through Okun's law.

c. are negatively related to one another: in the United States when the cyclical unemployment rate increases by 1%, this leads to a decrease of ½% in the output gap.

d. Answers (a), (b), and (c) are all correct.

11. According to the Fisher effect, changes in the expected inflation rate will

a. have little or no effect on the nominal interest rate.

b. cause both the demand and supply of loanable funds curves to shift in the same direction.

c. cause both the demand and supply of loanable funds curves to shift, but in opposite directions.

d. have no effect on the equilibrium quantity of loanable funds.

e. Answers (a), (b), and (c) are all correct.

f. Answers (a), (b), and (d) are all correct.

g. Answers (c) and (d) are both correct.

h. Answers (b) and (d) are both correct.

12. Which of the following statements is true?

a. The Fisher effect states that the expected real interest rate is unaffected by the change in expected inflation.

b. Borrowers and lenders should base their decisions on the real rate of interest and not the nominal rate of interest.

c. Anticipated inflation can impose real costs on the economy.

d. Statements (a), (b), and (c) are all true.

e. Statements (a) and (b) are both true.

f. Statements (a) and (c) are both true.

g. Statements (b) and (c) are both true.

13. The relationship between changes in the output gap and changes in the unemployment rate is less than one-to-one because

a. companies often meet changes in the demand for their product by changing the number of hours their current workers work.

b. the availability of jobs affects the number of people who are looking for jobs.

c. the rate of growth in labor productivity tends to accelerate during times of economic prosperity and decelerate during times of economic adversity.

d. Answers (a), (b), and (c) are all correct.

14. Which of the following statements is true?
    a. Moderate inflation may be the result of politicians pursuing too low an unemployment rate for the economy prior to an election.
    b. Moderate inflation may be the result of an aggregate supply shock to the economy.
    c. Moderate inflation is easily brought under control through a process called disinflation.
    d. Statements (a), (b), and (c) are all true.
    e. Statements (a) and (b) are both true.
    f. Statements (a) and (c) are both true.
    g. Statements (b) and (c) are both true.

15. Which of the following statements is true?
    a. The short-run Phillips curve is a vertical line with the horizontal intercept equaling the NAIRU.
    b. The short-run Phillips curve depicts the negative relationship between the unemployment rate and the inflation rate.
    c. An economy with a low rate of unemployment is an economy that has a shortage of labor and other resources, which leads to falling prices.
    d. Statements (a) and (c) are both true.
    e. Statements (b) and (c) are both true.

16. Debt deflation
    a. occurs when there is deflation, and the value of the borrower's debt is reduced due to the falling aggregate price level.
    b. occurs when borrowers reduce their aggregate spending, because the deflation increases the debt burden that borrowers experience.
    c. reduces the impact of the deflation on the level of aggregate demand, thus restoring the economy to its potential level of output in a timely manner.
    d. affects only lenders and not borrowers.

17. An economy will experience a liquidity trap when the Fed
    a. refuses to expand the money supply, even though there is an increased demand for money in the economy.
    b. refuses to expand the money supply in order to raise nominal interest rates to an acceptable level.
    c. finds that it cannot reduce nominal interest rates, even if it engages in open-market purchases of Treasury bills.
    d. adopts a target inflation rate of 0%, and successfully achieves this target.

18. When the central bank finds that it cannot use monetary policy to reduce the nominal interest rate, it must be the case that
    a. the economy is operating in a liquidity trap.
    b. the central bank has reached the zero bound
    c. the money market is in disequilibrium.
    d. Answers (a), (b), and (c) are all correct.
    e. Answers (a) and (b) are both correct.
    f. Answers (a) and (c) are both correct.
    g. Answers (b) and (c) are both correct.

19. Expected inflation

   a. does not impact the short-run or the long-run Phillips curve.

   b. is the rate of inflation that workers and employers expect in the near future.

   c. and the unemployment rate are the most significant factors affecting the rate of inflation in an economy.

   d. Answers (a), (b), and (c) are all correct.

   e. Answers (b) and (c) are both correct.

Use the following graph to answer the next three questions. In this graph $SRPC_1$ is the short-run Phillips curve for this economy when the expected inflation rate equals 0%.

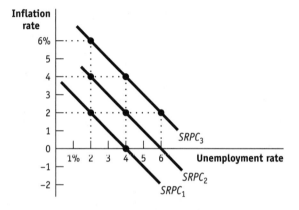

20. Using the graph, we know that the short-run Phillips curve ($SRPC$) equals $SRPC_2$ when the expected inflation rate equals

   a. 0%.

   b. 2%.

   c. 4%.

   d. 6%.

21. Suppose the inflation rate is 4% and this economy finds that its unemployment rate equals 3%. What is the NAIRU for this economy, given this information?

   a. 0%

   b. 2%

   c. 4%

   d. 6%

22. Suppose the policymakers for the economy depicted in the graph decide to pursue an unemployment rate of 2%. This will

   a. cause accelerating inflation in the long run.

   b. lead to rightward shifts in the $SRPC$, with each shift reflecting the expected inflation rate.

   c. cause equilibrium wage rates to fall.

   d. Answers (a), (b), and (c) are all correct.

   e. Answers (a) and (b) are both correct.

23. Which of the following statements is true?
    a. Zimbabwe in June 2008 had the world's highest inflation rate.
    b. The inflation rate in June 2008 in Zimbabwe was lower than the inflation rate in Germany during 1922–1923.
    c. During the German hyperinflation after World War I, German firms paid their workers several times a day so that these workers could spend their earnings before they lost value.
    d. Statements (a), (b), and (c) are all true.
    e. Statements (a) and (c) are both true.
    f. Statements (b) and (c) are both true.

24. Which of the following statements is true?
    a. In the short run, an increase in the money supply will increase the aggregate price level but will not alter the level of real GDP.
    b. In the long run, an increase in the money supply will increase the aggregate price level but will have no effect on the level of real GDP.
    c. In the long run, an increase in the money supply will cause nominal prices and nominal wages to increase by the same percentage as the percentage increase in the money supply.
    d. Statements (a) and (c) are both true.
    e. Statements (b) and (c) are both true.

25. Indexation of a contract implies that the contract has been written so that the terms of the contract are
    a. adjusted for changes in inflation.
    b. not affected by changes in the level of consumer price index.

26. Governments that run large deficits can
    a. reduce the size of the deficit by raising taxes.
    b. reduce the size of the deficit by reducing spending.
    c. finance the deficit by printing money.
    d. Answers (a), (b), and (c) are all correct.

27. A positive output gap implies an unemployment rate
    a. above the natural rate of unemployment.
    b. below the natural rate of unemployment.

28. Which of the following statements is true?
    a. Okun's law states that there is a direct relationship between the level of unemployment and the output gap.
    b. Okun's law finds that an increase in the output gap of 2% reduces the unemployment rate by approximately 1%.
    c. Okun's law was discovered by President George W. Bush's chief economic advisor.
    d. Statements (a), (b), and (c) are all true.
    e. Statements (b) and (c) are both true.
    f. Statements (a) and (c) are both true.

29. A negative supply shock will, holding everything else constant, cause the aggregate price level to
   a. increase and the aggregate level of real GDP to decrease in the short run.
   b. decrease and the aggregate level of real GDP to decrease in the short run.
   c. increase and the aggregate level of real GDP to increase in the short run.
   d. decrease and the aggregate level of real GDP to increase in the short run.

30. Disinflation in an economy is
   a. easy to accomplish and relatively painless for people living and working in this economy.
   b. difficult to accomplish and typically results in reduced production of real GDP and high rates of unemployment

■ ANSWER KEY

Answers to Problems and Exercises

1. a.

Real inflation tax	Inflation rate	Real money supply
$ 5 million	5%	$100 million
6 million	5	120 million
12.80 million	8	160 million
14 million	7	200 million
20 million	10	200 million

b. The real inflation tax will increase. When the inflation rate increases, then the purchasing power of the money supply is reduced: this is equivalent to a tax on the value of all money held by the public. In the table shown here in part (a) you can see this illustrated when the real money supply equals $200 million: when the inflation rate is 7%, the real inflation tax is $14 million, and when the inflation rate is 10%, the real inflation tax is $20 million.

c. If the real inflation tax is falling, this indicates that the purchasing power of the money supply is being eroded more slowly. This can only be true if the inflation rate is lower than its previous levels. Again, this is illustrated in the table shown here.

d. There is a trade-off between the inflation rate and the money supply for a given constant level of real inflation tax: the real inflation tax can be constant with an increasing inflation rate only if the real money supply is decreasing.

2. a. To calculate the price of the bread in 12 months use the following table to organize our answer.

Month of the year	Price of a loaf of bread
1	$ 4.00
2	8.00
3	16.00
4	32.00
5	64.00
6	128.00
7	256.00
8	512.00
9	1,024.00
10	2,048.00
11	4,096.00
12	8,192.00

b. To calculate the total increase in price for the period, we use the formula: percentage change in price equals (the current price − the base price) × 100/(the base price), or the percentage change in price equals ($8,192 − $2) × 100/2 equals 409,500%.

3. **a.** The nominal interest rate the Mary and Joe have agreed to in this contract is 5%, since the $50 interest payment represents 5% of the $1,000 loan.

b. We can calculate the real interest rate as the nominal interest rate minus the expected inflation rate: in this case, the nominal interest rate is 5% and the expected inflation rate is 3%, giving us a real interest rate of 2%.

c. If the actual inflation rate is 2%, then the real rate of interest that is paid on the loan is 3%, which is higher than the real interest rate that Mary and Joe thought they were agreeing to when they signed their loan contract. For Joe, the lender, this means that he is earning more than he anticipated from the loan. For Mary, the borrower, this means that she is paying back more dollars in real terms than she planned on when she signed the contract.

d. If the actual inflation rate is 4%, then the real rate of interest that is paid on the loan is 1%, which is lower than the real interest rate that Mary and Joe thought they were agreeing to when they signed their loan contract. For Joe, the lender, this means that he is earning less than he anticipated from the loan. For Mary, the borrower, this means that she is paying back fewer dollars in real terms than she planned on when she signed the contract.

e. If the actual inflation rate equals the nominal rate of interest, then the real interest rate is zero. When the real rate of interest equals zero, this represents a situation where the lender earns no real return on the money he or she has lent out, while the borrower is paying no real cost for the use of the money. The borrower wins, while the lender is hurt under this scenario.

f. No, if you knew what the actual inflation rate was going to be and it equaled the nominal interest rate for the loan, you would refuse to be a lender since the real return you would earn on the loan would be zero. If you made the loan, you would be giving up the use of your funds for the period of the loan without receiving any real compensation for the use of those funds.

4. **a.** The real interest rate will be unaffected by this anticipated inflation rate, since both demanders and suppliers in the loanable funds market will take this anticipated inflation into account.

b. The nominal interest rate will increase by 5 percentage points due to the increase in the anticipated rate of inflation of 5 percentage points.

c. Both the demand and the supply curves in the loanable funds market will shift upward (demand will shift to the right and supply will shift to the left) by the amount of the anticipated inflation rate: this will leave the equilibrium quantity of loanable funds unchanged in the market while increasing the nominal interest rate by the amount of the anticipated inflation. The following figure illustrates this.

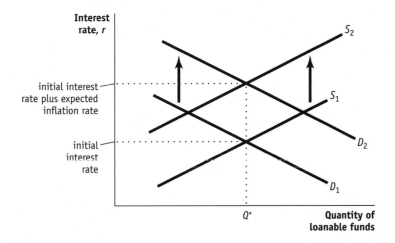

5. Disinflation refers to the deliberate pursuit by policymakers to bring down inflation that has become embedded in expectations. Here, policymakers pursue policy aimed at reducing inflationary expectations in order to reduce the increase in the aggregate price level. Disinflation may be very expensive economically, since it may result in significant decreases in real GDP in order to remove inflationary expectations from the economy. Deflation, on the other hand, refers to a fall in the aggregate price level. This deflation is not the result of conscious policymaking activity, but may prove difficult to remedy through policy if the economy is operating in a liquidity trap where nominal interest rates are equal to zero. In such a situation, monetary policy cannot be used to stimulate aggregate demand through lower nominal interest rates. So, even though disinflation and deflation both are concerned with either slowing down inflation or a direct fall in the aggregate price level, they represent different challenges to the policymaker.

6. In the case of a liquidity trap, the nominal interest rate initially is equal to zero and thus cannot fall any lower despite expansionary monetary policy. The following graph illustrates a liquidity trap, where *MS* is the nominal money supply, *MD* is the nominal money demand, and *r* is the nominal interest rate.

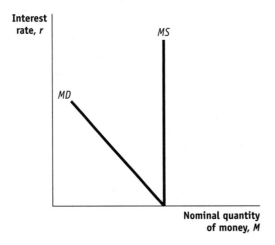

In the graph, when the central bank pursues expansionary monetary policy to shift the *MS* to the right, this will have no effect on the nominal interest rate since it is already at its minimal level of zero. Monetary policy cannot be used to stimulate the economy if the economy faces a liquidity trap.

7. When there is a deflation, prices in an economy fall. The effect of this fall in prices is to increase the economic burden of any preexisting debt, since the borrower's payments are not adjusted downward to reflect the deflation. Borrowers lose from deflation due to the increased real burden of their debt: this increased debt burden may lead them to be short of cash and force them to cut their spending sharply when their debt burden rises. Thus, deflation reduces aggregate demand, which deepens the economic slump that may, in turn, lead to further deflation. This reduction in aggregate demand due to the effect of deflation is referred to as debt deflation.

8. **a.** Point *D* best represents a recessionary gap for this economy since at point *D* actual real GDP is less than the potential level of real GDP.

b. The economy would produce at point *D* if there was a negative demand shock that caused the *AD* curve to shift to the left so that it intersected the *SRAS* at point *D*. This is illustrated in the following graph.

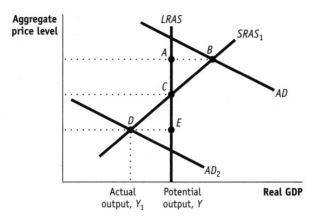

When a country produces a level of real GDP corresponding to a recessionary gap (Y_1 versus *Y* in the graph), this creates a negative output gap. According to Okun's law, a negative output gap will increase the unemployment rate above the natural rate of unemployment.

c. The level of actual unemployment exceeds the natural rate of unemployment due to the existence of cyclical unemployment.

d. At points *A*, *C*, and *E* the natural rate of unemployment and the actual unemployment rate are equal. We know this because the economy is producing at its potential output level, which is the level of output where the unemployment rate equals the natural rate.

e. Point *B* best represents an inflationary gap, since actual output at point *B* is greater than the potential output level of real GDP.

f. The economy would produce at point *B* in the short run given the *SRAS* if there was a positive *AD* shock that shifted the *AD* curve to the right so that it intersects the *SRAS* curve at point *B*. This is illustrated in the following graph.

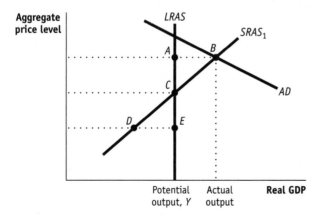

If the economy produces with an inflationary gap, this creates a positive output gap. According to Okun's law a positive output gap will decrease the actual unemployment rate below the natural rate of unemployment.

g. The rate of actual unemployment is less than the natural rate of unemployment since the economy will need to employ more workers in order to increase production beyond the potential output level of real GDP.

9.   **a.** If the level of real GDP increases by 2%, then the unemployment rate will fall by 1% to an unemployment rate of 4%. We can see this using the formula given in the text: unemployment rate = natural rate of unemployment − (0.5 × output gap) = 5% − (0.5 × 2%) = 4%.

   b. If the level of real GDP decreases by 3%, then the unemployment rate will rise by 1.5%, for an unemployment rate of 6.5%. To see this, use the formula given in part (a) and substitute in the relevant values.

   c. If the level of real GDP is initially $100 million, then an increase of real GDP to $105 million represents a 5% increase in output from its potential output level. Using the formula given in part (a), we can then calculate the new unemployment rate as 2.5%: as the level of real GDP increases, the economy will see its unemployment rate fall.

10. **a.**

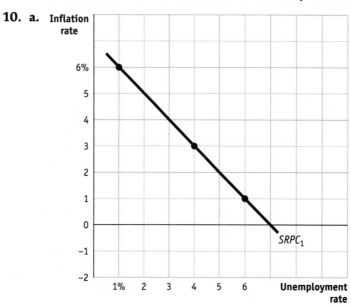

   b. Given $SRPC_1$, inflation equals 0% when the unemployment rate equals 7%. Over time people will come to expect inflation of 2%, and this will cause the $SRPC$ to shift up by this amount and people's expectations of inflation to rise to 4%. The new $SRPC$ will be $SRPC_2$, as illustrated in the following graph.

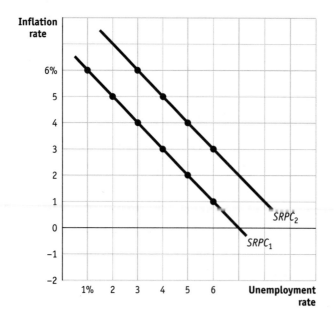

Of course, over time this will cause $SRPC_2$ to shift up reflecting higher inflationary expectations.

c. This country's NAIRU would be 5%. Effectively, we are looking for the $SRPC$ that has inflationary expectations of 0%, which we can illustrate as a downward shift of $SRPC_1$ where at any given unemployment rate, the inflation rate is reduced by 2%. We can illustrate this in the following figure as $SRPC_0$.

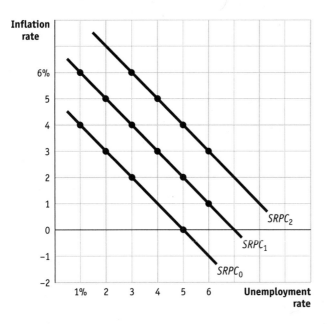

Remember that the expected inflation rate for $SRPC_2$ is 4%, the expected inflation rate for $SRPC_1$ is 2%, and the expected inflation rate for $SRPC_0$ is 0%.

d. For Funland the $LRPC$ will be a vertical line at a 5% unemployment rate. This is illustrated in the following figure.

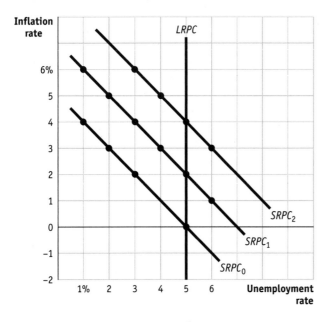

Answers to Chapter Review Questions

1. **Answer c.** High inflation is not the same as hyperinflation: economists distinguish between the two terms, calling any inflation rate in excess of 50%-per-month a hyperinflation. During periods of high inflation, people reduce their money holdings since the purchasing power of their money holdings falls due to the inflation. In the long run, the economy will produce at its potential level of output no matter what the level of the money supply.

2. **Answer b.** The classical model of the price level was used by the "classical" economists who wrote before the work of John Maynard Keynes. It is a model that ignores the short-run movements of the economy in response to a change in the money supply and instead focuses on the long-run adjustment process. It is a model that works particularly well when analyzing periods with high inflation, since these long-run adjustments are apt to be quicker than the economic adjustment that occurs when the inflation rate is relatively low.

3. **Answer d.** In periods of high inflation, the short-run *AS* curve adjusts quickly through wage and price adjustment: this causes the short-run *AS* curve to shift to the left due to the higher nominal costs associated with the high inflation in order to move the economy toward its long-run equilibrium.

4. **Answer b.** The Fed monetizes the government's debt when it purchases U.S. Treasury bills on the open market: this purchase has the effect of increasing the money supply in circulation in the economy. The adoption of fiat money by an economy does not lead to monetization of the debt: it is the actual use of this money issued by the government to purchase the debt that monetizes the debt.

5. **Answer g.** This term is covered in the text: it is a term dating from the Middle Ages that referred to the right to stamp gold and silver into coins and then charge a fee for making the coins: this right belonged to the medieval lords, or seigneurs. Today the term is used by economists to describe the government's right to print money. The U.S. government, through the Fed, engages in seignorage when the Fed makes an open-market purchase (which is a type of open-market operation) of Treasury bills.

6. **Answer g.** An inflation tax is the reduction in purchasing power that occurs during inflation. This inflation tax occurs when the government spends more than its revenue and turns to printing money to cover its deficit. This printing of money, by expanding the money supply, leads to inflation and a loss of purchasing power for people who hold money.

7. **Answer b.** The real inflation tax is equal to the inflation rate multiplied by the real money supply. Thus, for a given inflation rate if the real money supply increases, this must necessarily result in an increase in the real inflation tax.

8. **Answer c.** Unexpected inflation has no effect on real GDP and real income in the economy in the long run: the economy will return to its potential output level. However, the unexpected inflation will hurt some people while benefiting other people: borrowers will find that they are paying back dollars with less purchasing power. Hence, borrowers will benefit from the unexpected inflation while lenders will be hurt.

9. **Answer c.** When actual output equals potential output, the unemployment rate equals the natural rate of unemployment and not the natural rate of employment. During an inflationary gap, the unemployment rate is less than the natural rate of unemployment, since, when the economy is producing an output level greater than its potential output level, it is temporarily using resources at more than the normal rate. Thus, during a recessionary gap, the unemployment rate will be greater than the natural rate of unemployment, since there is a negative output gap and this is associated with unusually high unemployment. Actual output fluctuates around potential output in the short run: in the long run, actual output equals potential output due to full price adjustment.

10. **Answer b.** Cyclical unemployment and the output gap are inversely related to each other, and this relationship can be quantified by Okun's law, which in the United States estimates that for a 1% increase in the output gap there will be a reduction in the unemployment rate of one-half of a percentage point. Thus, a 1% increase in the unemployment rate would be associated with a 2% decrease in the output gap.

11. **Answer g.** When the expected inflation rate changes, this causes both the demand and supply curves for loanable funds to shift, but in opposite directions. For example, if demand shifts to the right then supply shifts to the left. The equilibrium quantity of loanable funds will be unaffected by this change, but the nominal interest rate will change by the amount of change in the amount of expected inflation rate.

12. **Answer d.** All three statements are straightforward statements found in your text.

13. **Answer d.** The relationship between changes in the output gap and changes in the unemployment rate is estimated by Okun's law, which finds that a rise in the output gap of 1 percentage point reduces the unemployment rate by about one-half of a percentage point. The reasons for this being less than a one-to-one relationship relate to how firms react to changes in the demand for their product, how workers respond to changes in economic conditions, and how the growth rate of labor productivity is affected by economic conditions. The text reviews each of these factors and its effect on the relationship between changes in the output gap and changes in the unemployment rate.

14. **Answer e.** Moderate inflation may be caused by politicians pursuing too low an unemployment rate due to using a target rate of unemployment that is lower than the natural rate of unemployment; or because of aggregate supply shocks to the economy. Eliminating moderate inflation through disinflation is a costly procedure, since it requires accepting a higher than normal unemployment rate in order to reduce inflationary expectations.

15. **Answer b.** The short-run Phillips curve is downward sloping and depicts the relationship between the unemployment rate and the inflation rate. It is not vertical: the long-run Phillips curve is vertical and intersects the horizontal axis at the NAIRU. An economy that has a low unemployment rate will typically see rising prices in the short run due to shortages of labor and other resources.

16. **Answer b.** Debt deflation is the reduction in aggregate demand caused by deflation. A borrower's existent debt is not reduced due to deflation: the borrower's real debt is increased during a period of deflation, since the deflation increases the real burden of the borrower's debt. Debt deflation reduces spending and therefore worsens the economic slump: the economy does not move quickly to its potential output level.

17. **Answer c.** The liquidity trap is a situation in which monetary policy cannot be used because nominal interest rates must stay at zero or above. Monetary policy is ineffective when the economy operates in a liquidity trap, since the nominal interest rate cannot fall below zero. The Fed could adopt a target inflation rate of 0% and not necessarily run into the liquidity trap: however, the Fed would likely choose a higher inflation target, since it allows them more room to adjust nominal interest rates as a way of stimulating aggregate demand.

18. **Answer e.** When the central bank cannot effectively use monetary policy to stimulate the economy, it must be at the zero bound, or the nominal interest rate must equal zero. When the nominal interest rate is at zero, then the economy is operating in a liquidity trap—a situation where monetary policy is ineffective. The money market can still be in equilibrium, even though monetary policy cannot be used to stimulate the economy.

19. **Answer e.** Expected inflation and the unemployment rate are the most significant factors affecting the inflation rate in an economy. Expected inflation is that rate of inflation that workers and employers expect in the near future. Changes in expected inflation cause the short-run Phillips curve to shift: increases in the expected inflation rate cause the short-run Phillips curve to shift up, while decreases in the expected inflation rate cause the short-run Phillips curve to shift down.

20. **Answer b.** $SRPC_2$ reflects a short-run Phillips curve drawn with an expected inflation rate of 2%. We know this since this curve has shifted up by 2% at every unemployment rate from the short-run Phillips curve that is drawn with an expected inflation rate of 0% ($SRPC_1$).

21. **Answer d.** The NAIRU is the nonaccelerating inflation rate of unemployment for the economy, or that level of unemployment where the inflation rate matches inflationary expectations. An unemployment rate below 4% requires ever accelerating inflation.

22. **Answer e.** The unemployment rate of 2% is below the unemployment rate that this economy can maintain while still avoiding inflation. If this economy tries to pursue an unemployment rate of 2%, this unemployment rate will be initially accompanied by 2% inflation. This inflation rate will then be built into inflationary expectations and the $SRPC$ will shift to the right. But, again, if policymakers persist in trying to achieve 2% unemployment, this will cause even higher inflationary expectations to be built into the $SRPC$, shifting the $SRPC$ further to the right. Thus, trying to achieve an unemployment level of 2% for this economy will lead to accelerating inflation in the long run along with shifts in the $SRPC$ in the short run. We can expect wages to rise with expectations of higher inflation and with higher actual inflation rates.

23. **Answer d.** These are all factual statements found in the text. The Zimbabwe inflation, although severe, was milder than the German hyperinflation of 1922–1923.

24. **Answer e.** In the short run, an increase in the money supply will cause the AD curve to shift to the right and for a given $SRAS$ curve this will result in the aggregate price level and the level of real GDP increasing. But, in the long run, an increase in the money supply will result in nominal wages and prices rising in order to restore the economy to the long-run level of real GDP (that is, to potential GDP). This will require that the percentage change in nominal prices and nominal wages equal the percentage change in the money supply.

25. **Answer a.** Indexation of a contract implies that the terms of the contract are adjusted when there are changes in the inflation rate. This means that the terms of the contract will be impacted by changes in the consumer price index since this index provides a measure of the inflation rate.

26. **Answer d.** Governments run deficits whenever their spending is greater than their revenue. They can reduce the size of the deficit by increasing the revenue they collect or by reducing the level of spending or by doing a combination of both of these options. When a government is unwilling to increase taxes or cut spending, they are forced to finance any deficit spending they incur by printing money to cover their budget deficit.

27. **Answer b.** When the output gap is positive, this implies that actual aggregate output is greater than potential output. When actual aggregate output exceeds potential output, this implies that the unemployment rate is below the natural rate since the level of production is greater than the potential output level.

28. **Answer b.** Okun's law was discovered by Arthur Okun who was the chief economic advisor to President John F. Kennedy. Okun's law states the relationship between the output gap and the unemployment rate: this is an inverse (and not direct) relationship since as the output gap increases, the unemployment rate decreases. When the output gap increases by 2%, this causes the unemployment rate to fall by about 1% point.

29. **Answer a.** A negative supply shock will cause the short-run AS curve to shift to the left. For a given AD curve this will cause the short-run aggregate price level to increase and the short-run aggregate level of real GDP to decrease.

30. **Answer b.** Disinflation involves eliminating inflation and inflationary expectations from an economy. Once an economy has developed inflationary expectations, the only way to reduce these expectations is to throw the economy into a major recession. Such a recession results in reductions in production as well as increases in the unemployment rate.

chapter 17(32)

Crises and Consequences

▌BEFORE YOU READ THE CHAPTER

Summary

This chapter discusses the difference between depository banks and shadow banks and how both types of banks are subject to bank runs. The chapter also discusses what happens during financial panics and bank crises and why these types of economic disruption result in severe and long-lasting impacts on the economy. The chapter also discusses the role of regulatory loopholes and the rise of shadow banking in the banking crisis of 2007–2009 and how regulatory frameworks seek to avoid another banking crisis.

Chapter Objectives

Objective #1. People face a trade-off between liquidity and the rate of return. Without banks people would be forced to hold large amounts of cash to meet their liquidity needs; as holdings of cash increase, the rate of return decreases. Banks allow depositors to have immediate access to their funds (addressing their liquidity needs) while simultaneously providing depositors interest on these deposited funds (addressing their desire for a return on their idle cash). Banks are able to do this through maturity transformation, where they transform short-term liabilities into long-term assets.

Objective #2. Shadow banks have grown since 1980. Shadow banks provide a higher rate of return to savers than depository banks. Like depository banks, shadow banks engage in maturity transformation: they use short-term borrowing to finance their investments in long-term assets. Shadow banks until recently faced little regulation, but due to their similarity to depository banks they were vulnerable to bank runs.

Objective #3. Banking crises occur primarily due to two reasons: shared mistakes and financial contagion. Shared mistakes refer to financial institutions making the same mistake of investing in an asset bubble. Financial contagion spreads through bank runs or a vicious circle of deleveraging. Unregulated banking institutions, like the shadow bank sector, are highly vulnerable to contagion. The most recent financial crisis in the United States was a result of a real estate bubble, the rise of a very large shadow banking sector, and a vicious circle of deleveraging.

Objective #4. Banking crises are a frequent occurrence throughout the world. After a banking crisis or financial panic, there is usually a severe downturn in the economy. Bank crises typically result in bank reform that aims to reduce the frequency of future bank crises or financial panic.

Objective #5. Financial crisis typically results in a prolonged and severe drop in economic activity in an economy primarily because of the credit crunch, the debt overhang, and the ineffectiveness of monetary policy. The credit crunch refers to the increased difficulty that consumers and businesses have in getting needed credit: credit markets freeze up in the wake of financial crisis and do not operate properly. The debt overhang arises out of the vicious circle of deleveraging in which the value of assets falls, leaving individuals and businesses with greater debt but diminished assets. Monetary policy is ineffective during a banking crisis as a means to fight negative demand shocks caused by a fall in consumer and investment spending.

Objective #6. During a bank crisis, the government tries to limit the damage from the bank crisis by serving as a lender of last resort and by guaranteeing bank liabilities. The government may need to nationalize banks and then later reprivatize them in order to slow or halt the spread of the bank crisis.

Objective #7. The development of shadow banking eroded the bank regulatory system that was put into place in the 1930s. Particularly the repo market, a primary feature of shadow banking that provides very short-term loans, was not regulated at the time of the financial crisis of 2007–2009. The shadow bank sector was subject to bank runs due to the use of the repo, the lack of regulation, and the fact that this sector was not part of the lender of last resort system.

Objective #8. The financial crisis of 2007–2009 started with a real estate bubble. This crisis was the most severe crisis since the Great Depression. Persistently high unemployment is likely to endure for many years as a result of this financial crisis.

Objective #9. The Dodd-Frank bill was passed by the United States Congress in hopes of preventing another financial crisis like that of 2007–2009. This reform bill provides for consumer protection, greater regulation of derivatives, regulation of shadow banking, and resolution authority for a variety of financial institutions.

Key Terms

maturity transformation the conversion of short-term liabilities into long-term assets.

shadow bank a nondepository financial institution that engages in maturity transformation.

banking crisis occurs when a large part of the depository banking sector or the shadow banking sector fails or threatens to fail.

Notes

Key Terms *(continued)*

asset bubble when the price of an asset is pushed to an unreasonably high level due to expectations of further price gains.

financial contagion a vicious downward spiral among depository banks as well as shadow banks: each institution's failure increases the likelihood that another will fail.

financial panic a sudden and widespread disruption of the financial markets that occurs when people lose faith in the liquidity of financial institutions and markets.

credit crunch when potential borrowers either cannot get credit at all or must pay very high interest rates.

debt overhang occurs when a vicious circle of deleveraging leaves a borrower with high debt by diminished assets.

lender of last resort an institution, usually a country's central bank, that provides funds to financial institutions when they are unable to borrow from the private credit markets.

repo a repurchase agreement in which a shadow bank sells an asset with the agreement that it will buy the asset back for a higher price a short time later.

■ AFTER YOU READ THE CHAPTER

Tips

Tip #1.   This chapter introduces new terms that you will want to spend time learning. These terms often are challenging for students, since they are terms related to the financial industry, and this industry may not be familiar to you. Mastery of these terms is important.

Tip #2.   This chapter discusses the vicious circle of deleveraging, and it is this concept that is essential for understanding why bank crises and financial panics can have such large and long-lasting impacts on the economy. A vicious circle of deleveraging begins when financial institutions find that they need to reduce debt and raise cash. This need may force these institutions into selling their assets quickly, and this often means that these assets must sell at deeply discounted (lower) prices. As the institutions sell these assets at reduced prices, other financial institutions' positions are hurt as well. Thus, creditors may stop lending to more and more institutions. The vicious circle of deleveraging leads to a downward spiral of asset prices, and this results in major impacts on consumer and business spending in the economy.

Tip #3.   Students are used to thinking about the term *banking* as referring to financial institutions that provide checking and saving accounts. This chapter introduces and develops the idea of the shadow banking system. It is critical that students understand the concept of shadow banking: shadow banking and commercial banks are both in the business of maturity transformation, but the shadow bank—unlike commercial banks—does not take deposits. Instead, the shadow bank uses short-term borrowing in markets, like the repo market, to finance its lending. Shadow banking has grown in both its size and its impact on the financial system in recent years. Prior to the financial crisis of 2007–2009, shadow banking was not regulated.

Tip #4.   There is a tendency to think financial crises are rare and unusual events. This chapter provides historical evidence suggesting that these crises are not that rare, and that they do cause major economic disturbances, particularly with regard to unemployment and production. Recognizing that financial crises do occur and have some common causes can help policymakers design better policies aimed at reducing both the frequency and severity of financial crises.

Tip #5.   It is important to understand the three reasons for why banking crises typically lead to recessions: (1) a credit crunch occurs, which reduces the availability of credit, (2) financial distress caused by a debt overhang occurs, and (3) there is a loss of monetary policy effectiveness. The loss of monetary policy effectiveness provides the primary explanation for why banking-crises recessions are so severe and why they last so long.

Tip #6.   It is important for students to realize that financial regulation is a long-standing policy in most economies. However, financial regulation periodically lags financial innovation, and for financial regulation to be effective it must be continually updated in order to maintain pace with a changing world.

WORKED PROBLEMS

1. Prime Bank has 500 customers who have each deposited $50,000. Prime Bank has kept 20% of these deposits as reserves to meet depositor demand for funds. The other 80% of Prime Bank's deposits have been used to make mortgage loans to individuals who have not deposited funds at Prime Bank. Each mortgage loan has a value of $200,000. To make this problem simpler, we will assume that each mortgage represents a loan made to a customer to finance the purchase of a residence that is initially selling for $210,000. Suppose that there is a real estate bubble in the economy, and home prices fall by 10%. Prime Bank asks that you help it understand the effect of this drop in prices on the value of its assets relative to the value of its deposits. In your answer, provide an analysis of the total level of deposits at the bank, the total reserves, the total amount of funds the bank has loaned out as mortgages, and the new market value of these loans, given the fall in home prices should Prime Bank decide to sell some of these mortgages. Analyze the impact of this real estate price decrease on the assets and liabilities of Prime Bank. As a simplifying assumption, assume that there are no costs to running the bank.

    STEP 1: Start by first calculating the level of deposits at First Bank, and use this information to then calculate the level of reserves and the dollar amount of mortgages financed at Prime Bank. Calculate how many mortgages Prime Bank will be able to make from this information.

    Review the section "Banking: Benefits and Dangers" on page 502 (Econ page 934).

    This is a mathematical exercise: since there are 500 customers who each deposit $50,000 at the bank, this implies that total deposits at the bank are equal to 500($50,000), or $25,000,000. Since Prime Bank holds 20% of its deposits as reserves, this means that reserves at the bank are equal to $5,000,000. The remaining $20,000,000 is used by Prime Bank to finance mortgages. If each mortgage is worth $200,000, then the bank has funds to support 100 mortgages.

STEP 2: Analyze the effect of the fall in real estate prices on the value of the mortgages held by Prime Bank.

Review the section "Banking: Benefits and Dangers" on page 502 (Econ page 934).

The homes that have been purchased with the mortgages issued by Prime Bank were initially valued at $210,000. So, at the time of purchase each home buyer provided $10,000 of the funds needed to buy the house, and the bank had loaned the home buyer the remaining balance of $200,000. Now that home prices have fallen by 10%, the value of the home can be computed as $210,000 − .1($210,000), or $189,000. Since Prime Bank holds 100 mortgages, this implies that the value of the mortgages according to the price that these homes are now selling for is equal to $18,900,000 instead of the original $20,000,000.

STEP 3: Analyze the effect of this real estate price decrease on the value of the assets and liabilities of Prime Bank.

Review the section "Banking: Benefits and Dangers" on page 502 (Econ page 934).

Before the real estate price decrease the value of assets at Prime Bank was equal to the sum of reserves plus loans or $25,000,000, while the value of liabilities at Prime Bank was equal to the value of deposits at the bank, or $25,000,000. After the real estate price decrease, the value of assets at Prime Bank is now equal to the sum of reserves plus the value of the mortgage loans following the price decrease, or $5,000,000 plus $18,900,000 for a total of $23,900,000. The value of liabilities at Prime Bank is still equal to $25,000,000. The effect of the real estate price decrease on Prime Bank is to make its liabilities greater than its assets: Prime Bank is no longer solvent.

2. The opening story details the demise of Lehman Brothers. Discuss how this story illustrates the vicious circle of deleveraging and how this vicious circle of deleveraging can be destabilizing to otherwise financially sound institutions.

STEP 1: Review what the term the *vicious circle of deleveraging* means before analyzing the Lehman Brothers story.

Review the section "Banking Crises and Financial Panics" on page 506 (Econ page 938).

The vicious circle of deleveraging refers to a phenomenon that occurs when a financial institution is under pressure to reduce debt and raise cash. Under these circumstances, the institution may be forced to sell assets quickly and at steeply discounted prices. This results in financial contagion, since other financial institutions that own similar assets will find that the values of these assets are negatively impacted by the decline in asset prices. As creditors reduce the amount of credit they are willing to provide, more financial institutions are forced to sell assets, reinforcing the downward spiral of asset prices.

STEP 2: Discuss Lehman's situation in September 2008, paying close attention to the assets it held and why these assets represented a potential problem for the firm.

Review the opening story "From Purveyor of Dry Goods to Destroyer of Worlds" on page 501 (Econ page 933).

In September of 2008, Lehman Brothers held a large number of subprime mortgages. These were mortgages made to individuals who had too little income or too few assets to quality for prime, or standard, mortgages. During the summer and heading into the fall of 2008, the real estate market in the United States saw housing prices decline. This decrease in price lessened the value of the investments that Lehman Brothers had in the housing industry. Lehman Brothers was rumored to have heavy exposure to housing price volatility, and this led to the firm having trouble getting short-term credit to finance its operations and trading. On September 15, 2008, Lehman Brothers declared bankruptcy. It was the largest bankruptcy in United States history.

STEP 3: **Discuss the impact of Lehman's bankruptcy on the financial system.**

Review the opening story "From Purveyor of Dry Goods to Destroyer of Worlds" on page 501 (Econ page 933).

Lehman's bankruptcy came as a big surprise to the financial system because the firm had hidden the magnitude of the problem it faced. Other financial firms holding securitized mortgages realized that their holdings of real estate loans were quickly falling in value, particularly as the default rates on these loans increased. In light of these troubles, credit markets froze as those with funds decided it was better to hold onto their funds rather than lend them, given the state of both the financial markets and the real estate market. This created a global credit crunch, and this inability to get credit resulted in dramatic declines in stock markets around the world. Lehman's collapse had triggered a financial panic and resulted in a severe recession.

3. For each of the following scenarios determine whether the scenario represents the concept of shared mistake, a credit crunch, financial contagion, debt overhang, or the ineffectiveness of monetary policy. Explain your answers.

   a. Sarah and her husband Mario in the early 2000s built several houses as speculation houses. They would borrow funds to build a house, then sell the house once the construction was finished. The real estate market was strong at the time, and they earned substantial returns on their investments. They continued to build these houses because they thought house prices would continue to rise. However, in 2007, they built a house and by the time it was finished they found that housing prices had fallen, and they were unable to sell the house for what they had put into building it. They also noticed that there were many similar houses on the market in similar subdivisions in their community.

   b. In the 1990s tech stocks became very popular, and their prices rose dramatically. At the end of the 1990s, tech stock prices fell dramatically.

   c. First State Bank finds that it has too much debt and needs cash. It is forced to sell some of its assets at a dramatic discount. This causes other firms holding similar assets to find the values of their assets falling, and as the value of these assets fall, these firms find that they need to reduce their debt and raise cash quickly. This puts even greater downward pressure on the price of these assets.

   d. Rumor is circulating that Second Street Bank has substantial exposure in an asset that is losing value in the market. Second Street Bank needs short-term credit to insure its own operations and lending, and it finds that its creditors are no longer willing to lend funds. Second Street Bank is not the only financial institution facing this problem; in fact, it appears to be endemic to the entire banking system.

   e. Lucinda bought a house for $200,000 in 2005. She financed this purchase with a mortgage for 90% of the value of the house. However, house prices have fallen since 2005 by 25%. Lucinda is now substantially poorer than she was when she first bought the house.

f. Since the financial crisis of 2007–2009, the unemployment rate has been very high and the level of production has been low in the United States. In the period immediately after the financial crisis of 2007–2009, the Federal Reserve pursued a policy of very low interest rates. But the economy at that time continued to have a high unemployment rate and aggregate production levels below the potential level of production.

STEP 1: Before characterizing each of the preceding scenarios, review the definitions of each of the given terms.

Review the sections "Banking Crises and Financial Panics" on page 506 (Econ page 908) and "The Consequences of Banking Crises" on page 510 (Econ page 942).

Shared mistake refers to the idea of many institutions (or individuals) making the same mistake of investing in an asset bubble. A *credit crunch* refers to a disruption in the availability of credit due to the disruption in the banking system. *Financial contagion* refers to a vicious downward spiral where each institution's failure increases the odds that another institution will fail. Financial contagion is usually accompanied by a vicious circle of *deleveraging,* in which institutions are under pressure to reduce debt and raise cash: this pressure results in assets being sold at a deep discount, and this discounting of asset values has an adverse impact on other institutions holding similar assets. *Debt overhang* refers to the situation where a vicious circle of deleveraging leaves a borrower with high debt but diminished assets. *Ineffective monetary policy* refers to a situation where monetary policy is not effective at fighting negative demand shocks: ineffective monetary policy often occurs during banking-crisis recessions.

STEP 2: Consider each of the scenarios and decide which of the preceding terms describes the scenario best.

Review the sections "Banking Crises and Financial Panics" on page 506 (Econ page 908) and "The Consequences of Banking Crises" on page 510 (Econ page 942).

a. The house construction business of Sarah and Mario illustrates the idea of shared mistakes: they erroneously believed that housing prices could only continue to increase, and when housing prices fell they lost money on their houses built for speculation. The fact that there were many houses for sale in the subdivisions illustrates that they were not the only ones to believe that housing prices could only move in one direction.

b. Tech stock prices were bid up beyond their worth in the tech stock bubble. This is another illustration of shared mistakes, whereby many people made the same mistake of investing in tech stocks, leading to a tech stock bubble.

c. This scenario illustrates a vicious circle of deleveraging, which is one of the identifying characteristics of a financial contagion. One firm's need to reduce debt and raise cash quickly results in many firms having problems with falling asset prices and an inability to secure needed credit.

d. Second Street Bank is suffering from a credit crunch. The bank is not able to get the needed credit, and as the credit situation tightens, more and more banks will need to reduce their lending. This will lead businesses and consumers to cut back on their spending, causing the economy to go into a recession.

e. Lucinda's situation illustrates the concept of debt overhang, where a vicious circle of deleveraging leaves a borrower with high debt but diminished assets. Lucinda still owes most of her mortgage, but the value of the house has fallen. This has increased her level of debt even though the value of her house is lower.

f. A key feature of banking-crisis recessions is that monetary policy is not very effective. Despite a very low interest rate, the monetary policy was not particularly effective in the aftermath of the financial crisis of 2007–2009. Monetary policy tends to break down after a banking crisis due to a lack of confidence on the part of banking institutions and an unwillingness on the part of consumers and businesses to borrow.

4. Your neighbor Sanjay exclaimed to you the other night, "I have lived through a number of recessions, but this recession is the worst I have ever seen!" Sanjay was speaking of the recession following the financial crisis of 2007–2009. Sanjay knows that you have been studying macroeconomics this term, and he would like you to help him understand why the recession following this crisis was so severe and why it has lasted so long.

STEP 1: Show how the financial crisis of 2007–2009 illustrates both shared mistakes as well as financial contagion.

Review the sections "Banking Crises and Financial Panics" on page 506 (Econ page 938) and the section "Regulation in the Wake of the Crisis" on page 515 (Econ page 947).

The financial crisis of 2007–2009 was preceded by a real estate bubble, in which real estate prices rose by more than 60% in the period after 2000 before they fell back down to levels more in keeping with their historical levels. As real estate prices fell, many homeowners found that the value of their homes had fallen below their mortgage amounts: these homeowners were underwater, owing more money than the value of the assets—their homes—were worth. Many of these homeowners went into default on their mortgages, and many homes were in foreclosure. Many of the loans to homeowners were subprime mortgages that were subsequently securitized with other mortgage loans. Shares in these securitized loans were sold to other investors who were highly exposed to losses from the bursting of the housing bubble. This led to financial contagion due to a vicious downward spiral of deleveraging, which worsened the recession and hindered economic recovery.

STEP 2: Identify the three main reasons that banking and financial crises lead to severe recessions.

Review the section "The Consequences of Banking Crises" on page 510 (Econ page 942).

There are three main reasons a banking and financial crisis can lead to a severe recession: (1) A credit crunch, whereby potential borrowers find they either cannot get credit or, if they can get credit, the borrowers must pay very high rates of interest for this credit; (2) debt overhang, whereby borrowers find that the pushing down of asset prices results in their having additional financial stress due to their continuing to have high amounts of debt, while the assets the borrowers hold have diminished in value; and (3) in the aftermath of a financial crisis, loss of monetary policy effectiveness as a means of restoring consumer and investment spending.

STEP 3: Discuss how the financial crisis of 2007–2009 created a credit crunch.

Review the sections "The Consequences of Banking Crises" on page 510 (Econ page 942) and the section "Regulation in the Wake of the Crisis" on page 515 (Econ page 947).

When the real estate bubble burst, it left many homeowners with mortgages that were greater than the value of their homes. As the homeowners went into default and foreclosure, the financial institutions holding these mortgages found that they were highly exposed to losses from the bursting of the housing bubble. Financial institutions became concerned about the solvency of other financial institutions, and that led to a freezing up of the credit markets. This situation was a classic illustration of a credit crunch.

STEP 4: Discuss how the financial crisis of 2007–2009 created a debt overhang.

Review the sections "The Consequences of Banking Crises" on page 510 (Econ page 942) and the section "Regulation in the Wake of the Crisis" on page 515 (Econ page 947).

After the housing bubble burst, many homeowners found that the amount they owed on their mortgages was greater than the value of their homes. These homeowners were "underwater", and their plight illustrated the debt overhang concept. Recall that debt overhang refers to a situation where the individual or institution has high levels of debt but diminished assets. As housing prices fell, this diminished the value of the homes (the assets), while leaving the debt owed (the mortgages) at the same level.

STEP 5: Discuss how the financial crisis of 2007–2009 created a scenario where monetary policy was largely ineffective.

Review the sections "The Consequences of Banking Crises" on page 510 (Econ page 942) and the section "Regulation in the Wake of the Crisis" on page 515 (Econ page 947).

Even though the Federal Reserve kept interest rates at very low levels after the bursting of the housing bubble, this did little to stimulate the economy. Many households facing high debt levels and decreases in the value of their assets were not in a position to increase their spending levels. In addition, many households had been adversely affected by the recession and the accompanying loss of jobs in the economy. Businesses were equally reluctant to increase their spending despite very low interest rates: household demand was not strong, and there was excess capacity in the economy. Thus, monetary policy implemented to increase consumer and investment spending proved to be ineffective.

Problems and Exercises

1. Suppose First Bank has 1,000 customers who have each deposited $10,000 at the bank. First Bank has kept 20% of these deposits as reserves to meet depositor demand for funds. The other 80% of First Bank's deposits have been used to make mortgage loans to individuals who have not deposited funds at First Bank. Each mortgage loan has a value of $100,000. For simplicity sake, let's assume that each mortgage represents a loan made to a customer to finance the purchase of a residence that is initially selling for $120,000.

   a. What is the total amount of deposits at First Bank, given the information provided?

   b. What is the total amount of reserves at First Bank, given the information provided?

   c. What is the total number of mortgages issued by First Bank, given the information provided?

Suppose a rumor circulates that First Bank may be unable to meet its financial obligations, and 50% of First Bank depositors demand their funds.

d. Given its initial level of reserves, will First Bank have sufficient funds on hand to meet the demand by these depositors for their funds? Explain your answer and provide a numerical value of the surplus or shortage of funds that First Bank will have, given this scenario.

e. To meet the demand for funds, First Bank decides to sell some of the mortgages it holds. Since First Bank needs funds immediately, it must sell these mortgages for less than their face value. Suppose that it sells each $100,000 mortgage for $75,000 to raise the necessary funds to meet depositor demands. How many mortgages will First Bank need to sell to raise the needed funds?

f. Consider First Bank's financial position after the sale of the mortgages in part (e). First Bank has sold mortgages to cover the demand for depositor funds. How many deposits (liabilities for First Bank) are still in the bank? Suppose that the remaining mortgages held by First Bank are now also valued at $75,000, the price First Bank has been able to sell mortgages for in the market. What is the value of the mortgages still owned by First Bank? Finally, what do reserves at First Bank equal?

g. Given your answers in part (f), is First Bank solvent (that is, do the value of assets exceed the value of liabilities) after it meets the demand for depositor funds that arises from the rumor?

2. A bank accepts deposits and uses these deposits to finance 30-year mortgages. How do these transactions represent maturity transformation?

3. What is shadow banking and how is it similar to the banking represented by depository institutions? How is shadow banking different from the banking represented by depository institutions? Discuss how shadow banking can be subject to bank runs.

4. Consider a bank run that becomes a financial contagion. Who loses when this happens? Explain your answer.

5. What kinds of bank regulation can policy makers impose to reduce the likelihood of banking and financial crises?

6. Briefly discuss the four major elements of the Wall Street Reform and Consumer Protection Act, otherwise known as the Dodd-Frank bill. In your explanation, discuss why each of these elements is important.

■ BEFORE YOU TAKE THE TEST

Chapter Review Questions

1. Which of the following statements is true?
   a. Commercial banks and investment banks refer to identical financial institutions.
   b. Commercial banks accept deposits from customers, while investment banks trade in financial assets but do not accept deposits from customers.
   c. Investment banks accept deposits from customers, while commercial banks trade in financial assets but do not accept deposits from customers.
   d. Commercial banks and investment banks both accept deposits from customers, but only investment banks trade in financial assets.

2. A subprime mortgage is
   a. a mortgage issued to a homebuyer who does not have sufficient income to qualify for a standard or prime mortgage.
   b. a mortgage issued to a homebuyer who does have sufficient assets to qualify for a standard or prime mortgage.
   c. less risky for the lender than a prime mortgage.
   d. Answers (a), (b), and (c) are all correct.
   e. Answers (a) and (b) are both correct.

3. A global credit crunch occurs when
   a. borrowers cannot find credit or they must pay very high interest rates for credit.
   b. lenders cannot loan money or they receive very low interest rates for any loans they do make.
   c. lenders are willing to loan money to borrowers, but borrowers refuse to take out loans.
   d. borrowers are willing to borrow money, but lenders do not have any money they can lend to borrowers.

4. Shadow banking refers to
   a. commercial banks that accept deposits and make loans.
   b. a wide variety of types of financial firms including investment banks, hedge funds, and money market funds.
   c. financial firms that, prior to the banking crisis of 2008, were not closely watched or effectively regulated.
   d. Answers (a), (b) and (c) are all correct.
   e. Answers (b) and (c) are both correct.

5. The existence of banks reduces the need to
   a. hold cash in the event of an unexpected financial need.
   b. balance the need for liquidity against the rate of return one can earn from interest-earning assets.
   c. have regulation of the financial industry.
   d. hold cash rather than using these funds to help pay for productive investment spending.
   e. Answers (a), (b), (c), and (d) are all correct.
   f. Answers (a), (b), and (d) are both correct.

6. Depository banks
   a. borrow on a short-term basis from their depositors and lend these funds on a long-term basis to others.
   b. borrow on a long-term basis from their depositors and lend these funds on a short-term basis to others.

7. Maturity transformation is done by
   a. depository institutions when they borrow on a short-term basis and lend on a long-term basis.
   b. shadow bank institutions even though these institutions do not take deposits.
   c. Answers (a) and (b) are both correct.

8. Shadow banks prior to the banking crisis of 2008 were
   a. not regulated and therefore did not need to meet capital requirements or reserve requirements.
   b. not regulated and could therefore offer their customers a higher rate of return on their funds.
   c. in the United States about 1.5 times larger, in terms of dollars, than the formal, deposit-taking banking sector.
   d. Answers (a), (b), and (c) are all correct.

9. A shadow bank is subject to a bank run if
   a. the shadow bank's lenders decide it is no longer safe to lend funds to the shadow bank, and the shadow bank finds it is unable to fund its operations.
   b. bank regulators fail to adequately evaluate the safety and soundness of the shadow bank.
   c. the government issues a warning that shadow banks are inherently unstable.
   d. Answers (a), (b) and (c) are all correct.

10. When many banking institutions get into trouble at the same time this is due to
   a. government regulations that prevent banking institutions from pursuing profitable business opportunities.
   b. these institutions making similar mistakes that are often due to the existence of an asset bubble.
   c. these institutions suffering from financial contagion in which the problems and difficulties of one institution spread to and create trouble for other institutions.
   d. Both answers (b) and (c) are reasons for banking crises.
   e. Answers (a), (b) and (c) all provide reasons for banking crises.

11. Which of the following statements is true?
   a. A "vicious circle of deleveraging" refers to the quick selling of assets that result in these assets being sold at a deep discount. This selling off of assets creates financial contagion, since other institutions holding similar assets will find that these assets have lost value.
   b. The shadow banking system is not prone to financial contagion.
   c. The shadow banking system, prior to 2007, was highly regulated.
   d. Lehman's was not affected by a "vicious circle of deleveraging."

12. A financial panic
   a. is a sudden and widespread disruption of financial markets that arises when people lose faith in the liquidity of financial institutions and markets.
   b. is typically accompanied by a banking crisis.
   c. could be the result of an asset bubble and a vicious circle of deleveraging.
   d. Answers (a), (b), and (c) are all correct.
   e. Answers (a) and (b) are both correct.
   f. Answers (a) and (c) are both correct.

13. From after the Civil War to the Great Depression,
    a. the United States rarely had bank crises.
    b. frequently had bank crises due primarily to the lack of regulation in the banking system.
    c. frequently had bank crises despite regulation of the banking system.
    d. had bank crises primarily because of the existence of a system of guarantees for depositors.

14. The banking crises of the early 1930s
    a. were milder than earlier periods of bank crises.
    b. resulted in about 40% of banks in the United States failing.
    c. were due to President Franklin Roosevelt proclaiming a bank holiday.
    d. resulted in GDP falling by a third and prices falling as well.
    e. Answers (b) and (d) are both correct.
    f. Answers (b), (c), and (d) are all correct.

15. Which of the following statements is true?
    a. From 1970 to 2007, there were only 10 "systemic banking crises" in the world.
    b. From 1970 to 2007, there were many "systemic banking crises" in the world, but most of these crises were in small, poor countries and most were not as severe as the U.S. Panic of 1873 or 1893.
    c. At the beginning of the 1990s, Finland, Sweden and Japan all experienced major banking crises that were the result of real estate lending.
    d. Statements (a), (b) and (c) are all true.
    e. Statements (a) and (c) are both true.
    f. Statements (b) and (c) are both true.

16. The "Celtic Tiger" refers to
    a. Portugal.
    b. India.
    c. Ireland.
    d. South Korea.

17. Banking crises are
    a. commonly associated with recessions.
    b. do not affect the overall health of the economy.
    c. typically not associated with long-running impacts on the aggregate economy.
    d. easily resolved within days of becoming apparent.

18. A severe banking crisis is characterized as
    a. a situation in which a large fraction of the banking system goes bankrupt or suffers a major loss of confidence.
    b. a situation requiring government intervention to bail out the banking system
    c. a situation that always leads to deep recession followed by a slow economic recovery.
    d. Answers (a), (b) and (c) are all correct.
    e. Answers (a) and (b) are both correct.

19. Banking crises typically result in prolonged recessions because of

a. the credit crunch that leads to a reduction in available credit due to the disruption of the banking system.

b. the debt overhang that arises as a result of falling asset prices that lead to a vicious circle of deleveraging; as this circle progresses, it leads to even greater decreases in asset prices. As asset prices fall, consumers and businesses cut back on their spending in order to reduce their debt and rebuild their assets.

c. the loss of monetary effectiveness as a means to stimulate aggregate spending in the economy.

d. Answers (a), (b) and (c) are all correct.

e. Answers (a) and (b) are both correct.

f. Answers (b) and (c) are both correct.

g. Answers (a) and (c) are both correct.

20. After a banking crisis, when the central bank expands the money supply in order to reduce interest rates and stimulate the level of aggregate spending,

a. banks tend to hold onto excess reserves rather than loaning out these reserves because the banks are worried about bank runs and/or a loss of confidence by their investors.

b. consumers and businesses are unwilling to borrow because of the financial difficulties caused by a loss in the price of the financial assets they hold.

c. even a very low interest rate may not be sufficient to encourage expanded economic activity.

d. Answers (a), (b) and (c) are all correct.

21. When financial institutions find they are unable to borrow from private credit markets,

a. the country's central bank may step in as a lender of last resort.

b. they may have to sell their assets at steeply reduced prices unless the central bank steps in and provides credit to them.

c. this may start a vicious circle of deleveraging.

d. the government may step in to guarantee the liabilities of these financial institutions.

e. All of the answers are correct.

22. Bank regulation was first recommended in

a. the 1930s, after the financial crash of 1929 that precipitated the Great Depression.

b. *The Wealth of Nations* (1776) by Adam Smith, when Smith compared the need for bank regulation to the need for fire standards in the building code.

c. 1980, when Ronald Reagan became President of the United States.

d. 1976, when Jimmy Carter became President of the United States.

23. From the 1930s until the crisis of 2007–2009, banking regulation addressed three primary elements:

a. deposit insurance, capital requirements, and interest rate ceilings.

b. deposit insurance, interest rate ceilings, and excess reserve requirements.

c. deposit insurance, capital requirements, and reserve requirements.

d. interest rate ceilings, capital requirements, and limitations of the types of assets that banks could hold.

24. When the government guarantees bank deposits via deposit insurance, this results in
    a. the risk that bank owners will engage in reckless behavior with these bank funds, since any loss is insured by the government.
    b. bank owners acting with greater caution, since they know that any adverse outcome of their decisions will cost taxpayers money due to the existence of deposit insurance.

25. Financial regulation broke down prior to the crisis of 2007–2009 primarily because of the
    a. rise of shadow banking.
    b. expansion of the commercial banking system.
    c. rise of the shadow banking system as well as the expansion of the commercial banking system.

26. A repo is
    a. a very long-term loan.
    b. a very short-term loan.
    c. a loan where the seller agrees to repurchase the asset from the borrower at a higher price.
    d. Answers (a) and (c) are both correct.
    e. Answers (b) and (c) are both correct.

27. The repo market prior to the crisis of 2007–2009
    a. paid a higher rate of return than traditional depository institutions did on their deposits.
    b. was used as a way for shadow banks to finance their speculative investments, since the shadow banks could borrow funds in the repo market, use these funds to purchase mortgage-backed securities, and then use these mortgage-backed securities as collateral for another repo trade.
    c. by 2007, the repo and other forms of shadow banking had grown larger than traditional depository banking.
    d. Answers (a) and (b) are both correct.
    e. Answers (a), (b) and (c) are all correct.

28. The shadow banking system in the 2000s
    a. had little safety net in the form of deposit insurance.
    b. did have capital requirements but these requirements were minimal compared to the capital requirements that conventional depository institutions had to meet.
    c. had no lender of last resort to turn to in the event of a bank run.
    d. Answers (a), (b), and (c) are all true statements.

29. When a homeowner is "underwater," this means that the
    a. value of the house is less than the amount owed on the homeowner's mortgage.
    b. value of the mortgage is less than the value of the house.
    c. institution providing the mortgage for the homeowner is insolvent; thus, the homeowner must find a new lender.
    d. homeowner has defaulted on their mortgage.
    e. home is in foreclosure in which the lending institution is in the process of reclaiming the house as the collateral on a loan that is not being paid back to the institution.

30. A subprime mortgage is a loan
   a. to people who would not qualify for a traditional, or "prime" mortgage.
   b. at a lower interest rate than a traditional, or "prime" mortgage.

31. The TED spread
   a. measures the difference between the interest rate at which banks are willing to lend to one another and the rate at which they are willing to lend to the U.S. government.
   b. by the summer of 2007 started to surge.
   c. had a sharp drop after the fall of Lehman Brothers in the fall of 2008.
   d. Answers (a) and (b) are both correct.
   e. Answers (a), (b) and (c) are all correct.

32. After the banking crisis of 2007–2009
   a. it was recognized financial regulation was a continuing process that could require regulations to change over time to keep up with financial innovations.
   b. it was clear that the traditional scope of banking regulation was too wide and there was need to constrict the expansion of bank regulation.
   c. it was evident that shadow banking did not need to be regulated.
   d. Answers (a), (b) and (c) are all correct.
   e. Answers (a) and (b) are both correct.
   f. Answers (b) and (c) are both correct.
   g. Answers (a) and (c) are both correct.

33. The Wall Street Reform and Consumer Protection Act, often referred to as the Dodd-Frank bill, addresses which of the following four key elements?
   a. consumer protection, derivatives regulation, limits on interest rates, and regulation of shadow banks.
   b. consumer protection, derivatives regulation, subprime lending limits, and regulation of shadow banking.
   c. consumer protection, derivatives regulation, regulation of shadow banks, and resolution authority.
   d. consumer protection, derivatives regulation, subprime lending limits, and resolution authority.

ANSWER KEY

Answers to Problems and Exercises

1. **a.** The total amount of deposits at First Bank is equal to the amount of each deposit ($10,000) times the number of depositors (1,000), or $10,000,000.

   b. The amount of reserves at First Bank is equal to 20% of $10,000,000, or $2,000,000.

   c. The total number of mortgages issued by First Bank is equal to the amount of money available for mortgages ($8,000,000) divided by the amount per mortgage ($100,000), or 80 mortgages.

   d. If 50% of First Bank's depositors demand their funds back, then First Bank will need 500($10,000), or $5,000,000 to meet this demand. Since First Bank only has $2,000,000 in reserve, the Bank will find that it has a shortage of $3,000,000.

   e. Since First Bank needs to raise $3,000,000 in funds to meet depositor demands, it will need to sell $3,000,000/$75,000 per mortgage, or 40 mortgages.

   f. Since 50% of depositors have withdrawn their funds from the bank, this implies that First Bank now has deposits of only $5,000,000. First Bank sold 40 mortgages to raise the needed funds to meet depositor demand, so it still owns 60 mortgages. If each mortgage is now valued at $75,000, this means that the value of First Bank's mortgages is now equal to 60($75,000), or $4,500,000. First Bank's reserves are now equal to $0, since the bank used the $2,000,000 it had in reserve plus the sale of 40 mortgages to raise the funds necessary to honor depositor demand for funds.

   g. First Bank's assets are now equal to $4,500,000 (the value of the mortgages it holds), while its liabilities are equal to $5,000,000 (the value of deposits at the bank). First Bank is not solvent.

2. The deposits made at the bank are short-term in nature: that is, the depositors place funds in the bank where these funds are available whenever the depositor demands them. These deposits represent liabilities to the bank, since the bank owes these funds to the depositors who made the deposits. The bank takes these funds and uses them to finance mortgages that have a maturity of 30 years: that is, the mortgage amount borrowed does not have to be repaid in full until 30 years have elapsed. These mortgages represent assets to the bank, since the bank owns these mortgages. The bank has transformed a short-term liability, the deposits, into a long-term asset, the 30-year mortgages. Maturity transformation is the conversion of short-term liabilities into long-term assets.

3. Shadow banking refers to a diverse group of financial firms including hedge funds, money market mutual funds, and investment banks. Like depository institutions, shadow banks borrow short-term funds and use these funds to create long-term assets. Shadow banks create long-term assets by borrowing funds in the short-run and then lending or investing these funds over the longer term. This process is referred to as maturity transformation. Shadow banks are different from depository institutions because shadow banks do not accept deposits. Shadow banks, like depository institutions, are subject to bank runs because both types of banking institutions provide the same economic task of allowing their customers to make a better trade-off between rate of return, or yield, and liquidity. If the shadow bank lenders decide that it is no longer safe to lend to the shadow bank, then the shadow bank will find this loss of credit means it can no longer fund its operations. Unless the shadow bank is able to quickly sell its assets to immediately raise cash, it will fail. This failure to get funds to finance its operations is what happened to Lehman Brothers.

4.   When a bank run occurs, many people are adversely impacted: the shareholders of the bank, the creditors of the bank, the depositors at the bank, the loan customers at the bank, and the bank employees. A bank run that spreads like a contagion affects many more people: it can cause a loss of confidence among depositors at other banks, and this can lead to a cascade of events that creates more bank failures and even a bank crisis. In a bank crisis, a significant portion of the banking sector ceases to function. Often a banking crisis also precipitates a severe economic downturn resulting in higher rates of unemployment and lower levels of aggregate production that persist for many years.

5.   There are two broad types of regulation that governments can implement to reduce the likelihood of banking and financial crises. Government can act as a lender of last resort so that financial institutions have a source of funds or credit when they are unable to borrow from private credit markets. This lender of last resort protects solvent financial institutions from engaging in fire sales to raise needed funds when the private credit markets are not functioning well. The government can also provide guarantees to depositors and others with claims on banks. These guarantees effectively mean that when a financial institution becomes insolvent, the government will step in and take on the bank's risk. When the government does step in, it often demands the temporary ownership of the bank until the government can "reprivatize" the bank. This guarantee is a method for restoring depositor confidence in troubled financial institutions.

6.   The Dodd-Frank bill called for consumer protection, derivatives regulation, regulation of shadow banks, and resolution authority.

Consumer protection was deemed necessary after the financial crisis of 2007–2009 because there was recognition that many borrowers prior to the crisis had accepted offers they did not understand. One of the goals of the Dodd-Frank bill was to reduce abusive financial industry practices while protecting borrowers.

The bill called for regulation of derivatives because these complicated financial instruments were seen as a means of concealing risk. The new legislation calls for more transparent markets in derivatives.

The Dodd-Frank bill legislated regulation of shadow banks in recognition that these institutions, although they did not fit the traditional definition of a bank, played a major role in the banking crisis. Shadow banks will be regulated with regard to their levels of capital and their investments.

The Dodd-Frank bill provided for resolution authority that empowered the government to seize control of financial institutions that require a bailout. This would be an extension of the government's resolution authority over not just depository institutions, but also over the shadow banking industry. Recognizing that government guarantees can lead institutions to take excessive risk, the provision for resolution authority allows the government to reduce its exposure to backing these overly risky institutions through the government's ability to seize these errant institutions if necessary. Knowing the government can do this will likely reduce risk taking on the part of financial institutions.

Answers to Chapter Review Questions

1.   **Answer b.** This is just a definitional question: commercial banks accept deposits from customers, while investment banks do not accept these deposits. In addition, investment banks trade in financial assets.

2.   **Answer e.** A subprime mortgage is a mortgage issued to a homebuyer who lacks the level of income and/or assets that would allow him or her to qualify for a standard or prime mortgage. Because the borrower lacks the income and/or assets to qualify for a standard mortgage, he/she represents a greater threat of defaulting on, or not paying back, the loan.

3. **Answer a.** In a credit crunch, borrowers would like to borrow funds, but they find it either impossible to get credit because lenders are unwilling to lend, or it is very expensive to get credit because lenders are only willing to lend at very high interest rates. In a credit crunch, lenders have funds but are reluctant to make these funds available unless they receive unusually high interest rates on the loans they make.

4. **Answer e.** *Shadow banking* is a term coined by Paul McCulley to refer to a diverse group of financial firms including investment banks, hedge funds, and money market funds that prior to the crisis of 2008 were not closely watched or effectively regulated. Commercial banks are not considered shadow banks; commercial banks are highly regulated.

5. **Answer f.** Banking reduces the need to hold cash in the event of a financial need because the existence of banks provides a means of borrowing funds if they are needed. In addition, the banking system provides liquidity for lenders while simultaneously providing a means for those individuals with surplus funds to make those funds available to those with productive opportunities but a deficit of funds. Thus, it is possible to have liquidity while earning an interest return on your assets because of the banking system. The banking system, however, does require regulation in order that asymmetric information issues like moral hazard and adverse selection can be addressed.

6. **Answer a.** Deposits at depository institutions are available at any time and are thus short term. Depository institutions lend out these funds to those seeking funds for productive purposes: these loans are due at some point in the future, but because they are not immediately due they are viewed as long term. This borrowing on a short-term basis and lending on a long-term basis is called maturity transformation.

7. **Answer c.** Maturity transformation refers to the conversion of short-term liabilities to long-term assets. Both depository institutions as well as shadow bank institutions engage in maturity transformation.

8. **Answer d.** These are all definitional or descriptive statements that are covered in the text.

9. **Answer a.** Shadow banks are in the business of maturity transformation: they borrow on a short-term basis and lend or invest longer term. If lenders decide that the shadow bank is not a safe place for their funds, then this mismatch between short-term borrowing and long-term lending can result in a bank run as other lenders decide they also do not want to place their funds at the shadow bank. Shadow banking, prior to the banking crisis of 2008, was not regulated. The government does not issue warnings about the stability of the shadow bank institutions.

10. **Answer d.** Banking crises are typically the result of an asset bubble or financial contagion. With an asset bubble, financial institutions make a similar mistake in valuing an asset at a level greater than its true value. With financial contagion, the financial problems of one institution spread to other institutions and create problems for these other institutions. Government regulation is not a source of banking crises.

11. **Answer a.** Answer (a) describes what happens when a financial institution is forced to sell its assets quickly in order to reduce debt and raise cash. These quick sales drive the price of these assets down, and other institutions holding similar assets find that these assets are no longer as valuable. This causes these institutions to need to similarly sell assets to reduce their debt and raise cash. The data suggest that Lehman's did suffer from a downward spiral of asset prices. The shadow banking system prior to 2007 was not regulated. The shadow banking system is especially prone to fear- and rumor-driven contagion.

12. **Answer d.** These are all true statements and are discussed in the text.

13. **Answer c.** Between the Civil War and the Great Depression, the United States had frequent bank crises despite the fact that banks were regulated. This regulation focused on reserves and capital but did not provide for guarantees for depositors. As a result, bank runs were common as were bank crises.

14. **Answer e.** The banking crises of the early 1930s were much more severe than earlier banking crises, resulting in GDP falling by a third and the overall level of prices also falling. During this period, about 40% of banks in the United States failed. President Roosevelt eventually declared a temporary closure of all banks—this was termed a "bank holiday"—in order to end the vicious circle.

15. **Answer f.** These are all descriptive statements that are discussed in the text of the chapter. From 1970 to 2007, there were no fewer than 127 "systemic banking crises" in the world. Most of these crises were in small, poor countries and were not as severe as the earlier panics of 1873 and 1893. The crises in Finland, Sweden, and Japan in the early 1990s were due to heavy lending into a real estate bubble.

16. **Answer c.** The term "Celtic Tiger" was used during the 1990s and 2000s to refer to Ireland and its economic success. Ireland's impressive economic performance, however, came to an abrupt halt in 2008 due to a huge banking crisis.

17. **Answer a.** Banking crises typically are associated with recessions and often severe banking crises result in prolonged, and significant, economic slumps.

18. **Answer d.** These statements are from the text: a severe banking crisis results in many bank failures, a loss of confidence in the financial system, the need for government intervention, and a prolonged and deep recession that lasts for an extended period of time.

19. **Answer d.** The severity of recessions following banking crises is typically explained by the credit crunch, the debt overhang, and the loss of monetary effectiveness. Economic activity slows as credit becomes difficult to get, consumers and businesses slow their spending in order to reduce their debt and rebuild their assets, and monetary policy is not effective in stimulating the level of aggregate spending.

20. **Answer d.** These are all reasons for why monetary policy is ineffective following a banking crisis. Banks fearful of bank runs or a loss of confidence by their investors will want to hold excess reserves in order to have more of a cushion against a bank run or reluctance on the part of investors to provide funds. The vicious circle of deleveraging reduces the value of financial assets held relative to debt: consumers and businesses will be reluctant to increase their spending until they have reduced their debt levels relative to the value of their financial assets. Finally, a low interest rate when consumers and businesses are recovering from a vicious circle of deleveraging may not provide sufficient incentive to get these groups to borrow and spend.

21. **Answer e.** When financial institutions cannot borrow from private credit markets, they must find a source of credit. This source of credit can come from these institutions selling their assets, but this sale of assets typically is only possible if the financial institutions offer these assets at greatly reduced prices. This selling of assets at fire-sale prices starts the vicious circle of deleveraging and worsens the balance sheet for all the financial institutions. The central bank can prevent this from happening by stepping in as a lender of last resort and providing a means of credit for solvent, but credit-strapped, institutions. For a financial institution where the value of the assets is insufficient to cover its debts, the central bank's willingness to lend as a last resort will not be sufficient to restore the public's confidence in the financial institution: in this case, the government may choose to step in and guarantee the institution's liabilities.

22. **Answer b.** Bank regulation goes back a very long way to 1776, when it was first advocated by Adam Smith. Although Adam Smith was a strong proponent of the free market, he recognized that bank regulation was necessary in much the same way that fire standards are necessary in the building code. There was more comprehensive banking regulation after the banking crisis of the 1930s. Deregulation of many markets occurred toward the end of the Carter presidency and continued, at a faster rate, during the Reagan administration.

23. **Answer c.** Banking regulation from the 1930s to the crisis of 2007–2009 consisted of three primary elements: deposit insurance on the funds deposited by bank customers, which effectively eliminated bank runs; capital requirements to reduce irresponsible bank behavior that might result from the existence of deposit insurance; and reserve requirements, which also aid in reducing bank runs.

24. **Answer a.** The existence of bank deposit insurance means that depositors no longer fear that their funds might not be safe at a banking institution: effectively, the deposit insurance reduces the occurrence of bank runs because of the guaranteed protection of depositor savings. However, when these deposits are insured, it creates an incentive for bank owners to engage in riskier behavior with regard to the use of these funds, since the bank owners know that these funds will be guaranteed by the government even if a speculative bet does not pay off. Bank owners know that the government, and therefore taxpayers, will cover the cost of any bad bet on their part.

25. **Answer a.** Financial regulation has traditionally been concerned with depository institutions. However, shadow banking also functions like depository banking because shadow banks engage in maturity transformation. It is the rise of shadow banking that has created the greatest problem in financial regulation.

26. **Answer e.** A repo, or repurchase agreement, is a very short-term loan whereby the seller of the asset (for example, a corporate bond) agrees to buy back the asset at a higher price a short time later. Often repos are sold back the next day. In effect, the seller makes a short-term loan to the buyer, with the asset being sold acting as collateral on the loan.

27. **Answer e.** The repo market prior to the crisis of 2007–2009 expanded, as many investors with excess cash put their funds in this market rather than in commercial banks. The repo market yielded a higher rate of return than that paid by depository institutions. Shadow banks recognized that they could use the repo market as a means to get short-term loans to purchase other assets, and then they could return to the repo market with these newly acquired assets and use them as collateral for additional loans.

28. **Answer d.** These are all descriptive statements about the shadow banking system in the 2000s prior to the financial crisis of 2007–2009.

29. **Answer a.** When a homeowner is "underwater", this means that the value of the house is no longer worth as much as or more than the amount owed on the mortgage. When a homeowner is "underwater", this often results in the homeowner being in default: that is, the homeowner may not be making mortgage payments sometimes because the homeowner has chosen to walk away from the property, and sometimes because he or she could not keep up with mortgage payments and could not sell the home for enough to pay off the mortgage. When a homeowner is "underwater", this may result in the home being foreclosed: the lending institution may repossess the home as a result of the failure of the homeowner to make mortgage payments. With a housing bubble, lending institutions may fail, as the value of the mortgage-backed securities that they hold fall in value.

30. **Answer a.** This is just the definition of a subprime mortgage.

31. **Answer d.** The TED spread definition is given in answer (a) The TED spread increased from the summer of 2005 until 2009 when the TED spread finally fell back to pre-crisis levels. The TED spread had a sharp spike after the collapse of Lehman Brothers in the fall of 2008.

32. **Answer a.** Bank regulation had failed to keep up with financial innovation, and this became evident with the banking crisis of 2007–2009 particularly with the recognition of the growth of shadow banking. In the aftermath of the banking crisis of 2007–2009, it was recognized that bank regulation would need to be extended to cover more than traditional banking and that shadow banking also needed to be regulated.

33. **Answer c.** The four elements of the Wall Street Reform and Consumer Protection Act are delineated and discussed in the chapter.

Macroeconomics: Events and Ideas

BEFORE YOU READ THE CHAPTER

Summary

This chapter discusses the limitations of the classical macroeconomics model and how it was not adequate for the economic problems posed by the Great Depression. The chapter also develops the primary ideas underlying Keynesian economics and presents an overview of the modifications of Keynesian economics that occurred in response to criticisms of this approach. The chapter then discusses the new classical macroeconomics and the elements of modern macroeconomic consensus, before addressing the main areas of dispute among macroeconomic theorists today. The chapter also discusses the Great Moderation Consensus that emerged prior to the financial crisis of 2008 and the heated debates among economists as to the best use of fiscal and monetary policy in the aftermath of this financial crisis.

Chapter Objectives

Objective #1. Classical macroeconomics focused on the long run, asserting that monetary policy affected only the aggregate price level and not the aggregate level of output. However, by the 1930s, the measurement of business cycles was a well-established subject, despite there being no consensus on a theory of business cycles.

Objective #2. The term macroeconomy was first used in 1933. Prior to the 1930s, the classical model of the price level dominated economic thinking about monetary policy. This model, based on the assumption of flexible prices, held that an increase in the money supply, holding other things constant, would lead to an equal proportional rise in the aggregate price level and no change in the level of real aggregate output. This model focused on long-run economic adjustments while regarding short-run economic adjustment as unimportant.

Objective #3. By the 1930s, the measurement of business cycles was well advanced even though there was no generally accepted theory of business cycles. The Great Depression served as a strong stimulus for economists to develop theories that could provide guidance for macroeconomic policies in the face of business cycle fluctuations.

Objective #4.   In the United States the history of business cycles goes back to 1854. Prior to this date the United States was primarily an agricultural economy: in such an economy, prices are flexible and, hence, the short-run aggregate supply curve is nearly vertical. This implies that demand shocks do not cause output fluctuations due to this price flexibility; any output fluctuation in an agriculture-dominated economy is due to aggregate supply shocks that are primarily the result of weather variation.

Objective #5.   Keynesian economics mainly reflects two innovations: first, it emphasized short-run effects of shifts in aggregate demand and their impact on aggregate output rather than the long-run determination of the aggregate price level; and second, it argued that changes in business confidence were the primary cause of business cycles. Keynes's economic ideas have been accepted across a broad part of the political spectrum. The main practical consequence of Keynes's work was the justification of macroeconomic policy activism: Keynes's work indicated that monetary and fiscal policy could be used to smooth out business cycle fluctuations.

Objective #6.   Keynes's work suggested that economic recovery requires aggressive fiscal expansion: this deficit spending creates jobs. In the 1930s, the modest increases in deficit spending were inadequate to end the Great Depression; however, the massive expansionary fiscal policy that occurred as a result of World War II was sufficient to create jobs in the short run and to prove that aggressive fiscal policy could result in economic recovery.

Objective #7.   Keynes suggested that monetary policy would be ineffective in depression conditions due to the liquidity trap where interest rates cannot fall below zero. Although this is true, Friedman and Schwartz persuaded many economists that the Great Depression could have been avoided if the Fed had acted to prevent a monetary contraction. Over time economists came to believe that monetary policy should pay a key role in economic management.

- Economic management of the economy through monetary policy instead of fiscal policy makes macroeconomics a more technical and less political issue.

Objective #8.   Monetarism asserts that nominal GDP will grow steadily if the money supply grows steadily. Monetarists believed that a steady growth rate of the money supply would prove more effective in smoothing out business cycle fluctuations than active policy intervention, since active policy intervention encounters lags in its implementation and effectiveness. Friedman advocated the pursuit of a monetary policy rule, a formula that determines the Fed's actions, rather than discretionary monetary policy. This view used the velocity equation, $MV = PY$, to suggest that as long as the velocity of money, V, was relatively stable, then a steady rate of growth of the money supply, M, would lead to steady growth of nominal GDP, PY. The Fed's experience with monetarism proved less than successful: steady growth in the money supply in the late 1970s and early 1980s did not ensure steady growth in the economy. Data reveals that the velocity of money shifted around erratically starting around 1980 due probably to financial market innovations. Despite this experience, economists believe that too much or too little discretion in monetary policy is counterproductive.

Objective #9.   In 1968, Friedman and Phelps proposed the natural rate of unemployment of NAIRU. They claimed that the apparent trade-off between unemployment and inflation would not survive an extended period of time with increasing prices; that is, the existence of inflationary expectations would lead the economy to continue to have inflation even with high levels of unemployment.

Objective #10.   The political business cycle results when politicians use macroeconomic policy to serve political ends. This can result in unnecessary economic instability.

Objective #11. New classical macroeconomics returned to the classical view that shifts in the aggregate demand curve causes changes in the aggregate price level but not the aggregate output level. This approach challenged the Keynesian idea that the short-run aggregate supply curve is upward sloping and instead argued that the short-run aggregate supply curve was vertical. This position was based on two concepts: rational expectations and real business cycle theory.

- Rational expectations is the view that individuals and firms make decisions optimally using all the available information. If this is true, then people will form their expectations about inflation not only by considering historical data, but also by taking into account any available information about government intentions with regard to trading off higher inflation for lower unemployment. The implication of this logic is that monetary policy can change the level of unemployment only if it comes as a surprise to the public.

- Real business cycle theory argues that slowdowns in productivity growth are the primary causes of business cycle fluctuations in the economy. Further research in this area has resulted in wide acceptance that some of the correlation between total factor productivity and the business cycle is the result of the effect of the business cycle on productivity, rather than the effect of productivity on the business cycle.

Objective #12. The Great Moderation Consensus is that monetary and fiscal policy are both effective in the short run, but neither can reduce the unemployment rate in the long run. Among macroeconomists there is broad agreement that monetary policy is an effective policy tool for stabilizing the economy, but that it cannot successfully reduce the unemployment rate below the natural rate of unemployment. Now, it is generally agreed that monetary policy is ineffective only in the case of a liquidity trap. In addition, most macroeconomists agree that discretionary fiscal policy should be avoided except in exceptional cases that call for activist government intervention in the form of fiscal policy.

Objective #13. Macroeconomics is a contentious field with much debate as to which policies are appropriate. There is broad agreement among macroeconomists that central banks should be politically independent, but these macroeconomists debate whether or not central banks should pursue formally stated inflation targets, what the level of formal inflation targets should be if the central bank adopts such a policy, and whether or not central banks should intervene to prevent extreme movements in asset prices.

Key Terms

macroeconomic policy activism the use of *monetary policy* and *fiscal policy* to smooth out the *business cycle.*

monetarism a theory of *business cycles,* associated primarily with Milton Friedman, that asserts that GDP will grow steadily if the *money supply* grows steadily.

discretionary monetary policy policy actions, either changes in *interest rates* or changes in the *money supply,* undertaken by the *central bank* based on its assessment of the state of the *economy.*

monetary policy rule a formula that determines the *central bank*'s actions.

velocity of money the ratio of *nominal GDP* to the *money supply.*

natural rate hypothesis the hypothesis that because *inflation* is eventually embedded into expectations, to avoid accelerating inflation over time the *unemployment rate* equals the expected inflation rate.

Key Terms *(continued)*

political business cycle a *business cycle* that results from the use of macroeconomic policy to serve political ends.

new classical macroeconomics an approach to the *business cycle* that returns to the classical view that shifts in the *aggregate demand curve* affect only the *aggregate price level*, not *aggregate output*.

rational expectations a theory of expectation formation that holds that individuals and *firms* make decisions optimally, using all available information.

new Keynesian economics theory that argues that market imperfections can lead to price stickiness for the *economy* as a whole.

real business cycle theory a theory of *business cycles* that asserts that fluctuations in the growth rate of *total factor productivity* cause the business cycle.

Great Moderation Consensus a belief in *monetary policy* as the main tool of stabilization combined with skepticism toward the use of *fiscal policy* and an acknowledgment of the policy constraints imposed by the *natural rate of unemployment* and the *political business cycle*.

Notes

AFTER YOU READ THE CHAPTER

Tips

Tip #1. This chapter requires you to be able to compare and contrast different macroeconomic theories. The following table provides a summary of these models. You will want to review each model and think about the focus of each model, and how the models differ with regard to their underlying assumptions and their policy implications.

	Classical macro	Keynesian macro	Monetarism	Modern consensus
Focus of model	Long-run determination of the aggregate price level	Short-run determination of the aggregate output level and the effects of shifts in *AD* on that level of aggregate output	Effect of money supply growth on the level of short-run aggregate output in the economy	Summarizing points of agreement among modern-day macroeconomists
Prices	Flexible in the short run and the long run	Flexible in the long run, but sticky in the short run	Flexible in the long run, but sticky in the short run	Flexible in the long run, but sticky in the short run

	Classical macro	Keynesian macro	Monetarism	Modern consensus
Unemployment	Model does not worry about unemployment: assumes that economy will produce at potential output level in both the short run and the long run, due to price flexibility	Unemployment possible in the short run due to leftward shifts in aggregate demand that lead to decreases in output and aggregate production less than the potential output level for the economy	Unemployment possible in the short run due to leftward shifts in aggregate demand that lead to decreases in output and aggregate production less than the potential output level for the economy	Unemployment possible in the short run due to leftward shifts in aggregate demand that lead to decreases in output and aggregate production less than the potential output level for the economy
Aggregate supply curve	Vertical in both the short run and long run, thus shifts in aggregate demand have no effect on the level of aggregate output	*SRAS* is upward sloping, so shifts in aggregate demand affect aggregate output and thus employment	*SRAS* is upward sloping, so shifts in aggregate demand affect aggregate output and thus employment	*SRAS* is upward sloping, so shifts in aggregate demand affect aggregate output and thus employment; *LRAS* is vertical at the potential output level for the economy
Shifts in aggregate demand	Focus on changes in money supply and how this shifts the aggregate demand curve and raises the aggregate price level	Changes in "animal spirits," or business confidence, cause shifts in aggregate demand; model emphasizes the importance of demand shocks	Shift in aggregate demand because of fiscal policy changes will have no effect on aggregate output due to crowding-out effect; shifts in aggregate demand affect aggregate output only if driven by changes in the money supply	Shift in aggregate demand possible because of changes in fiscal policy or the money supply
Effect of monetary policy	Increase in money supply leads to an equal and proportionate rise in the aggregate price level and no effect on aggregate output in the long run	Not particularly effective in depression conditions	Plays key role in economic management; GDP will grow steadily if the money supply grows steadily (a monetary policy rule)	Can be used to shift aggregate demand curve and to reduce economic instability
Policy ramifications	Economy in long run is at potential output: simply be patient for that result to occur	Legitimized macroeconomic policy activism: the use of monetary and fiscal policy to smooth out business cycles	Expansionary fiscal policy with a fixed money supply leads to crowding out: importance of monetary policy	Fiscal and monetary policy can shift the aggregate demand curve

Tip #2. A key issue underlying this chapter is the shape of the short-run aggregate supply curve. The classical macroeconomists thought the short-run aggregate supply curve was vertical; hence, shifts in aggregate demand curve could cause changes in the aggregate price level, but not changes in the level of aggregate output. Figure 18.1 illustrates this idea.

Figure 18.1

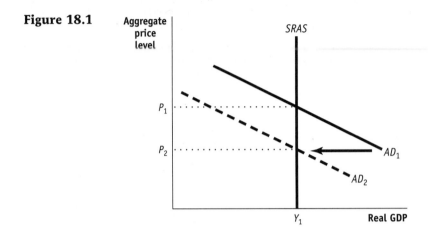

The Keynesian approach emphasized that the short-run aggregate supply curve is upward sloping and thus shifts in aggregate demand would cause both the aggregate price level as well as the aggregate output level to change. Figure 18.2 illustrates this idea.

Figure 18.2

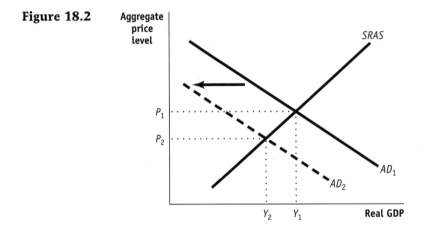

The monetarist approach concurred with the Keynesians that the short-run aggregate supply curve is upward sloping, but emphasized that fiscal policy would be relatively ineffective if the money supply was held constant due to the crowding-out effect. In addition, this approach favored the implementation of a monetary policy rule, thereby effectively reducing the scope of monetary policy.

The new classical macroeconomics returned briefly to the classical view that the short-run aggregate supply curve is vertical, but eventually found that economic data supports an upward-sloping aggregate supply curve rather than a vertical aggregate supply curve.

Tip #3. You will want to closely review the description of the modern consensus and be able to explain what this term means and how the modern consensus answers the five questions found in Table 18-1. The text provides a concise summary of these four approaches in Table 18-1. Review this table and the one given under the first tip in this section to reinforce the similarities and distinctions among these different approaches.

Tip #4. The following table provides a summary and comparison of four different macroeconomic approaches. You will find it helpful to study this table until you fully understand each of these approaches and how they differ from one another.

	Classical macroeconomics	Keynesian macroeconomics	Monetarism	New classical macroeconomics
Prices	Prices are completely flexible	Prices are sticky in the short run	Prices are sticky in the short run	Prices are completely flexible
AS curve	Vertical in the short run and the long run	Upward sloping in the short run	Upward sloping in the short run	Vertical in the short run and the long run; based upon rational expectations and real business theory
AD curve	Shifts in AD curve will cause changes in the aggregate price level but not the aggregate output level due to the AS curve being vertical: demand shocks do not affect the aggregate output level	Shifts in AD curve will cause changes in both the aggregate price level and the aggregate output level in the short run due to the AS curve being upward sloping: demand shocks affect aggregate output	Shifts in AD curve will cause changes in both the aggregate price level and the aggregate output level in the short run due to the AS curve being upward sloping: demand shocks affect aggregate output	Shifts in AD curve will cause changes in the aggregate price level but not the aggregate output level due to the AS curve being vertical: demand shocks do not affect the aggregate output level
Change in money supply	Shifts the AD curve and changes the aggregate price level but does not affect the aggregate output level; therefore, increases in the money supply lead to inflation	Shifts the AD curve and changes both the aggregate price level and the aggregate output level	Shifts the AD curve and changes the aggregate price level and the aggregate output level	Shifts the AD curve and changes the aggregate price level but does not change the aggregate output level; therefore, increases in the money supply lead to inflation
Emphasis	Aggregate output determined by AS and aggregate price level is determined by AD	Aggregate output and aggregate price level determined by the interaction between AD and AS; therefore, demand shocks can cause fluctuations in output	Monetarists hold that GDP will grow steadily if the money supply grows steadily	Aggregate output determined by AS and the aggregate price level is determined by AD
Business cycles	No real theory of business cycles since this model emphasizes the long run: no role for fiscal or monetary policy to smooth out business cycle fluctuation	Business cycles caused by changes in business confidence: advocates the use of monetary and fiscal policy to smooth out business cycle fluctuations	Importance of the appropriate growth rate of the money supply to avoid business cycles: advocates monetary policy rule since too much discretionary monetary policy may destabilize the economy	Assumption of vertical AS curve rules out business cycles: economic fluctuations in aggregate output are due to shifts in the AS curve
Short run versus long run	Short run viewed as unimportant: focus on long run	Short-run emphasis	Short-run emphasis	Short run viewed as unimportant: focus on long run

WORKED PROBLEMS

1. In agricultural economies, aggregate output and aggregate price level fluctuation in the short run are primarily due to shifts in aggregate supply because of weather. In contrast, modern, non-agricultural economies' aggregate output and aggregate price level fluctuations in the short run are due primarily to aggregate demand shocks. Use graphs to illustrate these business-cycle fluctuations in both agricultural economies as well as modern, non-agricultural economies.

STEP 1: Take time to reread the paragraph provided, paying particular attention to the idea that business-cycle fluctuations in aggregate output and the aggregate price level are driven by aggregate supply shocks in agricultural economies and, in contrast, these fluctuations are driven by aggregate demand shocks in more modern, non-agricultural economies.

Read the section "Classical Macroeconomics" on page 526 (Econ page 958).

In this step, you want to first realize that these are two very different perspectives on how fluctuations in output and the aggregate price level occur. This should suggest that separate graphs illustrating each of these perspectives would be helpful.

STEP 2: Draw a diagram illustrating short-run business cycle fluctuation in an agricultural economy where business cycle fluctuation is due to shifts in the short-run aggregate supply curve due to weather.

Read the section "Classical Macroeconomics" on page 526 (Econ page 958).

On this graph, you will want to label the initial aggregate output level and the initial aggregate price level. Then, on your graph illustrate how a shift in the aggregate supply curve to the left due to weather adversely affecting the ability of farmers to get their product to market causes aggregate output to fall and the aggregate price level to rise. On your graph, you can also illustrate how a shift in the aggregate supply curve to the right due to weather positively affecting the ability of farmers to get their product to market causes aggregate output to rise and the aggregate output level to fall. The following diagram illustrates how short-run fluctuations in the aggregate supply curve can cause business cycle fluctuations.

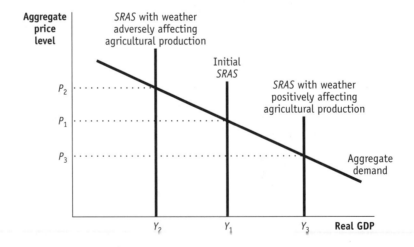

STEP 3: Draw a diagram illustrating short-run business cycle fluctuation in a modern, non-agricultural economy where business cycle fluctuation is due to shifts in the short-run aggregate demand curve.

Read the section "Classical Macroeconomics" on page 526 (Econ page 958).

On this graph, you will want to label the initial aggregate output level and the initial aggregate price level. Then, on your graph illustrate how a shift in the aggregate demand curve to the left due to a negative demand shock causes aggregate output to fall and the aggregate price level to decrease. On your graph, you can also illustrate how a shift in the aggregate demand curve to the right due to a positive demand shock causes aggregate output to rise and the aggregate output level to increase. The following diagram illustrates how short-run fluctuations in the aggregate demand curve can cause business cycle fluctuations.

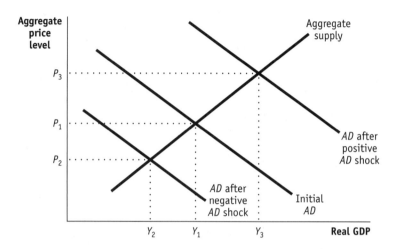

2. Classical economists argued that shifts in the aggregate demand curve in the long run would result in changes in the aggregate price level but would not change the level of real GDP. Keynes emphasized the short-run effects of aggregate demand curve shifts and how these shifts would alter the level of real GDP. Using graphs, illustrate these two approaches and provide an explanation for each of these conclusions. In your explanation, identify two ways in which these two approaches differed from one another.

STEP 1: Review the classical macroeconomic model and the Keynesian macroeconomic model and provide a verbal explanation comparing these two different approaches. In your explanation, identify two ways in which these two models differed from one another.

Review the section "The Great Depression and the Keynesian Revolution" on page 527 (Econ page 959) and Figure 18-2 on page 528 (Econ page 960).

One key difference between the classical macroeconomic model and the Keynesian was that the classical model emphasized the effects of shifts in aggregate demand in the long run on the aggregate price level, while the Keynesian model emphasized the effects of shifts in aggregate demand in the short run on the level of real GDP.

The classical macroeconomic model focused on the long run: although many classical macroeconomists would have agreed with the Keynesians that the short-run aggregate supply curve was upward sloping, they did not feel that the short run was important. The classical view was that the economy would operate at the long-run level of production, and any shift in the aggregate demand curve would only cause changes in the aggregate price level and not the level of real GDP.

In contrast, the Keynesian view focused on the short run and the impact of aggregate demand shifts if the short-run aggregate supply curve was upward sloping. Such shifts in the aggregate demand curve would cause changes in both the level of aggregate output and the aggregate price level.

A second key difference in these two perspectives was the emphasis that the classical model placed on the role of changes in the money supply in shifting the aggregate demand curve. The classical model, for the most part, ignored other factors that would shift the aggregate demand curve. In contrast, the Keynesian model argued that there were other factors, including changes in "animal spirits" (i.e., business confidence), that could cause shifts in the aggregate demand curve.

STEP 2: Draw a diagram of the classical view and provide a verbal explanation for this diagram.

Review the section "The Great Depression and the Keynesian Revolution" on page 527 (Econ page 959) and Figure 18-2 on page 528 (Econ page 960).

The classical view can be depicted as a vertical *SRAS*, since the classical perspective focused not on short-run fluctuations in aggregate output but rather on long-run attainment of full employment. Thus, if the aggregate demand curve shifted, this would only cause a change in the aggregate price level. The following diagram illustrates this idea.

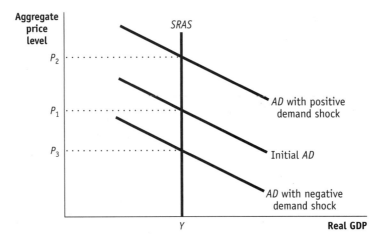

STEP 3: Draw a diagram of the Keynesian view and provide a verbal explanation for this diagram.

Review the section "The Great Depression and the Keynesian Revolution" on page 527 (Econ page 959) and Figure 18-2 and page 528 (Econ page 960).

The Keynesian view can be depicted as an upward sloping *SRAS*, since the Keynesian perspective focused on the possibility of short-run fluctuations on aggregate output due to shifts in the aggregate demand curve. Thus, if the aggregate demand curve shifted, this would cause a change in the level of real GDP as well as a change in the aggregate price level. The following diagram illustrates this idea.

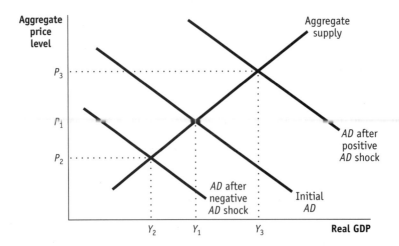

3. Milton Friedman and Anna Schwartz played a key role in convincing macro-economists of the importance of monetary policy and the possibility that monetary policy rather than fiscal policy could be used to manage the economy. Fiscal policy involves economic management by politicians, while monetary policy theoretically allows for economic management that does not involve political choices. Explain why fiscal policy involves political choices and how monetary policy could be detached from the political process.

STEP 1: Review what fiscal policy is and then explain how fiscal policy necessarily involves political choices.

Review the section "Challenges to Keynesian Economics" on page 531 (Econ page 963).

Fiscal policy is defined as changes in government spending or taxation designed to change the overall level of production in an economy. Anytime fiscal policy is contemplated or enacted it involves politicians making decisions about how the government should raise funds as well as how the government should expend its funds. These decisions are necessarily political: there will be disagreement about the right level of taxation as well as the right mix of goods and services for the government to provide. Due to the political nature of fiscal policy, this can make it difficult for the government to enact the economic management policy needed via fiscal policy.

STEP 2: Review what monetary policy is and then explain how monetary policy does not necessarily involve political choices.

Review the section "Challenges to Keynesian Economics" on page 531 (Econ page 963).

Monetary policy is defined as changes in the quantity of money in circulation designed to change the interest rate and affect the overall level of spending. If the central bank engages in monetary policy, the change in the interest rate that occurs affects everyone. This implies that economic management via monetary policy can be more of a technical issue rather than a political issue.

Problems and Exercises

1. Why did Keynes respond to the classical viewpoint by claiming that in the long run, "we are all dead"? Explain how his economic thinking about the macroeconomy represented a departure from the prevailing economic thought of the day.

2. How did the Great Depression provide an incentive for economists to develop new theories and new positions with regard to the efficacy of policy as a means of reducing business cycle fluctuations?

3. Briefly describe the two primary innovations in Keynesian economics. How did Keynes's work legitimize macroeconomic policy activism? Use the following graph to help illustrate your answer, and be sure in your answer to compare the Keynesian viewpoint with the classical viewpoint.

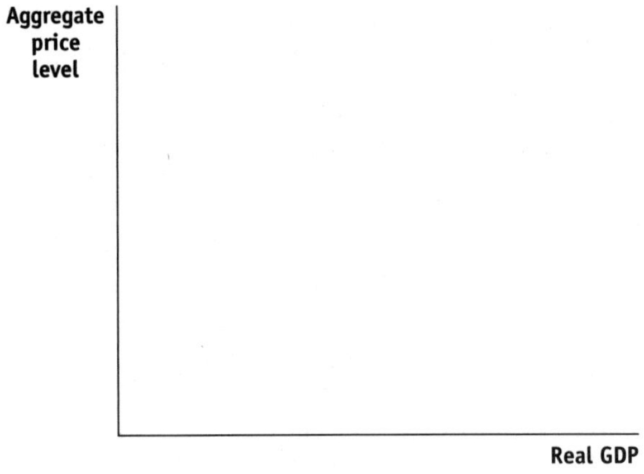

Aggregate price level

Real GDP

4. The new classical macroeconomics, developed in the 1970s and 1980s, challenged the Keynesian macroeconomic view that the short-run aggregate supply curve is upward sloping. What did the new classical macroeconomists propose with regard to the short-run aggregate supply curve, and what reasons did they give for subscribing to this viewpoint?

5. Although most macroeconomists agree that fiscal policy can affect the level of aggregate output in the short run, many macroeconomists do not support the use of discretionary fiscal policy as a method for smoothing business cycle fluctuations. Why, if fiscal policy is potentially effective, do these macroeconomists reject it as a policy tool? Is there any time that these macroeconomists would advocate the use of discretionary fiscal policy?

6. Why is it essential that central banks be politically independent?

7. Suppose the economy of Macroland reports a decline in output. The president of Macroland assembles a group of economic advisors to study this decline in output and to advise the government about appropriate policies to use to address this decline in output.

    a. The first advisor is a Keynesian macroeconomist. How would this advisor explain the decline in output, and what policy(ies) would this advisor suggest to return the economy to its potential output level? Graph an aggregate demand and aggregate supply diagram to illustrate your answer.

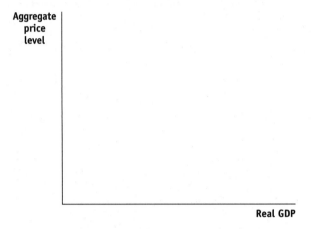

    b. The second advisor is a monetarist. How would this advisor explain the decline in output, and what policy(ies) would this advisor suggest to return the economy to its potential output level? Use an aggregate demand and aggregate supply diagram to illustrate your answer.

    c. The third advisor is an economist who accepts the viewpoints expressed by macroeconomists, in what the text terms, the modern consensus. How would this advisor explain the decline in output, and what policy(ies) would this advisor suggest to return the economy to its potential output level? Use an aggregate demand and aggregate supply diagram to illustrate your answer.

8. Use a diagram of the money market to explain why monetary policy is ineffective when there is a liquidity trap.

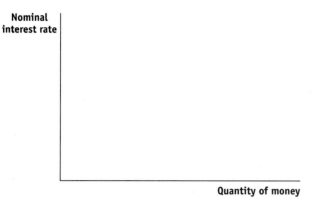

9. Why are the time lags involved in implementing discretionary fiscal policy of importance? In your answer be sure to present the monetarist view of these lags.

10. Some economists worry about the political business cycle and the use of activist macroeconomic policy for political gain. Why would economists worry about the use of macroeconomic policy for political gain?

11. How does the assumption of rational expectations support the new classical macroeconomics position that shifts in the aggregate demand curve affect only the aggregate price level and not the aggregate output level?

BEFORE YOU TAKE THE TEST

Chapter Review Questions

1. Which of the following statements is true?
   a. Macroeconomists believe the use of expansionary monetary policy is always an ineffective method for reducing economic recessions.
   b. Herbert Hoover was essentially a Keynesian macroeconomist at heart.
   c. The classical model of the price level holds that prices are flexible, and therefore the long-run aggregate supply curve is horizontal.
   d. Statements (a), (b), and (c) are all true.
   e. Statements (a), (b), and (c) are all false.
   f. Statements (a) and (b) are both true.
   g. Statements (a) and (c) are both true.
   h. Statements (b) and (c) are both true.

2. Which of the following statements is true?
   a. Prior to 1854, business cycles in the United States were primarily due to faulty economic policies made by government policymakers.
   b. Prior to 1854, the United States was primarily an agricultural economy, and any fluctuation in aggregate output that occurred could be attributed to aggregate supply shocks that were primarily weather related.
   c. Prior to 1854, the United States short-run aggregate supply curve was close to vertical due to price flexibility in an agriculture-dominated economy.
   d. Statements (a), (b), and (c) are all true.
   e. Statements (a) and (b) are both true.
   f. Statements (a) and (c) are both true.
   g. Statements (b) and (c) are both true.

3. The Great Depression
   a. reinforced prevailing economic views of the day that it was only long-run economic performance that was important.
   b. threatened both economic and political stability.
   c. illustrated that market economies produced consistently at the potential output level.
   d. Answers (a), (b), and (c) are all correct.
   e. Answers (b) and (c) are both correct.

4. Which of the following statements is true about Keynes's contributions to economic theory?
   a. In the long run, fluctuations in aggregate output are primarily due to fluctuations in aggregate demand.
   b. In the short run, the aggregate supply curve is upward sloping, and therefore shifts in aggregate demand will cause fluctuations in aggregate output.
   c. Shifts in the aggregate demand curve in the short run are primarily due to changes in the money supply.
   d. "Animal spirits" primarily affect aggregate supply in the long run.

5. Macroeconomic policy activism refers to

    a. the use of expansionary monetary policy to fight economic expansions.

    b. the use of monetary and fiscal policy to smooth out business cycle fluctuations.

    c. the idea that running large government deficits is never an acceptable means of eliminating business cycle fluctuations.

    d. Answers (b) and (c) are both correct.

6. Which of the following statements is true?

    a. In a liquidity trap, expansionary monetary policy can effectively raise interest rates.

    b. Friedman and Schwartz's work helped to prove the effectiveness of fiscal policy as a way of managing the economy.

    c. Friedman and Schwartz's work helped make macroeconomics a more technical, and less political, issue.

    d. Keynes made other economists aware of the limitations of macroeconomic policy activism.

7. Monetarism

    a. states that there is no relationship between the rate of growth of the money supply and the level of aggregate output in an economy.

    b. has nothing in common with Keynesian ideas.

    c. includes a strong belief in the efficacy of discretionary fiscal policy.

    d. maintains that most efforts of policymakers to reduce economic fluctuation actually result in greater economic instability.

8. When the central bank pursues a formula that determines its actions, this is called

    a. monetarism.

    b. a monetary policy rule.

    c. discretionary monetary policy.

    d. discretionary fiscal policy.

9. The NAIRU

    a. is equivalent to the natural rate of unemployment.

    b. hypothesis states that inflation eventually gets built into expectations, so that any attempt to keep the unemployment rate above the natural rate will lead to an ever rising inflation rate.

    c. states that once inflation is embedded in the public's expectations, it would continue even in the face of high unemployment.

    d. Answers (a), (b), and (c) are all correct.

    e. Answers (a) and (b) are both correct.

    f. Answers (a) and (c) are both correct.

    g. Answers (b) and (c) are both correct.

10. Which of the following statements is true?

    a. Activist macroeconomic policy lends itself to political manipulation.

    b. Adoption of a monetary policy rule by the central bank lends itself to political manipulation.

    c. Political business cycles reduce economic instability in an economy.

    d. Velocity, after 1980, was predictable and steady in the U.S. economy.

11. New classical macroeconomics

   a. holds that shifts in aggregate demand affected the aggregate output level and not the aggregate price level.

   b. incorporates rational expectations, the belief that individuals and firms make their decisions optimally using all available information.

   c. provides a logical argument that suggests monetary policy is ineffective as a method for stabilizing the economy.

   d. Answers (a), (b), and (c) are all correct.

   e. Answers (a) and (b) are both correct.

   f. Answers (a) and (c) are both correct.

   g. Answers (b) and (c) are both correct.

12. Real business cycle theory

   a. states that the correlation between total factor productivity and the business cycle is the result of the effect of the business cycle on productivity.

   b. states that fluctuations in the rate of growth of factor productivity cause the business cycle.

   c. states that fluctuations in the business cycle cause changes in the rate of growth of factor productivity.

   d. is a widely held view among macroeconomists today.

13. Expansionary monetary policy is helpful in fighting recessions, provided the economy is not operating in a liquidity trap, according to

   a. classical macroeconomics.

   b. monetarism.

   c. the modern consensus among macroeconomists.

   d. Answers (a), (b), and (c) are all correct.

   e. Answers (a) and (c) are both correct.

   f. Answers (b) and (c) are both correct.

14. Which of the following statements is true?

   a. According to the Keynesians, fiscal policy is ineffective in fighting recessions.

   b. According to the monetarists, fiscal policy is ineffective in fighting recessions.

   c. The modern consensus holds that discretionary fiscal policy is always acceptable.

   d. According to the classical macroeconomists, discretionary monetary policy is always acceptable.

15. True or false: "Aggressive monetary policy is effective in reducing the depth and extent of a recession."

   a. True   b. False

16. The classical model assumes prices are

   a. sticky and, therefore, both the short-run and long-run aggregate supply curves are vertical.

   b. flexible and, therefore, the short-run aggregate supply curve is upward sloping while the long-run aggregate supply curve is vertical.

   c. flexible and, therefore, both the short-run and long-run aggregate supply curves are vertical.

   d. sticky and, therefore, the short-run aggregate supply curve is upward sloping while the long-run aggregate supply curve is vertical.

17. If you were a classical macroeconomist, which of the following statements would you agree with?

    a. An increase in the money supply will result in an increase in the aggregate price level and will thus be inflationary.

    b. When the economy is in a recession, the government can reduce the recession by engaging in active monetary policy.

    c. The economy grows smoothly over time.

    d. Answers (a) and (c) are both correct.

18. In a primarily agricultural economy, demand shocks in the aggregate economy will

    a. result in significant output fluctuations.

    b. not affect aggregate output since the short-run aggregate supply curve in a primarily agricultural economy is very close to vertical.

19. Keynes argued that the focus of macroeconomists when there was a shift in aggregate demand should be on the

    a. aggregate price level.   b. aggregate output level.

20. "Animal spirits" refers to the

    a. effect of monetary policy on investment decisions.

    b. level of confidence that businesses have and how that confidence level effects spending decisions by firms and households.

    c. inappropriate policies enacted by Congress during the political business cycle.

    d. ability of the government through its spending policies to manage the economy and keep it from recession.

21. Mary and George, two economists, argue about the economic policy their government should pursue to help alleviate the current recession. Mary argues that the answer is for expansionary fiscal policy to provide a much needed spending stimulus to the economy, while George argues that this spending will only result in the crowding out of private investment spending. Which of the following statements best describes the economic perspective of these two economists?

    a. George adheres to the Keynesian model of the macroeconomy, while Mary favors the classical model of the macroeconomy.

    b. George favors the classical model of the macroeconomy, while Mary favors the Keynesian model.

    c. George favors the monetarist approach to the macroeconomy, while Mary favors the Keynesian approach.

    d. George favors the Keynesian approach to the macroeconomy, while Mary favors the monetarist approach.

22. Which of the following statements is true for the modern consensus in macroeconomics?

    I. Prices are flexible in the long run but likely to be sticky in the short run.

    II. Inadequate spending can cause short-run decreases in the aggregate output level.

    III. In the long run, the macroeconomy will produce at the full employment level of output.

    a. Statements I, II, and III are all true.

    b. Statements I and II are both true.

    c. Statements II and III are both true.

    d. Statements I and III are both true.

23. World War II demonstrated that

   a. fiscal policy was unnecessary if the country went to war.

   b. fiscal policy was ineffective if the country was at war.

   c. fiscal policy that was expansionary had the capability of creating jobs in the short run.

   d. the only way to get out of a deep depression was to go to war.

24. Keynes argued that

   a. the Depression could be eliminated with expansionary monetary policy since this would reduce the interest rate, and this reduction would result in higher levels of investment and consumer spending.

   b. ending the Depression required a focus on spending and the need for government to ensure that the level of spending was adequate.

   c. the Depression would end with the passage of time: we just all need to be patient and wait for the economy to move back to long-run equilibrium.

   d. luckily, during the Depression, the liquidity trap was not an issue and, therefore, monetary and fiscal policies would both work to end the Depression.

25. Discretionary fiscal policy

   a. due to implementation lags often ends up feeding a boom rather than fighting a recession.

   b. refers to the use of government spending and taxing policies used to smooth out the economy's ups and downs.

   c. without expansionary monetary policy will result in crowding out that limits the effect of the fiscal expansion, according to Friedman.

   d. Answers (a), (b), and (c) are all correct.

   e. Answers (a) and (b) are both correct.

   f. Answers (b) and (c) are both correct.

26. The president's economic advisors advocate that the president pursue economic policies that will result in an unemployment level of 4%. However, the NAIRU for this economy is estimated to be 5.5%. If the president implements these policies, this will

   a. lead to deflation.

   b. lead to inflation.

   c. lead to higher levels of unemployment than the NAIRU.

   d. move the economy to a higher long-run potential output level.

27. Monetary policy can

   a. change the level of aggregate output in the short run, according to macroeconomists who support the classical model.

   b. have no impact on unemployment unless the monetary policy is unexpected according to models that assume rational expectations.

   c. lower the nominal interest rate even when there is a liquidity trap.

   d. Answers (a), (b), and (c) are all correct.

   e. Answers (a) and (b) are both correct.

   f. Answers (a) and (c) are both correct.

▍ ANSWER KEY

Answers to Problems and Exercises

1. This classical model of the economy held that the economy, if it was in a recession, would self-correct and return to the natural rate of unemployment and the potential output level on its own. Keynes agreed with this assessment, but recognized that it might take time for the economy to return to this point: during the time that the economy failed to produce at the potential level of aggregate output, some people would be without jobs. Keynes felt that waiting for the long run to arrive in a situation of recession was not the only option: active government intervention in the form of fiscal and monetary policy could help smooth out business cycles. Keynes, by his emphasis on the short run and his use of an upward-sloping aggregate supply curve, was able to provide a model of the economy that illustrated the importance of the short run as well as the potential efficacy of fiscal and monetary policy in addressing business cycle fluctuations.

2. Prior to the Great Depression, the prevailing economic wisdom was that economies tended to full employment of their resources and that any change in the money supply would only result in changes to the aggregate price level, and not changes to the aggregate output level. The classical model of the price level based its analysis on a vertical aggregate supply curve for both the short run and the long run. With the onset of the Great Depression, economists found their conventional view of the macroeconomy tested: economists were forced to reconsider their model and to question the wisdom of using a model that emphasized only price level fluctuations, without regard to the possibility of aggregate output fluctuations. Thus, Keynes developed a model that considered the impact on the macroeconomy of a upward-sloping aggregate supply curve in the short run: such a model could model economic recessions and could also offer policy prescriptions for a depressed economy in the form of activist fiscal and monetary policy.

   After Keynes's work, other economists entered the discussion to question the limits of macroeconomic policy activism. In particular, Friedman revived interest in monetary policy, and his work led to a recognition that management of the economy could be shifted away from fiscal policy and toward monetary policy. This work meant that macroeconomics could be a more technical, less political, issue.

   The modern consensus reflects debate about and the study of macroeconomic issues. The modern consensus agrees that fiscal policy and monetary policy can each be effective in fighting recessions, but are unable to reduce unemployment in the long run. This consensus represents a melding of elements from both the classical model of the price level and Keynesian macroeconomics.

3. Keynes emphasized (1) the short-run effects of shifts in aggregate demand on aggregate output, rather than the long-run determination of the aggregate price level; and (2) that shifts in the aggregate demand curve could be caused by factors other than a change in the money supply. These other factors were lumped together as "animal spirits," or business confidence: Keynes emphasized that changes in business confidence were the primary causes of business cycles in the economy. Therefore, Keynes modeled the economy as having an upward-sloping short-run aggregate supply curve with a shifting aggregate demand curve. Thus, if the aggregate demand curve shifted to the left, this would lead the economy in the short run to experience not only falling price levels but also falling aggregate output and higher levels of unemployment. The following graph illustrates this idea.

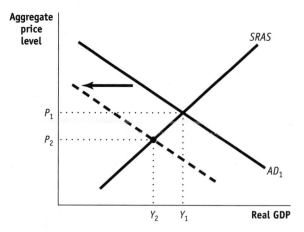

In contrast, the classical view held to a vertical aggregate supply curve (for both the short run and the long run) and thus, a shift in aggregate demand would alter the aggregate price level, but not the aggregate output level. The following figure illustrates this idea.

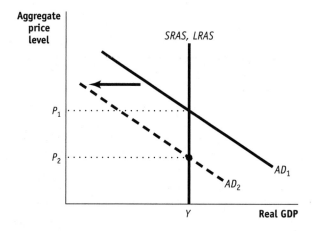

Keynes reasoned that activist fiscal and monetary policy could be used to offset these shifts in the aggregate demand curve, thus keeping the economy at its initial equilibrium. In fact, a failure to engage in activist policy could potentially cause the economy to operate in a recession or depression: Keynes provided a very strong justification for the role of government policy in reducing or eliminating business cycles.

4. The new classical macroeconomic model reverted to the classical view that the short-run aggregate supply curve was vertical: this implies that shifts in aggregate demand alter the aggregate price level, but do not affect the level of aggregate output. The new classical macroeconomic model based its conclusions on two arguments: rational expectations and real business cycle theory.

Rational expectations is the view that individuals and firms make their decisions based upon all available information, and people will therefore take into account not only historical information, but also government intentions with regard to future policy. Thus, any attempt by the government to trade off higher inflation in the short run in order to attain lower levels of unemployment will be noticed by individuals and firms, and this information will be included in the decision-making process. The new classical macroeconomics concludes that government policy to change the level of unemployment can only be effective if it is a surprise: this means that the government no longer can pursue intentionally policies to change the unemployment rate, since people will perceive their intent and act in a manner that eliminates the policy's effectiveness.

Real business cycle theory holds that fluctuations in the rate of growth of total factor productivity cause the business cycle. Rather than looking to shifts in aggregate demand as the cause of business cycle fluctuations (the Keynesian approach), the real business cycle theorists explained economic fluctuations as the result of variation in the rate of growth of total factor productivity. Subsequent research notes a strong correlation between growth rates of factor productivity and the business cycle, but does not identify the direction of causation.

5.   Discretionary fiscal policy is rejected as a policy tool by many macroeconomists, because they view it as often counterproductive due to the existence of lags in the implementation and effectiveness of this policy. They argue that by the time the discretionary fiscal policy is implemented and takes effect, the economy is often no longer struggling with the particular economic conditions the fiscal policy was intended to address. In addition, there is concern that the use of discretionary fiscal policy may contribute to greater business cycle fluctuations due to the political business cycle. These economists view the use of discretionary fiscal policy as having a limited role: they advocate its use when monetary policy is ineffective (in the case of the liquidity trap).

6.   Central banks, through monetary policy, exert strong influences on the macroeconomy. When a country's central bank is not politically independent, policymakers can adopt inflationary monetary policies that wreck economic havoc. Typically, this havoc is the result of excessive growth of the money supply. When a central bank is politically independent, it can maintain more appropriate money supply growth rates, thereby avoiding high levels of inflation and the resultant economic problems this inflation can cause.

7.   **a.** The Keynesian macroeconomist would explain the recession using an *AD-AS* diagram like the one depicted in the following graph.

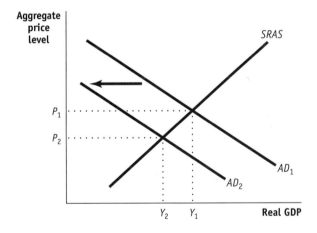

Output, Y, has fallen below its potential output level of Y_1 because of a shift in aggregate demand. The current level of production, Y_2, results in a higher level of unemployment. The Keynesian macroeconomist explains the cause of this leftward shift in aggregate demand as a change in "animal spirits," or a decline in business confidence. To remedy the situation, this economist proposes macroeconomic policy activism: the use of monetary and fiscal policy. In this case this policy should be directed at shifting the aggregate demand curve back to the right so that aggregate output can return to its initial level of Y_1.

b. The monetarist advisor would utilize the same diagram as the Keynesian economist to depict the fall in aggregate output. However, the monetarist would caution that expansionary fiscal policy would not restore the economy to Y_1 if the money supply is held constant. The monetarist reasons that the increase in spending (or decrease in taxes) by the government while stimulating aggregate demand will also stimulate money demand. With no change in the money supply this increase in money demand will cause interest rates to rise: the rise in interest rates will crowd out investment spending so that the increase in spending due to the change in fiscal policy will be off-set by an equal decrease in investment spending. The monetarist would therefore emphasize the inability of expansionary fiscal policy to address and correct the recession. The monetarist would advise steady growth of the money supply in order to generate steady growth of aggregate output.

c. This third advisor could also use the diagram in part (a) to explain the decline in aggregate output. This economist would assert that expansionary monetary policy could be used to shift the aggregate demand curve back to the right provided the economy was not operating in a liquidity trap. This economist would also advise that expansionary fiscal policy could also be used to shift the aggregate demand curve to the right.

8. The liquidity trap refers to a situation where the nominal interest rate has fallen to zero and, therefore, cannot be lowered further through expansionary monetary policy. Therefore, the Fed cannot stimulate the economy by expanding the money supply and decreasing the interest rate since the interest rate cannot fall lower than zero. The following figure illustrates the liquidity trap.

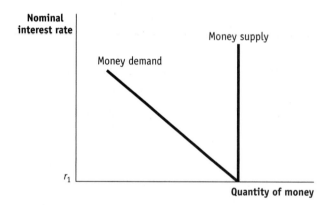

Note that in this figure, if the Fed were to engage in expansionary monetary policy, this would cause the money supply to shift to the right: but the interest rate cannot fall any further than zero, so this expansionary monetary policy would not stimulate investment and consumption spending.

9. Discretionary fiscal policy requires that the government first identify a macroeconomic problem and then pass the legislation to address this problem using discretionary fiscal policy. But it takes time for the government to recognize that there is a macroeconomic problem and then it takes more time for the government to write and pass legislation: meanwhile, the aggregate economy is dynamic and changing with this passage of time. Often discretionary fiscal policy is implemented after the economy has moved to a different part of the business cycle: the discretionary fiscal policy passed to combat recessionary concerns may actually be implemented during the boom part of the economic business cycle. Monetarists worry that these efforts by policymakers to smooth out the business cycle may actually make things worse due to these timing effects that occur because of implementation lags.

10. The political business cycle refers to the deliberate manipulation of the macroeconomy with the intent of reaching particular political outcomes. For example, the incumbent party in government may enact economic policies designed foremost to improve their chances at reelection: they attempt to manipulate macroeconomic policy to ensure that the economy is performing well at the time of the election. This manipulation for political gain may result in greater macroeconomic fluctuations than are optimal for the economy or for the individuals living and working in this economy.

11. The assumption of rational expectations holds that people will take into account any available information about monetary and fiscal policy. By building in this information, people will already adjust the aggregate supply curve to whatever they perceive to be the policy intentions of the government; hence, the short-run as well as long-run aggregate supply curve will be vertical, which means that the new classical macroeconomics ends up with the same results as those of classical macroeconomics.

Answers to Chapter Review Questions

1. **Answer e.** All of these statements are false. There is general consensus among macroeconomists that expansionary monetary policy is effective in reducing recessions. Herbert Hoover, during his presidency, held firmly to the belief that active intervention in the economy would only worsen the depression: this view reflected the viewpoint that aggressive monetary policy was dangerous and ineffective. In the classical model of the price level, prices are flexible and, hence, the aggregate supply curve is vertical and not horizontal.

2. **Answer g.** Prior to 1854, the U.S. economy was primarily an agricultural economy with flexible prices with little, or no, macroeconomic policy intervention on the part of the government. This implies that the short-run aggregate supply curve was close to vertical; hence, any fluctuations in aggregate demand would result in changes in the aggregate price level and no significant changes in aggregate output. Thus, any fluctuation in aggregate output, during this period, was the result of aggregate supply shocks which were primarily driven by weather.

3. **Answer b.** The Great Depression illustrated for economists that short-run economic fluctuations were important and that a theory to understand these fluctuations was needed. The Great Depression threatened economic stability due to the economic pain of extremely high levels of unemployment and the political instability that led to the rise of Hitler in Germany. Although some economists thought that a market-oriented economy was unstable, there were other economists that did not support this view.

4. **Answer b.** Keynes demonstrated that fluctuations in aggregate demand could cause short-run fluctuations in aggregate output. These fluctuations in short-run aggregate demand were primarily due to changes in "animal spirits," the term Keynes used to describe business confidence. Keynes focused on the short run and the effects of shifts in aggregate demand on a short-run upward-sloping aggregate supply curve.

5. **Answer b.** Macroeconomic policy activism is the use of monetary and fiscal policy to smooth out business cycle fluctuations. Expansionary monetary policy can be used effectively to reduce economic recessions. Large government deficits can be used to effectively fight economic recessions, but may worsen economic expansions.

6. **Answer c.** In a liquidity trap, expansionary monetary policy is ineffective, since interest rates can fall no further once they are equal to zero. Expansionary monetary policy, if effective, reduces interest rates. Friedman and Schwartz provided proof of the effectiveness of monetary policy as a way of managing the economy. Their work helped to shift macroeconomics from a reliance on fiscal policy to a reliance on monetary policy as a means of managing the economy. This shift meant that macroeconomics became a more technical issue instead of a political issue. Keynes proved there was a role for macroeconomic policy activism.

7. **Answer d.** Monetarism states that GDP will grow steadily if the money supply grows steadily. Monetarists, like Keynesians, believe that the short run is important and that short-run changes in aggregate demand can affect aggregate output as well as aggregate prices. Monetarism does not believe in the effectiveness of discretionary fiscal policy due to the fact that government perceptions about the economy often lag behind reality. Monetarists believe that the steady growth of the money supply will result in less economic instability and will prove better for smoothing out economic fluctuations than the pursuit of discretionary monetary or fiscal policy.

8. **Answer b.** A monetary policy rule describes the use of a formula by the central bank to determine its actions.

9. **Answer f.** The NAIRU is the same as the natural rate of unemployment, and the NAIRU hypothesis says that once inflation is built into expectations any attempt to keep the unemployment rate below the natural rate will lead to accelerating inflation. Thus, once inflation is embedded in the public's expectations, then that inflation will continue even if the unemployment rate is high.

10. **Answer a.** Activist macroeconomic policy does lend itself to political manipulation, since there is an obvious temptation for politicians to pump up the economy in an election year. One of the appeals of a monetary policy rule for a central bank is that it takes policy discretion away from politicians. Political business cycles increase economic instability in an economy. After 1980, velocity was highly unstable and therefore not predictable in the United States' economy.

11. **Answer g.** New classical macroeconomics returns to the classical model's vertical aggregate supply curve: a shift in aggregate demand, given this vertical aggregate supply curve, will cause the aggregate price level to change, but will have no effect on the level of aggregate output. Answer (b) is a straightforward definition of rational expectations, which is one of the underlying concepts in the new classical macroeconomics. If rational expectations is true (as is assumed in new classical macroeconomics), then individuals and firms will fully anticipate any planned monetary policy: thus, monetary policy is effective only when it is a surprise, and this implies that monetary policy no longer can be used to stabilize the economy.

12. **Answer b.** Real business cycle theory focuses on the rate of growth of factor productivity and how variations in this growth rate can cause business cycle fluctuations. Subsequent analysis suggests that there is a correlation between the rate of growth of factor productivity and business cycles, but the direction of causation between the two variables is difficult to fully determine. Today, this theory is felt to be limited in its explanatory value, despite its important contributions to our understanding of macroeconomics.

13. **Answer f.** Classical macroeconomics did not believe that expansionary monetary policy was effective in fighting recessions, while Keynesian macroeconomics believed it was of limited value. Monetarists do believe that expansionary monetary policy can be helpful in fighting recessions. The modern consensus is that expansionary monetary policy is useful, except when the economy finds itself in a liquidity trap where nominal interest rates equal zero and cannot fall any further.

14. **Answer b.** Table 18-1 (33-1) in your text provides a summary of the issues addressed in this question. Keynesians upheld the efficacy of fiscal policy as a method for fighting recessions, while monetarists believed that fiscal policy was not effective in fighting recessions. The modern consensus believes that discretionary fiscal policy is useful only under restrictive circumstances. The classical macroeconomists did not believe in discretionary monetary policy.

15. **Answer a.** The broad consensus among macroeconomists today is that expansionary monetary policy can be effective in reducing the extent of a recession.

16. **Answer c.** The classical model holds that prices are flexible, which results in the aggregate supply curve being vertical in both the short run and long run. An increase in the money supply causes an equal proportionate increase in the aggregate price level with no change in the level of aggregate output.

17. **Answer a.** Classical macroeconomists realized that the economy did not grow smoothly over time despite their focus on the long run and their assumption that the aggregate supply curve is vertical. They did believe that increases in the money supply would ultimately only result in an increase in the aggregate price level without any long-run stimulus to aggregate output. Classical macroeconomists did not believe in activist government intervention because they held that the economy would self-correct with time.

18. **Answer b.** In a primarily agricultural economy, the short-run aggregate supply curve is primarily vertical since the level of aggregate production in such an economy is agricultural commodities; thus, a rightward or leftward shift in the aggregate demand curve will not alter the level of aggregate production but will have a significant impact on the aggregate price level.

19. **Answer b.** Keynes, writing at the time of the Great Depression, argued that the classical model's focus on the aggregate price level was misplaced during times of economic recession that were due to inadequate spending. Keynes thought that economists needed to focus on the impact of shifts in aggregate demand on the aggregate output level and, hence, the level of unemployment in the economy.

20. **Answer b.** "Animal spirits" refers to business confidence and the effect of this confidence level on the business cycle: when businesses are less confident, they spend less, which results in households also spending less as their income falls.

21. **Answer b.** The classical model of the macroeconomy holds that shifts in aggregate demand that are the result of fiscal policy will have no effect on aggregate output but will affect the aggregate price level; the Keynesian model of the macroeconomy holds that shifts in aggregate demand that are the result of fiscal policy can cause short-run changes in the level of aggregate demand. Mary believes that an increase in fiscal spending will act to stimulate the economy (i.e., shift the aggregate demand curve to the right) and help diminish the recessionary economic impact, while George believes such a change in government spending will only lead to less spending by the private sector.

22. **Answer a.** All three of these statements are part of the modern macroeconomic consensus. The text discusses this consensus in detail.

23. **Answer c.** Fiscal policy can affect the aggregate demand curve in the short run: if fiscal policy is expansionary, it will shift the aggregate demand curve to the right, which will lead to a higher level of aggregate output and, therefore, a higher level of employment in the short run. Prior to World War II, it was not clear whether expansionary fiscal policy could increase the level of short-run employment, but with the war it became clear that this was possible.

24. **Answer b.** Keynes refuted the classical approach of relying upon the economy to move to long-run equilibrium: he reminded all that "in the long run we are all dead" and that, in the case of the Great Depression, it would be a very long time until the economy self-corrected and, in the interim, many people would be out of work and there would be substantial loss of production. Keynes instead argued for expansionary fiscal policy stimulus from the government: if the government could raise the level of spending to offset the decrease in spending by households and firms, then this would allow the economy to restore itself more quickly to full employment. During the Depression, the liquidity trap was an issue: interest rates were so low that the central bank could not stimulate the economy through reductions in the nominal interest rate.

25. **Answer d.** Government perceptions about the state of the economy often lag behind reality, which results in timing issues with regard to discretionary fiscal policy: often the policy that is implemented is designed to address recession but is not enacted and does not begin to affect the macroeconomy until after the recession has ended and the economy has moved toward an economic boom. Discretionary fiscal policy is designed to smooth out business cycle fluctuations but is less effective when not accompanied with expansionary monetary policy, since the increased spending by the government may crowd out spending by private firms and by households.

26. **Answer b.** If the NAIRU is 5.5% unemployment, then the attempt to lower the unemployment level below this amount will ultimately result in the raising of inflationary expectations: any attempt to keep the unemployment rate below the natural rate will lead to an ever rising inflation rate.

27. **Answer b.** Statement (a) is false, since the classical model holds that the aggregate supply curve is vertical: in the short run and the long run, the level of aggregate output is assumed to be constant. Statement (c) is false since the nominal interest rate cannot be lowered once the economy is in the liquidity trap with the nominal interest rate at the zero bound. Statement (b) is correct. The rational expectations assumption holds that the public takes into account all available information about monetary and fiscal policy: the only way that monetary policy can change unemployment is for that monetary policy to not be anticipated by the public.

19(34)

Open-Economy
Macroeconomics

■ BEFORE YOU READ THE CHAPTER

Summary

This chapter introduces the balance of payments and explores its measurement. In addition, the chapter considers the determinants of international capital flows and the role of the foreign exchange market and the exchange rate in the macroeconomy. The chapter explains the distinction between nominal and real exchange rates and emphasizes the importance of the real exchange rate in the current account. The chapter discusses different exchange rate regimes and contrasts fixed exchange rate regimes with floating exchange rate regimes. Finally, the chapter considers the effect of open economies on macroeconomic policy when operating under a floating exchange rate regime.

Chapter Objectives

Objective #1. The balance of payments accounts summarize a country's transactions with other countries.

- The balance of payments on financial account is the difference between a country's sales of assets to foreigners and the country's purchases of assets from foreigners during a given period of time. This is also referred to as the capital account. The financial account can be broken into subaccounts, including the private net purchases of assets by private individuals, and the official net purchases of assets, which represent transactions made by central banks.

- The balance of payments on current account is the difference between a country's exports and its imports plus net international transfer payments and factor income during a given period of time. Net international transfer payments is the difference between the payments foreigners send into the country and the payments that are sent out of the country to foreigners, while net international factor income is the difference between income payments received from foreigners and payments paid to foreigners.

- The sum of the balance of payments on current account (*CA*) and the balance of payments on financial account (*FA*) must equal zero. Thus, if *CA* is a positive number, then *FA* must be a negative number; conversely, if *CA* is a negative number, then *FA* must be a positive number.

Objective #2. A modified circular flow diagram can illustrate the flows between a country and the rest of the world.

- One flow represents the payments that are counted in the balance of payments on current account: here, the rest of the world sends payments into the country for goods and services (this would be payments for the country's exports), factor income, and transfers, and the rest of the world receives payments from the country for the goods and services (this would be payments for the country's imports), factor income, and transfers.

- A second flow represents payments that are counted in the balance of payments on financial account: here, the rest of the world sends the country payments for assets the world purchases from the country, while the country sends the rest of the world payments for assets it purchases. The country's balance of payments on financial account is a measure of the capital inflows or the amount of foreign savings that are available to finance domestic investment spending.

- Since the total flow into the country must be equal to the total flow out of the country, this implies that the balance of payments on current account plus the balance of payments on financial account must equal zero.

Objective #3. The merchandise trade balance, or trade balance, is the difference between a country's exports and imports of goods. It does not include the value of services traded.

Objective #4. Countries can pay for their imports by selling assets that create liabilities, obligating the country to pay for these goods and services at some point in the future.

Objective #5. The loanable funds market can be used to illustrate capital flows between countries. Provided investors think that a foreign asset is as good as a domestic asset and a foreign liability is as good as a domestic one, funds will flow from a country with a low interest rate to a country with a high interest rate until the difference between the interest rates in the two locales is eliminated. That is, the capital flows will equalize the interest rate between the two countries.

- A country that has capital inflows must have a matching current account deficit, and a country that has capital outflows must have a matching current account surplus.

- The financial account reflects the movement of capital and the current account reflects the movement of goods and services: movements in the exchange rate ensure that the balance of payments, the difference between the current account and the financial account, equals zero. The exchange rate is the price at which one currency trades for another currency.

- International differences in the demand for funds reflect underlying differences in investment opportunities. International differences in the supply of funds reflect underlying differences in savings across countries.

Objective #6. In recent years, the United States has had a massive current account deficit with resultant huge capital inflows. This capital inflow was attributed to the financial crises that caused investors to be unwilling to invest funds in poorer countries, which prior to the financial crises had been the recipients of substantial capital inflows. In addition, many governments started amassing large levels of foreign exchange reserves: this led these countries to have massive capital outflows that primarily flowed into the United States.

Objective #7. Currencies can be exchanged for one another in the foreign exchange market. This market determines the exchange rate, or the price for which two currencies exchange. When one currency becomes more valuable in terms of another currency, we say that the first currency has appreciated. When one currency becomes less valuable in terms of another currency, we say that the first currency has depreciated.

- The foreign exchange market brings together demanders and suppliers of currencies, and it is the interaction of this demand and supply that determines the equilibrium exchange rate. For instance, in the foreign exchange market for dollars, the demanders in this market are giving up foreign currency in order to acquire dollars. Their demand for dollars is influenced by the price they must pay for these dollars: this price is the exchange rate expressed as foreign currency per dollar. In the foreign exchange market for dollars, the suppliers of dollars provide dollars in exchange for the foreign currency; the supply of dollars they provide to this market depends on the price, or the exchange rate, they receive for those dollars. In the foreign exchange market, for dollars as the exchange rate increases, holding everything else constant, the quantity demanded of dollars will decrease, while the quantity of dollars supplied will increase. The equilibrium exchange rate is that exchange rate for which the quantity of dollars demanded equals the quantity of dollars supplied in the foreign exchange market.

- When there is an increase in capital inflows into a country, this increases the balance of payments on financial account. An increase in a country's exchange rate makes imports more attractive and exports less attractive for this country: this leads to a reduction in the balance of payments on current account for that country, which exactly offsets the increase in the balance of payments on financial account for that country. To generalize, a change in the balance of payments on financial account for a country must generate an equal and opposite reaction to that country's balance of payments on current account.

Objective #8. The real exchange rate is the exchange rate adjusted for international differences in aggregate price levels. The real exchange rate of country X's currency to country Y's currency equals the nominal exchange rate of country X's currency for country Y's currency times the ratio of the aggregate price level in country Y to the aggregate price level in country X. Equation 19-4 in your text provides an example of this calculation. The nominal exchange rate is the exchange rate unadjusted for inflation.

- The current account responds only to changes in the real exchange rate, and not to changes in the nominal exchange rate. A country's products become cheaper to foreigners only when that country's currency depreciates in real terms, and a country's products become more expensive to foreigners only when that country's currency appreciates in real terms.

Objective #9. Purchasing power parity refers to the nominal exchange rate between two countries at which a given basket of goods and services would cost the same in each country. Nominal exchange rates almost always differ from purchasing power parities. Sometimes this difference is due to systematic differences; for example, prices are lower in poor countries because services tend to be cheaper in poor countries than they are in rich countries.

Objective #10. The real exchange rate affects exports and imports. When a country's real exchange rate rises, or appreciates, that country's exports fall and its imports rise. When a country's real exchange rate falls, or depreciates, that country's exports rise and its imports fall.

Objective #11.   Recall that money is not a good or service but is instead an asset whose quantity is controlled by government policy. Thus, government through its policies can influence the nominal exchange rate. There are a variety of exchange rate regimes that countries have adopted: these exchange rate regimes represent different rules governing policy toward the exchange rate.

- When the government keeps the exchange rate against some other currency at or near a particular target, this is referred to as a fixed exchange rate.

- A country follows a floating exchange rate regime when it allows the exchange rate to fluctuate wherever the market takes it.

- There are other exchange rate regimes besides a fixed exchange rate and a floating exchange rate that lie somewhere between these two choices. For example, there are managed exchange rates where the government adjusts the fixed exchange rate often in order to avoid wide swings in its value; or there are exchange rates that float within a target zone but are prevented by the government from deviating from that zone.

Objective #12.   Under a fixed exchange rate regime, the government can affect the exchange rate through five primary activities.

- The government can affect its country's exchange rate by buying or selling currency in the foreign exchange market: this is an exchange market intervention. In order to engage in an exchange market intervention, a government must hold foreign exchange reserves, which are stocks of foreign currency that the government can use to buy its own currency when it needs to support its own currency's price. A large part of capital flows represents governmental transactions: these purchases and sales of foreign assets by governments and central banks support their currencies through exchange market intervention. When the government buys its currency, holding everything else constant, this will increase the value of its currency.

- The government can implement exchange rate intervention through its monetary policy. To support the exchange rate, the government can increase its interest rate, which will encourage increased capital flow into the economy and, therefore, an increased demand for that country's currency. Holding everything else constant, an increase in a country's interest rate will increase the value of its currency.

- The government can affect the exchange rate by reducing the supply of its currency in the foreign exchange market. Governments can achieve this reduction by limiting the right of their citizens to buy foreign currency through the imposition of foreign exchange controls. Holding everything else constant, imposition of foreign exchange controls increases the value of a country's currency.

- Thus, if the value of a country's currency in the foreign exchange market is lower than the target exchange rate, the government can prevent depreciation of its currency by buying the country's currency, by pursuing a higher interest rate via its monetary policy, or by imposing foreign exchange controls.

- If the value of a country's currency in the foreign exchange market is higher than the target exchange rate, the government can prevent appreciation of its currency by selling the country's currency, by pursuing a lower interest rate via its monetary policy, or by imposing foreign exchange controls that limit the ability of its citizens to sell their currency to foreigners. All of these actions, other things equal, will reduce the value of the country's currency.

Objective #13.   A fixed exchange rate provides certainty about the value of a currency. A commitment to a fixed exchange rate by a country is also a commitment to not engage in inflationary policies. Maintaining a fixed exchange rate requires the country to hold large quantities of foreign currency, and these holdings typically are a low-return investment. Use of monetary policy to help stabilize an exchange rate may also require a country to forego other goals like the stabilization of output or the control of the inflation rate. In addition, the use of exchange controls, like import quotas and tariffs, distort incentives for importing and exporting, and may lead to increased transaction costs due to bureaucratic red tape and increased corruption. In short, the pursuit of a fixed exchange rate eliminates uncertainty but limits monetary policy and may require the adoption of exchange rate controls, while the pursuit of a floating exchange rate leaves monetary policy available for stabilization but creates uncertainty for businesses.

Objective #14. A reduction in the value of a currency that previously had a fixed exchange rate is called a devaluation. A devaluation is a depreciation that is due to a revision in a fixed exchange rate target. An increase in the value of a currency that previously had a fixed exchange rate is called a revaluation.

- A devaluation makes domestic goods cheaper in terms of foreign currency; thus, a devaluation leads to higher exports and lower imports and, therefore, an increase in a country's balance of payments on current account. A devaluation acts as a stimulus to aggregate demand and can, therefore, be used to reduce or eliminate a recessionary gap.

- A revaluation makes domestic goods more expensive in terms of foreign currency; thus, a revaluation leads to lower exports and higher imports and, therefore, a decrease in a country's balance of payments on current account. A revaluation acts as a contractionary force on aggregate demand and can, therefore, be used to reduce or eliminate an inflationary gap.

Objective #15. Under a floating exchange rate regime, a country retains its ability to pursue independent monetary policy, but the use of monetary policy will affect the exchange rate, which in turn will affect the level of aggregate demand in the economy. Monetary policy in open economies has an effect beyond the effect we have described in closed economies.

- For example, a decision to use monetary policy to reduce the interest rate will lead to higher investment spending, but it will also provide less incentive for foreigners to move funds into the currency, which will reduce the demand for the country's currency. There will also be an increase in the supply of currency as people exchange the domestic currency for foreign currency due to the incentive to move funds abroad since the rate of return on loans at home has fallen relative to the rate of return on loans in other countries. Together these two effects cause the domestic currency to depreciate, and this depreciation leads to an increase in exports, a decrease in imports, and an overall positive impact on aggregate demand.

- Economic events in an economy also impact other economies. Changes in aggregate demand affect the demand for goods and services produced abroad as well as at home: holding everything else constant, a recession leads to a fall in imports and an expansion leads to a rise in imports. The link between aggregate demand in one country and aggregate demand in another country helps to explain why business cycles are often synchronized between different countries. A floating exchange rate regime is thought to limit the effect of aggregate demand in one country on aggregate demand in another country due to the behavior of the foreign exchange market: when there is a reduction in foreign demand for goods and services, this leads naturally to a depreciation of the domestic currency. This depreciation reduces the fall in the level of exports while simultaneously limiting the increase in imports. The overall impact of the movement in the exchange rate is to lessen the decline in the level of aggregate demand.

Objective #16. Many European countries adopted the euro as their currency beginning in 1999. However, some countries chose not to adopt the euro, including Britain. Adoption of the euro increased international trade and led to more productive economies for those countries adopting the euro, but adoption of the euro also meant that these countries gave up their ability to have an independent monetary policy. Britain was unwilling to lose its independent monetary policy since this would limit its ability to use policy to correct macroeconomic problems.

Key Terms

balance of payments accounts a summary of a country's transactions with other countries, including two main elements: the *balance of payments on current account* and the *balance of payments on financial account*.

balance of payments on current account (current account) transactions that do not create liabilities; a country's *balance of payments on goods and services* plus net international transfer payments and factor income.

balance of payments on goods and services the difference between the value of *exports* and the value of *imports* during a given period.

merchandise trade balance (trade balance) the difference between a country's *exports* and *imports* of goods alone—not including services.

balance of payments on financial account (financial account) international transactions that involve the sale or purchase of assets and, therefore, create future liabilities.

foreign exchange market the market in which currencies can be exchanged for each other.

exchange rate the price at which currencies trade, determined by the *foreign exchange market*.

appreciation a rise in the value of one currency in terms of other currencies.

depreciation a fall in the value of one currency in terms of other currencies.

equilibrium exchange rate the *exchange rate* at which the quantity of a currency demanded in the *foreign exchange market* is equal to the quantity supplied.

real exchange rate the *exchange rate* adjusted for international differences in *aggregate price levels*.

purchasing power parity (between two countries' currencies) the nominal *exchange rate* at which a given basket of goods and services would cost the same amount in each country.

exchange rate regime a rule governing policy toward the *exchange rate*.

fixed exchange rate an *exchange rate regime* in which the government keeps the *exchange rate* against some other currency at or near a particular target.

Key Terms *(continued)*

floating exchange rate an *exchange rate regime* in which the government lets the *exchange rate* go wherever the market takes it.

exchange market intervention government purchases or sales of currency in the *foreign exchange market*.

foreign exchange reserves *stocks* of foreign currency that governments can use to buy their own currency on the *foreign exchange market*.

foreign exchange controls licensing systems that limit the right of individuals to buy foreign currency.

devaluation a reduction in the value of a currency that is set under a *fixed exchange rate regime*.

revaluation an increase in the value of a currency that is set under a *fixed exchange rate regime*.

■ AFTER YOU READ THE CHAPTER

Tips

Tip #1. This chapter introduces new vocabulary. You will want to learn the definitions and be able to apply these definitions. The chapter introduces an abundance of new terms. You will want to thoroughly understand concepts like the exchange rate, appreciation of a currency, depreciation of a currency, devaluation of a currency, and revaluation of a currency. You will need to think carefully about how changes in the exchange rate affect a country's level of imports and exports. You might find the following table a helpful summary of these relationships.

Appreciation of country X's currency ⟶	Country X imports more, exports less
Depreciation of country X's currency ⟶	Country X imports less, exports more
Devaluation of country X's currency ⟶	Country X imports less, exports more
Revaluation of country X's currency ⟶	Country X imports more, exports less

Tip #2. It is important to understand what an exchange rate is and how changes in the exchange rate affect the country's balance of payments. An exchange rate is the price of one currency in terms of another currency. When a country's exchange rate increases, or appreciates, this makes its domestically produced goods relatively more expensive than goods produced by other economies. This will decrease exports and increase imports for the domestic economy: the balance of payments on current account will decrease, while the balance of payments on financial account will increase.

Tip #3. You will want to be thoroughly familiar with the terminology and the relationships represented in the balance of payments. The balance of payments (illustrated in Figure 19-1 of your text) shows the flow of money between national economies. It illustrates why the balance of payments on current account must equal the balance of payments on financial account. It illustrates the relationship in a domestic economy between the payments from the rest of the world for goods and services, factor income, and transfers, and payments to the rest of the world for goods and services, factor income, and transfers.

Tip #4. You will want to understand the distinction between fixed and floating exchange rate regimes and the advantages and disadvantages associated with either type of exchange rate regime.

WORKED PROBLEMS

1. You have the following information about Macroland's transactions in 2011. Macroland exports $1,800,000 worth of goods and services to other countries while importing $675,000. Macroland makes payments of $525,000 to factors of production located outside of Macroland while receiving payments of $450,000 from foreigners for factors of production located inside of Macroland. The government of Macroland sells $350,000 worth of assets to foreigners, while the government of Macroland buys $925,000 worth of assets from foreigners. Private citizens in Macroland purchase $405,000 worth of assets from foreigners, while private citizens sell $750,000 worth of assets to foreigners. Net transfers in Macroland for the year are −$280,000 and consist primarily of remittances sent from Macroland to other economies. You have been asked to calculate Macroland's balance of payments for 2011, including Macroland's current account and financial account. You have also been asked to calculate the net value of each category of payments in Macroland's balance of payments. Finally, you are asked to summarize your findings by organizing this data in the following table.

	Payments from foreigners	Payments to foreigners	Net
1. Sales and purchases of goods and services			
2. Factor incomes			
3. Transfers			
Current account [(sum of (1) + (2) + (3)]			
4. Official asset sales and purchases			
5. Private sales and purchases of assets			
Financial account [sum of (4) + (5)]			
Total			

STEP 1: Review the definitions of current account and financial account.

Review the section "Capital Flows and the Balance of Payments" on page 550 (Econ page 982) and Table 19-2 on page 551 (Econ page 983).

The current account is defined as the country's balance of payments on goods and services plus net international transfer payments and factor income during a given time period. The financial account is the difference between the country's sales of assets to foreigners and the country's purchases of assets from foreigners during a given time period.

STEP 2: Calculate the current account and explain your calculation.

Review the section "Capital Flows and the Balance of Payments" on page 550 (Econ page 982) and Table 19-2 on page 551 (Econ page 983).

To find the current account for Macroland in 2011, add together net exports plus net factor income plus transfers. That is, the current account is equal to (exports − imports) + (factor income paid by foreigners to factors in Macroland − factor income paid by Macroland to factors located outside of Macroland) + transfers. Remember that exports refer to the dollar value of goods and services sold to foreigners, while imports refer to the dollar value of goods and services produced outside of the country but sold to residents of the country. Thus, the current account for Macroland in 2011 is equal to ($1,800,000 − $675,000) + ($525,000 − $450,000) + (−$280,000), or $920,000.

STEP 3: Calculate the financial account and explain your calculation.

Review the section "Capital Flows and the Balance of Payments" on page 550 (Econ page 982) and Table 19-2 on page 551 (Econ page 983).

To find the financial account for Macroland in 2011, add together the sum of the official sales and purchases of assets and the private sales and purchases of assets. Official sales and purchases of assets are equal to the difference between payments from foreigners for these assets minus payments to foreigners for these assets. In this example, official sales and purchases of assets is equal to $350,000 − $925,000, or −$575,000. Private sales and purchases of assets are equal to the difference between payments from foreigners for these assets minus payments to foreigners for these assets. In our example, private sales and purchases of assets are equal to $405,000 −$750,000, or −$345,000. Summing these two figures together, we get that the financial account for Macroland for 2011 is equal to −$920,000.

STEP 4: Compare the current account and financial account and comment on why these two values should be quite similar to one another.

Review the section "Capital Flows and the Balance of Payments" on page 550 (Econ page 982), Table 19-2 on page 551 (Econ page 983) and Figure 19-1 on page 550 (Econ page 982).

In the example, the value of the current account plus the value of the financial account sums to zero. That is, the current account is equal to the negative of the financial account. This is true since the flows of money into an economy must balance with the flows out of an economy. Macroland receives a flow of money into its economy as payments for goods and services sold abroad, as payments for the use of factors owned by people in Macroland, as transfer payments, and as payments to Macroland for assets bought by foreigners. Macroland has a flow of money going out of its economy as payments for goods and services produced outside of Macroland but consumed in Macroland, as payments to factors of production owned by people outside of Macroland, as transfer payments, and as payments to the rest of the world for assets. Review Figure 19-1 in your text on this topic.

STEP 5: Fill in the given table using the calculations you have made.

Review the section "Capital Flows and the Balance of Payments" on page 550 (Econ page 982) and Table 19-2 on page 551 (Econ page 983).

Here is the completed table based on the calculations done in Steps 2 and 3.

	Payments from foreigners	Payments to foreigners	Net
1. Sales and purchases of goods and services	$1,800,000	$675,000	$1,125,000
2. Factor incomes	525,000	450,000	75,000
3. Transfers			−280,000
Current account [(sum of (1) + (2) + (3)]			920,000
4. Official asset sales and purchases	350,000	925,000	−575,000
5. Private sales and purchases of assets	405,000	750,000	−345,000
Financial account [sum of (4) + (5)]			−920,000
Total			$0

2.   Suppose there are two countries in the world, and each of these countries has its own loanable funds market. Initially, there are no capital flows between the two countries even though both countries view the two country's assets as being equally safe. The current loanable funds market for each country is provided in the following graphs, and you have been asked to comment on the current equilibrium interest rates in the two countries, given there are no capital flows. You should provide a set of graphs illustrating the equilibrium interest rates in the two countries. Then, you are asked to comment on what will happen to interest rates in these two countries if capital flows are allowed. You are asked to provide the intuition behind your response.

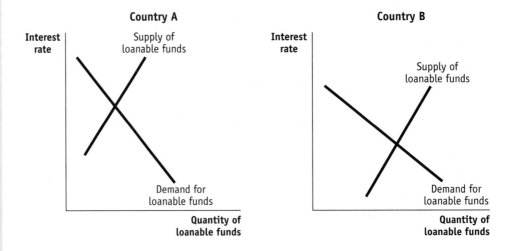

STEP 1: **Identify the equilibrium interest rate in each country's loanable funds market.**

Review the section "Capital Flows and the Balance of Payments" on page 550 (Econ page 982) and Figure 19-3 on page 556 (Econ page 988).

If there are no capital flows between these two countries, then the equilibrium interest rate in each loanable funds market will be the interest rate that equates the quantity of loanable funds supplied to the quantity of loanable funds demanded. The equilibrium interest rate in country A is higher than the equilibrium interest rate in country B. The following graph illustrates these two equilibrium interest rates.

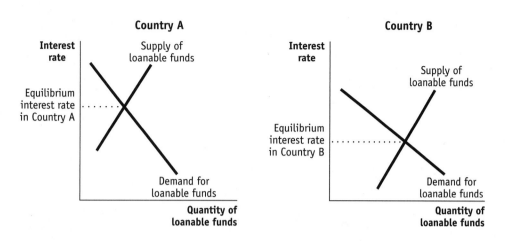

STEP 2: Explain the effect of allowing capital flows between countries.

Review the section "Capital Flows and the Balance of Payments" on page 550 (Econ page 982) and Figure 19-4 on page 557 (Econ page 989).

If these two loanable funds markets open to capital flows, funds will flow out of country B, where the equilibrium interest rate is low, into country A, where the equilibrium interest rate is high. As funds flow into country A, we can anticipate that the interest rate in country A will decrease, since there will be more funds available at each interest rate, while, as funds flow out of country B, we can anticipate that the interest rate in country B will rise, since there will be fewer funds available at each interest rate.

STEP 3: Analyze the effect of allowing capital flows on the interest rate in the two countries.

Review the section "Capital Flows and the Balance of Payments" on page 550 (Econ page 982) and Figure 19-3 on page 556 (Econ page 988).

As capital funds flow out of country B into country A, we see that both interest rates adjust. In country A, the interest rate decreases to r_3 (illustrated in the following graph). In country B, the interest rate increases to r_3. This adjustment continues until the interest rate reaches that level where the total quantity of loans demanded by borrowers in the two countries is equal to the total quantity of loans supplied by lenders in the two countries. The following graph illustrates this concept.

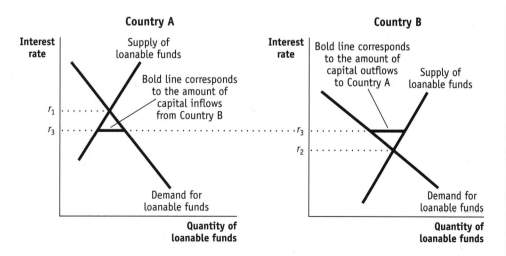

3. The exchange rate between the United States and Mexico is initially 10 pesos per dollar. If the exchange rate changes to 12 pesos per dollar, how does that change the relative prices of goods in the two countries? Identify which currency has appreciated in value, and explain what this means. Identify which currency has depreciated in value, and explain what this means. Finally, a friend asks you, given the new exchange rate, if this is a good time to visit Mexico or whether it would be better for her cousin in Mexico to visit your friend in the United States. Your friend wants a simple answer as well as an explanation for your answer.

STEP 1: Evaluate the effect of this change in the exchange rate on the United States dollar and on the Mexican peso, relative to the other currency.

Review the section "The Role of the Exchange Rate" on page 560 (Econ page 992).

Initially, someone holding pesos could trade 10 pesos for a dollar, while someone holding a dollar could trade this dollar for 10 pesos. After the exchange rate changes, the person holding pesos finds that it takes 12 pesos to get a dollar: from their perspective, the dollar has gotten more expensive. After the exchange rate changes, the person holding the dollar finds that the dollar buys 12 pesos instead of the initial 10 pesos: the dollar has greater purchasing power. From both perspectives, the dollar has gotten more valuable and the peso less valuable.

STEP 2: Review the definition of appreciation as it applies to currency, and then identify which currency has appreciated. Make sure you explain your choice of currency.

Review the section "The Role of the Exchange Rate" on page 560 (Econ page 992).

Appreciation of a currency refers to the currency becoming more valuable in terms of other currencies. In this example, the U.S. dollar has appreciated since originally it was worth only 10 Mexican pesos and now it is worth 12 Mexican pesos.

STEP 3: Review the definition of depreciation as it applies to currency and then identify which currency has depreciated. Make sure you explain your choice of currency.

Review the section "The Role of the Exchange Rate" on page 560 (Econ page 992).

Depreciation of a currency refers to the currency becoming less valuable in terms of other currencies. In this example, the Mexican peso has depreciated since originally 10 pesos were worth a U.S. dollar and now 12 pesos are worth a U.S. dollar. It now takes more pesos to buy a U.S. dollar.

STEP 4: Decide whether your friend should travel to Mexico or stay home. Explain your answer.

Review the section "The Role of the Exchange Rate" on page 560 (Econ page 992).

Your friend should travel to Mexico, since the peso has depreciated. It is now cheaper to buy pesos, making the trip to Mexico relatively cheaper.

4. Suppose that the currency market for Mexican pesos and U.S. dollars is initially in equilibrium, with 10 Mexican pesos trading for one U.S. dollar. Your friend reads that there has been a shift in demand for Mexican pesos due to a sudden increase in the capital inflow from the United States to Mexico. Using a graph, you are asked to evaluate how this increase in capital inflows will impact the exchange rate of Mexican pesos for U.S. dollars. You are also asked to comment on the effect of this change in the exchange rate on the Mexican and the U.S. economies. The following graph depicts the initial situation, where S is the supply of U.S. dollars, D is the demand for U.S. dollars, and XR_1 is the initial exchange rate of Mexican pesos per U.S. dollar.

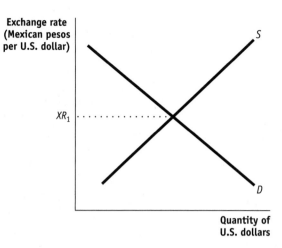

STEP 1: Identify the effect of increased capital inflows into Mexico from the United States on the demand for U.S. dollars curve.

Read the section "The Role of the Exchange Rate" on page 560 (Econ page 592) and Figure 19-6 on page 563 (Econ page 995).

Since the capital inflows are flowing into Mexico, this implies that there is reduced demand at every exchange rate for U.S. dollars because people will now want to hold Mexican pesos in order to fund their new investments in Mexico. The demand for U.S. dollars curve will therefore shift to the left, indicating that at every exchange rate fewer U.S. dollars are demanded. The following graph illustrates this idea: D_2 is the new demand for U.S. dollars as a result of the increase in capital inflows from the U.S. to Mexico.

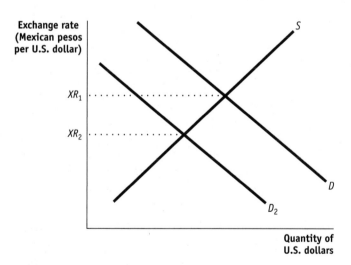

STEP 2: Identify the effect of increased capital inflows into Mexico from the U.S. on the supply of U.S. dollars curve.

Read the section "The Role of the Exchange Rate" on page 560 (Econ page 592) and Figure 19-6 on page 563 (Econ page 995).

As the demand for U.S. dollars shifts to the left there will be a movement along the supply of U.S. dollars curve resulting in a decrease in the exchange rate of Mexican pesos for U.S. dollars. As people want to exchange their U.S. dollars for Mexican pesos, they will find that each U.S. dollar purchases fewer Mexican pesos.

STEP 3: Identify the new exchange rate that is the result of this increased capital inflow into Mexico.

Read the section "The Role of the Exchange Rate" on page 560 (Econ page 592) and Figure 19-6 on page 563 (Econ page 995).

The new exchange rate is XR_2: since XR_2 is less than XR_1, this indicates that each dollar is now worth fewer Mexican pesos. The Mexican peso has appreciated against the dollar, while the U.S. dollar has depreciated against the Mexican peso.

STEP 4: Analyze what this new exchange rate means for both the U.S. economy as well as the Mexican economy.

Read the section "The Role of the Exchange Rate" on page 560 (Econ page 592) and Figure 19-6 on page 563 (Econ page 995).

As the exchange rate of Mexican pesos to U.S. dollars falls, this means that U.S. produced goods and services are now relatively cheaper than Mexican produced goods and services. This will lead to increases in U.S. exports and a decrease in Mexican exports. A fall in capital flows into the United States leads to a weaker dollar, and this decrease in the value of the dollar results in an increase in U.S. net exports. An increase in capital flows into Mexico leads to a stronger peso, and this increase in the value of the peso results in a decrease in Mexico's net exports.

Problems and Exercises

1. Use the following table of information to answer this question.

	Payments from foreigners (millions of dollars)	Payments to foreigners (millions of dollars)	Sales of assets to foreigners (millions of dollars)	Purchases of assets from foreigners (millions of dollars)
Goods	$200	$80	—	—
Services	50	20	—	—
Factor income	70	10	—	—
Transfer payments	10	20	—	—
Official sales and purchases	—	—	$100	$300
Private sales and purchases	—	—	80	80

a. Provide a definition or an equation for each of the following items.

(i.) Merchandise trade balance

(ii.) Balance of payments on goods and services

(iii.) Net international factor income

(iv.) Net international transfer payments

(v.) Balance of payments on current account

(vi.) Balance of payments on financial account

b. Given the previous information, compute the value of each of the terms given in part (a).

c. Explain why the sum of the balance of payments on current account and the balance of payments on financial account must equal zero.

2. The following graphs represent the loanable funds market in Macroland and Funland, the only two economies in the world.

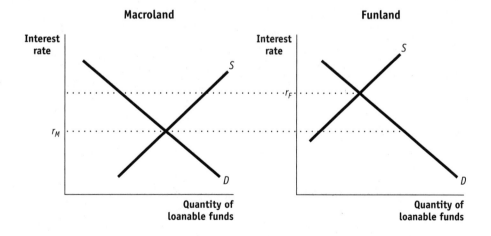

Residents in Macroland and Funland believe that foreign assets and liabilities are as good as domestic assets and liabilities.

    a. Given the two graphs, which country is likely to attract capital? Why?

    b. Given the Macroland graph, what do you predict will happen to the interest rate in Macroland over time? Explain your answer.

    c. Given the Funland graph, what do you predict will happen to the interest rate in Funland over time? Explain your answer.

    d. Briefly describe the capital flows between Macroland and Funland.

3.   **a.** Calculate the missing values in the following table.

	U.S. dollars	Funland dollars	Macroland dollars
1 U.S. dollar exchanged for			1.0500
1 Funland dollar exchanged for	0.0050		
1 Macroland dollar exchanged for			

Suppose that the preceding exchange rates change as shown in the following table.
b. Fill in the missing values for this table.

	U.S. dollars	Funland dollars	Macroland dollars
1 U.S. dollar exchanged for	1.0000	210.0000	
1 Funland dollar exchanged for		1.0000	
1 Macroland dollar exchanged for	1.0200		1.0000

    c. Which currencies appreciated against the U.S. dollar?

    d. Which currencies depreciated against the U.S. dollar?

e. Holding everything else constant, what do you expect will happen to the level of U.S. exports to Funland?

f. Holding everything else constant, what do you expect will happen to the level of U.S. exports to Macroland?

4. Suppose you are shown the information in the following table. Assume net international transfers and factor income equal zero for this problem.

Funland purchases of Macroland dollars in the foreign exchange market to buy Macroland goods and services	3.0 million Macroland dollars
Funland total purchases in the foreign exchange market of Macroland dollars	5.0 million Macroland dollars
Macroland sales of Macroland dollars in the foreign exchange market to buy Funland assets	1.5 million Macroland dollars
Macroland sales of Macroland dollars in the foreign exchange market to buy Funland goods and services	3.5 million Macroland dollars

a. Given the information in this table, compute the values in the following table.

Funland purchases of Macroland dollars in the foreign exchange market to buy Macroland assets	=	_____
Total sales of Macroland dollars in the foreign exchange market	=	_____
Macroland balance of payments on current account	=	_____
Macroland balance of payments on financial account	=	_____

Suppose capital flows to Macroland from Funland decrease and this causes Macroland's currency to depreciate against Funland's currency, holding everything else constant.

b. How will this affect the demand and supply of Macroland dollars in the foreign exchange market? Use the following graph to illustrate your answer.

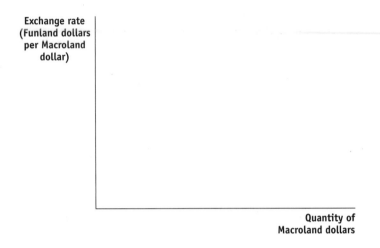

c. How will this depreciation affect Macroland's balance of payments on current account? Explain your answer.

d. How will this depreciation affect Macroland's balance of payments on financial account? Explain your answer.

5. Suppose initially the nominal exchange rate is 20 Macroland dollars per 1 Funland dollar, and the aggregate price index in both countries has a value of 100.

a. What is the real exchange rate expressed as Macroland dollars per Funland dollar?

b. Suppose the real exchange rate increases to 25 Macroland dollars per Funland dollar when the aggregate price index in Funland increases to 150. Assuming the nominal exchange rate is unchanged, what is the aggregate price index in Macroland?

c. Suppose the aggregate price index in Funland is 150 and the aggregate price index in Macroland is 125. If the nominal exchange rate increases to 25 Macroland dollars per Funland dollar, what is the real exchange rate?

d. If the real exchange rate measured as Macroland dollars per Funland dollar increases, holding everything else constant, what happens to the level of exports and imports in Macroland?

6. Suppose that currently the cost of a standardized market basket in Macroland is 300 Macroland dollars, while the same market basket in Funland costs 150 Funland dollars.

   a. If purchasing power parity holds for the two countries, what must the nominal exchange rate, expressed as Macroland dollars per Funland dollar, equal? Explain your answer.

   b. If the actual nominal exchange rate equals 4 Macroland dollars per 1 Funland dollar, what do you expect will happen to the nominal exchange rate over the long run, holding everything else constant? Explain your answer.

7. Compare and contrast the advantages and disadvantages of a fixed exchange rate regime and a floating exchange rate regime.

8. Suppose Macroland has adopted a fixed exchange rate regime and wishes to target the exchange rate to U.S. $2.25 for each Macroland dollar.

   a. The following figure represents the current situation in Macroland.

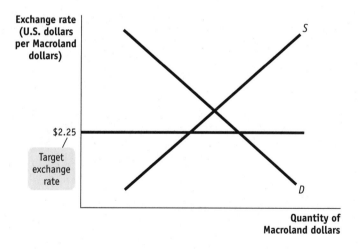

   Describe the situation depicted in this figure, given that Macroland would like to maintain a fixed exchange rate of U.S. $2.25.

   b. Given the graph in part (a), what policies are available to Macroland if it is determined to maintain the exchange rate at U.S. $2.25? Explain each option.

c. The following figure represents the situation in Macroland six months later.

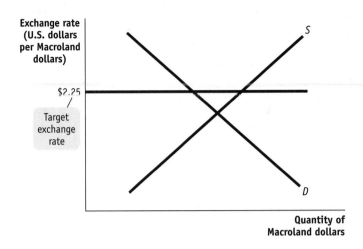

Describe the situation depicted in this graph, given that Macroland would like to maintain a fixed exchange rate of U.S. $2.25.

d. Given the graph in part (c), what policies are available to Macroland if it is determined to maintain the exchange rate at U.S. $2.25? Explain each option.

9. Suppose there are only two countries—Macrobia and Tacrobia—that investors view as being equally attractive for investment. Furthermore, suppose the loanable funds markets in these two countries can be described by the demand and supply equations given below:

Demand for loanable funds in Macrobia: $r = 10 - (1/100)LF$

Supply of loanable funds in Macrobia: $r = (1/100)LF$

Demand for loanable funds in Tacrobia: $r = 10 - (1/200)LF$

Supply of loanable funds in Tacrobia: $r = (1/300)LF$

In the equations provided, r is the interest rate expressed as a percentage (e.g., if the interest rate is 10%, then that would be expressed as 10 in the equation) and LF is the quantity of loanable funds measured in dollars. Currently the two countries do not allow capital inflows or capital outflows.

a. What is the equilibrium interest rate and quantity of loanable funds in Macrobia?

b. What is the equilibrium interest rate and quantity of loanable funds in Tacrobia?

c. If these two countries decide to allow capital flows, what do you predict will happen? Which country will provide capital outflows and which country will provide capital inflows? Explain your answer.

d. Suppose that at every interest rate, Tacrobia provides $200 of loanable funds to Macrobia. What will be the effect of this on the supply of loanable funds curve in Tacrobia? Write the new supply of loanable funds curve equation for Tacrobia.

e. Given the new supply of loanable funds curve you computed in part (d), what will be the new equilibrium interest rate and quantity of loanable funds in Tacrobia?

f. Suppose that at every interest rate, Tacrobia provides $200 of loanable funds to Macrobia. What will be the effect of this on the supply of loanable funds curve in Macrobia? Write the new supply of loanable funds curve equation for Macrobia.

g. Given the new supply of loanable funds curve you computed in part (f), what will be the new equilibrium interest rate and quantity of loanable funds in Macrobia?

h. Given your answers in parts (e) and (g), what do you predict about capital flows between these two countries?

10. Consider each of the following transactions and identify how the transaction would be categorized in the U.S. balance of payments accounts. For each transaction identify whether it would be counted as part of the balance of payments in the current account or the financial account. Lastly, identify whether the transaction will increase or decrease the relevant account.

   a. An American company purchases machinery that is produced in Germany by a German company.

   b. An American donates money to the foreign group organizing an international sporting event in another country.

   c. A French citizen purchases cheese produced in the United States.

   d. An American purchases 100 shares of a Swiss company.

▮ BEFORE YOU TAKE THE TEST

Chapter Review Questions

1. Which of the following statements is true?
   a. The balance of payments on goods and services is the difference between the value of imports and the value of exports during a given period.
   b. The merchandise trade balance includes the sale of goods as well as financial assets.
   c. A country's international transactions are tracked by the balance of payments accounts.
   d. Statements (a), (b), and (c) are all true.
   e. Statements (a) and (c) are both true.
   f. Statements (b) and (c) are both true.

2. The balance of payments on goods and services plus net international transfer payments and net international factor income
   a. equals the merchandise trade balance.
   b. equals the balance on payments on current account.
   c. equals the balance on payments on financial account.
   d. plus the balance of payments on financial account equals zero.
   e. Answers (a) and (c) are both correct.
   f. Answers (b) and (c) are both correct.
   g. Answers (b) and (d) are both correct.

3. For a hypothetical economy if the balance of payments on financial account equals –$100 million, then the balance of payments on current account must
   a. equal –$100 million.
   b. be greater than –$100 million.
   c. be less than –$100 million.
   d. equal $100 million.

4. The balance of payments tracks the
   a. flow of payments into a country from the rest of the world as well as the flow of payments from the country to the rest of the world.
   b. flow of payments for goods and services, factor income, and transfers in the balance of payments on current account.
   c. flow of payments for assets in the balance of payments on financial account.
   d. Answers (a), (b), and (c) are all correct.

5. Suppose that there are two countries with open economies. If the interest rate in the loanable funds market in the first country is higher than the interest rate in the loanable funds market in the second country, we can expect that
   a. this interest rate differential will continue if citizens in both countries view their domestic assets as comparable to foreign assets.
   b. this interest rate differential will be eliminated due to the movement of international capital flows.
   c. the supply of loanable funds in the first country will increase, while the supply of loanable funds in the second country will decrease.
   d. the supply of loanable funds in the first country will decrease, while the supply of loanable funds in the second country will increase.
   e. Answers (b) and (c) are both correct.
   f. Answers (b) and (d) are both correct.

6. Which of the following statements is true?
   a. A country that receives capital inflows will have a matching financial account surplus.
   b. The exchange rate is always measured as the price of a dollar in terms of the foreign currency.
   c. The more euros it takes to buy a dollar, the fewer dollars Europeans will supply.
   d. When a country's currency appreciates, exports fall and imports rise.

7. Suppose a U.S dollar trades for 0.9 euro. Which of the following statements is true?
   a. A euro trades for $1.11.
   b. If the exchange rate changes to 1 U.S. dollar in exchange for 0.95 euro, then the euro has appreciated.
   c. If the exchange rate changes to 1 U.S. dollar in exchange for 0.95 euro, then the dollar has appreciated.
   d. When the exchange rate changes to 0.95 euros per dollar, the United States will export more goods to European Union countries.
   e. Statements (a), (b), and (d) are all true.
   f. Statements (a), (c), and (d) are all true.
   g. Statements (a) and (b) are both true.
   h. Statements (a) and (c) are both true.

8.   An increase in capital inflows into a country, holding everything else constant, will
   a. result in an increase in net exports for the country.
   b. result in a decrease in net exports for the country.
   c. result in an increase in the balance on financial account for the country and an equal and opposite reaction in the balance of payments on current account.
   d. Answers (a) and (c) are both correct.
   e. Answers (b) and (c) arc both correct.

Answer the next two questions using the following information. Suppose the aggregate price level for a given market basket of goods in Macroland is 125, while the aggregate price level for the same market basket of goods in Funland is 150. Suppose that currently the exchange rate is 10 Macroland dollars for 1 Funland dollar.

9.   Given the previous information, what is the real exchange rate initially?
   a. 10 Macroland dollars for 1 Funland dollar
   b. 1 Macroland dollar for 10 Funland dollars
   c. 1 Macroland dollar for 1 Funland dollar
   d. 10 Macroland dollars for 10 Funland dollars
   e. 12 Macroland dollars for 1 Funland dollar

10.   If the aggregate price level of the market basket in Macroland increases to 150, what must the exchange rate be in order for the real exchange rate to be unchanged from its initial level?
   a. 10 Macroland dollars for 1 Funland dollar
   b. 1 Macroland dollar for 10 Funland dollars
   c. 1 Macroland dollar for 1 Funland dollar
   d. 10 Macroland dollars for 10 Funland dollars
   e. 12 Macroland dollars for 1 Funland dollar

11.   When the purchasing power parity rate is greater than the nominal exchange rate, then over time we can expect the
   a. purchasing power parity to fall.
   b. purchasing power parity to rise.
   c. nominal exchange rate to rise.
   d. nominal exchange rate to fall.

12.   Which of the following statements is true?
   a. When a country's currency undergoes a real depreciation, this causes exports to fall and imports to rise.
   b. Nominal exchange rates almost always equal the purchasing power parity rate.
   c. The current account is affected by changes in the nominal exchange rate as well as the real exchange rate.
   d. None of the statements is true.

13. If a government wishes to fix the value of a currency above its equilibrium value in the foreign exchange market, it can
    a. engage in monetary policy to reduce interest rates, thereby increasing capital flows into its country.
    b. reduce the supply of its currency by limiting the right of its citizens to buy foreign currencies.
    c. engage in selling its currency through exchange market intervention.
    d. Answers (a), (b), and (c) will all help the government to reduce the exchange rate to its desired level.

14. Suppose that in the foreign exchange market there is a shortage at the target exchange rate. We know that
    a. the quantity supplied of the country's currency is less than the quantity demanded for that country's currency.
    b. it is impossible to maintain the target exchange rate unless the government engages in exchange market intervention, changes monetary policy, adjusts foreign exchange controls, or pursues some combination of these three policies.
    c. maintaining a fixed exchange rate will limit the ability of the government to pursue stabilization policy.
    d. Answers (a), (b), and (c) are all correct.

15. A fixed exchange rate regime
    a. reduces uncertainty for businesses about the value of a currency.
    b. exposes a country to a potential bias toward inflationary policies.
    c. reduces the amount of foreign currency a country must hold.
    d. creates an incentive to pursue monetary policy to help stabilize the country's economy.

16. A devaluation of a currency, holding everything else constant,
    a. makes foreign produced goods more attractive to purchase in the domestic economy and, therefore, leads to an increase in imports in the domestic economy.
    b. decreases the balance of payments on current account.
    c. may be used as a macroeconomic policy tool since a devaluation stimulates aggregate demand.
    d. Answers (a), (b), and (c) are all correct.
    e. Answers (a) and (c) are both correct.
    f. Answers (b) and (c) are both correct.

17. Consider a country with a fixed exchange rate currently operating with an inflationary gap. Which of the following statements is true for this country?
    a. A revaluation of this country's currency will reduce its inflationary gap.
    b. A country with a fixed exchange rate regime has no macroeconomic policy tools available to it to combat an inflationary gap.
    c. A revaluation of this country's currency will increase exports and decrease imports, and this will help reduce the country's inflationary gap.
    d. Answers (a) and (c) are both correct.

18. When a country pursues an expansionary monetary policy, this will
   a. increase the level of investment spending.
   b. decrease the demand for that country's currency in the foreign exchange market.
   c. increase the supply of that country's currency in the foreign exchange market.
   d. Answers (a), (b), and (c) are all correct.

19. Which of the following statements is true?
   a. Demand shocks may originate from outside the domestic economy.
   b. Business cycles in different countries often seem to be synchronized, because changes in aggregate supply affect the demand for goods and services produced abroad as well as at home.
   c. A fixed exchange rate seems to lessen the impact of changes in aggregate demand in one country on the economic performance in other countries.
   d. Statements (a), (b), and (c) are all true.

20. Which of the following represents a payment from foreigners to the hypothetical economy called Macropedia?
   a. the dollar value of corn Macropedia imports from Cornucopia
   b. the dollar value of bicycles Macropedia exports to Pedal Land
   c. the fees engineering firms in Macropedia receive for bridge designs they provide to the foreign country of Islandville
   d. the fees companies in Macropedia pay to Islandville in compensation for the financial services Islandville provides
   e. Answers (a), (b), (c), and (d) all represent payments from foreigners to Macropedia.
   f. Answers (b) and (c) both represent payments from foreigners to Macropedia.
   g. Answers (a) and (d) both represent payments from foreigners to Macropedia.

21. Foreign exchange reserves are
   a. funds of one country's currency held by another country.
   b. funds of a country's currency that the government holds in case they need money unexpectedly.
   c. are sometimes used by a country to maintain a fixed exchange rate.
   d. Answers (a) and (c) are both correct.
   e. Answers (b) and (c) are both correct.

22. Which of the following statements is true?
   I. The sum of the balance of payments on current account (*CA*) and the balance of payments on financial account (*FA*) must equal zero.
   II. The balance of payments accounts illustrate the concept that the flow of funds into a country's economy must equal the flow of funds out of that country's economy.
   III. A country that imports more than it exports must by definition have negative capital inflows.
   a. Statements I, II, and III are all true.
   b. Statements I and II are both true.
   c. Statements I and III are both true.
   d. Statements II and III are both true.

23. In 2010, which of the following statements were true?

    I. The United States had a substantial current account deficit.

    II. China had a substantial current account deficit.

    III. Japan and Germany had substantial current account surpluses.

  a. Statements I, II, and III are all true.

  b. Statements I and II are both true.

  c. Statements I and III are both true.

  d. Statements II and III are both true.

24. Suppose the loanable funds market in Macroland is currently in equilibrium. Holding everything else constant, if capital inflows increase to Macroland, this will cause the equilibrium interest rate

  a. to decrease while the equilibrium quantity of loanable funds will increase.

  b. to increase while the equilibrium quantity of loanable funds will decrease.

  c. and the equilibrium quantity of loanable funds to decrease.

  d. and the equilibrium quantity of loanable funds to increase.

25. Suppose the loanable funds market in Macroland is currently in equilibrium. Holding everything else constant, if businesses in Macroland increase the level of their investment spending that is financed by borrowing, this will cause a shift in the

  a. supply of loanable funds curve to the right and a movement along the demand for loanable funds curve.

  b. supply of loanable funds curve to the left and a movement along the demand for loanable funds curve.

  c. demand for loanable funds curve to the right and a movement along the supply of loanable funds curve.

  d. demand for loanable funds curve to the left and a movement along the supply of loanable funds curve.

26. Which of the following statements is true?

    I. Fast growing economies often have greater demand for loanable funds than do slower growing economies since these countries often have greater investment opportunities.

    II. The supply of loanable funds in any particular country is impacted by the country's private savings rate: some countries have higher savings rates than do other countries.

    III. Between 2000 and 2010, the United States provided huge capital outflows to much of the rest of the world.

  a. Statements I, II, and III are all true.

  b. Statements I and II are both true.

  c. Statements I and III are both true.

  d. Statements II and III are both true.

27. Holding everything else constant, an increase in political risk in a country will most likely cause capital inflows into that country to

  a. increase.   b. decrease.

28. Suppose that currently the exchange rate is one U.S. dollar to 5 Mexican pesos. If the exchange rate changes to one US dollar for 10 Mexican pesos, then the peso has
   a. appreciated against the dollar.
   b. depreciated against the dollar.

29. Suppose there are only two currencies in the world: the U.S. dollar and the Mexican peso. Furthermore, suppose that the foreign exchange market for U.S. dollars is initially in equilibrium. If the demand for U.S. dollars increases, holding everything else constant, this will result in a movement along the supply of U.S. dollars curve and
   a. an increase in the peso–U.S. dollar exchange rate.
   b. a decrease in the peso–U.S. dollar exchange rate.

30. Holding everything else constant, if the U.S. dollar rises against the Mexican peso, then
   a. U.S. goods will look cheaper to Mexico.
   b. U.S. goods will look more expensive to Mexico.
   c. Mexico's goods will look cheaper to the United States.
   d. Mexico's goods will look more expensive to the United States.
   e. Answers (a) and (d) are both correct.
   f. Answers (b) and (c) are both correct.

◼ ANSWER KEY

Answers to Problems and Exercises

1. a. (i.) Merchandise trade balance = (exports of goods) – (imports of goods) = (payments from foreigners for goods) – (payments to foreigners for goods)

(ii.) Balance of payments on goods and services = (exports of goods and services) – (imports of goods and services) = (payments from foreigners for goods and services) – (payments to foreigners for goods and services)

(iii.) Net international factor income = (factor income payments from foreigners) – (factor income payments to foreigners)

(iv.) Net international transfer payments = (transfer payments from foreigners) – (transfer payments to foreigners)

(v.) Balance of payments on current account = (balance of payments on goods and services) + (net international transfer payments) + (net international factor income)

(vi.) Balance of payments on financial account = (sales of assets to foreigners) – (purchases of assets from foreigners)

b. (i.) Merchandise trade balance = $200 million – $80 million = $120 million

(ii.) Balance of payments on goods and services = $250 million – $100 million = $150 million

(iii.) Net international factor income = $70 million – $10 million = $60 million

(iv.) Net international transfer payments = $10 million – $20 million = – $10 million

(v.) Balance of payments on current account = $150 million + (– $10 million) + ($60 million) = $200 million

(vi.) Balance of payments on financial account = – $200 million

c. This reflects a basic rule of balance of payments accounting for any country: the flow of money into a country must equal the flow of money out of the country.

2. a. Funland will attract capital, because its equilibrium interest rate is higher than the equilibrium interest rate in Macroland.

b. Over time the interest rate in Macroland will rise due to capital outflows. Since Macroland initially has a lower equilibrium interest rate than Funland, some Macroland lenders will decide to send their funds to Funland to take advantage of the higher interest rate. Over time this will cause the interest rate in the two countries to equalize.

c. Over time the interest rate in Funland will fall due to capital inflows from Macroland. As funds from Macroland are attracted to Funland's loanable funds market, due to its initially higher equilibrium interest rate, this will cause the interest rate to fall in Funland. Eventually, the interest rates in the two countries will equalize.

d. Capital will flow out of Macroland and into Funland. Thus, Macroland will experience capital outflows, while Funland will experience capital inflows.

3. a.

	U.S. dollars	Funland dollars	Macroland dollars
1 U.S. dollar exchanged for	1.0000	200.0000	1.0500
1 Funland dollar exchanged for	0.0050	1.0000	0.0053
1 Macroland dollar exchanged for	0.9524	190.4762	1.0000

b.

	U.S. dollars	Funland dollars	Macroland dollars
1 U.S. dollar exchanged for	1.0000	210.0000	0.9804
1 Funland dollar exchanged for	0.0048	1.0000	0.0047
1 Macroland dollar exchanged for	1.0200	214.2000	1.0000

c. Macroland dollars appreciated against the U.S. dollar since in part (a), 1 Macroland dollar was worth 0.9524 U.S. dollars, and in part (b), 1 Macroland dollar was worth 1.0200 U.S. dollars.

d. Funland dollars depreciated against the U.S. dollar since in part (a), 1 Funland dollar was worth 0.0050 U.S. dollars, and in part (b), 1 Funland dollar was worth 0.0048 U.S. dollars.

e. U.S. exports to Funland, holding everything else constant, will fall because, as Funland's currency depreciates against the U.S. dollar, this makes U.S. products more expensive to the residents of Funland relative to Funland's products. Funland will export more to the United States and the United States will export less to Funland.

f. U.S. exports to Macroland, holding everything else constant, will increase since, as Macroland's currency appreciates against the U.S. dollar, this makes U.S. products cheaper to the residents of Macroland relative to Macroland's products. Macroland will export less to the United States and the United States will export more to Macroland.

4. a.

Funland purchases of Macroland dollars in the foreign exchange market to buy Macroland assets	=	2 million Macroland dollars
Total sales of Macroland dollars in the foreign exchange market	=	5.0 million Macroland dollars
Macroland balance of payments on current account	=	−0.5 million Macroland dollars
Macroland balance of payments on financial account	=	0.5 million Macroland dollars

b. The depreciation of the Macroland currency against Funland's currency will cause the demand for Macroland dollars to decrease at every exchange rate (measured as Funland dollars per Macroland dollars). This will, for a given supply of Macroland dollars, cause the exchange rate to decrease. This is illustrated in the following figure.

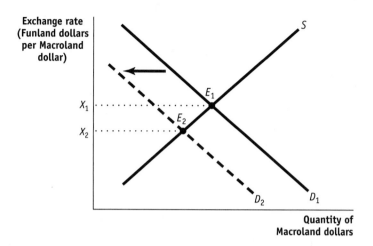

c. This depreciation of Macroland's currency against Funland's currency will cause Macroland's balance of payments on current account to increase, since Funland will now find Macroland goods and services relatively cheaper.

d. This depreciation of Macroland's currency against Funland's currency will cause Macroland's balance of payments on financial account to decrease, since any increase in Macroland's balance of payments on current account must be offset by an equal and opposite reaction in the balance of payments on financial account.

5. **a.** Real exchange rate in Macroland dollars per Funland dollar = (20 Macroland dollars per Funland dollar)(100/100) = 20 Macroland dollars per Funland dollar

b. To answer this question, we will want to use the equation:

Real exchange rate = (nominal exchange rate)[(price index in Funland)/ (price index in Macroland)]

Thus, 25 Macroland dollars per Funland dollar = (20 Macroland dollars per Funland dollar)[(150)/(price index in Macroland)], and solving for the price index in Macroland, we find that the price index in Macroland equals 120.

c. To answer this question, we will want to use the equation given in part (b):

Real exchange rate = (nominal exchange rate)[(price index in Funland)/ (price index in Macroland)]

Thus, the real exchange rate = (25 Macroland dollars per Funland dollar) [(150)/(125)], and solving this equation for the real exchange rate yields a real exchange rate equal to 30 Macroland dollars per Funland dollar.

d. When the real exchange rate increases this is an appreciation of Macroland's currency, and this appreciation will make Macroland's products more expensive to foreigners: Macroland will export less and import more when the real exchange rate increases, holding everything else constant.

6. **a.** If purchasing power parity holds in the two countries, then the price of the market basket in the two countries is 300 Macroland dollars equals 150 Funland dollars. This implies that the exchange rate must equal 2 Macroland dollars per Funland dollar or, equivalently, 1 Macroland dollar per 0.5 Funland dollar.

b. If the actual exchange rate is greater than the purchasing power parity exchange rate, one would anticipate that the exchange rate will fall over time, since nominal exchange rates between countries at similar levels of economic development tend to fluctuate around levels that lead to similar costs for a given market basket.

7. A fixed exchange rate regime provides certainty about the value of a country's currency: this certainty facilitates transactions between countries. In addition, adoption of a fixed exchange regime may help a country commit to not engage in inflationary policies. But, adherence to a fixed exchange rate presents challenges as well as benefits to the country. In order to fix the exchange rate, the country will find that it must hold large amounts of foreign currency: this is typically a low-return investment for the country. In addition, a country with a fixed exchange rate will find that it can no longer use monetary policy to pursue macroeconomic goals like output stabilization and control of the inflation rate. Finally, the adoption of a fixed exchange rate potentially distorts the incentives for importing and exporting goods and services.

A floating exchange rate regime neither requires the country to hold large amounts of foreign currency, nor constrains the country with regard to monetary policy. It does, however, introduce uncertainty about the value of the country's currency, and that may hinder the level of international trade between the country and other countries. A floating exchange rate does provide very clear price incentives for the determination of the level of exports and imports at any particular point in time.

8. **a.** In the graph depicted in part (a), Macroland finds that there is a shortage of Macroland dollars at the target exchange rate of U.S. $2.25 per Macroland dollar. That is, the quantity of Macroland dollars demanded exceeds the quantity of Macroland dollars supplied at the desired exchange rate.

b. When there is a shortage of Macroland dollars, the government of Macroland can intervene in the foreign exchange market and sell Macroland dollars and acquire U.S. dollars to add to its foreign exchange reserves. In addition, the government can act to reduce interest rates in order to increase the supply of Macroland dollars while reducing the demand for Macroland dollars. By reducing the interest rate, the government of Macroland will decrease capital flows into Macroland, thus reducing the demand for Macroland dollars, and increase capital flows out of Macroland, thereby, increasing the supply of Macroland dollars. Finally, the government of Macroland can impose foreign exchange controls that limit the ability of Macroland residents to sell currency to foreigners. Each of these policies will reduce the value of the Macroland dollar.

c. In the graph depicted in part (c), Macroland finds that there is a surplus of Macroland dollars at the target exchange rate of U.S. $2.25 per Macroland dollar. That is, the quantity of Macroland dollars demanded is less than the quantity of Macroland dollars supplied at the desired exchange rate.

d. When there is a surplus of Macroland dollars, the government of Macroland can intervene in the foreign exchange market and buy Macroland dollars and sell U.S. dollars from its foreign exchange reserves. In addition, the government can act to increase interest rates in order to decrease the supply of Macroland dollars while increasing the demand for Macroland dollars. By increasing the interest rate, the government of Macroland will increase capital flows into Macroland, thus increasing the demand for Macroland dollars, and decrease capital flows out of Macroland, thereby decreasing the supply of Macroland dollars. Finally, the government of Macroland can impose foreign exchange controls that limit the ability of Macroland residents to buy foreign currency. Each of these policies will increase the value of the Macroland dollar.

9. **a.** To find the equilibrium interest rate and quantity of loanable funds in Macrobia, you need to find the intersection of the demand and supply curves. Thus, the equilibrium interest rate is 5% and the equilibrium quantity of loanable funds is $500.

   b. To find the equilibrium interest rate and quantity of loanable funds in Tacrobia, you need to find the intersection of the demand and supply curves. Thus, the equilibrium interest rate is 4% and the equilibrium quantity of loanable funds is $1,200.

   c. Since the interest rate is higher in Macrobia than in Tacrobia, you would expect loanable funds to be attracted to the higher interest rate: Tacrobia will have capital outflows and Macrobia will have capital inflows until the interest rates in the two countries are equalized.

   d. If Tacrobia has capital outflows of $200 to Macrobia, this will cause the supply of loanable funds curve in Tacrobia to shift to the left by 200. This shift will be a parallel shift of the loanable funds supply curve since it is a constant amount of capital outflows irrespective of the interest rate. The new loanable funds curve is $r = (1/300)LF + (2/3)$.

   e. With the new loanable funds supply curve and the original loanable funds demand curve, we can solve for the new equilibrium interest rate and quantity of loanable funds in Tacrobia. This new equilibrium is at an interest rate of 4.4% and a quantity of loanable funds equal to $1,120.

   f. If Tacrobia provides Macrobia with $200 of capital inflows, this will cause the supply of loanable funds curve in Macrobia to shift to the right by 200. This shift will be a parallel shift of the loanable funds supply curve since it is a constant amount of capital inflows irrespective of the interest rate. The new loanable funds curve is $r = (1/100)LF - 2$.

   g. With the new loanable funds supply curve and the original loanable funds demand curve, we can solve for the new equilibrium interest rate and quantity of loanable funds in Macrobia. This new equilibrium is at an interest rate of 4% and a quantity of loanable funds equal to $600.

   h. Since the interest rates in the two countries are still different, you would expect capital flows to continue between the two countries until these interest rates are equalized. Because the new interest rate in Tacrobia is now 4.4%, which is higher than the interest rate of 4% in Macrobia, Tacrobia will have higher capital inflows and Macrobia will have higher capital outflows.

10. **a.** When the American company purchases machinery that is produced in Germany by a German company, this transaction enters the U.S. balance of payments current account as an import. This transaction will reduce the balance of payments on the U.S. current account.

    b. When the American donates money to the foreign group organizing an international sporting event, this enters the current account as a transfer payment to a foreigner. This transaction will reduce the balance on the U.S. current account.

    c. When a French citizen purchases cheese produced in the United States, this transaction enters the U.S. balance of payments on current account as an export. This transaction will increase the balance of payments on the U.S. current account.

    d. When the American purchases 100 shares of a Swiss company, this transaction is categorized as part of the U.S. balance of payments on financial account. The balance of payments on the U.S. financial account will fall.

Answers to Chapter Review Questions

1. **Answer c.** The balance of payments on goods and services is the difference between the value of exports and the value of imports during a given period. The merchandise trade balance does not include the sale of financial assets, but does include the sale of goods. The balance of payments accounts provide a set of numbers that describe a country's international transactions.

2. **Answer g.** By definition, the balance of payments on goods and services plus net international transfer payments and net international factor income equals the balance of payments on current account. In addition, the sum of the balance of payments on current account plus the balance of payments on financial account equals zero.

3. **Answer d.** The sum of the balance of payments on current account and the balance of payments on financial account must sum to zero: thus, if the balance of payments on financial account equals −$100 million, then the balance of payments on current account must equal $100 million.

4. **Answer d.** Figure 19-1 in your text reviews this concept: the balance of payments tracks flows of goods and services, factor income, transfers, and assets between a country and the rest of the world. Transactions involving goods and services, factor income, and transfers are measured in the balance of payments on current account, while transactions involving assets are measured in the balance of payments on financial account.

5. **Answer e.** If two countries are open to trade and allow capital to flow freely between them, then an interest rate differential in their loanable funds market will disappear quickly due to capital flows between the two countries. Capital will tend to flow into the country with the relatively higher interest rate and out of the country with the relatively lower interest rate. Thus, the supply of loanable funds in the market with the higher interest rate will increase, while the supply of loanable funds in the market with the lower interest rate will decrease: this will cause the interest rate to fall in the first country and to rise in the second country until the interest rate differential is eliminated.

6. **Answer d.** A country that has capital inflows will have a matching current account deficit. The exchange rate may be measured as the price of a dollar in terms of the foreign currency, or it may be measured as the price of the foreign currency in terms of dollars. The more euros it takes to buy a dollar, the fewer dollars Europeans will demand in the foreign exchange market for dollars. When a country's currency appreciates, this means that the exchange rate for that currency in terms of the other currency has risen: this increase in the exchange rate makes goods and services produced in the country whose currency has appreciated more expensive relative to goods and services produced elsewhere. This will lead to a decrease in exports and an increase in imports for the country whose currency has appreciated.

7. **Answer h.** If 1 U.S. dollar trades for 0.9 euro, this is the same as 1 euro trading for $1.11 (to see this, simply divide 1/0.9 to find how many dollars it takes to purchase 1 euro). If the exchange rate changes to 1 U.S. dollar in exchange for 0.95 euro, this means that dollars have appreciated and that euros have depreciated in value, since 1 dollar initially was worth only 0.9 euro and now is worth 0.95 euro. This means that a dollar has greater purchasing power in European Union markets and, therefore, imports of European goods to the United States will increase and exports of American goods to European Union countries will decrease.

8. **Answer e.** When a country has an increase in capital inflows, this causes the exchange rate to increase leading to an appreciation of that country's currency. With this appreciation of its currency, the country will find that its goods and services become relatively more expensive and, therefore, its net exports will decrease. Furthermore, the increase in capital inflows will cause the balance on financial account to increase, and this increase will be met by an equal, but opposite, reaction in the balance of payments on current account.

9. **Answer e.** To find the real exchange rate, we need to know the nominal exchange rate (in this case, 10 Macroland dollars per 1 Funland dollar) and the aggregate price level in the two countries. We can plug them into Equation 19-4 (34-4) in your text: real exchange rate equals (10 Macroland dollars/Funland dollars)(150/125) = 12 Macroland dollars per 1 Funland dollar.

10. **Answer e.** To find the exchange rate, we need to know the real exchange rate (in this case, 12 Macroland dollars per 1 Funland dollar) and the aggregate price level in the two countries. We can plug them into Equation 19-4 (34-4) in your text: 12 Macroland dollars per 1 Funland dollar equals (the exchange rate)(150/150). Solving for the exchange rate yields an exchange rate of 12 Macroland dollars per 1 Funland dollar.

11. **Answer c.** Purchasing power parity between two countries' currencies is the nominal exchange rate at which a given basket of goods and services would cost the same amount in each country. When the purchasing power parity rate is greater than the nominal exchange rate, we would anticipate that the nominal exchange rate must increase over time in order for the two countries to have similar costs for a given market basket.

12. **Answer d.** When a country's currency undergoes a real depreciation this causes exports to rise and imports to fall, since the depreciation reduces the price of the country's goods and services relative to the prices for goods and services produced in other countries. Nominal exchange rates almost always differ from purchasing power parity rates: the nominal rate tends to fluctuate around the purchasing power parity rate. The current account responds only to changes in the real exchange rate, not the nominal exchange rate: it is a change in the real exchange rate that alters the relative cost of domestic goods and services in comparison to foreign produced goods and services.

13. **Answer b.** When the government wishes to fix the exchange rate to a rate that is above its equilibrium value in the foreign exchange market, it must deal with the fact that there is a surplus of its currency at that desired exchange rate. The government can eliminate this surplus by buying its currency through an exchange market intervention; by pursuing monetary policy that raises its interest rate relative to the interest rates of other economies, thus increasing capital flows into its country (and increasing the demand for its currency); or by reducing the supply of its currency to the foreign exchange market through the imposition of foreign exchange controls.

14. **Answer d.** When there is a shortage at the target exchange rate, this indicates that the quantity demanded for the country's currency is greater than the quantity supplied of the country's currency. A government will find that it can maintain the target exchange rate, only if it is willing to give up its use of monetary policy for stabilization purposes and instead use monetary policy, exchange market intervention, and foreign exchange controls to pursue its target exchange rate.

15. **Answer a.** A fixed exchange rate regime benefits businesses by eliminating uncertainty about the value of a currency while reducing the ability of the government to use monetary policy as a means of stabilizing the economy. A fixed exchange rate regime reduces, in some cases, a country's bias toward inflationary policies, since it can send a signal to the foreign exchange market about the country's commitment to a stable exchange rate and decision to pursue noninflationary policies in the future.

16. **Answer c.** A devaluation of a currency is a reduction in the value of a currency that previously had a fixed exchange rate. This devaluation makes domestic goods cheaper in terms of foreign currency and will, therefore, increase the level of exports and decrease the level of imports in the domestic economy. This will stimulate aggregate demand in the domestic economy. The effect of these changes is to increase the balance of payments on current account.

17. **Answer a.** A revaluation of a country's currency will make domestic goods more expensive in terms of foreign currency and will, therefore, decrease exports while increasing imports. This will cause aggregate demand to decrease and, therefore, help the country reduce its inflationary gap.

18. **Answer d.** When a country pursues expansionary monetary policy, this causes the interest rate to decrease: this makes investment spending more attractive. In addition, the decrease in the interest rate also affects the foreign exchange market: the demand for the domestic currency will decrease since the domestic economy is now offering a relatively lower rate of return on their loans, and the supply of the domestic currency will increase because there is now a greater incentive to move funds abroad since the rate of return on loans in the domestic economy has fallen.

19. **Answer a.** Business cycles in different countries often seem to be synchronized, because changes in aggregate demand in one country often have an effect on the level of aggregate demand in other countries. Adherence to a floating exchange rate regime helps insulate countries from recessions originating from outside their economies, since the movement in the exchange rate limits the level of change in aggregate demand.

20. **Answer f.** Payments to Macropedia from foreigners are represented by dollars that flow into Macropedia. For example, the farmers in Macropedia will receive compensation from abroad if they export their agricultural commodity to another country; or the providers of a service will receive compensation from abroad if they provide their service to people residing in another country. Thus, answers (b) and (d) both represent flows of funds into Macropedia, while answers (a) and (c) represent flows of funds out of Macropedia.

21. **Answer d.** Foreign exchange reserves entail the holding of one country's currency by another country. For example, China and the major oil-exporting countries in 2007 held U.S. dollars. These dollars are sometimes used to help maintain a fixed exchange rate: for instance, if the exchange rate is depreciating, the country can buy some of its own currency using its foreign exchange reserves in order to keep the exchange rate from falling.

22. **Answer b.** Statements I and II state the same idea: if the sum of the balance of payments on current account (*CA*) and the balance of payments on financial account (*FA*) equal zero, then this implies that the flow of funds into a country's economy must equal the flow of funds out of that country's economy. If a country is importing more than it is exporting, this means that its balance of payments on current account is negative and, therefore, implies that its balance of payments on financial account is positive. When the balance of payments on financial account is positive, this implies that the country has positive capital inflows.

23. **Answer c.** The facts underlying this question are discussed in the chapter's Global Comparison discussion of "Current Account Surpluses and Deficit." This data is noteworthy due to the financial crisis that occurred during this period and the effect of this financial crisis on different countries throughout the world.

24. **Answer a.** An increase in capital inflows will cause the supply of loanable funds curve to shift to the right. This shift will cause a movement along the demand for loanable funds curve and result in a decrease in the equilibrium interest rate and an increase in the quantity of loanable funds.

25. **Answer c.** An increase in the level of investment spending that is financed through borrowing will cause the demand curve to shift to the right, since at every interest rate there is now greater demand for loanable funds. This shift will cause a movement along the supply of loanable funds curve as the interest rate rises in response to the increase in the demand for loanable funds.

26. **Answer b.** Fast growing countries typically offer many attractive investment opportunities because of their rapid growth rates. The supply of loanable funds curve for any particular country is impacted by that country's private savings rate: some countries have much higher savings rates than other countries. During the period 2000 to 2010, the United States was the recipient of huge capital inflows from much of the rest of the world, including China, Japan, and many Middle Eastern countries.

27. **Answer b.** When a country experiences an increase in political risk, this makes the country a less attractive place for foreign investors to send their wealth. An increase in political risk may entail the possibility that the government will seize foreign property and that possibility lessens the attractiveness of the country to foreign investors. When political risk increases, capital inflows decrease.

28. **Answer b.** Five pesos originally are worth 1 U.S. dollar, but when the exchange rate changes, five pesos are only worth $0.50 in U.S. dollars. The value of the peso in terms of U.S. dollars has fallen and, thus, the peso has depreciated against the U.S. dollar.

29. **Answer a.** When there is an increase in the demand for U.S. dollars, this causes the demand curve for dollars to shift to the right. The subsequent move along the supply of U.S. dollars curve will cause the equilibrium exchange rate of pesos to U.S. dollars to increase.

30. **Answer f.** If the U.S. dollar rises against the Mexican peso, this means that it takes more pesos to buy a U.S. dollar: this then implies that U.S. goods are now relatively more expensive to Mexico than they were before the dollar rose against the peso. If U.S. goods are now relatively more expensive to Mexico, then Mexico's goods are now relatively cheaper to those of the United States.